LABOUR IN POWER
1945–1951

LABOUR IN POWER
1945–1951

by

KENNETH O. MORGAN

CLARENDON PRESS · OXFORD
1984

Oxford University Press, Walton Street, Oxford OX2 6DP
London Glasgow New York Toronto
Delhi Bombay Calcutta Madras Karachi
Kuala Lumpur Singapore Hong Kong Tokyo
Nairobi Dar es Salaam Cape Town
Melbourne Auckland
and associated companies in
Beirut Berlin Ibadan Mexico City Nicosia

Oxford is a trade mark of Oxford University Press

Published in the United States
by Oxford University Press, New York

© Kenneth O. Morgan 1984

British Library Cataloguing in Publication Data
Morgan, Kenneth O.
    Labour in power, 1945-1951
    1. Labour party—Great Britain—History
    I. Title
    324.24107'09   JN1129.L32
    ISBN 0-19-215865-1

Library of Congress Cataloging in Publication Data
Morgan, Kenneth O.
    Labour in power, 1945-1951.

    Bibliography: p.
    Includes index.
    1. Great Britain—Politics and government—1945-1964.
    2. Great Britain—Economic policy—1945-
    3. Great Britain—Social policy.   4. Great Britain—
    Foreign relations—1945-   5. Attlee, C. R.
    (Clement Richard), 1883-1967.   6. Labour Party (Great
    Britain)—History.   I. Title.
    DA588.M637   1984   941.085'4   83-19290
    ISBN 0-19-215865-1

Typeset by Joshua Associates, Oxford
Printed in Great Britain
at the University Press, Oxford

For Jane—again

Preface

The Labour government of 1945-51 was, by any test, one of the most crucial in British history. Its impact upon the development of modern Britain, at home and overseas, was immense in almost every aspect. Like the governments of Peel, Disraeli, Asquith, and Lloyd George, and perhaps Gladstone's first term in office, the Attlee government wrenched the course of British history into significant new directions. The consequences were profound for Europe, the North Atlantic community, and the developing world, no less than for the political, social, and economic evolution of Britain itself. For perhaps the last time in the experience of the British people, a government was able to place its imprint upon external circumstances, rather than have to respond, passively or helplessly, to them. This may never happen again.

My interest in writing a general study of this important government has flowed naturally from my previous historical research and writing. Since publishing a biography of Keir Hardie some years ago, I have been fascinated by the history of the British labour movement, of which the Attlee government in many ways formed the climax. A book on the Lloyd George coalition of 1918-22 naturally led to an interest in comparing the very different consequences of the second world war for Britain after 1945. A survey of the history of Wales over the hundred years from 1880, including the growth of new regional policies after 1945, furthered my interest in wider social and economic changes in Britain as a whole during that period. Writing a history of the Attlee government has, then, long been an ambition of mine. The availability now of nearly all the public records for these six years, together with many other manuscript and printed sources, makes this an appropriate time at which to make the attempt.

My purposes in writing this book have been wholly scholarly. It is intended to provide a self-contained survey of a unique phase of British political and social history. The events described took place over thirty years ago, long before my undergraduate pupils were born. The Attlee years are as remote to them as are the equally contentious subjects of the Norman conquest or the English civil wars, which is how they should be. I have not written this work with any intention of passing judgement on the troubled history of the labour movement in Britain in the 1980s, any more than my book on the Lloyd George ministry of 1918–22 was intended to offer an argument on behalf of coalition or centrist government. In a future book, I may reflect on some aspects of the contrasts between the British left after 1945 and its successors today, between the socialism of Aneurin Bevan and of Tony Benn. But that is not my intention here. Nor, I trust, do I write from any conscious spirit of political partisanship.

What, however, I do openly declare at the outset is a commitment, even an enthusiasm, for the business of politics as such. I would endorse, both in general and in particular, the main lines of arguments in Bernard Crick's delightful essay, *In Defence of Politics*. For it seems to me that academics, especially in their learned journals (one of which I have the honour to edit), sometimes write about politics in a cloistered, negative, hyper-intellectual fashion that tends to distort the nature of political experience and activity. Historians are committed by instinct and professional habit to exalt the canons of rationality, continuity, and consensus. We tend to write, all too often, as if political life were, in reality, a prolonged tutorial or seminar, in which politicians are given good or bad marks by their intellectual superiors for the philosophic soundness or adequacy of their arguments. In this process, of course, the inherent value-judgements of the academic himself or herself are commonly ignored. Political life, in fact, is just not like that. My own involvement in constituency politics and political journalism on occasions in the past has, above all, confirmed for me that political truth possesses an intrinsically different quality from academic truth (which does not make it necessarily inferior), that political decisions are taken, often from instinct, in a confused turmoil of pressures and conflicts, with always the need to reconcile, to extract the basis of a working agreement, to relate the ideal to the practical realities, and to harmonize the desired end with the available, limiting means. Political judgements and decisions are not the product of relaxed, abstract speculation undertaken, almost for intellectual recreation, in a timeless continuum. They need to be understood in their own context and in their own terms.

This book is the first I have written in which the period is entirely one that I have lived through myself. I hope, however, that that has not led to any great distortion or substitution of personal, selective reminiscence for hard historical fact. I was, indeed, well below voting age when the Labour government fell from office in October 1951. As a child, I took a growing interest in political issues in the newspapers or on the radio. I was intrigued to notice that Wood Green, the North London suburb where we lived, was transformed overnight by redistribution from a rock-solid Conservative seat in 1945 to an equally secure Labour stronghold in 1950. But I had no record of political activity at that time. Nor had my parents, though I suspect that I provide a good illustration of the Butler–Stokes thesis on the generational factor in determining political sympathies. So far as my recollections of the 1945–51 period go, they provide, for what they are worth, confirmation of what a cousin of mine once wrote in another context:

Those years were not a return, but a revelation. They were lit by surprises; between 1945 and 1951 we saw not only the first pineapples and bananas of our lives, but the first washing-machine, the first fountain, the first television set. The world opening before us was not a pale imitation of one we had lost, but a lucky dip of extraordinary things we had never seen before.[1]

This was precisely my reaction, too, as a young schoolboy, brought up in a home of no particular affluence, initially in a village in mid-Wales, subsequently in a London suburb. Indeed, I would add professional football matches, test matches, and Christmas pantomimes and circuses to the new delights of the post-war years. For me as a child, the years 1945–51 were happy and fulfilling in every way. However, the historical records tell us that these were a time of austerity, constant crisis, and general gloom. As an historian, I have

[1] Susan Cooper, in Michael Sissons and Philip French (eds.), *Age of Austerity, 1945–1951* (Penguin edn., Harmondsworth, 1964), p. 57.

come to follow their view, although not without some reluctance and perhaps regret.

I have been exceptionally fortunate in all those who have helped me in the preparation of this book. I have benefited from the personal recollections of Lord Franks, Sir Harold Wilson, the Rt. Hon. Michael Foot, MP and Jill Craigie, Mr Sam Silkin, Mr Emrys Roberts, Mr Ivor Bulmer-Thomas, Mr John Parker, Sir Alec Cairncross, the late Rt. Hon. James Griffiths, and some civil servants of the Attlee years who prefer to remain anonymous. Among the many custodians of the valuable archives that I have been privileged to use, I must give pride of place to the ever-cheerful assistants at the Public Record Office at Kew, itself one of the technological wonders of the world and a monument to public enterprise. Stephen Bird, the archivist of the Labour Party, was an expert and immensely helpful guide through the riches of Walworth Road. I have also received kind assistance from Mr Donald Knapp and Miss Joan West of the Conservative Political Centre; Mr Gwyn Jenkins of the manuscript department of the National Library of Wales, Aberystwyth; Mr Richard Storey of the Modern Records Centre, University of Warwick; Miss Marion Stewart of Churchill College, Cambridge; and my colleague, John Kaye, archivist of The Queen's College. Among the many academic colleagues who have been most helpful I must mention Dr Henry Pelling of St. John's College, Cambridge, himself a titan amongst labour historians and my very distinguished predecessor here, for advice on sources; Lord Bullock for very generously allowing me to read the manuscript of his magnificent third volume on Ernest Bevin prior to publication; Philip Williams of Nuffield College for much help over the Gaitskell Papers; Sir Alec Cairncross for allowing me to read two important papers of his on the convertibility crisis and devaluation; Lord Blake, Provost of The Queen's College, for advice on Conservative Party sources; and Dr Deian Hopkin of University College of Wales, Aberystwyth, for information on Welsh sources. My old friend, Sir Henry Phelps Brown, generously read through the entire work in manuscript and added greatly to the perceptions of the book. Eva and Alan Taylor kindly commented on sections on foreign affairs, while Roger Louis notably added to my understanding of Middle East politics, on which he has himself a major book coming out shortly. My colleague and good friend, Alastair Parker, read several chapters to my great benefit, and removed several inaccuracies. I am also much indebted to Mr Peter Truscott's advice on several matters. None of these friends, of course, bears any responsibility for my conclusions or for the errors which doubtless remain. The Queen's College, Oxford, as often before assisted me from its research fund and gave me essential leave for writing. As always, Pat Lloyd was a prompt and infallible typist, while Ivon Asquith was the kindest and most reassuring of publishers.

Finally, on the personal side, I must thank my mother for her constant encouragement for my studies—including in the years 1945-51; our children, David and Katherine, for their good humour and forbearance; and most of all to my wife, Jane, for criticizing my text and suggesting new lines of inquiry, for putting up with years of marriage swamped by an avalanche of proofs, papers, and manuscripts, and for providing encouragement and inspiration throughout. For the second time, I dedicate a book to her. As Martin Luther observed in a somewhat different connection, I can do no other.

Oxford, May Day 1983   KENNETH O. MORGAN

Acknowledgements

The following people and institutions have very kindly granted me permission to quote from documents of which they hold the copyright: The British Library of Political and Economic Science (Dalton and Mackay papers); Churchill College, Cambridge (Alexander papers); Mrs Rosemary Donnelly (Desmond Donnelly papers); Dr Christopher Hill; Mr Stanley Clement-Davies (Clement Davies papers).

The author and publishers would also like to thank the following for kindly supplying photographs for use in this volume: The Labour Party Library; BBC Hulton Picture Library; Keystone Press Agency; UPI; Popperfoto; S. & G. Press Agency; Syndication International; BIPNA.

Contents

List of Plates
(between pp. 288 and 289)

1. Labour's two party chairmen during the general election campaign: Ellen Wilkinson, party chairman 1944-5 (Syndication International; photo: The Labour Party Library); Harold Laski, party chairman 1945-6 (S. & G. Press Agency; photo: The Labour Party Library).

2. The Labour Cabinet, 23 August 1945 (Keystone Press Agency).

3. (a) Herbert Morrison brandishing Labour's election manifesto, July 1945 (Popperfoto; photo: The Labour Party Library);
   (b) Ernest Bevin in the Foreign Office, 24 July 1946 (Popperfoto; photo: The Labour Party Library).

4. The Labour Party conference, Bournemouth, June 1946: Morgan Phillips, Herbert Morrison, Hugh Dalton (Syndication International; photo: The Labour Party Library).

5. (a) Post-war gaiety: a bathing beauty contest at Butlin's holiday camp, Filey, 1946 (BBC Hulton Picture Library).
   (b) Post-war gloom: queuing for rationed food in the bomb-damaged East End of London, March 1946 (BBC Hulton Picture Library).

6. Squatters in Abbey Lodge, central London, September 1946 (BBC Hulton Picture Library).

7. Cripps preparing his budget, April 1949 (BIPNA; photo: The Labour Party Library).

8. Morgan Phillips, Denis Healey, and Len Williams (photo: The Labour Party Library).

9. Labour Party conference, Blackpool, June 1949:
   (a) members of the National Executive outside their hotel: Griffiths, Attlee, Phillips, Greenwood, Morrison, Edith Summerskill, Laski, Shinwell (Syndication International; photo: The Labour Party Library).

1

The Long March to 1945

'Surely we can't go back to 1945? ', Professor Eric Hobsbawm protested on 15 July 1980, during a public debate with Tony Benn at Birkbeck College, London.[1] The Labour government elected in that historic year, he went on to explain, belonged to an earlier, almost primitive, phase of the evolution of the British labour movement. It had scant relevance to the problems that confronted British socialists in the 1980s. He did not, however, deflect Mr Benn from focusing attention on the experience of the Attlee government in 1945 as a radical model for contemporary democratic socialists to follow. Nor have these and similar injunctions prevented politicians and academics from turning, time and again, to the events of 1945–51 for their practical or dialectical purposes. Indeed, the Labour government of the Attlee years bids fair to rival the Liberal government under Asquith in 1905–15 as the most controversial in twentieth-century British history. Beyond that, however, as much the most successful exponent of the British variant of democratic socialism down to the present time, the Attlee administration is in grave danger of retreating from reality into the half-world of legend and fantasy. For Labour partisans, the government ministers of 1945 risk joining Keir Hardie, George Lansbury, and all the saints from the pioneering days of the movement, who for their labours rest. For their opponents or for the uncommitted, as generational and demographic change pushes the post-war years after 1945 into a penumbra of oblivion, the Attlee government, with its distant battles over ration cards, ground-nuts, or the nationalization of steel or sugar-refining, seems to be receding from history into pre-history.

Party politicians in the 1980s have tended to use the Attlee years for a variety of purposes and to promote a variety of objectives. Each tends to detect a different Labour government, one created in his (or her) own image. For many years

[1] Printed in *The Guardian*, 29 Sept. 1980.

after 1951, most politicians chose to view the Attlee government as the basis for a new moderate consensus, the source
of a post-war, post-imperial orthodoxy, founded on the
mixed economy, full employment, the welfare state, colonial
independence, and collective security based on the North
Atlantic alliance. Liberals took pride in the knowledge that
the inspiration for much of the Attlee consensus came from
two great Liberal theoreticians, Beveridge and Keynes. Conservatives after 1951, from the Butskellite era of the fifties
down to the Heath period of the early seventies, stressed
their anxiety to retain the essence of the achievements of the
Attlee government, including a goodly measure of public
ownership and other forms of state intervention. They could
delight in contrasting the 'sensible socialism' of Attlee
or Bevin with the wild excesses of Bevanism, or later of
Bennery and the nameless terrors of the neo-Trotskyist left.
In addition, Conservatives could draw a polemical distinction between the alleged consistency and firmness of
purpose of Attlee and his colleagues after 1945 with the
supposed rootlessness ('fudging and mudging' in Dr David
Owen's phrase) of later Labour leaders from Harold Wilson
to Michael Foot.

On the other side, of course, to the overwhelming majority
of Labour politicians after 1951, from Hugh Gaitskell on
the right to Aneurin Bevan on the left, whatever their differences over immediate domestic or foreign-policy issues,
the Attlee years at least were sacrosanct and beyond dispute.
The record of that heroic period, however unfulfilled or
shackled by financial constraints, was one in which all shades
of Labour opinion could take legitimate pride. Bevan,
while distancing himself from the specific policies of colleagues such as Gaitskell, over whose budget he had resigned
from the Cabinet in April 1951, never disowned the achievements of the Attlee administration in general. His political
testament, *In Place of Fear* (1952) contained no hint of
criticism of the record of the government in which he had
served for nearly six years. Indeed, he and the Bevanite
contingent continually urged the need to build upon the
sound base constructed by the 1945–51 government, for a
further socialist advance. Unlike the coalition of Lloyd

George in 1918–22, here was apparently a post-war administration which implied no badge of shame for those who had
participated in it. Meanwhile, in the political centre, the
Social Democratic Party, formed in early 1981, also made
much use of the image of the Attlee years. It saw the Labour
Party of that previous, creative period as a totally different
creature from the party of the 1980s. Leading Social Democrats, especially Dr Owen in his discussion of the origins of
the National Health Service, and Mrs Shirley Williams in her
political testament of faith, repeatedly sang the praises of
the 'responsible socialism' of 1945–51, broad-based, tolerant,
and humane, contrasted with the 'lurch to the left' to be
detected under Michael Foot, with the Bennites and Militant
Tendency as its main evangelists.[2] Indeed, Dr Owen ironically
commented, during a Blackwell's literary lunch in 1981,
that to criticize the Attlee government at all had become
'a sin against the holy ghost'.[3]

By complete contrast, for Tony Benn and the Labour
'hard left' of the 1980s, the Attlee government, or at least
the mood of the 1945 election and its immediate aftermath,
was commended precisely because it did embody that lurch
to the left, the only occasion in recent British political
history, perhaps since Cromwellian days, that such a seismic
transformation had occurred. In the debate with Professor
Hobsbawm referred to above, Benn hailed the spirit of 1945
in which Labour was 'able to mobilise young and old, left
and right, men and women, Scots, English and Welsh, the
trade union members and the Labour Party' in support of
'a clear policy of reform'. His 'arguments for socialism' in
the late 1970s and early 1980s were frequently punctuated
with nostalgic references to the heritage of the Attlee government—a government in which Mr Benn's father, as Lord
Stansgate, played a distinguished part. The Marxist playwright, Trevor Griffiths, in his television play, *Country*
(1981), seemed to echo some of Benn's themes by depict-
ing the mood of 1945 as one of near revolution, another
1789 with *jacqueries* of rebellious peasants pulling down

[2] Cf. Shirley Williams, *Politics is for People* (London, 1981), pp. 19–21.
[3] During a speech at a Blackwell's literary luncheon, attended by the present
writer, 27 Mar. 1981.

squirearchical barns and stables—even if the main thrust of
Griffiths's play was to depict the capitalist class, embodied
in a brewing dynasty, regrouping and fighting back almost
before the announcement of the 1945 election results had
died away. On the political right, Conservative ideologues
such as Sir Keith Joseph and even the Prime Minister, Mrs
Thatcher, tended to endorse Benn's conclusions, although, of
course, from a radically different perspective. 'Dry' Conservatives of this stern, unbending monetarist school saw in
the Attlee government the inauguration of thirty years of
collectivism and bureaucratic centralism which had led only
to economic decline, civic disintegration, and an erosion of
public morale. The new-style Conservatism heralded in 1979
(and triumphantly endorsed in 1983) aimed—by 'privatizing'
industries long brought under public control or ownership,
by reducing direct taxation and restoring the primacy of
market forces, by rolling back the frontiers of the state in
welfare, education, and the arts—to set the people free from
the socialistic servitude which the Attlee administration had
first imposed upon the nation.

This uncertainty among the politicians as to whether the
Attlee years marked the start of a new moderate 'Butskellite'
consensus or the false dawn of a new radical socialism, has
been mirrored by the range of conclusions reached by a
number of distinguished scholars who have applied themselves to investigating the social and political condition of
Britain after 1945. Arthur Marwick, in several works, has
been prominent among those who have viewed the record of
the post-war Labour government as largely a continuation
of the social blueprints of the war years, of Beveridge and
Uthwatt, of the 1944 white paper on employment and the
planning mechanisms adopted by the Churchill coalition
government during the war.[4] Conversely, Henry Pelling has
seen the effect of the war as relatively minor, even irrelevant
in some respects. He has preferred to link the policies of the
Attlee administration with longer-term changes in social and
economic ideas going back far into the inter-war period,
partly embodied in specific corporate experiments adopted

[4] Arthur Marwick, *Britain in the Century of Total War* (London, 1968),
pp. 327 ff.; *idem, British Society since 1945* (London, 1982), pp. 50 ff.

by the National government in the thirties, partly in policies worked out by the Labour Party itself after the *débâcle* of 1931.[5] Paul Addison, in a major study of wartime politics and social policies, has seen the Attlee regime as the legatees of the consensus of the second world war. The Labour movement, he has argued, was led after 1945 by the 'social patriots' who had dominated public life during the war. The parameters to Labour's post-war programme were set by the constraints faithfully laid down during the wartime consensus.[6] In a way, this view has been echoed by Marxist scholars such as Ralph Miliband and David Coates who have seen the Attlee government as essentially 'opportunist', dedicated to a sterile parliamentarism rather than to genuine socialist change. According to this interpretation, the years after 1945 were strictly non-revolutionary. Indeed, 'consolidation' as advocated by Herbert Morrison upon the national executive from 1948 onwards, partly so as not to upset the middle class, was built into the Attlee government's priorities and assumptions from the very beginning.[7] Alternatively, I. H. Taylor has seen the early period of the Attlee government, perhaps down to mid-1947, as marked by a sustained shift to the left, unique in our history, and a continuation of the wartime radicalism born in the atmosphere of Tobruk and Alamein. Only in the post-1947 era was this leftwards momentum checked, and even reversed, by a variety of forces, including external financial pressures and Labour's own internal party conflicts from 1951 onwards.[8]

None of these differing verdicts can in any way be derided or dismissed. Each has been fortified by detailed research and compelling argument. What they show above all—as does the varied rhetoric of the politicians—is the elusive, protean nature of the 1945-51 Labour government, and its centrality to the experience of the British people in the present century. What they suggest also is the urgent need of looking afresh at the Attlee years, in the light of the vast new sources

[5] Henry Pelling, *Britain and the Second World War* (London, 1970), pp. 297 ff.
[6] Paul Addison, *The Road to 1945* (London, 1975), pp. 270–8.
[7] Ralph Miliband, *Parliamentary Socialism* (London, 1961), *passim*.
[8] I. H. Taylor, 'War and the Development of Labour's Domestic Programme, 1939–45' (unpublished Ph.D. thesis, London School of Economics, 1977).

available. Several of the leading ministers of the Attlee government have left collections of papers that are relatively meagre: this is true of Bevin, Cripps, Morrison, Bevan, and, most characteristically of all, Attlee himself, whose archival legacy is typically reticent and impenetrable. One danger for the historian is of being unduly influenced by the colourful and immensely informative and entertaining diaries of Hugh Dalton, who risks being taken as a unique witness for the 1945–51 period, as does that equally beguiling remembrancer, Richard Crossman, for the years from 1951 to 1970. On the other hand, there are many other archives relating to figures perhaps of less central significance; there are abundant printed sources in the press and other literature; there are, of course, the oral recollections from several of the key participants, political and administrative, a unique if distinctly hazardous form of historical evidence. Film and radio archives and recordings, and simple popular oral tradition cry out for extended and systematic use. Above all, as noted in the Preface, the riches of the public records are now freely available for the six years down to 1951. With all the qualifications that must necessarily be attached to the public records as a *genre*, allowing for their inevitable built-in bias towards civil service notions of continuity, they provide an incomparable insight into policy formulation and decision-making for the Cabinet and other agencies of central government during the tumultuous years after 1945. Indeed, in the experience of the present writer, the records for the Attlee government after 1945 are distinctly fuller and more reliable than those for the myriad 'conferences of ministers' that composed the Lloyd George administration after the first world war. Armed with these resources, equipped with the inescapable hindsight which sheds perspective upon post-1945 Britain in the light of the thirty and more years that have followed that deceptively familiar era, scholars can now try to penetrate some aspects of the reality of the British experience between July 1945 and October 1951. The task of propelling Britain's most influential and effective Labour government out of pre-history and into history may now properly begin.

To a most unusual degree, the Attlee government was a child of its origins. To preface its history by a brief examination of the early pioneering years of the Labour Party is no mere exercise in antiquarianism or academic self-indulgence. On the contrary, the rise of labour from the days of Keir Hardie onwards was vivid in the minds of leading figures of the Attlee government. Most of them regarded themselves as being present at a climacteric of history, fulfilling an almost sacred trust bequeathed them by the pioneers of the party and the founding fathers.

From the start, there was a powerful feeling that the 1945 Labour government marked the end of an old phase, as much as it heralded a new beginning. As was frequently observed in the aftermath of Labour's electoral triumph, 'Keir Hardie would have been proud to have seen that day'. The Attlee government was essentially a cabinet of veterans, most of whom were in their sixties or even seventies. Their instincts were conditioned largely by the early history of their party in which they themselves had often played significant roles. For them, crises such as the first world war, the General Strike, or the split of 1931 were living realities. Clement Attlee himself, a typical late Victorian born in 1883, had joined the ILP in Stepney in January 1908 while active as a social worker in London's East End. He had served as mayor of Stepney in 1919 and had been a member of parliament continuously since 1922. Ernest Bevin, born in 1881, had been prominent in the 'new unionism' amongst the dockers during the Edwardian years, and general secretary of the Transport and General Workers, in effect, since 1918. For over twenty years he had been probably the most influential trade-unionist in the land. Politically, he had joined the Social Democratic Federation, a Marxist body, some time after 1900, although he had entered the House of Commons only in 1940 and never felt at ease in the parliamentary forum. Herbert Morrison, born in 1888, had become a socialist before the age of twenty, joined the SDF in 1907 and then the Brixton branch of the ILP in 1910. He had been prominent in local government as a left-wing (indeed, for a time, pacifist) socialist since before the first world war. Hugh Dalton, born in 1887, had joined the Fabians and the

ILP while an undergraduate at Cambridge in 1907. He seems to have been converted to socialism after seeing riotous undergraduates try to break up a meeting to be addressed by Keir Hardie, whose calm and courage in the face of this provocation deeply impressed the young scholar of King's.[9] Only Sir Stafford Cripps of the 'big five' in the Attlee team, born in 1889, had entered the Labour Party relatively late in life, at the age of forty, coming as he did from a wealthy west-country Conservative Anglican family. But even his involvement with the labour movement, legal and political, went back nearly twenty years in 1945.

Slightly younger members of the Attlee government had almost equally long memories and extensive careers of political involvement. Aneurin Bevan, born in 1897, the youngest of the new Cabinet ministers at the age of forty-eight, had been stirred, while a young miner in Tredegar, by the aftermath of the riots of Tonypandy, and the quasi-syndicalist gospel of the *Miners' Next Step*, published by the Unofficial Reform Committee in the Rhondda in 1912. Ellen Wilkinson, born in 1891, had been active in the co-operative movement, in women's trade-unionism and in feminist organizations since before the first world war. There were many other senior figures in the new Labour government in 1945, too—Emanuel Shinwell (who joined the ILP in 1904 at the age of twenty and who soon became an ardent admirer of the youthful rebel, Victor Grayson); George Isaacs, a socialist and printing workers' official since about 1906; Albert Alexander, a pioneer co-operator in Sheffield since well before the first world war; James Chuter Ede, a left-wing schoolteacher first elected to parliament in 1923; Tom Williams, an activist amongst the Yorkshire miners from the same period; Arthur Greenwood, a collectivist adviser of the Lloyd George cabinet secretariat in 1916; James Griffiths, converted to socialism while a young teenager in the aftermath of the religious revival that swept through South Wales like a torrent in 1904–5. All these, and many others, had records of intense political commitment that went back for forty years and more.

Several of the peers included in Attlee's ageing team were

[9] Hugh Dalton, *Call Back Yesterday* (London, 1953), pp. 45–6.

able to draw on even longer memories. Lord Stansgate (sixty-eight in 1945) had been, as William Wedgwood Benn, a Liberal east London MP elected in the halcyon year of the Liberal landslide of 1906. Lord Pethick-Lawrence (seventy-four in 1945) had been an ardent champion of the suffragettes (of whom his wife was a prominent member) and an opponent of militarism since long before 1914. The veteran of them all was Lord Addison, the seventy-six-year-old leader of the Lords from 1945 onwards, who had been elected as a Lloyd George Liberal in January 1910 after building up a distinguished career as an anatomist in the two decades before that. As the first Minister of Health in 1919–21, he was the only man to have served in both post-war administrations. He frequently drew upon his vast well of reminiscence of the earlier efforts at post-war reconstruction to chide or stimulate his colleagues in the Attlee government. He had switched to Labour in 1923 and had been one of the nine-man minority in the Cabinet which rejected MacDonald's proposed cuts in unemployment benefit in 1931. So, in every sense, history was very close to these men and women.

From its foundation at the Memorial Hall, Farringdon Street, in 1900, down to the crisis of 1931, the Labour Party did not greatly change in its fundamentals. It remained throughout its first thirty years essentially Keir Hardie's 'Labour alliance' of trade-unionists and political socialists, loosely affiliated on behalf of an ill-defined programme of workers' emancipation and representation. All the diverse theoretical strains itemized by Anthony Crosland in the *Future of Socialism* in 1956 were undoubtedly present in the early years of the Labour Party, along with others (for instance, Celtic nationalism or post-war technocracy) which Crosland omitted.[10] The 'socialism' of the party in this early period, such as it was, was largely shaped by the Independent Labour Party, to which a high proportion of the new Cabinet ministers in 1945 had at some stage belonged. The ILP was undogmatic, fraternal, a secular church with a powerful overlay from late-Victorian revivalist nonconformity. It was a movement

[10] C. A. R. Crosland, *The Future of Socialism* (London, 1956), pp. 81–7.

founded on the ideal of comradeship, and on ethical rather than economic considerations. 'Class war' notions were rejected; the ILP, in Keir Hardie's famous phrase, made war upon a system, not a class. On to this was grafted the administrative, utilitarian ethic of the middle-class intellectuals of the Fabian Society, which became especially important in policy-making from the first world war, when the Webbs and other Fabians were finally integrated into the main stream of the British Labour movement. Beyond these relatively small groups of socialists, there stretched the vast and (until 1919) ever-growing army of trade-unionists, affiliated to the party, and reaffiliated under the terms of the 1913 Trade Union Act which relegitimized the political levy on the basis of 'contracting out'. The unions remained essentially industrial in outlook, a defensively-minded pressure group and not much more. Until the first world war, this loosely-constructed coalition was not a serious challenger for political power. As the vocal champion of the Edwardian left, Lloyd George stole most of its clothes. The war, however, while deeply divisive and painful for the party, brought with it dramatic new opportunities. It offered the trade unions immense new power within a collectivized national wartime labour market. Part inspired by the revolution in Russia, the labour movement was impelled towards more radical and specific forms of socialism. In party political terms, there was the fortuitous (and ultimately decisive) split in the Liberal Party after the ousting of Asquith by Lloyd George. All this enabled Labour to emerge unambigously after the war as the decisive voice of the British left. In addition, the franchise reform of 1918, by raising the electorate from eight million to twenty-one million, and enfranchising millions of working-class males and almost all females aged thirty and over, gave a powerful democratic impetus to a class-based left-wing political party.

The end of the first world war saw the Labour Party remodelled under the 1918 constitution drafted largely by Arthur Henderson and Sidney Webb. But, despite the growing centralizing influence of Head Office in London and of Henderson as party secretary, the structure of the party remained incoherent, with the political leadership still under pressure from the massed ranks of trade-unionists outside parliament. Indeed, the 1918 constitution, by underwriting the dominance of the unions at all levels of the party, made the problems of leadership and of clear direction within the Labour Party as intractable as ever, as the general strike was to confirm. Nor, despite Clause Four (technically, Clause Three (a) in 1918), were the party's ideas significantly remodelled. Its foreign policy, symbolized in the 'brave new world' idealism of its new leader, MacDonald, after 1922, was powerfully shaped by an emotional and largely pacifist internationalism. Domestic policy was largely geared to a defence of the interests of the workers within a hostile capitalist environment. Far from being shaped by a belief that the advent of socialism was inevitable, as has sometimes been suggested, Labour's programmes in the twenties were dominated by the premise that the subjection of the working class under an unjust economic system would endure into a limitless and unforeseeable future. In particular, there was no distinctive Labour economic programme. The capital levy, of which Pethick-Lawrence was a major exponent, was quietly jettisoned by MacDonald's first Labour government in 1924. Not until the 1970s was the idea of a tax on wealth and capital assets seriously entertained by the party again. There was very little emphasis either on nationalization, Clause Four notwithstanding. Only the coal-mines were a serious candidate for public ownership, and, at least down to the mid-thirties, no precise or seriously-considered scheme for the mechanics of coal nationalization was introduced. Indeed, Shinwell was to complain, with some justice, that none existed even in 1945.[11] Tawney's early blueprint of 1920 was allowed quietly to gather dust. Nationalization of the land was left to Lloyd George's Liberals in the twenties. Indeed, the ex-Liberal, Addison, was viewed with some suspicion by MacDonald in 1929 when he flirted with the dangerous radical nostrum of land nationalization as part of a programme to regenerate British agriculture.[12] The bulk of Labour's economic and fiscal ideas were an

[11] Emanuel Shinwell, *Conflict without Malice* (London, 1955), pp. 172–3.
[12] Kenneth and Jane Morgan, *Portrait of a Progressive* (Oxford, 1980), p. 173.

inheritance from the 'new Liberalism' of pre-1914, with its emphasis on the phasing out of indirect taxation, the graduated taxation of earned income, attacks on vested interests, and remedies for the evil of 'under-consumption'. Several of the 'new Liberal' theorists of pre-1914—Chiozza Money, Norman Angell, J. A. Hobson amongst others—were now active in the Labour Party, or else were indirectly associated with it as Hobson was linked with the ILP's 'living wage' scheme of 1927. The impact of Edwardian economics lived on with them. No finer symbol of the Liberal past existed than Philip Snowden, Labour's unchallenged financial spokesman down to 1931, and a stern and doctrinaire advocate of the free-trade gospel of Cobden and Bright. Snowden's basic outlook was shared by Willie Graham, Labour's other major financial expert in the twenties, and by Henderson and other ex-Liberals prominent in the party. With Snowden installed as Labour's Chancellor of the Exchequer in 1924 and again in 1929 (having resigned from the ILP during the intervening years), it was clearly not going to be socialism in our time during a period of Labour government.

The débâcle of July–August 1931 marked the apotheosis of Labour's early phase, with all its limitations in terms of economic ideas and political coherence. Later interpretations, in paranoid vein, viewed the downfall of the second MacDonald administration on 23 August and the rise of an all-party so-called 'National government' in its stead the following day led by the same prime minister, in terms of the pressures of a bankers' ramp, the machinations of those in high places including the King and Montague Norman, and the vanity and treachery of MacDonald himself, reaching out for duchesses to kiss. In fact, what the supreme economic crisis of 1931 showed (as had the resignation of the highly original, if erratic and unstable Oswald Mosley from the government the previous year) was the total bankruptcy of the Labour Party in trying to produce a viable or intelligible programme to remedy unemployment or industrial stagnation. The trade unions, and their ministerial spokesman, Arthur Henderson, emerged in a somewhat heroic light, for their resistance to cuts in unemployment benefit—which, indeed had no direct bearing on the foreign exchange crisis of the time, caused by the banking collapse in Europe, and were manifestly unjust in themselves. But the crisis also demonstrated the defensive, relatively unconstructed outlook of the TUC as well, with the exception of a rare figure like Bevin. Long before the National government emerged so unexpectedly after MacDonald's audience at the Palace on the morning of 24 August, the Labour Party had thrown in the sponge. It presented a pathetic spectacle of indecision and intellectual emptiness. In the ultimate crisis of capitalism, Britain's supposedly socialist party had sabotaged itself. Perhaps, in the words of Churchill's cruel gibe a decade earlier, Labour was simply 'unfit to govern'.

After the trauma of 1931, a totally new phase began. It was to result in the emergence after 1935 of a cadre of parliamentary leadership, headed by the hitherto obscure figure of Attlee, with Morrison, Greenwood, and Dalton as his leading adjutants. Among the trade-unionists, Ernest Bevin became ever more dominant, at a time when the general council of the TUC exercised unprecedented influence within the Labour Party following the events of 1931. In the wings was the volatile and erratic figure of Sir Stafford Cripps. By the end of the thirties, Labour looked credible as a potential party of government as it had never done before. Yet, for much of the earlier part of the decade, Labour went through many gyrations. In the background, of course, were the continuing miseries of the unemployed, the marches of the hungry and the jobless symbolized by the pathetic procession from Jarrow in 1936. There was a marked heightening of political passions in a period marked by deepening crisis and polarization over both domestic and foreign policy. In the years 1932–4, Labour Party conferences resounded to calls for an overtly socialist programme, with perhaps a commitment to Brüning-type emergency measures to sustain a new Labour government against the pressures of the City, the civil service, and the court. Cripps, in *Where stands Socialism today?* (1933), advocated a centralized socialist state based on rigid party solidarity. The Socialist League for a time made some headway with demands for firmer commitment to nationalization and a programme of rigorous socialist planning on Stalinist lines. These pressures, which illustrated the continuing dynamic influence of grass-roots militancy in the constituencies within the 'federal hybrid' that the Labour Party really was, petered out after 1934. However, from 1935 onwards came new internal divisions over foreign affairs. Outside parliament, there were pressures for a Popular Front in alliance with the Communists and others on the left. Groups such as the Left Book Club and a variety of bodies concerned to promote the Republican cause in Spain gave impetus to this movement. Stafford Cripps remained its continuing advocate; as a result, in early 1939 he was to be expelled from the parliamentary Labour Party, along with Aneurin Bevan and George Strauss. Later, all three were to serve loyally enough as key Cabinet ministers under Attlee. In the parliamentary party and beyond, angry divisions between the pacifist strain embodied in George Lansbury (leader of the party after the 1931 election) and those like Dalton and the majority on the TUC who called for rearmament in defence of democratic socialism at home and abroad, continued to simmer. They boiled over at the celebrated Brighton party conference in 1935 when Lansbury was driven into oblivion as the result of a brutal, but devastatingly effective onslaught by Ernest Bevin.

Yet, from the Socialist League in 1932 to the Popular Front crusade of the later thirties, pressure to impel party policy decisively to the left was always rebuffed in the end. By 1939, the Labour Party at all levels, like the TUC, remained firmly under centrist or right-wing control. There were some victories for the left within the constituency parties, notably the successful agitation for an increase in constituency party representation upon the party's National Executive Committee from five to seven which came into effect in 1937[13]—and for which, indeed, there was a great deal to be said on general grounds. But wider radical pressures for a Popular Front, or any kind of commitment to what were perceived to be more extreme forms of socialism,

---

[13] Ben Pimlott, *Labour and the Left in the 1930s* (Cambridge, 1977), pp. 134–40. The first seven elected included three left-wingers, Cripps, Laski, and Pritt.

were always contained. Even the new constituency section
of the NEC, as enlarged from 1937 onwards, while providing
a niche for left-wingers such as Professor Harold Laski and
Ellen Wilkinson, was also largely dominated by centrist or
right-wing parliamentary figures like Morrison, Dalton, and
Noel-Baker. Clement Attlee was elected party leader in 1935
as the symbol of moderation, reformism, and gradualism. His
Labour Party in Perspective (1937) laid heavy emphasis
throughout on the constitutionalist nature of the party, and
its commitment to personal liberty. Indeed, Attlee's opponents in the leadership contest in 1935, Greenwood and
Morrison, were no less identified with centrist, mainstream
attitudes. When a split in the party did come in early 1939,
it was a very minor one. Cripps and Aneurin Bevan had
relatively few defenders after their expulsion, while the
left-wing weekly, *Tribune*, founded in 1937 largely through
heavy financial subsidy from Stafford Cripps, struggled hard
for survival. In the process of establishing its identity, it lost
from its editorial board one of its most articulate and
charismatic members, Ellen Wilkinson.

This remodelled leadership illustrated the new coherence
and realism within the ranks of British democratic socialists.
So, too, did the evolution of Labour's programme during the
thirties. In the domestic field, Labour for the first time
strove to fashion a credible, hard-headed social democratic
programme, free both from the time-worn Lib-Labism of the
Philip Snowden type, and from the more doctrinaire or
Marxist forms of socialism as advocated by the Socialist
League. The fruits were indicated in Hugh Dalton's influential
book, *Practical Socialism* (1935) and the youthful Douglas
Jay's *The Socialist Case* (1937). In both works, there was a
marked emphasis on technical, detailed policies for economic
planning, investment and capital reconstruction, in clear
contrast to the inspirational and vague character of Labour's
fiscal policies between the wars. The attempt was being made
to harmonize the British socialist tradition (especially its
powerful Fabian variant) with demand management and
counter-cyclical activity by central government, as proposed
by Keynes in the *General Theory* in 1936 and as implemented
by the Social Democrats in Sweden from 1935 and (perhaps

in a few areas only, such as regional planning) by the Roosevelt New Deal in the United States. One influential intellectual body was the 'XYZ group' brought together by the unconventional financial journalist, Nicholas Davenport at his elegant home at Hinton Manor near Oxford, from 1933 onwards.[14] It included such brilliant young university-trained economists as Douglas Jay, Hugh Gaitskell, and Evan Durbin, all of them close to Dalton, together with two notable Hungarian emigrés, Thomas Balogh and Nicholas Kaldor. Through a variety of publications in the thirties, culminating in Evan Durbin's powerfully argued *Case for Democratic Socialism* (1940), a distinctive, non-totalitarian socialist programme clearly emerged, subtly tailored to the British political tradition. A future Labour government would evidently have a much more effective fund of economic ideas from which to draw than would either of its predecessors. On the other hand, the radical thrust of Labour policies in the thirties should always be recalled: they were more than merely an echo of the cross-party 'middle way' consensus fashionable in the mid-thirties. The party as it emerged on the eve of war in 1939 was far removed from mere advanced Liberalism or the more humane versions of progressive Conservatism as espoused by Harold Macmillan and others. For instance, the activity of the Socialist Medical Association, headed by Dr Somerville Hastings, which forced the idea of a centrally-funded national health service on to the Labour party's programme in 1934, showed how a radically-motivated pressure group could push successfully for its own ideas even within so labyrinthine and cumbersome a structure as the Labour Party.[15] Again, *Labour's Immediate Programme* (1937) was a more challenging alternative to treasury finance and the budgetary orthodoxies of the National government than were the 'middle way' planning nostrums promoted by the 'Next Five Years' group. The Labour programme in 1937 included a wide range of industries and utilities destined for public ownership, along with extensive forms of public economic intervention, more

<hr />

[14] Nicholas Davenport, *Memoirs of a City Radical* (London, 1974); Douglas Jay, *Change and Fortune* (London, 1980), pp. 51 ff.

[15] See D. Stark Murray, *Health for All* (London, 1942).

precise schemes for social welfare and for the restoration of fuller employment. The gulf is only a narrow one between Labour's proclaimed manifesto in the later thirties and that presented to the voters in 1945.

The new precision in domestic policy was paralleled by a new realism in foreign affairs as well. Once again, a key figure was Hugh Dalton, bitterly anti-German and a dedicated supporter of rearmament from 1934 onwards. Following the Nationalist attack on the Popular Front government in Spain in 1936, backed by armed assistance from fascist Italy and Germany, it became more and more impossible for the Labour Party to maintain its neo-pacifist position. The TUC called loudly and repeatedly, notably through Ernest Bevin and its secretary, Walter Citrine, for armed resistance by Britain, France, and the League to German aggression in central Europe. The suppression of free trade-unionism and of Social Democratic movements in Hitlerite Germany and elsewhere was frequently emphasized. After the departure of the venerable Lansbury as leader in 1935, the old style of utopian pacifism had diminishing influence both in the political and the industrial wings of the labour movement, even though the parliamentary party continued perversely to vote against conscription and the arms estimates down to the spring of 1939. The Labour Party did not show up well during the Munich crisis—but still less so did the Chamberlain government which, after all, was actually in charge of the conduct of foreign policy. On such key issues as the defence of Czechoslovak national integrity and the necessity for an alliance with the Soviet Union, Labour's response was less ambiguous than that of Chamberlain and his colleagues. By 1939, in fact, Labour had cut loose from its belief in appeasement, either in its pre- or post-Chamberlainite forms. It had equally clearly shed the pacifism and the more sentimental aversion to voting for armaments in support of a capitalist regime, which had governed many of its responses from the start of the thirties. For the first time in its history, the Labour Party took an informed interest in problems of defence and national security. The new realism was illustrated by the pressure exerted from 1937 onwards by William Gillies and the International Department within Transport

House on behalf of increased armaments and collective action to defend socialism and democratic values.[16] The immediate impact of this was muffled by the instinctive hostility within the Labour ranks to Chamberlain's style of leadership and to the way his government appeared to be deepening the class division in the country by its divisive policies at home and abroad. But there was no doubt that in September 1939 Labour's National Executive and the TUC General Council would give an immediate endorsement to go to war against Nazi Germany, even if the NEC flatly refused to allow the party to serve in an administration headed by the hated Chamberlain. It was, of course, Labour's Arthur Greenwood, who was urged by Leo Amery to 'speak for England' on 3 September 1939. But the advice was unnecessary. In sober reality, his party had been doing so with positive effect for many months past through Attlee, Morrison, Dalton, and its other leading spokesmen. Just as the ghost of Snowden's Cobdenism had been exorcized in domestic policy, so that of muddle-headed internationalist utopianism had been in Labour's views on external and defence policies.

The second world war was the crucial watershed in the history of the British labour movement. For its leaders, for the trade unions, for constituency activists, it offered a totally new experience and an abiding moral point of reference. George Orwell in *The Lion and the Unicorn* (1941) hailed the effect of the war in demolishing the old class-ridden society and in demonstrating practical socialism at work. 'The war and the revolution are inseparable.'[17] Over forty years later in 1983, Michael Foot, now Labour's leader, was to point back to the war years as setting out the priorities for which British socialists still ought to strive. It was not, however, until the Labour Party entered the Churchill coalition in May 1940 that the full implications of the war for the British left emerged. Until then, the eight months of 'phoney war' in Europe were paralleled by an uneasy

[16] John F. Naylor, *Labour's International Policy* (London, 1969), pp. 193 ff.
[17] George Orwell, *The Lion and the Unicorn* (Penguin edn., Harmondsworth, 1982), p. 95.

relationship between the labour movement at home and Chamberlain's increasingly discredited regime. The unions continued to view warily attempts to secure the dilution of labour and the change of work practices in order to fulfil the vast new production of armaments that was needed, especially in relation to fighter aircraft. In any case, a government led by such time-worn and even despised figures as Halifax, Simon, Hoare, and Kingsley Wood, all flayed so devastatingly by Michael Foot and Frank Owen in *Guilty Men*, was hardly one that could plausibly embody the new cry for the imperatives of national unity. When major hostilities began with the disastrous campaign in Norway and the débâcle at Trondheim in April 1940, Morrison and the Labour Party chose to focus on the failure to mobilize manpower and resources with sufficient zeal at home. Even the Norway debate of 7–8 May 1940 was not at first intended by the Labour opposition as a vote of no confidence in the government, though as the debate took its course, with powerful interventions by Amery, Admiral Keyes, and Lloyd George amongst others, it rapidly became one.

The emergence of Churchill as prime minister on 10 May, indirectly as the result of Chamberlain's own tactical manoeuvrings at the time,[18] changed all that. The Labour NEC unhesitatingly voted (with one, unnamed, dissentient) to enter the government now. Attlee became deputy Prime Minister, and, in effect, Leader of the House. Ernest Bevin entered parliament to join the government as Minister of Labour and supreme director of economic planning at home. Morrison, Greenwood, Alexander, and later Dalton and Cripps, all occupied major posts in Churchill's administration. The TUC became enmeshed in the processes of social and economic strategy as never before, not even during the Lloyd George essay in corporatism in 1916–18. The government, the labour movement, the very mood of the nation were henceforth transformed.

Several major studies have been written of the profound changes that Britain underwent during the period of the Churchill coalition down to 1945, including an outstanding

[18] A. J. P. Taylor, '1932–1945', pp. 83–5, in David Butler (ed.), *Coalitions in British Politics* (London, 1978).

volume by Paul Addison. A variety of themes has been emphasized to indicate the wartime shift of mood. One was the new enthusiasm for centralized planning; it was endorsed by the Economic Section of the Cabinet which was heavily influenced by the ideas of Keynes. Apart from more formal measures such as the public control of the coal-mines, shipping, and the railways, there was also, beyond the sphere of central government, the overlapping operations of private bodies such as the Town and Country Planning Association, and even the British Medical Association—so notoriously resistant to state intervention in the past—in spelling out the agenda of a new post-war reconstruction. Even during the war years, the consequences of many aspects of this new respectability for planning were spectacular. Thus, the 1945 Distribution of Industry Act, pushed through by Hugh Dalton while at the Board of Trade under Churchill, began the process of regenerating and diversifying the socio-economic structure of old 'depressed areas' such as South Wales, Cumbria, the north-east, and industrial Scotland. Indeed, in the infrastructure created on a regional basis between 1940 and 1945, including the linking of the industrial base of areas like the Welsh mining areas with the operations of government ordnance and armaments plants, and extending the roles of trading estates, lay the seeds of the transformation of the once-derelict older industrial regions after the war.

In the social sphere, frequent emphasis has been placed on wartime blueprints such as the Barlow scheme for the redistribution of industry (itself a creation of the much-despised Chamberlain government just before the war) and the 1942 Uthwatt scheme for land use and town planning. In 1944, came the proposals of the Conservative Minister of Health, Henry Willink, for a national health service, with a new co-ordination of the hospital and local medical systems. Most spectacular of all was the Beveridge report for a comprehensive 'cradle to the grave' system of compulsory social insurance. Published in November 1942 it became a spectacular best seller and a major political embarrassment for Churchill and other Conservative ministers. Beveridge himself, an austere civil servant turned academic, was propelled into the limelight as a new 'people's

William'.[19] Henceforth, the main framework of the Beveridge proposals, including such novelties as family allowances, along with its ancillary assumptions of the need for full employment and a national health service, became the foundation of all detailed social planning and policy-making for the post-war world.

Other less tangible or measurable factors have also been itemized to help explain the wartime shift to the left. The egalitarian ethic imposed by rationing, controls, and the universal sacrifice of wartime at home and abroad is another common theme. Some commentators have laid stress, too, on the impact made by wartime evacuees from inner cities and industrial areas upon the consciences of rural and seaside communities with whom they were billeted—although much of the impact of evacuation was a distinctly transient phenomenon confined to 1939–40 alone. At the front, emphasis has often been placed on the radicalizing effects, or supposed effects, of military service, both in itself and through such institutions as the Army Current Affairs discussion groups which many Conservatives were later to blame for the huge swing to Labour at the polls in 1945. Certainly, it was taken as axiomatic by most commentators at the time of the general election that Labour's victory was largely the result of politically motivated servicemen casting their votes in Europe, or the African desert, or the jungles of Burma or Malaya, on behalf of a better world— one in which there would be no betrayal of the 'land fit for heroes' as had occurred (so it was widely believed) after 1918. Among the many varied apostles of wartime radicalism there have been listed the author J. B. Priestley, a kind of West-Riding Cobbett *redivivus* with his populist and evocative radio 'postscripts'; Tom Hopkinson's pioneering visual journalism in Hulton's *Picture Post*; and the folksy radicalism of Harry Bartholomew's *Daily Mirror*, from its influential current affairs commentator 'Cassandra' (Bill Connor) to the cartoonist Philip Zec (who met with Churchill's disapproval on at least one famous occasion) and ever-popular strip-cartoon heroine, 'Jane'. Finally, even the enthusiasm undeniably generated by the Red Army, especially during the period after the battle of Stalingrad

[19] See José Harris, *William Beveridge: a Biography* (Oxford, 1977), pp. 419 ff.

with the resultant pressure for a 'second front' in western
Europe in 1943, has also been cited as an essential element
of the radical (and, by implication, pro-Labour) tide of
opinion.[20]

It is, however, far more difficult to identify, still less
to quantify, these varied and sometimes conflicting forces.
Ever harder is it to relate these different economic, social,
cultural, and psychological pressures to the course of party
politics. The link, for instance, between Keynesian budgetary and currency techniques, and the economic thinking
of the Labour Party and the trade unions during the war is
far from clear. Many of these wartime measures, in any case,
were clearly identified as achievements of the Churchill
coalition as a whole; if anyone, the Prime Minister himself
should have drawn much of the credit. In addition, several
of the wartime proposals fell short of what Labour might
reasonably have demanded—and had been demanding
since the mid-thirties. The Willink scheme for a national
health service in 1944 included a series of concessions to the
BMA and the advocates of the voluntary and local hospitals, so that in the end much of the essence of it was
emasculated and the entire scheme fell by the wayside. There
is only a tenuous link between the Willink plan of 1944 and
the Bevan achievement of 1948. Again, the 1944 white paper
on unemployment, compared with the expectations aroused,
was a timid and unenterprising document. It was disappointing to Keynesian economists, and progressive Conservatives
in the Tory Reform group as well as to the Labour Party
(even though its authors included such Keynesians as
Robbins and Meade). In *Why not Trust the Tories?* (1944)
Aneurin Bevan violently condemned the white paper as a
surrender to market forces and private industrial and commercial interests. Many sober academic economists were to
agree with him. Again the political impact of short-term
evacuation of schoolchildren (much of which caused social
strain rather than social cohesion in the rural communities
which experienced it) or the shared delight in universal
ration cards or planners' 'red tape' are things that are hard

[20] Henry Pelling, 'The 1945 General Election Reconsidered', *Historical Journal* vol. 23, no. 2 (June 1980), p. 412.

to define, let alone to prove. The flourishing 'black market' to circumvent food rationing during the war suggests that the appeal of domestic sacrifice for the common good had its obvious limits. The political indoctrination conducted within the armed services through Ronald Adams's ABCA classes is probably a simple myth. In political terms, certainly, there were some interesting new developments, but largely outside the mainstream of party politics. There was the formation of the '1941 Committee', including a cross-party figure like Archbishop William Temple, and mavericks such as Victor Gollancz, Tom Wintringham, and Richard Acland. More significantly, there was the remarkable success of the Common Wealth Party, preaching a kind of Christian socialism, in by-elections from 1942 onwards, culminating in Wing-Commander Millington's astonishing triumph in Chelmsford, an old Tory stronghold, in April 1945.[21] Other by-election victories by progressive independents such as W. J. Brown at Rugby and Tom Driberg (the columnist, 'William Hickey' in the *Daily Express*) at Maldon may also be taken as clear pointers to a wartime mood for change. But remarkable by-elections had taken place during the first world war, too, admittedly then mainly for the benefit of the xenophobic or chauvinist right under the limited franchise obtaining prior to 1918. The relation between all these different developments and the future election prospects of the Labour Party remains open to dispute.

Nevertheless, in at least four main respects, the pressure for planning, equality, and reform during the second world war may be linked more specifically with the fortunes of the Labour Party. First, Labour ministers were uniquely associated with the triumphs on the home front. Ernest Bevin at the Ministry of Labour, with his general conduct of collective bargaining and the control of industrial production; Herbert Morrison (aided by his friend, Ellen Wilkinson) at the Home Office with his involvement in home defence and in repairing the ravages of the blitz in major cities; later on, Hugh Dalton at work on the Board of Trade in promoting regional development—these men, along with Attlee himself, bestrode the

[21] For the Common Wealth Party, see Angus Calder, *The People's War* (Panther edn., London, 1971), pp. 631 ff.

domestic scene between 1940 and 1945. The Cabinet Reconstruction Committee, with its advocacy of policies for
regional diversification and full employment, was dominated
by Attlee, Morrison, and other Labour figures. Butler was the
only leading Conservative active on the committee. Of
course, these Labour ministers were certainly not immune
from criticism. Morrison, for instance, was condemned by
Bevin in 1944 for pandering to the views of permanent
officials; Charles Key believed Morrison to possess 'an
election agent's mind and nothing else'.[22] Bevin's handling
of industrial relations was often fiercely attacked, as will be
seen. Even so, the clear outcome was that the perceived beneficial thrust of wartime planning and controls was largely
identified in the popular mind with the Labour ministers.
In the 1945 election campaign, Labour's party literature
was to make much of the work of Labour's representatives
in the winning of the war. The pamphlet on Ernest Bevin's
'Work in Wartime', for instance, adorned by a distinctly
Churchillian photograph of Bevin himself on the cover,
depicted him in relation to a succession of triumphs such
as the 'Bevin boys', industrial relations, social welfare, and
demobilization. A similar pamphlet on the wartime achievements of Herbert Morrison, with a consoling picture of a
pipe-smoking, down-to-earth Londoner on its cover, dwelt
on civil defence, the handling of children's problems, and the
protection of civil liberties in wartime through 18B and other
regulations. Of course, without the war, Attlee himself would
have remained virtually unknown to the mass public. Of the
Labour ministers, only Sir Stafford Cripps, fitted with difficulty into this wartime Pantheon. After all, he was technically an Independent until March 1945 when he rejoined
the Labour Party. After his visit to Moscow in 1942, Cripps
evidently had visions of wartime command at a time when
Churchill's reputation was at a low ebb after Singapore,
Tobruk, and other disasters. Lord Woolton found Cripps
in March 1942 to be in 'Man of Destiny' mood. 'The people
of this country were not going to continue to be satisfied
with representatives whose party loyalties took precedence

[22] Diary of Chuter Ede, 10, 11 Feb. 1944 (British Library, Add. MS
59698).

over their independence of thought and conviction.' Woolton concluded, 'The premiership is his goal.'[23] However, Cripps remained an outsider. His visit to India later in 1942 led to a serious deterioration of relations with Gandhi, Nehru, and other Congress leaders. The Cripps bubble finally burst after Alamein when Churchill felt safe in dismissing him from his post as Lord Privy Seal. Although he subsequently did good work at the Ministry of Aircraft Production, Cripps did not enjoy a good war. On the whole, it was mainstream figures such as Attlee, Morrison, Bevin, and Dalton, rather than a volatile maverick like Cripps, who were the residuary legatees of the war, and their party with them.

Secondly, the Labour Party was also ideally placed to take advantage of the wartime proposals in general, even ones that were treated with caution, or rejected, by Churchill himself. This especially applied to government commissions set up on an independent basis; the Welsh Reconstruction Advisory Council was dominated by the Welsh miners' MP, James Griffiths,[24] while Tom Johnston, that old Clydesider, almost single-handedly directed the formulation of regional economic policies in Scotland. In effect, Labour could behave like a party of government and a movement of opposition at one and the same time. There were always backbench critics such as Emanuel Shinwell and Aneurin Bevan who kept the flag of party independence flying during the headiest days of wartime consensus. Within the highest ranks of the government, Attlee himself was always profoundly aware of Labour's distinct political posture, and of the essentially transient nature of the wartime coalition. In 1943, he could chide Churchill for failing to take early action in endorsing the Beveridge scheme. Changes, he pointed out, were already taking place elsewhere in society, by agreement—on industrial planning, on housing, on the reorientation of the export trade. 'The people of Britain are prepared for considerable changes.'[25] The Labour Party

---

[23] Woolton diary, 3 Mar. 1942 (Bodleian, Woolton papers, Box 2).

[24] See material in James Griffiths papers, National Library of Wales, Aberystwyth, and Griffiths' article in *Wales* (July 1943), pp. 7–10.

[25] Attlee to Churchill, ? 1943 (Churchill College, Cambridge, Attlee papers, 2/2/7–9).

derived much party capital throughout from the entire Beveridge episode. The party could reasonably claim to have anticipated many of the key ideas contained in the report. In the party conference in Central Hall, Westminster, in May 1942, many months before Beveridge appeared, James Griffiths carried on behalf of the NEC a motion in favour of a comprehensive system of social security including family allowances and the nationalization of industrial assurance companies. The opposition of Arthur Deakin of the Transport and General Workers, who feared that family allowances might be used to curb wage advances, was swept aside.[26] In the Cabinet, Morrison emerged as a powerful advocate of the Beveridge proposals; he fought off efforts made by the Treasury to underline the financial dangers. On 16 February 1943 there came a rare break of the wartime consensus between the parties, when James Griffiths put down a motion calling for the immediate commitment of the government to the Beveridge scheme. In the end, 121 MPs voted against the government, 97 of them Labour. The remainder included David Lloyd George, that old social reformer, casting his last vote in the House of Commons. Only two Labour backbenchers voted with the government. Woolton, who observed the debate from the gallery, felt that 'the public has failed to realise that the possibility of such a scheme depends upon the absorption of almost the whole of the population into profitable employment', about which he was pessimistic. On the other hand, he acknowledged that the government spokesman, the austere figure of Sir John Anderson, 'made a complete mess' of his reply, while the popular mood in favour of Beveridge was beyond dispute.[27] On balance, the repercussions of Beveridge, like those of the 1944 white paper on Employment, were clearly helpful for Labour and added powerful impetus to the deliberations of its Policy Committee.

A third factor was the novel role of the trade unions. Of course, the unions had been deeply implicated in a corporate relationship with government and employers during the

<hr>

[26] *Report of the Forty-first Annual Conference of the Labour Party*, 25-8 May 1942, pp. 110 ff.
[27] Woolton Diary, 16 Feb. 1943 (Woolton papers, Box 3).

first world war, and especially under the Lloyd George regime after December 1916. There were many who urged that the wartime mood of consensus and industrial partnership should be continued far beyond the armistice. This article of faith was a major premiss for the more progressive supporters of the post-war Lloyd George coalition. But the new relationship between the unions and the government in 1914–18 was always superficial. The Treasury Agreement of March 1915 was always a one-sided one; in return for a promise not to strike, the unions gained virtually nothing in terms of curbs on profiteering. The miners were one powerful group who never accepted the Treasury Agreement, as the official strike by the South Wales miners in July 1915 indicated. There were always major flashpoints such as the restrictive effects of the 1915 and 1916 Munitions of War Acts, and the impact of conscription from 1916 onwards. The growth of rank-and-file movements within the miners in South Wales, along with the continuing rise of shop stewards amongst engineering and shipbuilding workers in Clydeside, Sheffield, and elsewhere showed the basic unreality of a belief in a wartime industrial consensus. After the armistice, the faith in a new-model industrial order proved within a few months to be a complete illusion.[28] The government turned itself into an anti-labour front, prepared to use troops in industrial emergencies, and to break its pledges on maintaining wartime controls. The handing back of the coalmines to the hated coal-owners was the ultimate expression of this change of stance by the Lloyd George coalition. During the inter-war period, the trade unions remained industrial outsiders, especially so after the 1926 general strike. They were removed from the close access to government they had appeared to enjoy between 1915 and 1918. Never was this more pronounced, or more damaging, than in the thirties when governments were anxious to build up a new agreement on the dilution of skilled labour to promote rearmament.

During the second world war, and its aftermath, it was all very different. This owed much to the massive presence

[28] See Kenneth O. Morgan, *Consensus and Disunity* (Oxford, 1979), on this theme.

of Ernest Bevin as Minister of Labour and all-purpose
director and co-ordinator in relation to domestic manpower
and production. Bevin's activities within this hitherto relatively feeble department of state were innovative and wide-
ranging. Indeed, he had made it a condition of his appointment by Churchill on 13 May 1940 that his ministry should
help to organize production and not merely supply personnel.[29] He acted boldly to raise wages and to improve working
conditions, most spectacularly in the 1942 Catering Wages
Act which he forced upon recalcitrant private employers. He
radically overhauled the procedures of collective bargaining.
Most important in this context, he enmeshed the trade-
union leaders (even a Communist like Arthur Horner, president of the South Wales Miners) in key processes of the
direction of production and control of the labour market.
Parallel with his efforts, Citrine, the secretary of the TUC
since before the time of the General Strike, became almost
an ancillary member of the government, with his blanket
membership of innumerable key committees. The trade
unions now became political and industrial insiders as
never before, prepared to accept even such disagreeable
measures as Order 1305 of May 1940 which prohibited
strikes in essential services and which, as will be seen later,
caused much acrimony in the later stages of the Attlee
government from 1948 onwards. It was Bevin's transcendent
and all-encompassing presence that kept this new authoritative role for the unions secure and enduring.

The consequences for the Labour Party were real, if sometimes indirect. Trade-union membership, and party affiliated
membership, rose rapidly. The organic relationship with the
political wing of the movement was strengthened by association in a common cause. New programmes were drafted
for several major unions—the winding up of casual labour in
the docks based on Bevin's Dock Labour (Compulsory Registration) Order of 1940; the draft 'miners' charter', including
nationalization of the mines and the five-day week, outlined
by the newly-created National Union of Mineworkers in
January 1945. The difference from 1918 was that this time
the unions were formulating demands as genuine participants

[29] Martin Gilbert, *Winston S. Churchill*, vol. vi (London, 1983), p. 331.

in government. This time, there were reasonable expectations that a post-war government, whatever its political complexion, would pay due heed to the pressure from organized workers, especially as it was believed that the deflation and mass unemployment of post-1918 would never again be allowed to recur. Of course, not all the results of this relationship for the unions, and of Bevin's own position, were harmonious. Industrial consensus, as ever, could be skin-deep. The more restrictive aspects of coalition policies, including the curbs upon strikes embodied in the notorious Regulation 1AA led to much bad blood. In the celebrated Betteshanger dispute in the Kent coalfield in 1942, there was even legal action taken against miners on strike. After uproar within the labour movement, Morrison had the men released from prison; Bevin then persuaded the government to take no further action. There were far more local industrial disputes in the war years than historians have yet realized. In 1942, 1943, and 1944 the days lost in industrial stoppages continued to mount, reaching a peak of 3,696,000 in 1944. The apprentice boys' strike in the South Wales coalfield in 1942-3 was one difficult local dispute to which attention has only recently been paid.[30] For all that, the general effects of the new wartime climate of labour relations were positive and beneficial, or were perceived to be. The renewed vitality of the Labour Party and its essential trade-union component was the consequence.

Finally, the war years do appear to have found the Labour Party much more buoyant in ideas and flexible in organization than were its opponents. Paul Addison has rightly pointed out the danger of believing that Labour won the 1945 election simply because of better organization.[31] There were far more Conservative agents, full-time and part-time, than Labour ones in that election, as there had always been. For all that, the Conservative Party manifestly found the second world war to be an uncomfortable experience. By

---

[30] Alan Bullock, *The Life and Times of Ernest Bevin,* vol. ii (London, 1967), pp. 267-8. The blame actually lay with the Secretary for Mines: see Appendix 6 to the Donovan Report, 1968, by Sir H. Emmerson. Cf. Stuart Bloomfield, 'The Apprentice Boys' Strikes of the Second World War', *Llafur,* vol. 3, no. 2 (Spring 1981), pp. 53-67.

[31] Paul Addison, op. cit., pp. 258-9.

1944 the executive council of the party's National Union was complaining of weakness in organization, and, perhaps, of a more subtle erosion in morale.[32] The chairman of the executive, Sir Eugene Ramsden, had expressed back in 1939 his dismay that many local constituency organizations had decided to close down their operations for the duration of the war, at a time when the Labour enemy was maintaining its machinery on full alert.[33] When Ralph Assheton succeeded Thomas Dugdale as party chairman in October 1944 he picked up this theme and voiced his anxiety at the shortage of agents and the rundown of organization in many parts of the country.[34] The *Evening Standard* recorded, shortly after VE Day, that there now existed only a hundred Conservative agents throughout Britain, compared with 385 in September 1939.[35] The problem was sufficiently serious for Churchill himself to address the party conference on 15 March 1945 on the need to repair gaps in party organization for the coming general election.[36] Nor had Conservative policy-making taken any visible strides forward. The central Post-War Problems Committee, with which Maxwell-Fyfe was involved, was neither energetic nor inspiring. The party in parliament felt that its leadership, with the exception of R. A. Butler and perhaps Oliver Stanley, was relatively out of sympathy with the new social enthusiasms of the age of Beveridge. The Tory Reform Association of backbenchers, which included such talented individuals as Lady Astor, Mavis Tate, and Lord Hinchingbrooke, became an isolated and disappointed pressure group. Several of its key members were to leave politics in 1945. Above all, the Conservatives still revealed at the top many of the divisions of the years of appeasement, and of the events that had led to Churchill's supplanting Chamberlain in May 1940. Anthony Eden, the Foreign Secretary from December 1940, had a difficult

---

[32] National Union Executive Council minutes, 27 July 1944 (Conservative Central Office).

[33] Communication from Sir E. Ramsden, 23 Sept. 1939, recorded in ibid., 8 Nov. 1944.

[34] Ibid., 8 Nov. 1944.

[35] *Evening Standard*, 30 May 1945.

[36] Percy Cohen, 'A History of the Conservative and Unionist Party Organisation' (1964), unpublished MS in Conservative Central Office, pp. 434 ff.

relationship with Churchill and with some other older colleagues. At various times, he was considering, in private discussion with Oliver Harvey of the Foreign Office, the prospect of a new centrist coalition after the war, headed by himself and Ernest Bevin, as representative of the 'steady aristocracy of trades unionists'. Alternatively, there was the possibility of a reconstructed, progressive Tory Party led by younger men such as Butler, Stanley, Lyttleton, and Eden himself.[37] Churchill, while transcendent as war leader and enjoying a more secure position as prime minister (through his position as elected Conservative Party leader in October 1940) than Lloyd George had ever enjoyed in 1916-18, was still isolated from the Conservative mainstream. He was a magnificent leader, a magnificent poster indeed during the campaign in 1945, but scarcely a reliable or contemporary figurehead for a revamped Conservatism in the new post-war world.

Labour, on the other hand, clearly had far more vitality and impetus. Of course, the party in wartime showed many signs of its old divisions at the top. Morrison and Bevin were were frequently at odds. Cripps was a perennial difficulty. Attlee himself was often criticized for his lack of dynamism, especially by Harold Laski. As late as February 1945, the *New Statesman*, perhaps at Laski's instigation, called for Labour to think again about electing 'a popular national leader and possible premier'.[38] The parliamentary party also knew several periods of disarray and internal conflict. The debate over Beveridge produced one in February 1943, with Bevin denouncing the treachery of his parliamentary colleagues. On 12 May 1944, Chuter Ede, Douglas, and Walkden agreed that 'indiscipline in the Party had seriously lowered its prestige during the past twelve months'.[39] Further trouble came at the party conference that December, when Aneurin Bevan led a fierce attack on the government and on the national executive for their policy of opposition to the

---

[37] Diary of Oliver Harvey, 4 and 25 Aug. 1942, quoted in John Harvey (ed.), *The War Diaries of Oliver Harvey* (London, 1978), pp. 146, 152.

[38] *New Statesman*, 24 Feb. 1945. Cf. Kenneth Harris, *Attlee* (London, 1982), pp. 205-6.

[39] Chuter Ede diary, 12 May 1944 (NL, Add. MS 59698).

left-wing ELAS movement in Greece. Ernest Bevin replied in
suitably blunt fashion, and it was a turbulent moment,
prophetic of many such after the war. Aneurin Bevan, in fact,
isolated on the backbenches but a dangerous critic, was prominent in many of the internal crises of the later war years.
On 28 April 1944 he launched a furious attack on Bevin and
on the trade-union leadership for their supine acceptance of
Regulation 1AA and the restriction of the right to strike.
Many of these complaints were voiced in his polemic, *Why
not Trust the Tories?* published that summer under the
pseudonym 'Celticus'; others frequently appeared in the
columns of *Tribune*. At a vital meeting of the party's
Administrative Committee on 16 May there were demands
by Sam Watson and other trade-unionists to have the party
whip withdrawn from Bevan again, as in January 1939.
However, the intervention of James Griffiths, Philip Noel-
Baker, and other conciliators managed to avert a rupture
on the NEC. Attlee and Greenwood having censured Bevan,
did not press the demand for his expulsion. Bevan himself
wrote stating, in somewhat qualified terms, that he would
abide by the party's standing orders.[40] At the party conference in December 1944, he was elected to the National
Executive for the first time, coming fifth in the constituency
section ahead of Dalton and Noel-Baker. Henceforth, with an
election coming up, Bevan was able to devote his intellectual
and oratorical gifts to working harmoniously for a Labour
victory.

The history of the party conference and of the national
executive both illustrate the vitality of the Labour Party
during the war years. Indeed, party membership rose during
the war, from 2,663,000 in 1939 to 3,039,000 in 1945,
despite the movements of population and the loss of members to the armed forces. At the 1942 party conference,
there was the important acceptance, already noted, of a new
policy for social insurance, several months before Beveridge.
At the December 1944 party conference, an instructive episode
came when Ian Mikardo, on behalf of the Reading divisional
Labour Party, successfully moved a radical resolution on

---

[40] Administrative Committee of Labour Party minutes, 16 May 1944; NEC
minutes, 26 July 1944 (Labour Party archives, Walworth Road).

behalf of the transfer to public ownership of the land, heavy industry, and all forms of banking, transport, fuel, and power.[41] He attacked the National Executive (and its spokesman, Shinwell) for the vagueness of its pronouncements on public ownership; he was supported in this by the youthful James Callaghan, prospective parliamentary candidate for Cardiff South. Despite a plea from Noel-Baker, on behalf of the NEC, for a vote not to be taken, the executive was forced to surrender totally, and Mikardo's resolution was accepted without a division. Its implications for party policy were not immediately clear. The most important outcome, as events turned out, was that, on 11 April 1945, the Campaign Committee appointed by the National Executive confirmed that Labour would nationalize the iron and steel industry, along with coal, gas, electricity, transport, and the Bank of England. This decision to include iron and steel in the roster of candidates for public ownership followed pressure from Dalton and Ellen Wilkinson that the recent party conference decision be heeded; it was carried in the face of the resistance of Greenwood and Morrison, who cited the aversion of City friends to seeing public ownership extended to manufacturing industry.[42] No clearer indication could be found of the grass-roots vitality within the party surging up during the war years than this decision on steel nationalization.

The Policy Committee of the NEC was also exceptionally active in 1944 and 1945, especially so when Herbert Morrison became its chairman after being re-elected to the NEC at the 1944 party conference. By the end of 1944, precise policy documents had been drafted to cover full employment, housing, social security, a national health service, education, control of the banks, public ownership, and world peace; of these, only public ownership seems to have occasioned much dispute.[43] On 27 February 1945, Michael Young, the twenty-nine-year-old former general secretary of PEP, was appointed secretary of the Research Department;

---

[41] *Report of the Forty-Third Annual Conference of the Labour Party*, 11–15 Dec. 1944, pp. 160 ff.

[42] Hugh Dalton, *The Fateful Years* (London, 1957), pp. 432–3.

[43] Labour Party Policy Committee minutes, 1944 *passim*; 'Short-Term Programme' presented to NEC, 29 Oct. 1944 (Labour Party archives).

the editor of the journal *Planning*, he illustrated the growing links between the cross-party reconstruction enthusiasms of the war years and the advance of the Labour Party.[44] Evidently when the post-war election came, at the policy level at least, Labour would not be unprepared. Nor would its organization be deficient. The appointment in March of Morgan Phillips, a former Welsh miner, once a student at the old Marxist Central Labour College in Regent's Park, as party general secretary (in preference to George Shepherd, the national agent) proved an important move.[45] Thereafter, Phillips applied his formidable administrative talents to ensuring that electoral organization, including the registration of voters after the massive population movements of the war years, was in sound condition. Shepherd and his assistant Dick Windle were exceptionally active on this front, too, with several new agents now appointed. In this growing mood of party confidence, a stern attitude continued towards far-left deviationists such as D. N. Pritt, the Independent Labour member for Hammersmith North. Most other rebels, including Cripps in the end, finally came to heel.

'The Coalition is getting more and more threadbare', complained Geoffrey Crowther in *The Economist* in March 1945.[46] He went on to refer to the government's muddles and failures over social insurance, housing, and the production of coal. But, underlying these detailed policy matters, lay the belief that, with victory in Europe now assured, the days of the coalition government were rapidly coming to an end. Since mid-1944 there had been indications that there was growing tension between the major partners in the government. In July of that year, Attlee fiercely rebuked Churchill for making what he believed to be ill-informed and unhelpful comments on the relationship between Labour ministers and the National Executive—a theme later to emerge during the election campaign. 'I think that you underrate the intelligence of the public and I do not share your belief', Attlee wrote magisterially.[47]

---

[44] NEC minutes, 27 Feb. 1945.   [45] Ibid., 22 Mar. 1944.
[46] *The Economist*, 24 Mar. 1945.
[47] Attlee to Churchill, 3 July 1944 (Churchill College: Attlee papers, 2/12/13).

The NEC had committed itself to the view that Labour should strike out on its own once the war was over, and should on no account participate in any continuation of the coalition.[48] With memories of 1918, let alone of 1931, the NEC could do no other. But the precise timing and method of Labour's departure—whether it would be deferred until Japan as well as Germany was defeated, for instance—was left uncertain. In early 1945, political tension continued to mount. Churchill's address to the party conference in March struck a clear partisan note, even though it included pleas to Labour and the Liberals to stay in the coalition for some time longer. More notable still, Ernest Bevin, often associated in the press with centrist or coalitionist views, delivered a strong speech at Leeds on 7 April, when addressing the Yorkshire Regional Council of the party; it seems to have been a deliberate attempt to rebuff Churchill's attempts to drive a wedge between major trade-union leaders and others in the Labour Party. Bevin trounced the Conservatives in general and Beaverbrook in particular. He stung Conservatives with the tart observation that it had been neither a one-man government nor a one-man war.[49]

When victory was achieved in Europe on 8 May 1945, the coalition rapidly fell apart. There was some public fencing between Churchill and Attlee over the political consequences. Churchill urged the Labour ministers to remain in his government until the end of the war with Japan, or for eighteen months, whichever was shorter. But on 10 May the Labour ministers accepted Bevin's formula that they should remain in office simply for the length of that parliament. However, when Attlee returned to Britain from the conference in San Francisco on 15 May he had a private discussion with Churchill in which the possibility of Labour's remaining in the coalition until the end of the war against Japan was at least kept open. Churchill formed the impression that Attlee 'would do his best to keep us together'.[50] But events had moved beyond the control of the party leaders. In a succession

---

[48] Labour Party Policy Committee minutes, 11 May 1945.

[49] Alan Bullock, *Ernest Bevin*, vol. ii, pp. 367–70.

[50] Labour Party Policy Committee minutes, 11 May 1945; Kenneth Harris, op. cit., p. 250.

of meetings, reaching a climax on 18–20 May during the party conference held at Blackpool, the NEC, under the chairmanship of Ellen Wilkinson, reached a clear view that Labour should leave the government forthwith and that Attlee should communicate with Churchill to this effect. The precise balance of voices on the NEC is not recorded. It is known that Attlee, Bevin, and (more surprisingly) Dalton were all opposed to an immediate departure from the coalition. But Morrison, with political antennae sensitively aware of the mood of the party, spoke strongly against. So, too, and with much effect, did Willie Whiteley, the chief whip.[51] Aneurin Bevan also spoke firmly in favour of a swift resignation. In addition, at a meeting with Attlee, Bevin, and Whiteley on the evening of 19 May, Morgan Phillips and other officers of the party—including Ellen Wilkinson herself—argued strongly for a clean break. The next day, Attlee and all the other Labour ministers resigned. They urged Churchill, however, to avoid 'a rushed election', on the pattern of the notorious 'coupon' election of November 1918, since the register was manifestly inadequate and most candidates, many of them servicemen, were not known to the electors. Churchill, who was nettled by what he felt was a breach of faith on Attlee's part, rejected this at once. As premier of an interim 'caretaker' government, consisting entirely of Conservatives and their National Liberal allies, he called for an election on 6 July, with the results to be announced three weeks later when all servicemen's ballots had been collected.[52] In fact, Churchill's position was generally a reasonable one. Three weeks had been allowed, in addition to the normal seventeen days between dissolution and poll. The general election of 1945 was anything but a rushed affair. In effect, it lasted almost six weeks. It provided ample opportunity for the electorate to form a considered view of the kind of government it wanted for the post-war period.

The general election got off to a stormy start. Much of

[51] NEC minutes, 9–21 May 1945.
[52] NEC minutes, 20 May 1945. See also Attlee to Churchill, 21 May 1945; Churchill to Attlee, 22 May 1945 (Public Record Office, PREM 4/65/4) for the public exchange of correspondence.

the turbulence arose from the activities of Professor Harold Laski, an eminent political scientist at the London School of Economics, who, by mischance perhaps, had been elected party chairman in succession to Ellen Wilkinson at the Blackpool conference. He bombarded Attlee with a fusillade of observations during the early part of the campaign, mainly to the effect that Labour ministers should in future be bound by the edicts of the National Executive on policy matters. He urged that Attlee and Bevin should attend the international conference at Potsdam, after being invited by Churchill, as observers only; they should in no way commit the party or a future Labour government on an international settlement. He compounded these activities by writing to Attlee just after the party conference to inform him that his leadership was 'a grave handicap to our hopes of victory at the coming election'. Attlee lacked, so Laski told him, 'a sense of the dramatic, the power to give a lead, the ability to reach out to the masses. . . .' Laski drew the remarkably inappropriate parallel of Churchill replacing Auchinleck by Montgomery just before Alamein, and suggested that removing Attlee now would have the same positive effect.[53] Attlee, one may surmise, would not have been flattered to have his talents compared with those of Auchinleck; in any case, his own demon of driving ambition, however meek in expression, goaded him on. In a memorable rebuke, Attlee eventually told Laski that 'a period of silence on your part would be welcome'. Churchill tried, naturally enough, to turn what Attlee called 'the silly Laski business' to electoral advantage. In his final election broadcast, he poured scorn on Laski as 'this hitherto almost unknown person' who had suddenly leapt into prominence. He taxed Attlee on the extent to which the Labour members of parliament were dictated to by party apparatchiks on the National Executive. In reply, Attlee rebuked Churchill effectively enough for his ignorance of the working of the Labour Party's machinery; the Labour Party leadership was no more bound by the NEC now than it had been when it took office back in 1940.[54] But later

[53] Laski to Attlee, 14 June 1945 and ? June 1945 (Labour Party archives, LAS/38/20–21).
[54] See Glanville Eastwood, *Harold Laski* (London, 1977), pp. 120–4 for

observers may perhaps conclude that Churchill had a distinctly better case than contemporaries at the time were
led to believe. The relationship between the parliamentary
party, the National Executive, and the 'movement' beyond
has been fluid throughout Labour's history; the precise
location of ultimate sovereignty at any given time has been
anything but clear-cut. In the 1980s, the Labour left were to
make precisely those claims on behalf of the NEC and the
party conference—with much success on key issues—that
Churchill had suggested in 1945. In the heat of battle in June
and July 1945, however, less academic considerations prevailed. The calmness of Attlee's response won the day. As
McCallum and Readman have observed, he resembled a placid
batsman dealing effectively with the deliveries of a brilliant
but erratic bowler.[55] Churchill's bodyline attack was thus
repelled. The episode added greatly to Attlee's prestige with
the electorate as a whole.

In fact, the disputes over Laski were not typical of the
1945 election campaign. Laski himself was somewhat
removed from the limelight when he entered a writ for libel
against the *Nottingham Guardian* on 20 June, followed by
one against the *Newark Advertiser* on the 22nd. More heat
was generated, as is well known, by Churchill's far more
extraordinary accusation, in his first radio election broadcast on 4 June, that a Labour government would introduce
a kind of Gestapo into Britain, 'no doubt humanely administered in the first instance'. Following the recent uncovering
of the horrors of Belsen and Buchenwald, this observation
might be considered tasteless in the extreme; *The Times* and
The Economist both condemned it roundly.[56] But whether
the less fastidious electors considered Churchill's gibe to be
much more than the usual rough-and-tumble of electoral
debate is doubtful. The Conservative standing in the Gallup
Polls tended to improve after Churchill's broadcast of 4 June,

aspects of Laski's role at this time. Also Churchill to Attlee, 15 June and 2 July
1945, Attlee to Churchill, 2 and 3 July 1945 (PRO PREM 4/65/4).

[55] R. B. McCallum and Alison Readman, *The British General Election of
1945* (London, 1947), p. 175.

[56] *The Times*, 5 June 1945; *The Economist*, 9 June 1945, which described
Churchill's allegations as 'pernicious nonsense'.

admittedly from a previously very low level. Attlee's first broadcast, while inevitably far more laconic and self-effacing in tone, introduced in its turn the spectre of 'a second-hand version of the academic views of an Austrian professor, Friedrich August von Hayek', author of *The Road to Serfdom*, who, he claimed, was Churchill's inspiration. This suitably Germanic—and elaborately pronounced—nomenclature was Attlee's riposte to the Tory bogey of the Jewish academician, Laski.[57] Other fiery broadsides also were delivered. Bevin, in an aggressive onslaught, condemned the Tories for introducing 'the politics of the gutter' into the campaign. Aneurin Bevan and Emanuel Shinwell, both discreetly kept off the air, toured the constituencies to denounce the squalor and immorality of Toryism. On the Conservative side, there were violent anti-socialist tirades from Lord Beaverbrook and Brendan Bracken, Churchill's unfortunately selected personal advisers, though Conservatives were also to point out that Beaverbrook had afforded a platform for left-wing propagandists such as Michael Foot, J. B. Priestley, and the cartoonist, David Low, over the wartime period.[58]

These excitements soon petered out. By the second week of June, when the election campaign proper was under way they were largely forgotten. It was overall a quiet contest, perhaps the most tranquil of the century. Speeches and pamphlets focused in a thoughtful fashion on housing, education, unemployment, national insurance, and other social themes. The emphasis throughout was on domestic aspects, rather than on the wider questions of world peace and international reconciliation. So, in fact, had been the emphasis in the alleged 'hang the Kaiser' election in 1918. There was now a general belief on the Labour side that, while the campaign was going very well, Churchill's personal charisma would nevertheless ensure a Tory victory, if a narrow one. Dalton, Ede, Bevin, even Bevan all suspected that Churchill was unbeatable this time.[59] On the Conservative

[57] *The Listener*, 14 June 1945, prints Attlee's broadcast.
[58] A. J. P. Taylor, *Beaverbrook* (London, 1972), p. 566.
[59] Dalton, *The Fateful Years*, p. 463; Chuter Ede diary, 23 July 1945; Bullock, op. cit., p. 389; Michael Foot, *Aneurin Bevan*, vol. i (London, 1962), p. 507.

side, the *Evening Standard*'s political commentator, William Allison, declared that 'electioneering experts of mature experience' (unnamed) predicted 'a comfortable majority' for Churchill and his team.[60] Herbert Morrison, the chief tactician in Labour's campaign and an exceptionally shrewd judge of the national mood, felt unable to offer a prediction though he sensed that a Labour victory might be in the making.[61] There was in fact plenty of evidence to sustain this view. The Gallup Poll showed a consistently large lead for Labour, even though it diminished during the campaign. On 18 June it recorded a Labour lead of 45 per cent to 32 per cent over the Conservatives. On 4 July, on the eve of voting (recording a sample taken on 27 June) the Labour lead was 47.0 per cent to 38.5 per cent. But these soundings were little regarded in the pre-Nuffield age. The polls appeared in the Liberal *News Chronicle* whose own political correspondent, Stanley Dobson, nevertheless pronounced confidently on 26 June that the result would be 'a stalemate' with perhaps some gains for the Liberal Party. There was evidence, too, that Churchill was less popular with the electors, now that the war was over in Europe. His major meeting, at a half-empty football stadium in Walthamstow, north London, was disrupted by fierce Labour heckling, and much of his speech had to be abandoned.[62] For all that, Churchill's stature and towering reputation, with his photograph exploited on every Conservative hoarding, and much use and abuse of the term 'National' for the benefit of his party, seemed to be insuperable assets. The newspaper press, other than the *Daily Herald* and *Daily Mirror*, was not pro-Labour, and seemed obsessed by Churchill: as luck would have it, two prominent Labour cartoonists, Low in the *Standard* and Vicky in the *News Chronicle* were ill during the campaign, their pencils temporarily stilled.[63] On the Labour side, and even in *The Times*, there was a pervasive belief in a red scare, or 'bogey', perhaps whipped up by the

[60] *Evening Standard*, 30 June 1945.

[61] Bernard Donoughue and G. W. Jones, *Herbert Morrison* (London, 1973), p. 338.

[62] *The Times*, 4 July 1945.

[63] W. Harrington and P. Young, *The 1945 Revolution* (London, 1978), p. 173.

Beaverbrook press, which would alienate the uncommitted voter from the Labour Party, as in earlier 'stunts' like the Zinoviev letter of 1924 or the Post Office savings bank scare of 1931. In the *New Statesman*, Kingsley Martin concluded that it would be 'a close thing',[64] but that Labour must keep its guard well up right to the end.

When the results were declared on 26 July (allowing for separate polls on 12 and 19 July in Lancashire towns affected by 'wakes weeks', for public holidays in Scotland, and for the collection of servicemen's ballots from distant theatres of war) they were, as Chuter Ede observed, 'unbelievable'.[65] In one of the rare seismic landslides of British electoral history, Labour was returned with 393 seats against 210 Conservatives and allies, and a mere 12 Liberals.[66] The disparity in votes cast was less great but still considerable: Labour polled 11,967,000 (48.0 per cent) against 9,972,000 (39.6 per cent) for the Conservatives. In all, there were 203 Labour gains. For the first time, Labour became totally predominant in major cities such as Birmingham, Liverpool, Manchester, and Leeds. Such local peculiarities as the Protestant proletarianism of Liverpool were overridden in the tidal wave: here, eight seats out of eleven fell to Labour and the Braddock machine. There were sweeping gains, too, in dormitory and suburban seats in the south-east, and the east and west Midlands, with unexpected progress in many rural areas as well. In East Anglia, for instance, Labour carried six seats out of seven in Norfolk. Tory ministers in the outgoing 'caretaker' government fell like the autumn leaves at Vallombrosa —Grigg, Bracken, Amery, Hore-Belisha, Macmillan, and Sandys were amongst the casualties. The party chairman, Ralph Assheton, was himself defeated at Rushcliffe. Labour suffered only two defeats, one to a Liberal in Carmarthen, another to a Communist in Mile End. The whole feel of the electorate seemed to have changed overnight. Over two million middle-class voters had voted Labour, many for the

---

[64] *New Statesman*, 23 June 1945 (the 'Critic' column).

[65] Chuter Ede diary, 26 July 1945 (BL, Add. MS 59701).

[66] For analyses of the results, see McCallum and Readman, op. cit., and Margaret Cole, *The General Election of 1945 and After* (Fabian Research pamphlet, 1945). There were also elected 2 Communists, 3 ILP, 1 Common Wealth, and 17 heterogeneous Independents.

first time. In 1935, only John Parker's seat at Romford had provided Labour with a large outer London constituency; now there were dozens in Labour hands. No longer would Labour be associated uniquely with single-industry areas like mining villages, textile or steel towns, or the potteries. Suburbia and mixed residential commuter constituencies had fallen in the deluge, too, as had cathedral cities like York, Lincoln, and Winchester. Labour's agents reported to the NEC after the campaign that only 'health resorts' and seaside towns were now required for a complete coverage.[67] Yet Lowestoft and Yarmouth had swung Labour's way; would Tunbridge Wells itself survive? The reactions at home and abroad were suitably apocalyptic. In America, the results provided a sensation, accompanied at first by some alarm which later dissipated.[68] Conservatives were thunderstruck by the débâcle, though Churchill himself seems to have reacted in a more restrained and generous fashion. In many Foreign Office and diplomatic circles, there was pervasive gloom. Alexander Cadogan lamented man's base ingratitude which could dismiss the hero, Churchill, on the morrow of his triumph.[69] Orme Sargent, shortly to become Cadogan's successor as head of the Foreign Office, looked forward pessimistically to 'a Communist avalanche over Europe, a weak foreign policy, a private revolution at home and the reduction of England to a 2nd-class power'.[70] In Labour circles, in old industrial areas such as Durham or South Wales, there was passionate rejoicing. There was a recount at Abertillery, just to confirm that the Tory had in fact lost his deposit.[71] A spiritualist recorded that the spirit of Keir Hardie (*ob.* 1915) had communicated its congratulations, together with warnings of problems that lay ahead.[72] As the uncharismatic

---

[67] NEC minutes; Elections Sub-Committee report, 18 Oct. 1945. It might be noted that Labour performed less well in Lancashire textile towns: Bury, Darwen, and Stockport stayed Conservative.

[68] Material in FO 371/44661–2.

[69] David Dilks (ed.), *The Diaries of Sir Alexander Cadogan, 1938–45* (London, 1971), p. 772.

[70] Piers Dixon (ed.), *Double Diploma: the Life of Sir Pierson Dixon* (London, 1968), p. 166.

[71] Cliff Prothero, *Recount* (Ormskirk, 1982), p. 57.

[72] Diary of Mrs Hedley Dennis, Abercynon, 26 July 1945.

Attlee went to Buckingham Palace to take office as the first
prime minister of a majority Labour government on the evening of 27 July—'quite an exciting day' as the new premier
recorded[73]—the establishment of that Jerusalem for which
the founding fathers had striven, at such personal sacrifice,
seemed close at hand.

Interpretation of the Labour election victory in 1945
has become a familiar pastime for historians and political
commentators ever since. With the plethora of new material
available, a number of negative conclusions can be reached.
It was not mainly the result of the servicemen's vote. Only
60 per cent of servicemen voted at all (1,701,000 in total),
owing to difficulties in sending out and collecting voting
forms. They were only a small fraction of those 25,000,000
who went to the poll, even though it was believed by Labour
candidates such as Leah Manning at Epping and George Wigg
at Dudley that those servicemen's votes that were recorded
went overwhelmingly Labour's way.[74] Nor can Labour's
victory be attributed to superior electoral organization. Ralph
Assheton and the principal agent, Sir Robert Topping, had
worked hard to have Conservative election agents released
from the armed forces, and the organization geared for
battle. The majority of Labour's agents in 1945, as always,
were inexperienced, last-minute recruits. The débâcle in
1945 cannot reasonably be placed at the door of Conservative Central Office. Also, to attribute the results to personal
or fortuitous episodes such as Churchill's 'Gestapo' broadcast
is facile, as has been seen. There is no evidence that the Tory
cause suffered from this gaffe, however tasteless. Nor can a
'swing of the pendulum' theory be seriously advanced. The
political pendulum has not in fact swung with any regularity
from side to side in the present century—witness the years
of relative Conservative ascendancy from 1918 to 1939, and
again from 1951 to 1964. There was no premonition of a
Labour victory at the polls prior to 1940. Had there been
a peacetime election in that year, it seems highly probable,
judging from the by-election results in the period January-

---

[73] Kenneth Harris, op. cit., p. 264.

[74] George Wigg, *George Wigg* (London, 1972), p. 113; Leah Manning, *A Life
for Education* (London, 1970), p. 164.

September 1939, that Chamberlain would have won it on a prosperity ticket, as the man who had brought recovery at home along with peace in our time. If the 1945 general election is regarded as revenge for the thirties, for Jarrow, Munich, and the means test, it was a much-delayed and indirect revenge, one not anticipated in Labour or trade-union circles, even during the 1945 campaign itself.

The Labour victory, in short, can only reasonably be projected against the circumstances of the war years, reinforced by the new realism in Labour domestic and foreign politics in the thirties. Labour was uniquely identified with a sweeping change of mood during the war years, and with the new social agenda that emerged. It was noted by observers how large a part the housing shortage played in the 1945 election; so, too, did the need for economic policies to prevent a return to mass unemployment. As has been noted, a variety of factors enabled Labour to exploit the vogue for planning and egalitarianism during the war, and to turn them to electoral advantage in a way impossible for the Conservative members of the late coalition. The Liberals, of course, were the victims of long-term forces of social, religious, and political decline; among their fallen candidates was Beveridge himself at Berwick-on-Tweed, along with their leader, Sir Archibald Sinclair, in Caithness. Labour alone seemed to understand and project the new mood. It reinforced it by bringing its own traditional supporters out to vote in unprecedented numbers, and by breaking down old parochial or ethnic barriers in cities such as Birmingham, Liverpool, Cardiff, or Leeds which had long held back the Labour cause. It was a victory for which the party had well prepared and organized in the latter stages of the war; yet it was a victory which left its leading figures stunned and for a moment almost overwhelmed. James Griffiths, a Welsh miner who was to go to the department of National Insurance in the new government, echoed the bewilderment widely felt amongst his own people at the deluge of 1945: 'After this—what?'[75] Shattered by unexpected triumph and yet buoyed up by unprecedented opportunity, the new Labour government devoted its energies and its talents to providing a credible, lasting answer in the post-war society.

[75] *Parl. Deb.*, 5th ser., vol. 318, 7158: speech by James Griffiths, (6 Feb. 1946).

2

The Framework of Politics,
1945–1951

For a party supposedly dedicated to the concept of the brotherhood of man, the Labour Party has had a singularly unfraternal history. Even considered against the adversarial and internecine character of British politics as a whole, Labour's record has been remarkable. In the early years, Hardie, MacDonald, Snowden, Henderson, and others were constantly at odds with their followers and friends, as well as with themselves. The Labour administrations of 1924 and 1929 were plagued by acrimony and lack of trust, even before the ultimate calamity of August 1931. In more recent years, the diaries of Richard Crossman and Barbara Castle, and the biographical revelations of Susan Crosland, have cast a somewhat lurid light upon the personal and political struggles within the party leadership in the 1960s and 1970s. After the 1979 election, especially in the contest between Denis Healey and Tony Benn for the deputy leadership in the autumn of 1981, Labour became a byword for internal conflict and an endless sequence of stabs in the back and elsewhere in the body politic, a condition from which Michael Foot strove to rescue it. The leadership contest after the 1983 election brought renewed acrimony in some quarters.

The Attlee years from 1945 to 1951, however, are something of an exception. More than at any other time in the party's stormy history, the dominant mood was one of unity. This extended from Downing Street to the humblest of party workers in the constituencies, down the pit and on the shop floor. Until the resignation of Aneurin Bevan and Harold Wilson over the charges imposed on the National Health Service in Gaitskell's budget of April 1951, there was remarkably little overt tension at any level of the administration or the movement. There was a total contrast to that constant sniping which plagued the 1924 government and which destroyed that of 1929–31. There was a marked difference, too, from the subtler erosion of morale that took place after 1964. Throughout the party, whose affiliated and individual membership bounded forward during these six years, there was an unmistakable commitment to the achievements of the government. Even in the damaging civil war within the party after 1951, both the Gaitskellite right and the Bevanite left took retrospective pride in their connection with the Attlee administration. None of them disavowed his or her record as a minister. There was an overriding mood of enthusiasm for the Labour government, and a visible pride. One notable instance, as will be seen, was the extraordinary by-election record of the administration, in which no seat was lost between August 1945 and October 1951, other than a freak Conservative gain (on a very low poll) in the working-class Camlachie division of Glasgow in January 1948, where local tensions between Labour, Communists, and the old ILP rump on Clydeside complicated the picture. Despite all the troubles of the time—austerity and rationing at home, wars and surrenders overseas, a mood of general gloom and of almost unbearable burdens—party morale remained at a uniquely high level. Rising membership (well over a million individual members by 1952) meant increased mass enthusiasm, not a concerted attempt to take over the party at the local level by a small group of militants. There remained a broad confidence, right down to October 1951, that the government was carrying out its manifesto pledges and fulfilling its mandate. The encroaching economic difficulties of the post-war years were viewed as unforeseeable misfortunes or as consequences of the war, rather than resulting from misjudgements by the government. The record poll of nearly fourteen million votes that Labour obtained in the October 1951 general election—albeit an election that Labour narrowly lost—was a fitting commentary on this saga of unity.

Between 1945 and 1951 the Labour movement was dominated by the Cabinet. Its leading personalities exercised a sustained and unique ascendancy over the government, the party, and its supporters. It was a relatively large Cabinet of twenty in July 1945, but five ministers clearly stood out.

At the summit were Labour's self-styled 'big three'—Attlee, Bevin, and Morrison.[1] Between them, they represented a matchless combination of experience at all levels of government. Clement Attlee had been Labour's leader for nearly ten years at the time of his assumption of the premiership on 27 July 1945. Yet amongst the general public, he had been, until the election campaign, an almost obscure figure. He was no orator, while his apparently diffident public manner, the clipped tones and deliberate understatement reminiscent of a retired bank manager or the headmaster of a minor public school, hardly created any sense of charisma or drama. During the war, since he had been largely a chairman of committees within Churchill's coalition, without any department of his own to run, he was overshadowed by colleagues such as Bevin and Morrison. Indeed, Morrison had even proposed that Attlee's position as party leader should be confirmed by the parliamentary party on 27 July 1945, just before Attlee took up the King's commission to form a government. Naturally, the election campaign, and the public jousting with Churchill, had much increased the general public's familiarity with the retiring Mr Attlee. Yet in July 1945, far more than Bonar Law in 1922, he could truly be classified as Britain's Unknown Prime Minister. The enigma largely remained over the next six years, while Attlee's laconic and unrevealing reminiscences, and destruction of many of his private papers, ensured that he would remain largely impenetrable to posterity as well. But it is transparently clear that he was a powerful, active, and, in the main, effective prime minister. Jo Grimond has called him 'a pragmatic paternalist', which is evidently not meant as a compliment. He was undoubtedly far more than merely a chairman of the Cabinet. Particularly in the 1945–6 session, he frequently intervened in Cabinet at length, and with extreme decisiveness, especially on foreign policy and in matters concerning India, where (as a member of the Simon Commission back in 1927–30) he had a special expertise. His initiatives were frequently of a radical and innovative nature; Kenneth Younger could

[1] See J. T. Murphy, *Labour's Big Three: a Biographical Study of Clement Attlee, Herbert Morrison and Ernest Bevin* (London, 1948).

later describe him as 'the extreme outside left member' of the Cabinet.[2]

The economic crisis of the summer of 1947, as will be seen, turned into a political crisis, and Attlee himself was almost toppled from power. Despite his skill in outmanœuvring Cripps and Morrison, and dividing them from each other, the impression remains that Attlee's position thereafter was more withdrawn. The pipe-smoking, silent, remote figure whom Sir Harold Wilson and others beheld at the head of the Cabinet table was reborn. In major crises—devaluation of the pound in August 1949, even more the disastrous chain of events that led to Bevan and Wilson's resignation from the Cabinet in April 1951—Attlee remained passive and offered no lead. He exemplified in his own meekly ambitious person the old Roman tag that if you remained silent you were believed to be a philosopher. Nor did he supply any new initiatives in policy in most areas; in economic matters he seemed particularly at a loss, especially after the departure of Cripps. It may be surmised whether in this later phase he had any real impact over decision-making, save for the critically important exceptions of the war in Korea and the new rearmament programme between December 1950 and March 1951. With Bevin ailing and later succeeded by the less effective Morrison at the Foreign Office, Attlee's influence over British foreign policy, from the North Atlantic to the Persian Gulf, continued to be a powerful one. Attlee had his limits, intellectually and in terms of human relations. For all that, his influence within the government was visible and pervasive. He remodelled the Cabinet structure as no one had done since Lloyd George—and with far more permanent effect. Indeed, in a series of reflections dating back to 1932, he had given a unique degree of consideration to the mechanics of Cabinet government, long before he reached Downing Street.[3] An interlocking system of permanent committees, with the Prime Minister and the inner Cabinet at the apex

---

[2] Jo Grimond, 'Attlee: What did he really achieve?', *Sunday Telegraph*, 2 Jan. 1983; transcript of interview with Kenneth Younger, 27 Dec. 1961, p. 77 (Nuffield College Library).

[3] Kenneth Harris, *Attlee*, pp. 401–5. Since writing this chapter, I have read a valuable unpublished paper by Peter Hennessy on Attlee's committee structure.

was created: a vast range of committees of departmental ministers, often under the chairmanship of non-departmental ministers, came into being. In all, Attlee created a record 157 standing committees and 306 *ad hoc* committees (GENs). The most important standing committee on the home front was the Lord President's, chaired by Morrison, to deal with economic planning. In the late summer of 1947 it was effectively replaced by the Economy Committee, linked to the Production Committee. In external affairs, the crucial body was the Defence Committee, presided over by Attlee himself. Significantly, no Foreign Affairs Committee emerged at any stage. Not all Attlee's innovations in the structure of Cabinet government were successful. The Lord President's Committee was a failure. In housing, there was a lack of co-ordination and key decisions fell between a variety of departments. Nevertheless, the system magnified the authority of the deceptively modest, almost unassailable man at the top. So, too, did his subtle, almost invisible, authority over the parliamentary party and the movement in the country. The more patriotic electors could reflect that this socialist leader had been a patriotic and courageous infantry officer in the first world war, at Gallipoli and elsewhere; in his early years in the House, he was known as 'Major Attlee'. Other than in the brief crisis of August–September 1947, his position down to October 1951 remained impregnable; the government derived much of its authority and dignity from his reassuring presence. As a Labour peer, Lord Calverley, wrote to the Prime Minister in October 1949, 'You really are our match-winner.'[4]

Attlee's two outstanding associates were Ernest Bevin and Morrison. Bevin, physically imposing and temperamentally aggressive, had the presence and personality that Attlee lacked. He gained, almost by accident, the key post of foreign affairs. As will be later seen, he dominated this department as few had done since the time of Palmerston, to impel British external policies into dramatic new directions with powerful consequences for Britain and the world. He went to the Foreign Office unexpectedly, since the position originally marked out for him was the Treasury. It

---

[4] Lord Calverley to Attlee, 11 Oct. 1949 (Bodleian, Attlee papers, Box 5).

was almost certainly the difficulty of Bevin's working harmoniously with his arch-rival, Morrison, on the home front, and not the alleged influence of George VI, which saw the posts of Bevin and Dalton reversed, with Bevin transferring to the Foreign Office. His impact on the conduct and style of British foreign policy will be considered at length in later chapters. From the point of view of the cohesion of the Labour movement, Bevin's essential role was as the leading representative and voice of the trade unions. There were only six trade-unionists in Attlee's Cabinet at the outset: they included relatively second-rank figures such as George Isaacs, George Hall, and Jack Lawson whose influence beyond their departments was negligible. By October 1951, the number of trade-unionists in the Cabinet had fallen to only four. But with Bevin always present at the apex of power, the voice of trade-unionism rang loud and clear, if not always with grammatical precision. Partly because of this, Attlee gave Bevin unique latitude in meetings of the Cabinet. Bevin would be allowed to digress at length on a variety of foreign and domestic themes. At key moments of difficulty on the home front, for instance in trying to gain TUC support for the Prices and Incomes white paper of February 1948, which implied a wage freeze, Bevin would play a crucial mediating role. He always had much to say on housing, manpower policy, demobilization, labour relations, and food production, as well as on foreign policy and defence. His loyalty to Attlee, including in the crisis of August–September 1947, was beyond question. He embodied in his own titanic personality the solidarity of Labour. With Bevin present at the summit, the loyal support of the trade-union movement for the government, even when having to accept such stern medicine as a wage freeze, devaluation of the pound, or modified direction of labour, was assured.

No less indispensable was Herbert Morrison, another man of immense executive ability, whose rivalry with Bevin was a pathetic and unnecessary feature of the Attlee government. Morrison's major experience had been as a dominant local government leader on the LCC and as architect of the London Labour Party in the twenties and thirties. However, he had also served as a Cabinet minister under MacDonald in 1929-31, and had run Attlee close in the leadership contest of 1935. Morrison did not inspire universal affection. Colleagues saw him as ambitious for the supreme office; civil servants often saw him as erratic and ignorant of economics; critics in parliament felt he had the talents of an election agent, a Tammany Hall boss or perhaps a patron in local government—not a bad Mayor of Hackney in a lean year. In some ways, to paraphrase Bevin's famous *bon mot* on Bevan, Morrison was his own worst enemy, a man with a wretched private life, and close friendships only with a few associates such as Ellen Wilkinson (who was probably his mistress) and Maurice Webb. For all that, Morrison's role in the 1945 Labour government was many-sided and quite indispensable. He commanded the admiration even of such a left-winger as Laski. Indeed, he took on such a variety of tasks that it undermined his health; at key moments (notably in early 1947) he was out of action with heart trouble. Morrison was, first and foremost, Leader of the Commons, arguably the most subtle and adroit figure ever to occupy that vital post. Along with Addison, the Leader of the Lords, and Willie Whiteley, the chief whip, he ran the Legislation Committee which ensured a steady flow of programmed legislation, session by session, from 1945 to 1950, beginning with a torrent of over seventy bills in 1945-6 to keep the new members busy and happy, but tapering off in 1948-9 as the election came near and the logic of 'consolidation' took its effect. The Wilson government of 1964-70 could well have done with a Morrison to run the House and keep the legislative machine running so smoothly. Morrison was also the key link with the Parliamentary Party, who, by suspending standing orders in the 1945-51 period, kept an atmosphere of comparative harmony and tolerance within the parliamentary ranks throughout that time. He was a vital figure in the party machine as well, close to Morgan Phillips. As a leading member of the National Executive, a member of the International Sub-Committee and eventually the chairman of the crucial Policy Committee, he was decisive in framing Labour's programmes, and thus in an ideal position to promote the cause of moderation and of 'consolidation' from late 1947 onwards.

In addition, Morrison, often derided as a somewhat mindless machine politician, was also something of a party theoretician, with considerable intellectual gifts in the understanding of the mechanisms and realities of power. His work, *Socialization and Transport*, in 1933 supplied Labour with its only conceptual blueprint on how actually to nationalize major industries. Indeed, Morrison held the field alone here since Labour had no other viable plan to offer, for all the intellectual authority of Tawney, Cole, Laski, and others. Least successful of Morrison's operations was his chairmanship of the Lord President's Committee, which directed economic planning until superseded by the Department of Economic Affairs under Cripps in September 1947. Economic long-term strategy then passed to Edwin Plowden and the permanent Planning Council, with which Morrison never really had a satisfactory relationship. The subtleties of macro-economic ideas tended to pass him by. He kept his distance from the Keynesians in the Economic Section of the Cabinet Office, and preferred to rely on maverick figures such as Max Nicholson, once of PEP, now the head of the Lord President's secretariat. Nor was he much of a success at the Foreign Office from March 1951; Dean Acheson's unduly harsh view was that Morrison's appreciation of world events had never progressed far beyond earshot of Bow bells.[5] Nevertheless, Morrison emerges as the one pivotal and quite indispensable member of the Attlee government, ubiquitous, authoritative, optimistic to the end, perhaps the opponent that the Tories most respected and feared.

The other members of the inner Cabinet, Hugh Dalton and Sir Stafford Cripps, were less consistently central to operations, and underwent very different experiences. Dalton became Chancellor of the Exchequer in July 1945, instead of going to the Foreign Office as he had anticipated. To the Treasury he brought a powerful academic mind versed in domestic public finance (though perhaps less so in international financial problems), a high reputation as a party theoretician in *Practical Socialism*, a powerful European reputation in the Socialist International, where his obses-

---

[5] Dean Acheson, *Present at the Creation: my Years at the State Department* (London, 1970), p. 505.

sive anti-Germanism struck a receptive note, and a booming, extravert personality. He made it his business to cultivate young members of parliament in 1945 (always men rather than women), such as Evan Durbin, James Callaghan, George Brown, John Freeman, and, above all, Hugh Gaitskell. These warm friendships evidently compensated for an unhappy, childless marriage. Dalton also had—indeed, revelled in— a reputation for intrigue and was somewhat distrusted for it. Desmond Donnelly wrote to Aneurin Bevan in April 1951: 'like Morley said of Lloyd George [*sic*], the others like Dalton wouldn't know a principle if they saw one'.[6] In 1945–6, Dalton was a transcendent, almost unbearably confident figure, associating the Treasury and a cheap money policy with economic expansion and social welfare, taking a vigorous and refreshing line on foreign-policy issues from Germany to Palestine. In 1947 it all went disastrously wrong. Dalton seemed to misjudge the financial crisis over the convertibility of sterling that summer; in November, he leaked, quite incomprehensibly, budget details to a journalist before announcing them to the House, which led to his resignation. Although he returned as a member of the Cabinet in mid-1948 and remained powerful both on the NEC and at the Council of Europe at Strasbourg, where he headed the British delegation, Dalton's high noon as one of Labour's central ministers passed for ever in 1947.

Conversely, Stafford Cripps achieved a steady progress through these years. He was a powerful, if remarkably orthodox and non-socialist, president of the Board of Trade. In addition to much involvement in the export drive, in regional employment policies and the whole panoply of measures in relation to increasing industrial production, Cripps also played a major role in India, where he headed the Cabinet mission in February–June 1946. Cripps's main period of authority dated from September 1947, which will be considered at length later on. From that time, until his resignation through chronic ill health in October 1950, he controlled virtually single-handed the main lines of Labour's efforts at economic recovery. Here it is sufficient to say

[6] Desmond Donnelly to Aneurin Bevan, 14 Apr. 1951 (National Library of Wales, Donnelly papers, Box 3).

that this austere, eccentric figure, a high-minded high
Anglican of evangelistic inclinations, became firmly entrenched from the start as part of Attlee's inner Cabinet,
with traditional personal links to Bevan and the Tribunite
left as well as with the party centre and right. Only Bevin
perhaps of all the Cabinet ministers more consistently
enhanced his reputation as a statesman and a guiding moral
force throughout these six years.

Beneath the five major figures, there were more shadowy
men who served as chairmen of committees as well as departmental ministers. A remarkable personality was the septuagenarian Lord Addison (born in 1869), Secretary for the
Dominions until October 1947, then Lord Privy Seal, leader
of the House of Lords throughout. His position was based
on two elements—a unique record of ministerial experience
under Asquith, Lloyd George, and MacDonald in the past;
and a close personal relationship with his Buckinghamshire
neighbour, Attlee. 'Clem' and 'Chris' often enjoyed discussing
cricket and weightier matters over a cup of afternoon tea
in the Buckinghamshire countryside. In the Cabinet, Addison
was viewed as 'a wise old man' whom Attlee allowed to
intervene at length on health, housing, agriculture, defence
policy, and many other issues on which he had ministerial
expertise.[7] Another important chairman was James Chuter
Ede, a somewhat austere former schoolmaster, Home Secretary, and, in March 1951, Morrison's successor as Leader of
the House. A. V. Alexander was a further chairman of committees, mainly on defence; the Defence Committee established in December 1946 proved to be a crucial body as
international crises multiplied. In addition to long ministerial
experience at the Admirality, Alexander was also a vital link
with the Co-operative movement of which he was much the
most dominant member. The Lord Chancellor, Jowitt, a
former Liberal and National Labour man, a very conservative minister on all topics and relatively unimpressive in the
Lords, was another much used as chairman of co-ordinating
committees. Finally, Arthur Greenwood was a pathetic case
of a senior figure who destroyed himself. He was a former
deputy-leader of the party. He served as Lord Privy Seal up

[7] Interview by the author with Sir Harold Wilson, 15 Dec. 1978.

to October 1947 and played a leading role as chairman of the Cabinet Social Services. He was a major architect both of the National Health Service and of National Insurance. Here was a man of social compassion and of proven administrative skills. But he ruined himself through drink. In 1947 he departed to the wings for ever. A powerful intellectual force in the Cabinet was thus needlessly lost.

This was, as has been observed already, a distinctly elderly Cabinet. *The Times* noted in October 1947, after a ministerial reshuffle, that Bevin, Ede, Isaacs, Attlee himself, Shinwell, Jowitt, Alexander, and Dalton were all in their sixties, while Cripps and Morrison were in their late fifties. It was true that the even more venerable Pethick-Lawrence and Stansgate had left the government; yet when Arthur Greenwood had been removed from the post of Lord Privy Seal, ostensibly on grounds of age, he was replaced by the seventy-eight-year-old Addison who was ten years older! Not until October 1947 did Attlee introduce younger blood, when Harold Wilson went to the Board of Trade at the age of thirty-one (thereby entering the Cabinet), and the forty-one-year-old Hugh Gaitskell moved to Fuel and Power. Otherwise, Attlee may reasonably be criticized for keeping some unimpressive ministers in office without clear reason: George Isaacs, an elderly trade-union official who lingered on at the Department of Labour until January 1951 is one example; George Hall (another veteran trade-unionist), at the Colonies and then (outside the Cabinet) at the Admiralty is another. There was much unrewarded talent on the backbenches, some of which smouldered in occasional rebellion. Nor was it, by instinct, a Cabinet of radical or novel ideas. A. V. Alexander was an old-fashioned imperialist in his outlook on defence and colonial questions, while ministers as senior as Morrison or Bevin often held views on the Commonwealth which hardly took account of the political, military, or financial realities after 1945. Some ministers were outstandingly conservative in their departmental assumptions. Ede was no innovator at the Home Office. His 1948 Criminal Justice Bill was in many respects a disappointment, especially for his refusal to abolish capital punishment (a view which he later reversed when in opposition in the fifties). Not only backbench penal reformers such as Sidney Silverman were disappointed with him; so, too, were government colleagues such as Cripps, Bevan, and Griffiths. Nor did Ede radically overhaul the police or their procedures, despite the 1946 Police Act; in response to pressure from the Police Federation, Trenchard's old Police College at Hendon was not reestablished, while the fabric of local government was left undisturbed as it had been since created by the government of the Marquess of Salisbury back in 1888. Ellen Wilkinson and her successor, George Tomlinson, were to prove similarly unadventurous at the department of Education, especially over comprehensive secondary education and the public schools. Other random, litmus-test issues, indicators of radicalism in British politics in the post-1945 period also saw the Attlee government hesitant or hostile. No action was taken over apartheid in South Africa or to improve the civic and social status of coloured immigrants from the Commonwealth at home. The Cabinet did discuss, on 20 March 1950, the problems encountered by West Indian immigrants over jobs, housing, and racial discrimination, but no legislative action was proposed. Nothing whatever was done to overhaul the system of government in Northern Ireland, for all its proven gerrymandering by the Protestant Unionist ascendancy. On capital punishment, the Cabinet was reckoned in 1948 to be in favour of retaining the death penalty, by eleven to five. In elevating the status of women, this was not an era of reform either; no action was taken to effect equal pay for women civil servants or schoolteachers, despite repeated motions to this effect at party conference. Even on the abolition of fox-hunting, which aroused traditional enthusiasm in left-wing circles on social as well as humanitarian grounds, many trade-union ministers defended it as a popular pastime in mining areas, while Tom Williams, the Minister of Agriculture, supported fox-hunting as valuable in assisting food production.[8] On these variegated tests, therefore, the Attlee government does not emerge, on the whole, as a body of committed or instinctive radicals.

The left in the Cabinet was. relatively powerless. Ellen Wilkinson, of Jarrow march and *Tribune* fame in the thirties,

[8] *The Times*, 25 Feb. 1949.

was a cautious Minister of Education, as has been noted,
though it should be added that 'red Ellen' was in poor health
much of the time and died of an overdose of drugs (probably
accidentally) in early 1947. The left was otherwise represented in the Cabinet only by Emanuel Shinwell, the Minister
of Fuel and Power, and Aneurin Bevan, Minister of Health,
with perhaps that old Marxist ideologue, John Strachey,
joining them later (outside the Cabinet) when becoming
Minister of Food. Shinwell and Bevan could certainly act
together with powerful effect. For instance, they fought the
terms of the American loan in December 1945.[9] They were
both fierce critics of Bevin's policy in Palestine. They also
jointly endorsed the need for an incomes policy, including
a public board to regulate wage movements, as part of a
socialist policy for the planning of manpower. But Shinwell
and Bevan never really got on personally. When Shinwell
moved to the War Office (outside the Cabinet) in October
1947 he became increasingly right-wing in his assumptions,
especially on foreign and colonial questions: during the
Korean War, he was a leading sabre-rattler and a close intimate
of Field Marshal Montgomery. Aneurin Bevan alone kept
the flag of left-wing socialism aloft throughout—which gave
him a matchless authority amongst the constituency parties
and in party conference. On several occasions, his wounding
assaults on the Tory enemy ('lower than vermin' and the like)
earned him rebukes from Attlee, who had often thought of
him as a future Labour leader. Bevan certainly had many
points of dissent from the rest of the Cabinet. In foreign
affairs, as has been noted, he attacked the American loan
terms, and was a constant critic on Palestine. At home, he
fought with much determination to keep the government
committed to the nationalization of iron and steel in 1947.
Later on, he threatened resignation more than once over the
housing cuts, and over prescription charges on the Health
Service in the autumn of 1949. Yet Bevan was never seriously
close to leaving the government down to the end of 1950.
Indeed, his warm relationship with Cripps ensured that he
stayed on, right through the difficult period after devaluation, which he came strongly to endorse. In foreign affairs,

[9] Cabinet Conclusions, 6 Nov., 3 Dec. 1945 (PRO, CAB 128/4).

the growing intransigence of the Soviet Union often led him into a marked hawkishness on many issues, notably the Berlin airlift in 1948. In general, he supported Ernest Bevin's major decisions in foreign policy; Bevan had no sympathy whatsoever with the far-left fringe headed by Zilliacus, whose expulsion from the party in 1949 he supported. At home, he strongly backed the Cabinet's decision in 1948 and 1949 to use troops and emergency procedures to deal with unofficial strikers in the docks, who, he believed, were being disloyal to a democratic socialist government. In June 1948 he urged the Cabinet Emergencies Committee to take up wide powers 'in order to deal with any trouble that might arise if relations between troops and strikers became strained',[10] and he won his point. He was an energetic member throughout of the Cabinet Emergencies Committee. In May 1947 he had urged the use of possible legal steps by the Attorney-General against stevedores who were taking unofficial action to prosecute those responsible for 'the instigation of illegal strikes'.[11] Bevan's attitude to a socialist government was one of loyalty and solidarity, reinforced by realism. Meanwhile, the weekly, *Tribune*, edited jointly by his wife, Jennie Lee, and his close friend and later biographer, Michael Foot, generally preached loyalty throughout the period down to the end of December 1950, when serious differences between Bevan and his colleagues finally began to surface. In addition, Bevan proved himself an excellent administrator (except perhaps in some aspects of finance, such as the funding of the hospital service): he was a visionary who was also an artist in the uses of power. He was as committed to the success of the 1945–51 Labour government as later left-wing ministers were ambivalent in 1974–9. More broadly, Bevan's philosophy was that the talisman of power should be taken up and exploited, wherever it led. He was no virgin who cherished the purity of the barren wilderness. He had ironically urged his ILP wife in the thirties to seek the refuge of a political nunnery.[12] He sought power for the British left, and he used

[10] Minutes of Cabinet Emergencies Committee, 28 June 1948 (CAB 134/175).

[11] Ibid., 1 May 1947 (CAB 134/175).

[12] See Jennie Lee, *This Great Journey* (London, 1963), p. 116.

it at the Cabinet table with much brillance and effect for the advance of democratic socialism.

The Cabinet, particularly the inner group of Attlee, Bevin, Morrison, and, later on, Cripps, remained firmly in control at all levels of the party down to mid-1950. Very rarely were major government decisions taken without this inner group, together or in part, being involved. The outstanding exception to this generalization—a very dramatic one—was the decision to devalue the pound in August 1949. This was effectively taken by three young ministers, the thirty-three-year-old Harold Wilson, and Hugh Gaitskell and Douglas Jay, the last two not even members of the Cabinet. Attlee, Bevin, and Morrison were on the sidelines; Cripps was, or had been, actually hostile. Once the decision to devalue was taken, however, Cripps adopted it as a vital component of his economic strategy. The traditional pattern of power within the Cabinet then reasserted itself. Only the strain of office which impaired the health of Morrison, Cripps, and (fatally) Bevin lessened their influence to any degree. The coherence and unity of the Labour government, unique in the history of the movement, stemmed ultimately from their authority.

The Parliamentary Labour Party presented few problems of management for the government down to 1951. It began in 1945 with a highly loyalist chairman and vice-chairman, the respected Scottish veteran, Neil Maclean, and Morrison's close associate, the ex-journalist, Maurice Webb. There was a huge array of no less than 259 new Labour MPs in July 1945: Dalton and Ede sang the praises of these vigorous young recruits. Dalton listened with enthusiasm at the Young Victors' Party to the economic expositions of Gaitskell, Wilson, Crossman, Freeman, Blackburn, and others.[13] Ede noted that 'the new party is a great change from the old. It teems with bright, vivacious servicemen. The superannuated TU official seems hardly to be noticeable in the ranks.'[14]

[13] Dalton papers (British Library of Political and Economic Science), 9/1/8.
[14] Chuter Ede's diary, 28 July 1945 (BL, Add. MS, 59701).

Margaret Cole's assessment, written for the Fabian Society, was that only about 150 of the 393 (later 394) Labour MPs were genuine working men and women, with 119 union-sponsored and 23 financed by the Co-operative Society. On the other hand, there were 44 lawyers, 49 university lecturers and schoolteachers, 25 journalists, 15 doctors, even 18 company directors and businessmen on the model of Richard Stokes at Ipswich. Only eight of the twenty-one women Labour MPs were 'working housewives'. In 1966, Harold Wilson was to en-counter many problems in keeping control of so huge an army of supporters, many of them articulate, aggressive representa-tives of the professional middle class, lecturers, social workers, and the like. In 1945–51 there was little such difficulty.

Much of this was due to the wise arrangements devised by Herbert Morrison. He divided the MPs up into seventeen policy groups to provide them with specialist interests, and perhaps simply with something to do other than waste time at the Commons bar. To preserve a bridge with ministers, who might otherwise become too remote, a Liaison Com-mittee was set up, with Carol Johnson as secretary. To en-courage an air of tolerance and fraternal harmony, standing orders were suspended for the entire parliament. It was assumed that Labour MPs would provide their own self-discipline. It was a method that William Whiteley, the shrewd and experienced Durham miner who served as chief whip, warmly endorsed. On balance, these arrangements had a positive effect. There was some criticism of the policy groups. Dalton always claimed that his own Finance Group was a powerful forum of ideas, including as it did such carefully-selected young men as Durbin, Gaitskell, Callaghan, Mallalieu, George Brown, and later Douglas Jay, along with Willie Glenvil Hall, the Financial Secretary to the Treasury, and a Quaker of intellectual outlook.[15] By complete con-trast, Ernest Bevin's Foreign Affairs Group was a disaster. Under the chairmanship of the old Union of Democratic Control veteran, Seymour Cocks, it included such garrulous and difficult fellow-travelling left-wingers as Platts-Mills, Zilliacus, Solley, and Warbey, who used it to denounce Bevin on such issues as Greece, Spain, Indonesia, and relations with

[15] Hugh Dalton, *High Tide and After* (London, 1962), pp. 22–3.

the Soviet Union. Bevin treated this body with anger and contempt. He once publicly called Platts-Mills a traitor during a Group discussion, and put moderate members like Kenneth Younger in an impossible position. Younger fairly concluded that 'the Foreign Affairs Group was reduced to a very angry and virtually impotent body'.[16] The Civil Aviation Group also generated some ill will, especially between the minister, Lord Winster (who was finally moved elsewhere), and Frank Bowles, a solicitor who sat for Nuneaton.[17] In the summer of 1947, there was pressure from MPs to have the specialist groups replaced by new area bodies, which would improve the flow of opinion between the government and the parliamentary party, and provide closer links with party members in the constituencies. This duly came about. On balance, the parliamentary party usually did what it was told, partly because of these new arrangements, more generally because of a broad harmony of outlook, and agreement over priorities, between backbenchers and members of the government.

Of course, there were periodic rebellions by varying groups of MPs. On home affairs, the first signs of dissent emerged over the domestic implications of the American loan on 13 December 1945, when twenty-three backbenchers (including Callaghan, Barbara Castle, Edelman, Cove, Michael Foot, Jennie Lee, and Grenfell, a broad spread covering many shades of party opinion) voted against the government. Of these, Callaghan was PPS to John Parker at the Dominions Office, and Barbara Castle PPS to Cripps at the Board of Trade. Callaghan resigned, but Barbara Castle, with Cripps's blessing, stayed on. However, this was a special issue. Many ministers, including Dalton himself, shared doubts about the American loan and perhaps welcomed a bloodless show of protest. This episode was brushed aside without acrimony. So, too, was a minor revolt on Griffiths' National Insurance Bill in May 1946 when thirty-two Labour MPs, led by Sidney Silverman and Barbara Castle again, attacked the bill for the inadequacy of its maintenance allowances for the sick and the unemployed. In fact, Griffiths made some concessions and improved the benefits accord-

---

[16] Kenneth Younger transcript interview, pp. 10–11.
[17] Letter from Ivor Bulmer-Thomas to the author, 19 Oct. 1982.

ingly. There were frequent onslaughts by W. G. Cove and other representatives of the National Association of Labour Teachers against the failure of first Ellen Wilkinson and then Tomlinson to press on with comprehensive secondary schools.[18] The 'Keep Left' group in April 1947, headed by left-wingers such as Mikardo, Crossman, Foot, and Barbara Castle, but also including some later pillars of the right such as Woodrow Wyatt and Harold Lever, made something of the need for more vigorous socialist planning and new policies to cope with unemployment in the regions, but this did not lead to any significant parliamentary revolt. There were also brief rebellions against aspects of Cripps's 1949 budget with its pegging of the level of spending on food subsidies, and the threat of prescription charges. But the membership of all these rebellions was extremely varied and none had much impact on government policy—nor perhaps was expected to have.

In fact, the only domestic PLP revolt seriously to embarrass the government arose in February 1948 over an issue that was agreed to be a strictly non-party affair, a matter of conscience, namely the suspension of capital punishment for five years. Led by Sidney Silverman, a sufficient number of Labour members voted against the government (with old Howard Leaguers in the government such as Cripps and Bevan showing their sympathy by abstaining) so that Silverman's amendment was added to the Criminal Justice Bill that Ede introduced. The Lords then struck out the amendment, and Ede was left with the delicate task of using the party whips to ensure that his bill was saved, to avoid a constitutional confrontation on difficult terrain. In technical terms, this meant urging the House not to insist on its amendment. With the full resources of the whips brought to bear, the suspension of the death penalty was struck out, though it was a close-run thing. Quite apart from the widespread repugnance towards the barbarities of the rope felt amongst Labour members and ministers at this time, there was a general mood of discontent in the spring of 1948 over the higher taxes in Cripps's budget, the Nenni telegram, and many foreign-policy questions. However, the issue passed

[18] See Caroline Benn, 'Comprehensive School Reform and the 1945 Labour Government', *History Workshop* 10 (autumn 1980), pp. 197–204.

over, with a royal commission under Sir Ernest Gowers appointed at the end of 1948 to consider the future of the death penalty. It may be concluded generally that the Labour government had little difficulty in retaining the loyalty of its parliamentary backbench following on domestic questions down to, and well beyond, the 1950 general election.

Foreign affairs aroused a more persistent outcry. From the early months of the parliament, there were groups of mainly left-wing Labour MPs anxious to snipe at Bevin's policy. Fifty-eight signed a motion on Indo-China and Indonesia in October 1945, sent personally to Attlee. By early 1946 two distinct groups had crystallized. One, a smaller body of fellow-travelling, anti-American left-wingers, headed by Platts-Mills, Zilliacus, Solley, Hutchinson, and Warbey, consistently demanded a closer relationship with the Soviet Union and a loosening of ties with the United States. The larger, and far more influential body, which included Crossman, Driberg, Mikardo, and Foot, sought a more neutralist 'third force' position, between the other two major powers. A contemporary French commentator, Bertrand de Jouvenel, distinguished (not very accurately) between 'the pacifist head of Crossman and the Russophil head of Zilliacus'.[19] The two groups came together, to some degree, in the first serious challenge to the government from the backbenches, a foreign affairs amendment to the address in November 1946, calling for 'a socialist alternative' to the two superpowers. In all, 56 backbenchers signed this amendment, mainly on the left, but including several others not normally included on the party's leftward fringe, and some straight pacifists such as Rhys Davies and Reginald Sorensen. They included five PPSs (Barbara Castle, Bruce, Haire, Wigg, and Mallalieu). In the debate in the Commons on 18 November, Crossman made a vigorous attack on the government's 'drift into the American camp'; about 70 MPs abstained on a motion which the government won by 353 votes to none. Approximately 120 Labour MPs in all were unaccounted for. In a separate amendment, 45 Labour MPs were among the 55 who voted against the government on the continuation of peacetime conscription.[20] All this caused much

---

[19] Bertrand de Jouvenel, *Problems of Socialist England* (London, 1949), p. 13.
[20] *The Times*, 19–20 Nov. 1946.

concern at the time at the highest level, including a lengthy discussion of the foreign affairs amendment at the Cabinet on 8 November, with Attlee himself expressing alarm at such a public show of discontent, and Shinwell in part justifying the dissentients.[21] At the 1947 party conference in Margate, Ernest Bevin was furiously to denounce this 'stab in the back' while he had been away in New York at the Council of Foreign Ministers. But this revolt also petered out. There were as yet no signs of an organized opposition on the backbenches. Similarly, varied protests about the government's policy on Palestine, inevitably led mainly by Jewish MPs and by pro-Zionists like Crossman, or anti-partitionist attacks by Roman Catholic and other MPs on the Ireland Act of 1949 were sporadic and of little wider significance, even though four PPSs (Beswick, Mallalieu, Mellish, and Rogers) were dismissed for voting against the government over the Ireland Bill in May 1949.

Indications of a more organized revolt on foreign affairs came in April 1947 when the 'Keep Left' group was formed; it consisted, as has been seen, of fifteen MPs, mainly anti-Communist left-wingers such as Crossman and Foot. Seven of them were journalists. While 'Keep Left' pressed for socialist policies at home as well, the main thrust was to urge a new foreign policy, independent of America and the eastern bloc. In many cases, this led to an enthusiasm for a united western Europe, as a third force under democratic socialist leadership. There were pressures for new initiatives in Palestine, Greece, and the eastern Mediterranean generally as well. A small group of 'Keep Left' MPs, with Ian Mikardo as secretary, began to meet regularly in the House, and to record minutes of their meetings, with some editorial encouragement from *Tribune*.[22] But the 'Keep Left' group soon lost their momentum in 1948 with the Communist 'coup' in Czechoslovakia, followed by the Russian blockade of Berlin and the resultant Allied airlift, and later the defection of Yugoslavia from the eastern bloc. These events divided the 'Keep Left' members and drove Foot, Crossman, and others into a staunch support of Marshall Aid and the

[21] Cabinet Conclusions, 8 Nov. 1946 (CAB 128/8).
[22] Mark Jenkins, *Bevanism: Labour's High Tide* (London, 1980), pp. 44 ff.

creation of a North Atlantic alliance for defence purposes.
By late 1949 the 'Keep Left' group, for this and more personal reasons, had largely broken up. It was virtually a cipher
in the 1950 general election. Another distinct episode came
in April 1947 when seventy-two Labour MPs voted against
the government on the proposals for peacetime national
service, with pacifists such as Rhys Davies and Victor Yates
joining the conventional left. On this occasion, a very rare
one, the government gave ground to its critics. Alexander,
the Secretary for Defence, persuaded the Cabinet as a gesture
to reduce the period of conscription from eighteen months
to twelve. It was against the advice of all the Chiefs of Staff;
Montgomery wrote to Alexander in disgust that the motives
were 'purely political'.[23] A Labour peer told Alexander that
the government 'had capitulated to the backbenchers',[24]
which was partly true. But the revolt over conscription,
which later went up to eighteen months after all, and later
still to two years, was henceforth easily contained.

On balance, such rebellions as did present themselves
over foreign affairs were dealt with firmly by Attlee and his
colleagues, with little danger to their authority. Two distinct, and divergent, issues arose in April 1948 with some
common elements in the MPs involved. The more controversial arose when twenty-two members, organized mainly by
Tom Braddock and Konni Zilliacus, a veteran left-winger
from League of Nations Days, sent a telegram of support to
Pietro Nenni, the leader of the pro-Communist socialist
group in the Italian elections, instead of backing the right-
wing socialists under Saragat. The actual telegram may have
been drafted by Geoffrey Bing, a left-wing barrister and old
campaigner for civil liberties.[25] In retrospect, this seems a
trivial issue for a test of party orthodoxy, but Attlee and
Morrison, the NEC, and the Labour press in the form of the
Daily Herald and *Tribune* angrily denounced such fellow-
travelling irresponsibility. The party executive demanded a

---

[23] Montgomery to Alexander, 9 Apr. 1947, annexed to Cabinet Conclusions,
3 Apr. 1947 (CAB 128/9).
[24] Lord Winster to Alexander, ? July 1947 (Churchill College, Cambridge,
Alexander papers, 5/12/11a).
[25] Robert Jackson, *Rebels and Whips* (London, 1968), p. 68.

reply from each of the twenty-two which would promise
categorically that they would desist from such disobedience
in future.[26] Otherwise, they would be excluded from membership of the party. Zilliacus urged S. O. Davies, the left-wing
miners' member for Merthyr, that they should reply indivi-
ually to the NEC, but in identical terms; 'this would keep our
group together while formally meeting the NEC's demand
for individual replies'. Morgan Phillips found this unacceptable.[27] There was evidently a more sustained attempt to
organize the left-wing critics of foreign policy at this time,
since Zilliacus and Driberg were in correspondence earlier
in March, to help frame a neutralist foreign affairs amendment. Zilliacus threw out with scorn a compromise proposed
by the veteran, Seymour Cocks, as mere 'Bevin-and-water'.
'Are we', Zilliacus asked rhetorically, 'already mercenaries
who are prepared to be dragged behind American big business into a world war?'[28] However, the twenty-two rebels
were, in the main, less pugnacious than Zilliacus. Faced with
the might of Transport House, they mostly wrote in contrite
terms, giving assurances of their future conduct in terms such
as to satisfy the party leadership. At the same time, Platts-
Mills, an irreconcilable on the left, was expelled from the
party by the NEC. The other issue in April 1948, the stated
intention of over seventy Labour MPs, notably the Australian
enthusiast for federalism, R. W. G. ('Kim') Mackay, to attend
the Hague conference organized by the Council of Europe,
did not occasion such difficulty. Despite all reproof from on
high, over fifty Labour MPs did attend the Hague conference
on 7 May to hear inspirational addresses by Churchill and
others. They were duly rebuked by the party leadership and
the NEC.[29] But since no formal commitment to a united

[26] National Executive Committee minutes, 28 Apr. 1948; *Daily Herald*,
21–2 Apr. 1948; *Tribune*, 23 Apr. 1948. *Tribune* described the Nenni telegram as
'an act of sabotage against the declared policy of the party'.

[27] K. Zilliacus to S. O. Davies, 29 Apr., 3 May 1948; Morgan Phillips to Davies,
28 Apr. 1948 (University College of Swansea, Davies papers). Morgan Phillips wrote
that a collective reply from the rebels could not be regarded as satisfactory, with
a number of members 'acting as a group in organised opposition to Party policy'.

[28] Zilliacus to T. Driberg, 8 Mar. 1948 (Christ Church Library, Driberg papers,
L2).

[29] National Executive Committee minutes, 28 Apr. 1948; R. W. G. Mackay
papers (British Library of Political and Economic Science, 8/3).

Europe could possibly result, and since the eventual Council of Europe at Strasbourg was kept as an attenuated body which did not threaten British national sovereignty, the European issue was not pursued by the NEC. Probably, the party leaders even welcomed an opportunity to appear even-handed by berating some right-wing or centrist members over European unity while disciplining the left over the Nenni telegram.

The conclusion must be that revolts over defence and foreign affairs again occasioned the government little embarrassment. Even when three Labour MPs actually voted against the North Atlantic Treaty Organization on 12 May 1949, all three (Tom Braddock, Ronald Chamberlain, and Emrys Hughes) continued as adopted parliamentary candidates for the next election, approved by Transport House. The rebels were mostly open to conciliation. In the cases of such as Driberg, Crossman, and Foot, they shifted their emphasis a good deal in the wake of hardline Soviet politics from February 1948 onwards; Mikardo and Bing were somewhat tougher in attitude. The dissenters were usually anxious not to be cast in the roles of fellow-travellers or crypto-Communists. Equally, they were concerned not to repeat the pacifist errors of the years of appeasement in the thirties. The handful who remained irreconcilable were picked off without much difficulty by the party leadership: Morgan Phillips recorded the details in Transport House in a bulky file of papers (GS 34/5) headed 'Lost Sheep'. On 28 April 1948, the New Zealand barrister, John Platts-Mills, was expelled by the NEC without a vote. His expulsion was fortified by a large dossier of fellow-travelling, pro-Soviet, or other deviationist pronouncements he had delivered over the past two years. He informed a press conference that 'Bevin has put Britain on the road to war.'[30] Providentially, there was a far right-wing rebel to be expelled at the same time. This was Alfred Edwards, a trade-union member for the steel town of Middlesbrough, and a vigorous critic of steel nationalization and other aspects of government policy. Edwards, indeed, had given trouble for many months past. He had been reported in the right-wing press as declaring that strikes should be made totally illegal, while he expressed

[30] Ibid., 12 May 1948; *Manchester Guardian*, 18 May 1948.

a general hostility towards further nationalization and civil service 'red tape'.[31] Neither Platts-Mills nor Edwards was allowed to speak in his own defence at party conference in May 1948. Noel-Baker, the chairman of the conference at Margate the previous year had denied Edwards a platform then also. He blandly explained to another MP that Edwards had not been called solely in his own interests. 'I think he would have been howled down. I wanted to protect him from that. . . .'[32] At any rate, the expulsions of Platts-Mills and Edwards in 1948 were accepted by the party with little demur and warmly applauded in the pages of *Tribune*.

In 1949, there were three more expulsions, all of far left-wingers. All were clearly expelled on policy grounds, in terms of the views they had expressed and the company they had kept for some years past, not on the technical organizational grounds on which the proposed expulsion of Militant Tendency was based in October 1982. In May 1949, after years of rebellious and generally tiresome behaviour, Konni Zilliacus was expelled from the Parliamentary Labour Party for his pro-Soviet outlook on foreign affairs. His expulsion was accompanied by documents, carefully compiled by Sam Watson, which alleged a run-down state of organization in his local party at Gateshead.[33] Zilliacus could hardly complain; he had taken part in 41 per cent of the public rebellions against the party whips since August 1945. In early 1950 he was expelled from individual membership of the party as well and finished up bottom of the poll at the February general election. Along with Zilliacus, Leslie Solley, another barrister and Profumo prizeman of the Inner Temple, also on the far-left fringe, was also expelled from the parliamentary party; he had participated in 37 per cent of the public revolts since 1945, a record beaten only by Zilliacus. On 27 July 1949, the journalist, Lester Hutchinson, was also expelled from the party, and his prospective parlia-

[31] *Evening Gazette*, 31 May 1947.
[32] Philip Noel-Baker to Geoffrey Cooper, MP, 9 June 1947 (Churchill College, Cambridge, Noel-Baker papers, 2/85).
[33] National Executive Committee minutes, 18 May 1949; Sam Watson to Morgan Phillips, 22 Feb. 1949 (Labour Party archives, GS 34/5). The motion was moved by Attlee and seconded by Sam Watson; it was carried after a more moderate motion, proposed by Shinwell and Laski, was defeated.

mentary candidateship for Middleton and Prestwich was
annulled. Hutchinson blithely observed that his expulsion
came as no surprise to him since he had been abroad when
the previous cases had been under review; he felt certain that
the government's foreign and economic policies were leading
to catastrophe.[34] None of these three expulsions caused more
than a temporary *frisson*; Solley (in Thurrock) and Hutchinson (at West Walthamstow, where he faced the opposition of
no less than Attlee himself as candidate) were both heavily
defeated in the February 1950 general election. The existence of Zilliacus, Platts-Mills, Solley, and Hutchinson as a
small band of Independent Socialist members, along with
D. N. Pritt (whose applications for readmission to the party
were always contemptuously rejected) caused the government little concern. However, other frequent rebels such as
S. O. Davies, Tom Braddock, and Emrys Hughes were
treated more leniently. After the 1950 general election,
Labour's tiny majority made rebellion even less attractive to
those contemplating it, though Silverman, S. O. Davies,
Hughes, and others occasionally tried. A far-left splinter
group, 'Socialist Fellowship', started by Ronald Chamberlain
and Tom Braddock, was proscribed after attacks on government policy in Korea in 1950-1. Even men such as Ellis Smith
and Fenner Brockway found it too extreme.[35] Tom Braddock
was not endorsed as parliamentary candidate in 1951 and only
re-emerged later as Labour candidate in fighting the forlorn
hope of Kingston-on-Thames in 1959 and 1964. In general, the
leadership remained easily in command. There was nothing at
this period remotely resembling the parliamentary disarray that
was to follow the Bevanite controversies from 1952 onwards.

Again, all levels of the party hierarchy and machine found
the Cabinet and leadership comfortably in control. Morrison
kept a close and wary eye on matters of organization,
through his membership of the International Sub-Committee,
and still more through his role on the Policy Committee

---

[34] Ibid., 27 July 1949; *The Times*, 28 July 1949; S. Berger to Morgan Phillips,
15 June 1949 (Labour Party archives, GS 34/5).
[35] *Socialist Outlook*, Sept. 1950.

from 1948 onwards. His position was much strengthened by the powerful position of Morgan Phillips who emerged in these years as the most authoritative general secretary Labour had known since the early days of Arthur Henderson in 1911. He kept a close control of party organization at the local and regional level. For instance, he gave his eventual blessing to the formation of the Welsh Council of Labour, with Cliff Prothero as secretary, in February 1947, despite Labour's traditional suspicion of Celtic separatism.[36] Also Phillips was much involved in the disciplinary processes as well. It is clear from the party archives that Phillips brushed aside a good deal of grass-roots disaffection in the unions and in the constituency parties. A torrent of protest against Labour's foreign and defence policies, the wage freeze, and the handling of Platts-Mills and Zilliacus was simply smothered by the urbane and resourceful general secretary in Transport House. Undoubtedly left-wing complaints in the 1980s that the party right wing was as active in the forties in manipulating party policy, as it was vocal in protesting against similar left-wing methods later on, find much support in the records of the party. In his eyrie in Smith Square, Morgan Phillips enjoyed a broad synoptic view of opinion at all levels in the party. He used it to bolster up the position of the leadership at every turn. He was as zealous in bringing the Nenni telegrammers to heel in April 1948, as he was in forcing Bevan and Wilson into a position of isolation after their resignation from the government in April 1951. He used his influence to secure the defeat of Communist candidates in union elections. By 1949 there were signs also that Phillips was emerging as political analyst and part-time philosopher. In effect, he backed up Morrison in his call for 'consolidation' rather than frightening off the middle class with higher taxes or more socialism.[37] He could call on the services of exceptionally talented officers such as Denis Healey, secretary of the International Department at Transport House from February 1946 on-

[36] National Executive Committee Organizational Sub-Committee minutes, 15 Jan. 1947.
[37] See Phillips to Attlee, 19 July 1949 (Bodleian, Attlee papers, Box 2).

wards,[38] and Michael Young, head of the Research Department, both men of immense intellectual drive. Dick Windle headed a vigorous cadre of agents and party organizers. Morgan Phillips was generally a most formidable ally for Attlee and his team.

The National Executive, which Phillips administered, was easily controlled by the parliamentary leadership throughout the six years 1945 to 1951, with assistance from their trade-union allies: this was despite Morrison's professed anxiety, as expressed to Attlee, to avoid ministers 'running the show'.[39] It was leading government ministers—Attlee himself, Morrison, Dalton, Shinwell, Bevan, Noel-Baker, Griffiths—who dominated the NEC and its ancillary sub-committees. In no sense could the NEC be regarded as a rival to the parliamentary leadership, still less was it dictating to it. In the short term, therefore, Attlee's reassuring replies to Churchill during the 1945 campaign were confirmed, though not later. Laski's motion on the NEC on 24 July 1946, that relations between the NEC and a Labour government in power should be re-examined, was voted down by 10 votes to 7; the last echoes of the controversies of a year earlier were thus stilled. Working intimately with the parliamentary leaders were the trade-union figures who provided the clear majority on the NEC—along with several trade-unionists in the women's section of the executive as well. Such trade-union giants as Arthur Deakin of the Transport Workers, Tom Williamson of the General and Municipal Workers, and Sam Watson, the influential secretary of the Durham Miners, powerfully backed the government ('their' government) on virtually all issues, and ensured it a guaranteed automatic majority. There was some trouble in November 1946 when it was noted that two members of the NEC, Mrs Barbara Ayrton Gould, and Joe Reeves, a Co-operative Society member, had signed the foreign affairs amendment criticizing Bevin's conduct of foreign

[38] See B. Reed and G. Williams, *Denis Healey and the Politics of Power* (London, 1971), pp. 48 ff.
[39] Morrison to Attlee, 21 June 1946 (Bodleian, Attlee papers, Box 9).

policy.[40] But this was a rare episode, and neither Gould nor Reeves was rebellious again. Members of the left were few in number. Aneurin Bevan, of course, who regularly topped the poll in elections to the constituency section of the NEC, was a Cabinet minister, and in no position to revolt against his ministerial colleagues even if he wished to do so. He did move a motion on 27 April 1949, seconded by Michael Foot, that Zilliacus's expulsion be reconsidered, though his reasons for doing so were purely procedural: he argued that Zilliacus had had no opportunity of expressing his views. In fact, Sam Watson's counter-motion that Zilliacus and Solley be thrown out forthwith was carried with ease. It is clear, in any case, that Bevan had no principled objection to Zilliacus's expulsion as such. He wrote to a leading North Wales trade-unionist to this effect:

I have no doubt that Zilliacus ought to go because of his close associations abroad with the enemies of Labour and Social Democracy. He has on many occasions made himself out to be the representative of the Labour Party, and it was essential to strip him of all pretensions to the title. I, of course, agree that members of the Party must have the right to agitate for changes in policy . . . but Zilliacus had consistently broken decisions arrived at over and over again, and had passed beyond the bound of all reasonable toleration.[41]

For Bevan, here again unity and solidarity were the crucial touchstones. The only other left-wing figure at all continuously on the NEC in these years was Professor Laski. In fact, he was far less prominent after his notorious phase of chairmanship in the 1945 general election, and somewhat in the shadows after his unsuccessful (and costly) libel action against two obscure Nottinghamshire newspapers in which it had been suggested that he favoured revolutionary methods. By 1948, Laski, too, was a more mainstream, almost centrist figure. He led the executive's justification of peacetime conscription at the 1947 party conference—citing the need to resist Hitler before 1939. He was also foremost amongst those seeking to expel Lester Hutchinson in 1949,

---

[40] *The Times*, 18 Nov. 1946.
[41] Bevan to Huw T. Edwards, 20 June 1949 (National Library of Wales, Edwards papers).

with the backing of Herbert Morrison.[42] Laski was certainly no crypto-Communist, then or earlier. His roots were always firmly in the mass labour movement. There were, otherwise, only two left-wing figures at all on the NEC prior to the 1950 party conference. Michael Foot served between 1948 and 1950; he could make little impact, in the face of the trade-union block vote, and retired in 1950 to concentrate on editing *Tribune*. Tom Driberg was elected in 1949, but he was a lone, and eccentric voice, prone to lengthy journalistic excursions overseas. There were few premonitions on the NEC during these years of the tidal wave to the left that took place in the cantankerous party conference at Morecambe in 1952. In the Attlee period, the National Executive was yet another firm prop for the government.

The annual party conference, purportedly the instrument of policy-making as laid down in the 1918 constitution, was as docile and impotent as ever in its history in these years. Ian Mikardo pronounced it in *Tribune* to be 'as dead as the dodo'.[43] The June 1946 conference, declared the journal, with little apparent resentment, was little more than 'a victory parade' for Attlee, Bevin, Bevan, and other ministers.[44] There were some critical speeches on foreign affairs and on Palestine, but the leadership, aided by the trade-union block vote, had an easy ride. Margate in 1947 was somewhat more eventful. Bevin turned with ferocity on a motion which criticized his handling of foreign affairs, and condemned the 'stab in the back' in the House of Commons motion the previous November. His compendious speech swept all opposition aside. A rare defeat for the NEC at this conference was almost fortuitous. Aneurin Bevan, normally the darling of the delegates, was defeated over the abolition of tied cottages, which the agricultural workers demanded, as he was to be again in 1948.[45] The Margate conference

---

[42] National Executive Committee minutes, 23 Feb. 1949.
[43] *Tribune*, 28 May 1948.
[44] Ibid., 14 June 1946.
[45] Resolutions on housing at Margate conference, 1947 (PRO, HLG 102/60).

was not an easy one for Bevan who also faced criticisms of his housing programmes from Luke Fawcett of the Building Workers. Bevan loftily declared that his policy would in no way be influenced by an emotional spasm of this kind. Thus he took precisely the view of the role of party conference that Keir Hardie and MacDonald had done in the past, and that Wilson and Callaghan were to do in the future. On balance, the expected troubles at Margate (with Gladwyn Jebb of the Foreign Office carefully processing beforehand for Bevin's benefit the various critical resolutions) did not materialize.[46] Scarborough, the setting of the May 1948 party conference, was less difficult still. Bevin's foreign policy was endorsed by over 4,000,000 to 224,000, with the aid of the trade-union battalions commanded by Deakin, Williamson, and others. It was, commented the *Manchester Guardian*, 'a terribly dull conference', with little serious discussion of any issue; the *Financial Times* referred to the 'apathy, even boredom' of the debates.[47] Attempts to defend the rights of Platts-Mills were crushed. The *New Statesman* pointed out that the conference was overshadowed by the serious implications of austerity, economic crisis, and Marshall Aid; there was none of the careless rapture of 1946.[48] The 1949 party conference at Blackpool on 6–10 June was dominated by the likely advent of a general election. Criticism, therefore, was even more muted than before. At least, Cripps, the Chancellor of the Exchequer, did speak this time—in the previous three conferences, as a non-member of the NEC, he had been totally silent. The Foreign Secretary had an easier ride than ever; Dalton noted from the platform 'the almost complete absence of criticism of Ernest Bevin'. Herbert Morrison's presentation of the economic policy document, *Labour Believes in Britain*, with its clear commitment to a mixed economy and a retreat from the idea of nationalization, even of industrial assurance, was well received. The winding-up speech by Aneurin Bevan reaffirmed the place of private enterprise in a mixed economy,

---

[46] Memorandum by Gladwyn Jebb, 27 May 1947 (PRO, FO 371/67581B).
[47] *Manchester Guardian*, 21 May 1948; *Financial Times*, 22 May 1948.
[48] *New Statesman*, 15 May 1948.

albeit made more efficient by monopolies and restrictive practices commissions and the like, and by new injections of public investment. 'The language of priorities', observed Bevan, in a famous if Delphic remark, 'is the religion of socialism.'[49] The delegates were suitably overwhelmed.

The party conference, then, gave the leadership less trouble than at any other time in Labour's history. It was carefully orchestrated by Morgan Phillips and the conference rules committee, which suppressed or artfully 'wove together', Roosevelt-fashion, any critical amendments or resolutions. But in any event there was a mood of overriding harmony with what the government was doing, however electorally unpopular its financial austerities might prove to be. Thus Sam Watson for the NEC in 1949 had no qualms in asserting the right of conference to determine policy at suth a time;[50] it was the Labour left who resisted this doctrine then. The usual roles were therefore quite reversed. Major disputes in Cabinet, notably over the nationalization of steel in 1947, never reached the conference floor or the ears of the delegates. The one possible leader of rebellion might have been Aneurin Bevan, as he was to be from 1952 onwards. In fact, he had every reason for remaining loyal to the Cabinet's programme, as has been seen. Bevan in 1945–51 was the apostle of realism in both domestic and foreign policy; political freedom was, after all, 'the by-product of economic surplus',[51] which the socialist government was endeavouring to maximize. Keeping party conference docile, and minimizing the disruptive effect of theories of internal party democracy, were a vital part of that necessary process.

At all these levels, in the control of Transport House, in the command over the National Executive, and in the loyalty or docility of the annual party conference, and the grass-roots

[49] See Michael Foot, *Aneurin Bevan*, vol. i (London, 1962), pp. 259–62 for a vivid description.
[50] For some qualms about Watson's view, see Huw T. Edwards to Aneurin Bevan, 13 June 1949 (National Library of Wales, Edwards papers).
[51] Aneurin Bevan, *In Place of Fear* (London, 1952), p. 61.

constituency parties whose voice it was, an essential ingredient
for the party leader was the firm support of the Trades
Union Congress. In every segment of the party's operations,
the relationship of the trade-union leadership, especially of
the big unions, to the political wing of the movement was
closer than at any stage. The tone was set by the TUC's 'big
three', all firmly on the party right, all aggressively hostile
to left-wing or fellow-travelling deviationism whether within
the union rank and file or in parliament. Arthur Deakin of
the TGWU, Tom Williamson of the GMWU, and Will Lawther
of the NUM, commanding nearly two and a half million
votes at party conference were a massive trio who bestrode
the labour world like so many colossi. Deakin, a Welshman
who had succeeded Bevin as general secretary of the Transport Workers during the war and on a permanent basis from
1945, was bitterly anti-Communist like his predecessor, and
deeply loyal to the leadership.[52] His quarterly reports to his
union executive were a sustained commentary on the
dangers of 'Communist activity'.[53] He had his doubts over
aspects of government policy, notably proposals that there
might be a 'ceiling' on income or some other kind of wage
restraint. But he kept his protests largely submerged, and
in any case markedly changed his views from 1947 onwards.
In 1948 his was a dominant voice at the TUC urging acceptance of the government's White Paper which implied a wage
freeze. Tom Williamson, briefly an MP in 1945, took the
General and Municipal Workers even more decidedly to the
right. Like Deakin, he was a staunch supporter of Bevin's
foreign policy in all theatres. The National Union of Mineworkers, as re-formed in January 1945, contained many
regions that were traditionally militant, notably South
Wales, Kent, and Scotland. Indeed, a leading Welsh Communist, Arthur Horner, became general secretary of the NUM
in 1946. However, the president of the NUM, Will Lawther,
aided by the powerful presence of Sam Watson, leader of the
Durham miners, kept the mining block vote firmly cast for

[52] See V. L. Allen, *Trade Union Leadership* (London, 1957), for a study of
Arthur Deakin.
[53] These are included in the records of the Transport and General Workers'
Union, Modern Records Centre, University of Warwick, 126/T. & G./1/1/24–29.

the administration and the majority on the NEC. 'Unofficial' movements of miners, protesting against the policy of their right-wing leaders in Yorkshire and their left-wing leaders in South Wales, were checked, though not without some difficulty. Nor did Arthur Horner prove to be obstructive. Indeed, he was a major architect of the new Miners' Charter negotiated with Shinwell in 1946, including the long-prized objective of the five-day week and a standardized day wage structure. Horner may have been a Communist, but he was also an economic realist of independent judgement, a good Welshman, a democrat, and, in his way, a patriot. In effect, he lent the Labour government almost as much effective and consistent support as did his right-wing colleagues, Lawther and Watson. In 1947 Horner was even offered a post on the National Coal Board, which he turned down after some reflection: that would have been the Marxist poacher turned gamekeeper indeed.[54]

Another mighty union consistently supportive of the government was the Engineering Union, the AEU. Its formerly left-wing president, Jack Tanner, was now a far more centrist figure, an advocate of party loyalty and a champion of relating wage advances to improvements in productivity. In 1946 he led the opposition to the affiliation of the Communists; in 1948, he was foremost in denouncing Platts-Mills and Zilliacus, and in defending Bevin's foreign policy. The National Union of Railwaymen was somewhat less quiescent. Its general secretary, Jim Figgins, was considered to be on the left and often voted with left-wing critics at TUC and Labour Party conferences on behalf of motion for a 'socialist foreign policy'. The NUR was also, as the spokesmen of relatively low-paid workers, generally hostile to the wage-freeze policy in 1948–50 and helped to reverse it at the 1950 TUC.[55] For all that, the NUR was by no means a troublesome partner for the political leadership either. Its twelve sponsored MPs in the 1945–50 parliament (eleven after

---

[54] Arthur Horner, *Incorrigible Rebel* (London, 1960), pp. 182–4. Horner here emphasizes his good relationship with his fellow Welshman, Arthur Deakin.

[55] Records of the Executive Committee of the National Union of Railwaymen, Modern Records Centre, University of Warwick, MS 127.

February 1950) were all firmly on the party right. Its later general secretaries, Jim Campbell and Sidney Greene, presided over a steady drift rightwards. It maintained a stern opposition to the leftish postures of its small craft-union rival, ASLEF, representing the train drivers. The shop workers' union, USDAW, was also more divided in its views, and Walter Padley (elected MP for Ogmore in 1946) had to fight hard as president against Communist or far-left elements. However, with the assistance of his strongly anti-Communist general secretary, Alan Birch, he had won the battle by 1948, and USDAW joined the union giants in consistent loyalty to the government.

With the big guns usually firing in the same direction, the more radical leadership of smaller unions such as the Fire Brigade Union or craft bodies like the printers' union, NATSOPA, could be largely overridden. One clear test was the firm rejection by the TUC in 1946 of proposals, largely a legacy of the war, that Labour should form a 'progressive unity' front with the Communists. Another was the British TUC's decision not to affiliate with the Communist-led World Federation of Trade Unions. On all aspects of policy, the major union leaders regarded it as their moral duty to endorse the views of the political leaders, as mediated by the NEC. At annual party conference, the union block vote was notorious for its undemocratic, but automatic, operation, to ensure a majority for the platform, with very rare exceptions such as Bevan's defeat over tied cottages in 1947. On the NEC, the union representatives, especially in the union section chosen at the party conference, were firm in their support for moderation, and for the stern disciplining of left-wing rebels. The brief fluttering of revolt over foreign policy in November 1946, with Joe Reeves of the Co-operative Society involved, was almost a unique occasion. More important still, union leaders such as Deakin and Williamson acted as brokers between the political movement and the trade-unionists in the country. This was to prove of critical importance in March 1948 when a trade-union delegate conference managed to achieve union support for the wage-freeze proposals, which were anathema to many unionists, especially those representing the low-paid in service industries.

In 1949, the TUC managed to hold the line in upholding a wage freeze even when devaluation of the pound against the dollar pushed up the cost of living for working people. The unions were as stern in promoting industrial discipline as political. Deakin in particular was violently hostile to 'unofficial' movements against the TGWU leadership, especially among the stevedores on the docks. In the London dock strike of June–July 1949 he was as vehement as the government in urging emergency measures against unofficial strikers, including the use of troops and the prosecution of strikers if necessary. Four strike leaders (Constable, Dickens, Saunders, and Blomberg) were dismissed from the union, while others, including Jack Dash, were debarred from holding office, following a union committee of inquiry.[56] In 1950, rebellious unofficial strikers amongst the Smithfield Market drivers in June and the London busmen in September were severely rebuked.[57] It seemed at this time that, building on the new relationships of the war years, the unions were yoked with the government as quasi-employers, inextricably bound into a new corporate order, a compromise between state socialism and capitalism.

This intimate symbiosis between the unions and the Labour Party cannot be explained simply in terms of the personal authority of men such as Deakin and Lawther, however influential the offices they held. It must be admitted, of course, that the advent of more left-wing union secretaries like Frank Cousins and Jack Jones in the fifties and sixties, was to change the stance of even so loyalist a body as the Transport Workers' Union, Bevin's own creation. But the main causal factor was the community of outlook between the ideas and instincts of the Labour Party and the TUC at every stage, from 1945 onwards. The unions had important spokesmen in the government, including the dominant figure of Bevin. Indeed, twelve out of the twenty members of Attlee's Cabinet in July 1945 were of working-class origin

[56] Report and conclusions of Special Committee of Inquiry into the London Unofficial Dock Strike, 1949 (ibid., 126/T.& G./1/127); file of London dock strike (LAB 10/940).
[57] Report of the Special Committee of Inquiry into the Unofficial Strike in Smithfield meat market, 21 Aug. 1950 (loc. cit.).

(Attlee himself, Dalton, Cripps, Ede, Jowitt, Addison, Stans-gate, and Pethick-Lawrence being the eight exceptions). The unions had a significant share of the parliamentary party: they had about 120 union-sponsored MPs (34 for the miners, 17 for the TGWU being the largest groups), and 111 even after the general election of February 1950, even if many of them were silent or inarticulate. The government's responsiveness to the unions was demonstrable from the start. Among the very first measures that the government took on board in 1945 was the repeal of the hated 1927 Trades Disputes Act, with its attack on the political levy, and restrictions on the unions' right to picket or take sym-pathetic industrial action. 'Contracting out' on the 1906 basis was restored. Shawcross, the Attorney-General, dis-missed in remarkably blithe and offhand fashion suggestions from the Conservative side that the unions' unrestrained ability to picket might now lead to mass intimidation or other forms of abuse.[58] He compared them with Churchill's radio broadcast about Labour introducing a 'Gestapo'. Nationalization of major industries, full employment policies, the building up of the welfare state, the successful achieve-ment of demobilization, regional development in depressed areas—these were precisely the TUC's objectives, too. In return for union discipline and loyalty, the government left the pattern of wage negotiations to the traditional procedures of free collective bargaining, and relied for the most part on voluntary methods of wage restraint. Union Cabinet ministers such as Bevin and Isaacs resisted efforts by Shinwell and Bevan for a centralized planning of the wage structure.[59] It all worked reasonably well at least until 1950 when, in addition to discontent over Korea and other aspects of foreign and defence policy, there was mounting trade-union disaffection over the wage freeze, and also over the effects of the wartime Order 1305 which forbade strikes. Thereafter, much of the old serenity disappeared, with union leaders on the NEC protesting against attacks from Bevan and others on the left. For most of the time, though,

[58] *Parl. Deb.*, 5th ser., vol. 419, 192 ff. (12 Feb. 1946).
[59] Cabinet Conclusions, 14 Mar. 1946 and 11 Apr. 1946 (CAB 128/5); minutes of Lord President's Committee, 29 Mar. 1946 (CAB 132/1).

the Labour government's unity was based, more than at any other time in history, on the projection of a traditional programme of protection for the working class, and recognition of the unions as a new estate of the realm. There was nothing remotely resembling the disaffection of key sections of major unions and their alliance with middle-class constituency activists that appeared from 1957 onwards in the guise of CND and other forms. Secure in its mass proletarian base, Labour's army of true believers could march serenely on.

So far, the discussion has concentrated solely on the internal structure of the Labour movement—the Cabinet, the parliamentary party, the machine, the national executive, the annual conference, the relationship with the unions. But there remains to be considered the external framework as well, the extent to which the institutional fabric of the nation obstructed or assisted in Labour's socialist advance. The Labour Party's political opponents—the fortunes of Conservatives, Liberals, Nationalists, and Communists—will be examined at length in a later chapter. But what of the supposedly hostile constitutional structure itself? Did the mould here remain unbroken? At least since the events of 1931, Labour politicians had made much of the view that the system itself—the monarchy, the House of Lords, the civil service, the City and attendant capitalistic institutions, the sources of information and communication—were hopelessly biased against a Labour government. Even if the demands made by Cripps and others in the 1932-4 period for some kind of initial phase of emergency government by decree had faded away, there remained a pervasive belief among Labour supporters that their government would never receive fair play, and that the odds against a successful implementation of democratic socialism within a hostile capitalistic society were quite insuperable.

In fact, any failures by the Labour government between 1945 and 1951 can hardly be blamed on pressures from the institutional framework that it inherited. The monarchy, for instance, provided no obstacle of any significance. King George VI had viewed the advent of the meek and prosaic Mr Attlee in July 1945 with some equanimity. The King could pride himself in the belief that his influence had ensured that Bevin rather than Dalton went to the Foreign Office, even if Attlee's own testimony confirms that other factors (notably the personal rivalry between Bevin and Morrison) were really responsible. The King, of course, had scant sympathy with the socialist policies introduced by his ministers, and proclaimed in successive King's Speeches to the House of Commons. As Gaitskell observed at a later stage, the King was 'a fairly reactionary person'.[60] On the other hand, there was nothing effective he could do to obstruct Attlee's flow of legislation, even had he wished to do so. The monarchy, at the most, retained the power to choose a prime minister, if that was in doubt, and no such problem occurred between 1945 and 1951. The King, indeed, lent a veneer of tradition to such momentous changes as the transfer of power in India (with which his relative, Mountbatten, was intimately concerned), and the transformation of the old Empire into a multiracial Commonwealth of more equal partners. The King had an excellent personal relationship with Attlee, himself also a 'fairly reactionary person' in private inclinations from Haileybury days. The Prime Minister would amend the King's Speech to allow for the sovereign's speech defect.[61] Attlee was supposed to have shown emotion in public for the first time on hearing of the King's death in early 1952. Amongst the general public, King George and Queen Elizabeth remained very popular, especially after their decision to stay on in London during the wartime blitz. The royal wedding of their daughter, Princess Elizabeth, and Philip Mountbatten in 1947 was greeted with rejoicing as unrestrained as had been the jubilee of George V during the Tory years in 1935. The 165 votes cast, mainly by Labour MPs, to reduce the allowance to Princess Elizabeth on the civil list by £5,000 in December 1947 provided a very rare episode of dissent.

[60] Philip Williams, *Hugh Gaitskell* (London, 1979), p. 251.
[61] See J. W. Wheeler-Bennett, *King George VI* (London, 1958), pp. 647 ff. It might be argued that the King's relationship with Attlee was too good, since the coming royal tour of Africa influenced the timing of the 1951 general election, perhaps with fatal consequences for the Labour Party (see below, p. 480). In October 1950, 'armed violence' was substituted for 'aggression' to help the King read his speech out (A. Johnson memo., 21 Oct. 1950, CAB 21/2248).

Republicanism was never a political factor of any significance between 1945 and 1951, save for a few flourishes by mavericks such as Emrys Hughes. The Attlee years were unhindered by the existence of a hereditary monarchy, and indeed helped to democratize it slightly and thereby give it new life.

The House of Lords was naturally viewed with suspicion and resentment by the Labour Party. It was an anachronism based on heredity; it contained a built-in right-wing majority. It still retained substantial powers, notably the ability to delay a bill, other than a money bill, that had been passed through the Commons for a period of up to two years. As will be seen, in due course, the government introduced a new Parliament Bill in the autumn of 1947 to curb the period of delay to one year only, in order to facilitate the passage of steel nationalization before the next general election. This measure became law in 1949. At the same time, it cannot be seriously claimed that the government was greatly embarrassed by the presence of the upper house between 1945 and 1951. The seventy-odd measures of legislation passed in the 1945–6 session alone make the point. A vital factor was the authority and respect attached to Lord Addison, the Leader of the Lords and a political figure of great seniority who had served intermittently in Cabinet since 1916.[62] In his earlier years, Addison had been sometimes touchy and abrasive, and not always beloved by his civil servants. In his late seventies, buoyed up by a happy second marriage and his friendship with Attlee, Addison was a benign and genial figure who handled the passage of controversial legislation with much dexterity, while maintaining an atmosphere of cordiality in the upper house. He built up a warm personal relationship with Lord Salisbury, the Leader of the Conservative peers, and with other political opponents such as Lord Swinton (with whom he had served in government in 1921). He also welded together the small band of Labour peers— who included such talented figures as Pakenham and Listowel, as well as veterans such as Stansgate, Pethick-Lawrence, Ammon, Nathan, and Hall. He acted as mentor and guide to the Labour peers in keeping the government's legislation flowing smoothly in a chamber nominally hostile to everything

[62] See Kenneth and Jane Morgan, *Portrait of a Progressive*, pp. 252 ff.

that the Labour Party represented. Pakenham was startled
when in full flow to receive a curt note from Addison in-
structing him to take his hands out of his pockets.[63] Addison's
qualities were considerable. But the main reason, of course,
why the Lords presented no serious difficulty to the Attlee
government lay in the political situation. It was impossible
to argue that a government with a majority of more than
150 in the Commons did not have a mandate to pass measures
such as nationalization, social reform, and the like. Nor did
the Tory peers seriously argue the point. They did not offer
any real resistance to government legislation until a lengthy
fight over the Transport Nationalization Bill in 1947. Much
more trouble came, as will be seen, over iron and steel
nationalization in 1948-9 but this issue was shrewdly chosen
since it was known that government supporters were divided
amongst themselves and that there had been lengthy disagreements within the Cabinet. Nor did the public seem at
all enthusiastic. Otherwise, the Lords roused themselves
only over the relatively non-party issue of the 1948 Criminal
Justice Bill, which they severely amended, including the
striking out of Silverman's backbench amendment to have
capital punishment suspended for five years. The government
gave way, a major factor being the sympathy with the Lords'
point of view of Morrison, Ede, and other ministers. Otherwise, the Lords took their medicine like sportsmen and
gentlemen between 1945 and 1951 and caused little trouble.
In return, they were subjected to no internal reform of any
kind. There were somewhat desultory negotiations in 1947-8
between Conservative, Labour, and Liberal figures on a
possible overhaul of the composition of the Lords.
Clement Davies, the Liberal leader, submitted plans for
a new second chamber of 300, with perhaps 100 'Lords
in Parliament' (male or female) nominated on a life-
membership basis.[64] Addison reported to Mackenzie King,
the Canadian Prime Minister, that agreement had been
reached on abolishing the hereditary right to attend and

    [63] R. J. Minney, *Viscount Addison: Leader of the Lords* (London, 1958),
pp. 43-4.
    [64] Memorandum by Clement Davies, 1947 (National Library of Wales,
Clement Davies papers, C/1/35).

vote, and on a fairer distribution between the parties in the upper house.[65] But these talks were always speculative and led nowhere. On the powers of the Lords, there was no agreement. Neither Attlee nor Morrison considered the reform of the Lords' composition to be a leading priority. Morrison told Clement Davies that 'we should try to maintain continuity and not set up something new and different from the past'.[66] No change in the composition of the Lords occurred until—significantly enough under a Conservative administration—the passage of the bill of 1957 to establish life peerages.

The influence of the civil service between 1945 and 1951 is a more difficult subject. Again, Labour mythology had it that a right-wing, public-school-trained bureaucracy would secretly undermine or resist radical reforms proposed by a socialist government. 'Jack Wilkes' (George Strauss MP) voiced this fear in *Tribune* early on, and Edward Bridges complained to Leslie Rowan, the Prime Minister's secretary, about attacks on the Cabinet Office by J. P. W. Mallalieu in the Labour press.[67] This is a theme hard to uncover since the evidence varies somewhat from department to department. A weaker minister such as Isaacs at Labour or Wilmot at Supply (and perhaps Wilkinson at Education) was more susceptible to civil service dictation than a powerful figure like Aneurin Bevan, who found his permanent under-secretary, Sir Arthur Rucker, to be an invaluable ally in framing and forcing through the National Health Service in 1946. On balance, evidence of civil service obstruction of the activities and policies of the Labour government is very hard to uncover. There were, indeed, many instances of radical impulses at work within the civil service machine. One important instance, perhaps unexpectedly, is in the Treasury where Dalton and then Cripps worked closely with such progressive advisers as Robert Hall, a man with an active

---

[65] Addison to Mackenzie King, 9 Apr. 1948 (Bodleian, Addison papers, Box 137); cf. *Parliament Bill, 1947: Agreed Statement on Conclusion of Party Leaders,* Cmd. 7380 (1948).

[66] Clement Davies memorandum, 1947 (Davies papers, C/1/35).

[67] *Tribune,* 11 Jan. 1946; Bridges to Leslie Rowan, 19 Nov. 1946 (Dalton papers, 9/2/68), referring to an article in *Tribune* on 15 Nov. 1946.

socialist background, R. W. ('Otto') Clarke, and Austin Robinson. There was, in any event, in the Treasury as elsewhere in Whitehall, a powerful commitment to economic change and planned reconstruction after the stagnation of the thirties, and the new initiatives of the war years. This was even more emphatic amongst the Keynesians in the Economic Section of the Cabinet Office, where James Meade, a member of the old XYZ group, was director until late 1947. In the argument over whether to devalue in 1949, younger officials such as Robert Hall and 'Otto' Clarke finally won the day over those like Bridges, the permanent secretary to the Treasury, and Cobbold, the Governor of the Bank of England, who advised the Chancellor to resist devaluation and to cut public expenditure severely instead. That did not prevent Cripps, on one excitable occasion, telling Gaitskell that his Treasury officials were all old-fashioned liberals who were trying to prevent him from carrying out what Gaitskell termed 'socialist [sic] policies'.[68] This is a judgement by Cripps for which neither the available printed evidence nor the recollections of many of those involved lends support. Elsewhere, there were important progressive influences in other departments, notably the cases of John Maude at the Ministry of Education under Ellen Wilkinson, with his determination to raise the school-leaving age, and Andrew Cohen, the so-called 'King of Africa', at the African division of the Colonial Office under Creech-Jones.[69]

Two areas of somewhat wider interest are the Foreign Office and the Cabinet Office. In the Foreign Office, there were powerful voices calling for an implementation of traditional policies, including the maintenance of Britain's imperial power in the Middle East and a hostile attitude towards the role of the Soviet Union. Sir Orme Sargent, even more than his predecessor as permanent undersecretary, Sir Alexander Cadogan, whom he succeeded in early 1946, was an influential and conservative voice. But the instincts of Sargent and other civil servants and diplomats

---

[68] Hugh Gaitskell's diary, 3 Aug. 1949.
[69] See letter by Lord Redcliffe-Maude to the *Guardian*, 28 Aug. 1982; Robert Blake, *A History of Rhodesia* (London, 1977), pp. 250 ff. Cohen became under-secretary at the Colonial Office in charge of African affairs in 1947, at the age of 38.

chimed in precisely with the inclinations of Bevin and Attlee themselves. It would be impossible to argue, for instance, that the policy of the Labour government in the Middle East, and more especially Palestine, was the consequence of a pro-Arab lobby of Foreign Office officials forcing their views insidiously on a reluctant or confused minister. Bevin was just not that kind of person; never in his career had he been anyone's puppet or poodle. He evolved, in his curious, intuitive fashion, his own very clear ideas, and he pushed them through with regard to Germany, Greece, the relationship with the United States, western defence, and other crucial matters. There were Foreign Office voices in 1949-50 calling for a more cordial British response to the movement for European integration, and to the 1950 Schuman Plan for a European coal and steel community, but Bevin and the Labour government reached their own, largely negative, conclusions. There was, in any case, a range of views within the Foreign Office (as within the Treasury), from liberals such as Gladwyn Jebb and Frank Roberts urging in 1946 the need for renewed attempts to achieve a viable working relationship with the Soviet Union,[70] through the open-minded pragmatism of Strang, Makins, or Warner, to the more ideological interpretations offered by Brimelow. The cold war was not a creation of the Foreign Office mind; nor were the latter's views predictable or monolithic. Bevin, as ever, was his own man, and the government took its own decisions, in the light of what it felt was Stalin's intransigence and the international realities.

The Cabinet Office had two important secretaries in this period, Sir Edward Bridges (who served until early 1947, as well as being permanent secretary to the Treasury), and then Sir Norman Brook. Bridges had strong views on streamlining the machinery of government. This brought him into frequent conflict with Morrison who accused Bridges of wanting him to be over-dependent on the Treasury and to

---

[70] e.g. Jebb memorandum on Truman doctrine, 19 Mar. 1947 (FO 371/ 67582A). For instances of Brimelow's more ideological approach, see memoranda in FO 371/56780 (on the Russian reactions to Churchill's Fulton, Missouri, speech, Feb. 1946) and minute of 8 Mar. 1946 in FO 371/56780 (on Anglo-Soviet relations, 1946).

'tack the economic planners (like Plowden) into the Cabinet Office'.[71] With Dalton, Bridges had a good relationship, as evidenced by his being dispatched to Washington in late 1945 to renegotiate the American loan after Keynes had run into difficulties. Norman Brook, another powerful intellect, had much influence in preparing the framework of emergency government in 1945-6 so that the government would be equipped to deal with possible industrial disturbances, but this was strictly in line with government views, including those of the key figure of Bevin. As secretary, Brook sent in a stream of proposals, mostly on the cautious side, to Attlee in 1948-9 on topics including capital punishment, the nationalization of steel, and the stimulation of the export trade.[72] But it would be impossible again to argue that right-wing influence within the Cabinet Office pushed Attlee and his colleagues in a conservative direction they did not intend. Indeed, the civil service expertise and practical knowledge afforded by experienced operators such as Bridges or Brook were vital in steering the government through many desperate crises, notably the near-disaster over the convertibility of sterling in August 1947. To these should be added the imperturbable, ubiquitous figure of Leslie Rowan, Attlee's principal private secretary, who had served Churchill in a similar capacity during the war. Rowan's calm efficiency became legendary in Whitehall, while his chairmanship of the Overseas Negotiations Committee played a crucial role in extracting the country from the terrifying balance of payments deficits of 1947. In return for its loyalty, the civil service was not subjected to any significant change. Here again, Attlee and his colleagues were institutionally conservative. No major restructuring of the civil service, or of its relationship to government departments, took place between 1945 and 1951. There was the novelty of Plowden and the Economic Planning Council in the summer of 1947,

[71] Morrison to Edward Bridges, 8 July 1947 (Nuffield College, Morrison papers).
[72] Brook to Attlee, 21 July 1948 (PREM 8/839) on capital punishment; Brook to Attlee, 29 May 1948 (PREM 8/1489, pt. 2) on steel nationalization; Brook to Attlee, 30 June 1949 on exports (PREM 8/1412). Also instructive is Brook to Attlee, 25 Feb. 1950, on the extent to which Labour should continue in office after the 1950 general election (PREM 8/1166).

but they, too, were brought within the comforting aegis of the Treasury by Cripps by the end of the year. Bevin did nothing to overhaul the composition or the recruitment to the Foreign Office, despite incessant sniping from the left. The civil service, like the monarchy and the House of Lords, cannot be made a scapegoat for the non-fulfilment of the socialist millennium.

The City, and financial institutions in general, played an even more sinister role in Labour demonology, inevitably so for a professedly socialist party with memories of 1931 and the covert activities of Montague Norman and the House of Morgan well in mind. Assaults on the 'spivs' or parasites of the City were grist to the mill of Labour left-wingers, including Aneurin Bevan on occasion, during the years after 1945. Of course, the City was unsympathetic to national-ization and other assaults on private enterprise, to the redistributive tone of Hugh Dalton's budgets, and to the all-encompassing power of the state. Dalton wrote, in scornful Lloyd-Georgian terms, of the apprehensions of the 'flapping penguins' in Threadneedle Street, who failed to understand the logic of his cheap money policy or such initiatives as the flotation of 'Daltons'. On the other hand, the City, no less than the civil service, was neither monolithic nor blindly ideological. Neither the City nor the central clearing houses wanted a return to the stagnation of the inter-war years. There was much enthusiasm for reconstruction and the formation of new capital within the City also, especially as it felt assured by the collaborative attitude taken towards private industry and the business world shown by Cripps at the Board of Trade. There were always minority elements within the business world which were distinctly sympathetic to Labour, like the economists who hovered round Nicholas Davenport at Hinton Manor. There were also businessmen such as Lords Latham and Southwood in the '1944 Associa-tion', friendly with younger politicians such as Gaitskell and Jay; they were headed by the former Labour MP, Sir Valentine Crittall, later Lord Braintree. This body lived on, retaining its links with Gaitskell, until it dissolved in 1960.[73]

[73] Material in Gaitskell papers (Nuffield College F/24), especially G. de Freitas to Attlee, 6 Nov. 1945, and Attlee's reply. When the 1944 Association was

By 1947, certainly, the financial press was full of criticisms of socialist policies and of Labour mismanagement. The *Financial Times, The Economist*, and the *Investors' Chronicle* had all conceived a powerful hostility towards Hugh Dalton. It was especially virulent in the case of Geoffrey Crowther, editor of *The Economist*, once thought to be a distinctly left-wing figure. The financial press rejoiced in Dalton's progressive, agonizing discomfiture in 1947, culminating in his resignation from the Treasury in November. Cripps and his 'once and for all' (and very mild) capital levy in his 1948 budget provoked some exaggerated abuse in City circles, too.[74] But relations were much restored during the Cripps regime, and the City's view of the Labour government throughout was by no means one of unthinking Pavlovian hostility, as left-wing critics ironically noted. The Stock Exchange showed few signs of politically-motivated speculation against a Labour government, especially one that declined to tax dividends or undistributed profits to any marked extent. The devaluation crisis in 1949 was brought about by an American recession and speculation in Belgium and other foreign lands, not by the activities of financiers at home. When the Labour government fell in October 1951, there was an immediate fall in share prices which took several months to reverse itself.[75] Despite the temporary campaigning against nationalization by 'Aims of Industry' in the 1950 general election, the City did not seriously impair Labour policies either. So far as the government was obstructed by capitalist pressures in terms of speculation and capricious movements of capital, sluggish investment and lack of business co-operation at home, it had the weapons in its own hands to redress the situation. It could not take refuge in anti-capitalist demonology, if it refused to employ them. Nor did it do so.

Beyond the financial world, the institutional forces of at least the early phase after 1945 were broadly sympathetic to

wound up in 1960, Raymond Mais declared that it had lost its way by becoming 'too political' in the fifties.

[74] *Financial Times*, 7 Apr. 1948.
[75] Ibid., 3 Nov. 1951.

Labour. The post-war mood will be considered at more length, in social, cultural, and psychological terms, in a later chapter. But it may be noted that, at least at the outset, the newspaper press contained broad elements of support for the government, despite Bevan's celebrated attack at a rally before the 1948 conference at Scarborough on 'the most prostituted press in the world . . . owned by a gang of millionaires'.[76] There were the pro-Labour tabloids, the brilliantly effective *Daily Mirror*, and the duller, union-sponsored *Daily Herald*, to counter the Tory mouthpieces of Beaverbrook, Rothermere, and Kemsley. Of the three serious daily newspapers, the *Manchester Guardian* was broadly in sympathy with the government throughout, in line with the C. P. Scott 'Lib-Lab' tradition, while its editor since 1944, A. P. Wadsworth, was a great admirer of Ernest Bevin and a critic of Churchill. *The Times* was also for a time remarkably pro-Labour in 1945–7 under the editorship of R. M. Barrington-Ward (who died in 1948). It began to change its tone (and then only partially) during the economic troubles of 1947. By 1950, however, it had clearly veered towards its traditional allegiance to the Conservatives. In the middle range, the Liberal *News Chronicle*, like its sister the London evening paper, the *Star*, may be counted as broadly sympathetic to Labour (and most certainly anti-Tory) during these six years, especially under the editorship of Gerald Barry. If its leading articles offered a somewhat sententious form of Liberalism, it featured such pro-Labour journalists as Ian Mackay and Robert Lynd; its famous cartoonist, Vicky, was a committed socialist; while the 'Arkub' strip cartoon for children was deftly orchestrated by the veteran Labour MP and cartographer, J. F. Horrabin. Of the Sunday press, the *Observer*, especially when edited by the literary critic, Ivor Brown, up to 1948, was generally on the moderate left, while the *People* and, even more *Reynolds News* (which featured columns by left-wing journalists such as Tom Driberg MP and the far-left foreign affairs specialist, Gordon Schaffer) were firmly pro-Labour. The extent to which the press was political at all in this period requires some care in definition; it has been suggested that after 1945 the old-style 'political press' of

[76] *News Chronicle*, 17 May 1948.

nineteenth-century usage effectively disappeared.[77] But it may reasonably be concluded that the fourth estate, like other more established estates of the realm, viewed the onset of a Labour government in 1945 with some equanimity, and a fair measure of enthusiasm. This applied also to the weeklies. In addition to Kingsley Martin's highly individualist, but clearly left-wing, *New Statesman*, and the generally loyalist if radical *Tribune* (with Jennie Lee, Michael Foot, and George Strauss on its editorial board, and George Orwell amongst its writers until 1946), even *The Economist* was sympathetic to Labour down to mid-1947. Geoffrey Crowther, though critical of Dalton's performance at the Treasury, gave such innovations as the early nationalization measures and the National Health Service an enthusiastic welcome. Here, too, the omens were not unfavourable.

The general view that emerges, then, is of the institutional framework of the time, both in terms of internal party cohesion and external structural restraints, as being generally favourable to Attlee's government at the start of its tenure of power. Naturally, like all governments, it found the unity did not last, though its 'state of grace' certainly endured much longer than the twelve months initially allowed himself by President Mitterrand when he launched the new socialist administration in France in 1981. The odds were not unduly weighted against the Labour government. On balance, they were generally in their favour. By 1948, the picture was beginning to change, as it usually does in time with all governments. As will be seen, the official Conservative opposition was becoming revitalized and a more effective alternative. The whole national psychology showed some sign of changing at that period, too. Within the Labour Party itself there was more grass-roots disaffection building up over these six years, over foreign policy above all, but also on such issues as wage restraint and the fate of Zilliacus, than the anodyne record of party conferences would suggest. Sir Hartley Shawcross hinted as much to Attlee in 1947.[78] The evidence of one major study, however, indicates that

---

[77] Stephen Koss, *The Rise and Fall of the Political Press in Britain* (London, 1981), p. 17.

[78] Shawcross to Attlee, 1 Aug. 1947 (Bodleian, Attlee papers, Box 9).

only in 88 constituency parties was there anything like a consistent pattern of radicalism or criticism.[79] In general, the constituency parties lined up alongside the unions in demonstrating party unity. There was also growing trade-union rebellion visible by 1948, not only amongst far-left elements within the dockers or the power workers but amongst more mainstream unionists including the engineers and the railwaymen. The disaffection that led to the constituency parties' revolt against the National Executive, from 1952 onwards, and the mass union revolt behind some aspects of Bevanism in the fifties can be detected in embryo beneath the surface façade of unity in 1945-51. So, too, can the infiltration of Communist or Trotskyist elements within the Labour League of Youth, which led to its being disbanded later on. What can be said is that these forces for discord and factionalism were more than countered by the elements of harmony between 1945 and 1951. There was a genuine partnership within the Labour movement, and a relative lack of serious obstruction in the wider institutional fabric beyond. To a degree unique in the history of British Labour governments, and indeed unusual in the record of any administration this century, there was a background of consensus for the British variant of 'socialism in one country'.

[79] Jonathan Wood, 'The Labour Left in the Constituency Labour Parties, 1945-51' (University of Warwick, unpublished MA thesis, 1977).

3

Priorities and Policies:
Nationalization and Industry

The public ownership of the means of production and distribution had been prominent in the Labour Party's programme since Sidney Webb's famous socialist clause had been
inserted into the party constitution in 1918. In the early
thirties, it was renumbered as 'Clause Four', and 'exchange'
was added to the list, referring specifically to the joint-
stock banks. But until 1945, the meaning of this commitment to nationalization in practical terms was most uncertain.
In the twenties, Labour made little of the subject. Only the
nationalization of the coal-mines appeared on party manifestos down to 1929, and the second MacDonald government elected in that year made no effort to implement it.
The only schemes in existence for the precise method of
nationalization of coal were those drafted by Frank Hodges,
then secretary of the Miners' Federation of Great Britain,
and by the economic historian, R. H. Tawney, at the time of
the Sankey Commission back in 1919–20.[1] Otherwise,
Labour tended to regard nationalization more as an aspiration, of a somewhat utopian kind, than a specific method of
tackling economic and industrial problems. After 1931,
the party's commitment became far more precise. There were
documents such as the TUC's *Public Control and Regulation
of Industry and Trade* in 1932, with which Bevin was closely
identified. There were more detailed studies of the nationalization of major industries conducted by Labour Party study
groups and such research organizations as the Fabian
Research Bureau. In addition, there were some more concrete
models that emerged in the thirties, such as the proposals
for the public ownership of electricity supply offered by the

---

[1] Frank Hodges, *Nationalisation of the Mines* (London, 1920); R. H. Tawney,
'The Nationalization of the Coal Industry' (Labour Party pamphlet, 1919),
reprinted in Rita Hinden (ed.), *R. H. Tawney: the Radical Tradition* (Pelican
edn., London, 1966), pp. 123–43.

McGowan committee appointed in 1936, and the Central Electricity Board that was already in existence. *Labour's Immediate Programme* in 1937 outlined a specific list of industries or utilities ready for nationalization, a list which closely anticipated *Let us Face the Future* in 1945. It itemized the Bank of England, the coal-mines, electricity, gas, railways, and 'other transport services', together with vaguer statements about the public ownership of land. Significantly, machine tools, and iron and steel, both discussed earlier, were now left out. The joint-stock banks, much in the public eye after the events of 1931, were also quietly omitted, despite the *Programme*'s bold statement of the need for a Labour government to control the levers of finance.

During the war, there was some watering down of the 1937 programme. Land nationalization disappeared altogether, in favour of the ideas for the control of land use and development put forward in the 1942 Uthwatt report and later implemented by Lewis Silkin in the 1945 government. Nationalization of the joint-stock banks continued to be an absentee. However, a notable addition, as has been seen, in April 1945 was the nationalization of iron and steel, following the unanimous adoption of the Mikardo resolution in favour of public ownership at the 1944 party conference. Morrison's reluctance was overruled by Dalton and others. In addition, the war years saw sweeping moves towards the control or near-nationalization of major industries, including coal, electricity (already mostly in public hands), and shipping. There was also the Heyworth Committee with its eventual report in December 1945 calling for the public ownership of the gas industry, and further schemes under the 'Swinton Plan' for non-competing public airways corporations. The 1945 Labour manifesto, therefore, contained a precise and unambiguous list of industries and services ready for ownership by the nation. Indeed, the single most striking difference between the Labour Party's programme in 1945 and that in all subsequent elections down to 1979 is the centrality of nationalization in its overall grand design.

The purpose of nationalization, though, was less clearly outlined in 1945. Although earlier proposals, especially for coal nationalization, had concentrated on the relationship of public ownership to better industrial relations, to considerations of social justice and perhaps the redistribution of wealth, the emphasis in 1945 tended to be largely on considerations of efficiency, on ageing industries such as coal or the railways which had 'failed the nation', or else on institutions such as the Bank of England or Cable and Wireless which must be integrated for planning purposes with a national policy of investment and re-equipment. The economic rather than the social rationale for nationalization predominated in Labour rhetoric in 1945, especially when applied to more modern industries such as civil aviation. Gaitskell rammed home this point in his controversial lecture, *Socialism and Nationalisation*, in 1956.[2] In any case Labour did not wish to imply that it was interested only in nationalizing failures for sociological or humanitarian reasons, even if that was often the impression made on the neutral observer.

There was, then, a clear list in 1945. To some degree, there also existed a clear operative model. This was Herbert Morrison's blueprint, outlined in *Socialization and Transport* in 1933, based on his own plan for the London Passenger Transport Board in 1931, for an autonomous public corporation. In the face of the opposition of Bevin and other trade-union leaders, Morrison had made this the basis of the nationalization schemes due to be carried out by a future Labour government. Draft proposals in 1933 for a National Transport Board, Electricity Board, and Coal Board translated the Morrisonian vision of the public corporation into practical form. Twelve years later in 1945, there was little significant change to report. Morrison's corporate model has been much criticized since, not only from the far left. It has been condemned for effecting only a technical or superficial change in the traditional forms of private ownership, replacing an irresponsible board of private capitalists with an almost equally autocratic board of public bureaucrats. But it should be said that Labour's strategists had come up with no credible alternative scheme. Morrison's vision held the field alone, while there were already existing examples of the public corporation in the form of the British Broadcast-

---

[2] Hugh Gaitskell, *Socialism and Nationalisation* (Fabian Tract 300, July 1956), pp. 18 ff.

ing Corporation, the Central Electricity Board, and the London Passenger Transport Board dating from before the war. Certainly, there was no coherent scheme for workers' control in existence; indeed, as will be noted, the unions themselves did not welcome a system which made them half-bosses and compromised their historic function of defending the wage-earner against his employer. Men like Deakin and Williamson were content with a number of unionists being placed on the boards of nationalized industries. Morrison alone, therefore, had had the sustained intellectual energy to provide a workable model of public ownership. In introducing the Civil Aviation Bill on 6 May 1946 he was to provide a public justification for the corporate method of nationalization.[3]

The specifics of Labour's proposed public ownership schemes remained vague in the extreme, as Shinwell amongst others was later frequently to complain. The details of organizational structure, finance, the compensation of private stockholders, pricing policy, the system of consultation with the workers, the relation to the consumer, domestic and industrial—all were left studiously vague. Walter Citrine, secretary of the TUC and later head of the Electricity Board, was justified in complaining that the method by which industries would in fact be taken into public ownership 'had not been thought out with any precision'.[4] The answers were still being worked out piecemeal in many cases long after 1951. Even so, in the heady atmosphere of 1945, with a background of wartime collectivism and controls on which to draw, and widespread goodwill for a fundamental break with the old, discredited system of capitalist ownership, these details did not seem greatly to matter. The Labour government in 1945 was bent on implementing socialism as it conceived it, in place of the stagnation and unemployment of the past. Nationalization was generally agreed to be the vital mechanism in the achievement of this historic objective.

Between 1945 and 1949 a steady stream of measures formed the centre-piece of the government's programme.

---

[3] *Parl. Deb.*, 5th ser., vol. 422, 604–5 (6 May 1946).
[4] Lord Citrine, *Two Careers* (London, 1967), p. 263.

The Bank of England, civil aviation, cable and wireless, and coal in 1946; railways, long-distance road transport, and electricity in 1947; gas in 1948; iron and steel in 1949—this was a roll-call of achievement which, it was believed, would bring new lustre to the socialist cause. To these ought to be added the Cotton (Centralized Buying) Act of 1947, and the major powers of development at home and abroad included in the 1947 Town and Country Planning Act, and the Colonial Development Corporation. In almost every case, something like the corporate model was introduced; internal democratization was kept strictly limited.

However, until 1948 when the general momentum in favour of nationalization slowed down, with the manifesto pledges of 1945 largely fulfilled apart from iron and steel, and with markedly less enthusiasm for pushing on with public ownership into new fields, the precise method of nationalization actually adopted provoked remarkably little argument within the Labour Party. The trade unions were content to ensure that basic union demands for the workers in specific industries, such as the Miners' Charter drafted by the National Union of Mineworkers, were put into effect. Beyond that, there was little pressure for innovation, and the Morrisonian corporate prototype was not significantly challenged. The unions appeared content with their subsidiary role, satisfied that, under a Labour government, a nationalized industrial sector, however it was run, would ensure economic advance and social justice for the wage-earner and his family. When Sir Stafford Cripps, in a moment of appalling frankness in October 1946, observed that a major reason why workers' control or even copartnership could not be considered for nationalized industry was because the workers as a whole were not competent, at least in the realms of management, this gaffe provoked remarkably little uproar.[5] In practice, Deakin, Lawther, and other union leaders had no aspirations for a managerial role, as distinct from the indirect corporate association implied in such bodies as the Dock Labour Board. They wished the adversarial character of labour–management relations to continue. In effect, therefore, criticisms of the workers' incompetence

[5] *The Times*, 28 Oct. 1946.

or ignorance, however tactless (and, of course, quite un-proven) could be ignored. The general test lay in economic criteria, that major industries and services in private hands had 'failed the nation', and should be brought under public ownership because that necessarily implied public control and economic planning. The basis was technocratic, not doctrinaire. Even in 1945, most advocates of public owner-ship were drawing a line between the method of nationaliza-tion, and the objective of socialism. The one was short-term, instrumental, and probably finite. The other was long-term, ideological, and perhaps postponed to an indefinite future.

The first wave of bills came in the lengthy session of 1945–6, processed by the Cabinet's Legislation Committee under the chairmanship of Morrison. This included the Bank of England, civil aviation, cable and wireless, and coal-mining. By the autumn of 1946, all were on the statute book, as part of the seventy-five measures that the government swept through in that astonishing first year of socialist rule; electricity was shortly to follow. None occasioned any major dissent. The government, armed with a huge majority, piloted these complex measures through both houses with much ease.

The Bank of England enjoyed a unique role in Labour demonology, with memories of Montague Norman's free-wheeling operations in 1931 vividly in mind. Hugh Dalton, the Chancellor of the Exchequer, who had special respon-sibility for the nationalization of the Bank, had been a junior minister in MacDonald's second ministry and had, therefore, a keen personal involvement with that earlier crisis. In fact, from the start it was clear that Dalton's pro-posed reform was essentially technical and institutional.[6] In no respect was it intended to lead to an overhaul of British central financial institutions, let alone of the banking and clearing-house system. His early pronouncements in August 1945 indicated the limitations of his proposals, as well as hinting at the weakness of the advertised National Invest-ment Board which had loomed so large in Labour's financial

[6] See Dalton, *High Tide and After*, pp. 32–50; R. A. Brady, *Crisis in Britain* (Cambridge, 1950), pp. 43 ff.

blueprints in the thirties. The latter, as visualized, seemed to be little more than a revamped version of the old Capital Investment Board, instead of the broad planning instrument contemplated before the war by the young economists of the XYZ group and by Douglas Jay in *The Socialist Case* (1938). The main changes in the Bank of England proposed by Dalton's Act—which passed the Commons swiftly enough before the end of the autumn session in 1945—were that former bank stock should be exchanged for government stock, at 3 per cent interest only, and that a Court of Directors, consisting of a Governor, Deputy Governor, and sixteen directors nominated by the Chancellor of the Exchequer, should replace the old Court of Directors appointed by private stockholders. Beyond this, Clause 4 of the Act empowered the Treasury to give directives to the Bank, as necessary, 'in the public interest'. It was a moderate enough form of public control. In fact, the structure and personnel of the Bank's Court of Directors did not show much change. Only one of the directors, George Gibson, a trade-unionist, was a direct Labour nominee—and, as luck would have it, he had to resign during the furore over the Lynskey corruption tribunal in 1949. There was no real control exercised over the clearing banks, nor over capital movements internally or externally. Partly for this reason, the Conservatives offered only token opposition. Indeed, Churchill himself, with memories of 1925 and 1931 fresh in his mind, declared in his opening speech as Leader of the Opposition in August 1945 that he would not oppose the bill. The Opposition put up little fight on the second reading; one unorthodox Tory, Robert Boothby, actually voted with the government. The main purpose of the nationalization of the Bank of England was as a reassuring therapy for Labour members, a symbol that the bank could no longer sabotage a Labour government as it was felt to have done in 1931. In practical terms, Lord Catto, a very conservative figure, remained scarcely less independent as Governor after nationalization than he had done under the old regime. For the government, real control over financial movements lay rather with measures such as the 1947 Exchange Controls Act and its successors, with the operations of the Capital Issues Committee, and with broader curbs on investment through local and national government, rather than through the limited changes involved in nationalizing the Bank. As has been noted already, the private joint-stock banks were left quite unaffected. Bank nationalization, wrote Nicholas Davenport in his memoirs, was 'a great non-event'.[7] At the very start, therefore, the limits to the government's programme were apparent, along with the qualifications attached to public ownership within an economy that, especially with hard times forecast by Keynes and other experts, was expected to remain largely in private hands.

Cable and Wireless was a second measure of public ownership that went through in 1946. It was a largely technical proposal which aroused little public interest. The opposition did not divide on the second reading. That did not prevent Dalton, when introducing it on 21 May, injecting a note of drama—'Yesterday it was coal; today it is cables. The Socialist advance, therefore, continues.'[8] The idea of setting up an integrated telecommunications network between Britain and the Dominions had been accepted in a Commonwealth conference during the war in 1944. As Dalton pointed out, the Dominions had expressed concern that a public utility corporation should be set up in Britain, for the co-ordination of imperial cable and wireless services. The main change now was that the operating company should be owned in its entirety, amounting to some thirty million of £1 shares, by the government-controlled company. In fact there was already a government share of £2,600,000 in the equity so no new principle was being introduced. There was also the factor, highly acceptable to the Conservative benches, that Commonwealth interests dictated such a move. The transfer, therefore, of Cable and Wireless Ltd, a company set up in 1929, into public hands, was a swift and painless operation which produced again little or no dissent or debate.

The nationalization of civil aviation, which also took effect in the 1945–6 session, was again straightforward and relatively uncontroversial. Wartime plans emanating from the Conservative Lord Swinton had already made out the case

---

[7] Nicholas Davenport, *Memoirs of a City Radical*, p. 160.
[8] *Parl. Deb.*, 5th ser., vol. 422, 201 (21 May 1946).

for an integration of the smaller companies emerging in the thriving field of international and internal air services. BOAC had existed since March 1940, a product of the last phase of 'Tory socialism' of Neville Chamberlain's government. Morrison, who introduced the Civil Aviation Bill in May 1946, took pleasure in citing former Tory arguments against the idea of wasteful private competition in air services.[9] The transition from the Swinton scheme to the government's fully centralized system was a small one. The main feature was the Labour government's decision to create three new corporations, a remodelled BOAC, the British European Airways Corporation and a South American Airways Corporation (later to be merged with BOAC in 1949). The bill went through the Commons without much trouble, though there were some harsh words from Frank Bowles (disappointed, perhaps, at failing to gain office) and some Labour backbench technocrats in the party's Civil Aviation group at the expense of Lord Winster and Ivor Thomas, the ministers handling the bill.[10] There was some cross-voting in the committee stages, and Winster was later to be removed to another department. There was some temporary protest from Swinton and other Tory peers in the House of Lords. Addison told Dalton with glee of the 'terrific hub-bub' generated amongst their lordships by the Civil Aviation proposals, with 'Swinton & co. gesticulating in incoherent indignation'.[11] Despite this, the bill swept through with ease. In later years, the overwhelming merits of the forms of civil aviation ownership adopted seemed somewhat less clear. The Cabinet's Civil Aviation Committee in 1948, chaired by Addison, criticized some aspects of the new arrangements, notably the lack of co-ordination between the Ministries of Civil Aviation and Supply, and between both and the newly-formed BOAC.[12] There were also criticisms of the purchasing policy followed by the new Corporations, especially in relation to heavy passenger aircraft. Even so, there was again general goodwill towards a new nationalization

[9] *Parl. Deb.*, 5th ser., vol. 422, 201, 596 ff. (6 May 1946).
[10] Letter from Ivor Bulmer-Thomas to the author, 19 Oct. 1982.
[11] Hugh Dalton diaries, 1 Nov. 1945 (Dalton papers, I/33).
[12] Cabinet Conclusions, 15 July 1948 (CAB 128/13).

scheme, felt to be necessary for an integrated and efficient transportation system, while the Commonwealth registered their warm enthusiasm. Addison, as chairman of the Civil Aviation Committee and (until October 1947) Dominions Secretary, monitored both aspects. There were impressive physical legacies, too, such as the new London airport at Heath Row.

Another measure that may conveniently be taken here, which again produced a broad consensus of agreement and generated little controversy, was the nationalization of electricity. This finally was to pass on to the statute book in August 1947. The Central Electricity Board, created as far back as 1926, already offered an acceptable model for corporate public control, with the wholesale distribution of electricity taken over by a public body. Beyond that, the McGowan Committee in 1936 had set out an unassailable technical case for public ownership on grounds of efficiency, as a way to integrate the national grid system and ensure an effective nation-wide distribution of energy from electricity, with an interconnected transmission system operating on a standard voltage. A large proportion of the electricity services, amounting to 60 per cent of supply, was already under municipal control, covering 277 out of 491 generating stations even before the war. There was, therefore, no great argument when a full-scale transfer to national control was undertaken. A British Electricity Authority was set up under the chairmanship of Lord Citrine, former general secretary of the TUC, and fourteen area boards functioning on a federal basis. Considerations of a technical kind prevailed throughout; suggestions by James Griffiths that Wales should have a distinct electricity board of its own on national grounds were rejected by Morrison.[13] Any opposition to the bill was mollified by the remarkably generous terms of compensation given to private stockholders, whether companies or individuals, and the full reimbursement made to local authorities for their electricity undertakings. Yet again, a broad measure of goodwill prevailed.

[13] 'A Note on the Electricity Bill, 17 Dec. 1946', CP (46) 462 (CAB 129/15).

The climax of the government's first phase of nationalization was the momentous and historic proposal to nationalize the coal-mines. With the background of ancient controversy within the coal industry and of tense labour relations going back to 'Black Friday' and the General Strike, this was potentially a more explosive issue. It is indicative of the climate in 1945–6, in the first twelve months of a democratic socialist government, that very little significant opposition in fact came from the Conservatives. Indeed, Anthony Eden's speech, in the second reading debate, offered little more than token criticism, while Clement Davies for the Liberals warmly supported the bill. It was universally acknowledged that the inheritance of industrial relations between coal-owners and miners was an appalling one, coloured by decades of class confrontation. It was acknowledged, too, that the private coal-owners were perhaps the least defensible sector of the capitalist world, especially after their response to the 1926 General Strike and the victimization that followed it, which had fuelled long and bitter memories in mining districts. There had been a variety of previous proposals for a closer integration of this vital industry, so central to the nation's economic performance and, for many years, to its export trade too. The Reid Committee in the latter stages of the war had recommended the overhaul of all pit operations above and below ground, the elimination of smaller pits, and the reorganization of mining on the basis of new large-scale units. The wartime Minister of Fuel and Power, Gwilym Lloyd George, himself by far the least radical of this famous dynasty, had endorsed the Reid proposals. He had also in 1943 suggested to the Cabinet that the government actually take over the pits during the war period, but Churchill had personally vetoed this.[14] On the other hand, the argument from consensus can be overdone, here as elsewhere. Coal is a clear instance where Labour's own ideas, or perhaps instincts, pushed the Attlee government beyond the tentative arrangements proposed during the coalition period. In any case, the coal-owners' own scheme, the plan by Robert Foot published in January 1945, fell far short of anything that could strictly be termed public ownership or even control.

[14] Memorandum to the Cabinet, 7 Oct. 1943 (WP 446).

The basis under the Foot scheme would remain the private system, while the Central Coal Board visualized would be confined to colliery owners alone.[15] This feature, apart from any other, made it totally unacceptable to the National Union of Mineworkers and the Labour Party.

What, however, Labour's alternative blueprint for a nationalized coal industry really included remained veiled in uncertainty. Wags claimed that all Emanuel Shinwell, the new Minister of Fuel and Power in 1945, could find when he ransacked the archives of Transport House was a pamphlet by James Griffiths written in Welsh. This was, no doubt, an exaggeration (and Griffiths' pamphlet, *Glo* [Coal], was an excellent one), but it did suggest the intellectual void at the heart of Labour's proposals for nationalization. In fact, the Morrisonian model of the central corporate board was again set up, with a National Coal Board under the chairmanship of a former coal-owner, Lord Hyndley of Powell Duffryn. Only two members of the NCB at first were trade-unionists, Citrine, former secretary of the TUC, and Ebby Edwards, the secretary of the NUM. Both resigned their previous posts to indicate that they were serving on the Coal Board as individuals only. The industry was divided up into eight new regions, rather than following the old districts. They served as intermediaries between the Board and the forty-eight local areas or colliery groups. The emphasis, for all Shinwell's claims on behalf of administrative decentralization, was on a highly unified financial and organizational structure. There was little difficulty in getting through this complex measure, conceived, as Sir Norman Chester has pointed out, 'virtually from scratch'.[16] The only criticism came from some Labour members hostile to the generous scale of compensation to the private stockholders which amounted to a total of £164,000,000 in government stock. More significant for Labour supporters was the successful agreement with the NUM over the Miners' Charter, embodying the five-day week. No single measure in the earlier phase of the Attlee government aroused more genuine or spontaneous enthusiasm

[15] *The Economist*, 27 Jan. 1945.
[16] Norman Chester, *The Nationalisation of British Industry* (HMSO, 1975), p. 1003.

than did the nationalization of the coal-mines. On Vesting Day, 1 January 1947, there were mass demonstrations of rejoicing in mining communities from South Wales to Nottingham, Yorkshire, Durham, and Fife, as the flag of the NCB replaced the ensign of the old, discredited private coal-owners.

Yet, in reality, problems within the coal industry were mounting up even as these celebrations were taking place. The ability of the coal industry, whether under private or public ownership, to make a significant impact upon a growing and dangerous coal shortage was causing Attlee, Dalton, Morrison, and others much concern in the latter months of 1946.[17] So, too, was the evident shortage of manpower in the pits. Shinwell himself, eventually, came to share these fears. There were also apprehensions about the loss of output allegedly resulting from the implementing of the five-day week and extended holiday provisions under the Miners' Charter. Labour relations proved especially difficult in so centralized and vast an industry, with inadequate delegation of authority at the local level in the various coal regions. In the summer of 1947, Grimethorpe and other pits in South Yorkshire were to demonstrate that strikes and industrial disturbances in the coal industry were by no means a thing of the past. Unofficial strikes and an alarming rate of absenteeism, especially in South Wales, were testimony to the problems inherited by the ageing coal industry, whatever its new structure of ownership. There was much rank-and-file criticism that wages were being held down by the NUM's voluntary acceptance of compulsory arbitration, at a time when the government's policy was deliberately to keep down the selling price of coal. In May 1948 Sir Charles Reid was to resign from the National Coal Board in protest at what he held to be its managerial inadequacies and excessive centralization.[18] Even with the historic achievement of the public ownership of coal, therefore, the aspiration of the miners for half a century, the expectations attached to nationalization as a vital component of the socialist, or even simply a socially just, order remained far from fulfilled.

[17] e.g. Attlee to Dalton, 21 Nov. 1946 (Dalton papers, 9/2/76).
[18] *New Statesman*, 22 May 1948.

The impetus on behalf of nationalization was kept up in the session of 1946-7. Apart from putting the electricity bill on the statute book, the two main proposals in this session, also major parts of the Labour manifesto in 1945, were road and rail transport. There was somewhat more controversy surrounding the Transport Act of 1947, in part no doubt because the government was running into other difficulties at the time, especially financial. The Transport Act, in addition to nationalizing the railways, also took road haulage into public ownership. A British Transport Commission, following the models of the earlier bills, offered an integrated system of road and rail transport, both passenger and freight, with the object of avoiding duplication and wasteful competition. Railway nationalization produced little dissent. There was already a high degree of concentration in the industry, dating from Sir Eric Geddes's measure passed under the Lloyd George coalition back in 1921. Churchill himself had been an advocate of railway nationalization at that period, on grounds of efficiency. The National Union of Railwaymen was passionately in favour. British Railways, therefore, began its somewhat troubled history in 1947 with much goodwill, and even with fraternal noises of co-operation between the NUR and the train-drivers' union, ASLEF. Road haulage, however, generated somewhat more controversy. Indeed, from 1947 onwards, the conventional historians' wisdom that public ownership, as proposed in 1945, was so broadly accepted that it went through with little opposition or protest, is clearly in need of much modification. The Opposition fought the Transport Bill hard in the Commons. They focused on the threat to the liberty of the small road operator, the so-called 'C Licence' holders whose activities covered distances of less than forty miles. Many government supporters themselves were unhappy about this aspect of the bill, defended in somewhat stolid fashion by the Minister of Transport, Alfred Barnes, a leading figure in the Co-operative movement. Douglas Jay later admitted that its inclusion in the Transport Bill was a mistake, since it constituted an invasion of private liberty and, if implemented, would have discredited the idea of public ownership with the community at large.[19] A long struggle took place in the committee stage of the Transport Bill in the Lords, which roused itself for the first time in trying to resist a major item of government legislation. The Cabinet's Socialization of Industries Committee for some while resisted any change over C Licences (which covered some 350,000 vehicles).[20] In the end, after discussion in the Cabinet, with Morrison for once apparently on the more radical side, the government gave way on C Licences on 13 March.[21] The Transport Act then passed on to the statute book without too much difficulty. The issue of C Licences, however, was not forgotten. The transport unions made the valid point that the number of C Licences tended to rise sharply after 1947. It increased again by about 100,000 after December 1949, to reach a total of 766,578 in June 1951.[22] To this extent, therefore, the public, integrated nature of the new transport system was far from complete.

The final measure in this wave of nationalization came in 1948 with the public ownership of gas. Here, as in the case of transport the previous year, the opposition produced much more spirited resistance. Hugh Gaitskell, Shinwell's successor at Fuel and Power, needed stamina and determination to see the bill through all its stages. In the face of over eight hundred Conservative amendments, the government responded by forcing the committee on the Gas Bill to sit through two consecutive nights in May 1948, a total of fifty consecutive hours without a real interval. Gaitskell confided to his diary his resentment of the Opposition's tactics of delay and obstruction, and especially the speeches of Brendan Bracken. 'I find it hard to hide my distaste and keep my temper.'[23] The affair generated much party rancour, reinforced by physical strain. Gaitskell enlivened the third reading debate by comparing Bracken's 'screeching, raucous voice' to that of

[19] Douglas Jay, *Socialism in the New Society* (London, 1962), p. 298.
[20] Minutes of the Socialization of Industries Committee, 8 Mar., 9 May 1946 (CAB 134/687).
[21] Cabinet Conclusions, 13 Mar. 1947 (CAB 128/9).
[22] Proceedings of the Executive Committee of the National Union of Railwaymen, December quarter 1951 (University of Warwick, Modern Records Centre, MS 127).
[23] Hugh Gaitskell diaries, 23 Apr., 1, 18 June 1948 (Nuffield College Library).

Hitler, which led to uproar. In retrospect, the Conservative fury kindled by the Gas Nationalization Bill seems almost absurd. As with electricity, there was in existence an impartial and respected blueprint for the gas industry, in this case, the Heyworth Committee, set up by Gwilym Lloyd George during the war, which had reported in December 1945. Its idea of a supervisory national board could be fitted without much difficulty on a gas industry already with a high degree of municipal ownership of many years' standing. At any rate, the outcry over gas soon blew over, and in 1948 another milestone in the record of nationalization was safely achieved.

Despite these troubles over road haulage and gas, this sustained programme of public ownership, involving almost a fifth of the economy, went through, in general, without much difficulty or dislocation. Much has been made by transatlantic commentators such as Robert Brady and Harry Eckstein[24] of the existence of blueprints from the wartime and pre-war years to explain the relative ease of the government's victories, and this is valid enough. But the gulf between, say, the Reid proposals for coal or the Swinton scheme for civil aviation, and the measures introduced by the Labour government was a significant one. It is clear that the government managed to defuse some potential criticism by well-chosen concessions, for instance over C Licence road operators, or over the compensation paid to private stockholders in coal, gas, and electricity (which, in retrospect, seems almost inconceivably generous, especially in relation to coal). But the general conclusion must be, when reflecting on the nationalization measures put on the statute book between August 1945 and August 1948, that the champions of private enterprise had only limited zest for the fight, or belief in their case in the various industries and utilities proposed for public ownership. In the aftermath of war, with its thrust towards collectivism, in the new era of planning, rationalization, and integration that Labour seemed to embody, a radical transformation in the economic structure was put through in peaceful, almost

[24] Brady, *Crisis in Britain*, pp. 41 ff; H. Eckstein, *The English National Health Service* (Cambridge, Mass., 1959), pp. ix–x.

uneventful, fashion. As will be seen, several of the problems that emerged in the newly-nationalized industries were self-imposed in decisions taken by the government over pricing and other matters. The nationalization measures of 1945–8 did not arouse any passionate enthusiasm—save in the case of coal, then as now always a special case—but neither did it arouse any passionate defence on behalf of the old, discredited regime.

These measures, then, went through with a relative absence of party contention. They went through also without much debate or dissension within the government. The Cabinet's Socialization of Industries Committee, chaired by Morrison, and including Dalton, Cripps, Shinwell, Barnes, and Winster, was a relatively tranquil and harmonious body. Discussion over such issues as the fate of the C Licence holders was not cantankerous. But the case of the nationalization of iron and steel was totally different. Indeed, the very issue of steel pointed to deep uncertainties about the role of national-ization as such within the government's priorities. It was to deal an insidious blow, both to the government's national-ization programme and to the wider reputation of Attlee and his colleagues, from which neither really recovered.

The Labour Party had never shown the same enthusiasm for the nationalization of iron and steel that it had felt towards coal, transport, gas, or electricity. It had not figured in Labour's manifestos in the thirties. As has been seen, it was a late insertion in the manifesto of 1945, much resisted by Morrison at the time. Even after the general election, it was acknowledged that iron and steel would not be immediate candidates for action, comparable with coal or the Bank of England. Indeed, circumstances in relation to iron and steel made it a very different case from all the other industries and utilities proposed for nationalization. Unlike the other cases, this was a foray into manufacturing industry. Engineer-ing, machine tools, and new and other potentially con-tentious areas in the metallurgical trades would be brought into consideration as a result. Again, the steel industry had made a good recovery from the depression of the thirties, fortified by tariffs against foreign steel imports and by a highly cartelized structure within the industry. Its record of production and profitability during the war years was reasonably good. It was hard to argue that steel was 'failing the nation' in the way that the railways or coal could be said to have done. Again, unlike the cases of coal or the railways, there was only a limited enthusiasm among the steel workers for nationalization. Indeed, the workers in the steel industry were notoriously non-militant, and the record of industrial relations since 1919 (other than 1926) had been generally good. Harry Douglass (due to become its secretary in 1953) could tell Attlee in 1947 that the Iron and Steel Trades Confederation was anxious for 'full and immediate nationalization'.[25] On the other hand, Lincoln Evans, the right-wing general secretary of the Iron and Steel workers from 1947 to 1953, was a consistent spokesman against nationalization on the NEC. In 1950, he was to spell out his views to Morgan Phillips at some length, while protesting that Morrison had publicly misrepresented the attitude of himself and other leading union members. 'Public ownership schemes of this kind were no solution to the problem of our present economic difficulties, and had very little relevance to such matters as our trading prospects in the world, the balance of payments, or, indeed, to making ourselves economically independent by 1952. These statements were accepted without reserve by our people.'[26] The thrust for steel nationalization, therefore, was not backed by any decisive pressure by workers in the industry.

On the other hand, it was acknowledged very widely that the steel industry was in urgent need of reorganization and new capital investment after the war, especially with its crucial role in both exporting industries and in domestic house and factory construction.[27] Many steelworks were inadequate, with ancient blast furnaces, coke ovens that were too small, plants which were wrongly sited and competed

[25] Harry Douglass to Attlee, 23 Aug. 1947 (PREM 8/1489, part 1).
[26] Lincoln Evans to Morgan Phillips, 2 Oct. 1950 (Labour Party archives, GS 23/1).
[27] For an effective exposition of this case, see W. Fienburgh and R. Everly, *Steel is Power; the case for Nationalization* (London, 1948). Also cf. Duncan Burn, *The Steel Industry, 1939–1959* (Cambridge, 1961).

with one another in inefficient fashion. The immobility within the industry had been illustrated in Ebbw Vale in Aneurin Bevan's own constituency. The Steel Federation of owners, under the chairmanship since 1935 of Sir Andrew Duncan, had been notoriously restrictive in its ownership structure. The result was that a steady rise in steel prices between 1935 and 1945, with consequent heavy costs throughout manufacturing industry, gave a profit to firms great and small, efficient and inefficient alike. It was not only socialist zealots who regarded a major overhaul of steel as imperative. Some of Sir Andrew Duncan's own pronouncements bolstered the case. *The Economist*, an opponent of steel nationalization even though it supported public ownership elsewhere, admitted that the private steel companies needed a major shake-up, to be properly integrated and re-equipped. 'Something pretty drastic, by almost general consent, needs to be done to the steel industry if it is to be made efficient.'[28] It drew attention to decisions taken in the last months of the Churchill coalition in 1945, to this end, notably establishing a huge new Steel Company of Wales works and tin-plate strip mill, on a green field site at Port Talbot in South Wales, as a result of a merger of four private firms including Richard Thomas and Baldwin. The steel industry's future was unsettled. Nor were the steel owners beloved within the steel-making world. 'Jarrow' was an emotive cry for Labour critics of the steel bosses as were 'Tonypandy' or 'Featherstone' in the case of the coal-owners.

When the government's first proposals emerged in April 1946, they were cautious and tentative. John Wilmot, the Minister of Supply (outside the Cabinet), who had responsibility for steel nationalization, had been considered a man of the left, perhaps even a pacifist, in his younger days. He had won the historic Fulham by-election for Labour in the heady days of 1933. Now, however, he was a somewhat reluctant nationalizer, and in frequent touch with Sir Andrew Duncan and Steel House. Herbert Morrison always maintained his opposition to steel being nationalized, while other senior ministers tended to join him, as Britain's financial

[28] *The Economist*, 28 Apr. 1946.

problems and the need to promote exports and manufacturing production, free from partisan bickering, mounted up. Wilmot's memorandum, considered by the Cabinet on 4 April 1946, reaffirmed the ultimate commitment to nationalization, but proposed to defer matters until 1947–8.[29] In the interim, a new Steel Control Board would be set up in consultation with the private steel owners, to supervise developments and planning, and to prepare an eventual scheme for actual nationalization. Even at this stage, there was hesitation within the government about the need for nationalization at all. Morrison repeated his well-publicized doubts. Bevin, though committed to nationalization of steel, seemed to feel that a prolonged period under the Steel Control Board would be desirable before that took effect. Attlee himself emphasized the general economic difficulties facing the government, and also drew attention to the severe legislative burden already facing the Cabinet and the Commons. He preferred that steel be left over until the 1948–9 session, with gas and other measures to be given priority. Even Shinwell, more surprisingly perhaps, long considered a figure on the left, was doubtful about the idea of steel nationalization. As Minister of Fuel and Power, he felt much concern over the shortage of coking coal for steel production. On the Socialization of Industry Committee in March he had asked whether 'efficiency might not be secured by leaving the Industry in private hands and subjecting it to an investigation similar to those being carried out in other privately owned industries by the Board of Trade Working Parties'. On the other side, Dalton and Bevan urged that there should be no delay in pushing ahead with public ownership. Cripps and Ellen Wilkinson, the member for Jarrow, also upheld nationalization, as did A. V. Alexander, normally a right-wing minister but also a member for the steel citadel of Sheffield.

The outcome was that an Iron and Steel Control Board was set up as a strictly interim measure. Wilmot presented it as a prelude to nationalization. In fact, it soon became evident that he and other ministers increasingly viewed it as an alternative to nationalization. The Steel Board seemed

[29] Cabinet Conclusions, 4 Apr. 1946 (CAB128/5).

to work well, and production rose rapidly under its aegis in 1946-8. Even Dalton himself admitted that Duncan, 'a great executive', had become an effective advocate for the steel owners, though he added that 'He [Duncan] led this industry into a situation in which nationalisation became inevitable.' The first year of the Iron and Steel Control Board showed a record level of 14,316,000 tons annual rate of production, over a million tons higher than twelve months earlier.[30] The output target of 12,500,000 tons for the year had been met with great ease. There was, in addition, an admirable system of labour relations in the industry, following the general establishment of the forty-eight-hour week and new joint consultative machinery. No major strike had occurred since 1926.

In these circumstances it was not surprising that Wilmot's new moves in early 1947 largely confirmed the present position, even though he himself insisted that 'no passive reproduction of the *status quo* is contemplated'. The Cabinet discussed steel on 17 April 1947, and a considerable division of opinion emerged.[31] Several ministers urged that gas nationalization be given preference over steel, especially with those other vital components of the fuel industry, coal, and electricity, already nationalized. Some ministers urged again that steel was a great problem. 'The Steel Bill . . . broke new ground and raised difficult and complex issues; it would be keenly opposed by the industry; and it would cause bitter controversy in Parliament. In particular, it might become an issue between the two houses of parliament.' The case was urged that what was at issue was whether, rather than when steel was to be nationalized. Attlee summed up in favour of gas nationalization being included in the legislative pro-gramme for 1947-8 and for steel to be left out.

Later in April, Wilmot produced his new scheme for the steel industry, a compromise measure which would indeed nationalize it, but leave the structure of the existing private companies intact, with the government exercising the

---

[30] Dalton memorandum on Iron and Steel, May 1946 (T 228/74); *The Economist*, 15 Nov. 1947.
[31] Wilmot memorandum, 6 Mar. 1947 (T 228/74); Cabinet Conclusions, 17 Apr. 1947 (CAB 128/5). Also see minutes of Cabinet Committee on Future Legislation, 4 Mar. 1947 (CAB 134/298).

compulsory purchase of shares. Shinwell protested that under this scheme 'it would be difficult to maintain that it was being effectively socialised'. Other ministers demurred on one ground or another, but on 28 April 1947 the Cabinet granted Wilmot leave to introduce a bill on the basis of his Cabinet paper.[32] But the issue remained in much doubt. From 24 July onwards, the Cabinet began a lengthy series of debates on the merits of steel or any other nationalization, at this time or in the future; virtually every minister took part and opinions were recorded by name in the Cabinet minutes.[33] The entire debate was overshadowed by a growing economic crisis over convertibility, the loss of reserves, and the desperate balance of payments crisis of that tense summer. In the background, too, was Attlee's apparent waning of authority in the face of the financial and political hammer-blows that were raining down on his once seemingly impregnable government.

Morrison and Wilmot led those anxious to preserve a kind of half-way house that fell short of outright nationalization. They presented a joint document (CP (47)212) to the Cabinet, to this end. Attlee himself gave them general, though somewhat guarded, support. Ernest Bevin, previously a staunch opponent of the 'steel barons', now placed his massive weight carefully on the fence, anxious to defer a decision until the autumn. A complicating factor for the Foreign Secretary was that he and the British government were already committed to the public ownership of the steel industry in the Ruhr in the British zone of occupied Germany. It was hard to argue the case for nationalization in Germany, while denying it in Britain itself. Tom Williams, Minister for Agriculture, was an advocate of compromise on Morrisonian lines. So, too, was George Isaacs, the Minister of Labour, as was Alexander, the Minister of Defence, another minister of working-class origin who had somewhat changed his stance. Addison, the Leader of the Lords, also opposed steel nationalization, then or later; he argued that the case was weaker than, say, for nationalization of the land which as an old agrarian radical he had himself

---

[32] Ibid., 28 Apr. 1947 (CAB 128/50).
[33] Ibid., 24 July, 31 July, 7 Aug. (CAB 128/10).

supported in the past. The Lord Chancellor, Jowitt, endorsed
Addison's view that 'a well thought-out bill' should be
deferred until 1950—in other words, that it should be
postponed until after the next general election. But there
were important voices on the other side. Aneurin Bevan was
especially vehement. 'A decision not to proceed with the
socialisation of the iron and steel industry in 1947–8 would
dishearten and divide Government supporters.' Indeed,
Bevan's line, in general, followed that urged in the columns
of *Tribune* and the *New Statesman* by focusing less on the
arguments in terms of productive efficiency and more on
the place of steel nationalization as a guarantee of the government's long-term commitment to socialism.[34] Of course,
Bevan also sat for a steel constituency. Dalton, the Chancellor
of the Exchequer, was another consistent supporter of steel
nationalization, mainly on general socialist grounds. So, with
perhaps less vigour, was Cripps at the Board of Trade, an old
ally of Bevan's, though now rapidly moving to the right on
many issues. Lesser figures such as John Strachey, the Minister
of Food (outside the Cabinet), George Tomlinson, the
Minister of Education, and Arthur Creech-Jones, the Colonial
Secretary, also endorsed the nationalization proposals.
Shinwell, after many gyrations, also finally declared his support for Dalton and Bevan, though prepared to accept Morrison
and Wilmot's CP 212 as an interim measure. A civil servant,
W. S. Murrie, now listed three ministers as being in favour of immediate nationalization (Bevan, Tomlinson, Strachey); seven
favouring CP 212 (Morrison, Alexander, Jowitt, Addison,
Pethick-Lawrence, Isaacs, Wilmot); eight wanting a postponement (Inman, Dalton, Cripps, Ede, Creech Jones, Shinwell,
Williams, Barnes), with Bevin stating no clear view, and Attlee
veering towards postponement. The issue remained delicately
balanced, however, perhaps depending on Attlee's own response to divisions within his government. The final Cabinet
discussion on 7 August was overshadowed by the growing convertibility crisis in which foreign exchange and gold and dollar
reserves were fleeing the country at a quite terrifying rate.[35]

[34] e.g. *Tribune*, 10 Oct. 1947; *New Statesman*, 9 Aug. 1947.
[35] Memorandum by W. S. Murrie for the Prime Minister, 4 Aug. 1947, 'top
secret' (CAB 21/2243); Cabinet Conclusions, 7 Aug. 1947 (CAB 128/10).

Morrison's compromise plan was now rejected. Attlee
summed up in favour of the Cabinet remaining committed to nationalization, but deferring the issue until
1948-9. Even Dalton now admitted that steel nationalization would have to be delayed, and that a place in the
1948-9 session would be more appropriate. Tomlinson,
Ede, and, most influentially, Ernest Bevin, supported
Dalton's view. Bevan, Strachey, and the fading figure of
Arthur Greenwood insisted that steel should still be pressed
forward in the coming 1947-8 session, but this cause was now
a lost one.

To placate Bevan and other critics, it was agreed that a
Parliament Bill would be introduced in 1948 to reduce the
delaying powers of the House of Lords to one year only.
It would, therefore, ensure that a steel bill brought in during
the 1948-9 session could be passed through all its stages in
parliament, and reach the statute book, before the next
general election. On this basis, Bevan reluctantly withdrew
his opposition, since the future of nationalization was
guaranteed. Soon afterwards, Wilmot, who had created a
poor impression by his inability to stand up to the steel
owners or to impose himself on his civil servants, was dismissed by Attlee—'he had to go'.[36] His replacement at
Supply in October 1947 by George Strauss, an old Tribunite
left-winger with knowledge of the scrap-metal business, was
thought to be a symbol of the government's resolve in
pushing on with steel nationalization in the end. It was
ironic that, in time, Strauss was to be criticized even more
fiercely than Wilmot had been, by Dalton and others, for
his pusillanimous approach to steel nationalization. Strauss,
so Dalton unfairly concluded in characteristic style, was 'a
rich Tory pretending to be a left wing Socialist. He never
wanted to nationalize iron and steel and kept on trying to
run away.'[37] In 1950 Dalton had to resist Strauss when he
tried to postpone the vesting date of steel nationalization
by six months in case Britain had to introduce legislation
under the Schuman Plan—a scheme for the French and
German coal and steel industries which, as will emerge, the

[36] Kenneth Harris, *Attlee*, p. 343.
[37] Dalton diary, 4 Jan. 1951 (Dalton papers, I/39).

Labour government opposed as did the bulk of officials in the Foreign Office and the Treasury.

In Strauss's hands, the proposals for steel nationalization that finally emerged did not allay the fear felt on government benches. Hilary Marquand, the Minister for Pensions, had written to Dalton in 1947 about the problems. 'This was the first manufacturing industry to be nationalized. What is suitable for an extractive industry like coal-mining or service industries like transport, gas and electricity need not necessarily be best for manufacture.'[38] He suggested, as a model, the federal structure prevalent in General Motors in the United States—an analogy which would have caused alarm in Labour circles if it had become public knowledge. At any rate, Strauss's eventual scheme (based on CP(48)123) in October 1948 followed the main lines of Wilmot's earlier scheme in taking over 107 companies for public ownership, employing 200,000 workers and with a total issued capital of £195,000,000: though, in fact, only 92 companies were to be nationalized in the end. All the main processes—the obtaining of iron-ore, the production of pig-iron and steel ingots, and the hot rolling of steel—would be involved. Vesting day for the industry would be 1 May 1950.[39] As both supporters and critics of the bill noted, the general structure of the privately-owned steel industry, including its overall selling and trading organization, would be left intact. The bill would take over companies *en bloc*, not reorganize or restructure the industry, at least in the first period of nationalization. In short, it would be relatively easy for a future Tory government to denationalize if it wished. By deliberate intent, the government had selected the least disruptive or wounding method of reforming the steel industry. For all that, a vigorous and lengthy party controversy ensued. The government pushed on with steel nationalization in the Commons first in 1948 and then, when it was rejected by the Lords, a second time in 1949. The entire issue became very complicated with the deteriorating relations between the two houses of parliament over the passage of the Parliament Bill at the same time. Morrison

[38] Hilary Marquand to Dalton, 26 Mar. 1947 (T 228/74).
[39] Cabinet Conclusions, 7, 14 June 1949 (CAB 128/12).

presided over a group of ministers, including such varied figures as Addison and Jowitt from the Lords, Bevan, Strauss, and Whiteley, the chief whip, to consider the difficulties in October 1949.[40] Against all this was a growing background of political tension as it became obvious that this was the last of the government's nationalization proposals, with a general election now looming up. Indeed, it became uncertain whether the government would in fact succeed in getting steel nationalization on to the statute book by early 1950, while the achievement of vesting day in May 1950 looked increasingly remote. In the end, as will be seen, a deal with the Opposition peers saw steel nationalization become law at the end of 1949 with its operation delayed until after the next general election. The actual merits or demerits of steel nationalization in terms of its effects upon industrial production or the economy generally faded from view.

The lengthy debate over steel, and the government's well-publicized uncertainties, drew attention to the flagging momentum of the push for nationalization in general. The extent of open disagreement amongst government supporters, once the general strategy of having a Parliament Bill in 1947–8 and an Iron and Steel Bill in 1948–9 was accepted, was very small. Steel constituency members from the Tawe to the Tyne duly lined up on behalf of the government in debates. Morrison and other dissentients maintained a public front of loyalty to the decisions of the Cabinet; Addison offered the Lords a passionate defence of the transcendent merits of steel nationalization. A rare maverick like Alfred Edwards in Middlesbrough East, as has been seen, was expelled from the party in 1948 for his opposition to steel nationalization. He was to stand again for Middlesbrough East in the 1950 general election, this time as a Conservative; he was easily defeated by Hilary Marquand. Another who left Labour over steel was Ivor Thomas, a talented and highly intellectual junior minister who sat for Keighley. Following a period of retreat and contemplation with the Anglican community at Murfield, he resigned the Labour Whip in October 1948, and sat henceforth as an Independent. His resignation statement criticized steel nationalization as

[40] Morrison to Attlee, 30 Oct. 1949 (PREM 8/1489, pt. 2).

'dogma run mad'. For this, he was booed by Labour members, and assailed by cries of 'dirty dog' from Dr Morgan, a Lancashire backbencher and medical adviser to the TUC. In his later book, *The Socialist Tragedy* (1949), Thomas cited steel nationalization as a prime instance of the doctrinaire cast of mind which now gripped the Labour Party. He, however, was an unusual figure. He coupled his attack on steel nationalization with criticisms of public ownership even in such apparently uncontroversial areas as cable and wireless. He later told the present writer that he believed he should never have joined the Labour Party at all.[41] Like Alfred Edwards, he stood as a Conservative candidate in February 1950, for Newport in Gwent, but also without success. Later he was to become active, as Ivor Bulmer-Thomas, in such causes as the preservation of historic parish churches, and to write a very distinguished book on British party politics. But, apart from these isolated rebels, the government, as has been seen, faced criticisms at the highest level. It is difficult to discover any specific statement by Attlee himself, in Cabinet or elsewhere, on the practical merits of nationalization of steel, nor does his biographer provide one. Within the Treasury, Plowden and the Planning Council strongly resisted nationalization as upsetting to a major industry vital to the balance of payments. He 'respectfully submitted' to Cripps that it 'was an act of economic irresponsibility'.[42] Norman Brook suggested to Attlee that it would be said of the steel bill 'that it removes the profit motive and puts nothing in its place'.[43] More surprisingly, Robert Hall, normally on the left, was another key Treasury aide unenthusiastic about nationalization and fearful of American criticism.[44] Edward Bridges questioned whether the harmony sought in industry over the new production drive would survive contention over iron and steel.[45] On the Conservative side, opponents naturally pointed to the wider ramifications of steel nationalization since firms such as

[41] Thomas, *The Socialist Tragedy*, and letter to the author, 19 Oct. 1982.
[42] Plowden to Cripps, 24 May 1948 (PREM 8/1489, pt. 2).
[43] Norman Brook to Attlee, 29 May 1948 (ibid.).
[44] Robert Hall to Brook, 25 May 1948 (ibid.).
[45] Memorandum by Bridges, 28 Mar. 1946 (ibid.).

Guest, Keen and Nettlefolds extended their activities far into engineering and other areas. It was only a handful of left-wing Labour MPs, notably Ian Mikardo, who suggested the logic of following up steel nationalization with further measures in the engineering, machine tools, or aircraft construction industries.[46] It all indicated how the tide of opinion was on the turn.

It was during the general Cabinet turmoil over steel in the summer of 1947 that the retreat from further long-term measures of sweeping nationalization beyond the accepted list of 1945 can be seen to begin. Even as early as March, Lyall Wilkes MP had recorded that the interest in nationalization was 'negligible' in his constituency of Newcastle Central. As always, the retreat was headed by Herbert Morrison. In a major debate on the NEC Policy Committee on 25 November 1947, he strongly criticized the document, 'Socialism and Private Enterprise' that the Committee had produced.[47] 'We definitely do not want to nationalise the small man—the shop round the corner. . . . We must take care not to muck about with private enterprise, merely for the purpose of being spiteful.' Two trade-union representatives, Harold Clay and George Chester, both attacked the document for being too antagonistic to private enterprise, while Dr Edith Summerskill criticized the plan to nationalize the distribution of food. Even Aneurin Bevan, while taking a far more buoyant view of the benefits of nationalization of steel and other industries, condemned the document as 'too abstract in approach' and called for a more pragmatic attitude towards each particular service or industry. 'What we have to do is to create a framework within which private enterprise can operate efficiently.' The price mechanism was perpetuating inequalities of income, while a full employment policy made it more difficult for private capital to function. James Griffiths, while generally supporting Bevan, called for a more selective policy of nationalization 'as we approach 1950'.

[46] Ian Mikardo, *The Second Five Years: a Labour Programme for 1950* (Fabian pamphlet, 1948).

[47] Policy Committee minutes, 25 Nov. 1947, recording a discussion on the document 'Socialism and Private Enterprise' (RD 69). Wilkes was writing in *Tribune*, 28 Mar. 1947.

It was indeed on a strictly more selective basis that the party did proceed in 1948 and 1949. It had long been acknowledged implicitly that most of manufacturing or other industry would not be altered in its organizational structure at all. Cripps, for instance, had made it clear that nationalization was not contemplated in the cotton industry. Reinvestment in new plant and machinery would be achieved through the existing private mill-owners. Cripps's paper to the Cabinet back in August 1945 had urged that the government make it clear to the textile industry that it was not the intention to nationalize the industry in the present parliament, apart from centralized buying procedures contemplated for cotton.[48] This had led to some questioning from other ministers, notably Bevan, who urged that the government must be able to intervene in the spinning section of the cotton industry if necessary. The issue caused an early resignation from the government, that of Ellis Smith, Cripps's left-wing undersecretary at the Board of Trade. Smith's explanation to his Stoke constituents in January 1946 was somewhat obscurely phrased, but he did urge that 'the cotton industry be nationalized' and its surplus stocks taken in hand by the government as part of a planned global policy for production.[49] Smith was later to lead a left-wing splinter group, 'Socialist Fellowship'.

Where Cripps led, in 1947 and 1948 Morrison followed, both on the NEC's Administration of Nationalized Industries Committee, and on the Industries for Nationalization Committee. He was chairman of both, with Bevan, Dalton, Griffiths, and Laski also members in each case. In both committees, the general drift of the argument, not only from Morrison himself, was that an empirical approach should henceforth be adopted, that it should be recognized that industries already nationalized had shown some unresolved problems which should be cured before further sweeping measures of public ownership were attempted. Much more should be done to try to inform, with appropriate documentation and propaganda, a general public which appeared to be sceptical

[48] Cabinet Paper CP (45) 92, annexed to Cabinet Conclusions, 7 Aug. 1945 (CAB 128/1).
[49] *Manchester Guardian*, 14 Jan. 1946.

of the blessings of nationalization as achieved in the first three years of Labour government, quite apart from the controversial case of steel. Shinwell, indeed, now translated to the War Office, caused a minor sensation at a breakfast meeting of the Co-operative Congress on 2 May 1948 by declaring that there had been far too little detailed preparation in formulating schemes of nationalization and that 'the introduction of democracy in the running of industry' had not worked well.[50] These home truths, which merely repeated in public what Shinwell and others had been saying in Cabinet and on the Socialized Industries Committee for two years past (and which were undeniably true), led to vigorous complaints in the parliamentary party. James Callaghan sharply criticized Shinwell at a Parliamentary Labour Party meeting on 5 May for undermining public confidence in the nationalization already achieved. He in his turn was attacked by Dai Grenfell, who wrote to Attlee protesting at public attacks being made by 'men who have little experience or knowledge of the background of our movement'—hardly an accurate description of Callaghan, for all his relative youth.[51] The fact that Shinwell was currently chairman of the party gave his remarks all the more prominence. At a special meeting of the NEC on 12 May a contrite statement by Shinwell was generally considered to be 'adequate and complete' and the matter was dropped.[52]

But Shinwell's observations chimed in with a general mood of retreat from more nationalization. Labour's policy document, *Labour Believes in Britain*, in 1949, placed its main emphasis on the mixed economy, and marked an evident downgrading of the standing of nationalization in Labour's future priorities. On the various policy committees of the party, a number of candidates for nationalization emerged, and were eventually to appear on the famous 'shopping list' in the 1950 general election. Each was

[50] *News Chronicle*, 3 May 1948.

[51] *The Times*, 6 May 1948; *Daily Herald*, 6 May 1948; D. R. Grenfell to Attlee, 7 May 1948 (Bodleian, Attlee papers, Box 9).

[52] *The Times*, 13 May 1948; National Executive Committee minutes, 12 May 1948. Shinwell later returned to this charge on other occasions: e.g. *Report of 51st Annual Conference of the Labour Party*, held at Morecambe, 1952, p. 105.

governed, at least in part, by Morrison's insistence before the
NEC in October 1948 on the need for a moderate, sensible
approach. 'Ministers and the socialised boards must have time
for the development and clearly demonstrated improvement of
the industries, and [face] the problem of finding a list of social-
izations which will command fairly general public acceptance
or support', as coal or the railways had done in the past.[53]
On this basis, the cement industry emerged as a candidate
for nationalization in January 1949—though not the more
contentious brick-making industry. Soon cement was joined
by water supply, an area which was relatively uncontroversial
since there was already a large element of municipal ownership. Meat wholesaling, focusing on the market at Smithfield where there were currently several unofficial strikes,
also appeared somewhat mysteriously as a candidate in
mid-1949.

Much more controversial, and more electorally damaging
in the long run, was the inclusion of sugar-refining. This was
urged by the Agricultural Workers (with their concern with
sugar-beet production) but opposed by Lincoln Evans of the
steel workers who pointed out the good record of Tate and
Lyle both in terms of efficiency and of labour relations.[54]
However, the majority on the Policy Committee accepted
the view that Tate and Lyle effectively dominated the British
Sugar Corporation, with serious effects on the productive
capacity of sugar-beet factories and the efficiency of refineries. This was a tariff-protected private monopoly which
made large profits for Tate and Lyle, who owned 85 per cent
of the private refining capacity. There were, indeed, many
sensible arguments for the nationalization of sugar-refining:
Collison and Bradfield on behalf of the Agricultural Workers
itemized several of them. But, simply in terms of propaganda
and public relations, it was a foolish choice to be included
in Labour's shopping list. There was no sense among the
general public that anything was seriously amiss with the
sugar and syrup that appeared on their breakfast tables. The
famous 'Mr Cube', brandishing the sword of free enterprise,

    [53] National Executive Committee minutes, 27 Oct. 1948 (RD 173).
    [54] Labour Party Policy Committee, and RD 263 (on Sugar Refining),
Feb. 1949.

was a powerful illustrative ally for the Conservatives at the polls, and their allies in Fleet Street. No effective case for the nationalization of sugar was made out then or later.

Other, potentially more significant, candidates for national-ization were carefully omitted. Among them was the chemical industry.[55] It was indeed hard to argue against the proven efficiency of ICI in chemical production, in the export trade, or indeed in national defence. There was no case in its business practices sufficiently serious to raise the attention of the Monopolies Commission. Ever since the days of Brunner-Mond, ICI had been a good employer. Deakin and Williamson of the TUC potentates were both against national-ization of ICI, and so was Cripps. 'Keep Left' urged, with diminishing conviction, the case for further nationalization as a way of pushing on with the cause of more socialism. Ian Mikardo's *Second Five Years* (February 1948), published for the Fabian Society, urged the need to nationalize the joint-stock banks and industrial assurance companies, ship-building, aircraft construction, aero engines, machine tools, and some of the car industry relating to chassis and engine construction and assembly. He also called for nationalization by function, for instance of the bulk-buying of imported foodstuffs through the Ministry of Food.[56] But 'Keep Left' was less vigorous now, and its survivors more concerned with foreign policy and defence issues than in pumping new life into the cause of nationalization. Not even Bevan gave these demands more than token support. At the Dorking con-ference in May 1950, he was forthright in endorsing the mixed economy. The cause of public ownership languished accordingly.

A pivotal case of much general interest was that of the industrial assurance companies. James Griffiths and Aneurin Bevan, Ministers of Social Insurance and of Health re-spectively, although drawn from somewhat different wings of the party, acted together to press the NEC to adopt the nationalization of these companies as part of the extension of a comprehensive network of social security.[57] Griffiths,

[55] Ibid., RD 262, Feb. 1949.   [56] Mikardo, op. cit.
[57] Labour Party Policy Committee, 30 May, 7 July, 28 July, 24 Oct., 14 Nov. 1949. Also material in James Griffiths papers, National Library of Wales.

fortified by the intellectual backing of Richard Titmuss, argued powerfully that industrial assurance companies owned huge investments which were under no responsible control, and were unrelated to the new fabric of Beveridge-type social insurance created by the government. He and Bevan pointed out that the nationalization of the insurance companies had been mentioned in Labour's programmes in 1945 although not taken further after the election. But there were powerful opponents. Morrison opposed throughout on tactical grounds. He foresaw that the insurance agents, calling in at hundreds of thousands of private homes, would be a powerful propaganda factor working against Labour in the next election. 'The Pearl and the Pru' were dangerous enemies to stir up gratuitously. Cripps was also hostile. He told Dalton on 16 March 1949 that 'you will make a very profound mistake, perhaps even a fatal mistake, if you include industrial assurance as one of the items of nationalisation'.[58] Subsequently, when he attended the National Executive on 30 September, Cripps gave as his reasons the technical problems of trying to rationalize a scheme covering a hundred million existing policies. Even more important from the Treasury's point of view, such a scheme might upset the immense invisible exports derived from insurance operations in the United States, Canada, Brazil, and other countries.[59] Dalton eventually came to agree, especially when T. H. Gill, on behalf of the Co-operative Society, told the NEC that his society totally opposed a scheme that would mean the extinction of the thriving and profitable Co-operative Insurance Society. Cripps wryly told Dalton that 'the Co-op reason is as good as any as a get-out'.[60] In the end, with much reluctance, Bevan and Griffiths gave way. A proposal by R. Dinnage, a trade-union member of the NEC, was accepted which advocated 'mutualization' under which a certain proportion of insurance funds could be compulsorily invested in government securities. Improvements in terms of cash surrender and free policy values on discontinued policies could be brought about, without the extreme of a recourse

[58] Cripps to Dalton, 16 Mar. 1949 (Dalton papers, 9/7/9).
[59] National Executive Committee minutes, 30 Sept. 1949.
[60] Cripps to Dalton, 5 Oct. 1949 (Dalton papers, 9/7/56).

to public ownership. Also, the profits to shareholders could be limited to the amount distributed out of profits in the calendar year, 1948. This was what the NEC finally accepted, after lengthy debates, on 23 November 1949.[61] The 'mutualization' of industrial assurance, therefore, also appeared on the 1950 electoral shopping list. It is difficult to resist the view that this scheme embodied the worst of all worlds. It still aroused the predictable antagonism of the insurance companies, whose local agents became in effect unpaid Tory propagandists, without producing any obvious changes or benefits with which the voters could identify. On reflection, Dalton considered the entire haphazard shopping list of 1950, with such varied ingredients as water, cement, meat, sugar, and insurance, all stirred up together into an indigestible mixture, to be a disaster. It marked a retreat from nationalization which had been present in the government's psychology as early as the first debates on steel in April 1947. It heralded a twilight period of uncertain, half-hearted commitment, on the Bevanite left no less than on the Gaitskellite right, that endured until a new, and more specific and clearly-conceived party statement on public ownership—and the varied forms that it might now take—appeared with the joint endorsement of Gaitskell and of Bevan at the 1957 party conference.[62] Until that time, nationalization showed all the signs of unwilling temporary occupation in preparation for later withdrawal, rather than of ideological ground firmly secured.

The government's wider industrial policy, therefore, and its commitment to some kind of industrial planning, must be pursued in realms other than outright nationalization. It was true, as Shinwell pointed out to the Central Economic Planning Council in July 1947, that 'in an economy which was in process of socialisation, a break with the past must come in time if terms and conditions are to be regulated

[61] National Executive Committee minutes, 30 Nov. 1949. The draft paper, 'Industrial Assurance as a Public Service: Proposals for Mutual Ownership by Policy Holders', was then authorized to be drawn up.

[62] The document, *Industry and Society*, carried by 5,383,000 votes to 1,442,000 at the 1957 party conference at Brighton.

by industries rather than by geography and the vagaries of ownership'.[63] Nevertheless, the progress of industrial planning, and the specific measures of nationalization introduced between 1945 and 1948 seemed to be, more and more, programmes quite distinct from one another, indeed almost unrelated.

Since the great bulk of the economy would remain in private hands, much would depend on the kind of relationship struck up between the Labour government and industrial and business concerns which were run in the main by men who were its political opponents. The government's method, as operated mainly by Cripps at the Board of Trade, was essentially indirect, with an elaborate skein of consultation through the machinery of central government by 'sponsoring' departments of the Board of Trade, the Ministry of Supply, and others. This had particular relevance to the effort to direct private industry into the older depressed areas where regional diversification was a central objective. The actual administration of governmental controls was often delegated to trade associations. In some key industries, more direct methods were adopted to try to ensure new policies for manufacturing production and for labour relations. Cripps launched at the Board of Trade, in September 1945, the idea of 'working parties' in major industries. Cotton, pottery, hosiery, furniture, and the boot and shoe industry, all important in the export drive, were amongst the first to undergo these new arrangements, under which four representatives each from employers and unions and from the Board of Trade met to discuss aspects of efficiency in production and supply. In all, seventeen such working parties were set up in different industries by 1947. Private industrialists greeted these moves at first with some suspicion, viewing them as so many versions of unavowed or partial nationalization under the guise of joint industrial consultation. But it became clear that these working parties were purely consultative, self-contained, and finite in their powers, with no authority to direct the overall course of the industries they represented. Cripps himself took pains to reassure the

[63] Memorandum on the Extension of the Five-Day Week, 24 July 1947 (T 228/17).

Cabinet and private industry about their flexible, informal character.

In the financial crisis in the summer of 1947, Cripps moved towards a more positive form of industrial regulation. A new Cotton Board was created for the spinning industry, later transformed into a Development Council for the cotton industry as a whole.[64] It was followed by other Development Councils for some other sections of industry (wool and lace, furniture, jewellery and silverware, and clothing, each council containing equal numbers of employers and employees. A number of orders were also made under the 1947 Industrial Organization and Development Act, the last of which authorized a levy for research in the wool industry in November 1950. These Development Councils, Labour's main institutional innovation for dealing with private industry, were greeted with further suspicion and hostility by individual employers and by the FBI and its chairman since 1946, Sir Norman Kipping. They coincided with a somewhat deteriorating relationship between government and private industry in 1948–9 as a result of the controversy over steel nationalization, the activities of 'Aims of Industry' as a private-enterprise pressure group, and other factors. Labour supporters were also anxious that, on the union side, Joint Production Committees were being used by Communist shop stewards for their own purposes, as in the Scottish building trades.[65] In fact, it is clear that, here again, the degree of control exercised by the government over private industry, including such vital areas as the direction of exports, the levels of wages and profits, vital aspects of long-term investment, was very limited. The Development Councils had only a minor impact. The years of the Attlee government saw private industry greatly exercised by bureaucracy and 'red tape', and much public lamentation about creeping socialism in general. In practice, as left-wing critics frequently complained in the Labour press,[66] the regulation, let alone the indicative control of private industry by the government

[64] Note by Cripps on the Cotton Industry, 30 May 1946 (Lord President's Committee papers, LP (46) 136, CAB 132/6).

[65] Letter from John Taylor, Labour Party Scottish Council, May 1946 (LAB 10/591), IR 1144/1946.

[66] e.g. *New Statesman*, 5 Apr. 1947.

was never extensive. Nor was this in any way surprising. The government believed that it faced in 1945 a financial crisis of unparalleled severity—'a financial Dunkirk', as Keynes graphically described it. It believed that only in private industry could the managerial and technical skills be enlisted in order to meet the crisis. It drew extensively on experienced figures from private industry—men such as Edwin Plowden, Lord Hyndley, or S. J. Hardie, for its key planning advisers, or as chairmen or other central figures in nationalized industry. Clearly this was a government which thought at best in terms of partnership with industry, somewhat in the form of Roosevelt's NRA of 1933, and had no intention of harrassing private industrialists in their vital concerns. After all, even left-wing ministers such as Bevan and Strachey, while anxious for further nationalization in the future, were equally anxious to reassure private capitalists in the short term, to provide some kind of financial stability for the building of the democratic socialist commonwealth.

The government's relations with private, non-nationalized industry, then, were not marked by anything that could coherently be described as planning. That was not surprising since 'planning'—a protean and vague term which had led to much inconclusive debate in the United States during the New Deal period—was a conspicuous absentee in Labour's otherwise comprehensive election manifesto in 1945. Dalton, a highly orthodox Chancellor who had scant understanding of Keynesian economics, considered 'finance' to be in a quite separate compartment from economic planning. So far as Labour had a strategy of planning it was largely to renew and continue the physical and financial controls of wartime, to help exports, to direct industry towards development areas, and to direct the use of vital raw materials. It had nothing that resembled the *dirigiste* economic strategy of de Gaulle's 'popular front' government in France in 1945-6, building on the earlier socialist experiments of Blum's administration of 1936. Labour in Britain was not anxious to proceed further partly on doctrinaire political grounds: the 1947 *Economic Survey* drew a clear distinction between totalitarian and democratic forms of planning.[67]

[67] *Economic Survey for 1947* (Cmd. 7046), p. 5.

The last, which Labour always endorsed, enshrined the sacred principle of freedom of choice. Evan Durbin, a leading economic thinker, when spelling out the socialist approach towards dealing with the country's overwhelming economic problems, always emphasized that methods of compulsion, over labour or capital, were both impractical in operation and wrong in principle. It would restrict the freedom of the individual 'in order to carry through a programme one of whose main purposes is to extend that freedom. It shakes the principles on which democratic socialists rest their faith.'[68]

The main planning instrument appointed by the Cabinet was the Lord President's Committee, chaired by Herbert Morrison, and including Dalton and Cripps amongst others. This was always an uncertain instrument of central economic direction, as the record of its deliberations between January 1946 and September 1947 (when it lost most of its key functions) in the public archives clearly shows. Its themes were varied and haphazard; there was little consistent following up of one specific aspect of economic planning from one meeting to another. Certainly there was nothing on the lines of the Production Committee set up after the convertibility crisis of August 1947. Morrison's own relative inadequacy in economic matters, for all his extraordinary administrative skills and political acumen, was another difficulty. He preferred to rely on unorthodox advisers in the Lord President's secretariat, such as Max Nicholson and Alexander Johnstone, rather than turn to Keynesians like James Meade in the Economic Section of the Cabinet Office. In a major crisis, such as the balance of payments troubles of July 1947, his instincts let him down and left the government bereft. The Committee over which he presided, for instance, manifestly failed to produce a coherent policy for dealing with the coal shortage, which was anticipated as far back as May 1946, long before the harsh winter weather of 1946–7 savagely underlined the government's inadequacies. Nor did the Committee begin to anticipate, or discount, the serious

[68] Evan F. M. Durbin, 'The Economic Problems facing the Labour Government', in Donald Munro (ed.), *Socialism. The British Way* (London, 1948), p. 22.

effects of convertibility on the balance of payments and the huge drain on the dollar reserves, which had reached a critical point months before convertibility was due to come into effect in July 1947. On balance, the Lord President's Committee was inclined in key areas to argue against the case for planning.

A continuous effort, for instance, was made by Shinwell, when Minister of Fuel and Power, to have a planned policy for manpower. With the support of Aneurin Bevan and the left-wing press, he urged the need for a new machinery—far stronger than the inept National Industrial Conference of 1919, which emerged as an anti-labour rump—to regulate wages and the labour market. 'In the field of socialised industry the government would be unable to escape ultimate responsibility for the determination of wages and would find it very difficult to resist the argument that its employees should receive good wages irrespective of the effect upon production costs.'[69] This view argued for a new wages policy, including minimum wage rates in key industries, higher rates in unattractive industries, and an agreed policy of relating wage increases to acknowledged and proven increases in productivity. On 1 November 1946, Shinwell's paper on behalf of a kind of central wages tribunal was formally considered by the Lord President's Committee.[70] Shinwell argued that government intervention in the wage levels in different industries was now inevitable. With the co-operation of the unions, a national authority should be able to make recommendations to the government. He pointed out that the government already intervened indirectly, for instance in relation to agricultural wages. He had in mind, of course, the particular problem of coal-mining where a major problem continued to be the fall in manpower, especially of miners at the coal-face, owing to the greater attractiveness of wages in car factories and other establishments. There were less than 700,000 miners, while the government aimed at 730,000. Shinwell's view, which he continued to proclaim as late as 6 June 1947, would have extended the principle of planning into radical new directions. In the fight against the shortage

[69] Minutes of Lord President's Committee, 29 Mar. 1946 (CAB 132/1).
[70] Ibid. LP (46) 36 (CAB 132/1).

of labour, or bottle-necks in labour supply, wage regulation, in key industries such as coal, was vital to attaining broader economic objectives. In any case, economic direction was one and indivisible.

But the general bias of ministers was always against him. George Isaacs was consistently negative. As a trade-unionist, he had a deep commitment to preserving free collective bargaining. He warned Shinwell in January 1946 of the dangers of leading people to believe that, after coal nationalization, 'an entirely new system of wage negotiation will be set up, or that the Government of the day will control or influence wages settlements, or that for the future the workers will be in direct relationships with the state. A clear indication on the last question will have to be given when we come to debate the repeal of the 1927 Trade Disputes Act.'[71] A government which proclaimed its zeal for central direction in terms of production, investment, and exports would apparently have to restrain its enthusiasm where wages were involved. Bevin always upheld this view in Cabinet, too, as would be expected from another trade-unionist. Morrison, always genuinely concerned to limit the role of central government and to proclaim the virtues of free choice for the individual citizen, strongly resisted anything that could be taken to resemble the fixing of wages by ministers or their advisers. Cripps did show some early sympathy with Shinwell, but by the summer of 1947 he was talking of the problems of rising wage levels—by 1947 they were 27 per cent above the levels of 1939—and of creeping inflation which would damage the performance in exports. The need, he argued, was for voluntary restraint, backed up by government persuasion and propaganda to create the right climate, not for government direct intervention which might make the problems of inflation worse rather than better. Nor did a similar proposal by the Cambridge economist, Nicholas Kaldor, in 1950 meet with acceptance.[72] The whole discussion showed the casual, almost disengaged atmosphere

[71] Isaacs to Shinwell, 15 Jan. 1946 (LAB 10/586), IR/631/1946.

[72] When the Cabinet again discussed some kind of appeals tribunal for wages on 13 November 1947, Isaacs and other ministers again attacked the idea and no agreed Cabinet view emerged (CAB 128/12); Nicholas Kaldor, 'A Positive Policy for Wages and Dividends', 21 June 1950 (T 171/403).

in which the Lord President's Committee conducted its deliberations. Nor did it have a proper industrial or financial planning apparatus to back it up, other than the Economic Section of the Cabinet Office, inherited from the war. The Central Economic Staff attached to it was purely functional, concerned to provide background information and statistical digests. Morrison strongly resisted efforts to have an Economic General Staff created which would diminish the authority of the government, and viewed with disfavour efforts made by Bridges and Treasury officials to set up a new Central Planning Board in 1947.

Nor did the Treasury provide any serious initiative in the planning field at this early stage. Dalton's financial policy in 1945–7 will be considered at length in a later context, but it may be emphasized here that planning, of a Keynesian or other kind, was not a part of his world-view. The nationalization of the Bank of England, as has been noted, was a limited and technical change, with little relevance for economic planning. The nationalized Bank, for instance, would continue to decide the bank rate on its own initiative. The Investment (Control and Guarantees) Act of 1946 did give the Treasury powers to control new capital issues and promote public loans. But the National Investment Council which was set up was a shadowy body, with powers largely confined to co-ordinating bodies already in existence. It was far from the purposeful instrument visualized by the XYZ Group and by Dalton himself in the thirties. The Capital Issues Committee could approve or veto new issues on the capital market, above £50,000, but its powers, too, were limited. It could cover neither company savings, nor the investments of the joint-stock banks, by its very nature. Dalton did not use the budgetary method on Keynesian lines. His pursuit of low interest rates in 1945–7 was really dictated by other objectives, some of them not economic at all. His budgets did not use sophisticated methods of modern income analysis, while surplus purchasing power tended to be mopped up in leisure pursuits such as gambling and sport, rather than being used for productive ends. In short, the Treasury, like the Lord President's Committee, was not a body dedicated to the planned expansion of industrial production either. It tried to control private industry largely through exhortation, though Dalton's booming tones ensured that the exhortation would be voluble, and apparently bolstered by limitless resolution and self-confidence.

In the convertibility crisis of 1947, these major weaknesses in the direction of industry and financial strategy generally —weaknesses, for instance, which led to a remarkable absence of state direction in the critical field of exports down to September 1947—were clearly revealed. As will be seen later, they eventually resulted in an overhaul of the machinery of central government—the new powers of the Economic Planning Board under Sir Edwin Plowden announced in July 1947; the Department of Economic Affairs under Cripps in September; the new structure of Cabinet committees with the Economy, Production, and Priorities Committees all coming into being. The 1948 white paper on costs, incomes, and prices appeared to imply a new *dirigisme* in the course of central policy, though again with the collaboration rather than the coercion of the employers and the trade unions. The extent to which a new effectiveness did in fact enter governmental economic policy in the Cripps era from late 1947 was highly debatable, as will be examined later. By 1949 the retreat from planning, even in this qualified form, was under way. Here it needs to be emphasized that, even in its heyday in the first two years from 1945 onwards, when nationalization, controls, and collectivist regulation appeared to be irresistible, the Labour government's attempt to plan private industry through the Treasury and the Board of Trade, was half-hearted, indirect, and in many ways unsuccessful.

The absence of planning was evident, too, even in the public sector. Coal, gas, electricity, cable and wireless, civil aviation, road and rail transport, remained largely autonomous entities, directed by their own remote corporate boards. There was a lack of integration even within nationalized transport itself with much wasteful competition. No integrated energy or other policy seemed to emerge. There was endless conflict between Gaitskell and Citrine over the policy of the Electricity Board in 1948-9, with Gaitskell anxious to limit the Board's capital programme and Citrine apparently determined that domestic and industrial users should be permitted to burn as much electricity as they wished, whatever the cost.[73] This aspect has been used, even by many sympathetic to the government's overall aims, to suggest the general irrelevance of the policy of nationalization for the country's general economic performance. As has been seen, criticisms of several key features were voiced by ministers such as Shinwell and Morrison as early as 1947-8. The system of labour relations, for instance, and of consultation of the work-force, was acknowledged to have many imperfections, quite apart from specific disputes such as the Yorkshire coal strike of 1947 and troubles on the railways in early 1951. The use of emergency regulations by royal proclamation and of troops to unload ships or to man power-stations was not a good advertisement for a supposed new era in labour relations: Margaret Cole called for a new system of 'human relations' in the publicly-owned industries.[74] It was ominous, too, that in 1946 the government agreed to renew the hated Emergency Powers Act enacted by the Lloyd George government back in 1920. Even Ernest Bevin, who had campaigned passionately against the original Act in 1920, now accepted that it was necessary to keep the community protected during industrial emergencies; it could not, he thought, be construed as strike-breaking.[75] The government and the TUC made no effort to alter the adversarial character of relations between labour and management—even while, ironically enough, Britain was encouraging moves towards *Mitbestimmung* in western Germany at precisely this period.

Other criticisms of the nationalized industries also began to multiply. The method of compensating private stockholders seemed only to make the rich richer under a Labour government. This was particularly evident with the arrangements made for railway stock owners to be compensated on the basis of the wartime rental paid by the state. 'The railway take-over became a bonanza for the Stock Exchange', wrote Nicholas

---

[73] Philip Williams, *Gaitskell*, p. 174.
[74] Margaret Cole, *The Miners and the Board* (Fabian pamphlet, May 1949).
[75] Cabinet Conclusions, 28 Mar. 1946 (CAB 128/5).

Davenport.[76] The new nationalized industries were also attacked on grounds of efficiency. The financial losses incurred by the British Railways Board, the National Coal Board, and the Civil Aviation authorities in their early years from 1948 onwards, were emblazoned throughout the Beaverbrook and Rothermere press, to discredit the government and the very name of nationalization. There was also the question of simple productive efficiency. Quite unfairly, the National Coal Board, which came into existence on 1 January 1947, on the eve of prolonged wintry weather, was blamed for the massive fuel crisis which resulted and which almost brought industry to its knees. Many of these circumstances were purely adventitious. Yet even Aneurin Bevan, always the keenest nationalizer of those around the Cabinet table, admitted that public ownership needed to improve its performance in key areas, before further nationalization measures were undertaken. He, too, agreed with Morrison on the need for a vigorous campaign of public education to persuade the public that nationalization was a social good. This applied especially to Labour's supporters, whose doubts about nationalization in the run-up to the 1950 general election were notorious.

Nevertheless, many of these criticisms were unjustified, or else were the products of temporary adverse circumstances. The fuel crisis of early 1947, for instance, could not reasonably be blamed on nationalization at all. If anything, it reflected more on the inadequacies of the industry under private ownership in 1945–6. The problems, in any case, lay as much in transportation difficulties, made worse by the icy weather, as in defects in coal production. Again, the nationalized industries could easily have become more profitable. The government, in order to keep costs down and boost exports, persuaded these industries to follow a pricing policy below market levels. To encourage the wage freeze agreed with the TUC in 1948, a deliberate policy of keeping down railway fares for the passenger was pursued. House coal for domestic use (burned in grates by the working class, or in anthracite-fired boilers for central heating by many of the middle class) was ten to thirty shillings a ton less than it

[76] Nicholas Davenport, op. cit., pp. 180–1.

was on the world market. Gas and electricity charges in homes were also kept artificially low, despite Citrine's protests. Indeed, Citrine had difficulty in raising electricity charges for the domestic consumer at all in 1948, even though he claimed that the overall price per unit was lower than in 1938.[77] Without all these adventitious factors, all fully justified by the Treasury during the Cripps era, the various nationalized boards would have made handsome profits. Again, a burden of heavy interest charges made the balance sheets look unduly gloomy. The glowing financial success at this time of Cable and Wireless, on the other hand, made little impact on the general public, nor was it effectively deployed in Labour Party propaganda. In terms of efficiency, the gas and electricity supply industries were both soon to emerge as impressive models of public enterprise.

Other industries, of course, inherited decades of financial decline and of poor management by private capitalists. Coal was perhaps the leading example. However, the National Coal Board began in 1948 a powerful programme of capital investment, with impressive new developments like the Bwllfa 'horizon mining' project to link the famous militant town of Maerdy in the Rhondda Fach in South Wales with the Aberdare valley five miles away over the mountain.[78] New, modern machinery was being installed. New projects in terms of gas and chemical production, based on coal, were being developed. Despite all the problems of the industry, the heritage from the capitalist past, a serious shortage of manpower (only 698,000 miners at the end of 1951, increased somewhat by the unpopular introduction of Italian workers in South Wales), some difficulties through temporary stoppages and go-slow workings in the Yorkshire and South Western division, and (it must be added) problems created through loss of production under the Five Day Week of the 1946 Miners' Charter—despite all these problems, the nationalized coal industry began to thrive mightily. By 1952, the National Coal Board could report that it was now indeed profitable, and beginning to penetrate the export field again.

[77] Citrine, op. cit., p. 301.
[78] E. D. Lewis, *The Rhondda Valleys* (London, 1959), p. 271.

The total saleable output of coal (including open-cast) had risen from 190m. tons in 1946 to 222m. tons in 1951, after five years of nationalization, while output per manshift was the highest ever recorded.[79] The NCB's 'Plan for Coal' visualized 240m. tons' production by the sixties. The early fifties, indeed, were to prove the last thriving period that the coal industry experienced, before the cutbacks and closures of the later fifties and the subsequent period. Even so, if the coal industry still plays a major role in Britain's energy supplies in the 1980s, the achievements under nationalization must be given the credit. As for labour relations, if there were some problems after nationalization, they paled in comparison with the years under private ownership. Gas, electricity, civil aviation, cable and wireless, and steel all had excellent records of industrial relations after nationalization. The railways showed some discontent in 1950–1 but partly as a result of the wartime Order 1305, with its restrictions on the right to strike rather than of the specific conditions arising from nationalization. As for the coal industry, Grimethorpe or the South Wales go-slow workings, which generated such glee in the right-wing press, were as nothing by contrast with the hideous saga of industrial conflict with the private coal owners after 1918. Working conditions for miners improved beyond all recognition. Whatever the admitted inadequacies of the system of labour relations devised under nationalization, it would be impossible to dispute the enormous improvement in the climate of industrial relations—and of growing prosperity for the work-force—in the new age of public ownership.

In large measure, this was simply because of the symbolic fact of nationalization itself. As has been seen, Labour began to lose confidence in the idea of public ownership from 1948 onwards. Its election manifesto in 1950 contained the so-called 'shopping list' which was buried after the election. The manifesto of October 1951 was to call only in vague terms for new public enterprises when this would 'serve

---

[79] *National Coal Board: Annual Report and Statement of Accounts for the year ended 31st December 1951* (PP, 1951–2, viii), pp. 1 ff. The total of deep-mined coal rose from 181.2m. tons in 1946 to 211.9m. tons in 1951, an increase of nearly 17 per cent.

the national interest'. No particular candidates for this
operation were specified, and the entire document embodied
Morrisonian caution on the question. At the same time, it
is clear that Labour took some pride in what had been
achieved. Despite all the hostile propaganda from 'Aims
of Industry', the FBI, and Fleet Street, it was significant
that there was no general move by the Conservatives after
1951 to reverse the nationalization already achieved, apart
from the controversial case of steel, and the separate, limited
issue of road haulage. In effect, Churchill and his ministers
implicitly admitted the unfairness of many past attacks on
industries taken into public ownership in highly adverse
financial circumstances, and with, in the cases of the railways and the mines, a background of under-capitalization,
under-investment, and long-term failure. For the Labour
Party, nationalization, warts and all, was the main token
of its socialism for an otherwise reformist, moderate government. It marked, in effect, the end of an old debate. Key
aspects about the changing character of industry were left
on one side—the divorce of management and ownership
which, in the view of Anthony Crosland in 1956, made the
issue of public ownership increasingly irrelevant; the issues
ventilated in James Burnham's influential text on the
Managerial Revolution which shaped the thinking of Crossman and others on the Labour left.[80] This was a largely
insular debate, divorced from the world economic scene.
There was scant consideration of the relationship of the
British industrial economy, however owned, to the
industries of France and other nations in western Europe
which by 1950 were showing clear signs of becoming powerful competitors to Britain, with more modern plant and no
historic backlog of commitment to declining or derelict
communities. It was the demons at home that Labour wished
to exorcize in 1945. In large measure it succeeded, and with
somewhat more flourish than the later, almost apologetic

[80] Anthony Crosland, op. cit., pp. 462 ff.; also *idem*, 'The Transition from
Capitalism' in R. H. S. Crossman (ed.), *New Fabian Essays* (London, 1952),
pp. 48–9. Also see George Watson, *Nationalization: the End of an Illusion*
(Unservile State Papers, 1983), an attack on state monopoly. I am indebted
to the author for sending me this stimulating paper, with much of which I
disagree.

treatment of nationalized industry in the fifties and sixties might suggest. A vital step forward had been taken in the displacement of the old order, even if its successor was far from clear in 1951. Without nationalization above all, the morale and impetus of the 1945 Labour government could not have been sustained. For most members of the party and the movement, that was its ultimate justification.

4

Priorities and Policies:
The Welfare State

By the time of the general election of February 1950, the
main defence of the Labour government by its supporters lay
less in the achievements of nationalization or industrial
reform, than in the creation of the welfare state, including
full employment. The manifesto of 1950 proclaimed that
'Labour has honoured the pledge it made in 1945 to make
social security the birthright of every citizen. Today desti-
tution has been banished. The best medical care is available
to everybody in the land.'[1] More, it was argued that Labour's
social achievements between 1945 and 1950 marked the
climax of the steady growth of welfare services dating from
the work of Lloyd George at the Treasury between 1908
and 1915—work with which two Labour Cabinet ministers,
Lords Addison and Stansgate, had been involved as Liberal
MPs in those earlier days. Social reform—housing, health,
education, the conquest of poverty, ignorance, malnutrition,
and unemployment as personalized in Beveridge's 'five giants'
—had played a major part in Labour's rhetoric from 1918
onwards. Yet much of this had been relatively vague, even
when reinforced by the ideas of Tawney and other social
theorists. Indeed, much of the inspiration for the welfare
fabric as it existed prior to 1939 had come from Labour's
political opponents. A major impetus had derived from the
New Liberalism of pre-1914, voiced by men such as Hobson,
Hobhouse, and Rowntree in the press and in intellectual
circles, and spearheaded by Lloyd George and, for a time,
Churchill, in the Liberal government of Asquith. There had
also been important measures pushed forward by progressive wings of the Conservative Party: Balfour's Education
Act of 1902; some of the social legislation of the first world
war identified with Milner and his 'kindergarten' of youthful

---

[1] Labour election manifesto of 1950, printed in F. W. S. Craig, *British General
Election Manifestos, 1918–1966* (Chichester, 1970), p. 132.

imperialists; the reforms of the later twenties forced through
by Neville Chamberlain at the Ministry of Health; even some
measures of penal and health reform passed in Chamberlain's
otherwise unfortunate premiership in 1937–40—all were of
Conservative origin, with ideological roots that could plausibly be traced back to the days of Disraeli or even Peel. The
Labour Party, then, had no monopoly of social concern.
Labour's Immediate Programme, precise enough on industrial matters and employment, was vague on key social
issues, notably unemployment insurance and the idea of a
state medical service. A major new impetus, of course, came
from the wartime coalition, and especially from the Beveridge
report of November 1942. As has been seen, Labour in effect
appropriated the report as its own, especially as it chimed
in so closely with the policy declaration at the party conference earlier in the year. From 1943 onwards, Beveridge's
call for a reformed comprehensive system of social security,
from the cradle to the grave, became in effect Labour's
programme. National insurance would be merged with
a co-ordinated policy of social planning. Labour strongly
criticized the Churchill coalition's proposals for social insurance, published in 1944, especially over the scale of
benefits. The 1945 election manifesto was largely a re-
affirmation of key sections of Beveridge, with added emphasis on such old Labour themes as a national health service and
a big new housing drive. The more socialistic aspects of these
proposals, such as the possible nationalization of the hospital service, and the socialization of industrial assurance
companies, though mentioned in 1945, were played down.
Once Labour assumed office in July 1945, a new thrust
towards a comprehensive welfare service was assumed to be a
central objective. Indeed, one of the first executive decisions
taken was Dalton's agreement, when pressed by James
Griffiths, the Minister of National Insurance, to introduce
family allowances, on the lines demanded by Beveridge,
immediately after his budget in April 1946.

But a new and ambitious welfare system somehow
had to be paid for. Here was the supreme problem: for
the financial base was anything but secure. Beveridge's
projections had been made against optimistic economic

expectations of renewed growth and full employment after the war. In fact, in August 1945 the financial situation confronting Attlee and his colleagues was frightening in the extreme. The new government was presented in its first week in office, in early August, with a lengthy memorandum on the overall financial situation written by Keynes.[2] It was couched in terms of terrifying pessimism, with Keynes talking of a 'financial Dunkirk'. He spelt out, with characteristic clarity, the position confronting the nation—the vast burden of overseas indebtedness, the loss of overseas income owing to the sacrifice of the export trade and the sale of overseas assets, the huge rise in the cost of necessary imports, the threefold increase in the national debt. During the war, Britain had lost about £7,000m.—a quarter of its entire national wealth. It now faced a desperate situation in its international trade. The nation required imports that cost between £1,100m. and £1,200m. to maintain a wartime level of consumption; yet exports had been cut so severely during the war that they yielded a mere £400m. Only Lease Lend from the United States and mutual aid from the Canadian government had enabled Britain to pay its way at all: but these would end soon after VJ Day, cutting Britain off from £1,350m. sterling of vital assistance. Keynes outlined a probable payments deficit, even making the most favourable estimates about a recovery in exports, of £950m. in 1946, 550m. in 1947, and of £200m. in 1948. With extreme good fortune, Britain might be in balance in its overseas payment by 1949. Yet there would still be an accumulated deficit of £1,750m. over the three years after the war, notably the so-called 'sterling balances' of debts incurred with India, Egypt, and other Commonwealth countries. 'Where on earth is all this money to come from?', asked Keynes rhetorically. The only possible answer he could offer, in addition to a relentless concentration on the export trade, lay in substantial long-term aid, to the order of $5 billion, from the United States. Otherwise, any question of Britain retaining anything like great-power status abroad or of trying to maintain a tolerable standard

[2] Note by Dalton and memorandum by Keynes on 'Our Overseas Financial Prospects', 14 Aug. 1945, CP (45) 112 (CAB 129/1).

of living for its citizens at home would be totally impossible. Keynes's projection did at least assume that United States Lease Lend would linger on for a few weeks or months. In fact, President Truman announced the termination of this assistance to Britain as early as 21 August, only six days after the surrender of Japan. This was a cruel commentary on the wartime alliance against fascism, and a devastating bombshell for Attlee, Dalton, and their colleagues. Sir Isaiah Berlin in the British embassy in Washington spoke of fears that the American government was trying to 'jerk the rug' from under Britain's Labour government, to cripple it from the start.[3] Among many other problems, it all made an ambitious social programme by the incoming Labour government quite imponderable.

The creation of anything resembling the kind of welfare state outlined in Labour's 1945 manifesto, and proclaimed in a thousand speeches at the hustings, therefore, rested entirely on some kind of financial agreement being reached with the United States to ease the burden of indebtedness and deficit, and to give Britain a breathing-space to help with future recovery. In desperate mood, the Cabinet sent off a major delegation, headed by Keynes himself, to Washington early in September to negotiate this loan. Keynes arrived in America full of confident rhetoric. Bevin thought that you could almost hear the money jingling in Keynes's pocket as he spoke—though the Foreign Secretary shrewdly wondered whether it was really there. Keynes publicly declared that Britain was not a suppliant. In view of her many sacrifices on behalf of the free world since 1939 he expressed the hope that even an interest-free loan might be obtained. However, he was rudely disillusioned. Americans were hostile to the resumption of long-term debts on the European continent, on the pattern of those that had led to such difficulty after 1918. The prospect of lending money to a socialist government was even more unattractive to the US business world. The American Secretary of the Treasury, Fred Vinson, a Kentucky politician turned economist, was felt to take a simple, parochial view of the problem, while

[3] H. G. Nicholas (ed.), *Washington Despatches, 1941–45* (London, 1981), p. 609.

Will Clayton at the Department of Economic Affairs saw Britain's plight largely in terms of speeding up free world trade and multilateralism, on the basis of the currency and commercial arrangements outlined in the Bretton Woods agreement in 1944. President Truman himself was still feeling his way and unwilling to intervene. There was little meeting of minds between the two delegations, while the personal gulf that divided a cultured, sophisticated economist from King's, Cambridge, from a border-country politician like Vinson was unbridgeable. In addition, Keynes felt himself to be severely harassed by Dalton and the British government at home which, in Dalton's telegram to Keynes on 27 October, seemed to be forcing the British negotiators to press for $2.5 billion at 1 per cent for fifty years, terms that were simply unrealistic.[4] The discussions, therefore, soon struck barren rock.

Long before the end of October, Keynes was brutally aware that the hope of any interest-free loan was a chimera. The Americans insisted on commercial terms, probably 2 per cent, with attention paid to the sterling balances as well. Nor was the amount of the loan offered all that Keynes had hoped. The original expectation of $5m. dwindled to $4m., which was what Clayton and also the US State Department favoured. Vinson even proposed scaling it down further to $3.5m. A telegram from Keynes to Dalton as early as 18 October confirmed that the Americans were rejecting the idea either of a free grant or an interest-free loan, and complained at the lack of leadership being shown by Truman.[5] Attlee protested to Ben Chifley, the Labour Prime Minister of Australia, that 'the Americans are being difficult', especially with their implied threats to the system of imperial preference.[6] The rate of interest and the global total of the loan, however, could both be resolved in time. But further complications arose from Clayton's and Vinson's insistence on two other essential conditions. Both were governed by the

    [4] Dalton's telegram to Washington, 27 Oct. 1945 (PREM 8/35); D. Moggridge (ed.), *The Collected Writings of John Maynard Keynes*, vol. xxiv: 'Activities, 1944–1946: the Transition to Peace' (London, 1979), p. 568.
    [5] Keynes to Dalton, 18 Oct. 1945, NABOB 177 (PREM 8/35).
    [6] Attlee to Chifley, 32 Oct. 1945, T 167/45 (ibid.).

canons of nineteenth-century economic liberalism which
influenced the ideas of the US Treasury and State Department. The fact that these theories were of impeccable British,
indeed Manchester, origin did not make them more palatable
in London. The first was that Britain should enter into a
multilateral liberalization of trade, with a broad reduction
of tariffs, including the whittling down of the imperial
preferences fixed at Ottawa in 1932. The second was that
sterling should be made freely convertible into dollars and
other currencies. Keynes himself regarded this last as inevitable, even desirable,—'something we shall have to give away
de facto even if it is not given away *de jure*'[7]—and perhaps
underestimated the difficulties that would arise. But he did
resist a firm and early deadline being imposed. An ancillary
problem was American anxiety about the famous 'sterling
balances', which generated much heat over the years. These
balances had actually increased by no less than £700m.
during the war. The United States insisted that these debts
with Commonwealth countries (India and Egypt above all)
totally distorted Britain's position in relation to its reserves
and made a mockery of the eternal British pleas of poverty.
The British replied that no early action could be taken to
liquidate the balances, since they were basically debts owed
to the developing nations of the Commonwealth by the
mother country. For India, they were especially important.
Later mythology has made Keynes, then an ailing man, the
hero of the talks in Washington. It is clear from the public
record that in fact negotiations did not go altogether well
under his aegis, apart from an American agreement that only
$1 billion of the sterling balances (out of a total of $14 billion) would be released, which would be balanced by contributions to the central reserve from the overseas sterling
area. In order to help out Keynes (and also Lionel Robbins
whom Dalton thought 'rather hysterical' at this point), on
the suggestion of Burke Trend, Edward Bridges was dispatched
to Washington on 30 November. Negotiations at once
speeded up; indeed, as Dalton wrote, Bridges 'took command
and rallied our tired team'.[8] By the start of December, Keynes

---

[7] Keynes telegram to Dalton, 30 Nov. 1945, NABOB 419 (ibid).
[8] Dalton, *High Tide and After*, p. 84.

could outline the final American proposals. There would be a loan of $3.75 million with an interest charge of 2 per cent, to be repaid in fifty annual instalments, starting on 31 December 1951. There would be no waiver or escape clauses. Britain would consent to enter a general agreement on tariffs and trade. Convertibility of sterling would come into effect twelve months after Congress approved the loan.[9] It was the best that Keynes and Bridges could do. Now it all hung on the response of the Labour government in Britain.

The Cabinet held two anxious discussions on the terms offered by the Americans. They brought into the open the first serious divisions of opinion among ministers. But the outcome was never in doubt. Dalton urged the immediate acceptance of the terms as the best for which Britain could hope. Bevin and Morrison both took the same line, and argued that, without US aid of this kind, neither a revival of Britain's trade overseas nor social reform at home would be possible. The two dissentients were the two most left-wing ministers, Shinwell and Bevan, albeit on somewhat different grounds. In the Cabinet discussion of 29 November, Shinwell strongly attacked the commercial clauses attached to the loan.[10] 'They were incompatible with the successful operation of a planned economy in this country and would ruin our export trade.' Bevan, on political grounds, attached Britain's approaching the Americans as suppliant. The news of the Cabinet disagreement was then leaked by an American news agency. Dalton told the Cabinet on 3 December that the dissent of Bevan and Shinwell had been given wide publicity; Attlee mildly rebuked his ministers for an apparent breach of Cabinet confidentiality, but Shinwell and Bevan rejoined that their views were well known before they took office. Privately, the American banker, Henry Breck, complained to Keynes of the 'the present bitterness of feeling in England, and what I am afraid will be a corresponding bitterness over here, engendered by the coming debates in Congress'. Breck also attacked criticism of the outline terms by leading British Conservatives and by 'such a well-

---

[9] Memorandum by Dalton, 28 Nov. 1945, CP (45) 312 (CAB 129/5); Confidential annex to Cabinet Conclusion, 5 Dec. 1945 (CAB 128/2).
[10] Cabinet Conclusions, 29 Nov. 1945 (ibid.).

known friend of America as Geoffrey Crowther in the Economist'.[11]

The crucial Cabinet meeting took place on 5 December.[12] Dalton strongly defended the terms of the loan, with the firm support of Bevin, Morrison, Cripps, and Attlee himself, all the major figures in the government. Dalton reported that there had since been a further tightening of the screw, with the ending of restrictions on exchange control enforced by Washington, along with the freeing of the current dollar earnings of the sterling area, to continue for no more than fifteen months. But the result of turning the terms down, Dalton argued powerfully, would be a sharp reduction in the imports of food and raw materials, with a severe reduction in the standard of living of British people. Shinwell remained unrepentant. He attacked the length of the transitional period over exchange control restrictions. The Agreement as a whole 'was very unsatisfactory'. But, obviously, he was not going to resign, especially with coal nationalization under way. Aneurin Bevan was more conciliatory. He now saw that there was no alternative to accepting the draft agreement. The Cabinet announced its acceptance of the loan terms, without recorded dissent. The approval of the loan in parliament was now achieved without difficulty. As has been noted, on 13 December twenty-three Labour MPs, mainly moderate left-wingers such as Blackburn, Barbara Castle, Callaghan, Foot, Delargy, Jennie Lee, and Benn Levy, voted against the government. They were joined in the division lobby by over seventy Conservatives, many of them right-wing imperialists anxious for the future of imperial preference, others critical of the terms and the peril to the sterling area. The most passionate and persuasive Conservative dissentient was Robert Boothby who claimed that the loan would mean the end both of the sterling area and of the British Empire. Parodying Keynes's famous description of Lloyd George at Versailles, it was, he declared, 'an economic Munich', the result of the appeasement advocated by the beguiling 'siren' voice of Keynes.[13] However, Churchill and

[11] Henry Breck to Keynes, 5 Jan. 1946 (T 247/128).
[12] Cabinet Conclusions, 5 Dec. 1945 (CAB 128/2).
[13] *Parl. Deb.*, 5th ser., vol. 417, 468 (12 Dec. 1945).

the majority of Conservative MPs, while critical of the rate of interest exacted, the date of convertibility, and the reduction of imports that would follow, decided to abstain. Churchill's muddled speech seemed to argue that the loan was both deplorable and inevitable, at one and the same time. Interestingly enough, the far left strongly supported the government. Willie Gallacher, the veteran Communist member for West Fife, applauded the loan as giving the Labour government four years of respite to build socialism. He also applauded the radical upsurge he claimed to detect in capitalist America, notably in the unions of the CIO. Such far-left MPs as the two Communists, Gallacher and Piratin, together with D. N. Pritt, Zilliacus, Platts-Mills, Solley, Warbey, and S. O. Davies, all entered the government lobby. The loan was approved by the Commons by 345 votes to 98. Eight Conservatives actually voted with the government, as against 71 voting against and 118 abstaining. Soon after, assisted by a magisterial speech by Keynes, it passed the Lords as well. The furore of the debate on the US loan soon petered out. Keynes assured Will Clayton that, now that the parliamentary discussions were satisfactorily over, 'everyone here, including the critics in Government circles, is from now going to work loyally and whole-heartedly, to make a good job of policy along the lines which we have agreed'.[14] So it proved. The terms of the loan did not seem then, and certainly do not appear now with forty years' hindsight, to be unduly onerous. An effective interest rate of 1.6 per cent, allowing for the five-year period of grace down to December 1951, was not severe. Secure in its financial platform, at least for a time, the Labour government could now plan for the future. On the other hand, convertibility arrangements, which were eventually due to come into effect on 15 July 1947, twelve months after the US Congress finally approved the loan, were undoubtedly disastrous. There was an absurdly short deadline, with no contingency planning for the drain on reserves that might result from the obligation to convert sterling. As will be seen, the long-term outcome of the convertibility clause tacked on the loan on such doctrinaire grounds was to plunge the Labour government into its supreme crisis in the summer of 1947.

[14] Keynes to Will Clayton, 21 Dec. 1945 (copy: T 247/128).

This discussion of the US loan has been necessary here because, without it, the welfare state, built up between 1945 and 1951, would not have been possible. Without this lifeline from capitalist America, Labour Britain would have faced extremes of austerity and impoverishment, worse even than MacDonald and his colleagues confronted in 1931. The welfare services would have had to be cut back severely rather than expanded. Some of the criticisms voiced by Shinwell and Bevan assumed a degree of economic manœuvrability and commercial independence for Britain after the war that was quite unreal. At any rate, the debate ended for good in December 1945, and Bevan himself could apply his talents to creating that fabric of social welfare to which his party was committed.

Aneurin Bevan, indeed, was the key figure in the welfare programmes of the new government. His appointment to the Ministry of Health by Attlee in July 1945 was something of a surprise. In the Popular Front years of the thirties, and throughout the war he had been a stormy petrel, an incorrigible rebel. *Tribune* had been his private organ of dissent. He had been expelled from the Parliamentary Labour Party in January 1939 and nearly suffered the same fate in July 1944. Nor had he been particularly involved with problems of health and medicine as such during his time as miners' union activist and member for Ebbw Vale since 1929. On the other hand, no one could emerge from the crucible of the Welsh valleys unaware of how disease (especially lung disease), squalor, and environmental deprivation enshrouded the lives of the miners and others in the community. One aspect of South Wales society from the turn of the century had been the growth of a large array of workmen's health clubs and medical aid societies, often with the help of Miners' Federation funds through joint subscriptions to hospitals.[15] Bevan had himself served on the hospital committee of the Tredegar Medical Aid Society, as a young man in 1923–4. These private clubs were bitterly opposed by general practitioners who always resented the extent of lay control. The conflict between the professional status of

[15] See Ray Earwicker, 'Miners' Medical Services for the First World War: the South Wales Coalfield', *Llafur*, vol. 3, no. 2 (spring 1981), pp. 39–52.

the doctors and the social needs of a working-class community was already visible in microcosm. Nor was Bevan
totally innocent of specialist knowledge in medical questions.
The doctors themselves were probably misled by his cheerful
pronouncement at a dinner during his early months in
office in 1945 that 'I am a comparative virgin'. Bevan had
taken a close interest in health matters over a long period,
including the Clement Davies report on the anti-tuberculosis
services in Wales in 1939 which had outlined a terrible
picture of the effects of damp, insanitary housing, and inadequate social services for lung disease in the industrial
and rural parts of Wales. Bevan was also fully acquainted
with the arguments of the Socialist Medical Association,
a vigorous pressure group headed by a leading 'social
Christian', Dr Somerville Hastings MP, and Dr Stark Murray,
with its own journal *Medicine Today and Tomorrow*.[16] The
SMA had succeeded in forcing the idea of a non-contributory,
comprehensive state medical service on the Labour Party
programme in 1934, though the idea had not been taken
much further by 1939. The demands of the SMA gathered
momentum during the war, especially during the debates on
the abortive Willink health proposals in 1944. Bevan had also
close doctor friends, notably Dan Davies of Pontycymmer.
From South Wales, the new Minister inherited a broad synoptic diagnosis of the interrelated character of employment,
health, welfare, and the other components of a civilized
society. They left him with a deep scepticism of the vested
interests of middle-class pressure groups such as the medical
profession. Above all, he had a zest for power. He sought to
translate the socialist faith into practical and enduring reality.
In this, he was to prove an outstanding executive minister,
as Sir Arthur Rucker and other key civil servants readily
acknowledged. It was not a bad equipment to bring to bear
on a key welfare department in the heady days of Labour's
electoral victory in 1945.

Bevan's central task was the creation of a national health
service: this was to be his main preoccupation over the next
three years. Indeed, after the war, this seemed assured,

[16] See D. Stark Murray, *Health for All* (London, 1942) and files of *Medicine
Today and Tomorrow*, Radcliffe Science Library, Oxford.

following Beveridge, the Willink scheme, and other ideas for revamping the health and hospital services, including several put forward by the British Medical Association itself. Medical journals such as *The Lancet* and *The Medical Officer* were enthusiastic advocates of a complete reorganization of the health services on a national basis. With the American loan now secured, however controversially, these ambitions could now be fulfilled. There was general anticipation that a new publicly-funded health scheme would be a major priority for the Attlee government. The Socialist Medical Association, with Somerville Hastings again back in the House as MP for Barking, was active in promoting the cause of a salaried medical profession, a nationalized hospital service, new health centres, and the whittling down of the privileges of private medical practice, and such survivals as the sale of practices. A newly-conceived service would take its cue from the needs of the community alone. Bevan now applied his powerful intellect and energy to these and other matters, including the encouragement of medical education and research. In this context, he endorsed the idea of chairs of social medicine at medical schools. 'He thought it important that education on this subject should not be too abstract.'[17]

His early dealings with the British Medical Association in the latter months of 1945 were amiable enough. They were even more cordial with the presidents of the three royal specialist colleges (Surgeons, Physicians, and Obstetricians), especially with Lord Moran of the RCP, 'Corkscrew Charlie' to his admirers, a dexterous and politically-sensitive figure. Sir Alfred Webb-Johnson of the RCS would address the minister in correspondence as 'My dear Aneurin'. For Bevan was indeed a worldly, sophisticated figure, the confidant of Beaverbrook and Bracken, a habitué of the Café Royal. He liked to depict himself in later years as a natural aristocrat.[18] Like another earlier Welsh radical, who also had his troubles with the doctors, Aneurin Bevan, so often reviled in public

[17] Report of a meeting between Bevan and Socialist Medical Association deputation, 22 May 1946 (MH 77/63).
[18] See Janet Morgan (ed.), *The Backbench Diaries of Richard Crossman* (London, 1981), p. 429 (9 June 1955). Also see Crossman's account of Bevan's elegant, sophisticated style during a trip to Venice, ibid., p. 574 (14 Feb. 1957).

as an extremist and a demagogue, could in private 'charm a bird off a bough'.

But by November 1945, serious problems were beginning to mount. In part, this arose from the comparatively radical aspects of Bevan's draft bill which aroused the early suspicion of the BMA Negotiating Committee.[19] Indeed, the National Health Service is a prime exhibit in illustrating the danger of making too much of the continuity between the social consensus of the war years and the post-war Labour welfare state. Beveridge had its limits and, of course, was in any case not directly concerned with a national health service. The ideas of Henry Willink, Churchill's Minister of Health in 1944, especially in their final watered-down form, fell short of Bevan's later proposals in vital respects, notably on hospitals and health centres. Of course, even Willink's scheme had been severely mauled by the BMA and by important elements in the Conservative Party, including Churchill himself, for its alleged threat to the professional independence of the doctors. Bevan's draft scheme in October–November 1945 markedly increased the overall control of the Ministry of Health. He provided more encouragement for the group partnership of doctors in 'under-doctored areas' and for local health centres. He was clear that there must be a salaried element in the remuneration of the general practitioners, even though it was accepted that capitation fees would remain the chief component of a doctor's salary. Above all, there was a decisive commitment to the nationalization of hospitals, with the comprehensive reorganization of the hospital governing system, including the voluntary, cottage, and municipal hospitals, under regional boards accountable to the ministry. This last was something the Willink scheme had always resisted. A major factor in Bevan's case was the needs of Scottish hospitals, where more than a quarter of the voluntary hospital beds were in teaching hospitals and could not be excluded from the system.

When Bevan's memorandum on the structure of a national health service was first considered by the Cabinet on 18 October 1945 the nationalization of hospitals was the

---

[19] Dr C. Hill to Bevan, 8 Nov. 1945, and record of meeting of Bevan with Negotiating Committee of BMA (MH 77/119).

one issue which brought major disagreement.[20] Then, and
again in further Cabinet discussion on 20 December, Herbert
Morrison, with his long experience of local government on
the London County Council, led the resistance of those who
sought to preserve voluntary and municipal hospitals, under
local rather than national control. Morrison urged that there
was no authority in the party manifesto for such a proposal
(which was quite true). More powerfully, he urged the
importance of local and civic pride, and of voluntary enthusiasm in the running of hospitals. He pointed out the general
tendency of the government's programme to whittle away
the functions of the local authorities, to which Labour had
always had a powerful commitment: the projected gas and
electricity bills were likely to take away these services from
the local authorities as well. Morrison also criticized the proposal to make the cost of the hospitals a full charge on the
Treasury (to which Bevan had eventually got Dalton to
agree). 'There would be a very large transfer of liability
from the ratepayer to the taxpayer.' Morrison was backed
up by the Home Secretary, Chuter Ede, and to some extent
by A. V. Alexander, another Cabinet minister with a powerful civic instinct. But the great majority strongly backed
Bevan. Not only was this true of left-wingers such as Ellen
Wilkinson and Shinwell, but also of more centrist men like
Arthur Greenwood (an important figure as chairman of the
Cabinet's Social Services Committee) and Tom Williams, the
Minister of Agriculture. An authoritative voice on this subject
was that of Addison, once Lloyd George's Minister of Health
in 1919, and himself a notable architect of the welfare state.
In his pre-parliamentary days, Addison had been an anatomist
with an immensely high professional reputation; he was easily
the most distinguished doctor ever to enter politics. He had
also, in effect, founded the Medical Research Council in
1919. Addison now strongly backed up Bevan on the grounds
that a nationalized hospital system would greatly assist in
medical education, and in the training of nurses. His voice
carried much weight with Attlee who summed up strongly
in Bevan's favour. On 20 December 1945, with renewed
opposition from Morrison, and some murmurs from Dalton

[20] Cabinet Conclusions, 18 Oct., 20 Dec. 1945 (CAB 128/1).

about the effects of the block grant system, the scheme went through. The rest of Bevan's proposals, including the ending of the buying and selling of medical practices, had already been passed, without difficulty, on 3 December.

But the main reason for the problems that arose lay not in the unexpected extremism of Bevan's proposals. When they were published, their main outlines, including a framework of regional boards for hospital services, executive councils for medical service and a comprehensive element of public finance, won strong support, even from such notably non-socialist organs as *The Times, The Economist*, and *The Lancet*. The last-named thought the bill distinctly less revolutionary than the ideas originally put forward by Ernest Brown, a National Liberal, back in 1943. It was a flexible, if radical, measure dealing finally with an acknowledged social evil. 'It is in fact much less socialistic than was predicted a year ago.'[21] It was also, of course, less socialistic than the inflammatory reputation of Bevan as a left-wing firebrand might have suggested. The difficulty lay rather in the mulish resistance of the BMA, more especially its executive council headed by its elderly chairman, Dr Guy Dain, and its secretary, Charles Hill, who had won fame on the air as 'the radio doctor'. The Association was forced to admit that Bevan had made many concessions—ones much criticized by the Socialist Medical Association. He had made generous provision for both general practitioners and consultants within the framework of administration: the doctors would play a dominant role in the health insurance committees, for instance. He also ensured that the gulf between the GPs and the hospital service would continue, and even grow wider. He had left alone the system of private practice by specialists and the system of 'pay beds' in hospitals. The outcome would be that senior hospital consultants would be able to treat private patients in NHS beds. Bevan detested these last concessions, but had been advised by Moran that a mass exodus of doctors into private practice would otherwise be inevitable. Even the SMA came to accept this, with much reluctance. He also agreed that capitation fees, rather than a state salary, would become the basis of doctors'

[21] *The Lancet*, 15 Dec. 1945, 10 Nov. 1946.

remuneration. Nevertheless, the BMA Negotiating Committee still professed to regard the prospect of a full-time salaried medical service as lurking in the background; this would pose a fundamental threat to the professional freedom and integrity of the general practitioners. The BMA and its organ, the *British Medical Journal*, also claimed to view with alarm the new powers vested in the Ministry, and of the executive councils which would supervise GPs.[22] Dr Alfred Cox, absurdly, was even to denounce Bevan as a 'medical Fuhrer'. As early as December 1945, the Negotiating Committee of the BMA was to complain that Bevan's posture was one only of 'consulting' with them, rather than of true negotiation. The minister replied, with constitutional correctness, that ultimate responsibility could lie only with the elected democratic government and with parliament.

By March 1946, discussions between Bevan and the BMA negotiators had virtually broken down. A major factor in this was that the BMA and its council were overwhelmingly representative of wealthier suburban doctors, rather than of the broad spread of general practitioners up and down the land. Bevan was to find, as Lloyd George observed back in 1911, during the troubles over the National Insurance Bill, that a 'deputation of doctors was a deputation of swell doctors'.[23] The National Health Service Bill was carried overwhelmingly on the second reading (2 May 1946) by 359 votes to 172, the Liberals voting with the government. The six main features of Bevan's bill—the nationalization of hospitals; the new regional boards; the redistribution of doctors to cater for 'under-doctored areas'; the new salary provisions; the fee-paying patients allowed to specialists in hospitals; and the new health centres—were all generally commended. In the circumstances, it is surprising that the Conservatives divided the House at all, with Willink himself, ironically enough, moving a hostile amendment. The political mandate for the Health Service was incontestable. Yet now the BMA threatened the same campaign of

---

[22] Meeting of Bevan with BMA Negotiating Committee, 6 Feb. 1946 (MH 77/119); *British Medical Journal*, 30 Mar. 1946.
[23] Bentley Gilbert, *The Evolution of National Insurance in Great Britain* (London, 1966), p. 363.

intransigence and obstruction that they had offered to another Welsh reformer in 1911. The *British Medical Journal*
warned the doctors to be on their guard. The emollient
approach of this Welshman in office (like the Scotsman,
Ernest Brown, and the Englishman, Henry Willink, before
him) could not be lightly taken on trust. Like his predecessor, Lloyd George, Bevan was 'both a bard and a warrior'.[24]

The period from the summer of 1946 until the final capitulation of the BMA in May–June 1948 is an undistinguished
interlude in the history of the British welfare state. On the
other hand, it was a vital trial of strength for the Attlee
government and for the eventual reputation of Bevan
himself. In December 1946, after a ballot conducted by the
BMA and heavily influenced by its partisan projection of the
issues at stake, the general practitioners voted by more than
two to one against participation in the Health Service. The
issues that provoked especial criticism were the basis of
doctors' salaries, under which a salary element paid by the
state would figure alongside capitation fees, and the extent
to which doctors could be disciplined or coerced by local
executive councils.[25] After a further year of virtual non-
contact between the BMA and the Ministry, with the presidents of the royal colleges trying to build bridges between
the two sides, a further plebiscite conducted by the BMA
and published in February 1948 showed that only 4,735
of 45,549 doctors voting (on an 84 per cent poll) were in
favour of taking part in the Health Service.[26] The vote was
almost equally hostile in all regions of Britain, with marginally less hostility in Wales and Scotland than in England.
It seemed probable that the new Health Service would come
into effect in July shackled from the start by the refusal
of the nation's doctors and consultants to co-operate. In this
continuing impasse, Bevan himself struck the wrong note at
times. He failed to provide the specific, unambiguous reassurance that the doctors needed about their not being permanently enlisted by the state as a full-time salaried profession

[24] *British Medical Journal*, cited in Michael Foot, *Aneurin Bevan*, vol. ii,
p. 119.
[25] *British Medical Journal*, 25 Jan. 1947; *The Lancet*, 21 Dec. 1946.
[26] *The Lancet*, 21 Feb. 1948; *British Medical Journal*, 21 Feb. 1948.

yoked inextricably to the public service. In total exasperation, in a speech to the Commons on 9 February 1948, he
launched a fierce broadside at the BMA Committee as 'a
small body of politically poisoned people'. He denounced
the 'squalid political conspiracy' which had led to his proposals on medical salaries (now destined to be much aug-
mented after his acceptance of the Spens report) being so
misrepresented.[27] In fact, the links of Charles Hill in particular with the Tory Party were well known. Clearly,
though, such a ministerial pronouncement could only reduce
relations with the BMA to an even more glacial level of
frigidity.

But Bevan, never the most patient of men perhaps, had
been goaded beyond measure by the quite extraordinary
negativism of the BMA, an attitude which *The Lancet* and
many other responsible journals involved with public health
strongly condemned. There were the gravest doubts as to
whether the views of the ordinary GP were being fairly
represented by the BMA council. Henry Souttar, a past
president of the BMA who had resigned from the Association in protest in 1946, wrote in despair to Sir Arthur Rucker
on how the Association was frustrating 'a statesmanlike
attempt' to give practical effect to proposals which the
doctors themselves had been pressing on the government for
many years.[28] He incurred fierce personal attacks from
within the profession for his attitude, but he did not stand
alone. More significant in the long term, there was powerful
pressure by Moran, Webb-Johnson, and William Gilliatt, on
behalf of the royal colleges, to try to circumvent the public
intransigence of the BMA. Eventually, Moran wrote to Bevan
formally on 24 March 1948, in a well-publicized intervention,
conveying the view of the Physicians that the co-operation
of the general practitioners could be won if the Minister
made it crystal clear that no whole-time salaried medical
service would be brought in ever, either by legislation or by
departmental regulation. Bevan at once accepted this way
out. On 7 April 1948 he made a brief, and exceptionally conciliatory statement in the House. While all the central features

[27] *Parl. Deb.*, 5th ser., vol. 447, 35–6 (8 Feb. 1948).
[28] Henry Souttar to Sir Arthur Rucker, 5 June 1946 (MH 77/119).

of the NHS would be retained—the nationalization of hospitals; the regional boards and executive councils; the new municipally-run health centres; the redistribution of practices; the abolition of the sale of practices; the basic funding from the Exchequer—he affirmed that no whole-time salaried service would be introduced by regulation. He also promised that the fixed element of remuneration of £300 would last only three years, and then remain optional only. In effect, this, too, was to go in time, a final nail in the coffin of the hopes of the Socialist Medical Association. Bevan also confirmed that doctors would have complete freedom to publish their views on the running of the Health Service—not that this had ever been seriously in question. He now looked forward to an era 'of friendly co-operation'.[29] For the Opposition, Oliver Stanley gave Bevan's statement a warm welcome. Bevan had given nothing of major substance away beyond his original concessions. But the new precision of his statement about a salaried medical service turned the tide. The BMA welcomed it as 'affording the opportunity for re-examination of the points in dispute' and agreed to hold another plebiscite of its members.[30] After this, Dain's die-hard obstructionism seemed out of touch, even with grass-roots doctors' opinion. By June, a month before the NHS was due to be launched, without their waiting for the official advice of the BMA representative body, it was announced that 26 per cent of the English general practitioners had already joined the scheme. In Wales the figure was as high as 37 per cent, and in Scotland 36 per cent. Shortly after the Act came into operation, Bevan announced that 93.1 per cent of the population were now enrolled in the NHS.[31] The popularity of the service henceforth was never seriously in doubt. It was Bevan's, perhaps Britain's, finest hour.

Bevan's main preoccupation now was to ensure that the NHS that he had created would be given adequate funding. As he wrote, quite fairly, in his political testament, *In Place of Fear* (1952), he had given careful thought to the financial

[29] Moran to Bevan, 24 Mar. 1948 (ibid.); *Parl. Deb.*, 5 ser., vol. 449, 164–5 (7 Apr. 1948).
[30] *British Medical Journal*, 17 Apr. 1948, citing Dr G. Dain.
[31] *Parl. Deb.*, 5 ser., vol. 457, 1020 (4 Nov. 1948).

basis of the Health Service, and its actuarial soundness, and had ruled out any attempt to impose a contributory insurance system here.[32] But in fact, the financing of the Health Service proved to be a recurring problem, and one that somewhat harmed Bevan's reputation as an efficient social service minister. The hospital and specialist service was much the biggest item in the NHS budget: in 1950–1 it amounted to £238m. in a budget of £351m.[33] It proved especially hard to control financially, not least since executive direction lay not with the ministry, but with appointed regional boards under the terms of the NHS Act. The pharmaceutical charges were another very costly element in the budget. In fact, Bevan's preliminary estimate for NHS expenditure in the first year of 1948–9 proved to be a major underestimate. He had to rush in supplementary estimates of £53m. in 1949, an unpopular move with his colleagues at a time of severe retrenchment austerity under Cripps.[34] Morrison and other ministers complained that severe economies elsewhere, in capital investment for industry, housing, education, and other areas, were not being matched by any such sacrifices on behalf of the sacred cow of the Health Service. NHS estimates soared ever upwards from £228m. in 1949–50 to £356m. in 1950–1 and a projected £387m. in 1951–2, a figure that in fact was to be exceeded. Bevan, however, fought hard against any attempt to impose financial charges on the Health Service which, he claimed, would undermine the basic socialist purpose of the new scheme. After a severe tussle with Cripps, Bevan announced on 20 October 1949 that he accepted the principle of a shilling charge on prescriptions, but it was understood that there was no immediate likelihood of this being implemented.[35] Nor, indeed, did the Labour government ever do so, though Churchill's government hastened to impose a prescription charge, in 1952. In March 1950, as will be seen later, Bevan fought a further fierce battle with Cripps who now sought to impose a financial ceiling of £329m. on Health Service expenditure for 1951–2,

[32] Bevan, *In Place of Fear*, pp. 100 ff.
[33] Report by Sir Cyril Jones on the Financial Working of the National Health Service, 15 July 1950 (PREM 8/1486).
[34] Memorandum by Norman Brook, 29 Mar. 1950 (ibid.).
[35] Ibid.; Cabinet Conclusions, 20 Oct. 1949 (CAB 128/16).

and also to introduce charges on spectacles and dental treatment. Bevan told the Cabinet on 3 April 1950 that 'the abandonment of a free and comprehensive health service would be a shock to their supporters and a grave disappointment to Socialist opinion throughout the world'.[36] The issue was shelved in April 1950, aided by Bevan's close personal relationship with Cripps. However, under Gaitskell, a new and less experienced Chancellor in 1951, who was also a political rival of Bevan, the issue of Health Service charges suddenly re-emerged in the forefront of ministerial controversy. It led in time to Bevan's resignation and a severe undermining of the government's morale, perhaps with fatal long-term consequences for the history of the Labour Party.

The achievement of the National Health Service, however, should be viewed without judgement being blurred by the political disputes that led to Bevan's resignation in April 1951. It was obviously one of the government's outstanding triumphs, admired throughout the world, an immense landmark in the building of the welfare state. The solidity of the administrative and (despite the troubles of 1951) the financial structure of the NHS was confirmed by the Guillebaud Committee in 1956, as it was by historians subsequently. It should, however, be added that the arguments for a localized as against a nationalized hospital service were somewhat finely balanced; here Bevan's judgement must remain open to some doubt. Another conclusion is the Health Service's broad reasonableness, as *The Lancet* continuously insisted. A genuine compromise was effected, in 1946 as in 1911, between state direction and professional independence. In fact, it could be argued that Bevan went too far in giving the doctors and consultants a decisive place in the administration of the service, going in this respect somewhat beyond Willink's scheme during the war. The Socialist Medical Association, with its call for a salaried service, a vast extension of health centres, and an end to private medicine, voiced its disappointment in *Medicine Today and Tomorrow*, and its regrets at Bevan's relative lack of socialist zeal. A final verdict must be on Bevan's rare fusion, displayed effectively only in connection with the NHS perhaps, of the talents of

[36] Cabinet Conclusions, 3 Apr. 1950 (CAB 128/17).

the constructive reformer and the visionary. He always
sought power wherever it resided, even if you 'always saw
its coat-tails disappearing round the corner'. He proclaimed
the 'principle of action' which would make socialism prac-
tically effective.[37] The National Health Service, which still
endures despite much recent travail, is the finest of monu-
ments to his talents and his faith.

Conversely, housing, another of Bevan's departmental concerns at the Ministry of Health, is commonly thought to be a
blemish on his record. Certainly, there was recurrent criticism
at the time, from Ministry officials and politicians alike, of
the government's slow progress in house construction. After
1951, the Conservatives made much political capital by
achieving the target proclaimed in their election manifesto
of 300,000 houses a year: it was an achievement which really
made the reputation of Harold Macmillan, the Housing
Minister, and his assistant, Ernest Marples. Aneurin Bevan
himself gave hostages to fortune by once blithely observing
(and quite unfairly to himself) that he spent a mere five
minutes a week on housing during his period at Health.
Indeed, linking housing and health in the same department
was almost certainly a great administrative error by Attlee.
It made far more sense to include housing and local government within the same ministry, as occurred from January
1951 when Dalton went to a new Ministry of Local Government and Planning, leaving the Ministry of Health with
the problems of the NHS as its major concern. Housing and
local government went together far more naturally, since,
after all, it was the local authorities which mostly owned the
land and controlled the planning procedures for house-
building.

The housing programme of 1945–51 undoubtedly began
badly, especially in England. By November, a leading civil
servant was urging that 'it certainly looks as if the Ministry
of Health ought to try and increase the number of houses
started and reduce the time lag between authority to go to
tender and the beginning of construction. Scotland is making

[37] See Jennie Lee, *My Life with Nye* (London, 1980), e.g. pp. 234–5.

much better progress than England and it would be interesting to know the reasons for this.'[38] Labour's election propaganda in the 1945 campaign had placed a great emphasis on housing, and the perceived need for well over a million houses for working-class occupants, quite apart from the appalling heritage of slum property in inner-city areas, and the further problems of bomb damage in London and other major cities. Bevan was clear that the main emphasis should be on council houses built by the local authority with a high element of Treasury subsidy, that is, on houses for rent, rather than houses for private sale. He persuaded Dalton in October 1945 that the rent to be paid should remain at 10s. rather than 12s. as the Treasury preferred.[39] The emphasis also should be on permanent council housing of decent quality, rather than on a proliferation of temporary housing, 'prefabs' and the rest, which emerged in the aftermath of the war. Private house-building would be severely curtailed. Licences for private house-building would be granted only on condition that the house built was not resold for four years, and even then would be subject to price control. These defensible political priorities, concentrating on the desperate need of working-class occupants, were encumbered in practice by organizational defects in the running of the housing programme. The responsibility for the housing drive was diffused between several ministries—Health, Supply, Town and Country Planning, and Works, with the Scottish Office having its own responsibility north of the border. By April 1946, Attlee was successfully urging Bevan to consider the idea of a new Housing Production Executive to take control of the whole field of housing materials, the production of components, and the supply of labour, from these various departments.[40] There were also frequent conflicts over priorities in the demand for building materials such as bricks, timber, and steel between the competing needs of council houses, hospitals, schools, factories in development areas, and much else besides. The government seemed to find

[38] Memorandum by E. M. Nicholson, 6 Nov. 1945 (CAB 124/450).
[39] Record of discussion between Dalton and Bevan, 12 Oct. 1945 (T 161/1301).
[40] Attlee to Bevan, and others, 11 Apr. 1946 (PREM 8/232).

it difficult to create any effective instrument to co-ordinate
the supply of materials. The original Housing Committee of
the Cabinet, chaired by Greenwood, was replaced by a far
more formidable standing committee of the Cabinet, over
which Attlee himself presided, from December 1945 onwards, but it, too, failed to provide satisfactory co-ordinating
powers and was finally wound up in October 1947.[41] In addition, there were no agreed procedures to ensure that building
starts were kept in line with the available labour on a regional
or local basis. The total of half-built houses continued to
mount. By the end of 1946, indeed, of 953,000 men employed
in the building industry, only 200,000 were employed in
building new permanent houses, while 229,000 were occupied
in repairs, renovations, or conversions of existing houses.[42]

The complaints about housing policy, therefore, were
vocal at a very early stage. One powerful critic was Attlee's
private secretary, the economist, Douglas Jay (translated into
the Labour MP for Battersea in mid-1946). Jay strongly
attacked Bevan's procedures for tackling the labour shortages, and the Ministry's failure to announce any specific
target for permanent house construction. 'The picture is
gloomy', he told Attlee on 2 November 1945, 'and the
building of permanent houses is likely to remain the weak
point in the government's record for many months.'[43] He condemned the Ministry of Health's over-reliance on the local
authorities—a view reinforced in the Cabinet by Lord Addison who had had his own troubles with local-authority building programmes after the previous war in 1919 and whose
own Housing Act of that year had inaugurated the principle
of housing as a social service. Jay's putative solution was for
a new Housing Corporation to act in default of inefficient
local authorities, and for more direct building by the Ministry
of Works. He thought Bevan was 'very doctrinal' on this last
point.[44] The critics were later joined by Morrison in the
Cabinet, still smarting from his defeat by Bevan over the

---

[41] Minutes of Cabinet Housing Committee, 1945–7 (CAB 134/320).

[42] *Monthly Digest of Statistics*, May 1948.

[43] Douglas Jay to Attlee, 15 Oct., 2 Nov., 23 Nov., 7 Dec. 1945 (PREM
8/228). Curiously enough, Mr Jay does not refer to these cogent proposals of his
in his memoirs, *Change and Fortune*.

[44] Jay to Attlee, 15 Oct. 1945 (ibid.).

Health Service perhaps, who urged that the recruitment of
key workers such as miners and farm labourers was being
held back because of the shortage of suitable accommodation
in mining or agricultural areas. Bevan and Tomlinson, the
Minister of Works, however, were both opposed to novelties
such as a National Building Corporation. It would be 'unwise', thought Bevan, to create a new government building
organization at the present time. Neither the flow of labour
nor of building materials would benefit.[45]

Without doubt, early progress was very slow indeed. A civil
servant, E. M. Nicholson, wrote in exasperation on 12 February
1946 that 'at last houses are beginning to trickle out of the
building pipeline'.[46] But Bevan could announce that, at the
very most, only 20,000 permanent houses would have been
built in England and Wales by the end of January 1946,
a meagre haul indeed for six months of Labour government
committed to ending the housing shortage. Direct action by
homeless people, such as 'squatters' who occupied empty
office and other buildings in London and other cities, became
more widespread, and drew attention to the inadequacies
of the housing drive. On the other hand, the crushing burdens
that the government faced ought also, in fairness, to be given
due weight. There were ceaseless financial difficulties, culminating eventually in the severe cutback of local-authority
housing programmes from over 200,000 to 170,000 houses
in 1949. There were constant shortages of materials, notably
softwood and other timber, where the dollar shortages
made supplies from North America very erratic and where
Scandinavia could not make up the deficit. The problems of
the allocation of skilled labour were controlled by the
Treasury's 'manpower' budget and the arrangements of the
Ministry of Labour; they were far beyond the control of
Bevan at the Ministry of Health. They were much influenced,
for instance, by the success or otherwise of Isaacs at Labour
in speeding up demobilization from the armed forces in
1946. Bevan, in his frequent pressure for a national wages
policy, was well aware of the need for a new initiative in this
direction; he, of all ministers, cannot be blamed for bottle-

---

[45] Bevan to Tomlinson, 2 Aug. 1946 (ibid.).
[46] E. M. Nicholson memorandum, 12 Feb. 1946 (CAB 124/450).

necks over manpower. In addition to all this, the legacy of
the ravages of the wartime blitz imposed an enormous strain
on the resources available for urban development. One response to this was the programme of New Towns launched
by Lewis Silkin at the Ministry of Town and Country Planning in a major act in 1947, but this to some degree came
into conflict with the Ministry of Health's programmes.

In spite of all problems, in fact, there were clear signs in
the latter months of 1946 that a new urgency was being
injected into the housing drive, aided by the newly-created
Housing Production Executive created in April 1946 on
Attlee's personal insistence. Gradually demands ventilated
in the *New Statesman* and elsewhere for some new tier
of authority to take over the housing programme were shown
to be misconceived.[47] After all, only the local authorities
who had been deeply involved in council house-building since
1919 and who controlled the sites and planning machinery
were really competent to build houses, in the light of local
needs which they alone, as democratically elected bodies,
really understood. Despite an estimated need for 100,000
further building workers and problems about timber imports,[48] by the end of 1946, 251,000 new houses had been
approved, of which 188,000 were actually under construction. The number of half-built houses waiting for more
men or materials was drastically cut back. The total of
permanent new houses for England, Wales, and Scotland (but
excluding Northern Ireland) amounted to 139,000 completions in 1947, 227,000 in 1948, 197,000 in 1949,
198,000 in 1950, and 194,000 in 1951. To a grand total of
1,016,349 new houses completed in England, Wales, and
Scotland between August 1945 and December 1951 should
be added a further half million temporary homes, the conversion of existing premises into homes, and the repair
of war-damaged premises to make them again inhabitable.[49]
In the peak year of 1948, when the economy showed a
dramatic upwards swing, over 230,000 dwellings of all types

[47] e.g. *New Statesman*, 17 Nov. 1945.
[48] Memorandum on housing by A. Johnston, 14 Nov. 1946 (CAB 124/451).
[49] *Housing Return for England and Wales, 31st December 1951* Cmd. 8458
(PP, 1951–2, xxi, 1019 ff.): *Housing Return for Scotland, 31st December 1951*
Cmd. 8459 (PP, 1951–2, xxi, 1131 ff.)

were completed, and criticisms of the housing programme markedly subsided. Indeed, Gaitskell (under-secretary to the Ministry of Fuel and Power at the same time) urged Morrison in August 1947 that the materials absorbed by the house-building programme threatened to disturb the export drive.[50] Edwin Plowden, of the National Planning Board, was another who insisted at this time that pressure by Bevan and by Westwood, the Secretary for Scotland, for an immediate commitment to a global figure for house construction should be resisted. With 242,000 houses under construction in August 1947, and a further 100,000 tenders let, too much rather than too little seemed to be done in relation to housing now. Plowden urged that a moratorium should be imposed on further tenders outside mining and agricultural areas.[51]

Partly through pressure from Plowden and others in the Treasury, the total of houses built fell back somewhat after 1948, simply because repeated balance of payments crises and curbs on public investment in 1948-9 led to Bevan's house programme being reduced to well below 200,000. Bevan himself protested angrily, but, already engaged as he was in maintaining the funding of the National Health Service, he could hardly press for increased allocations for housing as well. In addition, mainly for political reasons with an election coming up, the restrictions on private building were somewhat relaxed. As a result, the building societies, whom Bevan had derided as mere 'money lenders', saw their credit operations rise sharply in 1948-50, though it should be said that they had flourished earlier during Dalton's regime of cheap money.[52] Bevan was also persuaded to relax the somewhat exaggerated standards he had set for council house design. On such matters as the provision of bathrooms and lavatories and the insistence on three bedrooms, Dalton scornfully commented that Bevan was 'a tremendous Tory'.[53] Perhaps, as a working-class aristocrat,

[50] Gaitskell to Morrison, 8 Aug. 1947 (CAB 124/452).
[51] Plowden memorandum, 11 Aug. 1947, and Plowden to Cripps, 30 Apr. 1948 (ibid.); cf. minutes of Cabinet Production Committee, 13 Oct.–18 Nov. 1947 (CAB 134/635).
[52] E. J. Cleary, *The Building Society Movement* (London, 1965), pp. 237 ff.
[53] Dalton, *High Tide and After*, p. 358. For an effective critique of Dalton's view, see Jennie Lee, op. cit., p. 160.

he simply had higher standards and more ambitious aspirations than his guilt-ridden, middle-class, university-trained
colleagues. These concessions were disliked by Bevan but
they probably gave renewed life to the housing programme,
and prevented housing becoming an electoral albatross in the
1950 and 1951 general elections as had at one time seemed
very probable.

The overall performance of the Labour government on
housing policy, therefore, was competent if not outstanding.
The credit rests only in part with Bevan. Hugh Dalton undoubtedly injected a good deal of new energy into housing
in 1951, at the new Ministry of Housing and Local Government, and house construction continued at a busy level
through all the financial problems of 1951 at the time of
the Korean War. The episodic progress of house-building
certainly showed up some of the inadequacies of the
government's machinery for the co-ordination of policy,
inadequacies for which the Ministry of Health was commonly, and often unfairly, blamed. It also showed the erratic
way in which priorities on the home front evolved, with
housing, along with health, regional development, the
restructuring of industry, and other themes occupying varying degrees of prominence during these six years. In the
light of the immensity of the financial and physical constraints upon the housing programme, however, criticisms
must be severely tempered. Of course, housing was a popular
and emotive issue which brought popular criticism upon the
government. The 'squatters' in the autumn of 1946 focused
attention on disused, under-used, or derelict buildings in
prime sites in inner-city areas. The need to evict homeless
'squatters' compulsorily from flats and hotels in central
London brought the government much unpopularity. The
housing problem, in all its many aspects, from the red tape
that bound up building contractors, to the environmental
limitations of the new council house estates, made excellent
copy for newspapers hostile to Labour. The backlog of
substandard housing, of course, was very far from removed
by October 1951. Shortages remained appalling, as did the
prevalence of dilapidated or insanitary houses and tene-
ments. Things were especially serious in Scotland, where

owner-occupiers were traditionally a small minority,[54] and not much better in Wales. Still, the government did manage to achieve the first major impetus in public housing since the days of the Wheatley Act at the time of the first Labour government in 1924. Furthermore, the main emphasis was placed squarely on those least fortunate, on working-class people without adequate housing and caught in huge waiting-lists, seeking housing at low rents, rather than on aspiring middle-class owner-occupiers who saw houses in terms of status and perhaps profit, as well as of security. The 'two nations' housing policy of the National Government in the thirties, with its boom years for private builders and developers, did not return. Of course, the government did not fulfil all its targets. Bevan's eventual figure of a minimum of 200,000 completions a year was scaled down by the Treasury as has been seen. For all that, the rehousing of several million people in new or renovated houses, at a time of extreme social and economic dislocation, was a considerable achievement. Housing, therefore, deserves its honoured role in the saga of Labour's welfare state.

Closely identified with the work of the Ministry of Health was that of the Ministry of National Insurance, a major department though not one accorded Cabinet rank in 1945. The minister here was another Welsh miner, James Griffiths, though one as firmly in the Labour mainstream as Bevan was on the left. His permanent secretary was his compatriot, Tom Phillips.[55] Griffiths had emerged during the war as Labour's expert and spokesman on social insurance. He drew in part on his own experience in the South Wales Miners' Federation of the inadequacies of provision for national assistance or compensation for industrial injuries. Griffiths' objective was basically the fulfilment of the Beveridge report. He had himself been a leading critic of the Churchill government in February 1943 for its failure to take an immediately enthusiastic and positive view of the report. In February

---

[54] Christopher Harvie, *No Gods and Precious Few Heroes* (London, 1981), pp. 70–2.
  [55] James Griffiths, *Pages from Memory* (London, 1969), p. 80.

1946, therefore, Griffiths introduced a comprehensive measure outlining the government's ideas on National Insurance.[56] One scheme of consolidated insurance would henceforth bring together insurance against sickness, unemployment, and old age, on a clear principle of universality. There would be a basic rate of 26s. for sickness benefit (compared with an existing rate of 18s. for six months only), with other benefits for wives or adult dependants and for children. The same rate would apply to unemployment benefit which continued for more than the statutory twenty-six weeks, on the basis of credits for the unemployed. Griffiths had ensured this last provision at a meeting of Cabinet on 17 January. There would also be implemented maternity benefits and widows' benefits, while family allowances (costed eventually at £59m.) would come into effect from August 1946. Retirement benefits would be raised to a basic rate of 25s. for a single pensioner and 42s. for a married couple, at what was believed to be a subsistence basis. Beveridge's proposals had been for lower rates of 24s. and 40s. respectively. In an echo of Labour's traditional viewpoint, dating from the days of the Webbs and the 1909 Minority Report, Griffiths claimed that his bill would enact the principle of 'a National Minimum Standard'. It would be administered directly by the state instead of through friendly societies. His compendious measure went into standing committee with scarcely a breeze of criticism to disturb it in three days of debate. Conservatives made little of the much-diminished role of the friendly societies: after all, they had received their *nunc dimittis* with Lloyd George's National Insurance Act of 1911. Butler's somewhat carping and negative opening speech stressed observations by Keir Hardie and others in the distant past on the active role of the Tory Party in promoting social reform. Nor did Labour backbenchers try to reactivate the Webbs' critique of Lloyd George's bill in 1911. They accepted the contributory principle of the financial basis of social insurance, however

[56] *Parl. Deb.*, 5th ser., vol. 418, 1733–58 (6 Feb. 1946). There is an interesting discussion in J. Hess, 'The Social Policy of the Attlee Government', in W. J. Mommsen (ed.), *The Emergence of the Welfare State in Britain and Germany 1850–1950* (London, 1981), pp. 300–8.

regressive in its social effects, as actuarily inevitable. Anyhow, the alternative was the hated 'dole'. In committee,
however, there were Labour dissentients, led by Sidney
Silverman and Barbara Castle, one of the government's PPS
ministers. They attacked the myriad of qualification and re-
qualification limits attached to the time for which benefits
would be paid. Even more, they focused upon the scale of
benefits which in key respects were below what Beveridge
had recommended. Clause 12, which included reference
to the exhaustion of benefits by unemployed men, was a
particular target, especially at a time when the rate of unemployment was rising sharply in South Wales, Scotland,
and the north-east of England.[57] Griffiths made some concessions in this direction, upgrading the scale of benefits
after a minor revolt in the division lobby by over thirty
Labour members joined by a few Liberals. Clause 12,
however, remained in the bill. The third reading went
through without a division on 30 May and the Act duly
received the royal assent on 1 August.

The National Insurance Act, most ably piloted through
by Griffiths, was a corner-stone of Labour's welfare schemes.
Indeed, it remained a basis of the welfare state for the next
thirty years or more. It was closely linked with the wartime
proposals, of course: certainly, the organic links here were
closer than between the Willink proposals for health and
Bevan's conception of the National Health Service. The old
policies did not disappear in their entirety. Some aspects
of the National Insurance scheme in its mode of operation
still retained features of the hated means test and the
'genuinely seeking work' provision with all their inquisitorial
features. But the Act of 1946, a measure which commanded
almost universal support, provided a comprehensive universal
basis for insurance provision that had hitherto been
unknown. It was backed in 1948 by two other important
measures that Griffiths also put through. The Industrial
Injuries Act extended the insurance principle to a major
category of areas previously omitted from the general insurance system. The benefits here, in response to union pressure, were much higher than for sickness or unemployment:

[57] See Silverman's amendment, *Parl. Deb.*, vol. 423 (23 May 1946).

45s. a week, as against 26s. The old socialist notion of making injuries a charge upon industry itself was quietly abandoned. Judicial tribunals were set up to adjudicate on disputes. The Miners' Federation in South Wales, under Griffiths's own presidency, had campaigned hard in the thirties on the injuries issue, especially with reference to silicosis and other lung diseases in mining areas. Also, the National Assistance Act of 1948, introduced by Aneurin Bevan, by instituting a broad framework of national assistance, dealt the final blow to the old poor law of nineteenth-century notoriety. A couple with no personal resources beyond their pension, and paying a rent of ten shillings a week, for instance, could have their income made up to fifty shillings a week by the new National Assistance Board. The total fabric of the National Insurance legislation of the Attlee government appeared to end an old argument and working-class grievance. It confirmed the new concept of social citizenship first outlined in aspects of Lloyd George's bill of 1911. It provided a comprehensive basis for social provision; for the next generation, legislation would focus largely on filling the gaps within its all-encompassing framework. The first major reform to follow was Richard Crossman's National Superannuation scheme under the Wilson government, which was to be swept away by the general election in 1970. Like the Health Service, the National Insurance provision was subject to erosion from the private sector. Private insurance schemes continued to flourish, and to multiply, side by side with the state scheme. The funds of industrial assurance companies remained outside the national framework; as has been seen in the previous chapter, it was hardly the fault of either Griffiths or Bevan that this particular weakness was not remedied by the nationalization of these companies. Despite this, the universalism laid down by the National Insurance system survived as the foundation of future social planning. As for Griffiths himself, his political stature rose steadily. He was to enter the Cabinet as Colonial Secretary in February 1950 and almost became Foreign Secretary a year later. The contrasting fate of the welfare reformers, Addison in 1921, Griffiths and Bevan in 1945, offers a pointed comment on the social priorities of Britain's two post-war administrations.

Social insurance was an area where the government was largely influenced by the blueprint bequeathed by its wartime predecessor. So, too, but with more negative results, was the sphere of public education. Labour felt a special commitment to Butler's Education Act of 1944. Not only was it, in part, the work of Butler's under-secretary, James Chuter Ede, himself a former schoolteacher who took a major role in the negotiation with educational, political, and religious pressure groups at the time.[58] Also, in Labour's view the Act of 1944 gave a totally new standing and prestige to the maintained schools by creating a comprehensive fabric of state secondary schooling. It was a kind of educational Beveridge. No minister felt more deeply committed to the Butler Act than did Ellen Wilkinson, the new Minister of Education in July 1945. She was herself a distinguished product of the grammar-school tradition, since as a girl she had won a scholarship to Ardwick Higher Elementary Grade School in Manchester. After a period as a pupil teacher (where she encountered the future Lord Woolton, then plain Fred Marquis, another trainee teacher),[59] she had gained a good honours degree in history under the great Professor Tout, an austere medievalist, but also a liberal-minded man with a suffragette wife. Ellen Wilkinson embodied Labour's instinctive faith in the grammar schools, the bright working-class child's alternative to Eton and Winchester. Years later, in October 1953, Crossman noted how Labour Party conference delegates were delegates were relatively conservative on educational matters. 'Nearly all the delegates either were at grammar school or have their children at grammar school, and are not quite so susceptible to the romantic Socialism of the 1920s.'[60] In any case, Ellen Wilkinson, 'red Ellen', a woman long honoured on the left as a kind of Jarrow version of La Pasionaria, had moved to a distinctly more centrist position in the party during the war years, and had become far more emphatically anti-Communist than during the Popular Front era. Her close personal relationship with Herbert Morrison also served to

---

[58] e.g. Chuter Ede diary, 17 Mar. 1944 (BL, Add. MS, 59698).
[59] Betty D. Vernon, *Ellen Wilkinson* (London, 1982), p. 8.
[60] Janet Morgan (ed.), *The Backbench Diaries of Richard Crossman*, p. 270.

reinforce an increasingly cautious stance on domestic matters. She was to show scant sympathy with pressure from the National Union of Teachers, or from the National Association of Labour Teachers and such Labour backbenchers as W. G. Cove, in favour of a multilateral or comprehensive system of secondary education. Nor did she accept the view common on the left that the tripartite division in the Butler Act into grammar, modern, and technical schools, with the enshrining of the notorious 'eleven-plus examination', was socially and educationally divisive. Her view seems to have been endorsed throughout the Cabinet, where such public-school products as Attlee of Haileybury, Cripps of Winchester, and Dalton of Eton lent their voices to the perpetuation of élitism. The main working-class representative in the Cabinet, Ernest Bevin, had also had much to do with the achievement of the Butler Act in 1944, though Bevin had been anxious to include provision for day continuation courses for children up to eighteen, and better technical instruction for trainees in industry. These views were widespread throughout the Labour Party. Wales, where Labour had almost swept the board in the 1945 election, was an old stronghold of the grammar schools. Had not Lloyd George once described Pengam Grammar School as the 'Eton of Wales'?[61] Local authorities under Labour control urged that the selective grammar schools should be sustained, with all the resources at the government's command, so that they could surpass the public schools by example and academic excellence.

In the Cabinet in the autumn of 1945 the main priority for educational reformers was certainly not the need for comprehensive or 'multilateral' schools. They were, indeed, an untried and unknown quantity. The main necessity appeared to be the raising of the school-leaving age to fifteen, as was later stressed by Ellen Wilkinson's PPS at the time, Billy Hughes, and by her chief civil servant adviser, John Maud. In the Cabinet in the very early days of the Attlee government, on 23 August 1945, less than a month after taking office, Wilkinson won the approval of the government for what she regarded as her prime educational objective

[61] Kenneth O. Morgan, *Rebirth of a Nation: Wales, 1880–1980* (Oxford and Cardiff, 1981), p. 106.

in the foreseeable future: the school-leaving age would be raised to fifteen, with no exemptions, on 1 April 1947, and to sixteen thereafter.[62] She was strongly supported by Bevin, Ede, and Bevan. Other ministers, headed by Cripps and also including (ironically enough) Morrison, were later to argue against her on 16 January 1947, urging that housing, factory building, and other priorities could reasonably take precedence over the training of more teachers and the building of more schools. But Wilkinson won her point; more, the educational budget was later raised significantly, to over £100m. for 1946. After this, Wilkinson became something of a scapegoat for educational reformers, for her commitment to the tripartite system of state secondary education, as enshrined in the Norwood report of 1943 and the Butler Act of 1944, and for her refusal to move on comprehensive schools. She was attacked, violently by W. G. Cove, more temperately by Margaret Herbison and Leah Manning, all of them teachers' spokesmen, in the Commons, and again at the 1946 party conference. Thereafter, Ellen Wilkinson provided no new initiatives, in some measure perhaps because of her failing health. She died of an overdose of drugs in February 1947. However, her successor, George Tomlinson, a former Lancashire weaver who remained at the Education Department until October 1951, followed a broadly identical policy. Down to the fall of the government, he resisted any attempt significantly to modify the 1944 structure for secondary schools. In fact, the tide of opinion both in the Labour Party and in the educational world was beginning to turn against him. Criticisms of the 'eleven-plus' examination, with its marked elements of unfairness, social and cultural, and of the inadequacies of the secondary-modern school (which the vast majority of children attended) despite the pledges included in the Butler Act about their academic quality, continued to mount. The National Association of Labour Teachers applied constant pressure, and in 1950

---

[62] Cabinet Conclusions, 23 Aug. 1945 (CAB 128/1) and 16 Jan. 1947 (CAB 128/9); Billy Hughes, 'In defence of Ellen Wilkinson', *History Workshop* 7 (Spring, 1979), pp. 157–60; Lord Redcliffe-Maud, *Experiences of an Optimist* (London, 1981), pp. 51–9; also letter from Lord Redcliffe-Maud in *The Guardian*, 28 Aug. 1982.

Alice Bacon, one of its less abrasive spokesmen, persuaded the party's National Executive to consider the question by setting up a working party.[63] Several local authorities were now seeking ministerial permission to try the experiment of a reorganized multilateral system; the rural county of Anglesey in North Wales finally put one into effect in 1951. The NEC working party set forth its proposals in February 1951 calling Labour to commit itself to comprehensive schools, and an NEC pamphlet in July 1951 made this henceforth official party policy. In the October 1951 general election, comprehensive secondary education was clearly one of Labour's more radical priorities, even though concealed in the vague wording of the manifesto by a call for 'greater equality of opportunity' in education. Grass-roots pressure, effective lobbying by NALT and the National Union of Teachers, growing awareness in urban localities of the inadequacies of the 1944 tripartite division as it worked out in practice, all played their part.

It is easy to see that, in the perspective of 1945, the comprehensive idea might have appeared risky and unfamiliar, especially given Labour's old commitment to the grammar schools as the avenue for self-improvement for working-class boys and girls. Some of the effects of the general establishment of the comprehensive system from the 1960s onwards met with criticism from educationalists and, more important, from parents for its effects upon academic standards. One feature of the general establishment of the comprehensive system in the 1970s was to be a mighty boom in private secondary and primary education, despite inflationary pressure on domestic budgets. For all that, it is hard to avoid the view that education was an area where the Labour government failed to provide any new ideas or inspiration. Anthony Crosland in *The Future of Socialism* in 1956 was to focus on education as a major cause of class division and of the maldistribution of rewards and opportunities for the working-class child. These were 'the most divisive, wasteful and unjust of all the aspects of social inequality'.[64] No serious

[63] *Report of the Annual Conference of the Labour Party*, 1950, p. 92; cf. Alice Bacon's comments at the Policy Committee meeting, 24 May 1950.
[64] Crosland, *The Future of Socialism*, p. 258.

discussion of the basic principles of educational policy
occurred at ministerial level once the raising of the school-
leaving age had been agreed in the first few weeks of the
government's existence in 1945. Nor was there any significant discussion within the party, until the NEC yielded to
pressure from NALT and others in 1949, and set up its working party. Elsewhere, too, Ellen Wilkinson and Tomlinson
were resistant to change. Direct grant schools were modestly
diminished, from 232 to 166. The public schools, long a
folk-symbol for the left of privilege and class division,
remained quite untouched. Even the Fleming proposals for
introducing a quota of 25 per cent of entrants to public
schools from non-fee-paying elementary schools were not
implemented at all after 1944, partly perhaps because of the
resistance of working-class parents to their offspring becoming social 'guinea-pigs'. Eton, Harrow, and the rest flourished
as never before, their charitable status and endowed income
quite unaffected by the Inland Revenue. Much of the cricket
programme at Lord's in the month of July was taken up with
public-school contests on the pre-war pattern of ostentation.
George Tomlinson was deeply impressed by a visit he paid to
Eton in 1947. He told the headmaster that, had he been a
pupil there (instead of at Rishton Wesleyan school, which
he had left at the age of ten) he could have guaranteed to
have won the battle of Waterloo himself.[65] The public-school
headmasters could sleep quietly at nights while such docile
reformers as these served under Attlee. At the apex of the
government, the Prime Minister took pride in the ministerial
advance of fellow old Haileyburians such as Christopher
Mayhew and Geoffrey de Freitas,[66] and the numerical
advantage of Haileybury over either Eton or Winchester in
his socialist administration.

The universities equally could feel no cause for alarm,
least of all Oxford and Cambridge. They also underwent
relatively little change after 1945, other than benefiting
from an extension of local-authority grants for students
to attend. The emphasis was still on the arts, rather than
science and technology. The total number of university

[65] Fred Blackburn, *George Tomlinson* (London, 1954), p. 6.
[66] Kenneth Harris, *Attlee*, p. 406.

students rose from 50,000 to 83,000, while, other than in
Wales and perhaps Scotland, their largely middle-class character continued undisturbed. Oxford and Cambridge, for all the
rigours of rationing and austerity, retained their pre-war
social cachet and class-based assumptions. They were fortified by Attlee's affection for Oxford, and Dalton's for the
rowing-club fraternity of King's. Oxford, in particular, newly
romanticized in Waugh's *Brideshead Revisited* (1945),
expanded its undergraduate population. It was still overwhelmingly drawn from the public schools, especially in
relation to male commoner undergraduates. The Robbins
report later showed that, as late as 1961-2, just 39 per cent
of Oxford undergraduate entrants came from state schools,
and a mere 25 per cent in Cambridge.[67] So higher education,
especially at the older universities, in general changed scarcely
at all in the years of Labour government, either in purpose
or in character. What Labour took most pride in, and
legitimately so, was the new impetus provided at the ele-
mentary level, the large increase in the school population,
the improved conditions for teachers (though equal pay for
women teachers remained as far away as ever, partly through
the gulf between the NUT and the National Association
of Schoolmasters), the new investment in school buildings,
and the expanded educational budgets that made all these
things possible. In this sense, the way was paved for the
educational boom of the fifties and sixties, although on the
basis of a structure of secondary and higher education
which offered little intellectual innovation or social intermingling. Not until the years of opposition after 1951 did
the Labour Party begin effectively to ponder these further
objectives of reform.

Labour's welfare state, then, was a mosaic of reform and
conservatism. Innovation in health and social insurance,
partial change in housing, relative quiescence in education
covered the spectrum of social policy. However, the total
picture of welfare provision cannot be viewed in isolation

[67] Cf. Arthur Marwick, *British Society since 1945* (London, 1982), p. 44;
Higher Education: Report, 1963 (Cmnd. 2154), para. 217, p. 80.

without a broader view of governmental policies designed to promote welfare, and, indirectly it was hoped, social equality. Budgetary policy, during Dalton's 'cheap money' era had a strong social component, including the financing of family allowances and national assistance, the easing of restrictions on house-building, and heavily subsidized rents for council house tenants. Food subsidies, by which large sums were paid from the Exchequer to food producers and suppliers, specifically to keep down the cost of living for poorer people, and thus to relieve any pressure on wage inflation, were manifestly redistributive in their effects. Not until 1949 did Cripps make serious inroads into food subsidies by imposing a limit of £465m. in his budget. But he, too, gave social expenditure a high priority throughout the era of so-called austerity. 'Fair shares', the ethos of wartime sacrifice embodied in post-war controls and rationing of foodstuffs and raw materials (taken further in the bread rationing introduced in July 1946 by Strachey) were always an intimate associate of the welfare society which Labour's legislation was concerned to implement. Where Conservatives emphasized self-help, Labour's rhetoric advocated the causes of social fairness, equality of treatment, and of providing a basic framework through the social services, perhaps at the expense of other forms of working-class expenditure.

A discussion of the welfare state, finally, cannot be concluded without reference to full employment. This had been an overriding theme for Labour during the 1945 election campaign, with an especial emphasis for the trade-union connection. Indeed, full employment had been Assumption C in the Beveridge report itself.[68] Labour's welfare provision after 1945, then, presupposed a nation fully demobilized, back at full-time productive work at home and in full and continuous employment. To a striking extent, this part of the social objectives of the government was triumphantly achieved between 1945 and 1951. Demobilization proved to be a difficult task for George Isaacs, the Minister of Labour. In addition to being pressurized by the Board of Trade and

[68] *Socialist Insurance and Allied Services*, Cmd. 6404, pp. 163–5. Also see A. Booth, 'The Second World War and the Origins of Modern Regional Policy', *Economy and Society* (11), 1982.

other departments to release key workers such as miners, building workers, skilled engineers, and the like, he faced contrary pressure from Bevin and the Foreign Office to slow down the process of releasing men from the armed forces so that Britain could meet its defence obligations in Germany and elsewhere. In the end, Isaacs coped well enough; between August 1945 and December 1946, the armed services were run down from over five million to just over one million. Further progress was held up by the insistence of A. V. Alexander, the Minister of Defence, that Britain's world-wide military commitments in the Middle and Far East and elsewhere, be rigorously maintained. The consequence was an acceleration of labour shortages, especially in skilled trades, and amongst coal-miners, and resultant obstacles both to full employment and production at peak capacity. Still, the government managed to weather the storm. Dalton continued in 1945–7 the wartime method of 'manpower budgets' in dealing with problems of labour supply. These greatly assisted in the distribution of manpower between different trades and industries, without lapsing into the unpopular policy of the direction of labour. The relation between the manpower budgets and a high level of employment in the period immediately after the end of the war is clear and direct. Indeed, Samuel Beer has urged that the shift from manpower budgeting under Dalton to fiscal budgeting under Cripps was perhaps the greatest single change in strategy for the Labour government during its six years in office.[69] This is an arguable case, though the point can be exaggerated, since it has already been noted that programmed economic planning was even less of a basic feature of policy under Dalton than it was to prove under Cripps.

It became clear during 1946 that the prized social objective of full employment was under strain, with signs that the scourge of unemployment was threatening to return to older industrial areas. The especially heavy rise of unemployment in South Wales, where traditional industries such as coal and steel were still working well below full capacity, brought anxious deputations from Welsh Labour MPs to interrogate Attlee, Cripps, and Isaacs. James Griffiths reinforced their

[69] Samuel Beer, *Modern British Politics* (London, 1965), p. 194.

pressure within the administration; they pointed out that unemployment in Wales had risen to over 66,000 by June, admittedly a total swollen by the inclusion of disabled workers.[70] In Scotland, unemployment reached over 60,000 in 1946, with a continuing pattern of over-dependence on the metal and engineering trades. Cripps had to tell his colleagues that unemployment was rising throughout all the development areas; even if far short of the appalling rate of the thirties, it was likely to reach over 250,000 by the end of 1946 for England, Wales, and Scotland.[71] The situation reached its nadir in February 1947, during the fuel crisis and the severe winter, when unemployment briefly reached alarming levels again, over a million at one grave point, and the three-day week became widespread.

In fact, though, the mass unemployment of the thirties was not to return. The fuel crisis passed, and, after the convertibility crisis of the summer of 1947, British industry entered upon a period of three years or more of rapid expansion. Industrial production soared high above pre-war levels, and by the end of 1948 the balance of trade was once again in surplus. Of course, much of this was due to the inevitable recovery of British manufacturing industry after the war, at a time when potential industrial rivals such as Germany were crushed by defeat and devastation. The spectre of serious competition from Japan and other Far Eastern countries was not yet menacing. The transition from Dalton's concept of thirties-style 'planned development' to Cripps's adoption of Keynesian demand management at the Treasury also had beneficial effects on employment policy. But much credit, too, was due to purposive government policy at the Board of Trade, by Cripps until September 1947 and then by his successor, the youthful Harold Wilson. Vigorous use was made of the Distribution of Industry Act of 1945, passed by the Churchill coalition in 1945, to bring new, modern industries to central Scotland, the north-east, the north-west and South Wales. The Board of Trade made ruthless use of

[70] Parliamentary Deputation on Unemployment in Wales, 1946 (PREM 8/272); Griffiths to Attlee, Mar. 1946, and Attlee to Griffiths, 28 Mar. 1946 (PREM 8/1569).

[71] Discussion of Economic Survey for 1947, Minutes of Lord President's Committee, 26 July 1946 (CAB 132/1).

Industrial Development Certificates to coerce firms into siting new plants in development areas rather than in the southeast or the east Midlands. It was argued that these policies were valuable for the latter regions as well by preventing congestion in new building and shortages of labour.[72] Financial inducements were also given to businesses newly located in Scotland, the north, or Wales, by the remission of rents or rates, or by interest-free loans. Encouragement was given, too, to trading estates, several of them based on wartime Ordnance factory complexes like those at Bridgend and Burry Port in South Wales. The result was that full employment became the proudest, and most justifiable, boast of Labour's social policies. From the start of 1948 onwards, the rate of unemployment fell consistently, to well under 2 per cent of the insured labour force. The north-east of England, which had known unemployment of 38 per cent in 1932, in 1949 showed a total of only 3 per cent; in industrial Scotland, the rate was 4½ per cent where it had once been 35 per cent; South Wales had an unemployment rate of 5½ per cent in 1948–9 when it had been crucified by a rate of 41 per cent in 1932, at the height of the depression. By October 1948, the *New Statesman* could record with pride that 443 new factories had been started in Development Areas, giving work already to 32,000, with a further 185,000 jobs to follow.[73] Even in Scotland, economically the least thriving area of the United Kingdom, other than Northern Ireland, 536 new factories were built in 1945–52 through the Scottish Development Agency alone, giving employment to 150,000.[74] Despite financial crises in 1949 and 1951, the situation did not greatly change. The rate of unemployment was a mere 1.8 per cent in October 1951 when the government fell. From Dundee to Swansea, mines, docks, factories, and engineering plants were throbbing with new life. Coal was again being exported, in modest quantities, from Newcastle, Cardiff, and Barry. It had been shown that deliberate government policy could significantly influence

[72] Douglas Jay, *Change and Fortune*, p. 213. Jay, with some justice, regards himself as the real architect of the post-war development policy for his work at the Board of Trade under Dalton in 1944–5.

[73] *New Statesman*, 30 Oct. 1948.

[74] Alec Cairncross (ed.), *The Scottish Economy* (Cambridge, 1954), p. 76.

the geographical spread of new industry and employment. Throughout all the vicissitudes of the 1947–51 period, the Labour government's most powerful claim to effective social engineering and to the unshakeable loyalty of its millions of trade-union supporters and their families, was that it was the party of full employment, the party which had exorcized for ever the ghosts of Jarrow, Wigan, and Merthyr Tydfil. Indeed, the shortage of labour and its speed of distribution were the major problems in 1947–51, rather than under-used capacity, wasted investment, long-term industrial contraction, human waste, and spiritual despair. Without this massive achievement, the welfare state would have been invalidated from the start.

The welfare measures of the Labour government did not, of themselves, produce a more egalitarian or open society. The profile of the class structure, or even simply of the distribution of wealth, showed relatively little change between 1945 and 1951. The government openly acknowledged the fact, as when Cripps in 1946 insisted on 'houses of the villa type' being built in the Development Areas, to cater for managers, skilled workers, and scientists. Bevan, who had at first 'refused to hear of' houses of more than 1,000 square feet being authorized, was eventually persuaded to agree, as was Key, the Minister of Works.[75] In part, as has been seen, the class division endured because the private sector in key areas of the social services remained vigorous—public schools, private insurance schemes, private medical and specialist services, a capitalist housing market and building industry. These areas were even expanding during the later period of the government. Morrisonian 'consolidation' led to greater encouragement for private house-builders, and emollient statements about the need to protect private education, and medical and insurance schemes as a guarantee of individual liberty. The erosion of the publicly-financed aspects of the social services, heralded in the dispute over NHS charges in the spring of 1950, and more fatally a year later, helped to consolidate the enduring resilience of the British

[75] See the file on 'Housing for Managers', 1946 (HLG 104/5).

class system. In addition, it was notorious that more affluent or middle-class people received substantial help from universal welfare benefits. This especially applied to benefits in kind rather than in cash, such as a free health service, free secondary-school places, and food subsidies. The opportunities in health or education for the middle class (for instance, in the way they were able to benefit from the eleven-plus examination through financial or cultural domestic advantages) enabled the gulf between them and manual workers to continue, if not grow even wider. The very extent and cost of the welfare state after 1945 meant that many of the new social reforms were financed by transfers of income within lower-income groups themselves, rather than by transfers from the rich to the poor.[76] Far more swingeing measures were required to turn Britain's welfare democracy into anything resembling a more classless society; assaults on inherited wealth and accumulated property; a new programme to extend social, sexual, and racial equality in education and housing; and curbing the endowed advantages of the private sector. Carr-Saunders and Caradog Jones, two leading academic sociologists, were far more emphatic on the existence of clearly-demarcated social classes, essentially based on occupation, when they published their work *Social Conditions in England and Wales* in 1958, than they had been in their earlier analysis of the social structure back in 1927, or in the second edition in 1937.[77] The economic as well as the social impact of the welfare state also appeared open to doubt. Until the sixties, Labour's hopes that the new benefits under the National Insurance and National Assistance Acts would be at subsistence level proved to be an illusion in the mildly inflationary economic conditions prevailing after 1945. Because the level of state benefits was so low, the means test became more and more pervasive. Detailed

[76] For excellent discussions of this aspect, see Asa Briggs, 'The Social Services', in G. D. N. Worswick and P. H. Ady (eds.), *The British Economy, 1945-50* (Oxford, 1952), pp. 365-80, and H. Glennester (ed.), *The Future of the Welfare State* (London, 1983). Also instructive are James Callaghan, 'The Approach to Social Equality' in Munro (ed.), *Socialism. The British Way*, pp. 127-52, and Roy Jenkins, 'Equality' in Richard Crossman (ed.), *New Fabian Essays*, pp. 69-90.

[77] A. Carr-Saunders, D. Caradog Jones, and C. A. Moser, *Social Conditions in England and Wales* (Oxford, 1958), pp. 115-25.

academic studies in the sixties by Peter Townsend, Brian Abel-Smith, and others documented the continuing prevalence of real poverty, notably among old people and larger working-class families. Voluntary pressure groups such as the Child Poverty Action Group and Shelter drew attention to the inadequacies of the social services and goaded governments to action.

But if the welfare state proved to have its limits, it offered an essential base for future social advance. It extended, at least in theory, a new concept of citizenship, universal and comprehensive. The statistics on school attendance and attainment, on the quality of housing, above all on the standards of health of the old, children, nursing mothers, and the disabled, testified to the enormous physical and social benefits that resulted. In addition, despite all the necessary qualifications that must be made, the Diamond Commission on the distribution of income and wealth, reporting between 1975 and 1979, provided incontestable evidence of the redistributive effects of welfare benefits, both in cash and to a lesser extent in kind. Cash assistance through pensions, family allowances, unemployment benefit, and the further addition of supplementary benefit meant, for instance, that the 20 per cent of the poorest households, who between them claimed a mere 0.9 per cent of the 'original' national income, rose to claim 7.5 per cent of 'disposable' income and 9.2 per cent of 'final income'. While the effect of public taxation, direct and indirect, was broadly neutral, welfare benefits had reduced social inequality by providing an income or 'social wage' for those who could not earn, or for families whose earning capacity had been interrupted. In the long term, therefore, fortified by increases in supplementary and other benefits under the Crossman regime in 1968–70, the welfare state had made some impact, almost by inadvertence, on social inequality and the maldistribution of real income.[78]

[78] *Royal Commission on the Distribution of Income and Wealth*, Report No. 1 (HMSO, 1975), Cmnd. 6171, Table 25, and Report No. 7 (HMSO, 1979), Cmnd. 7595, Table 3:1. I have benefited from reading an unpublished paper by Sir Henry Phelps Brown on this theme. Sir Henry's definitions are: 'original income' —all income from employment, self-employment and investments, with imputed

For the historian of the Labour government, the achievement in political terms that stands out was that social welfare was now largely identified with the Labour Party. More, unlike the hesitancy associated with nationalization or industrial policy, it was an achievement in which all wings of the party took uninhibited pride. It opened up new areas for advance which Labour could follow up at the Dorking conference of May 1950 and even in the hard years of internecine civil war in the fifties. This was shown by the pressure for comprehensive schools, for a revamped superannuation system (which involved a graduated, rather than a flat-rate, contributory system, and earnings-related benefits), and for the control of land for urban development. The welfare programme confirmed the political allegiance of the middle-class intelligentsia, the social workers, planners, and educationalists newly radicalized during the war. It ensured, too, that the social enthusiasms of the war would be sustained during the peacetime period. There was no Geddes Axe this time. The Treasury under Dalton and Cripps was a very different department from that run by Austen Chamberlain and Robert Horne in 1919–22. Beveridge, Utthwatt, and the rest were largely put into effect, despite some political harassment from doctors and other vested interests. By 1951, a plausible updated version of a land fit for heroes had been built on the scarred foundations of an ancient, war-ravaged community. From 1945–51 onwards, Labour's central political faith, its prime claim to be the unique custodian of the progressive idea, lay with its inextricable identification with the rise and decline of the welfare state.

rent of owner-occupied houses; 'disposable income'—original income *minus* direct taxes *plus* direct cash benefits, i.e. spending money; 'final income'— disposable income *plus* direct and indirect benefits in kind *minus* indirect taxes.

5

Priorities and Policies:
The New Commonwealth

Imperial and colonial policy had not been a conspicuous or impressive aspect of Labour's policies before the second world war. Of course, the party was instinctively anti-imperialist, especially in relation to India. Early pioneers such as Keir Hardie and Philip Snowden had been closely identified with the movement for independence from the Raj: Hardie had paid a memorable visit to Bengal in 1907 when he openly declared his sympathy with *swaraj*. Clement Attlee had been at first criticized in Labour ranks for appearing to compromise this unequivocal position by agreeing to serve on the Simon Commission on India in 1927-30. Egyptian nationalists in the Wafd Party, too, had looked to the Labour Party for guidance, despite the disappointments resulting from Sidney Webb's (Passfield's) tenure of the Colonial Office in 1929-31. During the twenties and thirties, young nationalist leaders from Asia and Africa—men like Krishna Menon and Pandit Nehru from India, Jomo Kenyatta from Kenya, Kwame Nkrumah from the Gold Coast, Dr Hastings Banda from Nyasaland—had moved in Labour circles in England, and had got to know Cripps and other leading party figures.[1] Prominent Labour politicians such as Lansbury, Ellen Wilkinson, and Harold Laski had joined Krishna Menon's India League in London in the thirties. At the same period was founded the 'Friends of Africa Committee', the beginning of Arthur Creech Jones's long association with African nationalism. But apart from a broad basic sympathy for colonial nationalist movements, Labour appeared to have relatively little positive or constructive to say. Down to the 1935 election, colonial or imperial themes had enjoyed little prominence in the party's manifestos or policy literature.

[1] See Hastings Banda (at the time, a doctor in North Shields) to A. Creech Jones, 26 July 1945 (Rhodes House Library, Oxford, Creech Jones papers, ACJ 7/1/33).

A vague call for 'an extension of the mandate system to colonial territories' was all that Labour had to offer in its party manifesto in 1935. Beyond that, there were only a few left-wing writers on colonial issues, writing on a purely individual basis. Of these, the most prominent was Leonard Barnes, a lecturer at Liverpool University, the author of such books as the *Duty of Empire* (1935) and *Empire or Democracy* (1939), and a member of the Labour Party Advisory Committee on Colonial Affairs. Only two backbench members of this Committee were at all active in parliament— Creech Jones and Wilfred Paling.[2] Others, such as Ellen Wilkinson, who had been involved with colonial issues in the early thirties, found their attention increasingly drawn to the European continent after the outbreak of the civil war in Spain.

During the years of the second world war, however, this major gap in Labour's ideas began to be filled. The credit for this belonged largely to an offshoot of the Fabian Research Bureau, whose secretary was the MP for Romford, John Parker, who had himself a keen interest in colonial questions. This group was the Fabian Colonial Research Bureau, founded in 1940. Its leading spirits were Dr Rita Hinden, a gifted and idealistic South African Jewish emigrée, later to edit the monthly *Socialist Commentary*, and Arthur Creech Jones, the Labour MP for Shipley. Creech Jones had been a conscientious objector during the first world war, and had been imprisoned for his beliefs. In the twenties, he was prominent in framing the economic policies of the Independent Labour Party, and was usually held to be on the party left. He was an uncharismatic figure: Attlee was later, quite unfairly, to refer to his tenure of the Colonial Office in 1946–50 as 'one of my mistakes'.[3] The fiascos of the groundnuts venture in Tanganyika did his reputation considerable harm, even though Strachey, the Minister of Food, bore the main responsibility. After Creech Jones lost his seat in the 1950 general election, his career as a leading politician was at an end: when he died in 1964 he was manifestly one of

[2] Partha Sarathi Gupta, *Imperialism and the British Labour Movement, 1914–1964* (London, 1975), p. 229.
[3] Kenneth Harris, *Attlee*, p. 446.

'yesterday's men'. Yet Creech Jones, today almost a forgotten figure, was a major influence in the political and intellectual history of the Labour Party in its most creative
period. With Rita Hinden, he provided the party with exciting new blueprints for a positive colonial policy, based on
long-term economic, technological, and educational development rather than on simple, negative anti-imperialism. He was
the main architect of the Colonial Charter, considered
(though not adopted) at the party conference in 1942. He
addressed himself, as no Labour politician had done before,
consistently and coherently to the long-term relationship
between the developed and undeveloped world, in terms of
aid, trade, and investment. Further, as Colonial Secretary
at a vital time from late 1946 onwards, Creech Jones was
able to translate many of these programmes into practical
reality. He was to prove the most influential Colonial
Secretary since Joseph Chamberlain—indeed, in constructive
terms, perhaps the most influential Colonial Secretary ever—
and a unique figure in the formulation of an intelligible,
credible policy for Labour for what later came to be termed
the third world.

It was crucially important that Labour did have a policy
for the Commonwealth and the colonies after 1945. When
hostilities ended with the surrender of Japan, the British
Commonwealth and Empire was as extensive as it had ever
been in its history. The surrender of Italian forces in Africa
and of Japanese forces in the Far East made its bounds ever
wider. In the Middle East alone, almost every country from
Iran in the east to Libya in the west, and in Africa as far
south as Eritrea and Abyssinia, had British troops in occupation. British power was recognized as transcendent throughout the entire Middle East, directly so in Egypt (where at
least 150,000 British troops were stationed at the end of the
war in 1945) and in Palestine, indirectly in Iran, Iraq, Transjordan, and the Arab territories in 'the Fertile Crescent'
and along the Persian Gulf. In Africa as a whole, Britain
remained much the most important territorial power from
the Cape to Suez. No territory had been ceded in the inter-
war years; no cession was on the immediate agenda after
1945. Indeed, as will be seen, there were serious proposals

by Bevin in 1945-6 that the British colonial empire in Africa should actually be extended further. Britain now proposed to the Council of Foreign Ministers that it take over the trusteeship of Cyrenaica and Tripolitania (modern Libya), and conceivably of Italian Somaliland in the Horn of Africa also, to form a Greater Somalia to include British Somaliland and the Ogaden.[4] In the Far East too, Britain was still a powerful military and naval force, with island possessions like Fiji, Tonga, and the Solomons in the south Pacific, major territorial concerns in Malaya, Sarawak, Brunei, and North Borneo, and important bases in Singapore and Hong Kong. Britain had insisted on reoccupying Hong Kong in 1945, under the terms of the old ninty-nine-year lease in spite of official American disapproval. Beyond these major territories, or proposed territories, Britain had scores of scattered possessions, colonies, or protectorates of one kind or another— the West Indies, so vital for sugar and other food supplies; British Honduras; British Guiana; the Falkland Islands far away in the south Atlantic; and a myriad of scattered islands from Ascension and St. Helena in the Atlantic to Mauritius, the Seychelles, and the Maldive Islands in the Indian Ocean. The economic, commercial, political, and strategic administration of all these innumerable colonial legacies was a prime concern for the Labour government in 1945, and its Colonial Office would inevitably be a major department of state.

In particular, there were powerful and deep-rooted nationalist movements in Egypt, parts of West Africa, and in much of Asia. The Indian subcontinent, above all, was aflame with communal tensions between the largely Hindu Congress movement and the Muslim League, complicating the already intensive pressures for independence from the Raj. The failure of the Cripps mission in 1942 and the subsequent internment of Gandhi, Nehru, Patel, and other Congress leaders during the war with Japan in 1943-5 made the problem of India even more explosive. Conversely, in Palestine, Arabs and Jews conflicted violently with the British mandate and with each other. In these grave

---

[4] Memorandum on 'The Future of the Italian Colonies and the Italian Mediterranean Islands', by Bevin and Hall, 30 Aug. 1945 (FO 371/50792), U/6967/51/G70; memorandum by Bevin, 10 Sept. 1945 (ibid.), U/6971/51/70G.

circumstances, a statesmanlike and consistent colonial and Commonwealth policy was a major priority for the Attlee administration, whatever its domestic preoccupations.

One outstanding feature of the Commonwealth policy of the Labour government after 1945 was its very close associations with the older white Dominions, Canada, Australia, New Zealand, and (until the end of 1948) South Africa. There were many reasons for this close relationship. On economic grounds alone, the Dominions were vital for Britain with their supplies of food and raw materials—meat from Australia, dairy products from New Zealand, wheat and timber from Canada. The Canadian role was also critical in trying to redress the desperate shortage of dollars in the post-1945 period. There were also major defence and geopolitical considerations including the strategic relationship with Canada and Newfoundland in the North Atlantic, the use of naval bases such as Simonstown in South Africa, and defence co-ordination in the Pacific with Australia and New Zealand following the peace treaty with Japan in 1946. The Labour government, therefore, made a priority of preserving intimate contact with the Commonwealth heads of government, and fully exploited the Crown connection during these years. From the Potsdam conference in July 1945 onwards, consultation with the Commonwealth nations continued to be frequent and intense. The Commonwealth ministers in Washington (now including India and Pakistan) would meet regularly in the British embassy under the chairmanship of Sir Oliver Franks in 1948-51, to formulate a common approach to world problems. The Dominions Office administered by the veteran Lord Addison until October 1947 was certainly not the sinecure that it had been sometimes assumed to be in the thirties. Indeed, the Office added to its importance after the transfer of power in India, Pakistan, and Burma. The rechristened Commonwealth Relations Office enjoyed, if anything, an enhanced role from October 1947 onwards when it was run by Philip Noel-Baker, later succeeded in February 1950 by Patrick Gordon-Walker.

One may surmise that the imperial role came naturally to the Labour leaders. Attlee, while capable of penning pungent Cabinet papers which called for imperial retreat and disengagement and the removal of outlying British bases in the new era of long-range air power, was also liable to respond to the call of empire. He was an old India hand; he retained his veneration for the Crown and the imperial connection, for all his socialism. In December 1950, he took pride in lecturing President Truman and his Secretary of State, Dean Acheson, on how the British understood Asian nationalism and the Oriental mind far better than they did.[5] Ernest Bevin was also stirred by the sentiment of empire, especially in the Middle East; he was alarmed at the spectacle of scuttle east of Suez from 1947 onwards. While pursuing a cautious role in Egypt, where he was anxious to reduce Britain's heavy military commitment in the 1946 negotiations, he was concerned also to reinforce her military and economic role in the Middle East, from the Persian Gulf northwards and westwards to Cyrenaica.[6] 'It is essential to our survival as a great power.' To this end, he pursued a calculated, long-term policy based on a more equal partnership with 'moderate nationalists' among the Arab states, in return for the military and economic advantages of a continuing British presence. Bevin also warmly endorsed the system of imperial preference in trade, while he was able to use the imperial connection as a useful dialectical weapon against the headier advocates of western European federal, or other, union in 1948–50. Herbert Morrison was another minister instinctively sympathetic to the majesty of the imperial mystique. In January 1946 he shocked many in the party by referring affectionately to 'the jolly old Empre'.[7] Over the Persian oil crisis in 1951, he was to be aggressive in urging the dispatch of British troops to Abadan to protect British oil installations, and service and technical personnel. Later on, in the 1956 Suez crisis, he appears to have supported Eden and the Consevative government in their policy of taking unilateral military action against Egypt without the support of the United States. Again, Albert Alexander,

[5] Record of Prime Minister's visit to Washington, 4–8 Dec. 1950 (PREM 8/1200 and FO 371/83019).

[6] Memorandum on 'Palestine: the present position' by R. I. Campbell, undersecretary of state, 29 July 1945 (FO 371/45376). A definitive forthcoming work on Labour's policy in the Middle East has been written by William Roger Louis.

[7] *The Times*, 12 Jan. 1946.

the Minister of Defence from December 1946, was throughout an advocate of retaining imperial positions in India and in Egypt, and of maintaining a world-wide defence posture. Hugh Dalton could talk derisively of the colonies as 'pullulating poverty-stricken, diseased nigger communities'.[8] Even Aneurin Bevan, the friend of Bracken and Beaverbrook, was a kind of Tory imperialist in some ways as Suez was to show in 1956.[9] And yet all these men were sensitive and realistic enough to recognize the new pressures for Commonwealth and colonial independence coursing through the British imperial domain, from republicans in Australia to nationalists in the Gold Coast, with renewed force after 1945.

The mood of the British public, too, while purged of the neurotic jingoism of Boer War days, was also capable of being excited by the majesty and pomp of empire. India was still a jewel in the British Crown in 1945. George VI still reigned as its emperor, even if he had never actually been there. Empire Day (25 May) remained a public holiday in state schools. The literature of the time—for instance, Enid Blyton's immensely popular and very numerous adventure stories for children written in the forties—was unashamedly colonialist, perhaps racialist, with clear assumptions of the cultural superiority of the Anglo-Saxon and other white races. School geography primers and atlases, with their extensive splashes of British red, reinforced the point by reindoctrinating a new generation of post-war children. The empire was further bound together by the resumption of Test matches in 1946. The first cricket team to tour England was an all-India team (in fact, the last of its kind) containing Hindus and Muslims alike; it was under the captaincy of the reassuring imperial figure of the Nawab of Pataudi, himself a pre-war Oxford University, Sussex, and England batsman. If this was not empire of the frenzied, federalized kind endorsed by Beaverbrook in the *Daily* and *Sunday Express*, with their Kiplingesque rhetoric and their call for Empire Free Trade, it was a broad and powerful enough sentiment to slow down the post-war transformation from empire into Commonwealth.

[8] Dalton diaries, 27 Feb. 1950 (Dalton papers, I/38).
[9] *Backbench Diaries of Richard Crossman*, p. 508 (5 Sept. 1956).

The relations between Britain and the white Commonwealth were marked by many difficult episodes and periods of crisis after 1945. But they were much assisted by the relatively cordial personal relationship that existed between the British Labour government, and the Labour Prime Ministers of Australia and New Zealand, Ben Chifley and Peter Fraser. Other Australasian statesmen, such as Herbert Evatt of Australia and Walter Nash of New Zealand, were also well known in British Labour Party circles, especially through the Fabians. In addition, Mackenzie King of Canada was strongly Anglophile. Immediately committed to the support of the mother country in September 1939, he became a close personal friend of Addison, the Dominions Secretary. In South Africa, a much more difficult case, the Prime Minister was still the veteran Field Marshal Smuts, a loyal ally in two world wars in the face of opposition from Afrikaner Nationalists, and a fervent advocate of imperial defence. He had actually served in Lloyd George's War Cabinet back in 1917. Men such as these made the Commonwealth links reforged after the war all the more natural and effective.

The centrality of the white Commonwealth for Britain's post-war future emerged at the Commonwealth Prime Ministers' conference held in London in April 1946, and at a further Commonwealth conference at Canberra in August 1947, when Britain was represented by Addison. At both, there arose the vital question of Commonwealth defence, especially in the Pacific, reinforced now by the need to dispose of former Japanese-occupied territories in the Far East and to conclude a peace treaty with the Japanese. The main concern in the London conference was the reorganization of Commonwealth defence arrangements, with a new Commonwealth Defence Committee to replace the old Committee of Imperial Defence.[10] Smuts here expressed his anxiety to Attlee at Bevin's proposals to withdraw British troops from Egypt. 'Our scattered Commonwealth, more than any other world group, depended for its life, effectiveness and influence on its communications, and Egypt was the

---

[10] Minutes of meetings of Commonwealth Prime Ministers, Apr.–May 1946 (CAB 133/86); Smuts to Attlee, 8 May 1946 (PREM 8/1388); record of Prime Ministers' meeting, 28 Apr. 1946 (FO 371/57178).

centre of them.' Without the British presence, Russia would gain a foothold in Africa and the Middle East. The newly-created Ministry of Defence in December 1946, a post held by Alexander, with the new Cabinet committee structure for defence matters, also had a powerful Commonwealth aspect. The economic aspects of the Commonwealth relations were even more central to Britain's needs. Long-term bulk purchase agreements were worked out for Canadian wheat and for meat and dairy products from Australia and New Zealand. In return, the Commonwealth was a vital market for British products, for steel and manufactured goods above all. It was specifically dispensed from the export premium on British steel. Altogether, the Commonwealth still took 41.5 per cent of British exports and re-exports in the boom year of 1950, compared with 26.5 per cent for western Europe and a mere 12.4 per cent for North and Central America. Trade and the flag were still intimately associated.

There was additionally the close involvement of the Commonwealth with the operations of the sterling area, although the two did not coincide. Canada, of course, was not a member of the sterling area; conversely, Iceland, Ireland, and Iraq all were. The protection of the sterling area and the 'sterling dollar pool', with its strong Commonwealth connections, was a vital theme both in the convertibility crisis in the summer of 1947 and the devaluation crisis two years later. In fact, the financial and commercial links with the Commonwealth indicated the frailty of many of the post-imperial ties. In 1947, Australia, South Africa, and India drew criticism from Britain for their failure to curb dollar imports, and the pressure that this produced for sterling. In 1949 it was the turn of the Commonwealth Finance Ministers to attack the British approach towards multilateral trade which led to the devaluation of sterling in September 1949. They had had to make heavy cuts in their dollar imports, for Britain's sake. There was much criticism that Cripps's unilateral decision to devalue the pound went beyond agreements reached at the Commonwealth Finance Ministers' conference two months earlier, and that there had not been any prior consultation.[11] By 1950, in fact, the links between the Dominions and mother country seemed less intimate. The defeat of the Labour governments in Australian and New Zealand general elections in 1949 made the relationship with the Attlee government somewhat less cordial. By now, too, there were many complaints that the growing association of Britain with the North Atlantic world, culminating in the formation of NATO in April 1949, was working against the cohesive structure of the Commonwealth as traditionally conceived. While the British government made much of the Commonwealth ties in its rhetoric when resisting pressures for a closer political or economic association with western Europe from 1948 onwards, in practice the British response to the Council of Europe, and later in 1950 to the Schuman Plan, was governed precisely by the imperatives of British domestic needs. By 1950, the Commonwealth as an entity looked and felt rather different. Canada was being sucked ever closer to its mighty neighbour across the 49th parallel. The new tendency in Australia and New Zealand was underlined in 1951 by the Pacific Security Agreement which marked a fresh link with the United States in hemispheric defence arrangements. South Africa, now under Nationalist government, seemed likely to flee the fold altogether. For all that, the importance of the Commonwealth connection in virtually every aspect of the foreign, financial, defence, and even domestic policies of the Attlee government (witness the anxiety of BOAC to 'fly Commonwealth' by purchasing Canadair passenger aircraft in 1948)[12] must always be borne in mind.

Two countries were always particularly difficult from the Commonwealth standpoint—South Africa and Eire. In relation to the Union of South Africa, the Labour government's early involvement was relatively cordial, as has been seen, with Smuts still installed as South African premier. On the other hand, Smuts wished to extract a high price for his loyalty—control over the High Commission territories

---

[11] Minutes of meeting of Commonwealth Finance Ministers, July 1949 (PREM 8/975).

[12] Memorandum by Addison on 'The Civil Aircraft Programme', 9 July 1948, CP (48) 179 (CAB 129/28).

(Bechuanaland, Basutoland, and Swaziland), and increased influence in East Africa and the Rhodesias. Its faith in Smuts led the British government in April–May 1946 to take the grave step of accepting his demand for the absorption of South West Africa into the Union of South Africa, and the winding up of the old mandate system.[13] For the next thirty years, in fact, turmoil in South West Africa (later renamed Namibia) was to plague the United Nations. The optimistic assessment made by the British government in 1946 was certainly not confirmed. Over the protected territories of Bechuanaland, Swaziland, and Basutoland, again the British government was anxious not to offend South African sensibilities. Even as late as 1950, this was a major factor governing the exclusion of Seretse Khama, the chief of the Bamangwato tribe in Bechuanaland, from his homeland after he had married a white English girl, to the dismay of South African racialists across the border. The South African link could have some sinister implications. In May 1946, John Parker, an able and liberal-minded undersecretary at the Commonwealth Office and government spokesman for the department in the Commons, was dismissed from the government. The occasion for this appears to have been Smut's anger at Parker's refusal to reprieve a Boer farmer in the protectorates convicted of murder three years earlier. But it was the culmination of months of displeasure by the South African government over Parker's opposition to its desire to acquire the protectorates, and also his efforts to persuade Smuts to sell coal to the Argentine to obtain maize that Britain could then sell to the Basutos during a maize shortage in southern Africa.[14] Relations with the Union of South Africa generally became much more tense from late 1948 when the bitterly anti-British Dr Malan, a pro-German sympathizer during the war, an Afrikaner identified, like his party, with the Volk consciousness and religious fundamentalism of the Dutch Reform Church, became the new Prime Minister of South Africa. Behind

[13] Cabinet Conclusions, 24 Apr., 13 May 1946 (CAB 128/5).
[14] Interview with John Parker in the *Guardian*, 24 Aug. 1982; letter from John Parker to the author, 24 Feb. 1982. Cf. Parker's book, *Father of the House* (London, 1982).

Malan were sinister elements such as the pro-Nazi Broeder-
bond. The Nationalists were to remain in unbroken power
and to extend the system of apartheid ever further, while
Smut's United Party, with its roots amongst English South
Africans in Natal and Cape Province gradually disintegrated.
In the discussions on a Central African Federation, involving North and Southern Rhodesia, and also Nyasaland, in
1949–51, a central argument, for instance from Percivale
Leisching at the Commonwealth Relations Office and
Andrew Cohen in the Colonial Office, was the need to provide a firm bulwark against the growing encroachment
and influence of a potentially hostile South Africa.[15] At this
stage, however, animosity towards South Africa and its
apartheid system did not figure prominently in the rhetoric
or the literature of the Labour Party. Between 1945 and
1951, cultural, educational, and sporting links with the
Union remained undisturbed, while the naval base at
Simonstown was a prized strategic asset. More ominously,
South African uranium was vital for the British nuclear
weapons programme.

Southern Ireland—also a concern of the Commonwealth
Office down to 1949—was another difficulty, with the free
movement of peoples between Britain and Eire, and the Irish
population resident in English and Scottish cities. In practice,
a vital accommodation was achieved in 1949 with the Act
that cut the vestigial ties remaining from 1922 that still
bound Eire to the Crown; a new Republic of Ireland came
into being. The continuation of the traditional Ulster Protestant stronghold of Northern Ireland, with all its acknowledged electoral gerrymandering and social discrimination
against the Roman Catholic minority there, caused much
anger amongst anti-partitionist Labour MPs, including some
from Lancashire with large Catholic elements amongst their
constituents. There was a substantial revolt by sixty-six
backbenchers and junior ministers against the government on
19 May 1949 over the continuation of the partition of
Ireland. But Labour generally ignored Northern Ireland and

[15] e.g. memorandum by Andrew Cohen on the 'Closer Associations' proposals
for Central Africa, 18 Apr. 1951 (CO 537/7203); also memorandum by Patrick
Gordon-Walker, 25 Apr. 1951 (DO 121/136).

left it to the Unionist rulers at Stormont. A very rare event in a by-election in County Down in 1946 was the direct participation of a candidate from the British Labour Party, Desmond Donnelly, who polled the remarkably high total of 28,000 votes.[16] The 1949 treaty went through easily enough. The Irish Dail, led by the Fine Gael premier of Eire, John Costello, had already passed an Act couched in similar terms. Since the basic arrangements of concern to Eire, citizenship, immigration, and trade, continued to be highly favourable to the south of Ireland, the North was ignored as before, and an era of happier relations between London and Dublin seemed to be inaugurated. The removal from office in February 1948 of de Valera, the veteran Fianna Fail leader, until he was elected president of the Republic in 1959, assisted in this process. The festering and acknowledged grievance of Northern Ireland remained a relatively minor issue, and not one seriously to disturb British foreign or Commonwealth relations.

The framework of relations between Britain and the White Dominions and Eire was a traditional one. Far more novel, indeed revolutionary, were the policies for African, Asian, and Caribbean colonies which impelled British history into radically new directions. In fact, there was little enough novelty during the regime of George Hall at the Colonial Office until October 1946. He was an elderly Welsh miner and one of Attlee's less inspired appointments. In any case, his major preoccupation was Palestine. His successor, Arthur Creech Jones, was a very different personality. As has been seen, he had long been a pioneer of new thinking on colonial policy. His successor as chairman of the Fabian Colonial Research Bureau, J. F. Horrabin, a noted cartographer as well as the joint founder of the Bureau's journal (significantly entitled *Empire*), continued to proclaim the Creech Jones/ Rita Hinden creed of economic development and constitutional reform. Indeed, under Creech Jones's regime, until February 1950, the Colonial Office took on a much more expanded, paternalist role than it had done before the

---

[16] Desmond Donnelly papers (National Library of Wales, Aberystwyth), Box. 1.

war. Its official civil service staffing strength increased by
45 per cent between 1947 and 1954, which became a para-
digm case for Professor Northcote Parkinson in illustrating
the 'law' of bureaucrats expanding to fill the space available.[17] The Colonial Office, of course, was hedged about
by the Foreign Office and the Treasury at every turn.
Still, it enjoyed in these years an excitement and an
economic initiative unknown since the days of the Boer
War. Development on a Chamberlainite or a Milnerite scale,
social imperialism on the grand 'Round Table' model' was
pursued relentlessly, from Jamaica to Tanganyika, by the
ragged-trousered philanthropists of the British Labour Party.

The first prong of Creech Jones's policy was the creation
of powerful new centrally-funded corporations to promote
colonial development. *Tribune* described this, not inaccurately,
as 'Fabianising the Empire'.[18] The two most significant
bodies set up were the Overseas Food Corporation, to promote the bulk buying of staple crops such as cocoa, cotton,
or tobacco from African, Asian, and Caribbean colonies, and
the Colonial Development Corporation, with a capital of
£100m. The latter became somewhat more controversial
since the losses in its first years (£4,500,000 in all) were
considerable. The government was attacked for profligate
'waste' as Lloyd George had been in the past. The calamitous
failures over the ground-nuts scheme in Tanganyika and over
the production of eggs in Gambia made the Corporation and
its energetic, left-wing chairman, Sir Leslie Plummer, easy
targets for right-wing critics and even something of a laughing-
stock. The eventual dismissal of Plummer in June 1950, by
Maurice Webb, Strachey's successor as Minister of Food with
a brief to clear up the mess over ground-nuts and eggs, led
to some protest from Driberg, Crossman, and other Labour
backbenchers.[19] The ground-nuts scheme (which had been

[17] C. Northcote Parkinson, *Parkinson's Law* (London, 1958), p. 13. Parkinson
gives figures of 1,139 staff in 1947 and 1,661 in 1954.

[18] *Tribune*, 4 July 1947.

[19] For the ground-nuts scheme, see Cabinet Conclusions, 13 Jan. 1947 (CAB
128/9); material on the East African Groundnuts Corporation Board, 1950 (CO
537/5876); and Hugh Thomas, *John Strachey* (London, 1973), pp. 245–56. For
the Gambia eggs scheme, see the enquiry into the CDC poultry scheme in Gambia
(CO 537/7184). On Plummer, see material in the Tom Driberg papers (Christ
Church Library, Oxford, L2) and *Daily Express*, 21 June 1950.

advanced £25m. from the Treasury by Dalton) was indeed a colossal exercise in mismanagement, with no real analysis of either the soil or the rainfall in East Africa. There was grave business incompetence throughout. It did the entire development concept fathered by Creech Jones immense harm. On the other hand, the powerful stimulus given by the CDC and its associated bodies to the economic growth of colonial territories in East and West Africa, in Tanganyika, Kenya, and Uganda, in Nigeria, the Gold Coast, Sierra Leone, and the Gambia, should be clearly noted. Of course, these schemes were marked by an obvious element of national self-interest as well. They were linked with Britain's economic needs, with the necessity of tying export-orientated mono-cultures in the colonies into the home economy, and also to protect the role of sterling through the 'dollar pool'. The operations of the 'pool' were severely criticized by many colonies, for instance, Malaya, the Rhodesias, the Gold Coast, or Ceylon, which tended to run up a surplus with the dollar areas but found it spent instead by Britain and other members of the sterling area through the multilateral pooling arrangements that existed. The way in which the sterling bloc operated often appeared as an unnatural obstacle to the real economic needs of the developing colonies. For all that, a purposive policy of long-term development, despite all the financial constraints of the time, was a notable extension of the British socialist tradition. Africa had become almost the greater Birmingham that Joseph Chamberlain had once visualized. An important episode in the later history of the Attlee government was the Colombo conference in January 1950, when Bevin travelled to Ceylon to represent the British government. Largely under his inspiration, six-year development plans were worked out under the 'Colombo Plan' for India, Pakistan, Ceylon, Malaya, Singapore, and British North Borneo. Of a total expenditure of £1,868m., Britain and the older Dominions would be responsible for up to £1,000m.[20] It was a valuable confirmation of the potentialities of economic association between the emergent Asian peoples and the mother country.

In political matters, Creech Jones pursued a vigorous

[20] Records of the Colombo conference, 9–15 Jan. 1950 (CAB 133/78–79).

programme of constitutional reform. By 1950, independence had been granted to territories as different as Ceylon, Newfoundland, and Malta. With varying degrees of success, he also tried to promote the idea of the federation of smaller territories, in Malaya, in the West Indies, and (in embryo only before 1950) in Central Africa. Of these, the new Union of Malaya was much the most successful, though the picture here was complicated by the war against Communist guerillas that flared up from June 1948 and which, among other dismal features, saw the murder of the High Commissioner, Sir Henry Gurney, in 1951.[21] Major constitutional reform was also promoted in West Africa, in the Gold Coast, and Nigeria above all, and more tentatively in the east and the south of the continent. Throughout, a powerful force in pushing on Creech Jones's policies was Andrew Cohen, the youthful left-wing head of the Africa Division of the Colonial Office, the so-called 'King of Africa'. The main initiatives were taken in areas of overwhelmingly black population such as the Gold Coast and Nigeria. In territories which contained substantial white settler populations, the Labour government was far more circumspect. In Kenya, the white paper of 1946 seemed to place white minority concern above African settlement in the 'White Highlands'. Bevin and Attlee, in any case, thought of Kenya as highly significant in terms of East African defence, especially the naval base at Mombasa. In Southern Rhodesia, with over 200,000 white inhabitants by the early fifties, reinforced by many emigrants from Britain fleeing from life under a socialist government, the British ministers were anxious to work closely with Roy Welensky and Sir Godfrey Huggins, and not to offend white sensibilities.[22] In West Africa, however, where white settlement was relatively negligible, the process of native self-government was taken dramatically forward. In the Gold Coast, political tensions were reinforced by the territory's dependence on a one-crop economy based on cocoa exports. Here, the Watson

---

[21] D. J. Goldsworthy, *Colonial Issues in British Politics, 1945–1961* (Oxford, 1971), pp. 17 ff. There is a succinct discussion of Malaya in P. S. Gupta, 'Imperialism and the Labour Government' in J. M. Winter (ed.), *The Working Class in Modern British History* (Cambridge, 1983), pp. 112–15.

[22] Robert Blake, *A History of Rhodesia* (London, 1977), pp. 273 ff.

Commission of 1948 recommended a major advance towards political independence. This policy was pursued vigorously by the new governor, Arden-Clarke, from 1949. The next year, a fresh constitution for the Gold Coast guaranteed an African majority in perpetuity. There were communal disturbances in Accra; the black African leader, Kwame Nkrumah, was temporarily imprisoned. For all that, his Convention People's Party captured thirty-four seats out of thirty-eight in the first elections, held in 1951. The Gold Coast was well on the way to complete independence by the time Labour left office.[23] So, too, was Nigeria, where the Richards Commission of 1948 visualized a new federal structure to accommodate the interests of the Ibo, Yoruba, and other tribes. A revised constitution in 1951 tried to balance the wishes of southern Nigerians with those of the pro-British Muslims in the north. Again, by the time of Labour's fall from power, Nigerian independence was within sight, with potentially a far more economically optimistic future than in the case of the Gold Coast, especially with its oil reserves. Other territories in Africa would not linger far behind. Creech Jones indicated that further changes were well under way in Sierra Leone, Uganda, Northern Rhodesia, Nyasaland, and Zanzibar by 1950.[24]

Less straightforward, as has been noted above, was the pressure, first effectively voiced at the Victoria Falls conference by white politicians in 1949, for a federation in Central Africa This would comprehend Southern and Northern Rhodesia, and the much smaller and poorer territory of Nyasaland, an area much permeated by the missionary activities of the Presbyterian Church of Scotland since the days of David Livingstone. Andrew Cohen, Percivale Liesching, and other Colonial and CRO advisers urged the need for a federal union of the three territories, partly for the economic motive of the closer development of mineral resources such as copper, partly for political reasons to

[23] See minutes of the meetings of the Gold Coast executive council, 1951 (CO 537/7174).
[24] Memorandum by Creech-Jones on 'The Labour and the Colonies' (Creech-Jones papers, Rhodes House Library, ACJ/4/4/2–5; Arthur Creech-Jones, 'British Colonial Policy with particular reference to Africa', *International Affairs*, xxvii, no. 2 (Apr. 1951), 176–83.

frustrate the supposed expansionist tendencies of the new Nationalist government in South Africa. It has been suggested also by Professor Gupta that the British nuclear weapons programme depended on secure supplies of chromium from Southern Rhodesia and that this was a major underlying factor. The Victoria Falls conference in 1949 was partly frustrated by the evident mutual antagonism of Creech Jones and Roy Welensky, the aggressive ex-boxer and former trade-union leader who was now Prime Minister of Southern Rhodesia. The manifest hostility of every significant leader of African opinion, especially Hastings Banda in Nyasaland, towards a federation that threatened to rivet permanent white domination from Southern Rhodesia upon its overwhelmingly black African neighbours was always present. Banda wrote to Creech Jones in 1951 that the Nyasaland African Congress believed it was planned 'to sacrifice them to please the European settlers of Rhodesia'. For all that, the chequered pursuit of the idea of federation in Central Africa was another, less happy, legacy of the Creech Jones era, although one followed up far more directly by his successors in office, James Griffiths and Gordon-Walker.[25]

Central African Federation was always a dubious proposition. The premiss of South African territorial aggression was never proven; the economic case was sketchily argued; the bypassing of black African opinion was a fatal flaw in the design. Nevertheless the general policy for the economic and political development of colonies in Africa and elsewhere was impressive enough. There was a vitality and dynamism about the Colonial Office in these years not known for over a generation, with development economists, academics, journalists, and other intellectuals, including many Africans and Asians (for instance Harry Lee, later Lee Kwan Yew, from Singapore), enjoying easy access to government ministers. In many ways, the Colonial Office in this period was the Fabian Colonial Research Bureau writ large. Certainly, it was an ornament in Labour's overall achievements. The

[25] Gupta, op. cit., p. 340; Blake, op. cit., pp. 243–63; Joint Memorandum by J. Griffiths and P. Gordon-Walker on 'Closer Association in Central Africa', 8 Oct. 1951 (DO 121/138); Hastings Banda to Creech Jones, 23 June 1951 (Creech Jones papers, ACJ/7/1/339–44).

architects of the powerful push to colonial freedom in the fifties and early sixties, with enormous implications for international relations and the association of the developed and underdeveloped nations, were without question Creech Jones and his somewhat unheralded and underestimated colleagues.

The Commonwealth and colonial policy of the Labour government, however, should not be assessed primarily by developments in the Gold Coast, Kenya, or the West Indies. It should not be judged by imperialistic assertiveness in upholding British outposts in the Indian Ocean or the Pacific, or in rebutting Argentine demands for an international tribunal to inquire into sovereignty over the Falklands, which appeared on Argentine postage stamps as the Malvinas.[26] The dispatch of HMS *Sheffield* to the south Atlantic in 1946 to deter part of President Peron's navy from approaching Falklands waters aroused little interest at the time. It should rather be weighed by two great retreats which dominated policy-making in these years, one a shambles and little short of a disaster, the other perhaps the most shining achievement of the Attlee government in any sphere of its operations. These were Palestine and India, both of which reached a critical phase in 1947. Detailed attention must now be paid to each in turn.

In Palestine, Britain inherited in July 1945 a hopeless tangle of commitments dating from the original decision to create a Jewish national home in 1917. Communal violence between the resident Arabs and Jewish immigrants had been mounting under the British mandate during the twenties and thirties. It reached a new alarming peak during the second world war, with the formation of two new Jewish para-military organizations, Irgun Zvei Leumi and the Haganah. The British government's white paper had proclaimed in 1939 that Jewish immigration to Palestine should

---

[26] See files on 'Argentine claims to the Falkland Islands', 1947 (CO 537/ 2456-7); Foreign Office memorandum on the Falklands and other Antarctic dependencies, 21 Oct. 1946 (Churchill College, Cambridge, Noel-Baker papers, 4/731).

be limited to 75,000 over a five-year period. In fact, this total, attacked by Zionists as quite inadequate, was never approached between 1939 and 1945. In the mean time, violence in Palestine continued to mount during the war years, culminating in the murder of Lord Moyne, the British Minister Resident, by the Haganah in November 1944. An extraordinary complex of factors helped to determine British policy in Palestine. There was, of course, the appalling fact of the holocaust of millions of Jews in Germany which gave a totally new dimension to the immigration question. There was the growing pressure of the Zionist lobby upon the government of the United States, especially on urban Jewish elements in the ruling Democratic Party. In the Middle East itself, there was the deeply sensitive position of Palestine strategically, with its vital importance for British naval and air networks, as well as the economic riches of the oilfields in Iraq, Iran, Saudi Arabia, and elsewhere on which British manufacturing industry depended. In the eyes of Zionists, this had made the British Foreign Office consistently pro-Arab and anti-Jewish in the thirties and during the war. Palestine should also be related to another deeply critical problem for Britain, that of Egyptian nationalism, fuelled by the presence of well over 100,000 British troops (five divisions) in the canal zone and the surrounding area, after the successful campaign in North Africa.

There was also a question of internal British politics. The Labour Party had had a profound connection with the Palestine question, since it was traditionally deeply committed to the Zionist cause. Poale Zion was actually affiliated to the Labour Party in Britain itself. Leading politicians such as Morrison and Dalton had strongly backed the Zionist position during the debates on the 1939 white paper. In addition, there were now important Jewish MPs in the government, Shinwell, Strachey, and Silkin prominent among them. In 1944, the party's NEC had called for Jews of the diaspora to be admitted to Palestine in such numbers as to become a majority there; a subsidized transfer of the Arab population elsewhere in the Palestinian desert was credibly proposed.[27] In the 1945 party conference and in the party

[27] *Annual Report of the Labour Party NEC*, 1944.

manifesto, Labour (Dalton in particular) had vehemently attacked the current restrictions on Jewish immigration, and had given almost blanket endorsement of the Zionist cause, even to the occasional embarrassment of Ben Gurion and the Zionist Labour Party. The revelations of the German concentration camps in 1945, and of the appalling atrocities committed against millions of innocent Jewish people, gave Labour's demands a new moral passion. It could well be assumed, therefore, that the advent of a Labour government in Britain would mean a different policy. Terence Shone, the minister to Syria and Lebanon, was only one diplomat fearful of a new pro-Zionist administration in Britain.[28] It was believed that the old pro-Arab policies of the Foreign Office would be reversed, and that a new deal would be offered to European Jewry.

In fact, Labour's policy once in office proved to be almost the exact opposite. This is usually linked with the outlook of Bevin as foreign secretary. Certainly, Bevin, who had little knowledge of the Palestine issue before he took office, dictated British policy there over the next three years. It was he, above all, who grappled with its implications for Britain's position in the Middle East, the relationship with the United States, and the military and financial problems of the British presence in Palestine in fulfilling the mandate. Bevin was not, and never had been, anti-semitic. But, without doubt, he was emotionally prejudiced against the Jews, as Foreign Office advisers of his at the time have admitted to the present writer. Bevin regarded the Jews as a religion rather than a nation. He never understood the driving force of Jewish nationalism, nor the emotional impact of the holocaust which had transformed the entire Palestine issue. He persisted in regarding ageing moderates such as Dr Weizmann as spokesmen for the Jewish cause when they were manifestly being overtaken by hardliners like Ben Gurion with their terrorist associates. On the other hand, some of the error in Bevin's policy lay in its style of presentation. He was monumentally insensitive in the handling of Jewish grievances, whether in press conferences or at Labour Party

[28] Terence Shone to Foreign Office, 14 Aug. 1945 (FO 371/45378), E5953/15/31.

conferences. His obsession with personalizing every dispute made matters far worse. References to the Jews 'wanting to get too much at the head of the queue' as far as immigration was concerned; pointed observations on the connection between anti-Semitism in America itself and American enthusiasm for exporting Jews far away to Palestine in vast numbers; heavy puns on the illumination afforded by the 'Israe-lites' during a power cut—these were examples of elephantine *gaucherie* which did relations between the government and Zionist sympathizers immense harm. The actual substance of Bevin's policy—his concern for balance and stability in the Middle East; his anxiety for a settlement acceptable to Arabs as well as Jews; his contempt for political pressures in America which urged unlimited and immediate mass immigration; his precise appreciation of the turmoil and bloodshed that would result if Arab Palestinians and Jews from Europe were thrust upon one another without guidance or control—was far more defensible. In practice, Bevin's view did not diverge substantially from the consensus that soon emerged in the Labour government. Attlee, in particular, gave Bevin's Palestine policy consistent support. The previous pro-Zionism of Dalton or Morrison never added up to much. They both signed, as early as 8 September 1945, a powerful Palestine Committee memorandum which broadly endorsed the Foreign Office case. It recommended a quota of just 1,500 Jewish immigrants a month.[29] Other friends of Zionism in the government, notably Bevan and Shinwell, and later Creech Jones and Strachey, never had a continuous involvement with the Palestine question and were in no position to challenge the expertise and influence of the Foreign Office. Bevin's policy, then, with all its tragic overtones, was far more than the emotional product of one prejudiced, insensitive personality. It summarized the measured response of the Attlee government as a whole to a political and communal problem virtually incapable of solution, one which has generated war and violence more or less continuously, from the early twenties to the tragedy in Beirut in 1982, and which still shows no sign of diminishing.

[29] Report of the Palestine Committee, 8 Sept. 1945, CP (45) 156 (CAB 129/2 and PREM 8/627).

By the autumn of 1945, Bevin was under pressure, both from American insistence on further large-scale Jewish immigration into Palestine, and from a series of violent raids by Irgun and by the smaller Stern Gang, in which personalities such as Menachem Begin (later Prime Minister of Israel) were prominent. Bevin's fury at the murder of British 'Tommies' was intense; but so, too, was his anxiety to try to involve the United States constructively in a solution of the Palestine dilemma. On 13 November 1945, he was able to announce to the Commons, as previously proposed to the Cabinet's Palestine Committee, the appointment of an Anglo-American committee of inquiry to examine both the Palestinian and European aspects of the case. The composition on the American side was overwhelmingly and uncritically pro-Zionist: James G. McDonald was especially fervent in this direction. The British representatives included such varied figures as the strongly pro-Arab Harold Beeley of the Foreign Office, and Richard Crossman, a backbench Labour MP of much volatility and intellectual brilliance, due to become a passionate critic of Bevin and advocate of the Zionist cause. His views soon changed from a broad sympathy with the Arab case to a warm commitment to Zionism, especially after touring the Jewish settlements in Europe. After much difficulty and internal disagreement, during a period in which violent incidents in Palestine continued and the Haganah openly assisted illegal immigration, the Committee produced an agreed report on 1 May 1946. It proposed the issue of 100,000 immigration certificates for Jewish immigrants immediately and continued immigration thereafter. However, it rejected both the idea of partition and turning Palestine into either a Jewish or an Arab state.[30]

The Labour government, despite pressure from a minority headed by Bevan in the Cabinet, and from Laski and others

[30] *Parl. Deb.*, 5th ser., vol. 415, 1927–32 (13 Nov. 1945); Bevin to Byrnes, 13 Oct. 1945 (PREM 8/627). Also Halifax to Bevin, 24 Oct. 1945 (ibid.), in which he announces that the Americans will participate in a joint Commission of Inquiry, but that the administration was much preoccupied by the Jewish vote in the New York mayoral elections on 6 November, 'as Byrnes has so frankly explained to me'. Also see Richard Crossman, *Palestine Mission* (London, 1947) and James G. McDonald, *My Mission in Israel* (London, 1951), for the committee of inquiry.

on the NEC for a more advanced policy, seemed prepared to accept these proposals, if without enthusiasm. Bevin, however, insisted that the admission of 100,000 Jews must be phased in gradually; the present rate of 1,500 a month was already troublesome to maintain. He and Attlee reacted violently to pressure from Truman and leading American Democrats to implement the quota of 100,000 immediately.[31] Indeed, Truman's statements seem only to have hardened Bevin's previously flexible attitude. On the other hand, there were the military and financial problems to be weighed in maintaining two or more infantry divisions and perhaps one armoured brigade in Palestine for an indefinite period, at a cost to the British taxpayer of perhaps £115m. to £125m. over the next ten years, at a time of already grave financial difficulties.[32] At the Labour Party conference in June, Bevin strongly resisted Zionist demands for a relaxation of policy on immigration, and for the establishment of some kind of Jewish state. In effect, the policy of the 1939 white paper was to be continued. He reacted with much contempt to Crossman's pro-Zionist criticisms. Instead of conciliatory diplomacy, the government appointed Lieutenant-General Barker to launch a far more vigorous policy of repressing the Irgun and the Haganah. The problem of Palestine now assumed a largely military aspect. A series of terrorist attacks by Jewish and Arab groups, with vigorous reprisals by the British army, culminated in the fateful blowing up of the King David Hotel on 22 July 1946. Ninety-one people were killed, British, Arab, and Jews. It was the work of the Irgun, led by Menachem Begin. This event heralded a new and more tragic phase in the disaster of Palestine, against a background of signs of anti-Semitism increasing in Britain itself as news of Jewish atrocities committed against British troops received massive press coverage.

Beyond the physical problems of maintaining law and order, it was unclear what kind of long-term political settlement in Palestine the Labour government actually visualized.

[31] Attlee to Bevin, 8 May 1946 (PREM 8/627).
[32] Chiefs of Staff Committee: Palestine. Anglo-American report: the Military Implications, 10 July 1946 (ibid.). The Chiefs of Staff at this time were Tedder, Cunningham, and Simpson.

On the Conservative side, Winston Churchill, an old friend of Weizmann and supporter of Zionism, was veering towards the notion of partition, or so he told Attlee privately. He suggested, in what Attlee's PPS called 'a clever, powerful and mischievous' speech in the Commons, that Britain might have to go to the UN and offer to give up the mandate.[33] By the end of July, the government itself was clear on only two points—that the recommendations of the Anglo-American Committee did not provide the basis for a stable solution; and that somehow the United States must be involved with a settlement. The outcome, as announced by Morrison to the Commons, was a revived version of the Colonial Office scheme, previously rejected by the Foreign Office but now viewed by it more favourably, for a kind of partition. There would be autonomous Arab and Jewish provinces, under a central Trustee government. A conference was called in London in September, with both Jewish and Arab representatives due to attend. However, the climate became steadily worse. Despite some support for the provincial autonomy scheme by American spokesmen in London, President Truman himself (though not personally sympathetic to the Jews) refused to back it. In Bevin's view, he had simply capitulated to Zionist pressure. Neither Jews nor Palestinian Arabs would agree to attend the London conference; only delegates from Egypt, Syria, Iraq, and the Arab League turned up. On the Jewish side, the old Agency leaders such as Weizmann, who sought a diplomatic solution, were manifestly being outvoted and out-talked by Ben Gurion, Rabbi Silver, and the younger, more militant supporters of the Irgun. Zionist sympathizers in Britain took some encouragement at this time by the replacement of George Hall at the Colonial Office by Creech-Jones, in the past an ardent supporter of Zionism.

The situation was complicated still further by American attempts to push forward the cause of unlimited Jewish immigration into Palestine, attempts fuelled by the coming mid-term elections for the US Congress in which the Jewish

---

[33] Churchill to Attlee, 2 July 1946 (Bodleian, Attlee papers, Box 4); Arthur Moyle (Attlee's PPS), memorandum summarizing Churchill's speech in parliament, 1 July 1946 (PREM 8/627).

vote in New York, Philadelphia, Chicago, and other cities was a powerful factor. A blatantly political speech by Truman on 4 October, which called for the immediate and unconditional admission of 100,000 Jews into Palestine, roused Bevin and Attlee to especial fury. Attlee, normally so restrained in the international diplomatic courtesies, dispatched a remarkably sharp rebuke to the American president. 'I am astonished that you did not wait to acquaint yourself with the reasons for the suspension of the Conference with the Arabs. . . . I shall await with interest to learn what were the imperative reasons which impelled this precipitancy.'[34] This reduced Anglo-American relations to a new, glacial level, at a critical period in the Foreign Ministers' discussions in New York. Bevin himself encountered anti-British demonstrations during his visit to the United States. In Britain, opinion seemed to be increasingly inflamed. The murder of British troops by Jewish terrorists was given ample coverage in Fleet Street. Another factor to generate Anglo-American tension was a violently anti-British play on Broadway, *A Flag is Born*, written by a Jewish playwright, Ben Hecht, who exulted publicly in the saga of the murder of British troops. Meanwhile the tragic toll of illegal immigration, murders, and acts of sabotage went on apace in the Holy Land itself.

In the first half of 1947, the Labour government staggered towards a solution. It became increasingly apparent that Britain was anxious to leave Palestine and to sacrifice its mandate. There were pressing financial reasons alone, stimulated by losses in the gold and dollar reserves long before the coming of convertibility. The fuel crisis in January and February made matters worse. A retrenchment in Britain's overseas commitments was vital to preserve foreign exchange and the stability of the pound. In addition, powerful precedents for an evacuation now existed. There was the British decision to remove its forces from Greece, announced to the American government in February 1947 and itself the origin of the so-called Truman Doctrine for Greece and Turkey. There was the even more cogent precedent of India. The British decision to evacuate its forces from the Indian

---

[34] Attlee to Truman, 18 Aug. 1946, T 418/46, and Attlee to Truman, 4 Oct. 1946, T 460/46 (ibid.).

subcontinent during 1948, a decision taken in February 1947, was now being quoted by Attlee and other ministers as a model for a similar retreat from Palestine.[35] The British government was also anxious to patch up differences with Washington somehow, in view of the urgent need for American financial and military assistance in western Europe. Beyond that, it was uncertain whether the British really regarded a military foothold in Palestine as especially crucial. There were already many difficulties with Egypt where the government of Sidky Pasha had broken off negotiations with Bevin in January 1947 over a British withdrawal from the Canal Zone. The main point of contention was the Egyptian claim for sovereignty over Sudan and the Nile waters. Bevin himself was anxious for an early settlement in Egypt, with Britain making more use of peripheral bases in Cyrenaica, for aircraft, and Aden, Bahrein, and British Somaliland for stores. He did not endorse the view of the Chiefs of Staff that a possible British withdrawal from Egypt made bases in Palestine the more necessary.[36] The overriding factor was that the imperatives, financial, military, and political, for a British evacuation were steadily mounting.

In February 1947, the Cabinet explored the various options at length.[37] Creech-Jones for the Colonial Office put forward a revised scheme for the partition of Palestine. There would be autonomy for Jewish and Arab districts, and the admission of 100,000 Jewish immigrants over the next two years. But this was rapidly seen to be impracticable. The Arabs would not accept any Jewish immigration at all; the Jews wanted a Jewish national state. Bevin himself pointed out that the views of the two delegations were quite irreconcilable, and Creech-Jones soon came to agree. The alternative was Bevin's own scheme, evolved by the Foreign Office, for a further five-year period of British trusteeship, as a preparation for an independent bi-national state of Palestine. At meetings of the Cabinet on 7 and 14 February, Strachey and Bevan led a small minority of ministers who

---

[35] Cabinet Conclusions, 7 Feb., 18 Feb. 1947 (CAB 128/9).
[36] Bevin to Attlee, 25 May 1946; Stansgate to Attlee, 10 Dec. 1946; Discussion of Bevin with Foreign Office officials, 10 Jan. 1947 (PREM 8/1388).
[37] Cabinet Conclusions, 7, 14, 18 Feb. 1947 (loc. cit.).

urged an openly pro-Jewish policy. They argued that the Jews, with their powerful socialist movement, would provide a democratic, dynamic element to invigorate the stagnant, paternal society of the Middle East and its sheikhs. However, it was Bevin's policy, strongly backed by Attlee, which prevailed. The one clear conclusion that seemed to emerge was that Britain herself could no longer provide a solution. On 18 February, Bevin told the Commons that the entire Palestine issue would now be referred to the United Nations.[38] The days of the mandate were evidently numbered. As in India, the scent of surrender was in the air.

In April, the matter was taken up by the United Nations which referred it to a committee of eleven states. The atmosphere was much inflamed by further acts of remarkable insensitivity by Bevin (whose health and temper were consistently bad at this period). The most notorious was the attitude adopted towards the US vessel, *President Warfield* (renamed the *Exodus*) dispatched from the United States, via southern France, towards Palestine, with 4,500 illegal Jewish immigrants on board. The *Exodus* became a symbol of hope for the entire Zionist community. In the end, Bevin decided to intercept the vessel; its passengers were sent back, after some manhandling, to the British zone in western Germany, back to the land of the concentration camps. The handling of the whole *Exodus* affair, admittedly a most delicate one, by the British government was extraordinarily lacking in perceptiveness and humanity. It made Britain even more hated in the Jewish world and in much of America. The Irgun replied with the execution of captured British soldiers in Acre. The climax in diplomatic terms came when the UN Committee finally came out in August with a proposal for the partition of Palestine into Jewish and Arab states, with Jerusalem under direct UN rule. Bevin, rightly, saw every kind of objection to this.[39] It would contain all the worst features of partition and of communal autonomy, co-existing with one another. It would enrage the entire Arab world, from Morocco to Iran, and would also mean a massive British military commitment for years to come at

[38] *Parl. Deb.*, 5th ser., vol. 433, 985–9 (18 Feb. 1947).
[39] Paper by Bevin, 18 Sept. 1947 CP (47) 259 (CAB 129/21).

a time of extreme financial crisis. The only solution that
Britain and Bevin could come up with was simply to leave.
Even pro-Zionists like Bevan were now anxious to be rid of
an impossible problem. On 20 September 1947, with little
dissent, the Cabinet accepted Bevin's view that the mandate
should be surrendered and British troops withdrawn from
Palestine by 1 August 1948.[40] Dalton strongly endorsed this
on financial grounds, while Attlee again stressed the parallel
of the withdrawal from India, where the transfer of power
had now taken place. No proposal of any kind for a political
settlement was made. In November, the UN General Assembly
endorsed a scheme for a partition, but this was being overtaken by events in Palestine. Virtual civil war was now taking
place between Zionist militants, and the so-called 'Arab
Liberation Army', initially formed with implicit British
support. On 14 May 1948, British troops finally withdrew
from Palestine. The Jews at once declared themselves to be
the *de facto* state of Israel under the premiership of Ben
Gurion. War between Arabs and Jews dragged on until
January 1949 when the UN managed to arrange an armistice.
Bevin on 29 January 1949 announced Britain's *de facto*
recognition of the state of Israel. The final armistice, due to
last just seven years, was concluded in July. Through the
biblical method of fire and sword, a Jewish state of Israel
had triumphed over Arab Palestinian opposition and British
diplomacy.

The entire saga of Palestine was a humiliating débâcle
for Britain, and for the Foreign Office in particular. It
brought Britain intense international odium, especially in
America. It also cost Britain many lives and much foreign
exchange. In the end, the blatantly pro-Arab views of the
Foreign Office were swept aside in a settlement in which
Britain simply abdicated. Unlike the settlements in India
in 1947 or in Egypt in 1954, no successor state was outlined
in the British decision to leave. There would simply be a
deliberate vacuum, to be resolved by armed violence—in
which, so the British thought, the tiny Jewish armies would be
swept into the sea by superior Arab numbers. Dalton believed
that Britain's support for the Arabs in 1948–9 would prove

[40] Cabinet Conclusions, 20 Sept. 1947 (CAB 128/10).

as futile, and as destructive to Commonwealth unity, as had been Lloyd George's support for the Greeks during the Chanak crisis in 1922.[41] Without question, Bevin's entire conduct of the Palestine question did his reputation, so towering in other spheres, immense harm, then and later. On the other hand, it is difficult to see any other viable policy which the Labour government could have adopted. The inheritance of rival commitments to Arabs and Jews, dating from the twenties, was impossible to reconcile. Indeed, the damage had been done with the original Balfour Declaration, with all its dangerous, inspirational vagueness, back in 1917. In Palestine, with ambiguous pledges both to Arabs and to the Jewish Agency, with extreme financial problems, with a military position that was untenable, Britain found its imperial role beyond its capacity. The will was lacking, too. The attitude of the American government, and the naïve insistence of the UN general assembly on a partition solution that was rejected on all sides, made things even worse. In Bevin's defence, it may at least be said that his insistence that any solution must be acceptable to Arab opinion, and that an imposed solution would lead to decades of bitterness and instability in the Middle East, has been borne out by later events. The eventual decision to leave Palestine was undoubtedly popular in Britain, and led to no serious loss of electoral support for the Labour government. The Zionist element in the Labour Party was always small, and was unable significantly to influence party policy in the House or on the NEC. A junior minister, C. R. Hobson, reported to Attlee in early 1949 that trade-unionist MPs resented those members who put 'Zionism before socialism', while there were also important pro-Arab MPs such as Richard Stokes and George Brown.[42]

By the start of 1948, in any case, Bevin and the British government were viewing the entire Middle East problem in new perspective. Lord Inverchapel, the outgoing British

---

[41] Dalton to Attlee, 13 Jan. 1949 (Dalton papers, 9/7/1).

[42] C. R. Hobson to Attlee, 27 Jan. 1949 (Bodleian, Attlee papers, Box 9). This followed abstention by some Labour MPs on a Commons vote on the government's policy in Palestine. Hobson, the Assistant Postmaster-General, was sponsored by the AEU.

ambassador in Washington, could report that the old problem of Jewish–Arab hostility was being superseded in Bevin's mind by the new Soviet threat to Middle East security, in which Anglo-American collaboration was absolutely vital.[43] The Foreign Office and the State Department were now anxious to produce a new co-ordinated defence strategy, focusing on protection of the Suez Canal, revision of the British treaty with Iraq, and new 'defence' treaties with Transjordan, Saudi Arabia, and the Yemen. In January 1948, too, Attlee could tell the New Zealand Prime Minister, Peter Fraser, that the difficulties with the Americans over Palestine were now being patched up.[44] Britain was trying to place a new emphasis on the social and economic development of the impoverished Middle East countries, rather than through imperialistic control based on military and air control, and symbolized by an outmoded military presence in Palestine. The argument was moving on. The British Labour Party, anxious to be rid of an impossible and appalling legacy, moved on with it.

Palestine, even so, could not be regarded as other than a disaster and a débâcle. India, the other great instance of imperial retreat, was by contrast projected as a kind of triumph. Labour had a long tradition of involvement with Indian nationalism, as has been seen, with a close connection with Krishna Menon's India League in the thirties. Labour's association with the mainly Hindu Congress movement had led it over the years to favour a unitary Indian state. The party viewed with disfavour the rise of the Muslim League, led from 1934 onwards by Mohammed Ali Jinnah. It saw it as a creation of the Raj in the thirties, designed to divide and rule the Indian subcontinent by playing on communal and religious antagonisms. The 'Socialist Clarity Group' (which included Albu, Warbey, and Gordon-Walker) saw the demands of the Muslim League as tantamount to

[43] Lord Inverchapel to the Foreign Office, 29 Jan. 1948, and copy of the topics raised by the British Chiefs of Staff mission with the US Chiefs of Staff (FO 371/68041).
[44] Attlee to Peter Fraser, ? Jan. 1948 (ibid.).

the creation of a 'Moslem Ulster'.[45] On the other hand, the 'Cripps offer' of 1942 had not been taken up, and had seriously worsened relations between Cripps himself and Congress leaders. The failure of the mission had been followed by the imprisonment of leading Congress figures including the saintly Gandhi himself. The succession of Wavell as Viceroy in 1943 inaugurated a new regime of partial repression.

But the new Labour government regarded itself as morally committed to speed up the process of independence for India, and perhaps for Burma and Ceylon as well. This was particularly the view of Attlee himself, whose special expertise on India dated from the Simon Commission. On India, the Prime Minister showed a decisiveness and passion unusual during his career. Usually so laconic and taciturn, the Prime Minister 'burned with a hidden fire' on Indian matters, wrote one of Mountbatten's aides.[46] Attlee appointed Pethick-Lawrence to the India Office, a septuagenarian but a figure long respected in Indian Congress circles. He had served on the Round Table Conference back in 1930. Of course, Cripps, too, remained a powerful influence on Indian policy. Indeed, Labour's initial move was to revive the Cripps proposals of 1942, with their promise of a constituent assembly. The Cabinet's India Committee, consisting of Attlee himself, Cripps, Pethick-Lawrence, Stansgate, Ellen Wilkinson, and Listowel, set out a programme for winter elections in India. But several obvious facts soon emerged. The Congress leaders would not accept a revamped version of the Cripps plan. The Muslim League continued to press for a separate Muslim state of 'Pakistan'. The Viceroy, Wavell, had poor relations with the Congress movement, and regarded Gandhi himself as 'a malignant old man'.[47] Clearly, therefore, some quite different kind of initiative was needed.

To supply one, Attlee announced in November that a Cabinet mission would be dispatched to India, consisting

[45] Labour Discussion Notes, 'A Policy for India', Mar. 1941 (Noel-Baker papers, 4/372).
[46] Kenneth Harris, *Attlee*, p. 381, citing Campbell-Johnson's diary. For an excellent recent account, published after this chapter was written, see R. J. Moore, *Escape from Empire* (Oxford, 1983).
[47] Penderel Moon (ed.), *The Viceroy's Journey* (Oxford, 1973), p. 185.

of Cripps, Pethick-Lawrence, and A. V. Alexander. It left
for India in February and stayed there until June, conducting intricate and long-drawn-out negotiations with
Congress and Muslim leaders. The Cabinet mission reflected
many shades of Labour opinion. Cripps was a strong supporter of the Congress viewpoint and a close friend of Nehru,
despite his experiences in 1942. He was obviously the
dominant personality of the three. Pethick-Lawrence played
a mediating role, though tending to support Cripps on most
major issues. By contrast, Alexander, a service minister
called in to monitor the aspects of imperial defence and
strategic planning, was an old-fashioned imperialist in many
ways, anxious to avoid the policy of 'scuttle'. He was not
prominent in the public negotiations and became known as
'the silent man' of the delegation.[48] To Alexander, Gandhi
was 'a mixture of saint, fanatic, astute lawyer and worthy
politician'.[49] A somewhat more detached view of the Cabinet
delegation was supplied by Major Woodrow Wyatt, a young
Labour MP present in India at the time, who eventually
served as personal secretary to Cripps and took some part
himself in negotiations with Jinnah and others. Wyatt recorded
that the struggle to get the Hindus and Muslims to agree was
equalled only by the struggle to stop some of the members
of the British delegation behaving idiotically. The officials
of the India Office were putting up a last desperate fight
since they held a rooted belief that British rule was really
good for India and somehow ought to be carried on. Wyatt
was critical of Alexander who, he claimed, felt that all
Indians were monstrous, perhaps because they didn't play
enough football: Alexander was a noted patron of Sheffield
Wednesday FC. Pethick-Lawrence was doing his best but
becoming constitution-bound. Fortunately, the delegation
was being held together by Cripps who took all the main
decisions and was doing magnificently.[50] Wyatt and other
observers agreed that one obstacle to success was Wavell, whose
political and intellectual limitations were much criticized.

[48] Alexander Diary of the Mission to India, Mar.-June 1946 (Churchill College,
Cambridge, Alexander papers, 6/2). Entry for 12 Apr. 1946.
[49] Ibid., 3 Apr. 1946.
[50] Woodrow Wyatt to Tom Driberg, 8 Apr. 1946 (Christ Church Library,
Oxford, Driberg papers, W/10).

However, by 29 April Wyatt had concluded that things so far were going well. Jinnah remained suspicious of the propaganda being so astutely put by Congress but was now more reasonable. His view of Alexander was now more favourable. For some little time, in Wyatt's view, he had been almost on the side of the angels, working to stop too much hustle. Cripps, he added, was still doing well.[51] Pethick-Lawrence told Attlee on 5 May that a good start had been made apart from Jinnah's symbolically refusing to shake the hand of the Congress president, Azad, another Muslim. Lawrence's confidence in Wavell, low at first, 'has grown all though my visit here'.[52] But by 11 May, the omens again were bleak. Alexander now was anticipating the 'final breakdown' of the conference at Simla. The cause would be the refusal of Congress to accept a legislature for the Muslim groups of provinces. Jinnah continued to insist on the territorial integrity of 'Pakistan'.[53] Then a letter from Gandhi on 20 May seemed to torpedo Cripps's proposals completely. The veteran Congress leader wanted, in place of a slow, complex process of constitution-making, a transfer of power to an independent provisional government at the outset, a government that obviously would be under Hindu domination. Alexander angrily commented that 'as a member of the British Cabinet I was not prepared to sit down under the humiliation of my country and therefore something better than a policy of scuttle would have to be thought up if that situation arose'.[54] Cripps was also very disturbed. The discussions became more and more heated. Alexander clashed with Patel and other Hindu leaders. Pethick-Lawrence and Wavell had a row over the precise powers to be exercised by the Viceroy during the period of interim government, and on whether to see a Congress delegation on a further occasion.[55]

On 11 June Alexander even threatened to return home on his own when Cripps and Lawrence urged the need to see

---

[51] Wyatt to Driberg, 29 Apr. 1946 (ibid.). Mr Wyatt tells me that he will be printing these letters in a forthcoming autobiography.

[52] Pethick-Lawrence to Attlee, 5 May 1946 (PREM 8/247); also Pethick-Lawrence to Attlee, 10 May 1946 (ibid.), and 7 Apr. 1946 (PREM 8/541 pt. 3).

[53] Alexander's diary, 11 May 1946.

[54] Ibid., 20 May 1946.

[55] Ibid., 3 June, 11 June, 24 June 1946.

Gandhi for one final effort at agreement.[56] In the end, none was possible. The Muslim League sought a grouping arrangement for those provinces such as the Punjab and Sind (mainly in the north-west of India) which had a Muslim majority. A separate executive and legislative would be created: in effect, this would mean a sovereign Pakistan. The Congress, by contrast, insisted on an early all-India government, elected on a broad democratic franchise, with no grouping of provinces. No consensus could be reached, Pethick-Lawrence told Attlee, either on the powers or the composition of any regional government that might be set up.[57] In despair, Cripps and his two colleagues merely presented their own scheme, and Attlee formally announced it to the House.[58] A three-tier system of government should be set up, with a union of India to deal with foreign affairs, defence, communications, and relevant areas of finance. Communal issues in legislation should require a decision by a majority of representatives present and voting. All other subjects would be vested in the provinces, with each province allotted seats proportional to its population, as a substitute for representation by adult suffrage. Any idea of Pakistan was ruled out. The Mission showed that there were minorities of anything from 37 to 48 per cent of non-Muslims even in the seven mainly Muslim provinces. The outcome was the creation of a new Interim Government, sworn in on 2 September, under the premiership of Pandit Nehru and dominated by the Congress. The Muslim League refused to participate in this assembly in any form, and renewed its call for Pakistan, free from the 'Hindustan' that was now being invented. Meanwhile, as in Palestine at precisely the same period, communal violence mounted, with 5,000 deaths in Calcutta alone on the League's 'day of direct action' on 16 August. Once again, British troops had somehow to preserve order in a society disintegrating into communal conflict.

By October, the Labour government's India Committee was talking in terms of early withdrawal. The apprehensions of the Chiefs of Staff about the Russian threat to the sub-

---

[56] Alexander's diary, 11 June 1946.
[57] Pethick-Lawrence to Attlee, 1 June 1946 (PREM 8/247).
[58] *Parl. Deb.*, 5 ser., vol. 422, 2109–2120 (16 May 1946).

continent were overruled. At every stage, the influence of Attlee himself was paramount. Every major decision was taken with his being intimately involved. There was, at this time, a vital parallel decision to speed up the process of independence in neighbouring Burma. This was a policy thrust by the government on Dorman-Smith, the recalcitrant governor of Burma (who was finally replaced by Brigadier Rance); it was concluded in negotiated form with the Burmese national leader, Aung Sang, in December. It was agreed then that Burma would be granted full independence during 1947.[59] The British government simultaneously was looking with more sympathy on the Muslim demands in India for some kind of separate statehood, even one that might involve two very distant territories in the far north-west and in eastern Bengal. There was also a growing commitment to move towards an early evacuation of British troops from the subcontinent. Salisbury, the Conservative leader in the Lords, denounced this, in a letter to Attlee, as 'betrayal and surrender'. Churchill preferred the term 'scuttle'.[60] In addition, the government was heading towards a break with Wavell. The Viceroy's 'Breakdown Plan' visualized a very early withdrawal, by 31 March 1948 at the latest. His views on the entire Indian problem seemed to be negative and pessimistic. On 17 December, Attlee told the King that he was contemplating the replacement of Wavell with the more dynamic and attractive figure of Louis Mountbatten who would conduct the crucial negotiations on the transfer of power. Alternatively, the idea of replacing Wavell with Cripps had been briefly considered.[61] On 8 January 1947, Attlee's view that there was a total deadlock was communicated to the Cabinet. Wavell sought 'a military evacuation from hostile territory'. The British government, by contrast, wanted 'a friendly transfer of power' from British to Indian authorities.[62] With

---

[59] *Parl. Deb.*, 5th ser., vol. 431, 2341–3 (20 Dec. 1946).

[60] Salisbury to Attlee, 18 Dec. 1946 (Bodleian, Attlee papers, Box 7); *Parl. Deb.*, 5th ser., vol. 431, 2350 (20 Dec. 1946). Churchill earlier observed that 'the British Empire seems to be running off almost as fast as the American loan'.

[61] Pethick-Lawrence to Wavell, 28 Sept. 1946 (PREM 8/541 pt. 6); Short to Cripps, 28 Nov. 1946 (CAB 127/150).

[62] Attlee's revised draft, CP (47) 1, considered in Cabinet Conclusions, 8 Jan. 1947 (CAB 128/11); Attlee's memorandum, 21 Dec. 1946 (PREM 8/541 pt. 8).

scant courtesy or pity, Wavell was dismissed at the end of
January. Mountbatten took his place, with full, indeed
unique, plenipotentiary powers to negotiate on behalf of
the British government as he saw fit.

The Cabinet remained broadly united thoughout this
critical period. Attlee did, indeed, issue a very rare rebuke
to Bevin. The Foreign Secretary had joined Alexander in
expressing alarm about Britain's hasty retreat from India.
He was anxious about the stability of the entire Arab world
throughout the Middle East. Cripps, Bevin wrote, 'is so pro-
Congress that a balanced judgement is not being brought to
bear on the importance of the Moslem world'. When the
British left India, they should do so on the basis of handing
over a going concern.[63] Attlee replied briskly that he was
being a realist, not a defeatist. The Indian Army simply could
not preserve order over a huge subcontinent. Indeed, it was
already transferring its loyalty from the Raj to the new
Interim Government. 'If you disagree with what is proposed,'
Attlee added, 'you must offer a practical alternative. I fail
to find one in your letter.'[64]

Thereafter, events moved very rapidly. On 18 February,
the Cabinet accepted Attlee's reiterated view on the urgency
of an early withdrawal. On the 20th, the Prime Minister
announced the decisions taken to the Commons.[65] Wavell
was being replaced by Mountbatten; he was evicted from
India as abruptly as Dorman-Smith had been in Burma. The
constituent assembly and provincial governments already
in being would continue to administer India, even though
the Indian religious communities were at odds about their
future. Finally, and most important, Britain would transfer
power into Indian hands and evacuate her forces no later
than 1 June 1948. There was some predictable criticism from
Churchill, but in general the reaction from parliament and
the country was favourable. Mountbatten's negotiations
with Indian leaders began on 20 March, and kept up a smart
pace throughout. It soon became apparent that June 1948
was far too leisurely a timetable for British withdrawal

---

[63] Bevin to Attlee, 1 Jan. 1947 (PREM 8/564).
[64] Attlee to Bevin, 2 Jan. 1947 (ibid.).
[65] *Parl. Deb.*, 5th ser., vol. 533 (20 Feb. 1947).

and that a date in 1947 must be substituted. Mountbatten now engaged in intense bargaining with the various spokesmen for the Congress, the League, and the Sikh community on behalf of a revised 'plan Balkan', under which the provinces would be able to vote simply whether to join India or a new Pakistan. In effect, partition was being proposed: on 27 May, after firm conduct of deliberations by Attlee, the British Cabinet endorsed this idea, one for so long rejected.[66] On 2 June, the various communal leaders in India accepted a plan which Nehru admitted would mean the 'Balkanization' of the subcontinent. A truncated Pakistan would come into being, and would receive dominion status along with India herself. Congress formally gave up its historic demand for a transfer of power with constitution-making authority granted to the Hindu majority, before India was actually to be partitioned. The timetable was relentlessly speeded up, until Mountbatten announced at a press conference on 4 June that 15 August 1947 was finally agreed as the date for the ending of the Raj. Ironically, this was an infinitely more hectic timetable than under Wavell's 'breakdown' plan (with its deadline of 31 March 1948), which Attlee and Cripps had condemned as defeatist and an undignified scuttle from responsibility. The divided body of the new Pakistan, based on part of Bengal in the east, and on much of the Punjab, Sind, North West Frontier Province, and other provinces in the north-west, would come into being, despite long-held British objections to its political, strategic, or economic viability. The Government of India Bill was carried on the second reading without a division on 10 July. Churchill absented himself from the debate, and the Conservative attack was led off, in moderate tones, by Harold Macmillan. On 15 August 1947, India and Pakistan formally became independent states, and full members of the Commonwealth. Ironically, this momentous event in British history, which terminated over three centuries of involvement and occupation in India, dating from the founding of

---

[66] Cabinet Conclusions, 27 May 1947 (CAB 128/9) and Attlee's statement to the House, *Parl. Deb.*, 5th ser., vol. 438 (3 June 1947). See Y. Krishnan, 'Mountbatten and the Partition of India', *History*, vol. 68, no. 222 (Feb. 1983), pp. 22–38.

the East India Company in 1600, passed by almost without notice. So riveted was public attention at that time by the financial crisis over convertibility, and the Cabinet's convulsions over steel nationalization, that Indian independence seemed anti-climactic.

The results in the short term were peculiarly brutal. There were violent events and many massacres especially in the Punjab with Sikhs and Muslims primarily involved. In all, perhaps half a million lost their lives. Large areas of the city of Delhi were destroyed. Kashmir, a territory whose status was in dispute with large Muslim and Hindu populations, was eventually partitioned by force of arms, with India keeping the lion's share. Churchill's lamentations in the Commons quoted a former Liberal Viceroy, and old Cabinet colleague, John Morley, on 'the sullen roar of carnage and confusion'. The assassination of Gandhi in early 1948 added to the appalling period of violence in the newly-liberated India. For all that, by mid-1948 the subcontinent had settled down; both the new India and Pakistan, headed by Nehru and Jinnah respectively, were political realities. In February 1949 it was agreed in the London Declaration that both could remain members of the Commonwealth, even though they had both acquired the status of republics. Burma had also gained its independence in 1947, as has been noted, while independence for Ceylon (Sri Lanka) was carried through, without controversy, in 1949, to complete the transfer of authority in south Asia. The preservation of strategic bases and communications links in Ceylon ensured that defence of the subcontinent would be maintained.

The communal carnage after the end of the Raj invested the early months of the newly-independent India and Pakistan with an aura of tragedy; but, long before the Labour government fell from office in 1951, the transfer was being seen in a very different light. Given the intermingling of religions and races in India, some kind of explosion was unavoidable, and it would have been militarily and financially impossible for the Indian Army to preserve any credible form of order. It would have been Palestine all over again, and on a far more terrifying scale. On the positive side, there was the swift decision to grant independence, in the end achieved through Mountbatten's diplomatic *carte blanche*, before the arbitrament of force had been brought in. The result was an enormous accretion of goodwill both in India and in Pakistan towards Britain itself, and also far more cordial relations within the Commonwealth which now became explicitly multiracial. Here indeed, is a sphere of policy where the difference of emphasis between Labour and the Conservative opposition was critical, even if not as stark as the baroque Victorian rhetoric uttered by Churchill himself might have led the unwary to believe. Since the Government of India Act in 1935 (indeed, since Montagu's time at the India Office in 1917–22), full independence for India was under active consideration by all parties—but there was no procedure and certainly no timetable. During the war years, the Raj had seemed almost to acquire a new authority and the empire itself to flourish anew, as the campaign against the Japanese proceeded.[67] The £1,300m. sterling balances that India accumulated in London between 1939 and 1946 confirmed the point. The nationalist demands of Congress, accordingly, became more aggressive. There was a real prospect of a vast holocaust in India after the war, with the British Army desperately trying to ward off the inevitable surrender. These events did not occur. That they did not forms a major triumph of statesmanship for the British government, and above all for Attlee himself. The major decisions at every turn—to set a precise date for the British withdrawal, to send Mountbatten to India with much enhanced powers—were decisions emanating directly from the Prime Minister himself. He dominated the India and Burma Committee throughout. In the final crisis, the elderly Pethick-Lawrence gradually withdrew from the forefront. Bevin was much less involved in India than in the Middle East and, as has been seen, was critical of aspects of the final withdrawal. Cripps, of course, was a dominating figure, and considered as a possible Viceroy in early 1947. Until Mountbatten's appointment he drafted almost every government policy statement on India. But his mission in 1946 had failed to placate Muslim fears, as his mission of 1942 had

[67] This controversial view is argued in J. Gallagher, *The Decline, Revival and Fall of the British Empire*.

inflamed the Hindus. Neither had produced a generally accepted constitutional framework. The plan of 1946 seemed almost to propose an India unified and federalized at one and the same time. Like Lloyd George's scheme for Ireland in June 1916, Cripps's vision of home rule could succeed only if each side held directly contradictory interpretations of what it implied. No other Cabinet minister had much expert knowledge on India. The parliamentary party and the NEC went along cheerfully with the decisions of the Cabinet and the India Committee. Without the special knowledge and passionate commitment of Attlee, therefore, the history of the British presence in Asia might have taken a far more alarming course. The gulf between Hindu and Muslim might have become so unbridgeable, their relations with the British occupying forces to untenable, that a Palestine-type solution based on prolonged civil war would have been the only outcome. Instead, the British left India with memories of the Mutiny and of Amritsar largely purged in a spirit of goodwill, a mood that endured through subsequent decades of difficult relations between India and Pakistan over Kashmir and other issues. India remained in the Commonwealth, contrary to the traditional views of Congress. In major respects, the new relationship brought the old European imperialist powers and the emergent nationalisms of Asia and Africa far closer together. When the record of the British Labour government is contrasted with the history of French decolonization, with prolonged warfare in Indo-China and later in Algeria over many years in the fifties, or with the way the Dutch left Indonesia or the chaos bequeathed by the Belgians in the Congo and the Portuguese in Angola, the British achievement in so immense and complex a domain seems the more remarkable.

Commonwealth and colonial policy, then, was a sphere where the Labour government had much that was positive to show, Palestine always excepted. The independence of India, in particular, became a beacon of freedom for emergent nationalist movements, and a kind of model for peaceful British withdrawal. The American author and politician,

Daniel Moynihan, once commented on the ideological links that bound nationalist movements in Asia and Africa to British social democracy, to the intellectual traditions of the London School of Economics and the *New Statesman*, to Laski and Tawney, and to the Labour Party to which so many Indian and African leaders at various times belonged. The transfer of power in India was central to this process of cultural transmission. However, as has been noted, it was part of a wider movement of modernization and emancipation, extending from relations with the white Dominions to the development and constitutional reform of colonial territories, in West Africa and south-east Asia above all. The concept of a new multiracial Commonwealth, with a more equal and flexible relationship to the Crown and mother country, was evolved. In 1945, 457 million people were under direct British sovereignty. At the end of 1951, the total had fallen to only 70 million. Despite contrary pressures from French Quebecois in Canada, from Afrikaners in South Africa, from republicans in Australia, this process of transformation continued. Indeed, India under Nehru was to become a leading champion of the new concept that the updated Commonwealth implied. During his talks with President Truman in Washington in December 1950, Attlee could make much of the joint influence that Britain and the new Commonwealth, with its powerful Asian membership, could exert on relations between the west and Communist China, during the worst period of the Korean War. He attached particular hopes to India which was, so he told the French Prime Minister, 'an outpost in Asia of European cultural and administrative traditions and influence'. In January 1951, the Commonwealth Foreign Ministers, headed by Sir Benegal Rau of India, were to exercise a joint mediating role between the Americans and Communist China.[68]

Professor Partha Gupta has rightly argued that an over-simplified or sentimental view of Labour's Commonwealth and colonial policy should not be taken.[69] He has shown

[68] Record of Attlee–Bevan talks, 2 Dec. 1950 (FO 371/83019) F/1027/6G; minutes of meeting of Commonwealth Prime Ministers, 11 Jan. 1951 (FO 371/92761), F K1023/26.

[69] P. S. Gupta, 'Imperialism and the Labour Government of 1945–51', loc. cit. pp. 99–126, for a most stimulating discussion.

how considerations of national and imperial self-interest, especially in relation to defence and to the needs of the British economy, helped to determine Labour's policy in Malaya, Ceylon, East Africa, the proposed Central African Federation, and elsewhere, between 1945 and 1951. The haphazard, and often unjust operations of the sterling area's 'dollar pool' were a frequent source of complaint from African and Asian colonies. The presence of significant white settler populations in places such as Kenya and Southern Rhodesia also acted as a check upon Labour's more enlightened aspirations. Nevertheless, we should not be surprised that Britain, like other European nations, did not take a wholly altruistic or unworldly view of its own national needs in the years after the war. Defence requirements could certainly be overridden, as happened with India. In general, the requirements of the mother country and of the developing territories under British rule seemed to flow in the same, beneficent direction.

The subsequent relationships of Britain and emergent territories during the years of Conservative government after 1951 were not always tranquil. Especially in areas of white settler influence such as Kenya and Southern Rhodesia, there were violent passages in the transition to independence. Cyprus brought years of bloodshed through British resistance to the demand for 'enosis' with Greece. So did Kenya in the Mau Mau period. The murder of prisoners at Hola camp was a particularly shameful episode. Nyasaland during the crisis over the Central African Federation was another potential cockpit. At various times in the fifties, leading nationalist leaders such as Archbishop Makarios, Jomo Kenyatta, and Dr Hastings Banda were all imprisoned at the behest of the British Colonial Office. Guyana was another difficult area in this decade, with its left-wing Prime Minister, Cheddi Jagan, expelled from his country. Despite all these problems, the process of colonial independence between 1951 and 1964 was relentless, especially during Macleod's period at the Colonial Office in 1959–61. Scores of formal ceremonies took place in different countries, with the bowing out of the old governor's regime and the running down of the Union Jack in favour of a national flag or emblem. By 1964, the

winds of change noted by Macmillan in 1960 were irresistible. The expulsion of South Africa from the Commonwealth
as a result of black African hostility was a notable milestone
here. Throughout, the legacy of the Labour government after
1945 provided the model and the inspiration. Colonial and
Commonwealth affairs did not figure consistently or prominently in the policies drawn up by the Labour Party
between 1945 and 1951. There were very few specialist
experts on colonial issues, while critics of colonial policy
such as Fenner Brockway were distrusted for an instinctive
left-wing anti-imperialism of Pavlovian predictability. In the
February 1950 election Creech Jones, the unsung hero of
many of these developments, lost his seat after redistribution.
Bevin told him that he had been 'too undemonstrative' and
that his great work was 'hid under a bushel'.[70] Attlee seems to
have shed few tears at the loss of one whom he regarded as a
weak link in his team. Creech Jones's reputation never
recovered; he was, it seemed, swept away in a torrent of
ground-nuts and Gambia eggs. Not until 1954, with the
foundation of the Movement for Colonial Freedom, did
Labour produce a powerful grass-roots pressure group concerned with colonial issues; not until then was there significant trade-union commitment on third-world questions.
Nevertheless, it may be that in more arcane or specialist
areas of policy in promoting colonial freedom and economic
development between 1945 and 1951 that the most significant of Labour's legacies for the future of the world can be
discerned. No aspect of its achievement glows more brightly
in the later twentieth century.

[70] Bevin to Creech Jones, 10 Feb. 1950 (Creech Jones papers, ACJ 7/1/43).

6

Priorities and Policies:
Foreign Affairs and Defence

Since the end of the first world war, the conduct of foreign policy was an area where the Labour Party, often against all the evidence, had prided itself on having a special insight and sensitivity. Labour could embody the decent, pacific instincts of ordinary people, free from the intrigues of multinational capitalism or the inbred world of public-school diplomacy. The first Labour government in 1924 was best remembered for Ramsay MacDonald's achievements in foreign policy—the Russian trade treaty and the truce in Franco-German antagonism. The second Labour government in 1929 had established the reputation of its Foreign Secretary, Arthur Henderson, as a pioneer of disarmament. French troops had been withdrawn from the Rhineland, and an agreement reached on reparations. Of course, Labour in the thirties had shown to the full the neo-pacifist illusions and confusions of men on the left, anxious to resist Hitler without recourse to massive armaments or the discredited methods of the 'system of Versailles'. Still, the party had in the end come through its travails of the thirties with more coherent, credible, and defensible positions on foreign policy and defence questions. During the war, Attlee, Dalton, Bevin, and other Labour ministers had been much involved in planning for post-war reconstruction, in which Britain was seen as playing a pivotal role, both as the centre to a world-wide multiracial empire, and as a broker between the United States and Europe, East and West. Although foreign affairs did not play a major direct part in the 1945 election campaign, expectations were high that Labour, especially with Bevin at the Foreign Office, would help launch a new, more secure, and peaceful international order. It would avoid the mistakes and recriminations that had helped to destroy similar hopes after 1918. In foreign policy, as in domestic, the advent of Labour to power in 1945 was thought to mean a propulsion of British history into radically new directions.

Labour's approach towards foreign affairs was highly important, if only because Britain was manifestly still a great power. It had won the war. It was one of the three peace-makers at Yalta and Potsdam, and a central participant in world events in every continent. The decline of Britain's international standing after 1945, in fact, has often been antedated by later commentators, both on the left and the right. Throughout the period 1945 to 1951, Britain was regarded as a decisive international influence, one of the 'big three' (assuming the exclusion of the French and Chinese), even if its encroaching and apparently interminable financial difficulties were reducing its status from the withdrawal from Greece in early 1947 onwards. Sir Oliver Franks, the most authoritative of British ambassadors to Washington, could tell Attlee in July 1950 that Britain, far from being 'one of the queue of European countries', was clearly 'one of two world powers outside Russia'.[1] The British government, like its successors perhaps down to that of Harold Wilson in 1964–70, accepted this as axiomatic. At the end of hostilities in 1945, Britain indeed occupied a major role in a way often forgotten later. It was British arms which received the surrender of sub-stantial German forces in Europe, the Italians in Abyssinia in 1941, and the Japanese in French Indo-China and the Dutch East Indies in 1945. British military and naval strength was vital in much of the Mediterranean, throughout the Middle East from Suez to Abadan, in southern and south-east Asia, throughout much of the Pacific, in the Caribbean, and, most critically of course, in central Europe and especially Germany. Britain also appeared to be a dominant financial power, as the centre of the sterling area, and the hub of the Common-wealth network of trade and investment. The role of the Labour government would, therefore, be of decisive signifi-cance in the shaping of the post-war settlement throughout the world. France was shattered, barely recovering from German occupation and internal division. Germany was defeated, divided, and prostrate. Other western European nations were only of minor account. Even the United States

[1] Sir Oliver Franks to Attlee, 15 July 1950 (PREM 8/1405).

was in potentially isolationist mood. It was determined on escaping from the shackles of the wartime alliance with Britain and on reconstructing its own, independent foreign policy on the basis of political non-alignment and economic liberalization. The new mood was heralded by the ending of Lease Lend on 21 August 1945, just six days after VJ Day. The demons which had kept America out of the League of Nations in 1920 and removed it from many of its international obligations between the wars, were still not exorcized. At the same time, Americans, under Truman as under Theodore Roosevelt forty years earlier, were bent on building up the Pacific and east Asia, notably China and Japan, as their sphere of influence. This left Britain and its Commonwealth confronting alone a newly expansionist Soviet Union in a variety of spheres from the Elbe to Afghanistan. The responses of the Labour administration to what was generally perceived to be a totally new, fluid international order would, therefore, be of crucial significance for the destiny of mankind.

In fact, foreign policy proved to be a source of contention for the Labour Party and its government henceforth. It evoked far more controversy and division than did domestic disputes over the precise balance between 'consolidation' and socialist advance, or such detailed matters as National Health Service charges or public ownership. In the period of opposition, from late 1951 perhaps down to the death of Gaitskell in early 1963, Labour largely disqualified itself as a credible party of government, because of fierce internal schisms over foreign policy and defence—over German rearmament in 1953–4; over SEATO and policy towards Communist and Nationalist China; most critically, over the atomic and hydrogen bomb, and Britain's independent nuclear deterrent in 1957–61; and, finally, over Britian's possible membership of the European Common Market in 1962. Like the Liberals after the end of the Boer War, Labour reunited its ranks only when it turned again to domestic economic and social issues. Many of these foreign-policy disputes in the fifties originated during the time of the Attlee government in 1945–51 and their roots must therefore be considered.

The personality and outlook of Ernest Bevin himself are

often held to have had much to do with this contention over foreign .affairs. Fortunately, we now have Alan Bullock's magisterial and authoritative third volume of his trilogy on Bevin as a sure guide through these difficult waters.[2] Certainly, Bevin was an unexpected selection for the Foreign Office in July 1945: the Treasury was the department originally pencilled in for him, with Dalton going to the Foreign Office instead. As the most influential trade-unionist of his generation, Bevin had largely been associated with domestic affairs in the past. On international questions, he had strong views, but in some key areas no great reserves of knowledge. He was passionately anti-Communist, as he had been while serving as general secretary of the Transport and General Workers. During the war, he had taken an outspoken part in the discussion of foreign affairs, notably over Greece where he belligerently defended the Churchill government's policy of opposing the left-wing ELAS movement. He took as axiomatic the preservation of the British influence in south-east Europe and the eastern Mediterranean. He was also instinctively committed to the Commonwealth relationship, and to a permanent military and economic involvement in the Middle East, a region to which he devoted careful thought on problems ranging from Suez to Persian oil. Towards the Soviet Union, his outlook was wary and suspicious, but not automatically hostile. Certainly, to regard Bevin's policy as a reproduction of an alleged anti-Communist, cold-war approach of the Foreign Office and its permanent officials is totally to misunderstand his personality and his psychological and intellectual dominance over that great department, as Lord Strang and others have been at pains to emphasize. There were of course important policy-makers in the Foreign Office, such as Sir Orme 'Moley' Sargent, permanent under-secretary from early 1946 in succession to Sir Alexander Cadogan, and a formidable critic of the Soviet Union. On the other hand, as noted previously, the attitudes within the Foreign Office covered a very broad political and ideological spectrum, from Brimelow to Jebb. On balance, the Foreign Office outlook was distinctly more anti-German than anti-Russian in the aftermath of Potsdam. In any case, Bevin was a dominant,

[2] Alan Bullock, *Ernest Bevin: Foreign Secretary 1945–1951* (London, 1983).

transcendent, creative force. As Alan Bullock has argued, he was the personal originator of foreign policy in the style of Canning, Palmerston, and Salisbury, the more so as Attlee himself largely gave his Foreign Secretary a free hand until ill health compelled a change of approach. As has been seen, no Cabinet Committee on Foreign Affairs ever emerged. Bevin's policy was not invented by a phantom army of Sargents, Warners, Furlonges, and Troutbecks; accounts of the 'origins of the cold war' between 1943 and 1947, which take the Foreign Office files too literally and unreflectively, go badly astray. Bevin's foreign policy was vividly his own. From the spring of 1947 onwards, its main outlines emerged with a new clarity, as the Council of Foreign Ministers lapsed into disarray from which Bevin strove to rescue it. From Palestine to Persia, from Germany to Australasia, British foreign policy in this crucial period of post-war transition bore the constant and unmistakable imprint of Bevin's personality and ideas. The particular kind of foreign policy that his government came to evolve was a response both to the challenge of unforeseen events and to the goading stimulus of Bevin's probing, if disorganized, mind. It was far from being the conventional wisdom of diplomatic orthodoxy.

A broad general cause for the disputes over foreign affairs that erupted after 1945 was the widespread belief in the Labour Party that the new government should adopt what was termed a 'socialist foreign policy'. The precise content of this was never particularly clear, but it certainly played some part in the rhetoric of the hustings in June–July 1945. In a powerful speech by the young Denis Healey, the candidate for Otley and an ex-Communist, at the 1945 party conference, he urged his party to support socialist revolution in the countries of western and central Europe. Healey was soon to succeed William Gillies at the important post of head of the International Department in Transport House in January 1946. Pressure for a 'socialist foreign policy', which would reflect in foreign affairs the same radical ethic manifest in Labour's social and economic policy at home, was a constant theme after August 1945, and a frequent cross for Bevin himself to bear. It featured in several early speeches in the new parliamentary session, such as that by Fred

Peart.[3] The main drift of those arguing for a 'socialist foreign policy' was that a socialist Britain should seek to remove the competitive, capitalist forces in the world that led to international conflict. To this end, Britain should pursue an 'independent' foreign policy, clear of entanglements with either capitalist America or Communist Russia. Whether, however, this meant Britain pursuing a completely isolationist course, playing a mediating role at the United Nations on behalf of world government, or trying to form some kind of middle 'third force' grouping, perhaps with socialist leaders such as Blum and Nenni in western Europe, was a good deal less clear. By 1947, many on the left were urging the cause of a united western Europe on precisely this ground, often with marked anti-American overtones. When, however, the Council of Europe actually created after the Hague conference in May 1948 showed a clear right-wing or Christian Democrat tendency, with Churchill himself very prominent, the enthusiasm of Labour back-benchers for a putative socialist united western Europe waned accordingly, apart from a few root-and-branch enthusiasts like R. W. G. Mackay. There were others in the party who seemed to think that the Commonwealth might serve as some kind of intermediate force in world affairs, especially when reinforced by independent India led by socialists such as Nehru and Krishna Menon. But this was an even more insubstantial dream. In effect, the departure of the Labour governments of Chifley in Australia and Fraser in New Zealand in elections in 1949 killed off what little vitality the notion ever had.

A perennial aspect in the advocacy of a 'socialist foreign policy' followed the old demands of the Union of Democratic Control in 1918—demands, indeed, which went back a good deal further, with their roots in the peace crusades of Cobden and others in the mid-Victorian radical left.[4] This implied a popular basis for foreign policy and open diplomacy, to create a people's peace after a people's war. There

---

[3] *Parl. Deb.*, 5th ser., vol. 416, 689–91 (22 Nov. 1945). Peart 'looked forward towards a Socialist Europe and a Socialist world'.

[4] The classic work on this theme, of course, is A. J. P. Taylor, *The Troublemakers* (London, 1957).

would be no 'power politics', no manœuvres along the old lines of the nineteenth-century balance of power, a detachment from entangling secret alliances with their identification with the building up of huge armed camps across the continents. The veteran Leonard Woolf, an old UDC propagandist during the first world war, actually called in 1947 (in a tract written under the auspices of the Fabian Society) for Britain to 'refuse absolutely to take any part in the wrangles and recriminations of the Security Council and Assembly'.[5] Indeed, the attitude of the advocates of a 'socialist foreign policy' towards the United Nations, a world organization certainly, but with the Security Council and the great-power right of veto built into it, was highly ambivalent.

The extreme utopianism of those such as Woolf cut little ice, even on the pacifist left. It was well rebuffed at the time by men such as W. N. Ewer, the diplomatic correspondent of the *Daily Herald* and a warm supporter of Bevin.[6] In practice, the advocates of a 'socialist foreign policy' came from two camps, as has been seen. The small fringe of fellow-travelling Marxists, with Zilliacus, Platts-Mills, Solley, and Hutchinson (all expelled from the party in 1948–9), was the hard core; —others came in from the far left such as William Warbey, Sidney Silverman, Tom Braddock, and S. O. Davies. A much larger grouping consisted of fifty or more backbenchers, including most of the 'Keep Left' group in 1947, headed by figures such as Crossman, Foot, Driberg, and Mikardo. Their object was rather a more independent policy, freed from American 'cold-war' pressures, and a more active support for nationalist, socialist, and democratic movements, in Greece, the Middle East, Indonesia, and elsewhere. It was this latter grouping that gave Bevin by far the most trouble, notably in the famous 'foreign affairs' amendment of November 1946. Bevin was frequently condemned, especially in the columns of the *New Statesman* and *Tribune* which enjoyed a virtual monopoly in the distribution of opinions in the party on foreign affairs. So, too, was Alexander at the

---

[5] Leonard Woolf, *Foreign Policy: the Labour Party's Dilemma* (Fabian publication, 1947).

[6] Critical comments by Ewer, appended to Woolf's tract, cited above.

Defence Ministry—'a tenacious supporter of the Bevin-Byrnes line', declared the *New Statesman*.[7]

These socialist critics, as was noted earlier, were amply represented in the Foreign Affairs group of the parliamentary party with which Bevin had such a stormy relationship. However, their membership was a shifting one; it was fatally divided by the events of 1948 including the Soviet blockade of West Berlin, which drove Crossman, Foot, and many others firmly into the pro-Bevin camp (in effect), through defending Marshall Aid, western European defence planning, and the formation of NATO. In practical terms, the foundations of the Labour government were never seriously shaken by dissent on the left over foreign policy. Attlee and Bevin were able to build up British armaments, renew conscription, and pursue a stern policy of resistance to the Soviet Union in almost every theatre, without much effective opposition. The apparently effortless series of victories for the government over its critics at party conference, however, and the ease with which Platts-Mills was thrown out of the party, should not mask a wider unhappiness (much reflected in conference resolutions which Morgan Phillips diligently suppressed in Transport House) about the direction which the government's foreign policy was taking. Even in 1951 there was an instinct that Labour's foreign policy ought by its very nature to be divergent from that likely to be followed by a Conservative government, for all the traditions of consensus and bipartisanship in foreign affairs. A Labour government should be more committed to world-wide reconciliation, disarmament, and a new international order than seemed to be the case. The constant applause for Bevin's policies from Churchill, Eden, and right-wing journals in Fleet Street, was deeply disturbing for many in the Labour Party, quite apart from the irreconcilables on the Marxist fringe. In the fifties after Labour's fall from power, these uncertainties broadened into a passionate debate over major aspects of foreign and defence policy which did the party prolonged, perhaps irretrievable, damage.

Bevin had himself given some ground to the advocates of a 'socialist foreign policy' at the outset of his period at the

[7] *New Statesman*, 12 Oct. 1946.

Foreign Office. He had implied that a Labour government would have a closer relation with the Soviet Union, and had spoken rhetorically of 'left speaking to left in comradeship and confidence'. In the aftermath of the war, with much popular admiration for the feats of the Red Army, this echoed the national mood. Bevin's first policy *tour d'horizon* in the Commons in August 1945 won the warm support of *Tribune*, save only for his references to Greece where it felt that his pledges about free elections ignored the fact that, politically, 'the dice were loaded against the left'.[8] It rapidly became clear, however, that any hope of Bevin providing comfort to left-wingers anxious for a warm, enduring relationship with Russia was quite illusory. Even in his first few days in office, during the Potsdam conference itself, Bevin's robust assertion of British pre-eminence in the Middle East and his vigorous rebuttal of Soviet claims to expand there aroused the admiration of such as Cadogan and Sargent. Bevin had 'sound ideas which we must encourage', recorded Cadogan, perhaps ominously, on 10 August 1945.[9] The first real test of Bevin's attitude came at the Council of Foreign Ministers meeting in London in September–October 1945, convened mainly to discuss the terms of peace settlements with Italy, Rumania, Bulgaria, Hungary, and Finland. The pattern became established, which the subsequent years were vividly to confirm, of conflict between the British Foreign Secretary and the Russian representatives, in almost every theatre under discussion, a deadlock leading to truculent confrontation on both sides. Long before it was formally so christened, the cold war was a chilling reality.

The Council of Foreign Ministers meeting in Lancaster House went badly almost from the start. It was obvious that the wartime alliance of Britain, the United States, and Russia was already under some strain. The very procedural issue of which nations should be represented at the peace treaty negotiations led to great difficulties; Molotov, the Soviet Foreign Minister, insisted that only the 'big three' and nations actually at war with each individual defeated enemy state should take part. In practice, this excluded France and

[8] *Tribune*, 24 Aug. 1945.
[9] Dilks (ed.), *The Diaries of Sir Alexander Cadogan*, p. 780.

China from all save the Italian settlement. On specific territorial issues, Bevin and Molotov found themselves at odds over the disposal of the Italian colonies in Africa, and also over the port of Trieste and the Dodecanese Islands in the Mediterranean. In Tripolitania, Britain resisted (as did Byrnes, the American Secretary of State, if somewhat more tentatively) Soviet claims for a ten-year period of trusteeship. In Cyrenaica, Britain demanded trusteeship for itself. Bevin had privately told the Cabinet that Cyrenaica, with its harbours at Tobruk and Benghazi, and several potentially important air bases such as Derna and Martuba, 'should be brought under British influence', and Soviet encroachment anywhere in North Africa resisted.[10] He also put forward a suggestion for international trusteeship, with Britain as acting trustee, over a kind of Greater Somalia, comprising Italian and British Somaliland, together with the Ogaden, in the Horn of Africa. Only Eritrea would not be absorbed, but would go in part to Abyssinia and to the Sudan. Not all these British claims were pressed with equal force, and there were several modifying factors. Some of the Dominions' governments were unhappy at British claims in North Africa. Dalton at the Treasury was anxious at the heavy cost of taking up the liabilities of Italian Somaliland and of Sheikh Idris el Senussi in Cyrenaica. Attlee, in an impressive memorandum on 1 September 1945, argued forcibly against the need for a massive British land commitment in the Middle East at all in the new era of air strike power. British Somaliland, the Prime Minister pithily added, 'has always been a dead loss and nuisance to us'.[11] The Americans also looked askance at the prospect of further encroachments by British imperialism, even in Labour guise, in eastern Africa and the eastern Mediterranean. Still, Bevin and his officials held firm against Russian counter-claims.

Equally, the London conference made no headway at all over the peace treaties with Rumania, Bulgaria, and Hungary. The status of Trieste, vigorously expounded by the Oxford

---

[10] Memorandum by Bevin and Hall, 'The Future of the Italian Colonies and the Italian Mediterranean Islands', ORC (45) 21 (FO 371/50792), U 6540/51/G70.

[11] Memorandum by Attlee on 'The Future of the Italian Colonies', 1 Sept. 1945 (CAB 129/1).

historian, A. J. P. Taylor, in *The Listener* on behalf of the Yugoslav cause, led to more deadlock.[12] A blunt exchange of views between Bevin and Molotov at the Soviet embassy on 23 September added to the tension. In public session earlier, Bevin even compared Molotov to Hitler—a wounding and clumsy charge which drew protests from Byrnes and for which Bevin later apologized. The climax came with a very bad-tempered meeting at the Soviet embassy on 1 October, in which disagreements over the Mediterranean and the Balkans were compounded when Molotov accused Britain of breaking faith over the disposal of the German fleet. Bevin for his part spelt out the growing number of issues on which Britain and Russia had failed to find common ground, including the role of France, and the future of every single Italian colony. Russia, declared Bevin, could not be allowed to sever 'the lifeline of the Empire' in the Mediterranean. To this Palmerstonian flourish, Molotov replied that Britain was seeking a monopoly of influence throughout northern and eastern Africa, from southern Somalia to the borders of Tunisia. Bevin concluded by regretting 'that so little progress had been made. Mr Molotov made some incomprehensible noise in reply.'[13] The emollient presence of Clark Kerr, the British ambassador to Moscow and a personal friend of Stalin, had no effect on these icy exchanges.

After this bad start, relations between Britain and the Soviet Union stayed frigid throughout that autumn; the Foreign Office expressed concern that the United States was failing to support Britain on key issues. Then, unexpectedly (and without prior warning), to his considerable annoyance Bevin heard that Byrnes had called a second Council of Foreign Ministers, to be held in Moscow in mid-December. Bevin listed his anxieties to the Cabinet on 6 December, the attempted exclusion of France and China prominent among them. He told Pierson Dixon that he feared Byrnes now wanted a settlement with Russia more

---

[12] *The Listener*, 27 Sept. 1945, with a riposte from David Thomson, 4 Oct. 1945.

[13] Record of meeting at Soviet embassy, London, 1 Oct. 1945 (FO 371/ 50922), U 9974/5559/G70.

or less at any price.[14] However, Bevin had to agree to attend
in Moscow. In any case, with the American loan now in the
balance, this was no time for Britain and America to be at
odds. In fact, the meetings at Moscow on 16–26 December
went rather better, at least on the surface. Compromises
were reached over the drafting of the peace treaties; the
western powers agreed to the recognition of Rumania and
Bulgaria, and some progress was also made over a settlement
with Japan in the Far East. In practice, the British view prevailed on several questions, especially on the status of France
and China at the peace talks. On the other hand, Soviet
control over much of eastern Europe, with Rumania, Bulgaria,
and Hungary now added to Poland, seemed to be confirmed.
It was an edgy conference, with Bevin often at odds with
Byrnes, notably over the latter's unexpected proposal that
Russia participate in international conferences for the pooling of information on atomic energy. This was at a time when
America and Britain were themselves in dispute over America's
apparent failure to honour the wartime Quebec agreement in
disclosing atomic information. In fact, there were signs of
divided counsels in Washington itself over Byrnes's handling
of the Moscow conference. It was shortly afterwards, on
4 January 1946, that Truman was alleged to have complained
to Byrnes that 'he was tired of babying the Soviets'.[15] Accurate
or not, this was the view echoed in many American east-
coast newspapers.

  In the early months of 1946, tense relations between
Britain's Labour government and the Soviet leaders persisted
in a wider variety of theatres. The apparent agreement reached
at Moscow in December did not improve the atmosphere.
Conflicts between Britain and Russia increased and multiplied
in Germany, Greece, the Mediterranean, the Middle East, and
the Far East. There were repeated assaults on Bevin and the
British government in the Soviet press, to which Bevin

[14] Piers Dixon, *Double Diploma: the Life of Sir Pierson Dixon* (London, 1968),
pp. 198 ff; record of teletype conversation between Bevin and Byrnes, 27 Nov.
1945 (FO 800/446), Conf. 45/9.
[15] Harry S. Truman, *Year of Decisions* (New York, 1955), pp. 551–2. There
has been much learned debate as to whether Byrnes ever actually received this
rebuke: see Jacques Barzun and Henry Graff, *The Modern Researcher* (New York,
1970), pp. 157–9.

responded with vigour. 'It seemed to have become the practice to make every importance [*sic*] international conference the occasion for vindictive attacks on British policy and British interests', Bevin complained to Vishinsky on 20 January.[16] The Foreign Office spread the view that Soviet hostility towards Britain was particularly inspired by the need to vilify a rival government that also claimed to be socialist. 'There was little to show that the Soviet Union still regarded Britain under a Labour government as an ally or even a friend', reported Sir Frank Roberts from Moscow. In historicist vein, Roberts went on to speculate whether the unyielding nature of Soviet ideology did not herald the modern equivalent of the religious wars that had torn Europe apart in the sixteenth century.[17] Thomas Brimelow, who had special responsibility for Russian affairs at the Northern Department, wrote to Bevin on 8 March that 'since the official designation of the present Soviet system is "socialist", it cannot be admitted that the British also have a socialist system'. The Russians, Brimelow claimed, dismissed Labour's nationalization measures as mere 'state capitalism'. C. F. A. Warner, the head of the Northern Department to 1946, confirmed that Russia was anxious to discredit British social democracy among the European working class.[18]

Relations between Britain and the Soviet Union seemed steadily to deteriorate. The growth of evident Communist control in a succession of eastern European states made matters worse. Russian aggressiveness and British insistence on an inflated world role could not, it seemed, be reconciled. Efforts by British diplomats to give new life to the wartime Anglo-Soviet alliance of 1942, by a new fifty-year alliance, were always rebuffed by Stalin. Bevin was bombarded from the Foreign Office with pessimistic diagnoses of the long-term ideological roots and urge for world expansion of the Soviet leaders, inherent in their Marxist-Leninist philosophy, even if suspicion of the Soviet Union should also be modified

[16] Bevin telegram to Foreign Office, 31 Jan. 1946 (FO 371/56780) N 1471/140/38.
[17] Sir Frank Roberts, dispatch to Foreign Office, 14 Mar. 1946 (FO 371/56763), N 4065/97/38.
[18] Minute by C. F. A. Warner, 14 Feb. 1946, minute by T. Brimelow, 14 Feb. 1946 (FO 371/56780).

by tactical flexibility and an adherence to the normal conventions of diplomatic intercourse. The *New Statesman* saw it as
an ominous sign of British hostility towards the Soviet Union
that Cadogan was replaced as head of the Foreign Office in
early 1946 by the equally conservative figure of Orme Sargent.
The new ambassador to Moscow, Sir Maurice Peterson, had
previously served terms as ambassador to Franco's Spain, and
Inönü's Turkey, a suspicious enough background to all on the
left.[19] Peterson certainly contrasted with his liberal intellectual predecessor, Archibald Clark Kerr, Lord Inverchapel,
who now went to Washington. However, such Foreign Office
and diplomatic pressures as there were—and they were
always modified by views such as those from Gladwyn Jebb,
a permanent under-secretary of state, who urged a more open
attitude towards Russia—were clearly pushing against an
open door as far as Bevin himself was concerned. This applied
equally to Bevin's under-secretary in the government,
Christopher Mayhew, and to Britain's dour Scottish spokesman at the United Nations, Hector McNeil. By March 1946,
Bevin's suspicions of Russian designs in most parts of the
world were almost unconquerable; they were fully shared by
Attlee, Morrison, and other leading Cabinet colleagues. A
celebrated episode occurred on 11 March 1946, in an obscure
American university in Fulton, Missouri. Here, Churchill
took the opportunity of a well-publicized degree ceremony
(and Truman's presence) to declare the existence of 'an iron
curtain' across Europe, extending from Stettin in the north
to Trieste in the south, and an inexorable division of the
continent into a Communist East and a democratic West. In
public, Bevin denied that Churchill's view reflected the outlook of the Labour government; he claimed that the Fulton
speech was a hindrance in his search for peace. In South Wales
on 16 March, he emphasized his own proposal, made as
recently as 21 February, for a fifty-year treaty of friendship
with Russia. But in private, Bevin viewed Churchill's speech
(of which he had been fully briefed in advance) with grim
satisfaction, and never disavowed its tone. It was noticeable,
too, that Attlee, in response to questions from Tom Driberg

[19] Cutting from *New Statesman* in FO 371/56780. For Peterson's first interview with Stalin, 28 May 1946, see PREM 8/349.

in the Commons, refused to condemn Churchill's speech, which had caused him little enough private grief. 'The government was not called upon to express any opinion of speeches delivered in another country by a private individual.'[20]

The next stage of the tense international drama was the latest round of Council of Foreign Ministers meetings in April–May 1946, held in Paris, since the French were now there represented by Bidault. This was another bad-tempered occasion. It was noticeable, however, that the combatants were somewhat differently composed. In the first two conferences, at London and Moscow, there had been a pattern of conflict and deadlock between Britain and Russia, with the Americans playing a mediating role, and, if anything, showing some sympathy with the Russians on broadly anti-imperialist grounds. At Paris, as at all future international conferences, however, it was America who bore the main brunt of Soviet hostility. This erupted over the renewed topic of the disposal of the Italian colonies, including the situation in Trieste, over Greece, over a settlement in eastern Europe, and a possible peace treaty with Austria. There was no agreement reached on any major question. Molotov enlivened the debates by attacks on Bevin's version of 'twentieth-century imperialism', as evidenced by large British military forces in Greece, Palestine, Iraq, Indo-China, and many other places.[21] Byrnes's proposal for a twenty-five-year non-aggression pact between the western powers and the Soviet Union was brusquely turned down by the Russians. Much attention focused on Germany now which increasingly seemed to reveal a stark division between western and eastern zones. Bevin returned to London depressed and unwell, with no positive achievement to show after a year of strenuous diplomatic endeavour.

However, further Council of Foreign Ministers meetings in Paris between August and October 1946 did at last make some progress. The Russians showed themselves prepared to be flexible over a settlement with Italy. They now agreed to

[20] *Manchester Guardian*, 18 Mar. 1946, for Bevin's speech; *Parl. Deb.*, 5th ser., vol. 420, 761 (11 Mar. 1946).
[21] Record of Council of Foreign Ministers at Paris, April–May 1946 (FO 371/53204).

reduce their claims for reparations to $100 millions. It was at last agreed that Trieste would become an international city under UN supervision, while the Dodecanese Islands would go to Greece. In return, Britain's phantom empire in Libya and Somalia disappeared from history. However, on the supreme issue of a German settlement, there was total dead-lock. Byrnes's proposals for a fusion of the various occupied zones met with relentless Russian hostility. It was to result in the end only in a fusion of the British and American zones, which made the polarization of Europe the more stark. Bevin explained to the House of Commons his ideas for the politi-cal and economic reconstruction of Germany, including the socialization of its basic industries. 'We are not ganging up with anybody, neither one side nor the other,' he insisted.[22] But his speech was listened to in silence on the Labour benches, and met with predictable fire from Platts-Mills and Zilliacus. A final conference of Foreign Ministers in New York in November–December 1946 did at last show some positive results, after Byrnes had threatened to dissolve proceedings. Molotov suddenly showed an unexpectedly conciliatory attitude; in rapid succession, peace treaties were signed with Italy, Rumania, Bulgaria, Hungary, and Finland. Commentators such as Walter Lippmann and Howard K. Smith have seen the New York conference as a possible opportunity for *détente*, subsequently undermined by combined American and Russian truculence.[23] But it is clear that any stabilization signified by these treaties, concluded with what were seen to be Russian satellite powers (other than Italy), masked a grow-ing divergence between the Americans and the Russians on Germany and all other major questions, with the British position unchanged. From the meetings at Paris in March 1946 onwards, the Americans had generally stood with the British on every major issue in dispute; so, too, in the main had the French Foreign Minister, Bidault. The breakdown of substantive negotiations with the Soviet Union that finally took place at the Moscow conference in March 1947 was fully in prospect. In short, 1946, so productive and hopeful

---

[22] *Parl. Deb.*, 5th ser., vol. 427, 1520 (22 Oct. 1946).
[23] e.g. D. F. Fleming, *The Cold War and its Origins*, vol. i (London, 1961), pp. 429–30.

a year for the Labour government's domestic programme of reform, was in foreign affairs a saga of failure, with disappointment and deadlock throughout.

During these tangled international meetings, the tension between the British and Soviet governments, their almost irreconcilable positions in every theatre under discussion, were dominating features of the diplomatic exchanges. It was this consistent anti-Soviet cast to Bevin's policy, apparently with little dissent from his Cabinet colleagues, that provoked criticism in the left-wing weeklies and on the Labour benches in parliament, and that led to the famous foreign-policy amendment to the Address in November 1946. Most Labour opinion oscillated between impatience with Stalin's obduracy and a utopian faith in world reconciliation; it led to a bewilderment and intellectual confusion faithfully mirrored by Kingsley Martin in the columns of the *New Statesman*. Its rival, *Tribune*, by contrast, with Michael Foot its main editorial contributor on foreign affairs, presented a more coherent outlook. There was certainly scant sign of anything that could remotely be termed a 'socialist foreign policy' in 1945–6, with the Labour government at odds with the Soviet Union in Europe and the Middle East, and seeking the active support of capitalist America. Attempts to preserve the Anglo-Soviet friendship of wartime soon seemed to evaporate. Mass Observation data in 1946–7 showed that anti-Russian sentiment was hardening. Even the visit of the Moscow Dynamo football team in the autumn of 1945 was far from a success; a controversial fog-laden match with an alleged Arsenal side (afforced by players from other teams) led to complaints of bad faith and foul play on both sides. By the start of 1947, attempts to breathe life into the promotion of a new Anglo-Soviet treaty were unconvincing. Sir Maurice Peterson had advised Warner to combine the exploring of opportunities for giving new life to the Anglo-Russian alliance with 'banging the Russians over the head as often as occasion may present itself', not the most cheerful of omens for a friendship treaty.[24] Bevin made a new attempt in February 1947 to try to work out a new treaty with the Russians, including military

[24] Sir M. Peterson to C. F. A. Warner, 15 Nov. 1946 (FO 371/56790).

provisions,[25] but the Americans were now clearly suspicious of any bilaterial arrangements, as counter-productive to Anglo-American collaboration over Germany and other issues. Neither Britain nor Russia showed much enthusiasm, in any case. Indeed, Bevin devoted part of a speech in the Commons to denouncing a new misinterpretation of the treaty of 1942 that had recently appeared in *Pravda*. His report to Attlee on the failure of the Foreign Ministers conference at Moscow in April—'saddening and sickening' —was fiercely anti-Soviet. Molotov's concluding speech was 'a product of an irascible mind'.[26]

In practice, the diplomatic exchanges over any Anglo-Soviet alliance were overshadowed by Byrnes's earlier proposal (taken up again for a time by Marshall, his successor at the State Department from January 1947), for a quadripartite treaty involving the 'big three' powers and France. By the summer of 1947, the British Foreign Office confirmed the general feeling of pessimism about any new treaty with the Russians. 'The breach between East and West', so Sir Maurice Peterson informed the Foreign Office Russia Committee, 'was held to be an accomplished fact.'[27] By now, the hostility of the Soviet Union towards the Labour Party and its key figures was almost total. Even Professor Harold Laski, the red bogey to Churchill during the 1945 election, was now being assailed in the Soviet press as 'a prop of bourgeois civilization' after his pressure on the French and Danish socialists to resist fusion with the Communists. G. D. H. Cole, another left-wing ideologue, was denounced in Moscow with equal fervour. The only genuine 'Labour left' that the Russians would acknowledge consisted of men such as Platts-Mills and Zilliacus who were soon to leave the party. In the Commonwealth Labour movement, that sound socialist, Dr Evatt, the Australian Foreign Minister, was denounced in *Izvestia* as 'the personal friend of Mr Churchill and the zealous flunky of

[25] Bevin to Attlee, 27 Jan. 1947 (FO 371/66362).
[26] Bevin to Attlee, 16 Apr. 1947 (FO 800/447), Conf. 47/7.
[27] e.g. dispatch from Lord Inverchapel to Foreign Office, 7 Feb. 1947 (FO 371/66363); James Byrnes, *Speaking Frankly* (London, 1947), p. 311; minutes of Policy towards Russia Committee, 14 Aug. 1947 (FO 371/66371), N 9549.

Wall Street'.[28] When the 'Keep Left' group issued its manifesto in April 1947, calling for a more sympathetic viewpoint
towards Russia and a modifying of cold-war postures, it
already seemed to be swimming against the tide of world
realities. By contrast, *Cards on the Table*, a vigorous pamphlet
by Denis Healey of the International Department in Transport House, published soon afterwards in May, indicated
growing support for Bevin and constituted a powerful riposte
to the fellow-travelling left.

In a number of cases, this Anglo-Soviet tension expressed
itself vividly. In each, it is significant that Bevin was able to
carry his Cabinet colleagues with him. The Middle East,
Greece and, above all, Germany emerged as flash-points in
1945–7 which confirmed the increasingly anti-Russian mood
of the Labour government.

In the Middle East, Soviet involvement after 1945 was
indirect and long-term. It was not until 1948 that Bevin
would consider the potential Soviet incursion here as more
damaging to British interests than was the instability in
Palestine caused by friction between Arabs and Jews. In one
region of the Middle East, however, Britain and the Soviet
Union found themselves early on in direct confrontation.
This was Iran, where, in Azerbaijan, on the northern border
with Russia, the Tudeh autonomists, who had clear Russian
backing, staged an open revolt against the Shah in November
1945. It was well known that Britain had been for years
heavily involved in Iran, in terms both of finance and military
equipment. British troops had collaborated with the Russians
in overthrowing the pro-German Reza Khan in 1941. The
change from Churchill to Attlee did not affect this tradition
of indirect imperialism. Thus a difficult situation built up,
with Russian troops remaining in northern Iran instead of
withdrawing, and Soviet pressure on behalf of an autonomous state of Azerbaijan which would clearly become a
Russian puppet. The Russian objectives were clear enough
—control of northern Iran, perhaps an oil concession in the
region, possibly even a long-term drive towards obtaining a

    [28] Sir Frank Roberts to Laski, 3 Oct. 1947 (FO 371/66372) N 11671/271/38;
Roberts to R. M. A. Hankey, 4 July 1946 (FO 371/56785).

warm-water port in the Persian gulf.[29] The Iranian opposition leader, Dr Mussadiq, destined to be a thorn in Britain's flesh to a far greater degree in 1951, sought to maximize internal dissension by proposing that the Iranian government enter into direct negotiations with Moscow over Azerbaijan.[30] In the event, the issue was decided on military grounds. Persian national forces offered stiff resistance to the Tudeh insurgents. The Russians decided to commit themselves no further, and in the light of firm American support for Britain, withdrew their troops in early May; the Tudeh were left to their own devices. Iran settled down again into its traditional client role of indirect tutelage, an intrinsic element in Britain's economic and strategic 'lifeline' as proclaimed by Bevin. The whole episode, however, added to the tension between Britain and Russia at a dangerous time. Although the Russians did not re-emerge significantly in the Middle East again until 1956, later events, culminating in the Soviet invasion of Afghanistan in 1979, were to confirm that Russian involvement in the region were long-term, if episodic in timing. Even in 1946, Qavam, the Iranian Prime Minister, was compelled to take three Tudeh representatives into his Cabinet. As far as the Labour government and Labour Party were concerned, apart from irreconcilables such as Platts-Mills, there was a general consensus in support of a firm policy here. Such leftish MPs as Crossman and Michael Foot endorsed a vigorous stand against Russian penetration and the rise of the Tudeh.[31] A broad harmony on foreign policy still survived.

Greece was a much more difficult and enduring problem. Since the British military intervention in December 1944, the government had been engaged in supporting the pro-monarchist and right-wing government of Voulgaris against the left-wing ELAS whom the Russians supported. Compared with Iran, Russian involvement was much more indirect, but instability in such a key region of the Balkans,

[29] See Gary R. Hess, 'The Iranian Crisis of 1945–46 and the Cold War', *Political Science Quarterly*, vol. 89, no. 1 (Mar. 1974), pp. 117–46.
[30] Telegram from Sir R. Bullard, Tehran, 10 Jan. 1946 (FO 371/52661) E 338/5/34.
[31] R. H. S. Crossman, 'The Third Force', *The Nation*, 24 Jan. 1948, pp. 93–6; Michael Foot's speech on 4 June 1946, *Parl. Deb.*, 5th ser., vol. 423, 1936.

adjacent to Soviet satellite states, inevitably stoked the fires of Anglo-Russian tension still further. As the right-wing regime in Greece remained entrenched, concern at the support that Britain was giving so notably un-socialist a system caused much alarm in Labour ranks, including many Labour MPs not normally associated with the left. The philhellene Noel-Baker, a Minister of State at the Foreign Office, was much troubled in conscience.[32] There was also the practical question of the extreme cost of the Greek civil war, which led to a large British military presence in Greece throughout 1945 and 1946, a total payment of £132m. to the Greek government at a time of extreme foreign exchange difficulties for Britain. In 1946, Bevin repeatedly announced his government's anxiety to withdraw its troops and promote the establishment of a broad-based coalition in Greece; but the situation showed no change. The position was complicated by Greek territorial claims against their northern Communist-led neighbours, Bulgaria and Albania, in northern Epirus and Thrace. The log-jam was broken in January 1947 by Britain's overwhelming financial problems, with a severe decline in the balance of payments and a drain on the US loan, accentuated by the fuel crisis. Dalton's repeated complaints at the cost of operations in Greece, hitherto beaten off by the Foreign Office, now met with Bevin's agreement. At the Cabinet on 30 January, Dalton argued that they should cut their losses in Greece, abandon a commitment which he costed at no less than an additional £50m., and withdraw British forces forthwith. Bevin now endorsed Dalton's view. 'I think Mr Dalton is justified. We get no help from the Greeks', he minuted.[33] The most Bevin would offer would be Britain continuing to provide the Greek Army with weapons and supplies. On 21 February, he told the US State Department officially that Britain was about to suspend military and economic aid to Greece, and also to Turkey. 'The U.S. Government will readily understand that in their existing financial situation H.M.G would not be justified in incurring any further expenditure on Greece, since Greece's needs for the next

[32] Material in Noel-Baker papers, 4/345.
[33] Dalton to Attlee, 11 Feb, with Bevin note (FO 371/67032); memorandum by Brook for the Prime Minister, 29 Jan. 1947 (CAB 21/2243).

year alone [which he assessed at £60–70m.] are so far beyond any sums which H.M.G. could possibly devote to this purpose.' He added that America must henceforth 'bear the lion's share' of aid to Greece.[34] This British announcement, presented as a bombshell by the American press, was no surprise to General Marshall and the State Department, which had long known of British anxiety about Greece.[35] America had already been taking an expanded role in the eastern Mediterranean, especially in Turkey. The American response, concocted between President Truman and Senator Vandenberg, the Republican leader of the Senate Foreign Relations Committee, took the form of the dramatic Truman Doctrine, proclaimed on 11 March. Its effect was that the United States would henceforth take over the burden of military aid to Greece, Turkey, and other potential victims of Soviet aggression. In due course, on 22 May, Truman signed a bill of $400m. of aid to Greece and Turkey.

Truman's Declaration was a controversial event. It was couched in highly ideological terms which announced a world-wide conflict between expansionist Communism and western free democracy. George Kennan was one important State Department aide who thought it too doctrinaire and inflammatory. In the British Foreign Office, Gladwyn Jebb fiercely attacked Truman's message as hasty and ambiguous, 'probably an amalgam of various drafts'. Later, in his memoirs, Jebb contrasted the impetuosity of the Truman Doctrine with the well-thought-out planning he detected in Marshall Aid. Truman, so Jebb argued, seemed to rule out the possibility of a country, such as France or Italy, going Communist by legal and constitutional means. An 'enduring struggle' was envisaged between the free world and godless Communism. In effect, Truman was ruling out the participation of Communist states, even Russia, as open members of the United Nations, and holding open the prospect of an aggressive America in its turn trying to impose the US way of life

[34] Foreign Office dispatch to Washington embassy, 21 Feb. 1947 (FO 371/67032) R 1900/50/G19; *aide-mémoire*, British embassy to US State Department, 4 Mar. 1947 (FO 371/67034) R 3190/50/19.

[35] J. L. Gaddis, *The United States and the Origins of the Cold War* (New York, 1972), pp. 346–52. The most detailed study of the origins of the Truman doctrine is still Joseph M. Jones, *The Fifteen Weeks* (New York, 1955).

throughout the world. The consequences for disarmament or effective international co-operation on economic aid would be disastrous.[36] But Jebb's view was countered within the Foreign Office by C. F. A. Warner, and also by 'Jock' Balfour, minister in Washington, who criticized Jebb's belief that Truman sought to incite the anti-Communist opposition within the Communist countries. Both of them stressed the need for America's being resolute now, after the feebleness shown towards totalitarian dictatorship before 1939. Hector McNeil, Britain's spokesman at the UN Security Council, told Jebb he was 'overpitching his case', while Bevin and Attlee both responded to Truman's message with warm enthusiasm.[37]

In any case, the Foreign Office resistance to a complete withdrawal from Greece did yield some fruit. Dalton protested to Attlee on 18 April that the Foreign Office was not being very understanding about Britain's international financial problems, nor being 'very ready to stand up to foreigners about money'. He added, 'I regard the Greeks as a poor investment for the British taxpayer.'[38] In fact, the deadline for Britain to reduce its forces to one brigade by 31 March 1947 was steadily pushed forward. In response to American pressure, this remaining British military presence continued in Greece until 1950, after the civil war was over. Britain also agreed to pay the cost of the British mission in Greece in sterling. In addition, military equipment up to a value of £2 million was made available to the Greek government. Throughout, the British government maintained a sternly belligerent posture towards both internal left-wing insurgence and external Russian involvement. The steady deterioration in Anglo-Soviet relations, the growing involvement of the USA, and the polarization of the world were merely confirmed.

The most vital case of all, however, was Germany. The instincts of the British Labour government in 1945 were to ensure that Germany, while restored socially and economically,

---

[36] Memorandum by Gladwyn Jebb, 19 Mar. 1947 (FO 371/67582 A) UN 2001/1754/78; Lord Gladwyn, *The Memoirs of Lord Gladwyn* (London, 1972), p. 202.

[37] Minutes by C. F. A. Warner, 25 Mar. 1947, and 'Jock' Balfour, 19 Apr. 1947; Hector McNeil to Jebb, 19 Mar. 1947 (FO 371/65782A).

[38] Dalton to Attlee, 18 Apr. 1947 (PREM 8/528).

could never again become a military threat to Britain as it
had done in 1914 and 1939. Bevin and Attlee were as one in
agreeing on the need to minimize the centralizing aspects of
any new German constitution, so as to weaken its potential
political unity. They agreed, too, on the need to ensure that
its economic strength was devoted solely to peaceful purposes, and on the necessity of disbanding finally its military
and naval resources. Hugh Dalton, perhaps the most viru-
lently anti-German of all the members of the government,
even sought a kind of Balkanization of Germany, along the
lines advocated by Vansittart in Britain, and the Morgenthau
plan in the USA, to deindustrialize Germany and reduce its
economy to a largely pastoral basis. The Labour government
added the further nuance that a major cause of German
aggression in the past had been the role of powerful cartelized monopolies in German industry, such as the Krupp
dynasty. In the British occupied zone, the objective was
said to be the public ownership of major industries, including
the coal-mines and steel works of the Ruhr. The general
mood was unsympathetic to Germany and its plight. When
the publisher, Victor Gollancz, attempted to get British food
supplies siphoned off to help the 'Save Europe Now' movement on behalf of starving people in Germany, Attlee gave
him scant comfort.[39] The British minister in charge of the
Control Office in the British zone, J. B. Hynd, was repeatedly
criticized as too pro-German. He was eventually dismissed in
April 1947. Ironically enough, his successor, the benevolent
Catholic peer, Lord Pakenham, was to display similar philan-
thropic tendencies, as might have been foreseen.

Nor was British Labour swayed by feelings of comradeship
with the revived Social Democratic Party in Germany. During
the war, SPD leaders in exile in London had met with scant
sympathy, either from politicians such as Dalton or from
Transport House, where William Gillies adhered to a stern
Vansittart-type blanket anti-Germanism.[40] After the war, the
Attlee government viewed with disapproval many of the

[39] Attlee to Gollancz, 17 Dec. 1945 (University of Warwick Modern Records
Centre, Gollancz papers, MS 157/3/SEN/2/8) and Attlee to Gollancz, 25 Jan.
1946 (ibid. 157/3/SNE/2/14).
[40] On this theme, see Anthony Glees, *Exile Politics during the Second World
War* (Oxford, 1982).

activities of the German SPD, and its new leader, Dr Kurt
Schumacher, himself a man whose health had suffered
gravely after years in Nazi concentration camps. Bevin and
other British ministers deplored the apparent nationalistic
spirit which led Schumacher and his colleagues to emphasize
the need for a unified Germany, and their frequent use (and
misuse) of the concept of *Reich* in speeches. When Denis
Healey arranged a British visit by Schumacher in 1948, it
was in the face of the disapproval of Dalton and other
leading figures in the Labour Party.[41] The possibility of
a re-emergent western Germany being led by a socialist-
dominated government (in fact, an eventuality not destined
to occur until 1969) aroused few emotions of comradeship
in Britain. Indeed, the narrow success of a right-wing CDU-
CSU government under Dr Konrad Adenauer in the first
German federal elections in May 1949 was greeted with
broad satisfaction by Attlee, Bevin, and their colleagues.

But there were other aspects of the German problem also
to be considered. There was the huge cost of maintaining
British forces in Germany—and also of keeping the German
population itself alive after the starvation and physical
destruction which had resulted from the later stages of the
war. Britain was committed to spending £80 million a year
on the occupied zone in Germany. It had also to supply
70 per cent of the food needs of the British zone, quite
apart from its own problems with raw materials and food.
Indeed, the introduction of bread rationing in Britain in
July 1946, which led to much argument in the British Cabinet,
was caused less by difficulties in Britain itself than by the
need to export wheat to Germany in such vast quantities at
a time of diminishing world supplies and bad harvests. The
pressures for minimizing the cost of the British presence in
Germany proved to be a powerful factor in discouraging the
Labour government from perpetuating the British presence
in Germany in order to ensure a democratized, disarmed,
economically self-sufficient, morally purged, and whole-
some German nation.

More pressing still, there was the inevitable tension

---

[41] B. Reed and G. Williams, *Denis Healey and the Policies of Power* (London,
1971), p. 73.

generated between Britain, the United States, France, and Russia, as the occupying powers both in Germany as a whole, and in the joint administration of Berlin. The British government and the Foreign Office may have begun with the pre-determined belief that a resurgent Germany represented the main threat to European peace after the war. Bevin's own instinctive anti-Germanism was not in doubt. In January 1947, he was to tell Zarubin, the Soviet ambassador, with every appearance of rough sincerity, 'A German was always a German. If he saw a chance of ruling again, his warlike spirit would come uppermost.'[42] Bevin, Dalton, Alexander, and others might insist on the dangers of an excessively central-ized, cartelized Germany again becoming a military threat or an arsenal for other countries, as in the thirties. In practice, the sorry saga of the Council of Foreign Ministers' meetings between September 1945 and July 1946 led to very different conclusions. By 3 May 1946, Bevin was presenting the Cabinet with the opinion that 'the danger of Russia has become certainly as great as, and possibly even greater than, a revived Germany'. The worst possibility of all for Bevin was a revived Germany making common cause with Russia, on the lines of the treaty at Rapallo in 1922. The conclusion that he drew was to retreat from the Potsdam position which had postulated the economic unification of Germany. Britain should not try to organize the British zone as a separate unit, which was economically impossible, but should work towards closer collaboration between the British, American, and French zones.[43] This view, although broadly endorsed by Attlee, was by no means universally acclaimed in the Cabinet on 7 May 1946. Dalton felt that the prospect of a reunited Germany should never be dismissed or discounted. Aneurin Bevan intervened to say that 'fears with regard to Russia seemed to be exaggerated'. Morrison, ironically enough, urged a more positive and progressive socialist policy in the British zone, including the nationalization of steel which he had strongly resisted for Britain itself. However, events were

---

[42] Memorandum of conversation between Bevin and Zarubin, 27 Jan. 1947 (FO 371/66363) N 1189/271/38.

[43] Cabinet Conclusions, 7 May 1946 (CAB 128/5), discussing Bevin's paper on 'Policy Towards Germany', 3 May 1946, CP (46) 186.

already turning against these influential dissentients. In the future, Dalton, Morrison, and even Bevan were to react strongly to the military, political, and ideological threat from Russia, not least in Germany, as constituting the chief danger to the fulfilment of that British democratic socialism which they felt was an inspiration to the world.

In Germany, the deadlock between Britain and Russia proved even more total than elsewhere. Eventually, Byrnes and the American government came to back up the British on every major issue. There were constant disputes with the Russians over the payment of German reparations from current production, and over Anglo-American attempts to have Germany considered as an integrated economic unit. There was also a separate French suggestion that the Ruhr, the Rhineland, and the Saar be detached from the rest of Germany altogether. By the summer, the Foreign Office view was that 'it is no longer to our interest to go on working for Germany to be treated as an economic and financial whole and for a central administration to be set up'.[44] Unless the Russians completely changed their stance, a division of Germany must result. The British and American governments were both convinced that the Russians intended to retain permanent control over the eastern zone, partly to build up their own armed strength. For economic and political reasons, therefore, it seemed vital to build up some kind of democratic alternative in the zones occupied by the western powers. A new development came on 3 May 1946 when General Lucius Clay, the American military administrator, told his Russian colleague on the Allied Control Council that deliveries of surplus capital equipment from the American zone to the Russian would be halted until the Russians agreed that Germany be administered as an entire economic unit, and accounted for reparations already abstracted from the eastern zone. From this time onwards, America took the lead in resisting Russian claims in Germany. Bevin moved rapidly to try to reinforce this new American firmness.[45] At the

---

[44] Foreign Office memorandum, 20 July 1946 (FO 371/55581) C 8825/130/G8.

[45] Bevin memorandum on 'Germany: the Next Steps', 24 May 1946 (FO 371/55588) C 1267/131/18.

Foreign Ministers' meeting in Paris on 9 July, he announced the objective of sharing the indigenous resources of the German zones. At least agreement had been reached in March on future German levels of industry between the four occupying powers. Now the economic aspects of the Potsdam agreement, long flouted by the Russians, should be implemented. Otherwise, Bevin talked, with studious vagueness, of 'organizing the British zone' including the spectre of nationalization of German industry. In effect, Bevin was signalling that the permanent division of Germany into east and west, regarded as unthinkable at the end of the war, now appeared to him increasingly inevitable.

As anticipated, Bevin's move stung both Byrnes and Molotov into a quick response. On 10 July, Molotov publicly attacked the western powers for trying to seek a permanent federalization of Germany for their own purposes. The following day, Byrnes countered by an offer to merge the British and American zones in Germany; the Soviet Union would be able to join in later, if it wished. After a brief discussion in Cabinet, Bevin told Attlee and Cripps formally on 25 July that it had been agreed to merge the American and British zones.[46] He followed up with suggestions for the pooling of all economic resources in the two zones, with the net deficit shared on an agreed basis between the British and American authorities. By September, plans were well advanced for the joint administration of food, agriculture, trade, industry, finance, and transport in the fused zone, together with common import and export policies.[47] It was piously hoped that the Russians and French would also join in these arrangements. In practice, only the French were likely to do so. Meanwhile, a speech by Byrnes at Stuttgart on 6 September was far more sharply anti-Russian in tone than anything he had ever previously uttered. A few days later, the US Secretary of Commerce, Henry Wallace, much the most pro-Russian member of Truman's administration, was abruptly dismissed from office by the American president, following his public objections to Byrnes's speech. Thus, the

---

[46] Bevin to Attlee and others, 25 May 1946 (FO 371/55589) C 8855/151/G18.

[47] Draft of Bevin speech, Oct. 1946 (FO 371/55593) C 12837/131/G18.

historic decision to merge the British and US zones came about, with the so-called Bizonia coming into being on 1 January 1947. Anglo-American differences on western Germany remained, notably divisions between Generals Robertson and Clay over a proposed central parliament, which Bevin thought too provocative to the Soviet Union at this stage. But henceforth there was broad accord between Britain and the United States over the main themes. It was agreed, for instance, that greater powers should be given to the *länder*, and new democratic constitutions came into effect for Bavaria, Württemberg-Baden, and Hesse in December 1946. Later the French zone was merged into Bizonia. Steps also proceeded, more slowly, towards a west German federal government democratically elected, with control over its own social and economic programmes; this eventually came about in May 1949. Protests by Schumacher, the German SPD leader, over the vital need for the reunification of all Germany were largely ignored by the British Labour government. Plans to nationalize the steel industry were quietly shelved, after American objections. In Germany as in Britain, 'consolidation' was henceforth to reign undisturbed.

The trend of policy in Germany was momentous in its implications. Bevin, wrote Oliver Harvey, noted that unifying the British and American zones, including the Ruhr, might force the Russians 'to lift the Iron Curtain' and open up the eastern zone.[48] In reality, it permanently institutionalized the division of central Europe into east and west. The river Elbe marked the physical existence of that 'iron curtain' of which Churchill had spoken in the Fulton speech. In this crucially important area, Anglo-American political and military collaboration became a reality. The prospect of the two English-speaking people being further 'mixed up together' in other parts of the world seemed inevitable, as tension with the Soviet Union continued to grow. The German settlement also ensured the permanent stationing of US troops on the European continent. The spectre of American isolationism was being eliminated. Taken with US support for British policies in the Middle East, and even more with the Truman doctrine enunciated for Greece and Turkey, the policy

[48] Minute by Oliver Harvey, 13 Aug. 1946 (FO 371/55591).

adopted in Germany made the polarization of the northern world as emphatic as in those religious divisions four centuries earlier of which Sir Frank Roberts, the minister at the Moscow embassy, had written. The clear mandate given to West Germany to develop its own industrial and fiscal policies, far beyond the Potsdam agreement of 1945 or the Levels of Industry Agreement of 1946, so that again it could emerge as a dominant economic force in the west, also had far-reaching implications for the post-war world. Even the rearmament of a revived western Germany was under discussion as early as 1948.

On balance, these changes were accepted by the Labour government and its supporters with remarkably little demur. The reduction of support costs in Germany was, of course, popular, especially with Dalton and Cripps. The spectacle of British people queuing miserably for rationed bread because of the need to send wheat to feed the defeated German enemy had not added to the Labour government's popularity in the summer of 1946. Left-wing critics of the notion of a divided Germany now turned, as did Crossman and others of 'Keep Left' persuasion, away from the chimera of a union of the western and eastern zones, to the idea of a west European 'third force' to keep a watchful eye on German militarism, and also to stand up to the Americans. By early 1947, the broad ranks of Labour MPs and government ministers now accepted the diagnosis offered by Bevin and the Foreign Office of irreconcilable Soviet hostility towards Britain. Pierson Dixon noted of the foreign affairs debate of 19 June 1947 that 'the whole House was soberly anti-Russian'.[49] This had been true for some months past. The Council of Ministers, torn by dissension in almost every theatre, confirmed the point. The stolid presence of Mr Molotov, in full negative flow at international conferences, did not encourage the revivial of wartime enthusiasm for the Soviet Union now, and only a few fellow-travelling Anglo-Russian 'friendship' groups tried to sustain it. Bevin's foreign policy chimed in with the stern anti-Communism of TUC leaders such as Deakin, Williamson, and Lawther, in their attempted purge of Communist unofficial strike leaders, in

---

[49] P. Dixon, *Double Diploma*, pp. 245–6 (19 June 1947).

their breaking of ties with the Communist-led WFTU, and their zeal for the rigours of the law in prosecuting Communist saboteurs in the field of industrial relations. Compared with these massive forces, the steady flow of grass-roots dissent from Bevin's cold-war policies that landed on Morgan Phillips's desk in Transport House could safely be dismissed, as it was brushed aside at party conferences. The realities of power, both the old realities of Britain's international and imperial position, and the new realities of ideological conflict between the Cominform and a democratic socialist government in the west, impelled Bevin and his colleagues towards a clean break with collaboration with the Soviet Union and the vain dream of a socialist foreign policy.

The logic of this relentless hostility towards the Soviet Union led in time to a new relationship between Britain and the United States. But there was nothing inevitable or predestined about it. There was long-standing hostility on the Labour side towards America as the stronghold of Wall Street and international finance capitalism. Pavlovian anti-Americanism was widespread on the Labour benches in 1945, with echoes of it in the pronouncements of Cabinet ministers such as Bevan and even Dalton. For their part, the Americans reacted to the news of the Labour victory 'with an astonishment reminiscent of Pearl Harbour'.[50] There were practical reasons for concern with American reactions to a Labour-ruled Britain, foreshadowed by Truman's decision to wind up Lease Lend in August 1945. In the loan negotiations that autumn, the American administration showed themselves less than wholly sympathetic to an ally who had fought and bled for their cause over six years. The severity of the terms imposed, notably the American insistence of liberalization of trade on purely doctrinaire grounds, was condemned on many sides in Britain, and not only on the left. An additional cause for British anger with the Americans was the failure of the administration in Washington to honour the wartime Quebec agreement to pool atomic information with Britain. This had led to difficult exchanges between Attlee and Truman in talks in Washington in November 1945. The passage of the

[50] Nicholas (ed.), *Washington Despatches*, p. 595.

McMahon Act by the US Congress in 1946 made matters far worse. Again, if there was suspicion of the motives of American capitalists by Labour supporters, there was, in the British Foreign Office, suspicion of American policy in almost every sphere. It was believed that American policy from Yalta to Potsdam had been naïvely anti-imperialist and unrealistically pro-Soviet. The replacement of Stettinius by the erratic and unpredictable Jimmy Byrnes at the State Department in July 1945 added to these fears. Further, there was a lofty belief amongst Foreign Office officials that the Americans were an unstable element, lacking the deep historical understanding shown by the British of complex issues in Europe, Africa, and Asia. As late as January 1947, C. F. A. Warner, assistant under-secretary and close to Sargent himself, was to write a memorandum for Bevin warning of the imminence of the Soviet threat. Warner chose to add, 'The Americans are a mercurial people, unduly swayed by sentiment and prejudice rather than by reason or even by consideration of their own long-term interests. Their Government is handicapped by an archaic constitution, some-times to the point of impotence, and their policy is to an exceptional degree at the mercy both of electoral changes and of violent economic fluctuations, such as might at any moment bring about a neutralisation of their influence in the world.'[51] Fortified by this patronizing approach and an ele-mentary lack of understanding of developments across the Atlantic, the Foreign Office regarded the United States at best as a volatile mediator, at worst even a potential adversary, as it had seemed to be in naval and other matters after 1918 as well.

Nevertheless Bevin's policy from August 1945 was clearly designed to promote a closer and more consistent relation-ship with the United States. In this crucial area, he showed an enterprise, and sometimes a delicacy of touch, manifestly lacking in other areas of his rough-hewn diplomacy. He was passionately anxious to eliminate the prospect of an isola-tionist withdrawal by the United States from European affairs, as had occurred so disastrously after 1919. The signs of isolationism were all around in August–September 1945.

[51] Minute by C. F. A. Warner, 6 Jan. 1947 (FO 371/66546) U 76/76/79G.

There was the decision so abruptly to cut off Lease Lend and the immediate start on a rapid demobilization of the US armed forces irrespective of the levels of the Red Army. The pressure to 'bring our boys back home' was irresistible: Truman himself wrote in alarm in October 1945 that the speedy demobilization of the 12 million US men and women under arms amounted to 'the disintegration of our armed forces'. Powerful isolationist sentiment was voiced by American Republican politicians as important as Senator Robert A. Taft of Ohio and ex-president Herbert Hoover; it helped towards large-scale Republican gains in the 80th Congress elected in the mid-term polls in November 1946. Walter Lippman argued that the USA should remain aloof equally from the Soviet 'iron curtain' and the British 'silken curtain'.[52] Nevertheless, Bevin laboured hard to ensure that British democratic socialism should not be bereft of American political and economic support in the world-wide troubles that assailed it. From February 1946 to March 1948, he had the assistance of an amiable and experienced ambassador in Washington, Clark Kerr, now Lord Inverchapel, even if one lacking either the political stature of his predecessor, Lord Halifax, or the intellectual authority of his successor, Sir Oliver Franks.

In the first year of the Labour government's period of office, there seemed no certainty at all of permanent American involvement in the European continent. Even if the second world war did not breed the disillusion amongst the American voters produced by the first world war, the factors compelling Americans to concentrate on their own national and hemi-spheric priorities were as powerful as ever. Gladwyn Jebb recorded in his memoirs that it was assumed in 1945 that American troops would remain in Europe for no more than twelve months after the armistice,[53] and this is confirmed in Foreign Office memoranda at the time. The immediate British concerns were to ensure American long-term aid, and US support for the British positions at successive Foreign Ministers' conferences. The first was eventually secured, as

[52] Truman, *Year of Decisions*, p. 509; Halifax to Foreign Office, 8 and 10 May 1946 (FO 371/51628).
[53] Gladwyn, *Memoirs*, p. 172.

has been seen; the loan was finally voted through the US Congress and signed by the President in July 1946. The latter objective was far harder to secure. In the first six months of the post-war period, Byrnes, the Secretary of State, showed much reluctance to endorse British views which carried marked imperialist overtones. This applied to the Italian colonies, Greece, and Indonesia above all. Attlee considered that Byrnes 'had no very clear understanding of the issues',[54] while Bevin and Byrnes always had an uneasy relationship. Byrnes himself was anxious to build on the alliance of the war years, and to avoid a divided world. At home, he sought bipartisan support, and worked closely with Republican senators like Vandenberg and Connally, to avoid the errors of narrow partisanship that Woodrow Wilson had lapsed into so fatally at the time of the 1919 Paris peace conference. But, increasingly, Byrnes's endeavours (fortified perhaps by his Irish ancestry) to keep his distance from Britain and act as a kind of mediating agency in the three major powers, led nowhere. Not even the growing Anglo-American tension over Palestine, which led to such fierce pressure from Jewish-Americans and other ethnic minorities within the Democratic Party, changed this basic position. Byrnes found himself under particular attack from the Russians in relation to eastern Europe where he was criticized for supposed American long-term designs on Poland, Czechoslovakia, and perhaps Hungary. Conversely, he was criticized at home for his weakness towards the Soviet Union at the Foreign Ministers' meetings in Moscow in December 1945, overtly by the Senate Foreign Relations Committee, more powerfully in private by Truman, and his Chief of Staff, Admiral Leahy. The President believed that 'Byrnes had lost his nerve in Moscow' and made far too many concessions.[55] In the winter crisis in Azerbaijan, however, Byrnes gave the British position on Iran consistent support. After studying plans of Russian troop movements towards Tehran in March 1946, he is recorded as saying 'Now we'll give it to them with both barrels!'[56] At the Paris peace conference in April–May 1946, he showed a far tougher

[54] Francis Williams, *A Prime Minister Remembers* (London, 1961), p. 172.
[55] Gaddis, op. cit., pp. 285 ff.
[56] Hess, op. cit., p. 135.

stance towards the Soviet Union than he had demonstrated hitherto. He was backed up by the Republican Senator Arthur Vandenberg in what one wit termed 'a second Vandenberg Concerto'. On such difficult issues as Iran, Cyrenaica, Greece, and Indonesia, the British and American positions were coming closer together. The appointment of as senior a figure as Averell Harriman as US ambassador to Britain in early 1946 underlined the centrality of the Anglo-American relationship. On Germany above all, the new mood in American foreign policy revealed itself, from General Clay's *démarche* on reparations to the Russians on 3 May 1946 onwards, and this became the key to the ever closer accord between Britain and the United States that eventually resulted.

The agreement to merge the British and American zones in western Germany, followed by Byrnes's belligerently anti-Russian speech at Stuttgart in September, gave a new impetus to this convergence of British and American policies. There always remained the eternal problem of Palestine as a complicating factor, and this was as far from resolution as ever at the start of 1947. Elsewhere, however, problems were diminishing; lengthy talks between Bevin and State Department officials in New York in November–December 1946 helped reduce them further. The Americans voiced open sympathy with the British government's obvious anxiety to withdraw from imperial control of India, and possibly of Egypt also. The radical nature of the Labour government's domestic programme caused less concern in American government circles than it did in the popular right-wing, isolationist press in the Mid-West or the west coast, while in any case Bevin and Attlee were talismans of Labour's enduring commitment to parliamentary democracy and individual liberty. Attlee himself, 'as British as Oxford, warm beer or cold toast',[57] seemed a totally reassuring figure. The emergence of a fused Anglo-American 'Bizonia' in Germany in January 1947 heralded a new closeness that soon spread to other spheres of common interest. General Marshall's succession to the State Department in January 1947, in place of Byrnes, greatly helped the new accord. At the Moscow Foreign Ministers' conferences in March 1947, there emerged a broad

[57] Nicholas, op. cit., p. 597.

identity of outlook between Bevin and Marshall on all questions. Marshall thought Bevin went too far in his proposals
for higher levels of industrial production in Germany. But
on other German issues—Russian reparations demands;
economic integration of the various zones of Germany; the
Russians' refusal to pool coal production in the Soviet zone,
and demands for special treatment of the Ruhr; Molotov's
insistence that the bizonal fusion of the British and American
zones be annulled—the two western powers found themselves at one. Other questions, such as the Austrian Peace
Treaty, remained as far from settlement as ever. Taken with
the Truman Doctrine for the eastern Mediterranean that
same month, the American commitment to a permanent
form of involvement, in resisting what was felt to be overt
Soviet expansionism in Europe and elsewhere, could no
longer be in doubt. Within the Labour Party, such residual
anti-Americanism as occasionally welled to the surface could
safely be discounted.

On the other hand, the precise form that this American
involvement would take remained unclear. There was no
immediate likelihood of any permanent military or political
commitment outside the special case of Germany. Nor did
Bevin base his policy on the presupposition that there would
be. In the first instance, partly to encourage later American
support, but mainly to ensure British leadership in whatever
initiative was taken in western Europe, Bevin was convinced
that the first priority was to enable Europe to organize itself
so as to build up its own military and economic power as a
deterrent to Soviet threats. In practice, this could only mean
starting with some kind of renewed alliance with France. This
was fraught with many complications. Any French government, even one headed by the veteran socialist leader, Léon
Blum, must be uncertain about concluding a military agreement with Britain before guarantees had been achieved about
the political future of Germany. In any case, French governments were notoriously unstable, and France was herself
in considerable political and industrial turmoil in the winter
of 1946-7 with the massive Communist Party an ever-present
threat to national solidarity. The Americans did not necessarily
view with enthusiasm an inbred alliance of two ancient,

imperialist western European powers, especially bearing in mind French reservations about German unification. The Soviet Union, of course, which Britain was currently courting over a possible renewal of the wartime treaty of friendship, might well consider that an Anglo-French alliance was directed against her. Much care, therefore, was taken by Bevin and the British ambassador, Duff Cooper, to project any future Anglo-French alliance in terms of dealing with Germany. Bevin laid down that any pact should be directed against future German aggression on the lines of the 1942 Anglo-Soviet treaty, rather than open up any wider understanding which might attract suspicion in Moscow and perhaps cause trouble from the French Communists as well. 'It was from the outset agreed that the Alliance should ostensibly be directed against renewed German aggression,' observed Sir Oliver Harvey, deputy under-secretary at the Foreign Office.[58] The Americans were placated by insistence that the Anglo-French treaty of 'alliance and mutual assistance' would help in promoting Byrnes's earlier plan for a Four-Power Treaty, including the Russians, and in the demilitarization and disarmament of Germany.[59] Bevin was anxious to appear broadly conciliatory to the French 'since they will have received a cold douche on levels of industry (steel)'; some reduction in the coal cuts proposed for the French zone of Germany was suggested, together with concessions on gold payments.[60] On 4 March Bevin travelled to the beach of Dunkirk where the Anglo-French treaty was solemnly signed at the very place where the British had conducted their famous retreat seven years earlier.

However, the return to Dunkirk did not necessarily lead automatically to any further degree of European integration, still less to any prospect of the United States involving itself in any vision of 'western union'. The Treaty of Dunkirk seemed to be a finite, self-contained episode, with no wider implications. Any tendencies towards European integration were rebuffed both by the Foreign Office and even more by

---

[58] Bevin to Duff Cooper, 23 Jan. 1947; memorandum by Sir Oliver Harvey, 11 Feb. 1947 (FO 371/67670) Z 1215/25/17.

[59] Foreign Office telegram to Paris, 3 Mar. 1947 (ibid.) Z 2214/25/17.

[60] Sir E. Hall-Patch to Roger Makins, 27 Feb. 1947 (FO 371/67672).

the Attlee Cabinet, by arguments which ranged from Britain's ties with the Commonwealth to the dangers of British political and economic sovereignty being imperilled by links with alien institutions of different legal pedigree.

The next phase in the American involvement in underpinning the foreign policy of the British Labour government came from very different origins. The economic stagnation of western Europe, including Britain which had serious balance of payments difficulties and faced a rapid running out of the US loan, caused much concern in US government circles. Marshall formally set up a committee in April 1947, under the chairmanship of George Kennan, to consider the general features of European economic recovery. In addition, there were important unresolved problems about Germany. The fusion of the British and American zones had left all the key economic questions unanswered. In the spring of 1947, there was still a desperate shortage of food, and widespread economic chaos in Bizonia; in April the Ruhr miners actually went on strike in protest against their food supplies. All the key economic issues remained unresolved—the costs of occupation, the levels of industrial production and of reparations, the direction of German exports. There was evidence of tension between Bevin, who sought a high degree of socialization in the economic policy, and the free-market enthusiasms of the American commander, General Lucius Clay. Another complicating element was tension between Clay, who was responsible to the US War Department, and Marshall in the US State Department. Clay had no wish to preside over a German economic collapse of 1930 proportions, that was not of his making. Some kind of rehabilitation of the German economy must be achieved, but one mutually acceptable in political terms to the two major western powers. Germany must be fitted into the wider framework of European economic recovery. In the light of these political and economic considerations, Secretary of State Marshall delivered a famous address at Harvard on 5 June 1947. It was to inaugurate a new era in the foreign policy of the United States and the history of the world. Its proposals for a long-term economic aid programme for Europe were vague enough. Denis Healey in Transport House thought it 'not much more than waffling aloud'.[61] No 'Marshall Aid' scheme as such was outlined in concrete terms, nor did Will Clayton, Marshall's emissary in Europe, offer any specific blueprint for economic assistance. On the other hand, Alan Bullock has rightly warned us against replacing one myth with another; Truman, Marshall, Clayton, Kennan, Acheson, and the other key American policy-makers evidently did recognize the Harvard speech as making a new departure in foreign policy, even if the end was not certain.[62] Undoubtedly, what happened next was that Marshall's speech was taken up with speed and zest by Bevin, and transformed into a new basis for the political, economic and, ultimately, military development of the North Atlantic world. It was perhaps his most important personal contribution to the conduct of British foreign policy. In the process, it had profound implications for the British Labour government and for the international philosophy of the Labour Party.

The very day that Marshall's plan was proclaimed at Harvard, Bevin moved into action. Key Foreign Office personnel drew up, within the next two weeks, a programme that involved Britain itself taking the lead, perhaps using the European Economic Commission as a basis, to turn the Marshall Plan into practical reality. Bevin himself outlined, later in June, a detailed plan for the consideration of the Cabinet for the closer economic relationship with western Europe.[63] Marshall had been careful to present his scheme as an invitation to eastern European nations as well, but it is obvious that Russian participation was discounted in London from the start. Equally, although Duff Cooper told the French Foreign Minister of the urgent need to avoid 'any impression of the formation of a western block', this was the predictable outcome of Marshall's speech. The organizational framework for the Marshall Aid scheme was always British, or to a lesser degree Anglo-French, and so it remained.

Over the next few months, Marshall's speech was transformed into a European recovery programme. After Molotov,

[61] Reed and Williams, op. cit., p. 72.
[62] Bullock, op. cit., pp. 403–4.
[63] Memorandum by Bevin for the Cabinet, 18 June 1947; record of conversation of Troutbeck, Makins, Hankey, and Radice at the Foreign Office, 5 June 1947 (FO 371/62399) UE 4781/168/53.

1 Labour's two party chairmen during the general election campaign: (*a*) Ellen Wilkinson (1944–5) and (*b*) Harold Laski (1945–6).

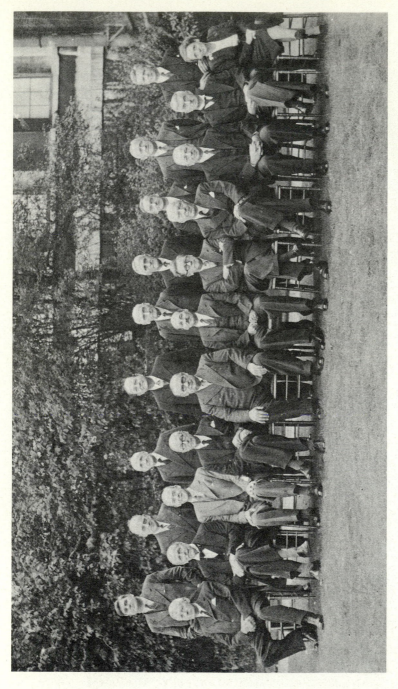

2 The Labour Cabinet, 23 August 1945: *seated, left to right*, Viscount Addison, Lord Jowitt, Sir Stafford Cripps, Arthur Greenwood, Ernest Bevin, Clement Attlee, Herbert Morrison, Hugh Dalton, A. V. Alexander, J. Chuter Ede, Ellen Wilkinson; *standing, left to right*, Aneurin Bevan, George Isaacs, Viscount Stansgate, G. H. Hall, Lord Pethick-Lawrence, J. J. Lawson, J. Westwood, Emanuel Shinwell, Tom Williams.

3 (a) Herbert Morrison brandishing Labour's election manifesto, July 1945,
(b) Ernest Bevin in the Foreign Office, 24 July 1946.

4 The Labour Party conference, Bournemouth, June 1946: Morgan Phillips, Herbert Morrison, Hugh Dalton.

5 (a) Post-war gaiety: a bathing beauty contest at Butlin's holiday camp, Filey, 1946;
(b) Post-war gloom: queuing for rationed food in the bomb-damaged East End of
London, March 1946.

6 Squatters in Abbey Lodge, central London, September 1946.

7 Cripps preparing his budget, April 1949.

8 Morgan Phillips, Denis Healey, Len Williams: Transport House *apparatchiks*

9 Labour Party conference, Blackpool, June 1949: (*a*) *left to right*, Griffiths, Attlee, Phillips, Greenwood, Morrison, Edith Summerskill, Laski, Shinwell; (*b*) singing 'Auld 'Lang Syne' at the end of the conference, *left to right*, Dalton, Bevan, Morrison, Tomlinson, Phillips.

10 Bevin conducting foreign policy: (*a*) Bevin and Molotov at the Foreign Office, 11 September 1945; (*b*) Dean Acheson, Bevin, and Robert Schuman discussing the Schuman Plan, Lancaster House, 11 May 1950.

11 Electioneering in February 1950: (*a*) Attlee greeting a constituent, West Walthamstow; (*b*) Dalton canvassing bus conductresses, Bishop Auckland, Durham.

12 Labour Party conference, Beatrice Webb House, Dorking, 20 May 1950:
Margaret Herbison, Patrick Gordon-Walker, Herbert Morrison.

13 Bevan and Phillips playing billiards at Filey holiday camp.

14 Harold Wilson and Sir Stafford Cripps leaving No. 10 after a Cabinet meeting, 10 January 1950.

15 Aneurin Bevan at the Ministry of Labour, 1951.

16 The 'Bevanites' elected to the National Executive (*left to right*, Mikardo, Driberg, Barbara Castle), Scarborough, 3 October 1951.

on behalf of the Russian government, had formally declined
any Soviet involvement in the Marshall proposals, during the
Foreign Ministers' conference which began in Paris on 27 June,
Bevin chaired a conference on European economic co-
operation from 12 July onwards: fourteen nations attended,
eight (all from eastern Europe, together with Finland)
refused. This conference outlined the need for a productive
effort to be launched by the European nations with new
attempts at internal financial stability, the maximum of
international economic co-operation, and the settlement
of the trading deficit with North America. These laudable
objectives were much to the delight of key US officials like
George Kennan.[64] He was anxious that the lead should come
from Europe, and preferably from Britain. A new Committee
of European Economic Co-operation was then set up, with
subcommittees on Food and Agriculture, Iron and Steel,
Energy and Power, and Transport.[65] It was due to hand in
its report by 1 September, a timetable of about six weeks
in all. The chairman of this committee was Sir Oliver Franks,
a notable civil servant at the Ministry of Supply during the
war, but now Provost of The Queen's College, Oxford. Like
Bevin, he was a Bristolian. On 30 June he had been given
leave of absence by the governing body of his college 'to
prepare a scheme for the comprehensive restoration of the
economy of Europe on the lines adumbrated by Mr Marshall,
the United States Secretary of State'. The Archbishop of
York sent his benediction on 3 July.[66] Among other things,
this move was to launch Franks on a major new diplomatic
career which was to take him to the Washington embassy in
May 1948.

Events moved rapidly thereafter. By the autumn of 1947 a
whole new infrastructure for western European co-operation
and recovery was in being. It was always carefully tailored to
the British view that economic co-operation should be
multilateral and functional in approach rather than a kind of

---

[64] 'Jock' Balfour to Foreign Office, 10 June 1947 (FO 371/62399); Dean
Acheson, *Present at the Creation* (London, 1969), pp. 234 ff.

[65] Record of Committee on European Economic Co-operation (CAB 133/13
and 133/46); minutes of British delegation (FO 371/62568–70).

[66] Minutes of the Governing Body, The Queen's College, Oxford, 30 June
1947 (consulted by permission of Mr J. M. Kaye).

economic integration as urged by the Americans and the French. In April 1948, President Truman formally signed the Economic Co-operation Act, which was followed by the establishment of the new permanent OEEC in Paris, the setting up of a European Payments Union, and the framing of a European Recovery Program under Paul G. Hoffman, as chief administrator with US Cabinet rank. So was launched a huge injection of economic aid over the long term into a number of western European nations. Initially, Britain, France, and the Benelux countries were the recipients; soon it extended to Italy as well. A total of four billion dollars was first specified for a fifteen-month period. Britain was a supreme beneficiary of Marshall Aid. In all, twelve billion dollars was assigned to European economic recovery up to 1 January 1951 when Gaitskell, then the Chancellor, felt able to announce that Britain no longer needed its quota of Marshall Aid, so rapid had been its economic recovery. There were occasional tensions with Paul Hoffman—for instance in his complaints about Britain's export performance.[67] The entire machinery for international payments and trading arrangements proved to be complicated and unpredictable, not least because the currencies involved were not convertible. For all that, it is inconceivable that the economic and social policies of the Attlee government could have survived without this massive platform constructed by a combination of American long-term economic self-interest, and British diplomatic initiative.

The political implications of the Marshall Plan were scarcely less momentous than the economic. The British Foreign Office view was that Marshall's proposals were 'sane and thoughtful', by contrast with the Truman Doctrine which was 'a panic measure'.[68] A clarity and coherence was now given to Bevin's grand designs in foreign policy which they had previously lacked during the wrangles with the Russians in 1945–6, and the endless imbroglio in Palestine. Now, suddenly, everything became transparently clear. As the Labour

---

[67] D. C. Watt, *Personalities and Policies* (London, 1965) pp. 53 ff. Hoffman also appears to have made known his dislike of the nationalization of steel.

[68] Minute by B. M. Bever, 20 Nov. 1947 (FO 371/61077) AN 4008/450/45.

government ran into mounting difficulties at home in the course of 1947, Bevin's foreign policy became transformed and triumphant. It chimed in with the doctrine of 'containment' now powerful in Washington, following George Kennan's famous anonymous article in the journal, *Foreign Affairs* in July. During the autumn of 1947, Bevin and a succession of French foreign ministers went much further in promoting closer economic collaboration, including several joint projects in Africa. Further, Bevin was talking in October of a possible new political grouping in the west, based on the Anglo-French *entente*, but including Belgium, the Netherlands, Luxembourg, Eire, Portugal, and perhaps Italy as well. Italy, after all, had joined the IMF and accepted Bretton Woods. A further prospect lay in discussions between the British and French chiefs of staff, limited in the first instance to the matters of the organization of land forces and the standardization of equipment.[69] The final Council of Foreign Ministers conference was held in New York in December. It led to a total breakdown between Russia and the western powers. To Bevin, this outcome was entirely predictable; it made the need for filling the political vacuum in western Europe all the more urgent.

At secret meetings at the Foreign Office on 17–18 December, Bevin outlined to Marshall and Bidault his vision of 'Western Union', what he termed 'a sort of spiritual federation of the West'. Any prospect of effective co-operation with the Soviet Union was now ruled out, and, with Marshall's enthusiastic blessing, the western European nations began to reorganize themselves. On 13 January 1948, Bevin formally told Marshall and Truman that Britain now envisaged a new political and defence arrangement between herself, France, Belgium, the Netherlands, and Luxembourg. In the first instance, this would take the form of a series of bilateral defence arrangements on the lines of the Dunkirk Treaty with France. Then, in a major speech in the Commons on 22 January 1948, Bevin publicly launched the idea of 'Western Union'.[70] He

[69] Minutes of Chiefs of Staff Committee, COS (48) 3rd, 7 Jan. 1948 (FO 371/ 67674); meeting of British Joint Staff Mission and US Chiefs of Staff, Jan. 1948 (FO 371/68041).
[70] Record of meetings of Bevin with Marshall and Bidault, 17–18 Dec. 1947 (FO 800/447); *Parl. Deb.*, 5th ser., vol. 446, 383–409 (22 Jan. 1948).

outlined the spread of Soviet influence in eastern Europe in terms almost identical with those of Churchill's 'iron curtain' speech at Fulton, Missouri. He recalled the refusal of Russia to join the European economic recovery programme, and the creation of the Comintern as a centre of international espionage, to punish Britain and France for launching the ERP. In terms much quoted later, Bevin spoke with unusual eloquence of the political, economic, and spiritual unity of western Europe. Developments in the western capitals were rapid from this point, and on 17 March 'western union' was put into practical form by the Brussels Treaty under which Britain, France, and the three Benelux countries engaged in mutual collective self-defence over the next fifty years. The Dunkirk Treaty with France in 1947 had formally named Germany as the potential aggressor. No such future enemy was specified at Brussels. Indeed, many commentators speculated that a revived Germany might itself become a leading member of Western Union in due course. The anti-Russian implications of the Brussels Treaty were obvious. For Britain, it marked a remarkable transformation in foreign policy compared with the quiescence towards western Europe that had endured, largely unbroken, since the end of the Peninsular War in 1812.

Nor would developments rest there. At the same time as the successful conclusion of the Brussels Treaty, negotiations were going on apace to create OEEC, the European machinery destined to implement the Recovery Program instituted by the Americans to distribute Marshall Aid. Further, there were now intense diplomatic moves, led by Sir Oliver Franks for Britain, to bring the United States into the new fabric of western European defence, an even more revolutionary development for American foreign policy than the Brussels Treaty had been for British. Gladwyn Jebb headed a powerful British delegation to Washington from 22 March 1948 onwards, from which the idea of a North Atlantic Treaty Organization, to deal with defence and security, would evolve. At first, there was still American reluctance to have a permanent commitment of troops and equipment three thousand miles away from home shores. But the pattern of events in early 1948—the *coup* by the Communists in Czechoslovakia in February; the threat of further Soviet pressure in Norway; the deteriorating situation in Germany which led to the Russian land blockade of West Berlin from 23 June and the western allies' reply of an airlift; the rift between Tito and Stalin which led to Yugoslavia's expulsion from the Cominform on 28 June—all pushed an increasingly receptive, anti-Soviet American public opinion in the one direction. Senator Vandenberg's resolution, giving approval in principle to American participation in North Atlantic defence arrangements, passed the Senate on 11 June, by sixty-four votes to two. American rearmament was sharply stepped up; a less publicized, but crucial, move at the same time was the siting of American B 29 long-range bombers in East Anglia. At a meeting at The Hague on 19-20 July 1948, the Brussels Treaty Foreign Ministers took a notable step forward, after Bevin had managed to placate the French who were fearful of American intentions and the possible domination of western Europe by the 'Anglo-Saxons'. In the autumn, the pressure from the Brussels Treaty powers for a long-term American military commitment became overwhelming. Bevin, Schuman, and Spaak gave the idea strong support at Paris on 25-6 October.[71] Secretary of State Marshall's support was not in doubt. In due course, the North Atlantic Treaty Organization was formally created at Washington on 4 April 1949. Henceforth, the United States was committed indefinitely to protecting the frontiers and social fabric of western Europe, despite the precepts handed down by all previous US administrations from the days of the Monroe doctrine. Britain for its part had taken a fundamental decision in strategy and defence policy. The polarization of the world between East and West was finally confirmed.

These historic and fateful events formed an extraordinary saga of achievement by Ernest Bevin. The period between Marshall's Harvard speech on 5 June 1947 and the coming into being of NATO in April 1949 is a period of sustained creativity such as few, if any, British Foreign Secretaries have produced since the time of the Elder Pitt. The passage

---

[71] Sir Nicholas Henderson, *The Birth of NATO* (London, 1982), pp. 44-6; record of the third meeting of the Consultative Council of the Brussels Treaty powers, Paris, 25-6 Oct. 1948 (FO 800/447), Conf. 48/3.

of time can give a kind of deceptive, seamless unity to British
and western European policy at this time. In fact, there were
frequent difficulties and periods of indecision or retreat, as
Sir Nicholas Henderson's recent work has reminded us.[72]
The transition from the economics of OEEC to the defence
arrangements of Brussels was a complex one, with differences
of outlook between Britain and France present all the time.
The inevitability of something like NATO emerging from the
concept of Western Union could also hardly be assumed. For
one thing, the US presidential election in November 1948,
which Truman quite unexpectedly won against all the odds,
could have altered matters in crucial respects. The military
and economic aspects of Western Union were always much
more precise than the political. Despite Bevin's rhetoric
about the unity of Europe in his speech on 22 January 1948,
the British government was extremely reticent in committing
itself to any specifically European political framework,
certainly one that was in any way federalist or integrationist.
Britain was always prone to cite the 'special relationship'
with the Americans as a countervailing argument.[73] The
initial venture on behalf of a united Europe at The Hague in
May 1948 took place against a background of freezing
indifference from Bevin and the Labour government, as will
be seen later.

   Even so, the transformation was achieved, with profound
consequences for the future of Britain, the United States, and
the western world. In terms of the internal history of the
Labour government, it is astonishing how little effective
dissent was expressed during this mighty change. The criticisms from 'Keep Left' evaporated in the summer of 1947. In
the debate of 22 January 1948, Richard Crossman, one of
Bevin's sternest critics, publicly announced his complete
change of mind over foreign policy. In the American liberal
weekly, *The Nation*, he condemned as 'insane' Russian offen-
sives against Britain in Iran and elsewhere, and called again
for a vigorous 'third force' in collaboration with the socialist
parties of western Europe.[74] Marshall Aid was a turning-point

---

[72] Henderson, op. cit.
[73] e.g. Bevin to Paris embassy, 30 Dec. 1948 (FO 371/79212) Z 67/1071/72.
[74] *The Nation*, 24 Jan. 1948.

in Labour attitudes towards American foreign policy. Naturally, it presented socialist Britain with an economic lifeline at a time of desperate financial difficulty, when the US loan of 1946, scheduled to last until 1951, had virtually been exhausted already. Beyond that, Labour spokesmen could contrast the dignified, constructive aspect of Marshall's Harvard speech with the 'cold-war' jingoism of Churchill in his oration at Fulton in 1946. The left could now call for Marshall Aid assistance to be diverted to assist industrial planning in western Europe—a theme congenial to French technocrats such as Jean Monnet—with perhaps the heavy industry of western Germany as well. In left-wing periodicals such as *Tribune* and the *New Statesman*, the sagacity and moderation of George Marshall were acclaimed, while Harry Truman, as a kind of US Attlee, the apostle of the Fair Deal and representative of the nearest American equivalent to the British Labour party, received a much-improved press. Labour's enthusiasm for Truman's electoral victory in the presidential election was almost complete.[75] The fellow-travelling utopianism of Henry Wallace found few supporters in the British Labour Party. By the same token, Labour's acceptance of inescapable involvement in the economic, political, and military orbit of the United States became ever more explicit. Any few doubts that remained were swept away by Czechoslovakia and the Berlin blockade, when even Aneurin Bevan was anxious to dispatch British tanks through the Soviet zone of Germany in the crusade for western democratic liberties.

The effect of Ernest Bevin's momentous period at the Foreign Office implied, therefore, a revolution in Britain's relations with the North Atlantic powers, with western Europe, and with the Soviet Union and its satellites. The relationship of Bevin's policy to the remainder of Labour's objectives is less clear. Labour claimed, with much justice, to be pursuing a radical programme at home, including nationalization, the welfare state, and policies for social equality. That such a socialist government could identify itself with a foreign policy which endorsed the Shah of Iran, a neo-fascist government

[75] e.g. *New Statesman*, 29 Jan. 1949; *Tribune*, 5 Nov. 1948.

in Greece, and men in western Germany who included former Nazis and all the old industrial dynasties virtually unreconstructed since the days of Hitler, was remarkable. Nor did 'a socialist foreign policy' seem to mean anything much when Britain preserved such consistently frigid relations with Russia and every socialist state east of the Oder-Neisse line. As has been seen, the conflict between Britain and the Soviet Union did not always arise through Soviet pressure on central Europe, even though in Germany Russian intransigence led Bevin into the novelty of the Bizone and permanent division of the country into east and west. Conflict also came with Russia in the Middle East, in North Africa, and in south-east Asia, where Britain's Labour government pursued a policy virtually indistinguishable from those of Conservative or imperialist administrations in the past. For the Labour government, the Middle East was Britain's strategic 'lifeline'; indirect client relationships with 'moderate nationalists' in Iraq, Transjordan, Iran, and elsewhere were to be preserved; social and economic development would be traded off for an enduring military presence; an aggressive policy was to be pursued over oil reserves in Iran and along the Persian Gulf. In addition, an uncomplicated nationalist view of British interests was taken in the Mediterranean, in the Horn of Africa, in the Indian Ocean, and along the Chinese littoral in the Far East. Again, in retrospect, it is a remarkable comment on the assumptions of Attlee, Bevin, and their colleagues, when in power—and on the intransigent response of the Soviet Union—that these forthright assertions of British predominance were accepted with such limited disagreement within the Cabinet or the parliamentary Labour Party.

What fused together the radical domestic programme and the strong, belligerent foreign policy which Bevin was allowed to conduct, was a general conviction in the Labour movement that Britain was still unquestionably a great power. In the United Nations, its natural forum was amongst the superpowers on the Security Council, not the minnows in the General Assembly. The international scene in 1945 gave such a view much support. Labour spokesmen from Attlee and Dalton to Bevan and Laski were committed to the view that Britain's experiment in democratic socialism made it an example of 'third force' reformism admired throughout the world. But Labour's leaders, with their abiding memories of the thirties, recognized that moral suasion and high principle were insufficient. A powerful factor throughout the post-1945 period was the belief that Labour must not lapse again into the quasi-pacifist illusions of the 'appeasement' era. In any case, 'appeasement' was held to be the work of Chamberlain and the 'guilty men' of Munich, not of the Labour opposition. Hence, men of the left such as Aneurin Bevan, and also Shinwell and Strachey, both of whom later went to service ministries, accepted the need for Britain to maintain a powerful army, afforced by national servicemen, a large navy to patrol the Atlantic, Pacific, and Indian Oceans, and a technically sophisticated air force. A network of military bases was maintained throughout the Middle East from Iraq to Cyrenaica. Despite Labour's old hostility towards armaments and arms manufacturers, in fact defence expenditure remained at a high level throughout the 1945-51 period. In 1946, at £1,736m., with almost 1,500,000 men and women in the services and supply industries, it took one-fifth of total gross national product. A. V. Alexander and Bevin were able to fight off Dalton's demands in January 1947 for major cuts in the armed forces; in the end, a moderate cut saw defence estimates fall from £1,064m. to £899m. in 1947, with a further reduction to £700m. in 1948.[76] After that, the Brussels Treaty, NATO, and ultimately Korea gave the military budget a further boost, to £780m. in 1949-50 and to £1,112m. for 1951-2. During the first winter of the Korean War in 1950-1, the proportion of the budget spent on national defence was to rise from 6 per cent to 10 per cent, until Britain was committed to a higher expenditure per head of population than was the United States. As will be seen, this was to produce grave dissension within the Attlee government. In general, the Labour administration, with occasional opposition from Dalton and Bevan, accepted the military aspects and financial costs of Britain's status as a great power. If troubles flared up in distant theatres such as Egypt

---

[76] Cabinet Conclusions, 17 Jan. 1947 (CAB 128/9); Dalton, *High Tide and After*, pp. 193-8; minute of Cabinet Defence Committee, 4 Aug.-29 Sept. 1947 (CAB 131/5).

or Malaya, it was accepted that a rapid dispatch of British land and air forces might follow.

Of course, Britain's role as a great power was increasingly shown up as an illusion. By 1947, her financial position was far weaker, the withdrawals from Greece, India, and finally Palestine, along with the convertibility crisis, confirmed the fact. Britain was manifestly subordinate to the United States, dependent on it for economic help through Marshall Aid, and for military technology and support through NATO. On the other hand, Britain exercised the political leadership of western Europe from 1945 down to the end of 1948, it retained an important role as head of the Commonwealth, and it exercised widespread financial influence through the sterling area. Its standing as a great power, so damagingly questioned, with self-fulfilling effect, after the Suez débâcle in 1956, was not in doubt in the 1945-51 period. Dean Acheson's remark in the sixties, that Britain had lost an empire but failed to discover a role, hardly seemed applicable to the era of Bevin. The British government and the British people, for all their economic difficulties, viewed their nation as one of the big three, and a unique political and moral force throughout the world. The departure of Churchill in 1945 notwithstanding, government and public in the Attlee years, for the last time in British history, were still able to cling to this reassuring, beguiling, deceptive vision of transcendence.

In one supremely ominous respect, Britain's awareness of itself as a great power expressed itself decisively after 1945, although with a total absence of publicity. This was the commitment of Britain to an independent nuclear weapons programme. Attlee viewed with much alarm Truman's unwillingness to share atomic information with Britain as promised at Quebec during the war. In discussions with Truman in Washington in November 1945, Attlee protested in vain at the American refusal to assist in the development of atomic plans. In fact, the McMahon Act, passed by the US Congress in the summer of 1946, gave permanent effect to America's decision not to co-operate with Britain on nuclear information or research.

The British government often talked publicly after 1945

about a nuclear power programme for peaceful purposes, to deal with the development of uranium for energy needs and the like. A programme of nuclear-fired power stations was publicly inaugurated. In secret, the talks were about atomic bombs. With the Americans refusing to act in partnership, Attlee and Bevin took the momentous decision to go ahead on their own with an independent British nuclear deterrent. After all, British nuclear physicists had been vital in developing the bomb in the first place. Secret research and experimental work began at Harwell from late 1945 onwards. This issue was never discussed openly. Certainly, it was never formally brought up before the Cabinet in the 1945–51 period. Most Cabinet ministers were left in apparent ignorance, though Gordon-Walker has written that he was aware of the existence of the British bomb and the need to use the Woomera testing range in Australia, as Commonwealth Secretary in 1950. The entire episode became a key exhibit in Richard Crossman's argument on the 'passing of Cabinet government', developed in the first edition (less forcibly so, perhaps, in the second) of a republication of Walter Bagehot's essay on the British constitution.[77] Significantly, key documents on this whole area have been reserved from historical inquiry, and only Professor Margaret Gowing's authoritative book provides information on the picture in general terms.[78] A secret Cabinet committee, GEN 75, had been in existence since late 1945 to deal with decision-making on atomic energy policy. It decided in December 1945 to concentrate on production of plutonium rather than on the U-235 extracted from uranium. The first nuclear reactors were built at Windscale, in Cumberland. An Official Committee on Atomic Energy was set up in 1946, with officials from the chiefs of staff secretariat, the Foreign Office, the Treasury, the Ministry of Supply, and the Dominions Office. Astonishingly enough, a key role until mid-1946 in atomic energy policy generally was played by Sir John Anderson, an Opposition front-bench spokesman and a strong critic of the

[77] Patrick Gordon-Walker, *The Cabinet* (paperback edn., London, 1972), p. 89; Bagehot, *The English Constitution* (Fontana edn., London, 1963), pp. 54–5,
[78] Margaret Gowing, *Independence and Deterrence: Britain and Atomic Energy*, 1945–52 2 vols. (1974). Only the first meeting of GEN 163 on 8 Jan. 1947 (CAB 130/16) is available.

government; his knowledge of developments was far greater than that of ministers of Attlee's Cabinet. A crucial meeting of GEN 75 took place on 25 October 1946, with Dalton and Cripps protesting fiercely, on financial grounds, against developing a British nuclear weapons programme. To the alarm of Portal, the Chief of Staff, the British bomb seemed about to disappear from history. Then Bevin, the Foreign Secretary, returned from a lengthy lunch engagement to sweep away the economists' reservations and bully them into submission. He argued that it was important for the Union Jack to fly over a British bomb.[79] In the same month, a new Ministry of Defence was created, under Alexander. In January 1947 GEN 75 was converted into GEN 163, a secret Cabinet committee consisting of Attlee, Morrison, Bevin, and Alexander, with Wilmot (later Strauss) the Minister of Supply, and Addison, the Dominions' Secretary.[80] Dalton and Cripps, both members of GEN 75, were significantly excluded. From this time onwards, GEN 163 was actively at work, directing scientific research in the production of a British atomic bomb programme.

The subsequent development of British nuclear weapons was dogged by difficulties of all kinds. In particular, there were constant problems with the Americans over the pooling of information and scientific collaboration. The *modus vivendi* on raw materials and technical co-operation, drawn up in January 1948, contained the grave flaw that Britain abdicated her right to be consulted over the Americans' future use of their own atomic weapons. More troubles came over security matters, with the arrest for espionage in February 1950 of Klaus Emil Fuchs, head of the theoretical physics division in Harwell, who had been spying for Russian intelligence. This was followed by the defection to Russia that September of Bruno Pontecorvo, another leading nuclear scientist, and the further defection of the diplomats, Guy Burgess and Donald Maclean, in May 1951. These events weakened American confidence in British security still further. In 1952, Churchill confirmed the decision of the Attlee

---

[79] See article by Peter Hennessy, *The Times*, 29 Sept. 1982, and minutes of Cabinet Committee on Atomic Energy, 25 Oct, 1946 (CAB 130/2).
[80] Gowing, op. cit., vol. i, pp. 21–2.

Cabinet committee to build Britain's own atomic bomb. But not until October 1952, when Britain for the first time publicly tested her own atomic weapons, over the Monte Bello Islands off the north-west Australian coast, did the Attlee government's decision become general knowledge to the Labour Party and the British public. By 1955, most Labour leaders seemed fatalistically to accept as accomplished fact both the existing atomic bomb programme and the further possibility of a British-made hydrogen bomb. As Arthur Creech Jones observed to Crossman about the bomb, 'the public assumed we'd got it already and that even if we hadn't we were bound to make it in a world as crazy as this'.[81]

The decision to go ahead with an independent British nuclear weapons programme and join the 'thermo-nuclear arms race', in conditions of such secrecy, later became a target for fierce condemnation, especially from CND in the late fifties. That a British Labour government could involve itself covertly in producing so horrendous an arsenal of destructive weapons seemed at variance with the moral and humanitarian instincts of a party calling itself, in any meaningful sense, socialist. How Aneurin Bevan and other later critics would have reacted in 1947 had they known of GEN 163 is pure speculation. It may be noted that one leading scientist, Professor P. M. S. Blackett, strongly opposed a nuclear defence policy in February 1947,[82] though most other scientists did not apparently share his scruples. There would, one assumes, have been bitter criticism in a world still stunned by the horrors of Hiroshima and Nagasaki. The very idea of Britain having an independent nuclear programme at all had been highly controversial throughout, not only on the far left. But this raised wider issues, still far from defined, let alone resolved, when Labour fell from power in 1951. It may be concluded here that Britain's nuclear weapons programme, whether a deterrent or not, was the logical outcome of Britain's assertive and highly self-conscious foreign

---

[81] *The Backbench Diaries of Richard Crossman*, p. 389 (23 Feb. 1955).

[82] Gowing, op. cit., vol. i, pp. 183–4. Professor Gowing records that no Cabinet Committee discussed Blackett's views, nor did Attlee offer any comment on them.

policy during the post-war years. Bevin's Union Jack waving over the bomb was a symbol of a wider independence. Lord Zuckerman has correctly observed that Attlee's decision to develop British nuclear weapons was taken solely to bolster the nation's political power, and with no knowledge of the military or scientific consequences.[83] Bevin insisted that it would be politically dangerous to leave the United States with a monopoly of atomic weapons, and Attlee shared this view to the full.[84] It was an outlook that carried conviction after 1945. Only after 1951, when difficult issues over rearming Germany and the future proliferation of nuclear armaments throughout the world loomed up, did division in the Labour Party become almost insupportable, and threaten to eliminate the party as a credible challenger for power. Until then, Labour ministers took comfort in the belief that socialism at home implied a vigorous policy of international leadership overseas; this must be underpinned by military strength. Labour's conduct of foreign affairs, with its nationalist overtones and surprising self-confidence, appeared the ultimate sign of a movement of protest that had adjusted itself to the realities and the torments of power. What moral capital was sacrificed in this process of adjustment remains a theme of painful controversy down to the present time.

[83] Lord Zuckerman, 'Europe in a nuclear shadow', *The Guardian*, 24 Jan. 1983.
[84] Minutes of Cabinet Defence Committee, 25 May 1950 (CAB 131/8). Bevin was replying to Tizard who had urged more emphasis on research rather than on the production of atomic weapons. Attlee's view was that 'we could not agree that only America should have atomic energy' (Francis Williams, *A Prime Minister Remembers*, p. 119).

7

The Mood of Post-War

Like the Lloyd George coalition after 1918, the Attlee government after 1945 claimed to reflect the social and psychological aspirations of the nation after years of total war. In 1918–22, the Lloyd George ministry believed itself to embody the wartime mood of consensus and social unity. This was expressed politically in a government of national unity, a playing down of party factionalism, and attempts to secure a permanent fusion of the Unionists and coalition Liberals. By contrast, the Labour government after 1945 made claims that were strictly partisan. It alone was seen as embodying the social enthusiasms and idealism kindled between 1939 and 1945, during what Orwell and others had viewed as truly 'a people's war'. There was ample evidence to justify this view—far more, indeed, than for the boasts of the Lloyd George government after 1918. The 1945 general election showed Labour to be uniquely in harmony with the wartime ethos that had brought Beveridge, full employment, social planning, and the idea of 'fair shares'. For many months, perhaps years, after the election, this identification of Labour with the national mood continued. Most by-election results actually showed a swing towards the government until March 1946, even after the 12 per cent swing from the Conservatives to Labour at the polls in July 1945. Local government results confirmed the parliamentary election returns as being far more than just a temporary upsurge of enthusiasm, unlike the marked reaction against the 'coupon election' visible in by-elections from early 1919 onwards in the earlier period. The local government elections of November 1945 showed Labour gaining over 1,000 seats throughout the land.[1] In January 1946, Labour stood 19 points above the Conservatives in the Gallup Poll (52½ per cent to 33½ per cent). In the borough elections of March 1946, Labour made further extensive gains, including on the London County

---

[1] *The Times*, 3–4 Nov. 1945.

Council which showed a final result of Labour 90, Conservatives 30, Liberals 2, and Communists 2. Even as late as the municipal elections of November 1946, Labour showed a further advance, with 257 gains as against 98 losses, and progress in southern England in such apparently unpromising terrain as Eastbourne. Labour's lead over the Tories in the Gallup Poll continued until August 1947. In November 1946, Morgan Phillips could legitimately claim that Labour was still 'on the offensive'.[2]

In the first year or so after the 1945 election, the Conservatives were still suffering from a kind of political shell-shock. It took a long while to recover from the trauma of the election. In parliament, the party offered little resistance to Labour's early measures, including its nationalization proposals. Churchill himself did not cut a very effective figure as Leader of the Opposition, especially when many of the early debates concerned technical, financial and economic matters in which he took little interest. He departed for a few months' vacation in America as early as December 1945, one result being the 'iron curtain' speech at Fulton, Missouri, in March 1946. When he returned, he was again an erratic Leader of the Opposition, liable to sudden, impetuous outbursts on Russia, India, or European unity which embarrassed his colleagues. Even at the time of the 1950 general election, Richard Law wrote to Beaverbrook that Churchill 'was hopeless as a leader of the opposition'.[3] Certainly, the extent to which Churchill was an electoral asset for his party must be open to some doubt, despite the semi-regal treatment he received in the press and on cinema newsreels. In working-class areas, he was sometimes received with the same glacial hostility of general strike days. Nor was Churchill effective in outlining the details of alternative Conservative policies. By May 1946 he had to rebut criticisms at the annual party conference and the council of the National Union at 'the supposed lack of Conservative policy'.[4] A privately-conducted poll in 1949 showed that the party would not

[2] *The Times*, 4 Nov. 1946.
[3] David Carlton, *Anthony Eden: a Biography* (London, 1981), p. 293.
[4] Minutes of the Executive Committee, National Union, 9 May 1946 (Conservative Central Office).

suffer if Churchill resigned as party leader.[5] The main burden of leading the Conservative attack fell on Anthony Eden. His relations with Churchill, dating from their different positions on foreign policy in the thirties, were always tense and awkward.[6] There were times, such as April 1946, when the gulf between the two men seemed almost unbridgeable. There were frequent speculations about Eden taking over the party leadership, for all his temperamental brittleness. Eden resented what he believed was Churchill's wilful, uncommunicative style as party leader, with intimates such as Lindemann counting for more than Eden himself; he attacked Churchill's hawkish outbursts on foreign affairs and his crude imperialism on India and Burma. At the top, then, the Opposition front bench was not a happy band of brothers. Other leading figures had fallen at the polls. Little initiative could be expected from such as John Anderson or Oliver Lyttelton to stem the sweeping tide of socialism. Lyttelton 'feared for his country' in the neo-revolutionary mood of August 1945, though he later calmed down.[7] Harold Macmillan somewhat increased the general distrust felt about his general stance as a front-bench spokesman. His maverick past reasserted itself in 1946 when he actually proposed changing the name of the Conservative Party, and flirted with possible ideas of coalition.[8] Not until he became Minister of Housing in 1951 did Macmillan build up a commanding reputation in Tory ranks. For the rest, the banner of opposition was held aloft most effectively by R. A. Butler on matters great and small, with help from Oliver Stanley, whose premature death in 1950 was a cruel blow. Otherwise, Conservative front-bench spokesmen were regularly outshone by their Labour counterparts in Commons debates, from the legalistic dialectic of Cripps, through the bombast of Dalton and the Cockney backchat of Morrison, to the rhetorical Welsh missiles launched by Bevan. To the general surprise, Attlee withstood Churchill's oratorical assaults with much ease.

In the country, the Conservative National Union and the

[5] Anthony Seldon, *Churchill's Indian Summer* (London, 1981), p. 39.

[6] Carlton, op. cit., *passim*.

[7] Lord Chandos, *Memoirs* (London, 1962), p. 329.

[8] *The Times*, 2 Sept. 1946, Macmillan proposed the alternative name, 'The New Democratic Party'.

local parties reverberated with criticisms of defunct organization and sagging morale. After the election, one victim was
the veteran party agent, Sir Robert Topping, who had to
resign. A new departure, however, came with the appointment of Lord Woolton as party chairman in July 1946, in
place of Ralph Assheton. While too much, no doubt, can be
made of Woolton's galvanizing effect on party organization,
there was certainly far more energy injected into Central
Office and the constituency parties thereafter. Party finance
was overhauled; the tally of trained, full-time agents rose
sharply; a membership drive sent party membership to well
over 2,200,000 by 1948.[9] A new stimulus came from a
committee on party organization set up under the chairmanship of the able Scots lawyer, Sir David Maxwell-Fyfe, which
produced an interim report in September 1948.[10] A useful
addition to Conservative strength, especially in Scotland,
came with the closer liaison with the Liberal Nationals, the
survivors of the Simonite split in 1931 who were renamed,
mysteriously, 'National Liberals' in 1948. This liaison was
achieved in the so-called Woolton–Teviot agreement of
October 1946, taking effect from 25 March 1947. Joint
associations would henceforth be set up in constituencies
where both parties were already in existence; the two parties
were merged in united opposition to the socialist enemy.[11]
By the end of 1948, the party undoubtedly showed more
vitality in the country, with Woolton placing the major
emphasis on a concentrated effort on two hundred marginal
constituencies, especially in suburban areas in the south-east
of England and the Midlands.

As regards Conservative policy, the party recognized its
own ideological vacuum after the election of 1945. In effect,
it made some attempt to emulate the methods of the Labour
Party, with its Labour Research Department, and the extra-
mural role of Gollancz books. In November 1945, the Conservatives set up an advisory committee on policy and political
education; C. J. M. Alport joined Central Office as head of

[9] J. D. Hoffman, *The Conservative Party in Opposition, 1945–51* (London,
1964).
[10] Lord Kilmuir, *Political Adventure* (London, 1964), pp. 157–9.
[11] Memorandum of conversation between Teviot, Mabane, and Woolton,
25 Oct. 1946; Woolton to Churchill, 26 Oct. 1946 (Woolton papers, Box 21).

the Political Education Department. Churchill also revived the old Research Department and appointed Butler as its head.[12] An important development in December 1946 was an unofficial Industrial Policy Committee, which included Butler, Stanley, Lyttelton, Macmillan, Maxwell-Fyfe, and some younger men. It produced the famous Industrial Charter of May 1947, offered to an enthusiastic party conference in Disraelian, 'one nation' terms. The Charter accepted the nationalization of the mines, railways, and Bank of England, and referred to new machinery for economic planning and the fixing of wages. There was also some talk of industrial copartnership. It was followed by an Agricultural Charter in June 1948 which broadly accepted the interventionism of Labour's 1947 Agriculture Act, with guaranteed price support for farmers. A mysteriously-entitled document, *The True Balance* (February 1948), dealt with women's questions. In 1948 also, Swinton College (the home of Lord Swinton, near Harrogate in Yorkshire) was opened as a centre for party political education; none had existed since the Bonar Law Memorial College at Ashridge before the war.[13] A revamped Research Department (merged with the secretariat) was also set up in November of that year. It enlisted such talented young men as Iain Macleod, Edward Heath, Reginald Maudling, and Enoch Powell. In later years, the Research Department, under Butler's tolerant patronage, became legendary as the symbol of the Conservatives' successful attempt to rethink and fight back.

Without doubt, the Conservative Party on the eve of the February 1950 general election was an infinitely more confident and lively body than it had been in 1947. Membership was going up fast; there was vigorous recruitment by the university Conservative Associations and by the party-throwing Young Conservatives, where attractive débutantes contrasted with the austere earnestness of the Labour League of Youth. Party conferences were aggressive, and fired by a firm belief that the next election would bring the Conservatives

[12] Percy Cohen, 'A History of the Conservative and Unionist Party Organisation' (unpublished MS, 1964), p. 448 ff; cf. John Ramsden, *The Making of Conservative Policy: the Conservative Research Department since 1929* (London, 1980).

[13] J. A. Cross, *Lord Swinton* (Oxford, 1982), ch. 7.

back to government, where they belonged. Many able young candidates were selected for 1950; apart from Heath, Macleod, Maudling, and Powell from the Research Department, there were Aubrey Jones, Lionel Heald, Christopher Soames, Robert Carr, and Pat Hornsby-Smith, all of whom won seats for the first time in 1950. The Industrial Charter seemed the centre-piece of a policy far more attuned to modern social and economic needs. And yet, it may be doubted how far this Conservative recovery was a complete one. The Industrial Charter was already much modified in the *Right Road for Britain*, published in 1949. The Charter played little part in the 1950 general election, less still in 1951; it and the Agricultural Charter were quietly buried thereafter. The organizational revival and the recovery of morale must be measured against repeated Conservative failures in key by-elections, even ones as promising as Gravesend in late 1947 or South Hammersmith in early 1949. Amongst the working-class electors, the party made little impact. In the years of Conservative government after 1951, the Tory revival of post-1945 had its legacy, notably in the emergence of men like Maudling, Heath, and Macleod to high office. The 'One Nation' group, formed in October 1950, was an important forum for new ideas. Up to 1951, however, the party remained in important respects lacking in initiative, out of touch with some new currents of social thought. Its hopes for beating Labour at the polls rested, as for all oppositions, on the government's mistakes or bad luck in economic policy. The Tory malaise after the 1945 general election was deep-seated. The party did not present, as yet, a convincing challenge for Labour or to the radical or leftward mood of the nation in the immediate post-war period.

The other political challenges to Labour can easily be dealt with. The Liberals were now in perilous, almost terminal, condition. They lost six of their remaining eighteen seats in 1945. Their leader, Sir Archibald Sinclair, fell at Caithness and Sutherland; their whip, Sir Percy Harris, lost their one remaining London seat at Bethnal Green; Sir William Beveridge himself was defeated at Berwick-on-Tweed. The Liberals, in fact, only numbered eleven, since Gwilym Lloyd George at Pembrokeshire stood as 'National Liberal and Conservative', and cut off all links with the Liberal parliamentary party. To confirm his drift to the right, he adopted the hyphenated form, Lloyd-George. He had always been the right-winger in the family: he had even served in Churchill's 'caretaker' Conservative government of May–July 1945. The remaining eleven Liberals bore a distinctly peripheral appearance. Six of them came from Wales, five in rural, mainly Welsh-speaking constituencies from Carmarthen to Anglesey, together with Professor W. J. Gruffydd, a Celtic scholar and poet who represented the University of Wales. The other five represented a handful of scattered rural areas, from Cornwall, through Dorset, across to Suffolk, up to Cumberland, and on to the Orkneys and Shetlands. One of the Welsh MPs, Clement Davies, had the thankless role of leading the parliamentary Liberal Party, in succession to Sinclair. In practice, the Liberals found the task of maintaining a credible middle position between socialism and Toryism almost impossible. Often the party seemed feeble and unable to decide its own intentions. An example was its voting for the second reading of the Trade Union Bill in April 1946—but then voting against the third reading, on the basis of very obscure logic from Clement Davies. The Liberals were to vote in conflicting ways on the second and third readings of several later bills. For some time, the party usually followed Labour members into the government lobbies. The Liberals voted for all the early nationalization programmes, for the National Health Service, for independence for India and Burma. But by 1948 there were complaints that the party was becoming obessionally anti-socialist and developing too close ties with the Conservatives. Clement Davies and Lady Violet Bonham-Carter were criticized for being unduly friendly with that old Liberal, Winston Churchill.[14] In Huddersfield West, there was by 1949 an effective pact between local Conservatives and Liberals to endorse the candidature of the Liberal, Donald Wade. In protest at these developments, three left-wing Liberal MPs, Lady Megan Lloyd George (Anglesey), Emrys Roberts (Merioneth), and Edgar Granville (Eye, Suffolk) all attacked Clement Davies for his right-wing stance; Dingle Foot warned against following the deviations of the 'Vichy Liberals'

[14] Material in Clement Davies papers, National Library of Wales, J3.

in the National Liberal Party.[15] Davies had to give repeated assurances that no merger between his party and the Tories was contemplated, and that he and his colleagues stood as Liberals 'without prefix or suffix'. But as the next general election approached, there were clear tensions in the party, as well as financial and organizational weaknesses. The outcome in February 1950 was Liberal representation falling to only nine, the Liberal share of the poll remaining at 9.1 per cent, and over three hundred lost deposits, which gave grist to the mill of music-hall comedians.

Throughout the post-1945 period, the Liberal tradition remained a vital element of British political and social culture. Much of the intellectual energy of the time came from Liberal luminaries such as Keynes and Beveridge. In the periodical press, in the universities, and the BBC, Liberals, often of pre-1914 vintage like Professor Gilbert Murray or Lord Samuel, still exercised powerful influence. There were the Liberal daily newspapers, the *Manchester Guardian* and the Fleet Street-based *News Chronicle* which tried, in their differing styles, to give heart to the faithful and to make sense of Liberal pretensions after 1945. Liberal commentators such as A. J. Cummings of the *News Chronicle*, operating from his eyrie in Bouverie House, Vernon Bartlett, the *Chronicle*'s diplomatic correspondent, or A. P. Wadsworth, editor of the *Manchester Guardian*, were respected figures. For all that, the party showed an accentuated picture of long-term decline, as it had done at least since the Lloyd George–Asquith split of 1916 (and even before that, in the opinions of historians who followed the diagnosis of the American-based George Dangerfield). If its 'strange death' had been visible prior to 1914, perhaps even in 1886, the party after 1945 offered a gloomy comment on the afterlife. Throughout the 1945–51 period, Liberals were always in danger of losing key figures to the big battalions of Conservatives or Labour. Gwilym Lloyd-George, as has been seen, was one defector. Liberal bankers and businessmen also tended to drift to the right in defence of free-market economics and in protest against the bureau-cratic menace of state socialism. So, too, did the distinguished

---

[15] Clement Davies to Lady Violet Bonham-Carter, 15 Nov. 1950 (Davies papers, J/3/45).

academic, Gilbert Murray, looking gloomily down on the state of Oxford and the world from the heights of Boars Hill. He voted Conservative in 1950 as did that old radical historian, Barbara Hammond, now equally defeatist, in 1951.[16] After the 1950 elections, four wealthy Liberal peers, Reading, Rennell of Rodd, Willingdon, and Cowdray, all joined the Conservative Party. Conversely, the Liberal MP for North Cornwall, Tom Horabin, had joined Labour in November 1947: he told Attlee that he was moved by the belief that another Tory government would be a disaster.[17] There were also persistent rumours that Lady Megan Lloyd George, the party's vice-chairman in 1949, would yield to persuasion from Morrison and Attlee and join Labour also.[18] She had always been firmly on the radical left, her father's true political heir. In fact, she remained Liberal until 1955. Her continuing rivalry with Lady Violet Bonham-Carter, echoing the ancestral split of 1916, helped to keep alive old Liberal divisions in Wales and elsewhere. Outside the House, Dingle Foot, Honor Balfour, and others of the Radical Action Group were thought ripe for a conversion to Labour; in time, Foot and Miss Balfour both took their famous names into the Labour camp. The overall impression was of the Liberals as a withering, somewhat impractical, third force. Party membership was static and somewhat elderly. Circulation of *Liberal News* was stationary at 30,000.[19] The party was still committed to ancient causes such as proportional representation, industrial copartnership, the rating or taxing of land values, and an unreconstructed Gladstonian view of free trade, while the real world moved on. Morgan Phillips could sleep comfortably at nights, even in relation to his native Wales, in the face of such challengers as these.

The Nationalist parties of Wales and Scotland were not a threat to Labour either. The efforts of Plaid Cymru in Wales

[16] Gilbert Murray to Clement Davies, 10 May 1950 (ibid., J/3/25i); Peter Clarke, *Liberals and Social Democrats* (Cambridge, 1978), pp. 283–90, describes Murray's extreme pessimism in his last years.

[17] T. L. Horabin to Attlee, 14 Nov. 1947 (Attlee papers, Bodleian, Box 9).

[18] *Manchester Guardian*, 13 Nov. 1948; material in Lady Megan Lloyd George papers, National Library of Wales, MSS 20475C and 20492A, notably Attlee to Megan Lloyd George, 1948–9.

[19] Lady Violet Bonham-Carter to Clement Davies, 9 May 1949 (Davies papers, J/3/6).

to make some impact on politics after the war, and to shed its reputation for a combination of linguistic nationalism, collaborationist pacifism, and neo-fascist Catholicism, bore some fruit. The youthful Gwynfor Evans made an impressive president of the party after 1945, following the aberrations of Saunders Lewis down to 1943. Plaid Cymru gained a vote of 20 per cent in a by-election in Aberdare in December 1946. Welsh Labour MPs and activists would cite the existence of Plaid Cymru as a cause for granting further recognition to Wales in the form of a Secretary of State, an elected council, or both, together with more vigorous policies to combat local unemployment.[20] But Plaid Cymru was a very small pressure group of mainly Welsh-speaking middle-class enthusiasts, strong in some schools and university departments of Welsh, and in eisteddfodic circles, weak among the working class in mining and other areas. In the 1950 general election, Plaid Cymru put up a mere seven candidates, all of whom lost their deposits. The nationalism of Wales was more widely diffused, for instance in a cross-party pressure group like *Undeb Cymru Fydd*, in the youth movement, *Urdd Gobaith Cymru*, and in the 'Parliament for Wales' movement launched in 1950 with some Labour and Liberal support. Similarly, in Scotland John McCormick's broad-based Covenant movement showed much more dynamism than did the Scottish Nationalist Party. The SNP lost its one MP, Dr McIntyre, in Motherwell in the 1945 election. Deposits were lost at Glasgow, Cathcart, at Kilmarnock and East Edinburgh in 1946, and Stirling in 1948. The SNP put up a mere three candidates in the 1950 election, all hopeless causes. Scotland and Wales were both overwhelmingly Labour territory; in areas like North and Central Wales and the Scottish Highlands, Labour was continuing to advance. The Nationalist challenge could at this stage easily be brushed aside.

Finally, the Communist Party remained the small, cantankerous splinter group it had been ever since its foundation in 1920. Two Communist MPs had been returned in 1945—

[20] Huw T. Edwards to Herbert Morrison, 27 Nov. 1946, and Edwards's open letter to Attlee and the Cabinet, 16 Dec. 1946 (National Library of Wales, Edwards papers).

Willie Gallacher in West Fife, and Phil Piratin, a newcomer, in Mile End. There were two Communist councillors elected to the LCC in the East End, in March 1946. At the start, the Communist strategy was to declare its warm support for Britain's experiment with socialism. On that basis, Gallacher and Piratin voted in favour of the US loan to Britain in December 1945. But by the end of 1946, the opposition of King Street and the *Daily Worker* to Labour's policies, especially to Bevin's anti-Soviet foreign policy, was total. The Communist Party now drifted into a phase of ultra-leftism in 1948, especially after the expulsion from membership of the Labour Party of Platts-Mills and others on the left fringe. The Communists seemed to be reverting to the old thesis of 'class against class' in their hostility towards the 'social fascists' of the Labour Party, from Attlee to Laski. A number of front organizations, such as the World Peace Committee's British section, sought to made inroads into left-wing Labour opinion, and to infiltrate Labour's youth section; the Communists now called for a new government of the left. In fact, the 1950 general election showed that the Communist Party, apart from local pockets of strength in London's East End, the Rhondda valleys, and Glasgow, was feeble in the extreme. All its 100 candidates were defeated, including Gallacher and Piratin. Ninety-seven lost their deposits. They could muster a mere 91,765 votes between them, 0.3 per cent of the total poll. Crypto-Communists such as Pritt in Hammersmith were similarly routed by Labour opponents. The *Daily Worker*'s readership slumped as did party membership and funds. From 45,435 officially claimed members in 1945, the total fell to 38,853 by May 1950. Five years of Labour government left British Communism more enfeebled and sectarian than ever. In the 1951 general election, they put up only ten candidates. More hopeful was Communist infiltration into major trade unions, including the dockers, the Welsh and Scottish miners, and the electrical workers. The main officers of the Electrical Trades Union were all Communists, headed by Frank Foulkes and Frank Haxell. There were eight Communists on the thirty-eight man Transport and General Workers executive body in 1948, including Bert Papworth. District committees of the

Amalgamated Engineering Union also had strong Communist representation. By 1949, Communist activity in the unions was causing the government, especially the Attorney-General, Hartley Shawcross, enough concern for them to consider prosecutions under the criminal law.[21] The Communist presence in these unions was undoubtedly of some significance, but largely because of specific circumstances in particular industries, local traditions in areas such as South Wales, or the organizational talents of men such as Jack Dash in London's dockland and Will Paynter and Will Whitehead in the Welsh mining valleys. The Communist Party itself did not benefit thereby. A senior Communist such as Arthur Horner, secretary of the NUM until 1960, derived his prestige as an industrial statesman, not as a party politician. So the Communist cause languished in Labour-run Britain, even while it flourished in the different circumstances of France and Italy, where the Social Democrats were divided and declining. On the far left, as on the far right, in the Liberal centre and the Nationalist fringe, Labour seemed able to repel all boarders.

In general, the mood of 1945 was perpetuated for some time to come. An intellectual and cultural climate continued that was sympathetic to the outlook of the Labour Party. The wartime period had emphasized the priorities of equality, social cohesion, the breaking down of old time-worn class barriers. George Orwell regarded the integration of the classes and the masses on the home front as the precursor of the socialist Commonwealth. Hitler and the blitz would achieve changes in society which had eluded all the efforts of Keir Hardie and earlier socialist pioneers. 'The blitz made comrades of us all', wrote the *New Statesman* nostalgically in 1950.[22] After the war, especially down to the end of 1946, Labour ministers made much of recalling this ethic of wartime sacrifice. The very idea of 'fair shares', Labour's master concept in 1945–50, exalted the virtues of common sacrifice

[21] Minutes of Cabinet Emergencies Committee, 12 Apr. 1949 (CAB 134/176); Shawcross to A. R. Harrison, 12 Dec. 1949 (LAB 16/97). For Communist Party membership, see Henry Pelling, *The British Communist Party* (London, 1958), appendix A, pp. 192–3.

[22] *New Statesman*, 16 Sept. 1950.

and communal effort, as opposed to private gain or selfish, commercial exploitation. As in the war years, the people would 'all pull through together'. A corollary was that this collective endeavour would be channelled by the central government, through powerful and revitalized local authorities, and a variety of public bodies and quasi-governmental institutions dealing with matters as diverse as regional economic development, the planning of new towns, or the promotion of the arts. The planners were in the ascendant, the new conquerors of mankind. The impress of strong government would force the notoriously individualist English (and the even more notoriously volatile Welsh and Scots) into a common mould. Whitehall, the civil service, the machinery of Fabian-style planning and control became exalted. In a famous phrase in Douglas Jay's first edition of *The Socialist Case* the gentleman from Whitehall knew best; he was the new Machiavelli or new Metternich of the age. It was noticeable, indeed, that Jay's second edition, published in 1947 with an approving foreword by Attlee, repeated this damaging phrase (p. 258). But it added a firm chapter at the close about the 'limits' to planning and the transcendent values of human freedom with much more force than in the 1937 version.

The mood that the government sought to foster was one of moral earnestness, almost Victorian in its intensity. Obedience to controls was publicly proclaimed as necessary to promote social welfare, full employment, and economic recovery. The new concentration on exports was given a moral aura. Further, its obverse—laziness, frivolity, 'go-slow' obstructionism, attempts to circumvent planning, controls, and rationing through the 'black market' or through mediators such as the 'spivs' of post-war folklore—were condemned with Savonarolan passion by government ministers. Not for nothing did Nicholas Davenport see this as a puritan régime of Cromwellian austerity prior to the restoration of the Churchillian Cavaliers.[23] The government now added to the roll of civil and criminal offences the notion of a 'social crime', as Hugh Gaitskell proclaimed when urging citizens to observe the regulations on petrol rationing. Evading the law on petrol supplies was social sabotage and, therefore, immoral.

[23] Davenport, *Memoirs of a City Radical*, pp. 80 ff.

A government, however, which made much of duty, moral earnestness, and respectability, embodied in the prim, puritanical form of Attlee himself, had to ensure that it, too, like Caesar's wife, was above reproach. When in 1948 rumours flew around that government ministers had been engaged in corrupt transactions with business intermediaries, receiving gifts in return for favours on governmental licences and contracts, the Cabinet reacted sternly. With rumours of another Teapot Dome or Stavisky scandal circulating in the press, the stern figure of Mr Justice Lynskey was appointed to head an investigating tribunal, with two senior barristers to assist him. This proved to be a fierce public inquisition.[24] It found its one public scapegoat in the pathetic figure of John Belcher, a former railway clerk and a junior minister at the Board of Trade. The one Labour man appointed to the directorate of the Bank of England, George Gibson, a former chairman of the TUC, also resigned as a result of the Lynskey inquiry. The fact that the main businessman involved, Sidney Stanley (originally Solomon Kohsyzcky, and later Schlomo Rechtand), was a Polish Jew who fled to Israel to escape British justice, helped to fan a mild populist anti-Semitism, already partly stirred up by events in Palestine. The Lynskey tribunal revealed only the most minor of scandals in high places, certainly nothing comparable with the Poulson affair of a later generation. The worst that emerged was that Belcher had been friendly with Stanley and had dropped a prosecution against the head of Sherman's football pools— another Jew as it happened. Compared with the Lynskey revelations, the Lloyd George era of 1918–22 seemed lurid in the extreme. Other ministers mentioned in the case, Hugh Dalton and Charles Key, Minister of Works, were able to exculpate themselves, though not without some slight difficulty in the case of Key. What is notable is the severity of the government's reactions. The Attorney-General, Shawcross, interrogated Belcher and his hapless wife with the unbridled ferocity he had previously reserved for Goering and Ribbentrop at Nuremberg. The Lynskey affair enabled the

---

[24] For the Lynskey Tribunal, see John Gross's chapter in M. Sissons and P. French (ed.), *Age of Austerity, 1945–1951* (Penguin edn., 1964), pp. 266–86, and H. T. F. Rhodes, *The Lynskey Tribunal* (London, 1949).

government to preserve its white sheet, to continue as the unassailable, if somewhat dull, apostle of public virtue and social morality. The congruence between the Attlee government and what were believed to be the intrinsic psychological and ethical components of the post-war mood, continued undisturbed. In the conventional sense, post-1945 Britain was not an especially religious nation. The Protestant churches, Anglican and more especially nonconformist, all felt the pressure of falling numbers and of secular challenges. The Church of England mourned the early death of Archbishop William Temple, a known Labour supporter. The Roman Catholics still rested largely on their Irish clientele in the big cities. The pronouncements of Archbishop Fisher and other Church dignitaries no longer attracted the awed submissiveness that had greeted Davidson or Cosmo Lang in the past. Even the drab Sabbath of Wales and Scotland was under some threat, with pressure for opening cinemas in Wales and golf-courses in Scotland. In this serious, if somewhat baffled, age, the moral religion preached by the government and its unimpeachable public servants, supplied the substitute secular gospel for which the people craved, or so it was fondly believed.

The extent to which the social changes of the post-1945 period fortified this post-war mood and assisted the long-term stability of the Labour government was much debated by party strategists in the 1945–51 period, and has been examined in minute detail by sociologists and psephologists ever since. It was generally acknowledged that British society had undergone a massive transformation during the war years, with the movement of the population into the armed services, into skilled work in factories, into coal-mines as 'Bevin boys' and in the countryside as 'land girls', and through the upheaval of the evacuation or emigration of school-children. Families had been split up; cherished landmarks had been uprooted. The stimulus of war to the economy had brought new life and full employment to the old depressed areas of Wales, Scotland, and the north. The post-war reconstruction, so Labour's planners believed, would not only ensure an enduring economic recovery; it would provide an indestructible social and generational platform for the permanent political ascendancy of the people's party. Toryism had died at Tobruk. Labour analysts pointed out their party's advance in most types of constituency and region. Instead of being based on old homogenous working-class communities such as mining villages, cotton towns, steel-making and pottery districts, working-class areas in the poorer parts of London, Manchester, and Glasgow, Labour could claim a national base. It had shown the capacity for growth in centres of light industry in the south-east and the Midlands, in suburban or commuter territory around great cities, in a range of rural areas from East Anglia to north-west Wales. Only the major agricultural counties of southern England, the west country and the Scottish Lowlands, and such centres of traditionalism as cathedral cities, market towns, spas, watering-places, and seaside resorts remained impervious to Labour's onward march. The economic drive launched by the government, notably through Cripps's regional policies at the Board of Trade, would, it was believed, ensure permanence for this new tide, and make Labour the natural majority governing party. After all, by the usual criteria, working-class people numbered something between two-thirds and three-quarters of the population.

Without doubt, the social changes in Britain between 1945 and 1951 did, in considerable measure, perpetuate the war-time transformation and take it further. But the extent to which the effects were necessarily favourable to the Labour cause was open to doubt. A close analysis of the social changes in the 1945–51 period is not possible, since no census was taken in 1941, and the comparison with 1931 is inevitably tenuous. The 1951 census, however, did confirm the wartime drift away from the centres of major cities, especially in the case of London and Liverpool, and also away from older industrial regions such as mining areas. This was spectacular in such places as Merthyr Tydfil and the Rhondda in South Wales, or the mining belt in Lanarkshire in Scotland. The growth of the suburbs, or of fringe communities on the edge of inner-city areas, such as Islington in north London, went on apace. By 1951, with the post-war housing drive and the new demand for service workers, skilled technicians, and minor civil servants, areas like Ruislip and Hayes and Harlington in Middlesex, Chigwell and Chingford in Essex, Chislehurst and Bexley in Kent, all had an explosive growth in their populations.[25] Every one of these areas was to emerge as a Conservative stronghold at general elections from February 1950 onwards: Churchill himself sat for Woodford in Essex. Not until 1964 did Labour show signs of winning back these suburban or domitory constituencies. In the inner-city working-class core, there were immense rehousing programmes in London, Birmingham, Cardiff, Liverpool, Manchester, Sheffield, Leeds, Newcastle, Edinburgh, Glasgow, and Dundee. Some of this could breed criticism elsewhere: the *New Statesman* discussed the resentment among skilled workers, in centres of light engineering and cheap housing in the Midlands and Greater London, at the excessive concentration of industrial effort and social investment in Teesside, Tyneside, Cumbria, Scotland, and South Wales.[26] The working-class character of these new housing estates, often accompanied by high-rise flat developments, was not in doubt. But the break-up of old, intimate, face-to-face communities often meant social dislocation, some disorder among the uprooted young, and by the mid-fifties a lessened commitment to an instinctive loyalty to the Labour Party. Even in solid mining areas such as Durham, Lanarkshire, and South Wales, there were signs of shifting values. Workers here often commuted long distances to work in engineering or other factories. The mining villages themselves, half-deserted in the daytime, lost some of their vitality. Working-class clubs, the world of the WEA and of close-knit community life began to lose some of their automatic adherence. Instead, there emerged a kind of shallow proletarian capitalism, based on the pub and the club, with the community noisily alive only in the evenings and on weekends. The rapid growth of working-class gambling after 1945, of massive spending on drink and tobacco, on the football pools

---

[25] *Census 1951: England and Wales. Preliminary Report*, p. xxi. The census went on to note that administrators, directors, and managers (406,190 in all) had risen by 15 per cent since 1931; schoolteachers (301,679) by 15 per cent; clerks, typists, and other administrative staff of all categories had risen to 2,132,135, of whom 60 per cent were female.

[26] *New Statesman*, 10 May 1947.

or horse- or dog-racing, products of the rising level of incomes and disposable savings in the Dalton and even the Cripps era, aided this movement away from more traditional working-class patterns of leisure. The Wigan of which George Orwell had written (in somewhat ambiguous terms) in the thirties was, after 1945, much more thriving with its people hard at full-time work, but also less integrated, and perhaps less attractive and alive.

Labour felt sure that people in major urban areas in large measure retained the simple, communal values that had sustained the party during the bad years in the thirties. But the diffusion of working-class people out from older ghetto communities into housing estates in new parts of suburban areas or the surrounding countryside might be taken as a solvent of older class-based political and social assumptions. An appeal to working-class loyalties could be combined with older aspirations such as the desire for domestic privacy and personal respectability, which the traditional semi-detached form of Bevan's post-war council estates, complete with three bedrooms, upstairs bathroom, and inside lavatory, helped to confirm. Again, industrial regions in the north, the north-east, Scotland, and Wales showed a far broader base of operations, with activity centred on converted wartime ordnance factories, on expanded trading estates, and on the introduction from 1946 onwards of new diversified, technologically advanced industries. Chemicals, rubber, electrical equipment, to a growing degree, car manufacture and its components, brought a new industrial revolution here, less painful than the first.[27] In old, once crucified, depressed localities, the population would be retained, the fabric of community and social life would be revitalized, and traditional Labour strongholds from Llanelli to Bishop Auckland kept in good repair. Full employment was a political, as well as a social imperative. A notable feature, too, was the increasing importance of female employment in new factories, as women workers built on the changes of the war years to secure more independent and interesting lives. But what tended to occur in many areas, as shown in an academic study of Banbury in

[27] See, for instance, Graham Humphrys, *Industrial Britain: South Wales* (Newton Abbot, 1972), for one area.

north Oxfordshire,[28] was rather a greater complexity of the social structure with the traditional three-tier social structure somewhat looser, and a new cadre of skilled workers emerging, hard to locate either in the working- or the middle-class world. Mark Abrams, writing about the late fifties, was to emphasize such long-term changes after 1945 as the growth of white-collar workers and the growth of the distributive and service trades at the expense of older manufacturing or extractive industry.[29] Another social imponderable was the impact of the new towns foreshadowed in Lewis Silkin's New Towns Act of 1946 which set up development corporations. In the course of the next ten years, overspill population from London was to migrate to the anonymous domain of Basildon, Bracknell, Hemel Hempstead, Hatfield, Stevenage, Harlow, and Crawley, with further movement to the older 'new town' of Welwyn Garden City. Large areas of Hertfordshire and Essex were beginning to lose their rural character for ever. In South Wales, there was to be Cwmbran in Monmouthshire; in the north-east, there was Peterlee and in Scotland, East Kilbride, Glenrothes, and Cumbernauld. All of these lay in the future when Labour fell from power at the end of 1951. But the very concept confirmed a loosening of older loyalties and political commitment as working-class families moved into new housing estates, a fresh environment, and new patterns of leisure and recreation.

In one important section of society, one much affected by wartime change, the political advantages for the Labour Party proved to be extremely limited. The countryside had dramatically revived after 1939, following the lean years of the thirties. This was partly a product, of course, of the massive emphasis on self-sufficiency in food production and modernized agricultural technology during the war. It was also a delayed response to the price supports for the farmers launched in the thirties, especially the Milk Marketing Board of 1933 which had much revived upland dairy farming, and other boards for eggs, bacon, and potatoes. These last were in embryo the work of the second Labour government in

---

[28] Margaret Stacey, *Tradition and Change: a study of Banbury* (London, 1960).
[29] Mark Abrams, 'Social Trends and Electoral Behaviour', *British Journal of Sociology* vol. xiii (1962), pp. 228–42.

1930-1 and of Christopher Addison, the Minister of Agriculture then, and now, of course, a prominent member of Attlee's government; but it is very doubtful how far the farmers gave Labour the credit. After the war, the urgent need to protect the balance of payments, to cut down food imports from the dollar areas, and to maximize agricultural and horticultural productivity led Labour to give a quite new emphasis on agriculture. Tom Williams, an elderly ex-miner from Yorkshire, who served as Minister of Agriculture from 1945 to 1951, presided over a dramatic improvement in agricultural conditions; they gave British farmers a degree of security and, in time, prosperity unknown since the golden age of high farming in the mid-nineteenth century. These changes chimed in with a renewed cult of the countryside noticeable in Britain after 1945, variously popularized in the broadcasts of Ralph Wightman; the radio play serial, *The Archers* (first transmitted in the Midland region in Whit week, 1950); the success of magazines like *The Countryman*; and the writings of A. G. Street. Urban Britons paid obeisance to the pastoral dream, as they had done throughout the industrial period of their history. Tom Williams's Agriculture Act of 1947 (helped through Cabinet by the advice and memories of Addison, hindered by criticism from A. V. Alexander, the Co-operative leader) was a dramatically effective measure. As Williams himself proudly claimed in the 1950 election, farmers had benefited from the guaranteed price and the annual price review, while guaranteed markets had absorbed agriculture into an effective system of economic planning. Farmers could be given production targets, while price guarantees ensured that they could invest with confidence in expensive plant and agricultural improvements. They would have assured markets, so Peter Self calculated, for about three-quarters of their produce. Instead of anxiety about the market, or the kind of long-term disaster as had occurred after the repeal of the Corn Production Act after the first world war in 1921, farmers could now concentrate on efficient methods of production.[30] The National Farmers'

---

[30] Lord Williams of Barnbrugh, *Digging for Britain* (London, 1954), pp. 155 ff.; *How the Labour Party has saved Agriculture* (Labour Party publications, 1951); Peter Self, 'A Policy for Agriculture', *Political Quarterly* vol. xix, No. 2 (Apr.–June 1948), pp. 138 ff.

Union had become another indirect agent for governmental planning. At the same time, tenant farmers received security of tenure, while the consumer was protected through the operation of food subsidies and the redistributive effects of deficiency payments.

Throughout the land, from the wheat fields of East Anglia, through the horticultural stronghold of the Vale of Evesham, and the hop fields of Herefordshire, to the hill farms of rural Wales, Cumberland, and the Scottish Highlands, farmers after 1945 experienced a growing prosperity, while improvements in water, electricity, and gas services, and in public and leisure amenities enormously enhanced the quality of rural life. So, too, did the provision of rural bus services contained in the 1947 Transport Act, although farmers also found that they could now afford private cars, often large ones. By 1950, indeed, there were criticisms that Labour's generosity to the farmers as a class was excessive, and that its relationship to a conservative pressure group such as the National Farmers' Union was too close. A Labour junior minister, Stanley Evans, member for Wednesbury in the 'black country' of the west Midlands, complained, in a memorable phrase, that farmers were being 'feather-bedded' at the taxpayers' expense. Williams rebutted the charge, and Evans duly lost his job at the Ministry of Food. But the new prosperity of the agricultural community, however evaluated, was beyond dispute. In spite of all this, it is clear that the voting inclinations of rural areas did not greatly change from their traditional conservatism. The English shires from Devon to north Yorkshire remained committed to ancient forms of political and social deference; the 'knights of the shire' were still a reality in Tory circles. Labour's only seat in the Scottish Highlands was the unusual case of the Western Isles, where Maurice Macmillan, as a native of Stornoway, enjoyed a strong personal following among the crofters. In rural Wales, Labour continued to make some headway after 1945. In time, Anglesey, Merioneth, and Pembrokeshire were to turn Labour in 1950-1, with Carmarthen following on in 1957. Conway was also, briefly, a Labour seat in 1950-1. But these advances owed something to the growth of new industries around the ports of Anglesey, the oil refineries of

Pembrokeshire, and in the quarrying heartland of Snowdonia. Welsh hill farmers still viewed the London-based (or Cardiff-based) Labour Party with suspicion. A special case was East Anglia, more especially Norfolk, four of whose county seats went Labour in 1945. The Farm Labourers' Union was very active here; indeed, pressure from sugar-beet workers was one factor in inserting the nationalization of sugar-refining on the 1950 party manifesto. But Labour won only three out of six county seats in Norfolk in 1950 (along with two seats in Norwich), only two in Suffolk, none at all in Huntingdonshire and Cambridgeshire, and only one county seat (Brigg) out of seven in Lincolnshire. In that election also, Labour's vote fell below 30 per cent in the Highlands, the Scottish Lowlands, Devon, Cornwall, and Sussex. The farmers' gratitude to Labour for their new prosperity was barely detectable in these returns. Labour's basic weakness in rural Britain continued—though admittedly a rural Britain whose population was in long-term decline and thus of lessened political significance.

Somewhat different results came for Labour in the two Celtic nations of Scotland and Wales. As has been seen already, the Nationalist parties in each, the SNP and Plaid Cymru, were small and struggling after 1945. The demand for independence, or for soverign dominion status within the Commonwealth, was as feeble now as throughout the inter-war years. Not since the Speaker's conference in 1919–20 had there been a serious plan for Scottish and Welsh home rule; there was no sequel now after another world war. Nevertheless, demands in both nations for further recognition or the redefinition of their political identities and nationhood were a continuing factor, and recognized as such from Attlee downwards. Attlee's own instincts, like those of Morrison, Cripps, and almost all his colleagues, were sternly centralist. Proposals for Scottish or Welsh devolution, even if only administrative, were thought to conflict with efficient socialist planning. In Transport House, Morgan Phillips viewed with reluctance any devolutionist demands coming either from his native Wales, or the Scots, while even pressure for greater recognition within the party structure for the Welsh and Scottish Labour Parties made limited headway.

Nevertheless, the relations between Wales and Scotland, and their dominant English neighbour, could not remain static. There were in fact some changes after 1945 which had important long-term consequences for the United Kingdom.

In Scotland, a massive impact had been made by Tom Johnston, the Secretary of State during the war years, who had now left to head the hydro-electric board.[31] But the impetus was not kept up after 1945. The Scottish Economic Committee newly set up lost its semi-autonomy, and in any case was a relatively feeble instrument. The Scottish economy as a whole showed only modest signs of growth after 1945, in marked contrast with the eventual economic transformation of South Wales. The main areas of expansion were evident not in manufacturing but in the service sector, in transport and distribution, in business and commerce, and in local government. Sir Alec Cairncross was to conclude in 1954 that 'the picture that emerges is one of an industrial economy that shows signs of lagging behind the rest of the country'.[32] In terms of manufacturing output, income per head, employment statistics, or social provision such as housing, Scotland lagged behind England. Its economy was still unduly dependent on the metal and engineering trades. Many of the upland rural areas were dormant economically, while even the coal industry, in Lanarkshire at least though not in Fifeshire or the Lothians, showed signs of contraction. A significant statistical commentary on Labour rule was that Scotland experienced a net loss of 177,000 people from the start of 1946 to the end of 1951. Of these, 97,000 migrated overseas, while another 79,000 went south of the border.[33] The migration was especially heavy among young adults. On the credit side, hydro-electrical development did arrest some of the age-long decline of the Highlands, while the rich pastures of the border country in the south prospered, both in arable and dairy farming. Edinburgh, with its arts festival inaugurated in 1947, continued to thrive as a cultural centre.

The Scottish Secretary of State in 1945, Joseph Westwood, an ex-miner, was perhaps the least impressive member of the

---

[31] Tom Johnston, *Memories* (London, 1952), pp. 147 ff.
[32] A. K. Cairncross (ed.), *The Scottish Economy* (Cambridge, 1954), p. 1.
[33] Ibid., p. 17.

Attlee Cabinet. His successor in the autumn of 1947, Arthur Woodburn, a former lecturer in economics, was a more effective minister, although as sternly centralist as his predecessor. Hector McNeil, the Secretary of State in 1950–1, was more positive still. Some minimal concessions were made by them to Nationalist pressure, including the powers given to the Scottish Grand Committee to deliberate on Scottish legislation, and to discuss the Scottish estimates. A new Scottish Economic Conference, chaired by Woodburn himself, was approved by the Cabinet on 11 December 1947, with the rider that it was important to resist the idea of any such body for Wales.[34] It excited little enthusiasm in Scotland. Despite Woodburn's efforts to deprecate its importance, pressure on the government for further national recognition of Scotland mounted. It focused not on the minute SNP but on the broad-based Covenant movement, headed by the charismatic figure of John MacCormick in 1947 after he had left the SNP. Its demands for Scottish home rule were supported by prominent personalities such as Naomi Mitchison and Sir John Boyd Orr. By 1950, the Covenant had attracted well over a million signatures. The government, however, brushed it aside. It offered no new initiatives other than increasing the already large number of civil servants in the Scottish Office in Edinburgh.[35] The Covenant reached a dramatic, or perhaps farcical, climax with the theft from Westminster Abbey on Christmas Day, 1950 of the Ancient Stone of Scone, a relic from the fourteenth century of symbolic significance. The 'stone of destiny' later turned up in Arbroath. Labour spokesmen tended to treat all this with some contempt, and it cannot be claimed that the Covenant movement damaged the party at the polls. Labour won 37 out of 71 Scottish seats in 1950, and 35 in 1951. Even so, the party's unresponsive attitude towards the aspirations of at least some Scottish men and women remained very much unfinished business in October 1951.

Welsh national feeling had more ground to make up. There was no Welsh Secretary of State, while the very concept of

---

[34] Cabinet Conclusions, 11 Dec. 1947 (CAB 128/13).
[35] See correspondence between Attlee, Hector McNeil, and John MacCormick, 1950–1 in PREM 8/1517.

Wales as a separate political entity had made scant progress
since the disestablishment of the Welsh Church in 1920. In
Wales, as in Scotland, Labour set itself up as the champion
of centralism. In Cabinet in 1946, this view was upheld by
Morrison in resisting a demand by James Griffiths, the
Minister of National Insurance and the effective voice for
Welsh aspirations in the government, for Wales to be made
a separate region under the nationalization of electricity.[36]
In fact, Welsh electricity supply was divided between one
board for South Wales and another that covered Merseyside
as well as North Wales (MANWEB). The nationalization
programme made few concessions to Welsh demands for
recognition: even the South Wales coal-mines appeared
in the 'South West division' under the NCB, to include a
few minor operations in Somerset. In a Cabinet paper of
January 1946, Morrison argued strongly against a Welsh
Secretary of State being created. This was partly on the
grounds that Wales allegedly 'could not carry a cadre of
officials of the highest calibre' and that 'the services of
high English officials would no longer be available'. The
remedy for Wales, as for Scotland, was to be made part
of a national economic plan, rather than being 'thrown
back on their own sectional resources'. Even the modest
idea of a Welsh permanent Advisory Council was rejected.
'It is difficult to devise a plan by which such a Council
would not become either a dead letter or a dilatory
nuisance.'[37] Attlee and Morrison rebuffed, in the course of
1946, demands by Welsh Labour MPs for a Secretary of
State. Attlee noted that 'the members adduced the usual
arguments as to nationalist aspirations etc. They also stressed
the economic difficulties which add fuel to the nationalist
fire at the present time'. D. R. Grenfell and W. H. Mainwaring, the spokesmen for the Welsh MPs, complained to
Attlee that the government seemed to 'repudiate entirely
the claims of Wales as a nation'.[38] It was also being dilatory

---

[36] 'A note on the Electricity Bill', 17 Dec. 1946, by J. Griffiths, CP (46) 21
(CAB 129/6).

[37] 'The Administration of Wales and Monmouthshire', 27 Jan. 1946, by
Herbert Morrison, CP (46) 21 (CAB 129/6).

[38] Correspondence between Attlee, and Grenfell and Mainwaring, 1946
(PREM 8/1569); also Labour Party archives, GS 9/2.

in dealing with rising unemployment in the valleys. In return, all the government would offer was some further co-ordination between civil servants in the regional offices in Wales that were distributed in different government departments. Also, some Welsh members would be added to the Cabinet Committee on the Machinery of Government, notably Bevan, Griffiths, Ness Edwards, and Hilary Marquand.[39] Of these last, Bevan was as implacable an opponent of any concession to Welsh separatism as he had been in the first 'Welsh Day' debate in the House in 1944. Morrison chose to reflect on the invention of some kind of Welsh coat of arms 'as a douceur to Welsh national sentiment', and consulted the Garter King of Arms on this grave issue. The government's whole response to Welsh demands, wrote *The Economist*, was 'disappointing'.[40] In the *New Statesman*, Kingsley Martin sharply attacked the government's negative attitude on Welsh questions. The party manifesto in 1945 had listed five main suggestions—a Secretary of State, a separate Welsh Broadcasting Corporation, an end to the forced transfer of labour from Wales, a new north-south trunk road to link up the principality, and a central body to plan the Welsh economy. 'All five have now been turned down in Westminister.'[41]

But Welsh national sentiment, like Scottish, could not be brushed aside so easily in London. Progress continued on various fronts. An annual Welsh white paper was published for the first time in October 1946, a compendious document that brought together the work of a variety of departments. It would direct attention to economic problems 'and away from vague talk on constitutional issues', said Morrison. The Labour Party itself made the striking concession in February 1947 of a Welsh Council of Labour, with Cliff Prothero as its first secretary; it merged the South Wales Council, formed in 1937 to combat Communist influence in the valleys, with a number of small branches in North Wales.[42] In 1948, there

[39] Attlee to Griffiths, 28 Mar. 1946 (ibid.).
[40] Morrison to Attlee, 24 Jan. 1946 (ibid.); *The Economist*, 2 Nov. 1946.
[41] *New Statesman*, 24 Aug. 1946. It was using, as a basis, the Welsh Labour Party's publication, *Llais Llafur*.
[42] Minutes of Lord President's Committee, 11 Oct. 1946 (CAB 132/1); Cliff Prothero, *Recount* (Ormskirk, 1982), pp. 61–3.

was further discussion in the Cabinet Home Services Committee of the idea of a Welsh Secretary of State. Morrison and Bevan again flatly opposed it. This time, however, they were led to propose an advisory council, drawn from both sides of industry. On Griffiths's suggestion, the powerful North Wales trade-union leader, Huw T. Edwards of the TGWU—a man strongly national, if not yet nationalist, in outlook—became its first chairman in 1949. The Council for Wales was always a somewhat feeble body. Morrison had vetoed the idea that a government minister might preside over its meetings. 'The difficulties which would arise between the Chairman and other Cabinet ministers would strengthen the demand for a Secretary of State for Wales.'[43] Griffiths was forced to commend to the House of Commons a council whose weak powers went largely against the thrust of his own wishes. Indeed, the Council of Wales was to prove for much of its lifetime (1949–66) something of the 'dead letter' that Morrison had envisaged, especially after Huw T. Edwards resigned its chairmanship in the late fifties following repeated jousts with Henry Brooke. Even so, the Council was a landmark in its way. Its inaugural meeting at Cardiff in May 1949, attended by Morrison for the government, had a sense of occasion. Those present included the almost nonagenarian preacher-poet 'Elfed' (H. Elvet Lewis), a nationalist from the *Cymru Fydd* (Young Wales) era two generations back. The Council for Wales soon focused public attention on unemployment, transport, and other crucial issues.[44] However, it could not suppress demands for more extensive national recognition. In 1950, the 'Parliament for Wales' campaign, *Ymgyrch Senedd i Gymru*, launched by *Undeb Cymru Fydd* much on the lines of the Scottish Convention movement, won support of five Labour MPs (one being the Merthyr Marxist, S. O. Davies), and gained for a time considerable public sympathy. In Wales, as in Scotland, Labour was to find that bounds could not easily be set to the march of a nation. However, with leading figures in its ranks like James

[43] 'The Administration of Wales and Monmouthshire', Oct. 1948, CP (48) 228 (CAB 129/30); Cabinet Conclusions, 15 Oct., 18 Nov. 1948 (CAB 128/13); correspondence between Morrison and Griffiths, Oct. 1948 (National Library of Wales, Griffiths papers C/2/6–11).
[44] Material in Huw T. Edwards papers.

Griffiths, and younger nationally-minded MPs such as Goronwy Roberts (Caernarfon), Labour could show a sensitivity in Wales, including on the question of the native language, that was less apparent in Scotland. The progress made in rural Wales by Labour in the general elections of 1950 and 1951, with patriotic MPs returned such as Roberts in Caernarfon, T. W. Jones in Merioneth, and Cledwyn Hughes in Anglesey, suggests that here Labour progressed, not so much on the basis of class as by being able to identify more effectively than before with the radical, cultural, and national aspirations of the Welsh people.

Throughout these post-war years, the class divide in Britain remained as pronounced as ever. George Orwell informed the American readers of *Partisan Review* of how little changed was the surface of British life, including the monarchy and the public schools, during the years of Labour rule. Social surveys revealed that the broad three-tier class system survived in ample measure, and that most citizens had little hesitation in placing themselves in one or other category.[45] Working-class life changed in its residential and cultural patterns, as has been noted, but it offered more material rewards than in the pre-war years of depression. Traditional entertainments flourished as never before. Mass spectator sport was never more thriving than after 1945. Football stadiums like Ibrox, Anfield, Villa Park, and Highbury regularly attracted over 60,000 spectators to home fixtures, crowds which were infinitely more peaceful than the much smaller attendances of the 1970s and 1980s. Violence at football matches was virtually unknown off the field, or on it (where the authority of the referee remained sacrosanct). Football proved to be one way of invigorating local folk culture; the success of forwards such as Len Shackleton of Sunderland and Jackie Milburn of Newcastle United rekindled the local pride of the 'Geordies' of the north-east, with their battle hymn, the 'Blaydon Races'. Cricket also flourished with huge crowds

[45] *Partisan Review*, May 1946, reprinted in Sonia Orwell and Ian Angus (eds.), *Collected Essays, Journalism and Letters of George Orwell*, vol. iv, 1945–50 (Penguin rev. edn., Harmondsworth, 1981), pp. 219–25. Also see F. M. Martin, 'Some Subjective Aspects of Social Stratification' in D. V. Glass (ed.), *Social Mobility in Britain* (1954).

flocking to see the batting exploits of Denis Compton and Bill Edrich in the golden summer of 1947, or to the triumphs of the visiting Australian team, under the legendary Don Bradman, a year later. Test matches, Wimbledon, the Derby, Cup Finals, had immense popular appeal, the more so with the publicity afforded on the radio, and increasingly from 1948 onwards on television as well. In Wales, rugby recaptured its pre-war glory, with the 'Triple Crown' success of 1950 suggesting another golden age. This flourishing of sport arose in part because of high levels of personal surplus income, as has been noted, with larger pay packets attracting resources that might otherwise have been used for public investment. In part, it arose because of the lack of other consumer choices. Sport, the cinema, the dance hall, flourished in a nation longing for an emancipation from wartime gloom and post-war austerity. They also appealed to a population which did not, in the main, possess a car, and could turn to only limited petrol supplies if it did. With rigid exchange controls, holidays abroad were very much a minority cult; only 3 per cent went overseas on holiday in 1947, contrasted with 43.7 per cent who took no holiday at all.[46] On the other hand, holidays in Britain, still largely based on the traditional seaside boarding-house, showed some inventiveness. The holiday camps were first pioneered by Billy Butlin, just before the war, in holiday resorts from Skegness to Pwllheli. They offered cheap package holidays ideal for working-class families, with their range of free popular entertainment on offer, their attention to children, and an atmosphere of cheerful, gregarious communality, perhaps reminiscent of the blitz. Holiday-makers, who queued with British fortitude for bread and meat in the shops, queued with equal enthusiasm for the processed pleasures of the holiday camps. Working-class contentment, based on the cohesiveness of the nucleated family unit, was one major factor in sustaining Labour's popularity with its own people. Among less contrived pursuits, ramblers and nature-lovers generally enjoy the benefits of Lewis Silkin's National Parks Act (1949) which created what came to be

---

[46] A. H. Halsey (ed.), *Trends in British Society since 1900* (London, 1972), p. 549.

called the Countryside Commission to protect areas of outstanding natural beauty. John Cripps, the son of Sir Stafford
and editor of *The Countryman* from 1947 to 1971, was one
of its later chairmen. There were ample forms of statistical
evidence to show that the workers benefiting from all this
were healthier, taller, and stronger, their wives happier,
their children better fed and educated, their old parents
better cared for and with ever-longer expectation for retirement. Compared with the almost total suspension of entertainment and mass pleasure during the war, the post-1945
period seemed for many people, especially for children who
had survived the blitz and evacuation, a halcyon period of
prosperity and fun. The drabness of post-1945 Britain is
often vastly exaggerated. Morrison's conception of the 1951
Festival of Britain, including the inventiveness, sparkle, and
gaiety of the Fun Fair at Battersea, chimed in with this
happy mood.

It was, in terms of dress, speech, and entertainment, a more
egalitarian society. Yet the middle class remained impervious
and impregnable. Indeed, the middle class clearly expanded
in size after 1945, reinforced rather than eroded by the
welfare state and social engineering. There were frequent
laments from middle-class people about the impact of rationing and cuts on living standards, including the effect of the
rising cost of living on middle-class budgets. A London
evening newspaper quoted one complainant: 'In 1939 on
£300 a year we ran a small car, we lived in a modern flat,
we threw occasional parties, we danced regularly, we had
all the cigarettes we wanted, we could even enjoy the
occasional pub crawl.' Now after the war, on £600 a year,
life could offer only an underground warren of a flat, a high
rent, no drink, few cigarettes, and the excitement of a weekly
outing to the cinema.[47] On the other hand, it was apparent
that, even in straitened circumstances (which included the
virtual disappearance of large categories of domestic servants),
middle-class people increased and multiplied. Indeed, Ian
Little has estimated that the wealthier middle class at least
probably improved their financial position absolutely between

[47] Quoted in Roy Lewis and Angus Maude, *The English Middle Classes*
(London, 1949), p. 207.

1945 and 1950.[48] Pressure for private housing, for places at
public schools (day and boarding), for membership of private
insurance schemes, continued apace. In addition, schoolteachers, lesser civil servants, junior managers, skilled workers,
and others were anxious to display their middle-class creden-
tials in terms of dress, diet, accent, and general social pretensions and life-style. Virginia Cowles, the American wife of a
Labour junior minister, Aidan Crawley, wrote *No Cause for
Alarm* in 1947, partly to reassure American readers of the
normality of life under socialism. From 1946 onwards,
indeed, Labour party strategists began to voice new appre-
hension about the need to conciliate the middle class, and to
show that Labour was more than an inbred proletarian army.
After the gains in suburban and commuter territory in 1945,
Labour viewed with concern the heavy slump in their vote
in the Kent commuter constituency of Bexley in a by-election
in July 1946, even with as able a candidate as Ashley Bramall
to hold the seat.[49] Evidently, the depressing impact of the
new Bread Units did not help. The losses in middle-class areas
in the county council elections in the autumn of 1946
aroused further anxiety. Labour was anxious to show that its
hostility to élitism (illustrated by Chuter Ede's refusal to
restore the Police Training College at Hendon after 1945,
following pressure from the Police Federation which represented 'the copper on the beat') was neither total nor
doctrinaire. In the autumn of 1947, Morgan Phillips sent a
questionnaire to key Labour agents of officials in different
parts of the country, in an inquest on Labour's losses in the
municipal elections. It drew a variety of responses; every
one in some sense reflected the grievances of middle-class
voters.[50] Cliff Prothero in Wales, J. T. Anson in Yorkshire,
W. Young in East Anglia, J. T. Baxter in Scotland, all referred
to middle-class disgruntlement, especially over the abolition
of the basic petrol ration in 1947 and the way in which the
AA and the RAC were able to sway motorists against voting

[48] Ian Little, 'Fiscal Policy' in G. D. N. Worswick and P. H. Ady (eds.), *The
British Economy, 1945–50* (Oxford, 1952), p. 174.
[49] *The Economist*, 27 July 1946, attributed the fall in Labour's vote at Bexley
to 'an incipient revolt of the middle class', and cited railway fares, bread rationing,
and 'red tape' as causes.
[50] 'Inquest on 1947 municipal elections' Labour Party archives, GS 14/5–6.

Labour. The rationing of bread and bacon was also said to be very unpopular. In the west Midlands, Jim Cattermole stressed the alienation of middle-class voters by Shinwell's remark to the effect that middle-class people 'didn't matter a tinker's cuss'. The logic of this view of Cattermole's was taken much further by Morrison in his campaign for 'consolidation' instead of further radical reform which might offend the salaried classes, as well as attempts by Attlee himself to suppress Bevan after his 'vermin' speech in July 1948. Labour could go to extreme lengths to present a moderate, or even frankly right-wing approach to middle-class electors. In the North Croydon by-election of March 1948, they fielded as their candidate that ineffably class-conscious man of letters, Harold Nicolson. After his defeat, he repaid Transport House for their support by commenting in acid terms in the *Spectator* on the petty snobbery of south London suburbia.[51] This came ill from the patrician owner of Sissinghurst Castle.

Class war doctrines were certainly not for public consumption. Morgan Phillips urged Attlee to pay careful heed to this aspect of the presentation of Labour policies in 1949, in the run up to the next election. Even in *Tribune*, the plight of the middle class was aired solicitously. Charles Hussey pointed in 1947 to the offence felt by teachers, journalists, bank clerks, civil servants, and other sensitive people over Shinwell's class-conscious diatribes. While these middle-class citizens had benefited from free education, health and insurance legislation, and the pegging of rents, their salaries, perhaps no more than £15 a week after tax, had been squeezed by inflation.[52] After the 1950 election, this diagnosis was taken further. Anthony Crosland, the new member for South Gloucester, wrote on how Labour had lost middle-class votes in marginal seats. Two main groups were specified. There were the lower ranks of the salaried class (teachers, minor civil servants, clerks), 'the only large social class which is absolutely worse off than it was in 1939'. Secondly, there were owners of small businesses (including garage proprietors,

---

[51] James Lees-Milne, *Harold Nicolson: a Biography*, vol. ii, 1930–68 (London, 1981), pp. 215–20; *Spectator*, 19 Mar. 1948.

[52] *Tribune*, 5 Sept. 1947.

road hauliers, small builders, horticulturists, shopkeepers) who felt threatened by nationalization, persecuted by controls and red tape, frustrated by petrol and other rationing. They needed more tax relief, more sympathy for the small trader, more understanding from a broad-based Labour government which required their support. Richard Stokes, the Labour industrialist who sat for Ipswich, bombarded first Cripps, then Gaitskell in 1949–50 with pleas to alleviate 'the plight of the middle class'. These he defined as people in the £750– £2,000 a year salary range, including technicians, managers, civil servants, and ministers of religion. Among his suggestions was a possible cut of a shilling in the standard rate of income tax. Cripps was not unsympathetic. He referred to 'the weak bargaining position of the average salaried worker', though in fact nothing was offered by way of relief.[53] Despite the apparent egalitarianism and collectivism of life after 1945, the resilience of middle-class people, and the persistence of their grievances, suggests that by 1950 the ethic of the war years was giving way to somewhat different imperatives— individual initiative, freedom of opportunity and movement, the priorities of a property-owning, home-owning democracy. This was reflected in the libertarian rhetoric shrewdly adopted by the Conservatives in the 1950 and 1951 elections— 'setting the people free'. Mark Abrams was to note how in the fifties traditional middle-class values, including an emphasis on privacy and on the home and family life, were being shared by white-collar workers and by more affluent skilled workers and their wives. Housewives were a frequent source of consumer criticisms of the Labour government, although the so-called Housewives League was probably too obviously a Conservative creation to be representative. The mood was subtly changing. Maurice Edelman wrote accurately enough that to be 'non-political in 1945 meant to be Labourish', but that to be 'non-political in 1950 meant to be Toryish'.[54] It was noticeable that J. B. Priestley's populist radio broadcast on behalf of the Labour Party in the 1950 general election seemed much less successful than a similar

[53] *Tribune*, 10 Mar. 1950. Paper by Stokes on 'The Incidence of Taxation on the Middle Class', 28 Nov. 1949, and memorandum by Cripps (T 171/400); paper by Stokes on 'The Plight of the Middle Class', 12 Oct. 1950 (T 171/403).
[54] *New Statesman*, 11 Mar. 1950.

effort had been in 1945. The social revolution after 1945, of which Orwell had dreamed, was giving way after his death in early 1950 to values remarkably similar to those which had troubled his conscience in the thirties. The Labour Party was unlikely to benefit from the consequences.

The cultural mood after 1945 is harder to assess. There had been many indications between 1939 and 1945 that a people's war was generating a new people's culture, with clear radical implications. The fostering of the popular interest in music and the arts during the war—events such as the lunchtime concerts by Dame Myra Hess during the London blitz, the release of the talents of war artists like John Piper and Graham Sutherland, the relatively classless cultural image projected on the radio from J. B. Priestley to the 'Brains Trust' (which featured Labour sages such as Drs C. E. M. Joad and Julian Huxley)—all suggested a release from the class-bound strait-jacket and unreflecting traditionalism which had held the arts back in Britain for much of the century. There were, indeed, signs that the immediate post-war period showed a continuation of this mood for change. A novel such as Evelyn Waugh's *Brideshead Revisited* (1945), with its tender treatment of upper-class life in Oxford and amongst the Catholic gentry of the north, seemed almost incongruous. The wartime CEMA gave way to the Arts Council in 1945, to patronize artistic work through interest-free loans. There followed an immense boom in music. By 1946, four major orchestras had been re-formed in London, the Royal Philharmonic under Sir Thomas Beecham, the London Philharmonic, the London Symphony, and, most influential of all perhaps, the BBC Symphony Orchestra. The BBC Symphony was the staple of the London Proms in the Albert Hall, which revived after the war with Sir Malcolm Sargent as conductor and impresario, complete with 'Land of Hope and Glory' as a patriotic finale. This advance in orchestral music was the more remarkable since London had no major concert hall after 1945, as the Queen's Hall had been destroyed in the blitz. A new generation of composers flourished, headed by Benjamin Britten, newly returned from America. His opera, *Peter Grimes*, which

opened in June 1945, just after VE Day, indicated a vitality
for British opera unknown since the frothy concoctions of
Gilbert and Sullivan. Another significant new composer was
Michael Tippett, a noted pacifist during the war. The London
theatre also went from strength to strength, with productions
ranging from the omnipresent Shakespeare to the works of
Christopher Fry, from the light-musical romances of Ivor
Novello to the grand opera featured at Covent Garden, where
the Royal Opera House reopened in February 1946. There
was also an immense boom in books, with over 200 new
publishing houses opening up, in the wake of the relaxation
of controls on paper. With Alan Pryce-Jones editing *The
Times Literary Supplement*, Peter Quennell, the *Cornhill*,
John Lehman, *New Writing*, and V. S. Pritchett as a superb
literary editor of the *New Statesman*, the literary scene
amongst the weeklies and literary journals was astonishingly
thriving. Transatlantic visitors gazed in awe at a war-ravaged
land which could still, almost effortlessly, play Greece to
America's Rome.

This early optimism led to a belief, held by Priestley
amongst others,[55] that a cultural revolution was in the
making, from which a social revolution and the dissolution of
class and institutional barriers would follow. There were one
or two overtly radical developments such as the periodical,
Politics and Letters, launched in Cambridge in 1947 by
Raymond Williams and Clifford Collins amongst others.
On the left flank, there were openly socialist experiments
such as Ted Willis's Unity Theatre, in open revolt against
the middle-class conventions that were believed to be holding
the British theatre in thrall. Perhaps even an English Brecht
could be visualized.

But the optimism and advance soon yielded to a more
cautious, perhaps pessimistic mood. By July 1947 Cyril
Connolly in *Horizon* was lamenting how the left-wing
idealism of Guernica and Munich days had evaporated. 'A
Socialist government . . . has quite failed to stir up either
intellect or imagination.' The sole socialist writer of any
note was Priestley, wrote Connolly (presumably discounting
Orwell), while 'the left-wing literary movement has petered

[55] Cf. J. B. Priestley, *The Arts under Socialism* (1946).

out'.[56] In December 1947, Connolly openly voiced his disappointment with what he saw as Attlee's intolerant and drab regime. 'A government which conscripts labour, cuts paper, prohibits book imports and does not even dare to propose the abolition of the death penalty . . . bears no relation to the kind of Socialism which many of us envisaged.'[57] Of course, Connolly is a singularly uncertain guide to the public mood; his personal opinions may not have been representative of anyone save himself, and his wider influence is open to debate. For all that, the intellectual and literary world does appear to show some turning against the premises of British socialism in some areas, perhaps as a reaction to Crippsian austerity, perhaps to the pressures of Stalinism and the cold war. Many of the left-wing pioneers of pre-war years concentrated their fire now on the evils of Communist totalitarianism rather than on the crimes of capitalism. Stephen Spender denounced it for its fear of innovation in ideas; his anti-Communism became increasingly vehement. Victor Gollancz, whose publishing house had been the prop for the Left Book Club in the days of the Popular Front, now condemned Godless and intolerant Communism.

The most striking case is that of George Orwell. His distinguished biographer, Bernard Crick, has rightly emphasized that Orwell remained a libertarian socialist until his death.[58] His attacks, in *Animal Farm*, while they aroused some nervousness from Aneurin Bevan and other colleagues in *Tribune*, had been directed at centralism and the suppression of free thought wherever they lurked. He remained a firm supporter of the Attlee government, and retained his personal links with the ILP and the far left. Even so, Orwell's own inclination after 1945 was to flee from the world of Hampstead intelligentsia to his own private retreat in the Scottish islands. *Nineteen Eighty Four* (1948) may well have had an ultimately socialist purpose. But the message of books is a matter of balance and tone. The balance in this book was manifestly to denounce the threat from centralization, state

[56] *Horizon*, vol. xvi, no. 90 (July 1947), p. 1.
[57] Ibid., vol. xvi, no. 96 (Dec. 1947), pp. 299–300.
[58] Bernard Crick, *George Orwell: a Life* (Penguin edn., Harmondsworth, 1980), especially pp. 561–71.

planning, and conformity as they currently impinged on human liberties. Orwell's work, however ludicrously misrepresented it may have been by right-wing critics in America as an attack on Attlee-style creeping socialism, may rightly be included with the anti-Communist drift of the cold-war years. From the thirties onwards, from the time of his traumatic experience in Catalonia, it was Stalin, not Hitler, whom Orwell always treated as the major threat to intellectual freedom and artistic integrity. Indeed, he never paid much attention to Hitler and fascism at all. In 1948, Orwell had been critical of the new anti-American tone of *Tribune*, which he attributed to Crossman's influence.[59] Orwell's writing and experience was part of a process that led Arthur Koestler and others to write in 1949 of Communism as 'The God that Failed'. More subtly political were the short stories by a promising new writer, Angus Wilson, published under the title, *Such Darling Dodos* in 1950, with their satirical comment on the assumptions of the pre-war left, and the post-war enthusiasm for socialism and the welfare state. Overtly reactionary in tone were the popular novels of Ivy Compton-Burnett, every one set in the idyllic lost world of the Edwardian upper classes, upholstered by deferential retinues of domestic servants.

Developments in the arts elsewhere also showed some drift away from the leftish passions of 1945. The theatre flourished mainly through productions of such conservative writers as T. S. Eliot. No significant new left-wing playwright emerged until John Osborne in the mid-fifties. Music flourished, as has been noted, but it is open to speculation what this implied. John Ardagh's suggestion that the musical renaissance in France in the 1970s marked a reawakening of private pleasures and fulfilment, in protest against the pressures and intolerance of a collectivist world, could conceivably be applied to post-war Britain too, though the argument is impossible to prove either way.[60] Newspapers and the weeklies showed something of the same movement. *The Economist*, for instance, moved away from the Labour

---

[59] T. R. Fyvel, *George Orwell: a Personal Memoir* (London, 1982), p. 158.
[60] John Ardagh, *France in the 1980s* (Penguin edn., Harmondsworth, 1982), p. 604.

camp after 1945. Lady Rhondda's once feminist *Time and Tide* moved to the right, its anonymous columnist, W. J. Brown, MP (famous for his aversion to evolutionist biology), moving right with it.[61] On the other hand, the high and rising circulation of Kingsley Martin's *New Statesman* after 1945, with easily the largest readership of all the weeklies, shows the continuing intellectual energy of the political-literary left, surviving from the thirties. What John Vincent has memorably termed the 'thin pink line from Fleet Street via Bush House to Golders Green'[62] stayed largely unbroken, and retained much of its cultural ascendancy until well on into the fifties. Elsewhere in the publishing world, the fate of Tom Hopkinson's *Picture Post* is symptomatic. During the post-war period, it continued its wartime tradition of crusading left-wing journalism. Labour MPs wrote for it; Ted Castle, husband of a left-wing Labour MP, was on the editorial staff. By 1950, however, the proprietor, Edward Hulton, had himself moved to the right, and even joined the Conservative Party early that year. After a skirmish with Hopkinson over the treatment of the war in Korea (including some sharply anti-American journalism from James Cameron), Hulton forced Hopkinson's dismissal as editor in October 1950.[63] Thereafter, *Picture Post*, by far the most important and original illustrated magazine ever published in Britain, went into a speedy decline and later folded up. The other main periodicals of this type, *Everybody's* and *Illustrated*, had always tended to be more right-wing in tone.

If the literary world shows something of a drift to the right, the fate of the cinema, by far Britain's most innovative cultural form, other than music, was somewhat different. It was *par excellence* the medium for mass entertainment: in 1946, one-third of the population went to the cinema once a week, and 13 per cent twice a week.[64] A series of British films during the war had suggested a new sense of experiment within this notoriously commercialized industry.

[61] My father was the chess correspondent of *Time and Tide* at this period, and was once rebuked (in my presence) for including too many games by Russians in his columns. The rebuke was subsequently ignored.

[62] John Vincent, reviewing Fyvel, op. cit., in *Sunday Times*, 29 Aug. 1982.

[63] Tom Hopkinson, *Of this Our Time* (London, 1982), p. 272.

[64] Arthur Marwick, *British Society since 1945* (London, 1982), p. 75.

To protect the native film companies, Harold Wilson at the Board of Trade imposed a heavy import duty on American and other foreign films in 1947–8, while Sir Wilfred Eady's National Film Corporation and its 'Eady levy' provided financial assistance. The main effect of this seems to have been to make socially realistic and highly intelligent films from France or Italy the taste of an esoteric minority of the avant-garde. The most striking British-produced novelties were the Ealing Studios comedies, made by the Boulting brothers from 1947 onwards. Films such as *The Lavender Hill Mob*, *Passport to Pimlico*, and *Whisky Galore* testified to the talents of actors and directors within the British film-making industry. Character-actors such as Alastair Sim, Stanley Holloway, and Margaret Rutherford became celebrities. On the other hand, these and other British films of the period tended to follow the traditional stereotypes in presenting a familiar, reassuring, tolerant, kindly British people to itself. Foreigners (especially Germans) were usually incomprehensible, funny, or even criminal; working-class British people were depicted in terms of patronizing ignorance. The British film industry, never more active than in the late forties, dealt essentially in the old folk clichés. It failed to generate new artistic forms, or to match either the social and political comment, or the visual imagination of the French and Italian films, or even the low-budget American films of the period. Orson Wells's *Citizen Kane* or Marcel Carné's *Les Enfants du Paradis* could not have been made in Britain between 1945 and 1951. Film documentaries, such as those of Paul Rotha, were, at least, much franker on social issues including the forbidden topic of class. Not until the later fifties did the British film industry show more enterprise and realism, especially in its treatment of working-class life.

The BBC, whose radio programmes flourished in this period, gave various forms of the arts much encouragement. This especially followed the creation of the Third Programme in September 1946. Broadcast music and drama were particularly effective. The television audience only became considerable from 1949, when the Alexandra Palace transmitter in north London was joined by Holme Moss for the

Midlands; television licences soon soared to a million in 1951–2. However, much of the nation's broadcasting was set in a conformist, or even Conservative, mould. News bulletins and election broadcasting arrangements were scrupulously impartial. On the other hand, news headlines were often slanted in an anti-Labour direction, while comedians such as Tommy Handley subjected vulnerable ministers like Shinwell and Strachey to a stream of abuse from which the Conservatives (especially the supra-human figure of Churchill) almost always escaped. Labour spokesmen such as Morgan Phillips also voiced concern about the anti-Labour bias in such discussion programmes as 'Any Questions', based in rural Conservative strongholds in the west of England. In these, the 'non-party' representative always appeared to be a right-wing figure like the farmer, Arthur Street. The controller of the Light Programme, T. W. Chalmers, blandly (and inadequately) retorted that 'the West Region possesses nothing like the political climate of Clydeside, Rhondda Valley or Middlesbrough'.[65] The televised play, *Party Manners*, which referred to Labour ministers imperilling national security by releasing the secrets of the atomic bomb, stirred up much controversy in 1950. Labour, and the BBC chairman of governors, Lord Simon, a Labour peer, caused the abandonment of a second showing.[66] Labour politicians from Morrison downwards felt that the BBC was no ally in projecting the ideas and values of their government.[67] In many ways, they were justified, perhaps even more when Churchill appointed Sir Alexander Cadogan to succeed Simon as chairman of governors, and Sir Ian Jacob as the new Director-General, in 1952. The BBC, like much else in the national culture, almost imperceptibly drifted away from the Priestley-type left-wing enthusiasms which had brought Labour into office in 1945.

[65] Asa Briggs, *The History of Broadcasting in the United Kingdom*, vol. iv: *Sound and Vision* (Oxford, 1979), p. 114.

[66] Ibid., p. 454.

[67] See Labour Party archives, GS 22/2 for discussions in 1950 between Morgan Phillips and Morrison, and Sir William Haley and Frank Gillard about 'Any Questions'. One complaint was that Raymond Blackburn appeared as a 'Labour' speaker after he had resigned from the Labour Party. Another concerned the impartiality of the chairman, Freddie Grisewood.

The main factor at work, though, may have been not that the art, literature, or communications media of the period were biased towards the Tories, but rather that much of their output was simply mediocre. This applied most forcibly in literature, where, in terms of novels and the drama above all, the later forties were an undistinguished period. W. W. Robson has called them 'one of the worst periods in English literature'.[68] T. R. Fyvel noted in early 1950 the absence of any surge of creative writing as had occurred after 1918. He linked this cultural decline with Labour's need for 'an intelligent and educated middle class minority'.[69] There were no major novelists during the Attlee years. The leading dramatists were men such as T. S. Eliot who had survived from an earlier era. The West End, wrote Fyvel with some exaggeration, was 'a commercialized desert'. Nor did English poetry show any great vitality. In the early fifties, the novelist Angus Wilson in *Hemlock and After* was to attack the cultural illusions of the recent past and, by implication, to suggest that the leftish attitudes of the period may have had much to do with them. The new young dramatists of the mid-fifties, such as Osborne and Arnold Wesker, were to go further and to link a decline in the arts with the lack of courage of the government in carrying out its socialist pledges. In the visual arts and architecture, the rebuilding of cities and other new urban developments largely ignored the architectural innovation and excitement of the thirties. The imagination shown, for instance, in Pick and Holden's planning of the London Underground in the thirties, did not often recur now. The 'new towns' and rebuilt cities, especially the City of London around St. Paul's which had largely been destroyed in the blitz, became a byword for drab austerity and uniformity. Many historic skylines and neighbourhoods were ravaged by the planners far more extensively than they had been by the *Luftwaffe*. Sir Patrick Abercromby and his fellow planners gradually lost the moral authority of the war years. It is true that the 1951 Festival of Britain, designed by the left-wing architect, Hugh Casson, did provide new encouragement and excitement for architects, designers, painters, and

[68] W. W. Robson, *Modern English Literature* (Oxford, 1970), p. 146.
[69] *Tribune*, 17 Mar. 1950.

sculptors. Robert Matthew's Royal Festival Hall on the South
Bank of the Thames was a marvellous centre-piece. Creative
artists such as the sculptors, Henry Moore and Barbara Hep-
worth, now became far more generally accepted. On the
other hand, the impulse generated by the Festival in 1951
contrasted the more starkly with the wasted opportunities
of the years since 1945. Artistic life under Labour Britain
was broadly disappointing. Other than in music, it showed
little capacity for growth or inclination to experiment.
Some important publications fell by the wayside. Connolly's
New Horizon closed down in 1950; John Lehman's *New
Writing*, which had once nurtured the talents of the young
Dylan Thomas, folded up around the same time. Nor was
post-1945 artistic or literary culture in any real sense classless. On the contrary, it was clearly the middle class who
flocked to the theatre (other than to Christmas pantomimes),
to the opera, to the arts festivals launched at Edinburgh in
1947 and Aldeburgh in 1948. It was manifestly to a public-
school or grammar-school, university-trained élite that the
BBC geared its Third Programme. Other than in Wales, where
the national eisteddfod was more truly classless and where
the international folk eisteddfod started beside the Dee at
Llangollen in 1947 broke new ground, working-class involvement in culture was mainly limited to the music-hall (now in
marked decline in the face of competition from the radio),
to the cinema (never more flourishing), and to the local
passion for the brass band or choral competitions in mining
and quarrying areas. Culture failed to bridge the class divide.
So far as it flourished after 1945, it can probably be related
to the middle-class recovery which has already been detected
elsewhere, and which so concerned the strategists of the
Labour Party.

The general picture of the mood after 1945, then, is of a
social structure still sharply divided, and under pressure from
middle-class aspirations and from a culture still traditional
in values. There was a veering away from the classless ethos
that the wartime years had suggested. Attlee's Britain was a
conservative, cautious land, reflecting the reassuring cricket-
loving, downbeat style of its Prime Minister. But it did not

feel itself to be a declining one. There was a rough strength about post-war Britain which contrasts with the declining self-confidence of the 1970s and 1980s. There endured after 1945 a powerful civic culture, a commitment to hierarchical and organic values, to Crown and parliament, to law and order, to authority however it manifested itself, from the policeman to the football referee. It was also a deeply patriotic society, one convinced of its own inner strength. The superiority of Britain was still broadly assumed. Such episodes as the famous football victory of Great Britain over a scratch team representing 'the Rest of Europe' by six goals to one in May 1947 proved the point to popular satisfaction. Painful defeats by Hungarians, Brazilians, and many others were still some way off, though the astounding defeat of England by, of all nations, the United States in the 1950 World Cup was a portent of declining standards. There was little enough overt discontent. The direct action of the 'squatters' was quietly suppressed by the authorities. Law and order prevailed in major cities. Murderers were officially, and cruelly, executed, amidst general approval. The frustrations of rationing were borne without undue demur. After all, British people were happy enough to be alive at all in 1945. There were signs of emigration to potentially more prosperous lands. Some migrated to Australia, New Zealand, or Canada after the war. The 'GI Brides' went to America with their soldier husbands and invariably stayed there. A disgruntled right-wing minority went to Southern Rhodesia in protest against the socialist policies of a Labour government. The British administration had to confront their aggressive spokesmen in the talks over a Central African Federation in 1950–1. But the vast majority stayed at home, happy in their homeland, proud to be British.

However, patriotism did not mean uniformity of outlook. On the contrary, the other striking feature of post-1945 Britain is the high degree of political consciousness and commitment. By-elections, the general elections of 1950 and 1951, all showed a very high turn-out. Electoral turn-out rose from 71 per cent in 1935 to 72 per cent in 1945, 83.9 per cent in 1950, and 82.6 per cent in 1951. Membership of the Conservative Party rose to over two million, and of the

Labour Party (swollen by trade-union affiliation, of course) to 5,849,002 by 1951. There was a high degree of political partisanship. Churchill still aroused some anger in the Welsh valleys. Morrison and others in 1951 derided the Conservative leader as a primitive 'warmonger'. Labour ministers, especially Bevan and Shinwell, aroused, in turn, far more fury from their Tory opponents than did, say, Tony Benn twenty years later. After his 'vermin' speech in July 1948, Bevan received packets of excrement through the post. He was physically assaulted by an enraged member in White's Club. The pacifist past of Morrison or the neo-Communist background of Cripps were stirred up to inspire Conservative militants. Anti-Semitism was sometimes openly encouraged, by right-wing controversialists. Colm Brogan, a Scottish Catholic, the brother of a famous Liberal academic, poured scorn on Labour's claim to be a British party at all. 'Think of Konni Zilliacus. The very name recalls the root and heart of Lancashire—Gold Flake packets in the Irwell, Old Trafford soaking in the rain.' Silverman, Messer, Levy, Orbach, Shurmer, Weitzmann, Swingler, Janner, and Shinwell (of course) were other names on which the author dwelt lovingly.[70] There was much latent anger and passion in British politics after 1945. Mass Observation data, private surveys by sociologists such as Mark Abrams, and BBC opinion analyses confirmed the very high degree of political commitment,[71] in which voters unhesitatingly proclaimed themselves Labour or Conservative, and with far more intensity than in far-off Gilbertian days of the divide between little Liberals and little Conservatives. Broadcasting added to the tendency by ensuring that political debate after 1945 was national, rather than local or regional, in emphasis. This reinforced the polarization of the time. The floating voter did not seem to be a major phenomenon: the point was to get 'our people' out to the polling booths. The British were

[70] Colm Brogan, *Our New Masters* (London, 1948), p. 20. Also see the same author's *Patriots? My Foot!* (London, 1949).

[71] Cf. Abrams, op. cit., 240–1. A high proportion of non-Conservative voters interviewed thought that a Conservative government would mean mass unemployment, an attack on the welfare state, and more strikes. Most non-Labour supporters feared that a Labour victory at the next election would mean an undermining of prosperity and more class-orientated legislation.

not in revolutionary mood after 1945—but they were fired by a clear sense of social and political objectives, and aware of the evident barriers that divided them from one another. The idea of a broad consensus after 1945 in which the National Health Service, nationalization and the retreat from empire commanded almost universal, bipartisan support, is perhaps a later construct which requires qualification. It does not conform to much of the record of events, to the personal recollections of those active at the time, or to the voters' contemporary conception of themselves. Britain, more than at any other time in the twentieth century, was an intensely political, if peaceful, culture in the 1945-51 period. That very commitment might yet help the Labour government, despite all the rightwards tendencies in social change, cultural movements, and the public psychology, in retaining power during all the challenges that lay ahead.

8

The Crises of 1947

Until the start of 1947, the Labour government seemed to be carrying all before it. It was strongly supported in by-elections and in local government contests. Apart from a temporary slump in July 1946 at the time of bread rationing and the Bexley by-election, it rode high in the opinion polls. The economy showed every sign of a boom in 1946, with exports making an excellent recovery, 111 per cent above the level of 1938. Exports of metal goods and chemicals were particularly impressive. Capital investment in industry resumed its growth after the erosion of domestic capital formation during the war, while employment remained at a high level apart from one or two trouble spots like South Wales. There was a massive programme of legislative achievement, with over seventy bills carried through parliament in the 1945-6 session, including much public ownership, the National Health and National Insurance bills, and the reform of the law on trade unions. Within the Labour Party itself, there was immense enthusiasm, and a broad mood of support for what the government was doing. The dominant figure in Labour's self-projection in this early phase was the Chancellor of the Exchequer, Hugh Dalton, a breezy, extravert product of Eton and King's, whose stentorian presence seemed to dominate the front benches. Even a routine measure such as the Cable and Wireless Bill could be invested with drama. Dalton's policy of 'cheap money' symbolized the new era, a total contrast to the deflation and retrenchment that had marked British policy at the hands of the Treasury after 1918. He warned his colleagues, in March 1947, that deflation would bring 'dear money, depressed trade, mass unemployment, cuts in wages and social services. It must be resisted with all our strength'.[1] His financial expansion on easy terms underlay the social reforms, the industrial reconstruction, and public investment projects of Labour's high

[1] Dalton's summary of the Budget for the Cabinet, Mar. 1947 (T 171/390).

noon. It was reinforced by an impressive technical mastery on the part of the Chancellor, himself the author of authoritative works on public finance. Dalton seemed to epitomize a radical government, confident in its priorities, at peace with itself and a wider world. He introduced his first budget in characteristic style in November 1945. He had much good news to impart to the taxpayers including a shilling cut in the standard rate of income tax. When he introduced his budget of April 1947, Dalton borrowed the title of a popular song of the time, and declared that he brought his proposals forward 'with a song in his heart'. The song had lingered on for the whole of the previous year.

By total contrast, 1947 was a year of almost unrelieved disaster. Dalton, in his own famous description, stigmatized it as 'annus horrendus'.[2] It began with the appalling wintry weather of early 1947 when unprecedented snow and ice severely accentuated a crisis of coal production which anxious ministers had long foreseen. Morrison had raised this as an urgent matter on the Lord President's Committee on 21 June 1946. Shinwell, the Minister of Fuel and Power, at first spoke in tones of some complacency, and implied that, after nationalization, crises in fuel production would be a thing of the past. He told the Lord President's Committee in July that the outlook was 'reasonably good'.[3] He discounted manpower and equipment problems in the mining industry, and the potential loss of production likely to follow the introduction of the five-day week under the 'Miners' Charter'. But the scheme of releasing miners quickly from the armed services was not a success. Will Lawther's presidential address to the NUM in June 1946 spoke of a 'coming catastrophe'. By November it was obvious that the fuel shortage was becoming alarming. On 21 November, Attlee warned Dalton about the problem, and set up a

---

[2] Dalton, *High Tide and After*, p. 187.

[3] *News Chronicle*, 22 Mar. 1946: 'Our mining difficulties are over', Shinwell observed at a press conference. Also minutes of Lord President's Committee, 19 July 1946 (CAB 132/1). However at the discussion of the 'Economic Survey' for 1947 at the Lord President's Committee on 26 July, other ministers noted that coal stocks at the start of the winter would be only 5m. tons above the safety margin and urged savings in consumption at electricity generating stations and elsewhere.

Cabinet Committee under Dalton himself, and including also Shinwell, Isaacs, and Barnes. Several Labour backbenchers, notably Douglas Jay, the new member for North Battersea, criticized the alleged lack of foresight, although George Wigg was to accuse Dalton of being 'personally vindictive' towards Shinwell.[4] In a normal winter, the problems would have been acute enough in the mines. But this winter was to prove abnormal, indeed the most severe of the century so far. From 20 January, freezing weather, fanned by a strong east wind, descended, and it remained bitterly cold, with much snow, for the next eight weeks. The result was calamitous. Coal stocks, already falling, slumped to below the four million tons level, which was regarded as the minimum for national survival. Coal could not be transported by rail or road; collier vessels from Newcastle, bringing coal to power stations in London and the south-east, could not put to sea. Shinwell told a stunned House of Commons on 7 February that many power stations had run out of coal, that much of industry would therefore have to close down, and that many domestic consumers would have to do without electricity for large parts of the day. The Conservatives coined the slogan, 'Shiver with Shinwell and starve with Strachey'.

The Cabinet's response to the crisis did not carry conviction. On 7 January there had already been a full discussion of the coal crisis by ministers. In addition to rapidly diminishing stocks as a result of manpower shortages and unexpectedly high consumer demand (607,000 tons a week, as against the 514,000 that Shinwell had forecast), there were mounting transportation problems in transferring coal stocks around the country. Cripps was delegated to draw up a plan of allocating fuel supplies, a plan based on Shinwell's estimates, which gave absolute priority to power stations and worked out quotas for industry.[5] The Cripps plan was a failure. Its operations were in any case blitzed by the massive snow falls later in January and throughout February. Factories were closed down; villages were cut off; livestock died in

---

[4] *New Statesman*, 29 June 1946, for Lawther's views; Attlee to Dalton, 21 Nov. 1946 (Dalton papers, 9/2/76); George Wigg, *George Wigg* (London, 1972), p. 127.

[5] Cabinet Conclusions, 7 Jan. 1947 (CAB 128/9); Dalton to Attlee, 11 Feb. 1947 and Shinwell's paper on 'The Coal Position', 21 Feb. 1947 (PREM 8/443).

thousands; people froze in their homes without even the radio as a solace since that, too, was a victim of the power crisis. Unemployment reached over two millions by the start of February. Not until March was there any visible improvement in fuel supplies; in the end, the government was rescued only by an improvement in the climate in late March. The whole episode was a devastating comment on a government which prided itself on its efficient planning. The Attlee administration's reputation was shaken to the core.

There were many other troubles at this time, too. The course of foreign policy aroused much dissent in the Cabinet, not least over Alexander's refusal to scale down the armed services. At an agonized Cabinet meeting on 17 January, Dalton, faced with Alexander's blank intransigence over the size of the army, talked of resigning and stressed the gap of 630,000 that still remained in the manpower budget. Alexander did agree to make some cuts eventually, with the armed forces reduced to 937,000 by March 1948 and 713,000 by March 1949. But these fell short of the 10 per cent in defence expenditure which Dalton regarded as the bare minimum. Two years after the war had ended, Britain still had well over a million men and women in the armed services (1,227,000 on 30 September 1947), and the costs in foreign exchange rose inexorably. The fierce fight over defence expenditure merged with other crises in foreign policy. Withdrawal from Greece was announced in February; at much the same time, the momentous decision to withdraw British troops from India was made known. Palestine was another area where, in due course, the Union Jack flew over an army in retreat, its task uncompleted. These withdrawals were by no means condemned; that from India met with much acclaim. But they suggested a government which, at one and the same time, maintained an excessive military commitment around the globe, and yet was being pressurized into a surrender of its great power status just the same.

Crises at home and abroad coincided with personal difficulties. Early in February the Cabinet was shaken by the death of Ellen Wilkinson, the much-admired Minister of Education after an apparently accidental overdose of drugs.

For much of the early part of the year, too, Morrison was unwell with heart trouble, the consequence of his trying to maintain so many thankless and demanding roles in the Cabinet, parliament, and party. Bevin's health was always an uncertain factor as he trekked to exhausting conferences around the world. Personal relations between Attlee, Morrison, Bevin, and Dalton were marked by intermittent bickering. Bevan and Shinwell were frequent critics. Somehow, the Cabinet never seemed quite to recapture its earlier spirit or cohesion thereafter. Heavy losses in the 1947 local government elections in November were to confirm the point. Labour's early returns showed 43 gains and 687 losses, with numerous defeats in Lancashire and the loss of control in Manchester and Birmingham. Of course, Labour losses were inevitable since the party was defending gains made in the heady mood of 1945, but they were severe nevertheless, and confirmed a slump in the vote in several by-elections.

The climacteric of Labour's troubles was reached with the grave financial crisis over the convertibility of sterling in August 1947, the worst Britain had experienced since August 1931. With Britain facing bankruptcy, the Cabinet was brought to its knees. Economic crisis led to political crisis, as will be seen, with new and unprecedented challenges to Attlee's leadership. It was never glad confident morning again. The strength and vitality of the Labour government fled, never really to return. Dalton's *annus horrendus* was crippling in almost every respect. In the end, the major casualty was to be the allegedly unsinkable Dalton himself. His reputation much damaged by the convertibility crisis, he had to resign in November after a leak of budget secrets. His career as a major figure came to an end. Much of the *élan vital* of the government went with him.

Before the convertibility crisis broke, there was much criticism within and without the government to the effect that the government had no real plan for the economy. *Tribune* and the *New Statesman* featured columns by left-wing back-benchers such as J. P. W. Mallalieu, or the Oxford economist, Thomas Balogh, who complained that the government had no real method for allocating either resources or manpower, and

that the whole economic strategy was haphazard and profoundly unsocialist.[6] But it was far from being the left alone
who offered these criticisms. No less vehement was a more
right-wing figure such as Evan Durbin, a junior minister who
attacked the half-hearted nature of the export drive.[7] The
Lord President's Committee under Morrison was seen as an
ineffective talking-shop, not an instrument for planning a
sustained industrial recovery. It is in this context that the
Cabinet arguments over steel nationalization between April
and July 1947 must be viewed, apart from the political
aspects of steel as a symbol of the commitment to socialism.
As the Cabinet fell into lengthy and heated arguments over
the merits of steel nationalization, with compromisers such
as Morrison and Wilmot ranged against nationalizers like
Dalton and Bevan, the Cabinet was churned up by its first
prolonged differences of opinion since it had taken office.
The final dispute between Morrisonian consolidation and
Bevanite socialist advance was clearly foreshadowed. In
time, as has been seen, the Cabinet went ahead with steel
nationalization in 1948, with a Parliament Bill to be introduced alongside it, to limit the Lords' veto and ensure that
steel nationalization would be carried through before the
next election. The whole affair left great uncertainty, not
only about the firmness of the government's socialist commitment, but about the general lack of direction in industrial
policy. In the crisis, Attlee's leadership seemed drifting and
indecisive. At a meeting of the parliamentary Labour Party
on 11 August there was unprecedented criticism of the
Prime Minister from MPs of all shades of opinion, for his
dithering over steel, for failure to cut the armed forces
sufficiently, and for a lack of drive in promoting economic
growth. Even at the summit, the Labour government henceforth seemed less obviously in command.

It would be misleading to emphasize unduly the government's failures and lack of momentum in 1947. There were
many legislative achievements in that year. The passages of
the Transport and Electricity nationalization bills were

[6] See Balogh's views in *Tribune*, 7 Mar. 1947; 'the government's weakness is
in central, as opposed to departmental, planning and policy'.
[7] Evan Durbin to Dalton, 12 Sept. 1946 (Dalton papers, 9/2/28).

impressive in themselves. Tom Williams's Agriculture Act was
a triumph, a far-sighted measure of economic and social
regeneration, with powerful beneficial consequences for the
farming community and for the consumer. Lewis Silkin's
Town and Country Planning Act was another important
measure, with greater powers for local planning authorities
over the environment, and a government levy on increases
in land values through development. The transfer of power
in India, while overshadowed by domestic financial worries
in August 1947, was by any test one of the great achievements of British imperial statesmanship. In foreign affairs,
as has been seen, 1947 was the year in which Bevin's policies
began to bear fruit with the Marshall Aid scheme and the
early origins of NATO. Nevertheless, the prevailing impression
for much of the year is one of discontent, of Cabinet disagreements, and of backbench revolts. Symbolically, the
Gallup Poll published in the *News Chronicle* in August found
that, for the first time since the general election, the Conservatives had overtaken Labour by 44½ per cent to 41 per
cent.[8] Only 38 per cent declared themselves satisfied with
the government's record to date, while 51 per cent were
dissatisfied: *Tribune* later countered that 'one of the imports
from America which this country can do without is the
Opinion Poll'.[9] But 1947 was truly a bleak, bad year.

The main causes were rooted in the economy. In 1946, there
had been much good news to record, with exports advancing
and industrial production rising impressively. The physical
controls of wartime were fruitfully retained, with the Board
of Trade directing industry to the former 'depressed' areas.
Dalton, that extravert parliamentarian, with a unique talent
for enraging his opponents as he took command at the dispatch
box, pursued an optimistic policy of 'cheap money'. This,
however, was hardly on Keynesian grounds, since a major
priority in his budgets from the autumn of 1945 to the spring
of 1947 was to keep the budget broadly in balance rather
than aim for a deficit. While prepared to consult him in
drafting the 1946 budget, Dalton had always been somewhat

[8] *News Chronicle*, 14 Aug. 1947.
[9] *Tribune*, 21 Aug. 1948.

wary of Keynes, both personally and intellectually. Indeed, he went to great lengths to see that the Treasury kept well clear of the Keynesians such as Meade and Stone at the Economic Section of the Cabinet Office. He rejected Meade's proposals for a financial survey for 1947–9, along with the existing manpower and materials survey. Dalton ensured that, while the Economic Plan and the statistics of national income and expenditure were done on a calendar year basis, January to December, the budget was prepared on the basis of the financial year, April to March. This meant that demand management through the budget was virtually impossible to integrate with economic planning. It also ensured that the Chancellor retained his solitary glory as the presenter of the budget in April. Cheap money meant that a large volume of treasury bills was issued which formed the basis of credit expansion by the banks. General interest rates were cut down to 2½ per cent, and treasury deposit receipts reduced to ⅝ per cent. In October 1946, Dalton followed the even bolder policy of replacing local loans with irredeemable treasury stock, bearing interest of only 2½ per cent. This venture added a new name to Stock Exchange jargon, since the stock was christened 'Daltons'. The Chancellor basked in glory at the Lord Mayor's banquet that evening. There were those who criticized the cheap money policy on technical grounds. It was complained that the net sales of securities intended for the large saver had fallen from £938m. in the period, April–November 1945, to only £108m. for the corresponding period in 1946.[10] 'Daltons' stock, indeed, proved to be a colossal financial disaster which revealed the Chancellor's lack of expertise in Stock Exchange matters. 'Daltons' were sold in vast quantities in January 1947, only three months after they were launched, and for a time there was a collapse of the gilt-edge market. However, 'cheap money' was generally popular. The smaller investor seemed happy enough. The stock-market flourished until the end of 1946 and the City basked under Dr Dalton's benevolent, optimistic regime.

Dalton's policy was obviously intended to avoid, once and

[10] For Meade's proposed financial survey, see Bridges to Trend, 14 Mar. 1947 (T 171/389); W. Manning Dicey, 'The Cheap Money Technique', *Lloyd's Bank Review*, New Series, no. 3 (Jan. 1947), p. 63.

for all, the bleak policy of deflation which had marked Austen Chamberlain's time at the Treasury in 1919-21, a policy which had led to the contraction of the money supply, a drift back to gold and monetary orthodoxy, and consequent severe unemployment in mining and other industries. Hence Dalton's Investment (Control and Guarantees) Act of March 1946 to give power to the Treasury to control all new access to the capital market, and his retention of the Capital Issues Committee, first set up by Sir John Simon in 1939. Dalton was also anxious to use Treasury resources to promote social reform and full employment, as in the early agreement to finance family allowances, to peg council-house rents (when pressed by Griffiths and Bevan, in each case), and to fund food subsidies at a high level. As has been seen, the basic danger, in Dalton's view, was of a return to deflation, rather than the threat of inflation. So he cut taxes, especially income tax; he refrained from a general attack on excess profits or capital gains, which might imperil investment. His first two budgets cut the total of taxation imposed by more than £500m. a year. These measures, which brought much pleasure to the City—those 'flapping penguins' whom Lloyd George and Dalton both derided—were accompanied by bold policies designed to assist the working class. As he told the Durham miners at Bishop Auckland in his constituency, he had provided generous subsidies to council houses of £16 10s. a house; he had helped local authorities in the conversion of old loans; he had given extensive assistance for development areas and rural communities; he had helped the boards of the nationalized industries in their borrowing. A block grant due to come in 1948 would further help the social services provided by the local authorities.[11]

Dalton, as has been seen, had been a major figure in the evolution of Labour's economic and foreign policies in the thirties; it could be argued that his main contribution to the Attlee government occurred long before he ever took office. But as an executor of policy he was an impressive figure, too. His overall philosophy had both a negative and positive side. In negative terms, he was anxious to pursue a cheap money policy to trim the influence of the Stock

[11] Dalton's draft speech, 20 July 1946 (Dalton papers, 9/2/25).

Exchange speculator, an alleged scourge of Labour governments in the past. His policy, so Dalton dramatically claimed,
meant the 'euthanasia of the rentier' (a phrase in fact
borrowed from Keynes). On the positive side, Dalton followed
David Lloyd George in seeing the Treasury as a potential
powerhouse of social reform. Since his days as a young
socialist in the Labour Research Department after 1918, he
was profoundly committed to fundamental improvements in
housing, health, education, and environmental planning.
There was another cause, too, all his own. Dalton, prejudiced,
cantankerous, and difficult as he could sometimes be, is
shown here at his warm-hearted, idealistic best. This was his
deep passion for the quality of life, and in particular a life-
long devotion to the English countryside. A start had been
made with Addison's National Parks scheme back in 1931 for
setting aside areas of outstanding natural beauty. Dalton's
second budget of April 1946 built on this by including a
provision for a National Land Fund, through which land
could be accepted in lieu of death duties and kept in perpetuity as part of the national estate for posterity to enjoy.
'There is still a wonderful, incomparable beauty in Britain, in
the sunshine on the hills, the mists adrift across the moors, the
wind on the downs, the deep peace of the woodland, the wash
of the waves against the white unconquerable cliffs which
Hitler had never scaled. There is beauty and history in all
these places'. Such frankly emotional language had not been
heard in a budget statement since the time of Lloyd George.
But Dalton's idealism and sincerity were beyond question.

Yet these admirable social objectives were being gained at
a cost. This cost was becoming increasingly insupportable.
It all rested on the loan negotiated with the United States
in December 1945. That loan, available from July 1946,
now began to run out at an alarming rate. A serious drain
of dollars began from the start of 1947. Basically, it was the
result of the world-wide shortage of food and raw materials
which left the United States as virtually the sole supplier.
It was made worse by the sharp rise in American prices in
early 1947 which Dalton later reckoned to have knocked
$1 billion off the value of the original loan. The dollar drain
was associated with a serious imbalance in the terms of trade.

A critical shortage of dollars was not redressed by adequate attention to exports to the North American market, while the British fuel crisis in January–February made matters much worse, by costing Britain perhaps £200m. worth of exports. In the first quarter of 1947, the balance of payments showed clear signs of turning against Britain. The most spectacular feature was the rapidly accelerating drain of dollars which went on to reach a new peak in the second quarter of the year. Indeed, the dollar drain in the first six months of 1947 swept away some $1,890m., more than half the original US loan of $3,750m. At that rate, the loan, intended to last Britain until 1951, would run out by mid-1948, or even earlier.[12]

This and other evidence made it transparently clear that Dalton's policy was leading to domestic expenditure outstripping the available resources; a crisis would not be far off. One ominous indicator from the market was the selling off of 'Daltons' stock at a large discount in January 1947. Dalton continued in the early months of 1947 to preach optimism and buoyancy over the general condition of the economy. His budget of April 1947 retained the cheap money policy, and budgeted for a nominal surplus of £269m. 'This is a good year for a good surplus.' The Chancellor seemed reluctant to accept criticisms, ranging from Durbin and Jay to the *Tribune* left, that the economy was lurching into disarray. Indeed, it may be that the general change in the nature of the financial problem in 1947, from domestic growth to international instability, was somewhat beyond even his formidable understanding. Francis Williams shrewdly observed in 1948 that Dalton 'moved more easily in matters of domestic than of international finance'. He had never acquired much facility in the arcane field of foreign exchanges and world-wide currency movements, comparable with his solid grasp of domestic taxation and budgetary techniques. One of his close aides told the present writer that Dalton was, at bottom, 'a financier rather than an economist',[13] an expert

---

[12] I am grateful to Sir Alec Cairncross for letting me see his unpublished chapter on the convertibility crisis.

[13] Francis Williams, *The Triple Challenge* (London, 1948), p. 158; private information.

on taxation, focusing on the estimates and balancing the budget, rather than knowledgeable in the planning of national production, investment, and distribution. He was no planner and no Keynesian. Dalton failed to move in time when the signs were apparent all around him. This was in line with the relatively optimistic advice he was being fed by the Treasury in early 1947. He and the government suffered gravely for it. Others were also to blame for the débâcle. The Lord President's Committee under Morrison failed to provide new directives to deal with the balance of payments problem in the spring of 1947. Attlee himself, authoritative on India and foreign affairs, had little original or instructive to say on financial questions. Neither from the nationalized Bank of England, nor—still less—from the City, was sensible guidance to be had. But it was the Treasury which bore the chief responsibility for handling the nation's finances at this time. It is the Overseas Department of the Treasury, and what Dalton later called its 'irrational optimism'[14] which stands, therefore, mostly to be condemned, along with the Chancellor himself.

In the spring of 1947, it became obvious that things were going seriously wrong. The temporary crisis associated with the fuel emergency and the resultant loss of production broadened into a more general decline. Certain rooted features of Dalton's policy were becoming more and more evident. The manpower budget was failing to cope with the wasteful use of manpower resources—though, admittedly, the Ministry of Defence was no help. There was a lack of assistance to industry over persistent scarcities of key materials or machinery; a fall in output and an increase in unit costs of production resulted, with serious effects on the balance of trade. In relation to the United States, the consequences were critical in the extreme, since Britain in 1947 was taking 42½ per cent of its imports from the new world but sending only 14 per cent of its exports there in return. In the second quarter of 1947, from 1 April to 30 June, there were signs of a major crisis. The volume of exports fell sharply, below even the level of the third quarter of 1946. Conversely, in May and June, imports were running at an annual rate of

[14] Dalton, op. cit., p. 257.

$6,600m. By the start of July, the dollar deficit had risen to $500m. a month.[15] Yet Dalton remained publicly optimistic throughout. The nation still remained insulated from the collapse of its trade with the United States by the cushion of what was left of the American loan. The government's only real initiative was the appointment of the new Economic Planning Board, to be chaired by Sir Edwin Plowden, in early July; it would include three trade-union members, including Vincent Tewson, the secretary of the TUC. But beyond that it is difficult to find in the Treasury papers for this period any particular indication that Dalton perceived, or was warned against, the extent of the holocaust that was coming. The Overseas Department of the Treasury, a shadow of its former self since the death of Keynes and notoriously secretive, consistently underestimated the dollar drain and had no adequate statistical apparatus at its disposal. Dalton's figures mostly came from the Bank of England, long after the event, and were usually wrong anyway. Sir Wilfrid Eady, his main Treasury adviser on overseas monetary movements, seems to have been out of his depth, contenting himself with ineffective calls for import cuts. The Chancellor himself chose to dwell on scares run in the Tory press, along with the perverse or doctrinaire anti-socialist Americans in Wall Street such as Bernard Baruch.

On top of this growing balance of payments crisis, there was the even more alarming problem of the convertibility of sterling, due to take effect on 15 July 1947, one year precisely from the passage of the US loan through Congress. This was one of the key conditions imposed on the British government by Vinson, Clayton, and the other unreconstructed liberals in the US Treasury and Trade departments back in December 1945. Indeed, the American loan would not have been forthcoming without it. Other conditions imposed—the commitment to a wider liberalization of trade, Britain's involvement in Bretton Woods arrangements, the threat to imperial preference—had provoked more

---

[15] Memorandum by Sir Edwin Plowden, 1 Aug. 1947 (T 229/103); Cabinet Conclusions, 29 July 1947 (CAB 128/9) and memorandum by W. L. G. B., 31 July 1947 (PREM 8/489, pt. 1); J. R. C. Dow, *The Management of the British Economy, 1945-60* (Cambridge, 1964), pp. 22-6.

controversy in December 1945. Even Keynes had seemed to think that convertibility was inevitable in the post-war world, although he did criticize its timing as a result of US pressure. Britain had since been taking steps to prepare for convertibility with a series of bilateral monetary agreements, starting with one with Belgium in October 1946. In fact, it is clear that the free convertibility of the pound into dollars in July 1947 was a monumental error, one forced on the government by American coercion. In happier times, it would have placed sterling under some strain. In the circumstances of July 1947, with gold and dollar reserves already running out, and the balance of payments so disadvantageous, it was totally un-bearable. Dalton publicly insisted that the effects of convertibility had been discounted, and that a modest programme of phased import cuts from the dollar areas, as announced by Morrison on 8 July, would deal with the problem. But he was to be rudely disabused.

The great day of 15 July 1947 came and went without any great excitement. There were 'no untoward events' reported *The Economist*. It felt that it was unlikely that there would be any special pressure on Britain's gold and dollar reserves, or on the exchange parity of sterling, in the near future. After all, the countries with which the bulk of Britain's balance of payments had been incurred had had the convertibility of sterling into other currencies for some while in any case.[16] *The Times* was equally content. Its 'city notes' of 16 July observed that the Americans had given an extended date of 15 September to allow other countries to complete their own convertibility arrangements at some leisure. This would avoid panic and prevent any great pressure on sterling.

Within a week, everything had changed. A huge outflow of capital hit the country, with a tidal wave of selling of stocks comparable to 1931. It was noticeable that the main casualty was government gilt-edged stock. By 19 July it was announced that Britain had had to withdraw a further $150m. of the American loan, making a total of $400m. for the first three weeks of July alone. It now seemed probable that the huge loan intended to run until the end of 1951

---

[16] *The Economist*, 19 July 1947. The *Financial Times*, 22 July 1947, declared that the markets were still 'idle and dull'.

would have been used up even by the end of 1947. The drain
on the dollar reserves was colossal. In the first week of
convertibility, the loss was $106m.; in the second, it was
$126m.; in the third, it was $127m.; in the week ending
16 August, it came to no less than $183m.[17] The Treasury
spelt out the rapid acceleration in the drain of dollars. In
the six weeks up to 14 August, it had averaged $115m. a
week, compared with $77m. a week in the second quarter
of the year.[18] Leakages in the capital account were occurring
on all fronts. Foreign holders of sterling on transferable
accounts could pay such sterling to any country in the world.
Through transfers to US accounts, they could put sterling
down in settlement of current transactions with the US, and
also obtain dollars for their sterling either on the New York
or the London stock-market. Everybody wanted dollars;
nobody wanted pounds.

Throughout the first three weeks of August, selling of
shares on the stock-market at home went on apace. A brief
rally on 1 August failed to be maintained; the value of
quoted government securities had fallen by £400m. in the
first two and a half weeks since convertibility of 16 July.
The *Financial Times* industrial share index had fallen by
9 per cent. On 11 August, the paper reported a 'cessation
of pressure to sell' and a brief rise in the industrial ordinary
share index. On the 13th, however, there was 'a fresh spasm
of weakness' both in Funds and Equities, with a sharp fall
in treasury bonds. On the 14th, British Funds 'went from
bad to worse', with falls of up to $1\frac{3}{4}$ on the day and a mood
of complete depression in the markets. On the 16th, it was
announced that gold shares—always a sure index of impend-
ing financial disaster—were buoyant, with the gold share
index rising to 4.81. However, the government broker was
having to intervene to buy Exchequer $1\frac{3}{4}$ bonds and National
War 2½ per cent bonds, which had fallen to a new low level.
As this broad collapse in stocks occured at home, the flight
of dollars abroad reached panic levels. Economists have
subsequently debated at length the causes of this cataclysmic
drain of dollars. Sir Alec Cairncross's authoritative view is

[17] Dow, op. cit.
[18] Memorandum by Dalton, 14 Aug. 1947 (PREM 8/489, pt. 2).

that convertibility in itself made only a marginal contribution to the dollar drain, even though it acted as a precipitant. More fundamental were the long-term deterioration in the current account throughout 1947, and a serious outflow of capital both outside and inside the sterling area, despite the exchange controls prevailing. The latter was especially marked in the case of South Africa, a politically sensitive country within the sterling area, which was undergoing a massive boom in construction and manufacturing at this time. There also appears to be much substance in Harold Wilson's conclusion, sent to Dalton in September after the crisis was over, that there had been speculation against sterling in foreign markets.[19] 'Leads and lags' in commercial credit caused a serious acceleration of the dollar drain in the first two weeks of August. In effect, prompt payment was made in sterling, while payment in foreign currency was delayed. Again, pounds were being converted into dollars in vast quantities in a country such as Belgium which enjoyed a creditor status with Britain. There were hints in Brussels of the pound's being devalued. Across the Atlantic, a rise in US interest rates in June and July speeded up the flight from sterling still further. With all these hammer-blows raining down, Britain seemed to be going bankrupt, and fast.

In this crisis, the Attlee Cabinet reacted with little less than panic. The Prime Minister offered no guidance; Bevin's attention focused rather on the economic negotiations with European countries after Marshall's Harvard speech. Morrison's Lord President's Committee was a broken reed. Strachey, Bevan, and other ministers, already angry about steel nationalization, spent most of their time fighting Dalton's proposed economies. When Dalton's revised plans for import cuts, notably in food, were resisted by other ministers, on 31 July he and Cripps offered their resignation; so, for different motives entirely, did Bevan. The Cabinet seemed totally lacking in direction. Finally, in desperation, Dalton dispatched

---

[19] Cairncross, op. cit.; R. N. Gardner, *Sterling–Dollar Diplomacy* (New York, new edn., 1969), pp. 311 ff.; 'Report on Balance of Payments Statistics', by Harold Wilson, 22 Sept. 1947 (T 236/1560). Dow, op. cit., pp. 24–5, takes a different view from Cairncross and Gardner.

a Treasury delegation headed by Eady to Washington on 18 August. The Cabinet had decided the previous day to halt convertibility: the task of Eady, a deft negotiator whatever his other limitations, was to obtain the best possible terms from the Americans for implementing this decision. Snyder, Vinson's successor at the US Treasury, was unsympathetic at first, not surprisingly so since Britain had done little to keep the Americans in touch with developments, Snyder told Eady that the $400m., which was all that remained of the US loan, had been frozen; America threatened to brand Britain publicly as a defaulter. However, the atmosphere improved thereafter, and on 20 August it was announced that the USA had agreed to convertibility being immediately suspended on 'an emergency and temporary' basis. On the following day, 21 August, the London Stock Exchange returned to something like sanity. Old Consols and treasury bonds were both 2½ per cent up on the day after 'action at last'.[20]

Following this shattering experience, Dalton took refuge in the public view that convertibility itself had been the real cause of the débâcle and that the Labour government had been the hapless victim of policies forced upon it by the US Treasury eighteen months earlier. *The Economist* and other periodicals and newspapers were inclined to agree. But it seems evident now that the convertibility decision, a calamitous error by any standards, was really superimposed on a long-term decline in the home economy (accentuated by the loss of export markets during the war), shown by the balance of payments and current account problems earlier in the year. As has been seen, it was not only the Americans who were fleeing from sterling in the crisis. Other non-sterling countries, including Argentina, on whose supplies of beef Britain critically depended, showed no confidence in Britain's ability to defend its currency or maintain its reserves. Belgium, as has been seen, was an important European country where foreign holders of sterling were selling fast, and Switzerland another. Within the sterling area itself, there was a net inflow of £180m. into South Africa in the course of 1947, almost all of it from sterling countries and

[20] *Financial Times*, 22 Aug. 1947.

partly caused by fears of a depreciation of the pound sterling. Compared with this, the fall in the sterling balances was relatively unimportant. The entire episode of convertibility in that sunny month of August 1947 tore the whole financial credibility of the Labour government into shreds. A huge effort would be required to rebuild its reputation, an effort that would probably be launched by Sir Stafford Cripps, the one minister who had come out with a clear policy during the crisis, even if a grim one. The message that the suspension of convertibility was only of 'an emergency and temporary nature' was for public consumption only. In December 1947, when Britain was able to draw on the remaining, now un-frozen $400m., which was all that was left of the original US loan, the American Treasury admitted that convertibility of sterling had been permanently abandoned. The pound was simply too weak for further adventures.

Beyond the immediate crisis, basic economic problems remained in full measure, especially the continuing dollar drain, the growing deficit in trade, and the balance of pay-ments weakness. No confidence could be placed in Dalton's optimistic nostrums. They had dissolved into the summer air. Henceforth a new policy had to be followed in finance, one with dire implications for the entire thrust of Labour's programme. There would be a much more serious attempt to cut costs by pursuing disinflation at home and sharply reducing dollar imports. On 16 October, Dalton and Cripps, now the Minister of Economic Affairs, circulated a joint paper to the Cabinet.[21] With the dollar drain expected to continue at the rate of $2 billion a year throughout 1948, they recommended savings of £175m. to reduce the gold and dollar deficit, of which £120m. would come from cuts in imports, including £75m. of food imports. In the end, after much furious argument in the Cabinet, a reduced programme of £66m. cuts in food imports was accepted. The unfortunate consumer thus faced still further reductions in basic rations of meat, fats, sugar, and other foodstuffs. It was estimated that the average calorie intake per person per day would fall to between 2,650 and 2,725 in the first half of 1948, com-pared with 3,000 in the last year of the war. The intake of

[21] This was CP (47) 283 (CAB 129/21).

protein would be especially diminished. The policy of austerity, usually linked with Cripps, actually began with Dalton's autumn budget of November 1947, with its heavy cuts in dollar imports, its sharp reduction of consumer purchasing power, and new rates of purchase and profits tax. On the other hand, the Cabinet abandoned an increase in tobacco duty in favour of a 1*d.* a pint increase in the price of beer. Other proposals rejected included a capital gains tax, dividend limitation, and supplementary estates duty. Additional cuts in government expenditure were resisted by the Cabinet. Food subsidies were frozen at the high level of £329m., whereas Bridges and the Treasury's Budget Committee had proposed on 17 September that there be draconian cuts in subsidies on basic foodstuffs from over £400m. to some £275m. Dalton minuted against Bridges's expressed fears of inflationary pressure—'Yes, and much better than unemployment!'[22] More generally, this budget heralded a much more concentrated emphasis on macroeconomic 'planning', with Plowden inaugurating a new approach of a *dirigiste* nature at the Economic Planning Board; a new white paper on costs, prices, and incomes was in active preparation. Morrison's Lord President's Committee had been supplanted by a new Economic Committee of the Cabinet. In September, a new Ministry of Economic Affairs was created under Cripps—in curious circumstances, as will shortly be discussed. The planning mechanisms of Plowden's board would henceforth be geared to Cripps's new department, rather than to the Treasury whose role in terms of broad industrial and export strategy would be much diminished.

In personal terms, there was, finally, the diminution of the reputation of Hugh Dalton himself. His authority was much shaken by the convertibility affair, to which he had responded belatedly and almost in panic fashion. It is striking that, in his diary for 1947, the actual word 'convertibility' does not once appear. His nervous system had also deteriorated with the extreme tension of the sterling crisis. Conversely, the star of Stafford Cripps had waxed at the

[22] Materials in Budget and Finance Bill papers, Sept.–Nov. 1947 (T 171/392–3).

same period, as the newly-created Ministry of Economic
Affairs confirmed. By 21 October, A. J. Cummings could
write in the *News Chronicle* that the government was better
placed to answer its critics on economic management than
it had been when parliament adjourned on 13 August. This
was. 'thanks in large measure to the ability and drive of Sir
Stafford Cripps'. What would have been Dalton's fate in
normal circumstances can only be a matter of speculation.
His November budget did not commend itself to financial
commentators. The *Financial Times* criticized 'its strangely
perfunctory air'.[23] Dalton's eloquence seemed to be sound-
ing the bugle of expansionist advance to cover a deflationary
retreat. In fact, the issue was decided by an extraordinary
personal indiscretion, when Dalton divulged some tax details
to a lobby correspondent of the London evening *Star*, just
before delivering his speech. Churchill reacted to this blunder
with much generosity, but Dalton and Attlee both reached
the conclusion on 14 November that Dalton must resign.
Cripps replaced him at the Treasury with all the powers
formerly accruing to the Ministry of Economic Affairs. The
press were unforgiving on Dalton's fall. A. P. Wadsworth in
the *Manchester Guardian* commented that 'Mr Dalton would
always yield to the call of popularity. Sir Stafford Cripps
will always listen to the call of conscience.'[24] The stock-
market responded positively, and so did the electors. Sir
Richard Acland (whose performance as candidate was sharply
criticized by Gaitskell)[25] held on to Gravesend in a difficult
by-election later in November. The swing against Labour was
only 6.8 per cent, much less than in recent by-elections in
Liverpool, Edge Hill, and West Islington.

Dalton's career in high office was far from over. Woodrow
Wyatt told Tom Driberg on 24 November that Dalton had
reappeared in the House and was just as intolerable as he was
before. Wyatt added that no doubt he would be back in the
Cabinet again in two or three months' time.[26] The forecast
was remarkably accurate, since Dalton reappeared at the

[23] *News Chronicle*, 21 Oct. 1947; *Financial Times*, 13 Nov. 1947.
[24] *Manchester Guardian*, 15 Nov. 1947.
[25] Hugh Gaitskell diaries, 4 Dec. 1947. 'What a bore he is!'
[26] Woodrow Wyatt to Tom Driberg, 24 Nov. 1947 (Driberg papers, W. 10).

Cabinet table in May 1948 as Chancellor of the Duchy of Lancaster, with a special responsibility for the Council of Europe due to be convened at Strasbourg in 1949. Dalton emerged, both at Strasbourg and at party conference, as the ebullient, prejudiced anti-German rogue elephant he had always been. But he was no longer a dominant figure, in the inner Cabinet or the party. An expansionist, part-inflationary policy had been cast aside, under extreme necessity. Dalton had fallen with it.

The economic crisis led to a damaging political crisis. Dalton's was not the only reputation to suffer in the convertibility affair. Herbert Morrison, too, just recovered from heart troubles, had seriously lost authority. The inadequacy of his Lord President's Committee was suggested by the creation of Plowden's Economic Planning Board, a departure which Morrison had long resisted. The establishment of the Economic Policy and Production Committees of the Cabinet in September 1947 showed that all the main economic levers were being taken from him. In any case, he was not a trained economist, and his diagnosis of the financial crisis of July had not impressed his colleagues. His inadequate programme of import cuts announced on 8 July had drawn some criticism. His biographers, who fairly point out that it was his first major speech to the House since his return from illness, emphasize that it was poorly delivered and uninspiring in tone—'a grim speech in a glum house'.[27] Meanwhile, Bridges and others complained that Morrison's political instincts were leading him to push personal cronies like Clem Leslie, the Planning Board's public relations officer, and Max Nicholson, who handled economic co-ordination, from within the Lord President's office.[28] It was hinted that the new Economic Planning Board was being hamstrung from the start by Morrison's political activities.

But the main criticism of Morrison lay rather in the obvious, physical fact that, as economic strategist, Leader of the House, party policy-maker, and much else besides, he was simply taking on too much, with grave effects on his health.

[27] Bernard Donoughue and G. W. Jones, *Herbert Morrison*, p. 408.
[28] Ibid., pp. 405–6.

His supreme talent as a leading minister remained beyond question. Apart from Morrison, however, there was also mounting criticism of Attlee. Growing during the arguments over steel nationalization, this reached a crescendo during the convertibility crisis. Cripps was now attacking the Prime Minister's lack of drive over exports to the dollar areas. Morrison was a frequent critic, too. Dalton also found the Prime Minister lacking in firmness. Even the normally loyal Ernest Bevin rumbled with anger at the failures in fuel production and over manpower policy. He also thought Attlee should be appointing more trade-unionists to the government. On the left, Aneurin Bevan reflected the discontent of the 'Keep Left' wing and of *Tribune* with the government's lack of socialist commitment, as shown over steel. The failure to cut down the defence budget, and the disasters in Palestine were other whips with which to flay the Prime Minister. On the right wing, Evan Durbin and Gaitskell thought Attlee's performance during the convertibility crisis was 'catastrophic'.[29] Durbin urged on Attlee a new energetic programme to reduce imports and reallocate coal, steel, and manpower, to assist exports and cut back on home consumption and building projects. The government must launch a supreme effort for the nation to help itself, since the dollar loan from America was due to run out in perhaps nine months' time.[30] But Durbin's views seemed to have little impact. Attlee remained impenetrable and impervious. His placid, durable qualities, invaluable in getting an agreed programme under way when things were going well, and in handling a fractious Cabinet of gifted prima donnas, seemed less appropriate for a new crisis which demanded energy and ideas. At the parliamentary party meeting on 11 August, Attlee was criticized on all sides. Cummings reported in the *News Chronicle* that Attlee had actually offered to resign, but had been dissuaded from doing so by Morrison and Dalton. 'He gives an impression that the situation is beyond his grasp.'[31] A left-wing group headed by Donald Bruce was said to be pushing the lost cause of

[29] Hugh Gaitskell's diary, 12 Aug. 1947.
[30] Durbin to Attlee, 23 July 1947 (Attlee papers, Bodleian, Box 9).
[31] *News Chronicle*, 23 May, 12 Aug. 1947.

Aneurin Bevan as prime minister. Others, more credibly, favoured Ernest Bevin. Pierson Dixon of the Foreign Office recorded in his diary that there were moves to form a coalition government, that would include Churchill and leading Conservatives. 'Personally I feel E. B. will find it hard to resist the lure of the premiership.'[32] Crises—or alleged crises —mounted all the time. There were industrial difficulties at this unwelcome moment. Miners at the Grimethorpe colliery in south Yorkshire went on strike over a two-foot increase in the daily stint for face-workers. The miners, reported Shinwell, 'were in ugly mood'. By 4 September 46 pits were affected in Yorkshire, of which 33 had totally stopped working at a time of extreme economic crisis. Appeals to the men by Shinwell, Lawther, and even Horner had no effect. Not until 16 September did this damaging affair peter out. The political rumours and counter-rumours were widespread; many of them were contradictory or manifestly false. The alleged Tory move to form a coalition under Bevin, for instance, is not revealed in the evidence available. But the increasing focus on Attlee's personal inadequacies as leader is clear beyond dispute. His speech in the Commons at the height of the financial crisis was correctly described as 'flat and disappointing'. 'It left a feeling of depression and unease', followed as it was by a performance at the dispatch box by Dalton marked by 'an almost total emptiness'.[33] A. J. Cummings on 12 August commented that Attlee was 'exhausted and feels deeply the humiliation of recent days'.[34] Meanwhile a by-election at Edge Hill in Liverpool was not going well: it was to register, on 11 September, a 10.2 per cent swing against Labour.

After the end of the immediate convertibility crisis on 20 August, moves began to seek a possible replacement of Attlee as prime minister. The main *dramatis personae* were Morrison, Dalton, and Cripps, although their ideas about a prospective successor for Attlee were very divergent. There had been an initial discussion between Bevin and Dalton after

[32] Dixon, *Double Diploma*, p. 246 (28 July 1947).
[33] *News Chronicle*, 8 Aug. 1947. The *Manchester Guardian*, also normally pro-government, spoke (8 Aug. 1947) of the 'widespread disappointment' caused by Attlee's and Dalton's speeches.
[34] *News Chronicle*, 12 Aug. 1947.

the Durham Miners' Gala on 26 July, but this had been ended by Bevin flatly refusing to usurp Attlee's place as leader. 'Who do you think I am—Lloyd George?' is one version of Bevin's reaction.[35] Then a new initiative was launched by Cripps on 5 September. He went to see Dalton with a proposal that they should jointly approach Morrison, with the idea of a joint request to Attlee to resign in favour of Bevin. Morrison was formally to propose Bevin as leader at a meeting of the parliamentary party. The extreme unlikelihood of Morrison ever acting in so self-sacrificing a fashion in order to promote the claims of his arch-enemy, Bevin, was evidently something that Cripps discounted, so firm was his resolve that Attlee should go forthwith. Dalton and Cripps were in broad agreement. But Morrison proved to be a far more difficult fellow conspirator when he met Cripps the following evening. While equally critical of Attlee, he refused to promote the cause of Bevin, but argued instead that he himself would be the most suitable replacement as prime minister. On 8 September, Morrison went further and wrote a letter, clearly intended for possible publication, in which he refused to involve himself in a *putsch* such as Cripps proposed. He reminded Cripps of the role of the PLP in choosing a party leader. He thus reverted to the position he had previously argued on 27 July 1945.[36] Cripps, therefore, went ahead on his own, and had a private meeting with Attlee on the evening of 9 September.[37] He proposed that Bevin would become prime minister, with Attlee as Chancellor of the Exchequer and Dalton at the Foreign Office. Morrison would become Lord Privy Seal, largely concerned with leading the Commons, while Cripps would replace Morrison as Lord President. It was an unconvincing package in many respects; nor did it have the overt concurrence of any of the ministers supposedly involved. According to the usual account, Attlee at once rang up Bevin and in Cripps's presence received Bevin's firm refusal to take part. Attlee also well knew how Morrison must react to such obvious demotion.

[35] For accounts, see Dalton, op. cit., pp. 239–40; Donoghue and Jones, op. cit., pp. 413–25.

[36] Morrison to Cripps, 8 Sept. 1947, Cripps to Morrison, 8 Sept. 1947 (Nuffield College, Morrison papers).

[37] Kenneth Harris, op. cit., pp. 348–9.

In a famous masterful response, he turned the tables on Cripps by offering him the supreme new post of Minister of Economic Affairs. Cripps would thus vault over both Dalton and Morrison in one giant leap. He accepted at once, persuading himself that the party and the country required his promotion. Indeed, he was almost certainly right. Morrison left for a holiday in the Channel Islands the next day in a mood of much disgruntlement hoping that there would be no remodelling the government in his absence.[38] The *putsch* was off. In view of the evident discord between the plotters, it had hardly been on in the first place. With Bevin firmly behind him, Attlee had scored a famous tactical victory.

In fact, the reshuffle that had long been required on general grounds did begin while Morrison was sunning himself on the beach in Guernsey. On 15 September, Attlee wrote to him informing him of Cripps's promotion to the new department, with power to supervise and co-ordinate the production programme for home and for export. There would also be set up a new Cabinet Economic Committee to take decisions on the working of the economic plan; the Lord President's Committee would thus lose its essential function. Attlee wrote sympathetically to Morrison on his many burdens, and proposed that he should succeed Greenwood as chairman of both the Legislation Committee and the Social Services Committee. Morrison would also have more time for leading the House, directing the party, and handling the non-economic side of the work of the Lord President's Committee.[39] Among other proposed changes, Addison would leave the Commonwealth Relations Office, but remain in the Cabinet as Lord Privy Seal and Leader of the Lords, as well as presiding in committee over Commonwealth problems. Other moves would be the removal of Shinwell from the Cabinet, and his dispatch to the War Office, with Gaitskell to replace him at Fuel and Power. Aneurin Bevan would be transferred from Health to Supply to take charge of steel nationalization. Morrison's reply on 19 September underlined all his doubts about Cripps's new ministry. He proposed Shinwell for the Commonwealth

---

[38] Donoughue and Jones, op. cit., p. 420.
[39] Attlee to Morrison, 15 Sept. 1947 (Morrison papers).

Office; shrewdly, he surmised that Bevan would be unwilling to move sideways to Supply. 'The iron and steel people have to be handled with decision and *care*',[40] Morrison observed, with recollections of earlier indiscretions in mind.

In the end, the new Ministry of Economic Affairs was announced to the world on 29 September, with Cripps to take over the Central Economic Planning Staff, the Economic Information Unit, and the Economic section of the Cabinet Office. Cripps would handle, not only domestic economic policy, but exports and overseas trade as well. Other changes followed, with Greenwood leaving the government altogether, along with Wilmot (who refused a peerage); Shinwell went to the War Office, but without Cabinet rank. He had at first refused to go, but had been encouraged to do so by Laski.[41] In Cripps's place at the Board of Trade came the remarkably youthful Harold Wilson, a thirty-one-year-old former Oxford economics don and wartime civil servant. Philip Noel-Baker entered the Cabinet, too, at the Commonwealth Relations Office. With the forty-one-year-old Gaitskell at Fuel and Power, the government thus had a much-needed infusion of younger blood. Conversely, the septuagenarian Addison retained a major role as Lord Privy Seal. George Strauss went to Supply, Bevan, who had refused to move, stayed at the Ministry of Health. Westwood was replaced as Secretary of State for Scotland by Arthur Woodburn. J. B. Hynd, the minister in Germany and Austria until the beginning of the year, and latterly Minister of Pensions, and Fred Bellenger, a junior minister at the War Office, also left the government. Attlee took the opportunity to promote a number of able young men in the lower reaches of the government, including George Brown, Patrick Gordon-Walker, Alfred Robens, Kenneth Younger, John Freeman, Arthur Bottomley, James Callaghan, Michael Stewart, and David Rees-Williams. The *New Statesman* was critical of the changes in general: they seemed to push the government towards the right, with the promotion of men such as Brown, Gordon-Walker, and (in Town and Country Planning) Evelyn King who was 'somewhat

[40] Morrison to Attlee, 19 Sept. 1947 (ibid.).
[41] Wigg, op. cit., p. 131; E. Shinwell, *Conflict without Malice* (London, 1955), pp. 186–7.

beyond the extreme right'; in fact, King was to resurface as a Conservative MP in 1964. More plausibly, the *Statesman* questioned why an able trade-union minister such as James Griffiths had not been promoted. On the other hand, the advance of leftish backbenchers like Callaghan and Freeman was felt to be an encouraging sign, while the move of that old Tribunite, Strauss, to Supply suggested that the government was in earnest over steel nationalization. The general verdict offered was that 'the old type of working-class leader gives way to the disinterested expert who had studied Keynes'.[42] It is difficult to characterize many of the ministerial changes in these terms, but no doubt the replacement of Shinwell, of impeccable Glasgow proletarian background, by the Wykehamist Gaitskell was some kind of symbol. Attlee's changes, in fact, went only a part of the way. The clean sweep that had been proclaimed still left Isaacs at Labour, Tomlinson at Education, and Barnes at Transport. Nor was any major reshuffle to follow for the rest of the government's term of office down to the 1950 election. For all that, the criticism of the government had led to a clear mood that changes were needed, and that heads ought to roll. Attlee had duly responded to it.

As a result, the balance of authority within the government was much altered. In the first place, the leftish element in the Cabinet was somewhat undermined, with the departure of Shinwell. Only Bevan stayed in as a left-wing critic, and he was too preoccupied over the finance of the National Health Service and the housing drive to cause great difficulty. Morrison had suffered an obvious rebuff. No longer was he supreme in economic policy-making. The new Ministry of Economic Affairs, along with the Cabinet's Economic Policy, Production, and Priorities Committees, had taken over that key role. His close friend, Maurice Webb, now chairman of the parliamentary party, wrote to Morrison on 1 October in some dismay about the Cripps *putsch*. 'I must say that I am very disturbed by it all. I do not like the erosion of your own power. . . . I wish you had not yielded up so much in the economic field to Cripps.' He hoped that rumours of Morrison's decline and fall would be 'nipped in the

[42] *New Statesman*, 11 Oct. 1947.

bud'.[43] In fact, Attlee handled Morrison with such tact, and the powers that he still retained were so numerous, that his disgruntlement soon disappeared. He remained a leading figure in party and parliament, while his call for moderation and 'consolidation' dominated Labour's outlook in the run-up to the 1950 general election. For all that, Morrison's star was no longer in the ascendant, any more than Dalton's.

As for the Prime Minister himself, his outmanœuvring of Cripps, and the astute fashion in which he managed to re-model the administration enabled him to recover much of his authority. By the start of 1948, any suggestions that he might be removed from the leadership were stilled. Even Bevan emerged as one of his supporters. But it was a some-what pyrrhic victory for Attlee. His control over the Cabinet was less automatic than in 1945–6 with Ernest Bevin his only wholly reliable supporter at the top level of government. Attlee somewhat retreated thereafter as a grey, almost anonymous, chairman and co-ordinator, much as he had been during the war. Only perhaps in the 1950–1 period, when Cripps was sick, Bevin was dying, and Morrison uncertain at the Foreign Office, and Attlee himself came to handle key aspects of foreign policy during the Korean War, did he begin to approach his earlier ascendancy. It was, perhaps, a sign then of the government's exhaustion. The spoils of battle obviously went to Sir Stafford Cripps, the symbol of the government's approach thereafter. As Chancellor, he took with him to the Treasury, on Dalton's downfall, all the new powers he had been given at the Ministry of Economic Affairs. His dominance on the home front was beyond question. His ascendancy also marked a change of tone and style in govern-ment's broad approach. The mood was now one of retrench-ment, not expansion, with the grim resolve of Cripps in place of the expansive buoyancy of Dalton. Instead of a somewhat profligate outward-looking policy, there was a stress on austerity, cut-backs, all the severities of a siege economy. A multilateral trading policy was replaced by adherence to a closed trading bloc, based on the sterling area and the European Payments Union. Bolstered externally by Marshall Aid, the Labour government went economically on the

[43] Maurice Webb to Morrison, 1 Oct. 1947 (Morrison papers).

defensive. Similarly, in its political approach, it was no longer on the attack, but anxious rather to retain ground won. From the autumn of 1947, after the hammer-blows of the *annus horrendus*, the government was beginning to lose the initiative.

9

The Cripps Era

From the economic and political crisis of August–September 1947, to the outbreak of the war in Korea in June 1950, the outstanding feature of the Labour government was the dominance of Sir Stafford Cripps. His ascetic personality, and its associated regime of 'austerity' gave this later phase of the government a legendary reputation, which, over thirty years on, has not wholly left it. Cripps's own political record over the years since 1931 had been decidedly curious. He had been supreme among the mavericks of British politics. His reputation for rock-firm consistency and reliability in the 1947–50 period must be measured against his erratic behaviour over previous years which had made him almost a pariah in public life. He had begun life as a conventional member of a Conservative, High-Church family: his father was a Tory MP. Not until he embarked on a successful career at the bar in his mid-twenties did he show a serious enthusiasm for socialism, and was elected to parliament as Labour member for Bristol East in January 1931. After the October 1931 general election, in which he was fortunate to retain his seat by just 429 votes, he moved rapidly to the far left. He advocated emergency government by decree by a future Labour administration, since it would otherwise be sabotaged by the City and the banks. In 1936–9 he was the main advocate of a Popular Front, and was expelled from the parliamentary Labour Party in January 1939, along with Bevan and Strauss. In this period, too, he founded and financed *Tribune*, as a weekly voice for the left. But during the war his outlook changed substantially. At the time of his mission to Russia in 1942, he appeared to have been transformed into a more centrist figure; there were rumours that he might be propelled into 10 Downing Street as the people's alternative to Churchill. During the war years, he quite lost his uncritical enthusiasm for the Soviet Union; instead, he became an apostle of the managerial style and of planning within a mixed economy, somewhat on the lines of Roosevelt's New Deal in the United States. He formally rejoined the Labour Party as late as March 1945. During the general election, his rhetoric was far from militant. He emphasized the need for industrial partnership and for 'good teamwork' between government, management, and unions on corporatist lines. At the Board of Trade from July 1945 onwards, his concern was with industrial and commercial efficiency rather than with socialist transformation. His working parties for textiles and other industries made no change in their structure or management, while he emerged as an outspoken critic of workers' participation in management. He was attacked for his caution in industrial matters by his left-wing PPS at the Board of Trade, Barbara Castle. As has been seen (above, p. 122), another Board of Trade junior minister, Ellis Smith, resigned in January 1946 because of Cripps's refusal to contemplate the nationalization of cotton spinning.

Yet Cripps's position in the Cabinet became an increasingly powerful one. At the Board of Trade he presided over a notable increase in the volume of exports. The negotiations over India underlined his centrality in the government's major policies, even if Attlee himself was the major architect of the transfer of power in the end. In the financial shambles of July–August 1947, Cripps alone emerged as a man who kept his head and offered a clear strategy for future policy. His announced programme for the boosting of exports on 11 September seemed to many to mark the turning of the tide, with the government at last taking resolute action. At the Treasury he was always a commanding, inspiring figure. Gaitskell marvelled at 'his amazingly keen intelligence' and 'superb self-confidence'.[1] To Cripps, this twice-born centrist, and ex-man of the left, nothing seemed impossible. At the Treasury from November 1947 onwards, he had a broad base of support. He won the confidence of business and the City. He made it plain that he was anxious not to upset the confidence of investors by swingeing attacks on profits and capital. At the same time, he retained a warm personal relationship with Aneurin Bevan, an old ally on the left from

[1] Hugh Gaitskell's diary, 16. Feb. 1948.

Popular Front days. He endorsed Bevan's views on steel nationalization, even if without enormous enthusiasm. More important still, he kept up a high level of social spending on health, housing, and other welfare services despite all the financial difficulties of 1948–50. The location of industry policy was maintained, even at the cost of exports on occasion. His aides thought him more fundamentally left-wing than Dalton ever was, and certainly more suspicious of the civil service presence. In early July 1949, Cripps complained privately to Gaitskell that his Treasury aides were all economic liberals who were preventing him from carrying through 'a socialist [sic] policy'.[2] Despite the heavy cuts made in investment, and all the sacrifices imposed on wage-earners during the regime of austerity, Cripps retained the support and confidence of the Cabinet throughout. He contrived, wrote the Spectator (3 June 1949) to be 'a theoretical socialist and a practical economist' at one and the same time. Over the devaluation of the pound in the summer of 1949, he was, for once, manifestly uncertain; but his eventual acceptance of the views of Gaitskell, Jay, and Wilson gave the advocacy of these young economist colleagues the mantle of authority. Cripps was an enormously powerful Chancellor, more authoritative than Dalton had ever been. He took over all the new planning machinery from the Ministry of Economic Affairs. He also exercised considerable influence over the operations of the Board of Trade, now under the energetic leadership of Harold Wilson. A memorandum of November 1950, just after Cripps had had to resign from the Exchequer through ill health, spelt out in detail the immense range of responsibilities that fell on the Treasury during the Cripps era. They included policy on the balance of payments, the rate of exchange, import controls and the export trade; budgetary and taxation policy, the control of government expenditure, monetary policy, and tariffs; wages, dividends, and investment programmes; and numerous associated fields such as foreign aid and development

[2] On 17 December 1948, Cripps persuaded the Cabinet Production Committee to turn down a plan to expand Ford's car plants at Dagenham and Langley, in the south-east, as it was in breach of the location of industry policy, even though Wilson and Strauss argued that it would boost exports (CAB 134/636); private information; Gaitskell's diary, 3 Aug. 1949. The '[sic]' is Gaitskell's.

assistance overseas.[3] Under Cripps, the Treasury regained all its old ascendancy in central government last enjoyed under Neville Chamberlain, or perhaps Lloyd George. No Chancellor has been so powerful since.

As Cripps's authority mounted ever greater in 1948 and 1949, there were many who felt that his power would be maximized with it. After Ernest Bevin, he was obviously Attlee's key minister. Indeed, as Bevin's health deteriorated in 1949, Cripps seemed almost the recognized Number Two in the government. Until his own health began to decline alarmingly in 1950, Cripps had certainly outstripped Morrison, while others such as Bevan were left far behind. Gaitskell commented engagingly in April 1948 on a dinner gathering at which Strauss, Strachey, Jay, Marquand, Wilson, and himself were joined by Aneurin Bevan. Cripps was the presiding figure. 'I could not help feeling', wrote Gaitskell, 'that Stafford was surveying his future Cabinet.'[4]

Stafford Cripps's dominance was, above all, intensely personal. It was the triumph of a powerful will over a flagging government. He remained an aloof figure. He had not stood for the NEC since 1938, and played no part in the Labour Party conferences of 1946, 1947, or 1948. He was never active in party circles. He embodied an air of unquenchable moral rectitude, reinforced by the patrician's contempt for the creed of materialism. The guiding star in Cripps's outlook was his profound commitment to the Anglican Church; he was located firmly within its High-Church wing. He was a deeply committed Christian, always liable to take time off during his Chancellorship to address schoolchildren and others on such topics as 'the Christian idea of citizenship'. 'The problem of the world today is a moral one', he told thousands of schoolchildren on New Year's Eve, 1948.[5] Churchill was one of many who found this air of Gladstonian moralism insufferable at times. 'There but for the grace of God goes God' was the famous jibe. When Churchill seemed to suggest that Cripps had broken faith with his friends and

---

[3] 'Major Responsibilities of the Treasury', Nov. 1950 (T 222/238).

[4] Gaitskell's diary, 23 Apr. 1948.

[5] *The Times*, 1 Jan. 1949. Also see press cuttings in Cripps papers, Nuffield College Library.

allies by changing his mind on devaluation in 1949, Cripps broke off all relations; he refused even to accept an honorary degree at Bristol from Churchill's tainted hands. He symbolized the idea of sacrifice, discipline, the call of conscience, the ascetic style. He favoured short skirts for women, instead of the fashionable 'new look', because this implied a saving in textile supplies. Cripps was a teetotaller and a vegetarian. He appeared almost to enjoy the austerity and self-flagellation that he exhorted the nation to adopt. He worked phenomenally long hours, with, among other results to his health, a severe tendency to insomnia. He would rise at 4.0 a.m. and then do three hours' work, before taking a freezing cold bath to stimulate himself for the hard day's slog that lay ahead. No greater contrast with the earthy hedonism of Hugh Dalton could be imagined than this inexhaustible pilgrim. His persona as Chancellor was bound up with his moral style. It thus became superimposed on the very image on the government. It was a curious, evangelical regime of Cromwellian severity, another rule of the saints, but it gave the Attlee administration fresh energy and self-confidence, a new belief in itself after the humiliating events of 1947.

Cripps operated a very different financial policy from that of Dalton. Even if the stark contrast, so often made, between the inflationist Dalton and the deflationist Cripps is something of a caricature, there was a marked shift in emphasis. Cripps was determined to end the somewhat irresponsible profligacy of the previous period, to get public expenditure under control, to relate spending programmes to the available resources, to have a carefully-costed budgetary stimulus, above all to get Britain to stand on her own two feet, without any dependence on American loans. Rising production and productivity, and the maintenance of full employment, were made possible only by a self-sufficient policy which concentrated on exports, the control of consumption and a programmed approach to national economic survival. No uncritical trust should be placed in other nations, either the countries of western Europe with their unstable fiscal methods, or on the United States, though collaboration with the latter was indispensable. The Cripps era, indeed, was marked by a degree of isolationism in economic policy and, as will be seen, in aspects of foreign policy as well. Britain and the sterling area should purge themselves, and look the world in the face. The broad intellectual presuppositions were Keynesian, with a reliance on budgetary policy and demand management that anticipates the 'Butskellism' of the fifties. Cripps, not Gaitskell or Butler, began the long reign of the Keynesians at 10 Downing Street down to 1979. Robert Hall, the director of the economic section of the Cabinet Office, then of the Treasury, spelt out the main strategy three years later.

The last Government adopted in 1947 and 1948 a revolution in British practice, when they [*sic*] took responsibility for maintaining full employment but avoiding inflation. It is the best argument in favour of this policy that this revolution passed almost unnoticed. The policy was accepted as the right one both in the country and abroad, except perhaps in countries like Belgium which have gone back to laissez-faire and are making use of employment as a method of economic regulation.

Any serious divergence from the Cripps policy, wrote Hall, 'would rightly be regarded as an abandonment of the principles of planning'.[6] Enshrined as a new conventional wisdom amongst the macro-economists, Cripps's policy swept all before it.

One of its outstanding features was a massive emphasis on exports. From the autumn of 1947, resources and manpower were diverted to the export trade as never before, to redress the balance of payments and to close the dollar gap. The emphasis was on quantity and rapidity of production. As James Callaghan, an acute political observer, wrote in 1948, 'production rather than unemployment was the main problem facing the government'.[7] The Board of Trade was given new powers, as were the various development agencies. The results were exciting and spectacular. The year 1948 was the most thriving that Britain had known since before the first world war. Mines, factories, and docks were throbbing with life. Unemployment virtually disappeared. Everywhere there were signs of a massive regeneration of industry with a great surge

---

[6] Notes on Budgetary policy by Robert Hall, 16 Mar. 1950 (PREM 8/1188).
[7] James Callaghan, 'The Approach to Social Equality' in Munro (ed.), *Socialism: the British Way*, p. 146.

in exports. Coal was once again exported in some quantities from Newcastle and Cardiff. The *Economic Survey* in 1949 was a hymn to the progress of the previous year, 'a year of substantial progress in nearly every part of the economic life of the United Kingdom'.[8] Exports raced ahead to a level of more than 150 per cent above that of 1938. They were recorded as being 25 per cent above those for 1947 and the largest in volume since 1929. Industrial production was 12 per cent above the level of the previous year. Coal output, while still disappointing to some extent due to manpower shortages, rose to 208m. tons; steel (still in private hands, ironically enough) saw a record level of production, from 12.7m. ingot tons in 1946 to 14.9m. in 1948. An output of 17½m. ingot tons for 1953–4 was confidently anticipated. The question of where these exports went was crucial. A happy feature of the year, therefore, was the progress made in capturing markets in North America, much assisted by the economic boom in the United States and Canada. Harold Wilson urged Cripps to think of setting a special export target for North America alone in 1949.[9] Gross capital formation rose from £2,040m. in 1947 to £2,352m. in 1948, though admittedly some of the increase was simply due to inflation. Harold Wilson's pronouncements to the Commons on the latest news of monthly exporting and foreign-trade figures became almost triumphant. Indeed, some ministers were now anxious that too many resources were being devoted to exports instead of to re-equipping basic industries at home.[10] In the course of the year, the balance of payments crisis of 1947 disappeared. Britain had been in deficit by £298m. in 1946 and by no less than £443m. in the awful year of 1947. By the second half of 1948 the deficit had been wiped out, and there was an estimated surplus of £30m. for the last six months of the year. It was a very narrow margin, but it clearly heralded that Britain, after the hammer-blows of the war and the financial débâcle of mid-1947 was once again paying its way, with only the

[8] *Economic Survey, 1949* (PP, 1948–9, xxix), Cmd. 7647, p. 511; cf. *The Economist*, 19 Mar. 1949.

[9] Wilson to Cripps, 3 Feb. 1949 (T 229/259).

[10] Minutes of Cabinet Production Committee, 23 July 1948 (CAB 134/636).

continuing imbalance of dollar payments as a major cause for concern. At least the desperate situation in late 1947, when Robert Hall could forecast a fall in the gold and dollar reserves to £272m. by the end of 1948 and their total disappearance by the end of 1949, was reversed.[11] Of course, a massive factor was the injection of assistance from Marshall Aid under the European Recovery Programme from the summer of 1948 onwards. Cripps told the Cabinet Economic Committee on 16 September 1948 that the allocation to the United Kingdom of $1,263m. for 1948–9 was 'unexpectedly satisfactory'.[12] But Marshall Aid was manifestly assisting a process of inherent recovery in an increasingly buoyant, growth-orientated Britain.

These achievements were often linked in the popular mind with the government's new emphasis on planning. There was the entire Plowden apparatus of the Central Economic Planning Staff, now attached to the Treasury. Added to this was the revamped Economic Section of the Treasury directed by Robert Hall, together with the Central Statistical Office, various regional boards concerned with the production and export campaign, and the Economic Information Unit under Clem Leslie. The Overseas Finance Department of the Treasury, which in Douglas Jay's view had been much the weakest section of the Treasury in Dalton's time,[13] was now overhauled. Wilfred Eady, who was not expert in foreign exchange matters, was transferred to the home department; he was replaced by the great statistician, R. W. ('Otto') Clarke, and the Prime Minister's secretary, Leslie Rowan, who had unrivalled talents in using the governmental machine. Coordination between the Treasury and other departments was provided by several interdepartmental committees of officials. They included the Overseas Negotiations Committee, chaired by Rowan; the Import Programme Committee, chaired by 'Otto' Clarke; and above all the Budget Committee, chaired by Cripps himself—which held many of its meetings (perhaps symbolically) at a secret rendezvous in a home for nervous invalids in deepest Sussex. At the ministerial level, there was the major instrument of the Cabinet Economic Policy

[11] Memorandum by Robert Hall, 12 Feb. 1948 (PREM 8/773).
[12] Minutes of Cabinet Economic Committee, 16 Sept. 1948 (CAB 134/216).
[13] Jay, op. cit., p. 171.

Committee which met almost weekly under the chairmanship of the Prime Minister; it held fifteen meetings between 9 October and 31 December 1947, and a further forty meetings in 1948. Its purpose was 'to exercise a general oversight' over economic planning, in Attlee's words.[14] The Prime Minister, Bevin, Morrison, and Cripps were its key members. Linked with it was the Cabinet Production Committee, chaired by Cripps, which dealt with the details of capital investment programmes, allocations of raw materials and manpower, the location of industry and, on occasion, wages and prices policy. It was in the Production Committee, wrote Douglas Jay, one of its members, that 'the main work was done'.[15]

The whole complex, interlocking machinery looked very much like the apparatus of co-ordinated, programmed planning. Morrison on more than one occasion spoke to the electors about 'a national plan'. In fact, it is clear that Cripps's main objective was to restore confidence in industry by partnership rather than by planned direction. He was anxious to govern by consent not through coercion. The National Investment Council, for instance, had meant little enough under Dalton; Cripps wound it up altogether. The Economic Planning Board under Plowden dealt with the short-term rather than the long-term shape of the nation's economy, though this was no doubt inevitable in the atmosphere of crisis in late 1947 and early 1948. The *Economic Survey* of 1948 did appear to herald a long-term planning of economic development and public investment for some years to come. By 1950, however, the *Survey* was devoid of any real suggestion that private industry should be 'planned' by government, while the nationalized industries largely went their own individual ways. The Surveys now spoke of 'guidelines' or long-range forecasts, rather than targets for industrial production and manufacturing capacity. Cripps noted that the Economic Surveys were not meant as a basis for economic planning: this was achieved by other means such as the annual review of the investment programme.[16] On balance, the Surveys preferred to place the

[14] Minutes of Cabinet Economic Committee, 9 Oct. 1947 (CAB 134/215).

[15] Jay, op. cit., p. 174.

[16] On this, see Jacques Leruez, *Economic Planning and Politics in Britain* (London, 1975), pp. 54–61; Cripps's note at a meeting of Cabinet Production Committee, 23 Jan. 1950 (CAB 134/644).

emphasis on patriotic endeavour for the common good rather than on the coercive imperatives of planning. The emphasis throughout 1948 and even more in 1949 was on loosening the restraints upon private business embodied in the physical and other controls of wartime. As a sign of the new encouragement given to private industry, there were the initial allowances for investment included in Cripps's 1949 budget. The *New Statesman* and *Tribune* were full of loud lamentation at the disappearance of established wartime controls; this was natural since, to the Labour left, the very concept of 'planning' was synonymous with the restrictions and controls bequeathed by the war years. These covered five broad areas —price controls, with particular reference to food; controls of production (such as the 'utility' scheme of clothing) and of consumption, including food rationing; export and import licenses, covering such matters as the export of machinery; centralized purchase of foodstuffs and raw materials; and modified labour controls through the Control of Engagement Order of October 1947.[17] The 'decontrol' policy of the Lloyd George coalition government in 1919–21 had long entered Labour mythology. Controls were an essential feature of the 'land fit for heroes' as visualized in 1945.

Yet, in spite of this, the Cripps policy of scrapping controls went on apace, stimulated in part by Morrison's belief that this would be popular at the next election, especially among the middle class. Harold Wilson's famous 'bonfire' of production controls on Guy Fawkes Day 1948 was followed by a further conflagration of scraps of paper in the spring of 1949, mainly involving the manufacture of consumer goods other than food. The *New Statesman* viewed all this with displeasure. It was a stern critic of the President of the Board of Trade's policy. As late as March 1951 it accused Harold Wilson of 'bland capitulation to rationing by price'. This was hardly just or accurate in view of the extensive price controls still operating. In fact, Wilson, joined by Bevan, had resisted

---

[17] e.g. *New Statesman*, 19 Mar., 4 June 1949. The various controls in existence are enumerated in 'Economic Controls: Long Term Powers', a report drawn up by a team of civil servants headed by Sir Bernard Gilbert and presented to the Lord President's Committee as LP (50) 16 (CAB 132/15). On labour it noted that the October 1947 Control of Engagement Order was becoming less effective, but the four other main types of control were defended.

Morrison's arguments for relaxing, or at least reviewing, governmental controls, on the Lord President's Committee in May 1950.[18] But certainly the dramatic stimulus to exports was achieved largely by a more vigorous and efficient system of incentives to private industry within the mixed economy, rather than through controlled planning, whether of the corporatist Monnet type that emerged in France in the late forties, or the more thoroughgoing mechanisms of socialist direction that Labour was supposed to favour.

The obverse of this concentration on exports was the remorseless cutting down of resources for the consumer at home. Rationing of food, clothing, petrol, and other commodities had continued since the end of the war. In the Cripps era, the system reached new extremes of severity. By 1948, the average citizen had to make do with a weekly ration of thirteen ounces of meat, one and a half ounces of cheese, six ounces of butter and margarine, one ounce of cooking fat, eight ounces of sugar, two pints of milk, and a solitary egg. There were some extra provisions for children. The housewife had to queue up at length for meagre rations of mixed quality. There were 'points' also for other foodstuffs which were in scarce supply, though such products as tinned fruit or sultanas could be obtained in exchange for 'Bread Units', illogically enough. Of course, many supplies were released by retailers through the much-denounced, but widely patronized, 'black market' to evade the rationing system. Bread rationing had been introduced on 21 July 1946 and the 'Bread Units' continued until July 1948, even though the system was manifestly ineffective. It seems to have meant, if anything, a rise in the consumption of bread, as well as the appointment of a standing army of bureaucrats to operate the system. After devaluation in September 1949, there was a reduction in the extraction ratio of bread. With supplies of more orthodox products in short measure, the shops featured, for a while, some exotic foodstuffs from non-dollar countries. Thus there appeared in the British diet such eccentric items as whale-meat steak, reindeer meat, and, most bizarre of all, snoek, a hitherto unknown, and largely

---

[18] Minutes of Lord President's Committee, 19 May 1950 (CAB 132/15); *New Statesman*, 10 Mar. 1951.

inedible, fish from the warm waters around South Africa which first arrived in May 1948. It all brought the government much unpopularity, not wholly without cause. John Strachey, who had followed the somewhat maladroit Sir Ben Smith as Minister of Food in June 1946, became the hapless target for wits in the press and on radio, for having to administer a severe food rationing programme with much of which he personally disagreed. Indeed, Strachey had to fight hard on the Cabinet Economic Committee for rations not to be diminished still further.[19] For his pains, he was abused on Tommy Handley's *ITMA* programme on the radio as 'Mr Streakey'. It was all thoroughly miserable, and probably added to the disenchantment felt with the government in the later part of its time in office. Mercifully, the rigours of food rationing abated somewhat in the course of 1948, with potato rationing ending in the spring, bread rationing in July, and jam rationing in December. The rationing of clothes and textiles (with the 'utility' control of production) was ended by Harold Wilson in March 1949; the petrol ration was doubled in the summer. For all that, severe rationing of all basic foodstuffs and of many other products was still very much in being at the time of the 1950 general election.

On the other hand, working-class people, by far the great majority of the population, seem to have accepted rationing as fair and as guaranteeing, along with free milk for schoolchildren and other welfare benefits, a higher basic standard of nutrition than had ever been known before the war. The brief débâcle of the derationing of sweets and chocolates in the summer 1949 confirmed the necessity of the rationing of basic foodstuffs. All the indices—for instance, the statistics of medical officers of health, or of school medical or dental officers—suggest that the standard of health and of robust physique steadily improved during the entire 1945–51 period, from infants, whose survival rates continued to improve, to old people, whose expectation of a long and happy retirement steadily lengthened. Seebohm

---

[19] e.g. minutes of Cabinet Economic Committee, 16 Sept. 1948 (CAB 134/216); Strachey to Attlee, 21 Aug. 1947 (PREM 8/489, pt. 2); memorandum by Strachey, 'The European Long-term Programme: the Food Implications', 17 Feb. 1949 (PREM 8/1412).

Rowntree's third and final study of poverty in York, published in 1951, testified vividly (and perhaps in exaggerated fashion) to the vast improvement that had taken place since the previous edition in 1936, let alone since the existence of that 'primary poverty' so devastatingly documented in 1901. Cripps, as has been seen, kept up a high level of expenditure on the social services; while food subsidies were pegged in the April 1949 budget at £465m., they still represented a formidable sum and did much to keep down the cost of living for working people. Most of the social services escaped the £122,500,000 cuts in public expenditure agreed to in October 1949. Cripps's imposition of a 'once and for all' capital levy, ranging from 2s. to 10s. in the pound on earlier investment income in his 1948 budget, while very modest, helped to encourage a sense of fairness and a belief that the rentier was suffering along with the working class. And, of course, full employment and relatively mild inflation were immeasurable boons to workers everywhere, for which much else would be forgiven. Labour's record in by-elections during the Cripps period was excellent, with even difficult seats like South Hammersmith in February 1949 all retained. In addition, as has been seen, the range of consumer choice was high, and getting wider. Football and cricket enjoyed unprecedented booms in the Cripps era, as did the cinema, the dance hall, and the holiday camps. Crippsian austerity was accompanied by its meed of gaiety and enjoyment. Working-class people accepted it with the more willingness, even if middle-class critics (notably the so-called Housewives League) vented their bourgeois scorn on Cripps and all his works.

The corollary of the control of consumption through rationing and austerity was some attempt at a control of wages and prices. This brought the government much difficulty. As has been seen, trade-union ministers such as Isaacs and Bevin had strongly resisted any attempt to interfere with free collective bargaining. Trade-union leaders as loyalist as Arthur Deakin reacted with horror to a wages programme that would mean in effect wage restraint, and thereby undermine the legitimate powers of the unions, their officials, and shop stewards. But here, too, the Cripps regime meant a considerable change. Deakin himself had begun to shift his

views in 1947. He became increasingly convinced, partly after
much travel overseas in 1946–7, that rising inflation was
fuelled by wage demands, which would result only in rising
unemployment.[20] He was also made aware of the need to
use wage restraint as a lever in dealing with manpower crises
in such undermanned industries as coal-mining. The government's white paper on personal incomes, costs, and prices
in February 1948, therefore, met with much less open trade-
union hostility than might have been anticipated. Even so,
its main demand, that there should be no increase in wages,
salaries, or dividends save in exceptional cases, went counter
to basic trade-union assumptions—and, indeed, to human
nature—and provoked some difficulty. Its operation might
result in wage stabilization being accompanied by an increase
in the cost of living, while artificial curbs on wage negotiations went against the entire thrust of collective bargaining as
the trade unions and employers had understood it for
generations. The TUC's economic committee expressed some
concern at the white paper and especially at Cripps's call for
a wage freeze, while there was a predictable outcry from
Communist officials in the ETU and other unions. Cripps's
negotiations with the TUC did not go very well, especially
his unwillingness to tax further profits or dividends; but he
was able to bring in the great authority of Ernest Bevin to
help him put the message across. In the end, on 24 March,
a conference of trade-union executive delegates at Central
Hall, Westminster, voted by the comfortable majority of
5,421,000 to 2,032,000 to accept a policy of a wage freeze
for the foreseeable future.[21] There was opposition from the
AEU, ETU, USDAW, and other unionists, especially those
representing the low-paid; but such a remarkable abdication
of their role by the unions was nevertheless unique in times
of peace, and without any further sequel since. Union sympathy was fortified by the budget in April when Cripps
combined a call for wage restraint with a capital levy on
former investment income, 'once and for all', on those whose
income exceeded £2,000 a year.

[20] V. L. Allen, op. cit., pp. 122 ff.
[21] Minutes of Economic Committee, 10 Feb. 1948 (CAB 134/216); *The
Times*, 25 Mar. 1948.

A wage freeze was now official TUC policy and was endorsed by the annual conference later in the year. The policy held in 1949 also, fortified by Cripps's success in gaining the support of well over 90 per cent of private firms in adopting a policy of dividend restraint on a similar voluntary basis. At the start of 1950, it was clear that there was difficulty in holding the line, with the rise in the cost of living resulting from devaluation in September 1949, and a special TUC executive committee endorsed a continuation of wage restraint now by only 4,263,000 to 3,606,000. Opposition was evidently mounting, and the further cost inflation produced by the outbreak of the Korean War and consequent shortages of raw materials finally turned the balance of TUC opinion. By a majority of 220,000 votes, the TUC in September 1950 voted down the wage freeze, with AEU, ETU, and USDAW now joined by the National Union of Miners. The TUC had already watered down the policy to produce a less rigid formula in June 1950. In fact, no great flood of wage demands resulted, though there was a marked upwards drift throughout 1951. But down to the fall of the Labour government in 1951, a broad policy of restraint in the pursuit of wage increases was followed by major unions. In effect, the wage freeze, with all its accompanying rigidities and distortions as is shown below (pp. 378–9), was continued with trade-union blessing for three vital years.

The stresses that inevitably resulted in a variety of industries led to a rise in industrial tension in many areas. The first three years of the Labour government had been remarkably peaceful on the labour front. There had been some awkward disputes. An early strike of dockers on Merseyside in October 1945 had seen over 40,000 dockers idle for the best part of a month, and 21,000 troops used to unload ships. The hated Emergency Powers Act passed by Lloyd George in 1920 was re-enacted, with the reluctant concurrence of Ernest Bevin himself. The Cabinet revamped its organization for coping with industrial emergencies in March 1946. Despite the protests of Aneurin Bevan, a permanent civil service emergency apparatus for handling major industrial disruption was created, under the chairmanship of Sir Frank Newsam. A further strike by road haulage workers in January 1947 led to the setting up of an Industrial Emergencies Committee of the Cabinet, under the chairmanship of Chuter Ede, the Home Secretary, not Dalton as Attlee had originally proposed. It first met in May 1947 with Ede, Alexander, Isaacs, Bevan, Barnes, Westwood, Strachey, and the Attorney-General, Shawcross, as its members, at a time of much unrest in the London docks.[22] There followed the damaging strike of Yorkshire miners at Grimethorpe and neighbouring collieries in August 1947. For all that, the period of the Attlee government down to mid-1948 was one of relative peace on the industrial front, as might have been anticipated. The intimate, organic relationship of the TUC with the government, with such figures as Bevin in the Cabinet, ensured a close harmony of outlook between unions and ministers. The government constantly showed its responsiveness to its natural working-class supporters.

The industrial scene, however, became more menacing during the Cripps period, from the summer of 1948 onwards, with the rise of more 'unofficial' strikes and more evidence of activity by Communist militants among stevedores in the docks and elsewhere. The 'wage freeze' programme gave a stimulus for local strike leaders to head revolts against quiescent, loyalist union leaders such as Deakin and Williamson who went along with the government's policy of wage restraint. But, of course, there were also real and specific grievances in several industries which enabled the wider discontent with a wage freeze to merge with particular problems such as the difficulties of the organization of casual labour in the docks. A serious unofficial strike in the London and other docks in May–June 1948 provided the first major test for both the union leadership and the Cabinet Emergencies Committee. A dispute over wage rates by eleven stevedores in 'Coe's Gang' on 27 May led to no less than 19,000 dockers being on strike by 23 June.[23] The government reacted sternly. With Isaacs away in the United States

[22] Attlee to Dalton, 13 Jan. 1947, Dalton to Attlee, 15 Jan. 1947 (PREM 8/673); minutes of Cabinet Emergencies Committee, 1 May 1947 (CAB 134/175, 176).

[23] See minutes of Cabinet Emergencies Committee, 21, 23, 28 June 1948 (CAB 134/175); special session of TGWU Executive Council 29 June 1948 (University of Warwick Modern Records Centre, 126/T. & G./1/1/26).

at the time, Bevin was as vehement as any in urging that the strike be broken so that the TUC line could be held. Troops were kept in readiness as strike-breakers, while the government's law officers drew up a revised list of regulations to deal with Communists and others involved with sabotage, trespass, the causing of sedition, or the incitement of disaffection. So much had views crystallized that Aneurin Bevan, previously a critic of the government's strike-breaking policies, was now as firm as any member of the Emergencies Committee in calling for tough action. 'It would be prudent to have wide powers in order to deal with any trouble that might arise if relations between troops and strikers became strained', he told the Committee on 28 June.[24] In the end, the government found it necessary for the first time to implement the terms of the 1920 Emergency Powers Act. A proclamation was issued by King George VI, and Attlee announced its passage in a broadcast on 27 June. The next day, the dockers began to return to work in London, Liverpool, and Birkenhead. The strike was over. 'Ministers agreed that this change in the situation was due to the issue of the Proclamation under the Emergency Powers Act, 1920, and to the speech which the Prime Minister had broadcast the previous evening.'[25] For all that, trouble in the docks continued, fanned by discontent over the wage freeze. Isaacs, the Minister of Labour, was in touch with Attlee early in 1949 about Communist involvement, or alleged involvement, in 'lightning strikes'.[26]

The most serious crisis on the industrial relations front came in May–July 1949, with a prolonged unofficial strike in the London docks. This had more obviously ideological origins than any previous dispute, since it began with a strike against Canadian shipowners by the Communist-led Canadian Seamen's Union. The vessel, *Beaver Brae*, was declared 'black'. This led to sympathetic action by London dockers who refused to unload Canadian ships and whose Communist or left-wing leaders put forward a call to support the Canadian Seamen's Union. An unofficial lock-out committee was set

---

[24] Minutes of Emergencies Committee, 28 June 1948 (CAB 134/175).
[25] Ibid., 29 June 1948.
[26] Isaacs to Attlee, 28 Feb. 1949 (PREM 8/1082).

up on 30 June. Between 23 June and 23 July, up to 15,650 dockers, mainly in London, were on unofficial strike in support of the Canadian seamen.[27] The government responded with accusations of Communist infiltration, and Isaacs, Shawcross, and Arthur Deakin all emphasized the role of ideological extremists such as the London dockers' leader, Jack Dash. The president of the Board of Trade, Harold Wilson, a Liverpool MP, told Isaacs that parallel strikes in Liverpool that June showed evidence of Communist involvement. The Communist Party was offering large sums of money to the Liverpool strike committee to continue the stoppage; but there were real grievances, too, 'on which the Communists were able to feed'.[28] The government responded toughly. The emergency led to considerable use of troops. The number of servicemen used as strike-breakers rose from 2,500 to 15,000 at the end of the strike on 23 July. Servicemen were reported to have unloaded 109,868 tons of imported goods from ships, and a further 29,261 for export. The Cabinet justified this partly on the grounds that the strike was in breach of the Dock Labour Scheme, but mainly that the public interest demanded that British trade be kept going at a vital time, with sterling under pressure. On 11 July, the King proclaimed a full state of emergency. A further aspect was a dispute between the elderly Lord Ammon, the chairman of the Dock Labour Board who was also a government whip in the Lords, and Attlee himself, over the government's handling of the affair. Ammon criticized the government for undermining the authority of the Board. 'The matter should be fought to a finish', he urged, with the government taking tough action against 'imported agitators'. The subsequent response of the Cabinet Emergencies Committee seemed inadequate to Ammon, whose reactions became increasingly angry. On 21 July he issued a press release in which he condemned the government for 'dillying and dallying'; this led the Cabinet to deplore officially his onslaughts on an administration of which he was, after all,

---

[27] Minutes of Cabinet Emergencies Committee, 21 June, 4, 6, 7, 20, 22 July 1949 (CAB 134/176); TGWU Special Committee of Inquiry 1949 (Warwick, 126/T. & G./1/1/28).

[28] Wilson to Isaacs, 13 June 1949 (LAB 10/832).

a member.[29] In fact, an attempt to extend the strike to Tilbury docks on 20 July failed. On 23 July the unofficial strike leaders in London urged a return to work, and peace of a kind returned to dockland. Ammon was dismissed, his career effectively over.

It is clear that there were many wider issues in the London dock strikes of 1949. The TGWU held its own inquiry which resulted in six out of the seven strike leaders being disciplined: Jack Dash, who was one of them, noted that all six were Communists. The TGWU inquiry declared that the strike 'was part of a wider plan, inspired from Communist sources, the object of which was to dislocate the trade of the country and so add to our economic difficulties'.[30] But Communism was not the root cause at all, even if less peripheral than one recent account has implied.[31] There were genuine fears about the working of the Dock Labour Scheme, with employers' demands that dockers work long periods of overtime; there was also much local criticism at the lack of responsiveness to local dockers' opinion about the entire Dock Labour Scheme. What had begun as a well-meant institution during the war to end the old problem of unregulated casual labour was breaking down. The TGWU was too vast and remote to handle local grievances, especially with Deakin so closely bound up with government policies as almost to be identified with the employers rather than with his own members. In such circumstances, Communist leaders such as Jack Dash inevitably gained in influence. In fact, the docks remained tranquil for a few more months. The Labour government had no further serious industrial troubles with which to contend until the strike of the Smithfield lorry drivers in June 1950, the high point of the use of troops under the emergency powers provision.

[29] Correspondence of Attlee and Ammon, July 1949 (PREM 8/1081); Attlee to Ammon, 5 July 1949 (University of Hull Library, DMN/1/12).
[30] Jack Dash, *Good Morning Brothers!* (London, 1969), p. 71; TGWU inquiry, 1950 and TGWU executive council minutes, 15 May 1950 (University of Warwick, loc. cit.); material on the Merseyside Seamen's Rank and File Committee and Communist infiltration (University of Warwick, National Union of Seamen's Records, 175/6/RF/1-6).
[31] P. Weiler, 'British Labour and the Cold War: the London Dock Strike of 1949' in J. E. Cronin and J. Schneer (eds.), *Social Conflict and the Political Order in Modern Britain* (London, 1982), pp. 146-78.

On balance, the industrial scene was generally peaceful during the Cripps policy of wage freeze. There were many points of friction amongst dockers, electricity power workers, and railwaymen, but they were seldom about wages. Rather they concerned issues like the Dock Labour Scheme or the anger felt in union circles at the continuance of Order 1305, that regulation of 1940 which forbade strikes and enforced compulsory arbitration. The element of Communist involvement was much exaggerated by Shawcross and other ministers during the 'red scare' atmosphere of 1949-50. In the London dock strike in 1949, General Robert Neville, a personal friend of Attlee's, recorded his view that 'the line of throwing the blame on the Communists has been overplayed'.[32]

The general effect of the wage freeze policy was remarkably successful in the fragmented, adversarial world of British labour relations, and a political triumph for Cripps. But the substance of that triumph is open to debate. The wage freeze was criticized for leading to distortions in the labour market.[33] It also, no doubt, led to the suspension of awards in many industries where wage increases were amply justified. It probably encouraged employers to try to circumvent the freeze by bidding for available labour through other inducements, including bonus payments and special overtime arrangements. This added to the effectiveness of shop stewards in bidding for local advances in piece-rates at the plant level. Indeed, the grievances of those whose wages were frozen under national arrangements, while their workmates secured benefits from local agreements, and the inequity of the differentials thus opened up, became a major factor in ending the wage-freeze policy in 1950. The fact remains, too, that wages did rise, albeit slowly, in the 1948-50 period, with prices rising under pressure of consumer demand and higher unit costs. It should be noted, too, that Cripps in 1948-50, unlike Selwyn Lloyd's 'pay pause' of 1961-2, did not interfere with arbitration awards in the public sector. The proportion of wages and salaries per unit of output rose, through the pressures of plant settlements, from a base of

---

[32] E. G. Cass (Attlee's secretary) to A. F. A. Sutherland, Ministry of Labour, 16 July 1949 (LAB 10/904).
[33] See B. C. Roberts, *National Wages Policy in War and Peace* (London, 1958).

100 in 1948 to 103 in 1950. It leapt to 114 in 1951 when the wage freeze period ended, and there was enhanced demand for labour under the new defence programme. The accumulated pressures of demand frozen during the restraint of 1948–50 led to rising wage levels and some internal inflation down to the time that the government fell from office. But, in the short term, after the convertibility crisis and in line with Cripps's need to hold the line at home in order to boost a titanic exports campaign, the pressure from wages was contained. On balance, it was a remarkable exercise in industrial consensus. Cripps won support not only from right-wing union bosses such as Deakin, but even from Aneurin Bevan in the Cabinet. The latter regarded a wages policy as an intrinsic part of a socialist economic strategy, and was prepared to take tough action in suppressing unofficial strike leaders who were endangering a Labour government, which provided a beacon of hope to the civilized world. Here, too, the line was held.

In the spring of 1949, the broad success of Cripps's strategy seemed to be assured. The mood of crisis and despair in August 1947 was forgotten. But already there were signs of more trouble, after the golden progress of 1948. Cripps's budget of April 1949 was described by *The Times* as 'stern, even brutal'.[34] The full rigours of austerity were maintained, with higher food prices likely as a result of the decision to hold the food subsidies at £465m., cuts in capital investment and limits to some spending on the social services, notably the housing programme. No taxes were reduced, apart from a token fall in the price of beer. The *Economic Survey* for 1949 looked to less expansion in that year, although gross fixed investment was projected to rise to £2,125m. compared with £2,005m. in 1948. Douglas Jay and Robert Hall both agreed that there was 'no immediate prospect of any general depression either here or in the United States'.[35] Then in the second quarter of 1949 it became clear that the balance of payments, so buoyant for well over a year, was again in

[34] *The Times*, 7 Apr. 1949.
[35] *Economic Survey* for 1949, p. 546; memorandum by Hall and Jay, March 1949 (T 171/397).

disarray. The business boom in the United States suddenly ended; this led to a sharp drop in dollar earnings. The fact that Cripps himself suddenly fell ill and eventually had to retire to a sanatorium in Zurich in July meant a grave loss of direction at a vital stage. The Cabinet's Dollar Drain Committee, chaired by Bridges, reported an increasingly alarming situation.[36] The gold and dollar reserves fell by $76m. in March 1949, with new raw materials purchased from the USA at a sharply increased price, and by $51m. in April. By 19 May, it was reported that the weekly rate of the dollar deficit was substantially above the projected target, and the outlook was gloomy. Between the first quarter of 1949 and the second, the drain rose from £82m. to £157m. In July, the situation got very much worse. The reserves fell by about $39m. in the week 10–16 July alone. They now totalled $1,564m. on 10 July: at this rate of decline, even with the boost from Marshall Aid, Britain's reserves would last no more than another forty weeks in all. The reserves continued to fall relentlessly, to $1,487m. on 27 July, to $1,439m. on 27 August, and on to a low point of $1,410m. on 3 September. There was a real spectre of national bankruptcy, as Cripps spelt out to the Cabinet Economic Committee on 17 June: 'a lot of items in the dollar balance [are] all going wrong at once'.[37] To add further to the mood of alarm, there was clear speculation against sterling in foreign currency markets, fuelled by the prospect of possible devaluation. Sir Alec Cairncross considers that the speculative, market factor was at least as important as the business recession in the United States in triggering off the exchange crisis in the summer of 1949.[38] Overseas buyers refused to take sterling goods, or else deferred purchases payable in sterling, through the expectation of the pound being devalued; while there was a steady leak of dollars which would normally have gone into the sterling area pool. The erratic mechanisms of the

[36] Reports of the Dollar Drain Committee, 14–28 July 1949 (T 229/230); Memorandum by Cripps on 'The Dollar Situation', 22 June 1949 (PREM 8/1412).

[37] Minutes of Cabinet Economic Committee, 17 June 1949 (CAB 134/220).

[38] Sir Alec Cairncross, 'The devaluation of 1949' in A. K. Cairncross and B. Eichengreen, *Three Devaluations of Sterling* (1983). This essay is an authoritative and invaluable account.

Commonwealth sterling dollar pool, with countries such as India and Ceylon taking increased dollar imports of food-stuffs, and Australia and South Africa spending very heavily (while in return the United States cut down its imports of Malayan rubber and tin) added to Britain's difficulties.

It seemed, then, that the triumphs of Cripps would count for nothing. The massive run on the reserves, and the accompanying fall in the exchange value of sterling appeared likely to drive the economy downwards to a point even below the panic moment of August 1947, with resultant severe cuts in imports, a fall in living standards, and possible mass unemployment as well through a slump in exports. Echoes of the dread days of 1931 were heard in Whitehall. The response of the Cabinet (especially Attlee himself) was most uncertain, and this uncertainty added to the mood of near-panic. Nevertheless, more firmness of purpose was eventually to show itself than in the convertibility crisis of August 1947. In the end, the events of 1949 were to result in a decisive and successful change of policy.

For some time, key economic advisers had been urging the cause of a devaluation of the pound. 'Otto' Clarke had been an advocate of this since the end of the war; he was joined in 1948 by Robert Hall, who subsequently converted Plowden and Roger Makins of the Foreign Office Economic Section. However, most voices spoke firmly against, including Bridges, the head of the Treasury, and Cobbold, the Governor of the Bank of England. Cripps himself was strongly against devaluation. 'It was neither necessary nor would it take place', he told foreign journalists in Rome in early May.[39] Partly he held this view on moral grounds, since he had already pledged the Commonwealth Finance Ministers and Britain's other trading partners that sterling would retain its parity with the dollar. In addition, as he told the Cabinet Economic Committee on 1 July, it was impossible to determine at what level devaluation should be carried, and whether that level should be maintained. Nothing would be more disastrous than an unsuccessful devaluation. Cripps was supported by Aneurin Bevan who argued that Britain's problems were due to a 'disequilibrium in the United States economy'. He added,

[39] *The Economist*, 7 May 1949.

'Devaluation, which was merely an attempt to transfer the crisis elsewhere, was a step in the direction of deflation and would be countered by an increase in United States tariffs.' Bevin, the Foreign Secretary, who had himself strongly supported the devaluation of 1931, was now more hesistant; he was anxious about the political aspects of relations between the sterling area and the dollar countries, with the US Treasury now showing open concern at the state of Britain's reserves and urging her to devalue immediately. Morrison preferred a sharp cut in public expenditure. But, he added sensibly, 'He would not welcome devaluation as a solution, but it was in fact taking place, and it might be better to devalue sterling as an act of deliberate policy than be forced to do so by outside pressure.'[40] Morrison's growing inclination towards devaluation was mirrored by a rapid shift of opinion both amongst civil servants such as Bridges and Max Nicholson and amongst economics ministers such as Hugh Gaitskell and Douglas Jay. Bevan and the left came to believe that devaluation might at least ward off other evils such as a rise in Bank Rate or swingeing cuts in public expenditure. Meanwhile, Cripps had an unsuccessful meeting with Snyder, the US Secretary of the Treasury on 9 July, in which American pleas for early devaluation were resisted. A hurriedly convened meeting of Commonwealth Finance Ministers in London immediately afterwards led to urgent calls for economy in dollar imports, and for cuts amounting to up to 25 per cent, whatever the cost for the poor peoples of Africa and Asia.[41]

On 10 July Cripps was still maintaining his stubborn opposition to devaluation. But at least he and the government were now prepared to discuss it, as part of a longer-term solution of relations between the sterling and dollar worlds. Cripps then left for a five-weeks' period of recuperation from illness in a sanatorium in Zurich. In his absence, earnest discussions took place amongst government ministers. Cobbold later told Attlee that he had discussions with Cripps before he left England, and that the Chancellor was now talking in terms of the vital need to associate the devaluation

---

[40] Minutes of Cabinet Economic Commiteee, 1 July 1949 (CAB 134/220).
[41] Record of Commonwealth Finance Ministers' Committee, July 1949 (PREM 8/975).

of sterling with strong action to combat inflationary pressure at home (which meant severe cuts) and to deal with the weight of the overseas sterling balances. Meanwhile Bevin floated the idea, not for the first time, of extending the sterling area to take in some of western Europe as well, as a protected trading area on an autarchic basis. Dalton and Bevan raised non-economic considerations such as the relationship of any possible devaluation to the date of the next general election. But the main initiative in this crisis came from younger ministers: Attlee himself offered no lead at all, and indeed scarcely seems to have understood the nature of the exchange problem. Harold Wilson later described him as 'tone deaf' on most economic questions.[42] Gaitskell, the Minister of Fuel and Power, and not even a Cabinet minister, quite unexpectedly emerged as the key figure, showing a vigour and decisiveness that helped to propel him into the Treasury within two years—and into the party leadership within six. On 17 July he seems to have become convinced that a considerable devaluation was essential, in view of the proven elasticity of British goods in dollar markets. His allies were Douglas Jay, another junior minister now converted to devaluation, and Harold Wilson, the thirty-three-year-old President of the Board of Trade, and a Cabinet minister whose view of devaluation was somewhat more circumspect throughout.

At a dinner meeting on 21 July, between a group mainly of economics ministers, Gaitskell, Strachey, Strauss, Jay, and (reluctantly) Wilson reached the clear view that devaluation was inescapable. They seemed to gain Bevan's support also: 'Nye was won over without great difficulty' wrote Gaitskell.[43] Dalton, previously an opponent of devaluation as a deflationary step, now came to agree with the general view. At a Cabinet meeting on 29 July, Attlee was given

[42] Cobbold to Attlee, 3 Aug. 1949 (PREM 8/976). It should be noted that Cobbold himself was an advocate of very severe cuts in public spending. Cf. Harold Wilson, *A Prime Minister on Prime Ministers* (London, 1977), p. 297.

[43] Gaitskell's diary, 3 Aug. 1949; see also Philip Williams, op. cit., pp. 198 ff. and Douglas Jay, op. cit., pp. 187 ff. Gaitskell and Jay seem to have come down in favour of devaluation in the course of separate Sunday morning walks on Hampstead Heath on 17 July. When Nicholas Kaldor talked to them on the 18th, he was preaching to the converted.

broad authority to take whatever financial measures were
thought necessary. Wilson was then deputed to carry a
message from the Cabinet (drafted by Douglas Jay, in fact)
to Cripps in his Zurich sanatorium. In effect, Cripps was
presented with an ultimatum by his colleagues which stated
that the drain on the reserves was so serious that the only
issues remaining to be discussed were the extent of the
devaluation, and the date—whether it would take place on
28 August or 18 September. Cripps seems to have given
weary agreement, on the understanding that no public
announcement would be made before he and Bevin went to
Washington in early September for the annual meeting of the
International Monetary Fund. He argued that to announce
devaluation unilaterally, with no prior consultation with the
Americans, would imperil the whole operation, especially as
his recent talks with Snyder had gone so badly. Cripps
added, 'He feels it is more necessary than ever to have an
early election'.[44] This meant an inevitable delay in a public
decision, while the haemorrhage on the reserves went on. A
meeting of ministers at Chequers on 19 August effectively
decided matters, with Attlee, Morrison, Bevin, Wilson, and
Gaitskell being joined by Cripps who had returned home.
Morrison had now become a clear advocate of devaluation
while Gaitskell recorded Bevin as 'swaying this way and
that'. Attlee went with the tide of opinion. That meant a
clear and unanimous decision by the Cabinet in favour of
devaluation, to be announced on 18 September; this was
endorsed at a full Cabinet on 29 August. The only other
major issue at stake was the extent of devaluation. Cripps
had not wanted to go below $3.00 to the pound at the
Chequers meeting on 19 August; Bevin favoured $3.20. But
the crisis in the dollar reserves now seemed so acute that the
rate of $2.40, a really massive change, was accepted in Cabinet
on 29 August.[45] At least Cripps's earlier view that the troubles
of sterling were temporary and the result merely of 'a mild
business recession' in the United States was being abandoned.

[44] Wilson to Attlee, from Zurich, 8 Aug. 1949 (PREM 8/1178, pt. 1), a MS
record of his talk with Cripps.
[45] Gaitskell's diary, 21 Sept. 1949 (a retrospect); Cabinet Conclusions, 29 Aug.
1949 (CAB 128/16).

Cripps and Bevin went to Washington at the start of September, sailing on the ship *Mauretania*, and told the American government that the British Cabinet had decided on an early and severe devaluation. This would reduce the pound by a third of its value by cutting its rate against the dollar from $4.03 to only $2.40. In addition, they placed a heavy emphasis on the need to maintain full employment and a high level of demand in the United States, on the American's altering restrictive measures which blocked ways by which Britain could earn dollars, the encouragement of overseas investment by the American and Canadian governments, and the establishment of international commodity agreements on such products as tin and rubber.[46] Loans from the Export-Import Bank, drawings from the IMF, and reciprocal tariff agreements were also mentioned. Apart from one or two minor squalls involving Bevin and Paul Hoffman, the Washington talks went remarkably well. The British ambassador, Sir Oliver Franks, whose own good relationship with Secretary of State Dean Acheson was notably helpful, reported to Attlee on 20 September on the foreign-policy implications. He emphasized 'the entirely new spring of goodwill and confidence' welling up in the United States and Canada. 'It was clear that the Americans decided to regard us once more as their principal partner in world affairs, and not just as a member of the European queue.' A permanent structure for remodelling the economic and financial pattern of the western world had been worked out in a spirit of goodwill.[47] This appears a reasonable, if optimistic, verdict. Cripps returned to Britain on 18 September, and announced in a radio broadcast on the evening of Sunday, 19 September, that the pound was devalued and would henceforth stand at only $2.40. There was some immediate reaction, notably from trade-unionists who feared that rising import prices would raise the cost of living, and from the *Financial Times* which argued, as others such as Roy Harrod have done since, that the devaluation had been far greater than was necessary. *The Economist* even argued that no level should have been fixed for the

---

[46] Draft brief for Ministerial Talks in Washington, Sept. 1949 (T 229/212).
[47] Sir Oliver Franks to Attlee, 20 Sept. 1949 (PREM 8/973).

time being.[48] It was generally agreed that some increase in the cost of living was inevitable. Nevertheless, Attlee was justified in claiming to Cripps on 21 September that devaluation had enjoyed 'a far better press' than might have been expected.[49] 'The antics of the market' had been generally condemned; indeed, industrial equities lost ground for some days because of vain fears of a 100 per cent excess profits tax. Almost all the government's supporters welcomed devaluation as the only way of ensuring rising production and full employment. The only alternative would be more serious cuts, high interest rates, deflation, and industrial stagnation. The government was helped in the three-day devaluation debate in the Commons by a brilliant speech by Aneurin Bevan, whom Attlee, in an inspired moment, had asked to lead off on the final day.[50] Bevan's rollicking performance made no specific reference to devaluation at all. He drew attention to improved indices of industrial production, and made much irrelevant comparison with Churchill's record in introducing the return to gold in 1925, and to Butler and Stanley's role in the new unemployment regulations in 1934. Bevan declared, perhaps with Churchill's ample form in mind, that he intended 'to prick the bloated bladder of lies with the poniard of truth'. This brilliant debating triumph, replete with onslaughts on 'the guilty men' of the thirties, helped on Labour's rapid acceptance of devaluation, and the successful achievement of another landmark in Labour's economic policy. The fact that devaluation must be accompanied by heavy cuts in public expenditure, which divided the Cabinet much more bitterly, was temporarily ignored.

In the event, the immediate consequences of devaluation were wholly satisfactory. The drain on the reserves was checked; exports soon began to flow again, especially to North America. The gold and dollar deficit shrank from $539m. in the third quarter of 1949 to a mere $31m. in the final quarter. Cripps's devaluation, however reluctantly carried out, appeared to be another in his record of successes, of plucking a kind of victory from the jaws of defeat.

---

[48] *Financial Times*, 19 Sept. 1949; *The Economist*, 24 Sept. 1949.
[49] Attlee to Cripps, 21 Sept. 1949 (PREM 8/973).
[50] *Parl. Deb.*, 5th ser., vol. 468, 309–25.

Economists have subsequently warned against attributing too much to the mere fact of devaluation; so did Treasury officials in 1950–1. The economic revival that followed owed a good deal to quite extraneous factors, notably the recovery of the American economy in 1950 which boosted British exports to North America, irrespective of the exchange rate. The severity of the devaluation in September 1949 seemed rather less easy to defend in the calmer economic climate of 1950. But governments can only be judged through their reaction to circumstances as they actually arise. Speed and decisiveness were essential in September 1949, with the huge outflow of the gold and dollar reserves. After devaluation, that outflow stopped, and then was markedly reversed. The first week after devaluation saw the reserves rising for the first time since May, from $1,410m. to $1,420m. By 19 October 1949 there had been a recovery of $360m. from the low point of early September, and Robert Hall pronounced that 'a very limited satisfaction' could be felt. By 10 November, Hall was recording the Treasury's puzzlement at the further rise to $1,565m., which implied a rise in every single week since devaluation. On 23 November, the total stood at $1,591m. which left the Treasury and the Bank of England 'a little nervous' as they were unable to explain so rapid an improvement. However, the rise in the reserves went on steadily, from $1,603.4m. on 30 November, to $1,656m. on 21 December, and $1,688m. on 31 December. It was clear that exports had leapt ahead after the announcement of devaluation, in the United States as well as Canada. Hall's doubts had all left him by 4 January 1950. 'We are now on the right path and should feel a legitimate satisfaction with what has happened.'[51] The Treasury concluded that the very low deficit in gold and dollars in the quarter from October to December 1949 was the result of a number of factors, partly the payment in sterling for sterling goods and services which had been purchased earlier in the summer and for which payment had been deferred, but also more beneficial long-term trends such as the resumption of purchases from Britain on a heavy scale by American importers. There

---

[51] Memoranda by Hall, 19 Oct. 1949–4 Jan. 1950 (T 229/230 and 229/231); Cairncross, op. cit., is conclusive on these matters.

had also been a general improvement in the sterling area gold
and dollar position after the British import cuts programme,
and comparable action agreed by other Commonwealth
nations within the sterling area in July.[52] The satisfaction of
the Treasury, so hard won, was confirmed by a growing
confidence in the Cabinet, especially since the programme of
cuts in public expenditure had now been agreed. The omens
for the economy seemed far more favourable at the start of
1950. Indeed, that year seemed likely to prove another
excellent one, with the balance of payments returning to a
clear surplus, and record levels of exports to the North
American continent and elsewhere. All the indicators were
suddenly set fair again. Devaluation, which could have been
a retreat as calamitous as that over convertibility in the
summer of 1947, seemed to set the seal instead on Cripps's
achievement in reinvigorating the economy, and in wrenching
it and the Labour government successfully into new directions.

Cripps's eventual decision to devalue flowed from a broad
belief on his part that Britain should try to pursue its own
self-contained programme of self-sufficiency, without over-
dependence on American aid. It had almost insular implications in terms of international trade and finance. Parallel
to this economic policy which canonized the sterling area,
and in some ways linked with it, there were some signs of
a more inward-looking tendency in foreign policy also at this
period. This, of course, must be severely qualified. The
period 1948–9 was one which saw Bevin build successfully
on the initiative achieved under the Marshall Plan and the
European Recovery Programme. The Brussels Treaty of
March 1948 saw Britain take the lead in stimulating western
European economic and defence co-operation. It led to the
founding of the North Atlantic Treaty Organization in April
1949, the permanent commitment of Britain to the Anglo-
American alliance, and the Americans to the defence of
western Europe. The creation of NATO followed several
grave episodes in international relations, of which much the

[52] Treasury draft of the Quarterly Announcement of the Gold and Dollar
Deficit, 31 Dec. 1949 (T 229/231).

most serious was the Russian blockade of West Berlin which began on 24 June 1948. This followed the British and American decision on 18 June to introduce currency reform in the western zones of Germany, as a prelude to the integration of Germany into plans for western European recovery, with an international authority (excluding Russia) to distribute coke, coal, and steel from the Ruhr. These developments, along with the western German federal constitution now being drafted, led the Russians to argue that western Germany was becoming a satellite of the capitalist powers. In the Berlin crisis, Britain was at one with the American government in organizing an airlift to beat the blockade, and in facing up to the Russians militarily. Eventually, the Russians ended the blockade in 1949 after 323 days, and thus suffered a marked international defeat. The Cabinet was unanimous in taking strong action throughout. Aneurin Bevan urged the sending of tanks across the Soviet zone to back up the airlift. Further events in 1948, including the breach between Russia and Tito's Yugoslavia (much admired in many leftish Labour circles for its Five Year Plan of 1947) added to the enthusiasm of many former 'Keep Left' sympathizers for the Attlee government's firm foreign policy. The re-election of President Truman in the United States, at a time when he was unusually popular in Labour ranks, was also helpful. Richard Crossman now became sternly anti-Russian and a strong advocate of the North Atlantic alliance. Michael Foot took a similar line in *Tribune*, and publicly rebuked Ian Mikardo, who resigned from the editorial board in protest of these cold-war views.[53] Clearly, in these and other respects, British foreign policy was not in the least isolationist. Down to the 1950 general election, the Labour government was firmly committed to an internationalist collective viewpoint.

In one important area, however, the partial isolationism of the Cripps era did assert itself. This was in relation to western Europe, when pressure for some kind of European unity built up in the early months of 1948. Bevin's famous speech of 22 January had made much of the concept of the political, economic, and even spiritual unity of Europe. British opinion

[53] *Tribune*, 27 May 1949; Mark Jenkins, op. cit., pp. 41–51.

seemed to be in strongly European vein, especially when the Brussels Treaty was signed in March. But it became clear early on that there was only the most qualified and hesitant support for European unity of a more integrated kind; this applied to the Foreign Office and its staff, the Cabinet, the Labour Party NEC, and the party throughout the country. However much socialists in France, the Low Countries, and Italy might urge that Britain should involve itself in a far closer relationship with its western European neighbours, it was clear that this conflicted with a deep, and in many ways well-founded, suspicion on the part of British socialists about the entire purpose and direction of the European movement. There were certainly many Labour MPs who were enthusiastic for western European unity in the winter of 1947–8. Several were left-wingers such as Crossman, Foot, Driberg, and Barbara Castle who saw a socialist-led western Europe as a kind of 'third force' in the world. G. D. H. Cole also committed himself for a time to this view, which was strongly upheld in France by the influential newspaper, *Le Monde*. A Europe Group of the Parliamentary Labour Party was formed on 2 December 1947 under the chairmanship of the Australian federalist, R. W. G. ('Kim') Mackay, with the right-wing J. B. Hynd as vice-chairman and the left-wing Christopher Shawcross as secretary. Leftish members included Warbey, Silverman, Mikardo, Crossman, and Foot, along with right-wing figures such as R. T. Paget and Aidan Crawley.[54] The Europe Group wrote to Bevin on 9 January 1948, urging the cause of a politically unified western Europe—partly as a way of solving the problem of a divided Germany, so it was argued.[55] The membership of the group was thought to number at least eighty by February, and Mackay himself conducted a crusade on behalf of federalism and integration with the zeal of a latter-day evangelist.

But all the tendencies in the party and the government were against such a policy. Bevin and Attlee had no sympathy with the notion of 'socialist foreign policy', as linked,

[54] Material in R. W. G. Mackay papers, Section 8, file 3 (British Library of Political and Economic Science); memorandum by Ernest Davies, 25 Feb. 1948 (FO 371/73095).
[55] Mackay papers, loc. cit.

somewhat unconvincingly, with European unity. Neither they nor their colleagues regarded a supranational authority of some kind in Europe as compatible either with Britain's parliamentary and legal tradition, or with the pursuit of socialist planning by a Labour government at home. The close relation with the Commonwealth countries in the sterling area and in terms of trade, and the need for Britain to maintain its special links with the United States were also felt to be major factors against an intimate bond between Britain and the heterogenous nations of western Europe, in most of whom capitalism remained largely unreconstructed. Bevin consistently insisted on the functional, piecemeal approach to collaboration with Britain's European neighbours: there should be 'no grand constitution' for Europe, he declared.[56] The terms of the Brussels Treaty were tailored accordingly. A memorandum on European co-operation in February 1948, drafted by Denis Healey of the International Department in Transport House, concentrated on the need for channelling economic aid through the European Recovery Programme and was non-committal on such issues as a western European customs union.[57] R. W. B. ('Otto') Clarke of the Treasury wrote to Roger Makins of the Foreign Office, 'I must say I think our two hours with Mr Healey were very well spent.'[58] In addition to these attitudes, there was also some simple xenophobia which readily came to the surface amongst leading Labour politicians, notably Hugh Dalton. Aneurin Bevan was another who never looked with enthusiasm on a European movement so lavishly patronized by his old adversary, Churchill. Cripps, anxious for Britain to pay its way and to regulate its own affairs untrammelled by outside commercial and economic considerations, was also generally hostile to the European idea. His basic loyalty was to the sterling area.[59] He noted that over 40 per cent of British exports and re-exports went to Commonwealth

[56] Record of meeting of Consultative Council at Quai d'Orsay, 25 Oct. 1948 (FO 371/73098) Z 8935/4416/72/G.

[57] Memorandum on 'European Co-operation within the framework of the Recovery Programme', Feb. 1948 (FO 371/71808).

[58] R. W. B. Clarke to R. Makins, 1 Mar. 1948 (ibid.).

[59] Cf. minute by L. Rowan of conversation between Cripps and Paul Hoffman, 28 July 1948 (CAB 134/232).

countries in 1948 as compared with only 25 per cent to western Europe.

When a number of socialist representatives from western European parties met in Selsdon Park, near London, on 21-2 March 1948, the hostility of the British delegation present was soon apparent.[60] It was vehement in the case of Dalton, and also the Labour Party's general secretary, Morgan Phillips. Equally eloquent was the fact that many leading ministers, including Bevan and Noel-Baker, voted with their feet by failing to attend. The main business at Selsdon was to discuss the forthcoming conference at The Hague on 7-8 May, convened by the European Unity movement of which Churchill had been made president, following flamboyant, if vague, speeches by him at Zurich and elsewhere. The British Labour Party made it crystal clear that it was not going to take any part in the deliberations at The Hague, and urged Labour MPs not to attend. In fact, a number did so when the Hague conference got under way, though fewer than had been anticipated. The meeting at The Hague was described by the British ambassador there as 'a personal triumph for Churchill'.[61] It was attended by eighteen former Prime Ministers and twenty-nine ex-Foreign Ministers, so the conference inevitably acquired a good deal of world attention. But Labour observers noted that the attendance was overwhelmingly representative of Conservative and capitalist groups. Gladwyn Jebb of the Foreign Office criticized movements that had 'as their chief characteristic an anti-Bolshevik crusade'.[62] It was noticeable, too, that the actual content of Churchill's speech diverted attention away from a federalist or integrationalist view of western Europe towards more limited objectives. The extreme views of federalists such as Mackay and Leah Manning were totally defeated. In practice, Churchill's view of western Europe was very close to the 'western union' that Bevin championed.

[60] Record of International Socialist conference at Selsdon Park, 21-2 Mar. 1948; Statement on European Unity by Morgan Phillips, Feb. 1948 (Labour Party archives, International Department).

[61] Sir P. Nichols to Bevin, 19 May 1948 (FO 371/73095) Z 4418/4416/72.

[62] Memorandum by Gladwyn Jebb, 24 Feb. 1947 (ibid.) Z 4416/4416/72.

Kenneth Younger was later to comment that Churchill's role in the European movement was 'one of the great frauds of history'.[63]

Nevertheless, the fact could not be denied that momentum had been created, and that the Hague conference did generate pressure for a closer political and economic relationship of the western European powers. A Council of Europe was to be instituted in Strasbourg which might herald a popularly-elected European parliament. There was an angry exchange of correspondence between Attlee and Churchill in July–August and again in November 1948 about the nature of the British delegation to the proposed European working party due to meet in Paris, whether it should consist of independent public figures as with the French and other continental delegations, or whether it should be primarily a political delegation dominated by spokesmen for the British government. Bevin urged Attlee not to yield to Churchill's 'somewhat bare-faced pressure'; nor did he do so. Attlee took some pleasure in reminding Churchill of all people, of the need to carry members of the Commonwealth, and also the United States, with Britain in any future European arrangements.[64] But the movement went ahead nevertheless, urged on by the US State Department for defence reasons. Dalton poured scorn on the Hague conference at the Labour Party conference in 1948 as 'a collection of chatterboxes'.[65] But this crude view had to be set aside. So had the *New Statesman*'s later dismissal of the Schuman Plan as the product of a conspiracy headed by the Vatican, the Ruhr industrialists, and the Comité des Forges.[66]

The Foreign Office view was generally suspicious, or hostile, towards the proposed Council of Europe. Roger Makins was one who distrusted its neutralist or, conceivably, anti-American overtones. He poured scorn on 'the contemporary American line that the UK were hanging back on European

[63] Kenneth Younger, interview transcript, p. 30.
[64] Churchill to Attlee, 27 July 1948 (FO 371/73096) Z 6319/4416/72; Attlee to Bevin, 28 July 1948 (ibid.) Z 6439/4416/72; Churchill to Attlee, 11 Nov. 1948, and Attlee to Churchill, 12 Nov. 1948 (PREM 8/986); Bevin to Attlee, 19 Aug. 1948 (FO 371/73097) Z 6925/4416/72.
[65] *The Times*, 20 May 1948.
[66] *New Statesman*, 10 June 1950.

co-operation and that we ought to go for closer political union—in spite of the political, financial and social instability of France and Italy'.[67] Sir Ivone Kirkpatrick was no more enthusiastic, while Gladwyn Jebb, as has been seen, was hostile to a European movement presented as an anti-Bolshevik crusade.[68] There were always other diplomatic voices. In particular, Sir Oliver Harvey, Duff Cooper's successor at the British embassy in Paris, was always a champion of European unity, and later anxious for Britain to endorse the Schuman Plan.[69] But these were the views of a clear minority. The views of the Foreign Office did no more than echo the hostility towards the Council of Europe consistently shown by Bevin himself. He remained the champion of the idea of an Atlantic alliance; the Brussels treaty and OEEC were essential bridges in achieving this. They would give the western European nations self-confidence and cohesion; but they could never deter Russian aggression by themselves, without American military and other support. Bevin always favoured a limited, gradual, functional approach to western European political and economic co-operation. He told the French Defence Minister, Paul Ramadier, himself an old Anglophile socialist, in October 1948 that he Bevin, 'was personally opposed to a European assembly which would raise false hopes and prove ineffective as an organisation'. He added that he wished to 'build up Western Europe in a solid way as we are now doing, e.g. in regard to defence and economics. . . . He had been frightened by The Hague and Interlaken resolutions, and did not think they could be translated very effectively into practical politics.' Ramadier demurred mildly and mentioned the need to dream. 'Mr Bevin replied that he had had dreams himself but as Foreign Secretary he had to keep wide awake.'[70]

Bevin went to complain to Ivone Kirkpatrick of the

---

[67] Minute by Roger Makins, 13 Sept. 1948 (FO 371/73097) Z 7391/4416/72.
[68] Minute by Ivone Kirkpatrick, 24 Aug. 1948 (ibid.) Z 7234/4416/72.
[69] e.g. Sir O. Harvey to Orme Sargent, 27 Jan. 1948 (FO 371/72929).
[70] Record of conversation between Bevin and Ramadier, 21 Oct. 1948 (ibid.). Bevin's alternative version was his view that dreaming was 'all very well provided that the awakening after the dream was not too much of a shock': record of conversation between Bevin and Schuman, 14 Jan. 1949 (FO 371/79214) Z 676/1071/726. The Inter-Parliamentary Union met at Interlaken in August.

tendency to multiply international organizations. He was anxious not to proceed 'one millimetre' beyond his original modest proposal for the role of the Council of Europe. There already existed the United Nations machinery, the Brussels Treaty machinery, and shortly the Atlantic Pact machinery. 'If we now add the complicated Council of Europe machinery, there will be no producers left in Europe and no potatoes for any of us.'[71] He urged Harvey in the Paris embassy not to show excessive enthusiasm for the European idea, and to delay the meeting of the working party to draw up the Council of Europe. 'There is a strong case for concentrating all our energy and determination in pushing through the Atlantic Pact first and proceeding to set up a Council of Europe when this has been achieved.' He believed the French had behaved 'neither considerately nor honestly'.[72]

The Labour government indicated its general approach when it appointed Dalton to head the British delegation to the working party set up to develop the idea of a Council of Europe. Dalton was notoriously amongst the most prejudiced and anti-European of all the Labour ministers. His colleagues on the British delegation were largely functionaries, Lord Inverchapel, Edward Bridges, the lawyer, Professor E. C. S. Wade and T. H. Gill of the Co-operative Society.[73] From the start, Dalton was concerned to eliminate dangerous sentences in the terms of reference of the working party which might suggest any commitment to federalism. 'But since the members of the Conference would be selected by Governments and responsible to Governments Dr Dalton did not think that additional safeguards would be necessary.'[74] He urged Attlee that the British delegation must not allow themselves to be 'hoodwinked, hustled or halted', presumably by foreigners.[75] This firm insularity was echoed by the Labour Party. In Transport House, Denis Healey drew up a cogent pamphlet, 'Feet on the Ground: a study of Western Union', in October

[71] Sir Ivone Kirkpatrick to Lord Inverchapel, 13 Dec. 1948 (FO 371/73101) Z 10350/4416/72/G; Kirkpatrick to O. Harvey, 28 Aug. 1948 (FO 371/73097).
[72] Bevin to Sir O. Harvey, 30 Dec. 1948 (FO 371/79212) Z 67/1071/72.
[73] Correspondence in PREM 8/986.
[74] Minute by E. Tomkins, Foreign Office, 7 Jan. 1949 (FO 371/97213) Z 233/1071/72.
[75] Dalton to Attlee, 3 Feb. 1949 (PREM 8/986).

1948. It emphasized the Bevin view, and argued that Britain was already the economic and strategic sheet-anchor of western Europe; it played the continental equivalent, under the EPU, of the role filled by the United States in relation to the Marshall Plan. The junior Foreign Office minister, Christopher Mayhew, urged Dalton to 'discard proposals for a European Federation or for a European Assembly with a mandate to prepare a Federal Constitution for Europe', so that the British idea of a Council consisting only of ministers of the states concerned could be adopted.[76]

Dalton's interpretation of the most limited view possible towards the Council of Europe dampened the enthusiasm of federalists. He urged that they should proceed with caution, rather than create a forum where 'people who were by temperament critics of government should be free to speak'.[77] He also pressed for the British view that the Council should proceed by bloc voting by each group of national representatives. In the Foreign Office, Gladwyn Jebb argued the essential incompatibility in key respects between the defence structure of the Brussels Treaty organization, with NATO grafted on to it, and the 'partly governmental and partly non-governmental' Council of Europe.[78] In the end, despite all Labour's prevarication, the Council of Europe did go ahead and held its first meetings at Strasbourg in September 1949. But it was clear that it fell far short of the federalist euphoria that was in the air at The Hague. Dalton wrote ebulliently to Attlee on 10 September that the convention had been extremely successful, with Churchill harming his own reputation and the Labour delegates, especially Aidan Crawley ('Definitely the best'), Edelman, Callaghan and Margaret Herbison doing well. Mackay remained 'a fanatical federalist' but had still proved himself quite useful. 'He was the nearest approach to a lone wolf in the Labour pack and we shall have to keep an eye on him.'[79] Not surprisingly, poor Mackay complained to Crossman at this time, 'I have put up with a great deal at the hands of Dalton & co. as you have suffered

[76] Mayhew to Dalton, 15 Nov. 1948 (ibid.).

[77] Dalton to Bevin, 20 Jan. 1949 (FO 371/79214) Z 586/1071/72.

[78] Notes for Foreign Secretary's speech by Jebb, ? 1949 (FO 371/79270) Z 2828/10719/72.

[79] Dalton to Attlee, 10 Sept. 1949 (Dalton papers, 9/7/45).

from the Labour Party.'[80] The Labour government and the
Foreign Office were well pleased with the low profile adopted
at first by the Council of Europe; it was a talking-shop and
little more.

The government seemed unconcerned that Strasbourg
added to some other factors in leading to some deterioration
in Anglo-French relations. The spirit of the Treaty of Dunkirk
seemed to have evaporated in the autumn of 1949 as *Le
Monde* complained. Bevin remained unmoved. Roger Makins
urged him that, when the foreign ministers met in Paris in
November, the French should be told flatly that the most
effective contribution made to western European strength,
apart from that from the United States, had come from
Britain, notably through the European Payments Union.
He and Bevin argued that complaints by the French, Belgians,
and Italians should be largely ignored, while the French anti-
Americanism over the growth of NATO and over the Anglo-
American financial talks in Washington in September should
be firmly corrected.[81] Thus British government policy
remained suspicious of European political union. It remained
so during the discussions over the Schuman Plan in 1950 and
again over the so-called European Army, to include contin-
gents from western Germany, in 1951. In fact, when Churchill
and the Conservatives returned to office, they proved no
more enthusiastic about political involvement in a united
Europe than their Labour predecessors had been. Britain
took no part in the lead-up to the Treaty of Rome in 1955.
Eden and Churchill in 1954–5 both made it clear that they
were opposed to an integrated Europe; nor would Britain
join the proposed European Defence Community. Labour's
insularity, without its socialist overtones, had become the
conventional wisdom. It remained so until a new European
impetus built up in the early sixties.

After Britain entered the Common Market in 1973, it was
a frequent complaint that the Labour government after 1945
lost a golden opportunity in failing to take the lead in
promoting European unity. This is not a view easy to sustain

[80] Mackay to Crossman, 10 Sept. 1949 (Mackay papers, Section 8, file 1).
[81] Brief by R. Makins for Foreign Ministers' meeting in Paris, Nov. 1949
(FO 371/79076).

from the evidence. The purpose of the Hague conference, befuddled by Churchill's magnificent but vague rhetoric, was far from evident. No clear model was worked out, then or later, about the constitutional, legal, or political relationship of the Council of Europe to the Westminster parliament. Nor was it explained how British social and economic policies would fit in with the very different notions entertained by the largely anti-socialist representatives in the European movement. Bevin, the Foreign Office, and the Labour Party (and, in practice, the Conservative Party) felt that the main priority was to build up co-operation in effective, practical, functional terms, through economic collaboration under OEEC and the EPU, and defence arrangements under the Brussels Treaty. The whole scheme would be outward-looking, linked with the larger programme of the alliance with the North Atlantic treaty powers. This was the main outline of British foreign policy down to 1951; as has been seen, it was the course generally followed by Churchill, Eden, and Macmillan governments in the fifties also. Irrespective of the merits or demerits of Britain's membership of the EEC in the 1980s, what emerged in the late 1940s was a far more imprecise and less constructive model. In practice, the move towards integration evolved largely in terms of the needs of France in its new economic incarnation under the Monnet Plan, and the newly-emergent German Federal Republic. Neither in its putative political design, nor in its trading or economic arrangements, did the European scheme fit easily into Britain's natural line of development. The anti-Europeanism, such as it was, of the Cripps era was a practical imperative as well as a partial reflection of a self-contained, insulated economy.

During these domestic and external preoccupations, the morale of the Labour Party went through many vicissitudes. There were many signs of stress in the party, and parliamentary revolts on Palestine, Ireland, and defence. The public pronouncements of class-conscious ministers such as Bevan and Shinwell caused much friction with trade-union MPs and others. In the constituency parties, discontent over Bevin's foreign policy or Cripps's wage freeze was markedly greater than ever appeared in the press. Yet the state of party morale remained high. There were periods of crisis. One came in October 1948 at a by-election in Edmonton, caused by the tragic death by drowning of Evan Durbin. There was a huge swing of 16.2 per cent against the government, the second biggest in the entire 1945–50 parliament. This was partially attributed to anti-Semitic campaigns against the Labour candidate, Austen Albu, though Dalton robustly attributed the swing to Albu's uncharismatic qualities as a campaigner.[82] But the general record in by-elections remained astonishingly good. The most tense of this period came at South Hammersmith in February 1949. The Conservatives were represented by Anthony Fell, a Roman Catholic in a constituency where the Catholic vote was considerable; Labour's candidate was W. T. Williams, a former Welsh Baptist minister. The Conservatives put in a massive effort, including a motorcade tour by Churchill himself. But Labour still held the seat with a reduced majority of 1,613. The result bore out many doubts felt in Conservative circles about Churchill's electoral appeal. It was considered a mistake for the party leader to involve himself too directly in a by-election campaign.[83] On the Labour side, Williams' victory strengthened a general feeling that the next general election was very far from lost. Subsequent comfortable Labour victories in the four remaining by-elections during 1949—at North St. Pancras, Sowerby, West Leeds, and South Bradford—confirmed this picture. Devaluation, far from being a political liability for Labour, seemed almost to have become an electoral asset.

In the late autumn of 1949, after devaluation, a political lull seemed to develop. The Labour government had to resolve a number of varied controversies at this period. All of them involved Aneurin Bevan and in some sense raised the burning question of the conflict between Morrisonian 'consolidation' and socialist advance as urged by the Minister of Health. Several of these have already been noted. The conflict over steel nationalization continued right down to the end of 1949. In the end, in November 1949, after anxious discussion between Addison and Salisbury, on behalf of the

---

[82] Dalton's diary, 21 Feb. 1951, in which he describes Albu as 'a bloody bad candidate'.

[83] *The Times*, 26 Feb. 1949.

peers on either side, the House of Lords agreed to pass the
Steel Nationalization Bill, on condition that vesting day was
delayed until July 1950, after the next general election
would be held. Morrison explained to Attlee that the outcome was in many ways a more favourable outcome for the
government than could have been expected.[84] Ironically
enough, the Parliament Bill, specifically introduced to ensure
that the Lords' delaying powers would be reduced to one
year only, was not required at all; it actually became law on
16 December, three weeks after the steel bill. The frequent
statement that the steel bill became law under the terms of
the 1911 Parliament Act is, thus, not correct. It was the
1949 Parliament Bill that did so.[85]

The disputes on the Party Home Policy Committee over
the 'shopping list' for nationalization were also finally
resolved in November 1949 with Bevan and Griffiths reluctantly agreeing to a watered-down form of the 'mutualization'
of industrial assurance. At least Bevan could take comfort
from the nationalization proposals that were itemized
including the unhappy case of sugar. There were also many
Cabinet arguments over the cuts in capital investment,
especially in the social services, after devaluation. These were
worked out laboriously as an aftermath of devaluation, rather
than an accompaniment to it, as Cripps had wanted. Cripps
first raised the spectre of prescription charges under the
National Health Service in October 1949. With much reluctance, Bevan accepted them on condition that the charges
should be accepted in principle only; in practice, the government never imposed them at all. Bevan took the opportunity
to declare against any suggestion that charges be imposed on
dentures or spectacles.[86] At the Economic Committee on
14 October he claimed that such charges on a free health
service would throw away much goodwill from the government's working-class supporters.[87] When Morrison on 20
October raised in Cabinet the need to consider charges for

[84] Morrison to Attlee, 31 Oct. 1949; Addison to Attlee, 4 Nov. 1949 (PREM
8/1489, pt. 2).
[85] The Parliament Bill was passed by the Commons in three successive sessions.
[86] Minutes of Lord President's Committee, 4 Nov., considering Bevan's paper
on the National Health Service, LP (49) 77 (CAB 132/11).
[87] Minutes of Economic Committee, 14 and 20 Oct. 1949 (CAB 134/220).

teeth and spectacles, Bevan retorted that, while he was prepared to review payments to specialists, a charge on appliances 'would involve a far-reaching departure from the basic principles of the scheme'.[88] The issue, so pregnant with future possibilities, went no further at this stage.

Bevan was also unhappy at the serious cuts in housing that followed Cripps's new policies. The housing programme, now at the peak of its achievement, bore the brunt of the post-devaluation cuts in public expenditure. It had been cut to below 200,000 a year; the allocations of softwood timber and steel would be reduced. He was anxious that the £35m. of cuts proposed should fall on houses built privately for owner-occupation, and that there should be no reduction in houses built by the local authorities. Attlee also received an angry letter from Bevan on 21 October 1949. It declared that, while the housing programme would be slashed by £40m. to £50m., the 'already gorged and swollen defence estimates' that Alexander had introduced would be reduced by no more than £30m.

A reduction in housing expenditure cannot be justified on the basis of the existing national emergency. Housing makes its own peculiar and essential contribution to economic revival. It has been agreed all through our discussions in the last few weeks that the increase in the export of goods and services following devaluation will change the pattern in the distribution of labour in the country and, therefore, more, not less, mobility in the labour force will be required. A reduction in the number of new houses will not decrease but increase the rigidity of the existing pattern and consequently make it more difficult to bring about a re-deployment of the labour force.[89]

Bevan rumbled with threats of resignation. He was in unhappy mood, with further problems surrounding the NHS supplementary estimates. But Attlee persisted, and the housing cuts went through. On the other hand, the Cabinet on 21 October rejected a proposal to reduce the milk subsidy by ½*d*. a pint, on straight political grounds. The total expenditure cuts, once projected at £300m. in practice amounted to only £122,500,000.

[88] Cabinet Conclusions, 20 Oct. 1949 (CAB 128/16); Bevan to Attlee, 2 Feb. 1950 (PREM 8/1239).
[89] Bevan to Attlee, 21 Oct. 1949 (copy in Alexander papers, Churchill College, 5/14/9b).

In the end, everything was somewhat messily patched up. It was just as well because the government was now confronted with a general election. There had been much debate amongst ministers about its timing. Cripps favoured an early election on tactical grounds, as did Bevan and the Tribunite left. Dalton noted on 19 July that Bevan 'spoke with his habitual force and warmth' to this effect. Morrison favoured an election delayed until the summer so that the economy could recover its equilibrium after the shock-treatment of devaluation and the latest round of expenditure cuts. The opinion polls (now much more noticed than in 1945) were not encouraging. Morgan Phillips advised Attlee on general electioneering grounds that the spring and summer would be best.[90] Gaitskell had sent a memorandum to Attlee during the Cabinet discussions on devaluation, urging either November 1949 or else June 1950 for the election. He marginally preferred the former since the higher import prices after devaluation would not yet have greatly affected the cost of living. An election any time between December and March would be 'most unwise'.[91] Attlee, as always, kept his own counsel, but appears to have been swayed by Cripps's moralistic view that the election must take place before the budget, which would otherwise appear to be an electioneering one, an impression which Cripps felt bound in conscience to resist. A meeting of senior ministers was convened on 7 December at Downing Street.[92] Cripps urged an early election; Morrison wanted one 'later', though he could not offer anything more precise. Bevin sent a note from Eastbourne saying that he had no views since 'he was no politician'. The majority seemed in favour of February rather than May or June. On 10 January, therefore, Attlee announced that a general election would be held on 23 February. An unexpectedly long period of notice was thus given, which would give the government's enemies time to develop their attack. For the first time since 1906, a general election was to be held during the depths of the winter.

[90] Dalton's diary, 19 July 1949; Morgan Phillips to Attlee, 19 July 1949 (Attlee papers, Bodleian, Box 2).

[91] Gaitskell to Attlee, 18 Aug. 1949 (Gaitskell papers).

[92] Donoughue and Jones, op. cit., p. 449.

The general election of February 1950 was a less intense or memorable affair than the campaign of 1945. It was even more tranquil this time; Churchill called it 'demure'.[93] Labour's tactics were to keep the temperature down and present the party as moderate and responsible. 'Consolidation' in the Morrisonian sense dominated Labour's style. Little was made of the pledge to nationalize the 'shopping list' of industries and services itemized in the manifesto. This applied even to Ian Mikardo's pamphlet for Allan Wingate Ltd, *The Labour Case*, which included a somewhat Delphic foreword by Herbert Morrison. Instead, Labour stressed economic recovery, welfare, and full employment. Morrison himself, who had a difficult contest in a marginal seat in Lewisham, emphasized Labour's appeal to the middle class, especially to professional and technical workers. He also urged that Labour 'put the family first'; a strong appeal was offered to housewives. The dampening down of excitement was helped by a deliberate policy of keeping Aneurin Bevan out of the limelight and off the air. Indeed, even Laski publicly rebuked Bevan in *Reynolds News* after the poll, for the damage done by the 'vermin' speech. The main tone for Labour was set by its star performer being Attlee himself. The Prime Minister delivered a long series of humdrum, but effective, speeches, in major cities and towns up and down the land, driven erratically hither and thither for 1,300 miles by Mrs Attlee in an ancient Humber saloon. The Conservatives naturally made much of Churchill. A speech of his at Edinburgh, which criticized Bevin's handling of foreign affairs and called for high-level talks with the Russians 'at the summit' attracted widespread attention.[94] But it was noticeable that the Conservatives placed less emphasis on Churchill's personal leadership and dominance than in the disastrous campaign of 1945. They offered a more collective image, with Eden, Butler, Macmillan, and others prominent in their attack. Some effort was made to appeal to Liberal voters; Churchill actually offered Lady Violet Bonham-Carter one of his party's twenty-minute election broadcasts (an offer which

[93] See H. G. Nicholas, *The British General Election of 1950* (London, 1951), especially pp. 90 ff.
[94] *The Times*, 16 Feb. 1950; *Manchester Guardian*, 16 Feb. 1950.

she was persuaded to turn down). The Liberals, meanwhile, were struggling with their disastrous decision to field almost 500 candidates, most of them in utterly hopeless seats, with grave financial consequences for their party.

The low-key nature of the campaign was emphasized by its being far more obviously than before a contest waged on the radio, and to a very limited extent, on television. Labour fielded a battery of major speakers. One of them was J. B. Priestley whose appeal to the middle-class conscience seemed less successful than that of 1945. The Conservatives replied with another populist, the 'radio doctor', Charles Hill of the British Medical Association. There was a general feeling amongst Conservatives that the tide was flowing in their favour in the south-east of England, especially in commuter-land, while Labour's strongholds in the north, Scotland, and South Wales seemed to be as firm as ever. The quiet character of the campaign did not imply apathy. On the contrary, it was generally agreed that there was an intense degree of public interest and partisan commitment. The Gallup Polls detected a small, and declining, number of 'don't knows'. Labour and Conservative party workers were active on the doorstep as never before. Tension was increased when the Gallup Poll showed that Labour recovered dramatically from being ten points adrift of the Conservatives in November 1949 (48 per cent to 38 per cent) to actually showing a lead on 30 January (45.5 per cent to 44.0 per cent). The eve of the poll confirmed this, with a narrow Labour lead recorded of 45 per cent to the Conservatives' 43.5 per cent, and the Liberals trailing at 10.5 per cent.[95]

The results declared were generally frustrating. On a huge poll of 84 per cent, Labour substantially increased its vote from 1945. It obtained 13,266,176 votes in all and captured 46.1 per cent of the poll compared with 12,492,404 votes and 43.5 per cent for Conservatives and allies, and only 2,621,487 votes and 9.1 per cent for the Liberals who lost over three hundred deposits. The results of the first night seemed to indicate the comfortable return of Labour to power, with a safe, if reduced, majority. All the old

[95] Gallup Polls were published in the *News Chronicle*, 20 and 30 Jan., and 10, 17, and 22 Feb. 1950.

working-class citadels in the East End of London, Lancashire, Yorkshire, and urban centres such as Birmingham, Coventry, Stoke, Derby, Nottingham, Sheffield, and Bradford, were as impregnably Labour as in 1945. There was certainly no evidence of a mass defection from the party here, whatever the rigours of austerity and the sacrifices made. But the next day revealed that the Conservatives were adding to their strength in rural constituencies all over England and Scotland (though not in Wales). Furthermore, the tendency of recent by-elections and local government elections for there to be a sharp swing back to the Conservatives in suburban constituencies was more than confirmed. There were far higher than average swings to the right in the London suburbs, Essex, the Hampshire ports, and North Lancashire. London suburbs such as Brentford, Chiswick, Croydon, Hendon, Heston and Isleworth, Ilford, Mitcham, Romford, Wembley, and Wimbledon all went Conservative, mostly by comfortable margins. The Conservatives also made headway in Birmingham, Liverpool, Manchester, and Glasgow. The tide had undoubtedly turned to some fair degree—but not sufficiently to deprive Labour of another term of office. With the distortions afforded by the electoral system, Labour's clear lead of almost a million over the Conservatives in votes cast resulted in an overall majority of only five. Labour ended up with 315 seats, the Conservatives and allies with 298, the Liberals with nine, and there were three others, including two Irish republicans who were unlikely to turn up very often. In the end, Labour fought a vigorous and united campaign. The party had been optimistic throughout; the standard warnings of 'over-confidence' were given to constituency activists. The far-left challenge had been extinguished, since the two Communists in West Fife and Mile End were beaten by Labour candidates, as was D. N. Pritt in North Hammersmith. The 100 Communist candidates averaged 2.0 per cent of the vote where they fought. Platts-Mills, Zilliacus, Solley, and Hutchinson all met with crushing defeats. In areas such as rural Wales and East Anglia, Labour still showed a capacity to retain ground recently won: witness the capture of five seats out of eight in Norfolk, for instance. The one Labour seat in Cornwall (Falmouth and Camborne) was held. Yet the

result was the most precarious of victories. Undoubtedly a
major reason for this was the effect of the redistribution of
constituencies. This had been put through by Chuter Ede in
1948–9 with scant regard for Labour's electoral prospects,
until he showed some belated concern for the undue tilting
in favour of rural constituencies that the Boundary Commissioners were undertaking.[96] In all, redistribution was calculated as having cost Labour at least 30 seats in all, or 60 in
terms of a majority over the Conservatives. In addition, the
distribution of votes contained the usual anti-Labour bias,
with the piling up of huge and unnecessary Labour majorities
in mining and other constituencies. Of the 60 largest
majorities, 50 were in Labour-held seats. It was a victory,
nevertheless. The voters had endorsed Labour's brand of
welfare democracy and economic growth. But it was an
ambiguous, unconvincing verdict: the Nuffield survey felt
certain that the returns constituted 'a mandate for moderation', however defined.[97] The immediate political future was
left most uncertain. The Labour right tended to blame
Bevan for alienating middle-class voters; he blamed the right
for not opting for an election in November. Morrison criticized Attlee's judgement in holding an election at such a
disadvantageous time in the depths of winter. When, once
again in July 1951, Attlee seemed likely to disregard Morrison's views about the timing of an election, Morrison harked
back to the events of February 1950, 'about which Stafford
and Nye were wrong'.[98]

The marginal victory of February 1950 may be taken as a
concluding verdict by the voters on the Cripps era. Many
blamed the austerity and severity of the period since the
summer of 1947 for the disaffection of the middle class and
floating voters, including housewives. It would be fairer,
however, to see Cripps's remarkable performance in holding
the government together at a time of a collapse of its policies
and morale as enabling Labour to pick itself up and pull itself
together, with a fighting chance of electoral victory next

---

[96] Chuter Ede, memorandum on 'Redistribution of Seats', 4 Mar. 1948 (HO
45/24249); Cabinet Conclusions, 8 Mar. 1948 (CAB 128/12).
[97] Nicholas, op. cit., p. 302.
[98] Morrison to Attlee, 6 July 1951 (Morrison papers).

time. After the Cripps regime, Labour's natural supporters remained in excellent heart, while there was a widespread belief that the economy was on the right lines. In May 1950, responding to a suggestion from Addison (to which Attlee gave some support) that the burden of taxation be reduced, Cripps drafted a paper which may serve as his economic testament.[99] He argued that a deliberate policy had been pursued since November 1947 of maintaining a high level of employment but avoiding the pressure of inflation. The budget had been used purposively—so he claimed—as an instrument of economic planning. The gap had been closed between public expenditure and the current value of goods available for consumption. Through taxation, the government had removed the difference between what people would otherwise spend, and what was available for them to buy. That is, it had provided the difference between the needs of investment and the amount of voluntary savings. This equilibrium had worked. Trade was almost in balance; the external situation was greatly improved. Inflation had been kept in check, yet the rigours of deflation had been avoided. Since current savings were insufficient to meet Britain's investment needs, the social and economic priorities inherent in government expenditure had to be funded by the Treasury and this meant a high level of taxes. Not all the diagnosis, perhaps, can be accepted. The absence of any reference to devaluation, where the Chancellor's touch had faltered, is noticeable. Later critics pointed to the declining rate of industrial investment under Cripps, compared with 1945–7, although a higher proportion of what investment there was did go into industrial plant and machinery rather than, say, into private housing. Still, a broad balance had been struck, nevertheless, between public provision and private consumption. When Cripps was to retire as Chancellor in October 1950, there were already problems lurking on the horizon, several of them the result of the Korean War and

[99] Memorandum by Cripps on 'Budget Policy', 15 May 1950 (PREM 8/1188). Cf. Notes on the Budget proposals by Addison, 10 Mar. 1950, in which he argued that the high level of personal taxation and capital investment cut into savings and produced social hardship; and Attlee to Cripps, 11 Mar. 1950 (T 171/400). 'We are extracting £600m. a year from people, simply to prevent them spending it', Addison observed.

the stockpiling of raw materials which led to renewed balance of payments difficulties. But a basis for economic recovery had manifestly been laid. Cripps was in many respects the real architect of the rapidly improving economic picture and growing affluence from 1952 onwards. In the 1947–50 period, he was indispensable for his party and his nation. He was the best of his time. It was tragic that the long-term benefits of the economic transformation he created at the Treasury were inherited in the fifties by other, less resolute hands.

10

The Second Attlee Government

Despite its small overall majority, there was no immediate sign of trouble for the Attlee government after the general election of February 1950. Most of the omens were remarkably favourable. Dalton felt that the Cabinet was, in general, perfectly harmonious. 'A few personal antipathies, Herbert v. Ernie, & Nye v. both—but bark worse than bite, and no real splits or resignation threats.'[1] The new Cabinet looked very similar to the old. Seven ministers of varying degrees of importance had fallen at the polls. The only Cabinet minister among them was Creech Jones, the Colonial Secretary, who lost at Shipley. In addition, Lewis Silkin had lost his seat after redistribution and had, surprisingly, failed to gain nomination in two other constituencies, in Sheffield and Islington.[2] The new Cabinet showed some changes. James Griffiths, a great success at National Insurance, was promoted to Cabinet rank as Colonial Secretary; Dalton went to the Ministry of Town and Country Planning; Shinwell returned to the Cabinet as Minister of Defence instead of Alexander; Gordon-Walker went to the Commonwealth Relations Office, with Noel-Baker moving on to Fuel and Power; Hector McNeil went to the Scottish Office in place of Woodburn. Outside the Cabinet, Maurice Webb went to Food, and John Strachey to the War Office. Among the high-ranking second tier of ministers, there was notable promotion for Gaitskell, who had distinguished himself during the devaluation crisis and who now became Minister for Economic Affairs, to help Cripps. Kenneth Younger became Minister of State at the Foreign Office, in place of Mayhew who had been defeated at South Norfolk. But the general balance of the Cabinet remained much as before. The weary titans of former years,

---

[1] Dalton's diary, 27 Jan. 1950.

[2] I am indebted to Mr Sam Silkin for information about his father. Mr Silkin points out that his father's health had suffered from piloting three major bills through parliament: he later went to the Lords.

Bevin, Morrison, Cripps, retained their old dominance. Bevan remained at the Ministry of Health, having turned down an opportunity to take the Colonial Office. Gaitskell criticized Attlee here. 'It only means the mess [on NHS finances] will not be cleared up.'[3] Some of the less impressive ministers, Isaacs, Ede, Barnes, Tomlinson, Strauss, remained undisturbed. The entire process of half-reshuffle had the unmistakable air of a government that expected to go to the country again quite soon.

However, for the moment, the government had to carry on, heedless of its tiny majority. It was agreed in Cabinet on 25 February that 'there could be no question of attempting to carry through any of the controversial legislation which had been promised in the Party's Election Manifesto. Very careful consideration would also have to be given to the content and presentation of the Budget.' Gaitskell urged Cripps privately to concentrate any tax relief on reducing income tax, 'particularly if, as I anticipate, we have another election within 6 months, and possibly within 3 months'.[4] Norman Brook explained to Attlee confidentially that he had omitted from the minutes any reference to a further appeal to the electorate, even though he realized that this might 'give some Ministers the impression that you have decided to carry on for a much longer period than you have in mind'. Attlee minuted his agreement.[5] In a Cabinet meeting on 2 March, Bevan protested at the unduly cautious wording of the King's Speech. He deplored any suggestion that the government's discretion in choosing suitable measures for the 1950–1 session should be limited. 'He would deprecate any reference in the Speech or in the Debate to the difficulties of the Parliamentary situation.' He also urged that there should be 'no signs of hesitancy' in pushing on with iron and steel nationalization, or in appointing suitable individuals for the Iron and Steel Corporation.[6] On this last point, the others agreed; but the general Cabinet view was

---

[3] Gaitskell's diary, 21 Mar. 1950.
[4] Cabinet Conclusions, 25 Feb. 1950 (CAB 128/17); also see minutes of Cabinet Future Legislation Committee, 6 Feb. 1950 (CAB 134/299); Gaitskell to Cripps, 10 Mar. 1950 (T 171/400).
[5] Brook to Attlee, 25 Feb. 1950 (PREM 8/1166).
[6] Cabinet Conclusions, 2 Mar. 1950 (CAB 128/17).

that the narrow majority would prevent the government from carrying through major legislative projects. This meant that the nationalization of cement, water, sugar-refining, and meat distribution, and the mutual ownership of industrial assurance companies were cast into limbo for ever. A compromise, anodyne King's speech was thus patched up.

In fact, the Cabinet remained united and in good heart for many months. The general mood was one of confidence, above all because the post-devaluation boom in the economy showed every sign of continuing. In 1950, there was another record year for exports, after the stimulus given on the exchange rate; the balance of payments moved strongly into surplus in the first two quarters of the year. The economic news, in fact, continued to be cheerful throughout 1950. The volume of industrial production was 30 per cent higher than in 1947; the volume of exports was 60 per cent above the level for that year, with the export of vehicles showing a particularly great increase. Over the year as a whole, there was a surplus of £229m. on the overseas balance of payments. There was no problem now of runs on the gold and dollar reserves as there had been a year before; there were even rumours that London might ask the IMF to sanction a higher rate for the pound against the dollar. Symbolically, at the end of the year, Hugh Gaitskell, then the Chancellor, was able to announce that Britain would make no further calls on assistance from Marshall Aid. 'The economic news is uniformly good these days,' wrote *The Economist* on 15 July, while investors 'face a more promising summer than they have known in recent years'.[7] If the country and the economy were in good heart, so, too, were Labour and its supporters. There were two difficult by-elections at this time, either of which could have reduced Labour's tiny majority of five to near-extinction. These were at West Dunbartonshire in Scotland where a by-election was held on 25 April, and at Brighouse and Spenborough in Yorkshire where a contest took place on 4 May. In fact, Labour held both these highly marginal seats; the swing from

[7] *The Economist*, 3 June, 17 July, 14 Oct. 1950; 'The Balance of Payments for 1950–1', report by Cabinet Programmes Committee, July 1950 (PREM 8/1412); minutes of Cabinet Economic Committee, 10 Nov. 1950 (CAB 134/224).

government to Opposition was minute, a mere 0.4 per cent in the case of West Dunbartonshire. In the 'spectacular' result in Brighouse, Labour whipped up an 85 per cent poll with eager canvassers pouring in from all over Yorkshire.[8] Other, less difficult, by-elections in Sheffield (Neepsend) in April and North-East Leicester in September were also won with ease.

This confidence was reflected in the Commons and the Cabinet. In parliament, the narrowness of Labour's majority and the intensity of the exchanges between government and Opposition only added to the fervour and unity of the Labour MPs. This notably reinforced their morale. Fired by anger with the Tory adversary, who came to use aggressive tactics in the form of tiring, late-night sessions and what Robert Boothby later called the policy of 'harrying the life out of them', Labour closed ranks and held firm. 'It looks as though those bastards can stay in as long as they like', Churchill was to complain after losing a division on steel nationalization by ten votes.[9] The Cabinet was similarly united. There was one serious eruption, over the contentious issue of the charges on dentures, spectacles, and appliances under the National Health Service. Cripps ventured this proposal, after having failed to obtain prescription charges the previous autumn. Bevan resisted furiously all assaults on his beloved Health Service. He opposed any attempt to impose a ceiling on health expenditure for 1950–1. Instead, he appointed an independent expert, Sir Cyril Jones, to conduct his own inquiry into the finances of the Health Service, with special attention for the expensive hospital service which took most of the budget. Two long and angry meetings of the Cabinet on 3 and 4 April 1950 saw Bevan in furious opposition to any deviation from the principle of a free health service. 'As regards prescriptions, he no longer favoured the proposal to impose a charge; he would prefer to seek economies by prohibiting doctors from prescribing proprietary medicines.' He added that the 'government's abandonment of the principle of a free and comprehensive health service would be a shock to their supporters and a grave disappointment to

[8] Sam Barker to Arthur Greenwood, 4 Apr., 5 May 1950 (Bodleian, Greenwood papers, 8, Box 2).
[9] Cf. *The Times*, 10 Mar. 1950; Dalton's diary, 7 Feb. 1951.

Socialist opinion throughout the world'. He pointed out that in any case they only had evidence for one year's working of the existing system. He was supported by Hector McNeil, the new Secretary of State for Scotland. Other ministers opposed him, while Cripps declared his flat opposition to any further supplementary NHS estimates. The only other choices were imposing charges or curtailing services, he declared. Attlee added his own concern about the escalation of costs.[10] In the end, on 6 April a satisfactory compromise was reached. A ceiling of £392m. was placed on NHS expenditure for 1950-1, while Bevan's own proposal of a Cabinet Committee to monitor the finances of the Health Service, month by month, was accepted. It was a powerful committee, with Attlee in the chair, and Morrison, Addison, Gaitskell, and Isaacs among its members.[11] The problem was a real one: no clear mechanism had yet been devised for checking the inflation of costs on hospital services and salaries, and on pharmaceutical charges. The Ministry had only minimal control over the spending of the local hospital boards. On the other hand, aided by the close personal relationship between Cripps and Bevan, the whole discussion was much less traumatic than was to occur over the budget proposals a year later. The tense personal atmosphere that arose between Gaitskell and Bevan then was noticeably absent, assisted by the government's broad agreement on other priorities. Gaitskell himself recorded in his diary in May that his own personal relations with Bevan were excellent at this time.[12]

There was a general consensus in the party at this period over the main direction in which the government was aiming. This emerged very clearly at the important conference, or seminar, held at Beatrice Webb House, Dorking, on 20-1 May 1950. Like an earlier conference held at Shanklin the previous year, it was attended by most members of the Cabinet, the National Executive, and leading trade-unionists, and was almost entirely

[10] Cabinet Conclusions, 3-4 Apr. 1950 (CAB 128/17).
[11] Minutes of Committee on National Health Service (CAB 134/519).
[12] Gaitskell's diary, 26 May 1950.

harmonious.[13] Morrison led off and his brand of moderate 'consolidation' dominated the discussions. He emphasized the losses at the last election, especially in middle-class areas of outer London and the south-east dormitory seats. There had been concern amongst the voters about taxation ('one of our weakest points' noted Morrison in his discussion paper), housing, and nationalization. He criticized the 'shopping list' in the manifesto, and urged that they should emphasize full employment and planning next time. A Transport House memorandum noted that 5 per cent of the middle-class vote had swung against Labour—but also that 29 per cent of the working class voted Tory. In the ensuing discussion, Attlee laid emphasis on the fact that many working-class voters were not yet converted to socialism. Shinwell urged that nationalization was only a means, not an end; health reforms, housing, and education were also major contributions to socialism. Cripps proclaimed the need for applying planning to private enterprise, and urged that greater equality of incomes should be achieved before taxation operated. Addison urged that planning and controls were as inherently socialistic as nationalization, no doubt reflecting his own experience during the first world war. Cautious contributions came from Isaacs and Greenwood, while Barbara Ayrton Gould, a member of the NEC, emphasized the need to win over middle-class constituencies, like Hendon North where she had just been defeated. Wilson stressed the basic contrast between Labour planning and Tory anarchy. The trade-union contributions, from Lincoln Evans, Jock Tiffin, and others, were notably moderate also. There was little enough dissent from the left, though Ian Mikardo had sent Morgan Phillips a memorandum from ten 'Keep Left' MPs and three former MPs, on the need for a capital levy and more nationalization. Their spokesmen at Dorking were not fractious. Michael Foot advocated greater equality and the further redistribution of wealth. Most influential of all, Aneurin Bevan urged the importance of retaining the commitment to nationalization (he claimed that Arthur Horner would win the Rhondda for

[13] The full account of the Dorking conference is recorded in the Morgan Phillips papers in the Labour Party archives, Walworth Road (GS 26/3). For the Shanklin, Isle of Wight, conference see *The Times*, 28 Feb. 1949.

the Communists if Labour dropped it). But he also stressed the need to reassure private enterprise concerns that Labour did not intend to nationalize them—a view that gave Morrison much private amusement. Time had evidently made consolidationists of them all. Morrison wound up with observations about the need to improve existing schemes of nationalization and to protect the needs of the consumer. He praised the party for its essential unity.

It was, indeed, a harmonious and happy gathering. A broad consensus emerged, as the 'confidential summary' listed it, focusing on the need for a broad-based, classless appeal, full employment, the improvement of existing nationalization schemes, planning without 'strangling the private sector', the further equalization of wealth including a possible levy on capital, an 'evolutionary and gradual' wages policy, with free collective bargaining backed up by arbitration. In effect, the whole Labour movement, from Morrison to Bevan, seemed at one in expounding a more dynamic version of consolidation, based on the mixed economy and planning through consensus, but with further advance well in mind also, such as a capital levy, more nationalization, and greater equality including in education. Attlee himself was pleased enough with Dorking. 'Went very well. The Surrey countryside was lovely', he told his brother, Tom.[14] His government seemed as cohesive and resilient as it had ever been. It certainly had not lost either its zest for power or its faith in victory.

The major policy issues that arose in the first half of 1950 did not produce any major division in the Cabinet. The two main preoccupations were both somewhat unexpected—the fate of Seretse Khama in the Bamangwato Reserve in Bechuanaland in southern Africa, and the problems of European economic integration focused on the Schuman Plan in May.

The Seretse Khama affair blew up when tension arose in the Bamangwato Reserve in the High Commission Territories, when its prospective chieftain, Seretse Khama married a white English girl, Ruth Williams, to the dismay of his tribe. A complicating factor was the personal rivalry between Seretse and his uncle Tshekedi, who had links with prominent

[14] Kenneth Harris, op. cit., p. 452.

British Conservative politicians but was unpopular in the reserve. The Commonwealth Relations Office handled the matter remarkably severely, in the case both of Noel-Baker and of Patrick Gordon-Walker, his former under-secretary who succeeded him at the CRO in February 1950, and who was perhaps the most right-wing member of the entire administration. From the outset, the adverse reaction to Seretse's marriage by South African Afrikaners was a major factor in determining the British government's response. Gordon-Walker's initial memorandum on the problem, in January when he was still under-secretary, emphasized Seretse's 'irresponsibility in marrying and provoking a crisis for the tribe'. It drew a sharp protest from Attlee himself. 'In effect we are invited to go contrary to the desire of the great majority of the Bamangwato tribe, solely because of the attitude of the governments of the Union of South Africa and Rhodesia. It is as if we had been obliged to agree to Edward VIII's abdication so as not to annoy the Irish Free State and the USA.'[15] Nevertheless, the Cabinet gave reluctant assent to the policy of the CRO. At a meeting with Seretse and his lawyer, Lord Rathcreedan, in London on 16 February, Noel-Baker and Addison both urged him that he must renounce his claim to the chieftainship of the Bamangwato and leave Bechuanaland.[16] Addison urged that direct British rule over the reserve was probably the best solution. When Gordon-Walker, the new Secretary of Commonwealth Relations, met Seretse and Rathcreedan on 6 March, he adopted a more brutal approach. Seretse must now leave, not only the reserve but also the Bechuanaland protectorate, and go to Britain forthwith. Gordon-Walker claimed that this would be for a trial period of only five years, but his tone seemed to suggest an almost indefinite period of exclusion.[17] Norman Brook later complained to Attlee that no 'native authority' was being proposed to take Seretse's place.[18] Seretse responded to Gordon-Walker's pressure with anger but with

[15] Geoffrey Cass to Patricia Llewelyn-Davies, CRO, 22 Jan. 1950 (PREM 8/1308).
[16] Note of meeting at the Commonwealth Relations Office, 16 Feb. 1950 (ibid.).
[17] Notes on meeting at Commonwealth Relations Office, 6 Mar. 1950 (ibid.).
[18] Norman Brook to Attlee, 11 Apr. 1951 (ibid.).

dignity; he protested that he was 'being kicked out of his own country'. Nevertheless, Gordon-Walker persisted; he made it clear that Tshekedi was also to be expelled from the reserve, since otherwise there would be pressure for the return of Seretse and his white wife.[19]

The whole episode was remarkable testimony to traditional attitudes in the CRO in the face of white settler influence and prejudice across the border in South Africa. It contrasted with the enlightened tone of policy in West Africa, where white settlers were few in number. Seretse appeared to be a manifest victim of British injustice, partly in response to pressure from Afrikaners in South Africa. Even when a judicial inquiry appointed by the Cabinet acknowledged the legality of Seretse's title to the chieftainship, it still recommended that he have the title withheld, since, otherwise, whites in South Africa and Southern Rhodesia would be affronted.[20] The deposed chieftain flew to London and lived quietly there for some years. In due course, he returned to the Bamangwato Reserve, with his wife, and spent the remainder of his brief life there in tranquility. Not surprisingly, there were several Labour backbench protests at the CRO's handling of the affair. They came mainly from left-wingers, headed by the veteran fighter for colonial liberation, Fenner Brockway. Perhaps there ought to have been a great deal more criticism. For all that, the CRO's policy was accepted by the Cabinet. Britain's ambiguous policy towards South Africa and also towards Southern Rhodesia and a proposed Central African Federation, remained unchanged.

A more immediate problem arose in connection with western Europe. In the early months of 1950, the course of European unity remained uncertain; the initiative that had led to the Council of Europe being established at Strasbourg

---

[19] Gordon-Walker memorandum, Jan. 1951 (DO 121/136). Also see telegram from Commonwealth Relations to South Africa, 21 June 1951 (CO 537/7222), in which it is stated that the return of Seretse to the Bamangwato Reserve, while still married to Ruth Williams, was unlikely to inflame the Union of South Africa now. But the Union could still make political capital out of it, and take economic and other action which would make the administration of Swaziland and Bechuanaland difficult and lead to a further crisis in Basutoland.

[20] Report of Judicial Inquiry, CP (50) 36 (CAB 129/38). The Cabinet decided to keep the report unpublished to avoid embarrassment.

had yet to be followed up; Britain and France seemed much at odds. Then on 9 May 1950, without prior consultation with either Bevin or Dean Acheson, Schuman, the French Foreign Minister, outlined a new scheme for a coal and steel community to integrate heavy industry in western Europe, including the German Federal Republic.[21] There was some sympathy in Foreign Office circles with the Plan. Roger Stevens of the FO hoped that the British government would 'adopt an attitude towards the French proposal which was neither hesitant or hostile'. He foresaw political advantages, especially since it would calm down French concern about Anglo-American plans for restoring industry in the Ruhr to private ownership.[22] Sir Oliver Harvey, in the Paris embassy, always an enthusiast for European integration, thought the Schuman scheme 'represents a turning point in European and indeed in world affairs'. He added, in a covering note to Strang in the Foreign Office, 'This is a never-to-be-repeated opportunity of getting a real move on in Europe. The French have made a startling, and indeed revolutionary proposal. . . . We really have the ball at our feet.'[23] Sir Ivone Kirkpatrick, while more cautious about 'third force' implications, felt the Schuman Plan might encourage the French to be less hesitant about the idea of integrating the German armed forces into a western defence structure.[24] In the Economic Section of the Cabinet, Robert Hall felt that 'my own view is that we have no option but to welcome the move and to wish for luck'.[25] He explained, in a later memorandum of 21 June, that British industry would benefit from a wider market and the stimulation of improved efficiency in western European industry. He was eager that Britain should join the new coal and steel community.[26] On the Opposition front benches,

---

[21] Record of conversation of Bevin, Acheson, and Schuman, 11 May 1950 (FO 371/85341) CE 2328/2141/181.

[22] Memorandum by Roger Stevens, 10 May 1950 (ibid.) CE 2141/2141/181.

[23] Memorandum by Sir Oliver Harvey, 19 May 1950 (ibid.) CE 2342/2141/181.

[24] Memorandum by Kirkpatrick on 'The French Plan from the Political Point of View', 11 May 1950 (ibid.) CE 2330/2141/181.

[25] Memorandum by Robert Hall, 11 May 1950 (PREM 8/1428).

[26] Memorandum by Robert Hall, 'The Schuman Proposals for Coal and Steel', 21 June 1950 (ibid.).

Churchill, Macmillan, and others gave a guarded welcome to the Schuman initiative, largely on political grounds.

But the response of the British Labour Party, from top to bottom, was almost entirely hostile. Bevin was bad-tempered from the start at having so major a *démarche* sprung upon him without warning: he disliked being hustled by Dean Acheson, who felt that here was a great leap forward towards western European integration. Bevin sensed instinctively that the Schuman Plan raised again the spectre of federalism, rather than the gradualist, functionalist method favoured by Britain. Cripps was scarcely more welcoming. He deplored the Plan as a move away from the idea of the Atlantic community and towards that of European Federation. He asked Monnet on 15 May for reassurance that there was no danger that the coal and steel community would turn into a capitalist cartel.[27] Negotiations with French representatives about the approach to be adopted in forming the community, held in late May, did not go well. On 2 June, the Cabinet reported negatively on the whole idea, aided by a powerful attack on the Plan by Kenneth Younger (a private pro-European deputizing for Bevin during one of his increasingly frequent periods of ill health). There was 'a real difference of approach between the United Kingdom government and the French government' which could not be glossed over by mere verbal ingenuity in the drafting of a communiqué.[28] Cabinet ministers felt that the general drift of such a plan would run counter to the policies of domestic planning of Britain's nationalized coal and steel industries by a Labour government. The new scheme would undermine the proposed pricing and investment policies for British industry. It would also work against the Commonwealth relationship: Britain's policy of selling steel abroad at an export premium, from which Commonwealth countries were dispensed, would not longer be possible. The United States would also, perhaps, have been offended. A further theme, developed later, was that an inward-looking western European coal and steel unit would not be able to

[27] Record of meeting between Attlee, Bevin, Morrison, Cripps, and Shinwell, 10 May 1950 (PREM 8/1201); record of conversation of Cripps and Monnet, 15 May 1950 (FO 371/85842) CE 2338/2141/181.

[28] Cabinet Conclusions, 2 June 1950 (CAB 128/17). Younger's private view was sympathetic to the Plan (Younger Interview, p. 27).

release the vast potential demand in the underdeveloped world. On a more local level, as Morrison told Kenneth Younger, 'It's no good—the Durham miners won't wear it.' This was the view of virtually the whole parliamentary party, too, apart from a handful of federalists such as Mackay and Leah Manning.[29] Some confusion was caused by the ill-timed publication on 13 June of *European Unity*, a pamphlet highly critical of the principles underlying the Schuman Plan, which was taken to be an indication of the views of the British government and Foreign Office, but which was, in fact, written by Denis Healey in Transport House. There were loud French protests at the 'insular and sectarian nature' of the British government's attitude.[30] Matters were not helped by the presentation of the Healey pamphlet at a press conference by Hugh Dalton, a virulent 'anti-European'. Finally on 25 June the Cabinet declared formally against participation in the Schuman Plan. This was partly because it would impose a supranational authority over British industry, partly because it would establish an industrial cartel 'on the pre-war restrictionist model'.[31]

There were angry interrogations from Eden and others on the Opposition front bench, which caused the government some parliamentary discomfiture. The new member for Bexley, Edward Heath, made a passionately pro-European maiden speech. But the Labour Party was solid in its opposition to the Schuman Plan. Attlee, Morrison, and Cripps firmly rebuffed the idea of creating a supranational authority to control British coal or steel, without democratic restraint. Bevin felt instinctively that such a Plan was not appropriate for Britain with its unique world-wide role and its special links with the United States. The proposed Schuman scheme might well become inward-looking, exclusive, and potentially anti-American. The Schuman Plan, in fact, went ahead; it was dominated by France and western Germany and shaped by the technocratic philosophy of Jean Monnet. Britain remained aloof. Conversely, by July 1951 the Chancellor,

---

[29] Donoughue and Jones, op. cit., p. 481; Manning, *A Life for Education*, p. 201.
[30] Material in Labour Party International Department archives; *The Times*, 14 June 1950.
[31] Cabinet Conclusions, 25 June 1950 (CAB 128/17).

Gaitskell, together with Noel-Baker and Robens, was inclining to the view of J. R. C. Dow of the Treasury that Britain should at least consider 'partial membership' of the coal and steel authority.[32] The episode did the government no harm. Schuman and the very notion of integration was anathema to most sections of British opinion, still stirred by isolationist memories of Dunkirk. Some talked darkly of the role of the 'Catholic black International'. There were excellent reasons for not joining in the Schuman Plan. It fitted in badly with British and Commonwealth economic priorities. It was not devised with Britain's industrial needs in mind; indeed, it is probable that Monnet and Schuman did not really expect Britain to join anyway. Alan Bullock has rightly argued that a decision to keep out of the Schuman scheme in 1950 did not pre-empt a decision to enter the EEC in 1955,[33] assuming that such a decision was desirable. The British government's strong response combined emotional xenophobia with economic good sense.

Apart from these excitements, the general political mood down to late June remained relatively hopeful in the government ranks. The administration proved its ability to govern successfully, even with so tiny a majority. The majority, in practice, tended to be somewhat larger than on paper, since the Liberals shied away from the thought of another early election, while three of them (Megan Lloyd George, Emrys Roberts, and Edgar Granville) voted regularly with Labour.[34] The skilled whipping of Willie Whiteley was also a reassuring factor. In all, Labour lost on only five of 234 divisions in this parliament. Even the bitterly-contested Iron and Steel Bill had been forced through, despite several close calls which saw the government whips having to ferry sick members through the division lobby, and frantic attempts to locate MPs abroad in such distant theatres as Korea or

---

[32] Report by J. R. C. Dow, 23 July 1951; memorandum of views of Gaitskell, Noel-Baker, and Robens, 24 July 1951 (PREM 8/1428); Cabinet Conclusions, 24 July 1951 (CAB 128/19).

[33] Bullock, op. cit., pp. 783–4.

[34] Clement Davies to Lady Violet Bonham-Carter, 15 Nov. 1950 (Clement Davies papers, J/3/45). See *News Chronicle* 25 Nov. 1950, reporting a speech by Lady Megan Lloyd George at Menai Bridge, which attacked Davies's 'Keep Right' approach.

Greenland. On balance, the Conservatives' harassing tactics
may have done more harm to themselves than to the government, in the eyes of a fair-minded public. Despite so small
a majority, despite a diminishing zeal for steel nationalization
on the part of George Strauss himself, the government was
putting public ownership into effect. The new British Steel
Corporation eventually came into being in October 1950,
with S. J. L. Hardie, former chairman of British Oxygen,
as its first head. Vesting day for the nationalized industry
was now scheduled for 15 February 1951. As has been seen,
the economic news gave much good cheer. The Minister of
Food, Maurice Webb, announced the end of 'points' rationing on 19 May. There were hopes of the early end of petrol
rationing, too. The government had its worries, chief among
them the continuing ill health of two key figures, Bevin and
Cripps. But on balance the omens seemed favourable. Gaitskell noted in his diary that Attlee's position in the government was stronger than it had ever been.[35] Labour looked
ahead to an early election, to be fought on the basis of rising
prosperity and a firm foreign policy, an election that Labour
could well win.

Then on 25 June the entire picture was transformed when
the North Koreans invaded South Korea across the 38th
parallel. Events in this remote, and hitherto little-regarded,
country in the Far East henceforth cast a sombre shadow
over the last phase of the Attlee government. From the
outset, Britain, as the chief ally of the United States, was
inevitably embroiled; in addition, of course, it had its own
real concerns in the Far East in Hong Kong, Singapore, and
the war against Communist insurgents in Malaya. On 27 June
1950 the Cabinet agreed, without recorded dissent, to
endorse US action in opposing Communist aggression in
Korea.[36] Britain then voted with the United States in the UN
Security Council when there was a seven to one vote in favour
of giving military aid to South Korea—a vote at which the
Soviet ambassador was providentially absent, and with
Yugoslavia as the sole dissentient. Lewis Douglas, the US

[35] Gaitskell's diary, 26 May 1950.
[36] Cabinet Conclusions, 27 June 1950 (CAB 128/18).

ambassador in London, urged Pierson Dixon that Britain should voice whole-hearted approval of American military and naval action. In fact, the British government at once released naval forces from Hong Kong in support of American troops in Korea. The Foreign Office telegraphed Sir Oliver Franks in Washington on 30 June to say that 'there would not be a more useful demonstration of the United Kingdom's capacity to act as a world power with the support of the Commonwealth'. It wished to use this as a lever with which to force the United States not to reduce ERP aid to Britain owing 'to certain preconceived and ill-founded notions about European integration'.[37] But this action on Britain's part was not enough. Sir Oliver Franks sent a magisterial handwritten personal note to Attlee on 15 July to urge that British land forces should also be sent to Korea. This action would demonstrate 'the quality of our partnership' and act as proof of the faith of other countries in the United Nations. Attlee used Franks's message, and the ambassador's personal stature, as a major argument in Cabinet on 25 July in favour of Britain's also sending land forces to Korea, as 'a valuable contribution to Anglo-American solidarity'.[38] The Chiefs of Staff had warned Attlee on 5 July against sending land or air forces to Korea: it would be 'militarily unsound', in their view. But with Bevin still away, convalescing after further illness, the Cabinet endorsed the Defence Committee's view that two infantry battalions should be sent from Hong Kong to Korea, quite apart from 19 Infantry Brigade. By 25 July, the Chiefs of Staff had come to share this conclusion, on political grounds. By November, there were two British brigades in Korea, with 29 Brigade also fighting there.[39] Henceforth, British involvement in the prolonged and bloody warfare up and down the Korean peninsular was intense. The courage of the 'Glorious Gloucesters' was later to pass into legend. Furthermore, in response to renewed US pressure,

[37] Sir Pierson Dixon memorandum, 28 June 1950 (FO 371/84081) FK 1022/30; FO telegram to Washington, 30 June 1950, No. 2980 (FO 371/81655).

[38] Sir Oliver Franks to Attlee, 15 July 1950 (PREM 8/1405, pt. 1); Cabinet Conclusions, 25 July 1950 (CAB 128/19).

[39] Prime Minister's Brief, 5 July 1950 (CAB 21/2248) and DO (50) 50; telegram from British government to heads of Dominions governments, 25 July 1950 (PREM 8/1405, pt. 2).

the Cabinet had agreed by the end of August to a much-increased defence programme of £3,400m. over the years 1950–4, which Cripps stated would be feasible. There was grave doubt expressed by Aneurin Bevan on 1 August. 'Our foreign policy had hitherto been based on the view that the best method of defence against Russian imperialism was to improve the social and economic conditions of the countries now threatened by Communist encroachment. The United States government seemed now to be abandoning this social and political defence in favour of a military defence. He believed that this change of policy was misjudged and that we should be ill-advised to follow it.'[40] However, Bevan's was a lonely voice of dissent; there was, in any case, no hint of resignation from him, while his hawkish attitude during the Berlin airlift was fresh in the memory. The huge increase in the defence budget went ahead, including an extension of the period of National Service from eighteen months to two years. As will be seen, the arms expenditure soared ever upwards, from £3,400m. to £3,600m. and then to £4,700m. by January. American voices called for a programme of as much as £6,000m. The entire foreign and defence policies were suddenly being recast, with grave consequences for its economic strategy and political future.

At first, this involvement in the Korean War did not produce much dissent in Labour's ranks, or disturb the over-all mood of unity, despite Bevan's protest recorded above. After all, there was Labour unanimity over the recognition of Communist China, while Bevin was firm in rejecting any notion that Britain was committed to defending the Chiang Kai-shek regime in Formosa.[41] When the government announced British support for the American action at the end of June, only a small handful of left-wingers, including S. O. Davies, Silverman, and Driberg, protested. Davies, and

[40] Cabinet Conclusions, 1 Aug. 1950 (CAB 128/18).

[41] See draft paper by R. H. Scott of the Foreign Office, 24 July 1950 (FO 371/83298) FC 1024/51, giving a joint Foreign Office–Commonwealth Relations Office view on behalf of implicit British involvement in Formosa in the event of a Communist attack. Bevin strongly dissented: 'any of these recommendations means a general war. If we are not careful, we might provoke it.' The Colonial Office shared Bevin's view, partly because of the large Chinese population in Malaya and Hong Kong: J. J. Paskin to M. E. Dening, 5 Aug. 1950 (ibid.), FC 1024/59.

his fellow Welshman, Emrys Hughes (the son-in-law of that old pacifist, Keir Hardie) alone voted against the government on the Korean issue on 5 July. Davies's stand brought support from all parts of Britain, including from a distinguished Oxford Marxist historian who assured the Merthyr MP that 'you are not without support in the Senior Common Rooms of the Home of lost causes'. A lone dissentient letter in Davies' postbag came from James Jackson, formerly of the Cardiff ILP, who declared roundly that 'a few public executions in Cyfarthfa Park would do the Merthyrites no end of good'. He linked Davies with Merthyr 'traitors' such as Keir Hardie and R. C. Wallhead in the past.[42] Otherwise, there was a remarkable unity about the government's policy. In *Tribune*, which had established links with Transport House since late 1949, Michael Foot staunchly defended the British support for the UN forces in Korea. Otherwise, he argued, Labour would lapse again into the futile appeasement of the Munich years. There should be 'no possibility of Communist aggression succeeding by reasons of Western appeasement'. Foot strongly condemned the actions of Sidney Silverman and others on the far left who wanted Britain to keep aloof. Despite the Chiang Kai-shek regime, despite Britain's recognition of Communist China, despite the Nationalist rump resident in Formosa, 'the aggression of the North Koreans was, and remains, an international crime of the first order'. *Tribune* acclaimed UN victories in South Korea in October; it drew contrasts between Labour's resoluteness now and the failure of previous Tory administrations to stand up to Hitler.[43]

In another episode, two left-wing Labour MPs, Ellis Smith and Fenner Brockway, resigned from the fringe movement 'Socialist Fellowship' on 5 July when that body declared against British participation in the Korean War. An incident of quite a different kind came on 4 August when Raymond Blackburn, the Labour member for Northfield, announced that he wished to resign from the party, in protest against

---

[42] Christopher Hill to S. O. Davies, 8 July 1950 (S. O. Davies papers, A16); James Jackson to Davies, 2 Aug. 1950 (ibid.), where the writer denounces the 'Zilly-Prittsky-Plattsky Gang'.

[43] *Tribune*, 30 June, 28 July, 6 Oct. 1950.

the government's defence policy. In a statement in the House on 13 September, he proclaimed his enthusiasm for a national government or a coalition, headed by Churchill. But the defection of the eccentric Blackburn, in a phase of transition from socialism to alcoholism, only served to rally other Labour members in defence of their government.[44] The Labour Party annual conference at Margate in October endorsed the British involvement in Korea by a huge margin. A left-wing motion critical of Bevin's foreign policy was rejected by 4,861,000 to 881,000. Aneurin Bevan who remained the star of the conference platform, launched a passionate plea for party unity.

But this euphoria could not last. There was growing anxiety about the strain being imposed by rearmament on the British economy. Further, it was against the instincts of the Labour Party to have Britain committed to an open-ended and bloody war in a faraway country. In any case, by November, the character of the war had changed. Instead of a defence of South Korea, which confined hostilities to that country, General MacArthur, in megalomaniac vein, had pushed on far into North Korea, and was advancing towards the Yalu river on the very borders of Manchuria. This posed a clear military threat to Communist China (which Britain had recognized *de jure* since 6 January 1950); the prospect opened up of a dramatic and dangerous widening of the original, limited war. Talk in American military circles of pre-emptive air strikes against Chinese bases in Manchuria and on the Chinese mainland added to Labour's unease. Concern reached its supreme pitch at the end of November. Chinese troops now entered the war in vast numbers, following MacArthur's offensive towards the Yalu. On 26 November they attacked MacArthur's forces and drove them back in headlong retreat. Most terrifying of all, President Truman at a press conference on 30 November appeared to envisage the possibility of the United States using the

[44] For the resignation of Smith and Brockway from Socialist Fellowship, see *Socialist Outlook*, July–Sept. 1950; Morgan Phillips to A. E. Parkinson, Wrexham, 8 May 1951 and to Joan Wicken, Stroud, and Thornbury, 13 June 1951 (Labour Party archives, GS 30/1 and 30/4). For Blackburn, see Raymond Blackburn, *I am an Alcoholic* (London, 1959), especially pp. 95 ff.; *The Times*, 5 Aug. 1950; *Parl. Deb.*, 5th ser., vol. 478, 1159–69 (13 Sept. 1950).

atomic bomb in the war in Korea. In a message to Congress on 1 December, he urged the appropriation of $1,050m. for producing fissionable materials for an American atomic weapons stockpile.

This added a new and alarming dimension, which caused anxiety throughout British government circles. Dalton, in particular, wrote to Attlee on 30 November 1950 that 'the latest events, so full of the gravest possibilities—including Truman's statement today on the atomic bomb—have convinced me that *you ought to fly out to Washington at once*—to confer with Truman.' It would reassure the party and the country, Dalton believed. Attlee could arrange this 'after clearing with Ernie and Herbert, without summoning the full Cabinet'; Bevin himself was in no fit condition to travel. The Foreign Affairs Group of MPs wrote in similar terms.[45] Later that day, the Cabinet duly agreed that Attlee should fly to Washington to confer with the American President. Publicly, it should not be presented that only the use of the atomic bomb would be on the agenda; the supreme command in Europe and international arrangements for raw materials should also be discussed. Roger Makins of the Foreign Office told the US chargé d'affaires that the visit of Attlee had arisen from an upsurge of feeling in the House of Commons. 'The President's statement about the use of the atomic bomb had precipitated suddenly a feeling of uneasiness about the conduct of the war in Korea which had been building up for some time.'[46] On 2 December, René Pleven and Schuman, the French Prime Minister and Foreign Minister, met Attlee and Bevin in London to convey French anxieties; it was clear that Attlee would be going to Washington as the emissary of the fears of western Europe, not merely of Britain alone.[47] On 3 December, then, Attlee flew to Washington with the CIGS, Field Marshal Slim and only one or two Foreign Office aides; he would be reinforced by

[45] Dalton to Attlee, 30 Nov. 1950 (Dalton papers, 9/9/108); J. B. Hynd to Attlee, 30 Nov. 1950 (Attlee papers, Box 9); Truman's statement to Congress, 1 Dec. 1950 (FO 371/81655), AU 1075/13; Dalton's diary, 30 Nov. 1950.
[46] Cabinet Conclusions, 30 Nov. 1950, 6.45 p.m. (CAB 128/18); record of conversation between Roger Makins and Holmes, US Chargé d'Affaires, 1 Dec. 1950 (FO 371/83019) F/1027/16.
[47] Record of Attlee–Pleven meeting, 2 Dec. 1950 (ibid.), F/1027/6G.

the powerful intellectual presence of Sir Oliver Franks in the Washington embassy. The foreign and defence policies, and indeed the overall history of the Labour government, would never be quite the same.

Attlee's talks with Truman and Acheson lasted daily from 4 to 8 December.[48] After a hesitant opening, Attlee and Truman struck up a good personal relationship. A wide range of themes was pursued; the discussion was not confined to Korea alone. In the first meeting on the 4th, Attlee urged the need for an early cease-fire in Korea, and emphasized the folly of excluding Communist China from the United Nations. As he had promised to do at the meeting with Pleven and Schuman, he stressed the importance of paying heed to Asian, more especially Indian, views of China. 'India was an outpost in Asia of European cultural and administrative traditions and culture.' For his part, Acheson was impressed neither by Attlee's arguments nor by his debating style. The Secretary of State urged that 'China was little more than a Russian satellite', and that this was no time to talk. On the 5th, Attlee again pursued the theme of relations with China. He urged that a demilitarized zone be created between the UN line in Korea and the Manchurian frontier, with a possible unified Korea in due course. Above all, he urged the need to detach, or try to detach, the Chinese from the Russians. A compromise over Formosa, which declined to accept the principle of Nationalist Chinese sovereignty over the island, was one major suggestion. Two meetings on 6–7 December were concerned wholly with economic matters, including attempts to obtain international action on the allocation and price-fixing of raw materials. Already the stockpiling of vital materials by the Americans and their consequently rapidly inflating costs were proving worrying for the British balance of payments. The final meeting between Attlee and Truman on 8 December saw Attlee again press the case for admitting Communist China to the United Nations; he declared against the idea of 'a limited war against China'. Acheson was again inflexible. He spoke of the danger of Korea and Formosa going Communist, with resultant

---

[48] Record of Truman–Attlee conversations, 4–8 Dec. 1950 (PREM 8/1200). I have greatly benefited from talks with Lord Franks on these and other matters.

danger to Japan and the Philippines. He and Truman argued against a policy of appeasement through concessions. Lord Tedder, the chairman of the British Joint Services Mission in Washington, who had joined the talks, argued that, on the contrary, an air war with China would mean a war with Russia also. The final communiqué tried to offer British opinion reassurance on negotiations with China, on the limits to the UN action in Korea, and on international control of raw materials. Little was said on paper about the atomic bomb, although Attlee felt satisfied with the private re-assurances he had received.

He returned to Britain on 11 December in a mood of some triumph. The Cabinet was told by him the following day that the Americans had accepted his warnings of war with China, even only a limited war with an economic blockade. Truman had been categorical that there was no intention of using the atomic bomb in Korea. The bomb, Truman had stated ambiguously, was 'in a sense a joint possession of the United States, the United Kingdom and Canada'.[49] Attlee was hailed in parliament and in the press as the bringer of peace, who had calmed down impulsive and ideological Americans, and pulled the world back from the brink of a wider war in the Far East. Kenneth Younger believed that both Truman and General Omar Bradley, the UN land commander in Korea, would have extended the war had it not been for Attlee's intervention. Attlee's arguments had been 'utterly devasta-ting. . . . One could almost see the atmosphere being deflated as he spoke.'[50] Ever since December 1950, Labour partisans have chosen to point the contrast between Attlee's quietly effective diplomacy and Churchill's flamboyant, but ulti-mately empty, rhetoric.

In many ways, the praise bestowed on Attlee was fully merited. Even Acheson agreed that relations between the two governments were more harmonious after the Washington talks. Trust had been restored. Attlee had applied a major element of sanity at a time of some panic. Henceforth, the United States would pursue a more measured policy in Korea with more regard for European and Asian opinion. The

[49] Cabinet Conclusions, 12 Dec. 1950 (CAB 128/18).
[50] Kenneth Younger, interview transcript, pp. 50 ff.

eventual clash between Truman and General MacArthur, which led to that mighty commander's dismissal in April 1951, owed something to the note of caution so unerringly struck by Attlee in December 1950. Franks's views on the closeness of the Anglo-American 'special relationship' had been fully confirmed. On the other hand, it is clear that, while Attlee received reassurance on the atomic bomb (which Truman had surely not thought of using in any case) on other issues—Formosa, the recognition of China and its later admission to the UN, or international policies on raw materials—the British Prime Minister achieved little real change in Truman and Acheson's policies. After all, Attlee was manifestly the spokesman of the weaker partner. Franks, who was present throughout, did not feel the talks marked any great turning-point in Anglo-American relations. Further, there were grave costs that accrued from the Washington talks. One central theme that emerged immediately was that the Americans, in response to perhaps moderating their action in Korea, expected the British defence programme, now standing at £3,600m., to be increased still further.

On 18 December, Attlee told the Cabinet of the need to accelerate the defence commitment.[51] The American chiefs of staff were talking even in terms of a £6,000m. programme over the next three years: virtually every Cabinet minister, from Gaitskell to Bevan, believed this was economically quite impossible. The one possible exception was Shinwell, in extremely hawkish mood at this time. But some acceleration was accepted as inevitable. Another alarming concession to be made in return for a renewed American commitment to western European defence—one due to cause much disarray in the Labour Party—was the agreement to German rearmament, or rather to 'German participation in the defence of Europe'. This had previously been opposed throughout the Labour movement. Bevin was hostile; so was Cripps. Dalton was almost pathological. 'I hate all Germans and regard them all as Huns', was his measured view.[52] But American pressure was overwhelming now. On 14 December, the British Cabinet agreed in principle to West German rearmament, and German

---

[51] Cabinet Conclusions, 18 Dec. 1950 (CAB 128/18).
[52] Dalton's diary, 'August 1951'.

participation in an integrated defence force in Europe. 'The Cabinet recognised that an effective German contribution was essential to the successful defence of western Europe.'[53] But it was also necessary to avoid needless provocation to the Russians, to reassure the German Social Democrats (who opposed rearmament), and to allay French fears about the threat from a rearmed Germany. The details of German rearmament were left to the future, with Dalton continuing his anti-Teutonic crusade. Bevin told the NATO Council on 18–20 December that a German contribution to western defence 'should not be rushed'. Not until September 1951, in the last weeks of the government, when Morrison was now at the Foreign Office, was a definite programme adopted for putting German rearmament into effect.[54] Here was an issue to plague the Labour movement throughout the early fifties. It was a direct legacy of the supposedly triumphant Truman–Attlee conversations in Washington.

Another problem to emerge was that Britain was becoming enmeshed, despite all the inclinations of Bevin and the rest of the government, in backing American positions in the Far East, however questionable. On the Chiang Kai-shek regime, on Formosa and the islands of Quemoy and Matsu, just off the Chinese mainland, there was little the British government could do except warn and exhort. Another embarrassing issue, which caused Attlee and his colleagues much difficulty, was the American insistence in January 1951 on pressing home a resolution at the United Nations General Assembly, which would brand China as an aggressor. The degree of hostility to this amongst Cabinet ministers varied a good deal. Bevin was concerned not to upset the Americans by taking too hard a line.[55] For this, Attlee seems to have rebuked him. Alexander and Jowitt took the American view 'like good old High Tories', while Shinwell was simply 'a wartime Blimp'.[56]

[53] Cabinet Conclusions, 14 Dec. 1950 (CAB 128/18).

[54] Bevin memorandum on meeting of NATO Council at Brussels, 18–20 Dec. 1950 (F 800/449); Younger to Attlee, 16 Aug. 1951 (PREM 8/1440, pt. 4); Cabinet Conclusions, 4 Sept. 1951 (CAB 128/20).

[55] Bevin to Attlee, 12 Jan. 1951 (FO 371/92067) F 10345/6; Kenneth Younger, interview transcript, p. 59; minute by Younger, 1 Jan. 1951 (FO 371/92756) FK 1022/6.

[56] Younger, interview transcript, p. 60.

Others, however, including Bevan, Ede, Dalton, Younger, and, most important, Attlee himself, were deeply unhappy at the 'brand China' resolution. A Cabinet meeting on 22 January left a final decision open. Bevan, Younger, and Ede wanted Britain to vote against; only Hector McNeil, the hawkish Scot, wanted to vote for.[57] Younger's view was contrary to that of the Foreign Office; Gaitskell reported Strang and Bridges as being 'horrified' by it. Strang expressed the Foreign Office view on 8 January that Britain 'had misgivings about entering upon a path which would begin with condemning China as an aggressor, and end in limited or unlimited war. The Americans were not to take it for granted that we should agree to support a resolution declaring China an aggressor.'[58] Gladwyn Jebb followed this cautious line at the UN, while a meeting of Commonwealth ministers on 11 January showed a general consensus hostile to the 'brand China' resolution. It endorsed instead the principles of the Cease-Fire Committee.[59] Dean Rusk had urged Sir Oliver Franks of the need for Britain to take part in at least an economic blockade of China. Franks was sympathetic but urged in return the need for America first to withdraw recognition from Chiang Kai-shek so as to carry Asian opinion with her.[60] Meanwhile the Chiefs of Staff, headed by Slim, urged Britain to endorse the 'brand China' resolution.[61] On 26 January, the Cabinet on balance was in favour of supporting a modified version of the American resolution, incorporating some modifications introduced in an Israeli amending resolution. In the event, on 28 January, the last-minute changes introduced enabled Gladwyn Jebb to vote for the US resolution which was carried in the Assembly by 44 votes to 7. But the whole episode was disturbing. It was widely taken as indicating that the Labour government was being swept along by ideological cold warriors in Washington, who linked China

[57] Cabinet Conclusions, 22 Jan. 1951 (CAB 128/19); Gaitskell's diary, 2 Feb. 1951. Addison persuaded Attlee, Ede and Williams to modify their views.

[58] Minute by Strang, 2 Jan. 1951 (FO 371/92756) FK 1022/10; cf. Confidential Annex to Chiefs of Staff Committee minutes, 8 Jan. 1951 (DEFE 4/39).

[59] Minutes of meeting of Commonwealth ministers, 11 Jan. 1951 (FO 371/92761) FK 1023/26.

[60] Telegram from Sir Oliver Franks to Foreign Office, 18 Jan. 1951 (FO 371/92761) FK 1023/24.

[61] Minutes of Chiefs of Staff Committee, 8 Jan. 1951 (DEFE 4/39).

and the Soviet Union in the same global diagnosis. The erratic sabre-rattling of the unstable MacArthur, the UN supreme commander, added substantially to fears that some kind of limited war against Communist China was being seriously considered.[62]

Most alarming of all was the eventual agreement to a far larger defence budget. This fell well short of the £6,000m. asked for by the American chiefs of staff. Even so, on 25 January the Cabinet reluctantly accepted a programme of £4,700m. over the three years, 1951–4.[63] This was a huge increase in the defence budget for Britain, with all its economic worries; it inflicted a heavier burden of defence spending per capita on the British people than was imposed in the United States herself. Aneurin Bevan strongly condemned in Cabinet the impact of the defence programme on the economy. He was sceptical of the advice given by the military about the Soviet threat. Russian steel production alone would not allow the Russians to sustain forces on so huge a scale. 'It would be folly for the democracies to adopt vast defence programmes which would put such a strain on their economies. . . . Rearmament should be approached with restraint, not with enthusiasm.' Bevan had not hitherto been a consistent critic of defence policy. He had, reported Younger, endorsed both NATO and Britain's possession of the atomic bomb, when the information eventually reached him. The previous November he had issued a statement declaring his support for the rearmament programme.[64] But his economic and political critique of the new defence programme foreshadowed new and graver disagreements.

In the Cabinet meeting of 25 January, Hugh Gaitskell outlined the costs of the programme (excluding stockpiling), which would mean an additional £500m. of expenditure in the first year, £800m. in the second year, and £1,000m. in the third and final year. The Chancellor spelt out the economic problems that the new rearmament programme would cause in such remorseless detail that he might almost

---

[62] Cabinet Conclusions, 26 Jan. 1951 (CAB 128/19); Gaitskell's diary, 2 Feb. 1951. For British fears about MacArthur, see FO 371/92813.

[63] Cabinet Conclusions, 25 Jan. 1951 (CAB 128/19).

[64] Younger, interview transcript, p. 63; *News Chronicle*, 23 Nov. 1950.

have been an opponent of it. No one, not even Bevan, put the
case for the prosecution so cogently. The terms of trade
would be turning against Britain in any case in 1951, stated
Gaitskell. There would be a desperate shortage of raw
materials. There was not likely to be much financial assistance from the United States. Exports and investments in
engineering, building, and textiles would be seriously affected.
New controls would be required to switch men and materials
from civilian to defence work, and some civilian building and
investment would be set back. There would be a net reduction in consumer living standards that would be felt keenly
from the autumn of 1951 onwards. In the face of this bill
of indictment, it is somewhat extraordinary that Gaitskell,
nevertheless, gave his backing to the defence programme
of £4,700m. with some enthusiasm—though on political
rather than economic grounds. Not an expert in foreign
politics, Gaitskell felt swayed by the need to back up the
Americans at almost all costs. As for his critics in the Cabinet,
he dismissed them privately as 'anti-American'; in the case of
Strachey, 'it was almost pathological'.[65] Griffiths and Ede
seemed to object on grounds of pacifist timidity. In the
Cabinet meeting on 25 January, Bevan and probably other
ministers resumed the attack on the economic consequences
of the arms programme. There would be a slump in exports;
a huge problem would result for the labour force; welfare
programmes like council house-building would be severely
affected. There would be a massive scarcity of raw materials
and of machine tools. This all meant a vast burden for the
economic fabric, and serious damage to almost every aspect,
in fulfilment of a programme whose very basis was unrealistic.
In addition to these points, all of which were later to be
proved substantially correct, it could be added that much
would depend on the performance of the steel industry, still
in some uncertainty, with vesting day for nationalization due
on 15 February. In spite of all this, a second Cabinet meeting
in the afternoon of 25 January took the fateful decision to
endorse the £4,700m. defence programme for 1951-4.
Morrison, Dalton, and Gaitskell all spoke in favour, as did
Attlee. Dalton noted in his diary, 'Our Own Arms Programme.

[65] Dalton's diary, 9 Feb. 1951.

This is being accepted, in its modified but still very impressive form, without much opposition either in Cab. or Parl. Party.'[66] The Cabinet then resumed its arguments about German rearmament. This transformed defence commitment, into which the Cabinet was stampeded in January 1951, marked a profound watershed in British political history. It instilled new elements of pressure and division within the government and the party. Its political and financial implications were to dominate British public affairs for a decade to come.

The troubles over the war in Korea, and the Cabinet controversies over the rearmament programme, served to exacerbate other divisions opening up in the party and the Labour movement in the latter months of 1950. Industrial relations were turning increasingly sour. In the TUC conference of September 1950, the policy of wage restraint was narrowly overturned, partly perhaps because of resentment at the dictatorial methods of Arthur Deakin. The miners joined the opposition, which was decisive. The pattern of tense labour relations continued, and added further to the strains racking the government at this time. There had already been industrial troubles in the summer. In June, a strike by Smithfield meat lorry drivers led to troops being used on a massive scale. At its peak, Chuter Ede reported to the Prime Minister that two to three thousand servicemen were being used to transport meat to and from Smithfield. Isaacs gloomily observed that 'the Communist Party was actively engaged in an attempt to disrupt transport in this country', and referred to recent disputes involving London busmen, dockers in London, Liverpool, and Hull, and the influence of the Polish dockers' union on their British comrades.[67] Indeed, with the international atmosphere made more tense after the outbreak of the Korean War, a stern anti-Communism gripped the mind of the government in dealing with industrial disputes at home as well. It should be added, however, that far more traditional

---

[66] Dalton's diary, 'mid-February 1951' note on 'Our Own Arms Programme'. The Cabinet minutes of 25 January do not attribute individual views, unlike those of 15 January.

[67] Memorandum on 'The Smithfield Strike' by Chuter Ede, 7 July 1950 (PREM 8/1538).

sources of conflict played their part in these strikes as well: the TGWU executive council was told that one cause of the London busmen's strike in September 1950 was the employment of women bus conductors or 'clippies'. The Union affirmed that it was union policy that women should be employed on buses 'only in those areas where men are not available'.[68] Two broad areas of union disaffection emerged at this time. One was the continuing strains imposed by the two-year-old wage freeze. The other, which loomed increasingly large in the latter part of 1950, was trade-union hostility towards Order 1305, originally passed in July 1940 and still in force. This attempted to stop strikes by forcing disputes to be settled by joint machinery, especially by a five-man National Arbitration Tribunal. The unions (notably the TGWU, NUGMW, USDAW, and AEU) had for long been in favour of the Order, as Ministry of Labour officials pointed out. Since a union need only be a party to a dispute over employment for the case to be referred to compulsory arbitration, unions could use statutory provisions to put pressure on employers to secure union recognition.[69] But the employer was not compelled to recognize the union if he paid the awarded rate. The Order also threatened trade-unionists with imprisonment if they withdrew their labour, and ignored its provisions. This was bitterly resented. Protests flooded in to Ede at the Home Office at its continued operation. Electricity workers in the AEU and ETU were especially vehement. So, too, were railway workers in the NUR. Communist strike leaders could exploit this feeling, although, without doubt, Order 1305 aroused deep feelings which had no connection with Communism or any other political philosophy.

The actual number of strikes in 1950 remained small: only 1,383,000 working days were lost in the year, the lowest in any year since the war. But, towards the end of the year, industrial troubles mounted up. The government was

---

[68] Report on special meeting between Finance and General Purposes Committee of TGWU executive council and section committee representing London busmen, 19 Sept. 1950 (University of Warwick, Modern Records Centre, 126/ T. & G./1/1/28).

[69] Memorandum on Order 1305 by R. M. Gould, Ministry of Labour, 4 July 1950 (LAB 10/975).

increasingly obsessed by the red menace. Shawcross, the
Attorney-General, meanwhile continued his inquiries into the
extent of Communist involvement in the London dock
strikes of June–July 1949, in conjunction with the Ministry
of Labour's Solicitor's Department.[70] Shawcross's findings
noted the role of Maletts, Goldblatt, and Blankenzee, three
Communists flown in from the Communist-led WFTU
transport section, to stir up trouble in London's dockland.
Citrine, the head of the Electricity Board, and Gaitskell
were earlier in consultation with Attlee over the role of the
'unofficial' Communist elements in disputes in London
power stations in December 1949.[71] Bevan added his view,
at the Cabinet Committee, that civil proceedings would be
more effective than criminal as a deterrent, as they had been
in the case of the miners.[72] In August 1950, Citrine and
Noel-Baker, Gaitskell's successor at the Ministry of Fuel and
Power, were urgently telling Attlee of the threat to electricity
supplies from Communist-led agitation in the ETU. Citrine
noted gloomily that 'Foulkes and another leading member
of the Electricity Trades Union had left for Moscow, no
doubt to get instructions.' Noel-Baker urged the Prime
Minister to remove 'active and suspected Communists' in key
positions in power stations, and to take action against any
sympathetic strike action that might follow.[73] Finally, in a
ten-day strike by North Thames Gas Board workers in
London gas stations, Shawcross took legal action against the
'unofficial' leaders. Ten of them, not all Communists by any
means, were prosecuted for a breach of Order 1305, and also,
as an additional refinement, for a breach of section 4 of the
Conspiracy Act passed by the government of Disraeli back in
1875. The men were sentenced to a month's imprisonment,
but on appeal it was reduced on 21 November to a £50 fine,
with six weeks to pay.[74] The episode added markedly to the
tension of the industrial scene, with the rare event of a
Labour government employing the criminal law to suppress

[70] Shawcross to A. R. Harrison, 12 Dec. 1949 (LAB 16/97).
[71] Citrine to Gaitskell, 23 Dec. 1941, Gaitskell to Attlee, 24 Dec. 1949
(PREM 8/1290).
[72] Minutes of Cabinet Committee, GEN 314, 24 Jan. 1950 (ibid.).
[73] Noel-Baker to Attlee, 3 Aug. 1950 (PREM 8/1275).
[74] *The Times*, 22 Nov. 1950.

workers who had been on strike. When the cabinet considered
the operation of Order 1305 on 15 January 1951, it was
decided to continue its existence, with Isaacs arguing in
favour, and Shawcross suggesting that fines rather than
imprisonment would be a more suitable form of penalty.[75]

At this critical stage, there was a change at the Ministry
of Labour. Isaacs was at last moved out of the Cabinet, and
became Minister of Pensions. The former Minister of Pensions,
Hilary Marquand, once a professor of economics at Cardiff,
succeeded his fellow Welshman, Aneurin Bevan, at the
Ministry of Health. Bevan moved at this crucial and sensitive
moment to the Ministry of Labour. It was something of a
mystery why Bevan agreed to this. No doubt, he was long
overdue for a transfer from Health, but Labour was hardly
promotion. Moreover, it involved all the central difficulties
of the distribution of manpower in pushing on with the
accelerated defence programme that Bevan had so strongly
attacked. Probably he felt that it was better to try to influence the defence programme rather than retire into the
wilderness. Anyhow, Attlee gave him no other choice.

Aneurin Bevan's time at the Ministry of Labour lasted
only three months from January to April 1951. But it is
a crucially important episode in his career, far more so than
historians have usually realized, and a vital period for the
history of the Attlee government. As has been noted, the
Ministry brought Bevan right up against all the difficulties
of operating the new defence programme. Further, at the
Ministry of Labour, he confronted the two most sensitive
of domestic issues—Order 1305, and the remnants of the
wage restraint policy. On both, he had a significant impact.
On Order 1305, he had urged talks with the National Joint
Advisory Council, which represented both sides of industry,
on 24 January, immediately after taking up his new post.[76]
Protests flooded in to his office about the effects of the
Order, not least the recent prosecution of the London gas
workers. In fact, the Order remained in existence, and Bevan

[75] Cabinet Conclusions, 15 Jan. 1951 (CAB 128/19); Memorandum on Order
1305 by Isaacs, 10 Jan. 1951 CP (51) 8 (CAB 129/46).

[76] Meeting of Bevan and Joint Consultative Commitee, 24 Jan. 1951 (LAB
10/994).

had the further mortification of seeing Shawcross prosecute a group of seven London dockers, who were subjected to a fine in February. At a meeting of the Parliamentary Labour Party, Bevan was publicly attacked on the issue.[77] He then began moves to annul the Order; but in fact it was his successor, Alfred Robens, who finally abolished it. Robens wrote to Frank Soskice, the Solicitor-General, on 1 June that 'Order 1305 itself has ceased to have the authority it enjoyed up to a short time ago because the Trade unions as a whole have ceased to support it. I can see little hope of gaining their support for any system of sanctions, however mild the penalty.' Robens and Soskice then drew up a new Order 1376, a milder decree, which omitted the prohibition of strikes and lock-outs. It gave the unions the best of both worlds: they could strike or take employers to Court instead. However, union men argued that it also contained the dis-advantage of making it less easy for a union to exert pressure on employers.[78] For Aneurin Bevan, Order 1305 was a desperately difficult issue at a delicate time in his relationship to the government. A nine-week strike by Short and Harland aircraft workers in Belfast in February–March, after ten shop stewards (seven of them Communists) had been dis-missed, added to his embarrassment.[79] Bevan as the hammer of the unions was an unfamiliar and unwelcome concept.

The remnants of the wage freeze came up with a threatened official national strike by the National Union of Railwaymen in February 1951, in pursuit of a 7½ per cent wage demand. As usual, the issue was obscured by rivalry between the NUR and the train-drivers' union, ASLEF. At a meeting with the union executive on 22 February, Bevan tried to keep aloof. It was not possible, he declared, for the government to become directly involved in wage negotiations 'which would bring the State and workers into collision'. At the Ministry, he urged all the unions to negotiate over the findings of a Court of Inquiry. 'It is essential that the process of

[77] Material in LAB 10/994.
[78] Robens to Soskice, 1 June 1951, Soskice to Roberts, 18 June 1951, memo-randum for Robens, 3 July 1951 (LAB 43/157); Cabinet Conclusions, 23, 26 July 1951 (CAB 128/20); G. Bain, *The Growth of White Collar Unionism* (Oxford, 1970), p. 175.
[79] Material in LAB 10/1030.

conciliation should be continued and any suggestion of discussion under duress removed.'[80] However, he was under attack from many trade-unionists, including one railwayman from Battersea who reminded Bevan of Lloyd George's imaginative gesture in settling the NUR strike in 1919. Indeed he himself had spoken critically of the inflexibility of the wage freeze, on the Economic Committee.[81] At the Cabinet on 22 February, there was a dispute between Bevan and Barnes, the Minister of Transport. Barnes wanted the government to stand firm on the British Railways executive's offer of 5 per cent. Bevan urged that more money could be found, and wanted the full 7½ per cent paid, since this would bring lower-paid workers up to a £5 weekly wage. In fact, most ministers agreed with Bevan; it was stated that railwaymen had not secured the minimum increases granted to other industries, while a national rail strike would have a crippling effect on the economy.[82] On 23 February, the dispute was settled. The railwaymen got their 7½ per cent, at a total cost to British Railways of £12m. There was much praise of Bevan for his skill in surmounting his first real hurdle at the Ministry of Labour, and much gratitude from Jim Figgins, secretary of the NUR.[83] The fact remained that the government had weighed in heavily on one side, and made a policy of wage restraint that much harder to achieve.

Bevan's period at Labour was a time of torment for him. He was truly to find it 'the bed of nails' that Ray Gunter later described in 1964. Bevan was torn, both over Order 1305 and over wage policy, between an instinctive sympathy for the workers and an urge for strong government and industrial discipline. It brought him some unaccustomed criticism from the left, and had a direct bearing on his later response to the issue of the National Health Service charges. Significantly enough, it was before a noisy audience of London dockers at Bermondsey on 3 April, some of whom were heckling him about the recent prosecution of dock

[80] Material in LAB 10/1021.

[81] John Polling to Bevan, 19 Feb. 1951 (ibid.).; minutes of Cabinet Economic Committee, 18 Dec. 1950 (CAB 134/224).

[82] Cabinet Conclusions, 22 Feb. 1951 (CAB 128/19); Barnes to Attlee, 21 Feb. 1951 (LAB 10/1021).

[83] *The Times*, 24 Feb. 1951; *News Chronicle*, 24 Feb. 1951.

workers under Order 1305, that Bevan made his off-the-cuff remark about not remaining a member of a government that would introduce Health Service charges.[84] His period at Labour brought ever nearer a crisis in his relations with the government and the party.

It is against this complex background—the war in Korea, the escalating defence programme, the troubles in industry—that the fateful dispute between Hugh Gaitskell and Aneurin Bevan over charges on the National Health Service must be viewed. Even at a distance of thirty years, this destructive and bitter conflict between the two most gifted and eloquent of the younger socialists of the day has many of the overtones of a tragedy. It had personal aspects, of course, as well as differences over policy. Gaitskell and Bevan always had a fluctuating personal relationship; temperamentally and intellectually, they were quite different. No doubt, there were simple class aspects to the gulf between a product of Winchester and New College, and a son of the pits of Ebbw Vale and Tredegar. But Bevan's intimates were invariably middle-class, rather than authentic working-class or trade-union spokesmen. After all, he moved in the circles of such as Beaverbrook and Bracken, as did his close political ally and later biographer, Michael Foot. Bevan always steered clear of the dullish trade-unionists who sat at the 'Welsh table' in the Commons dining-room. The gulf between him and Gaitskell was temperamental rather than sociological. Gaitskell's friends tended to be economists and administrators, university-trained for the most part; Bevan's were politicians, journalists, writers, artists on the fringe of Bohemia. As Bevan later told Crossman, he was basically an aristocrat, while Gaitskell was essentially a bourgeois. Yet in fact, for much of the time, the two men had a perfectly good relationship. There was no apparent reason why they should not collaborate politically as effectively as, say, Asquith and Lloyd George had done between 1908 and 1915, with similar positive effect. The problem was rather that their positions in the movement and the government inevitably

---

[84] *The Times*, 11 Apr. 1951. Little was made of Bevan's statement at the time.

propelled them into rivalry against each other, with Bevan, the older by eight years, resenting the progress of the younger, and politically less experienced man.

All the evidence suggests that Bevan was very disturbed when Gaitskell, with no Cabinet experience and after only five years in parliament, was appointed to succeed Cripps as Chancellor in October 1950. Dalton, whose protégé Gaitskell was, recognized Bevan's disappointment. Cripps, it was known, preferred Bevan. After five years of distinguished service, Bevan stayed on at Health, to wrestle with the intractable finances of the National Health Service. The ambitious Gaitskell acknowledged that Bevan felt 'humiliated' and that Harold Wilson, another economist of much ability who was ten years younger, still felt 'inordinately jealous'. But he made sure that he himself would be Number Four in the government, behind Attlee, Bevin, and Morrison, as Cripps had been.[85] Perhaps on balance, Harold Wilson, an economics Cabinet minister of three years' standing, had more cause for disappointment, but he was thought to have been less resolute than Gaitskell over devaluation in 1949. Bevan's resentment was reinforced in mid-March when Ernest Bevin, whose rock-like figure had held the Cabinet together in so many difficult passages, was finally moved from the Foreign Office by Attlee to become Lord Privy Seal. Bevin himself was upset by this dismissal—he was actually celebrating his seventieth birthday when the news broke—but his health had been deteriorating alarmingly for some time.[86] Indeed, he died a month later. To replace Bevin, Attlee considered Shawcross, Griffiths, and other possibilities; Bevin and Dalton both favoured Griffiths, a highly competent Colonial Secretary who was also a trade-unionist.[87] But Attlee felt compelled to appoint Morrison to a post he had long coveted. Morrison's qualities as Foreign Secretary will be considered in the next chapter. Suffice it to say here that this selection for the other major post in the administration, while he himself languished in the lower

[85] Gaitskell's diary, 3 Nov. 1950. Gaitskell notes that he celebrated his appointment by dancing in a Greenwich Village night-club.
[86] Kenneth Harris, op. cit., pp. 471–2.
[87] Dalton's diary, 19 and 20 Feb. 1951. He quotes Attlee as saying, with reference to Griffiths, 'we couldn't give all the key posts to the middle class'.

ranks of first Health and then Labour, added immensely to Bevan's sense of personal humiliation. Kenneth Younger would have favoured Bevan, who, he felt, would have been 'a rather right-wing and very solidly anti-Communist' Foreign Secretary.[88] This is an exaggeration, but without doubt Bevan would have brought a brilliance and genuine internationalism to the Foreign Office quite beyond the powers of Morrison. It all added to his sense of personal injury at a key time.

But it would be a calumny to the reputations of both Bevan and Gaitskell to see the dispute between them primarily in terms of personal advancement. They were genuinely divided over major policy issues—perhaps not on long-term objectives, but certainly on domestic and external priorities in the immediate future. It was put about by Attlee, Younger, Gordon-Walker, Shinwell, Dalton, and others, after Bevan's resignation in April, that he had objected solely to the charges proposed in Gaitskell's budget on dentures and spectacles provided under the NHS, and that only at the very end, almost at the time of his resignation, had he broadened the debate to object to the wider implications of foreign policy and the burden of the rearmament programme. This is not correct. Nor is Strauss's reported view that Bevan had offered no earlier criticism of the rearmament programme and that he, Strauss, was at first the only critic of it.[89] As has been seen, Bevan had made major pronouncements in Cabinet from 1 August 1950 to 25 January 1951, warning against the implications of the rearmament programme for the economy. He had argued, too, that the programme rested on quite false assumptions about Russian military and foreign policy, and the nature of the Communist threat in the Far East and elsewhere. No doubt, his criticisms were episodic —after all, he was a domestic minister—but their general thrust emerges clearly enough from the public record. Bevan's general discontent with the government's foreign and defence policy in the winter of 1950–1 was well known; he often

---

[88] Kenneth Younger, interview transcript, p. 67.
[89] Evidence quoted in Philip Williams, *Gaitskell*, pp. 247–8, and footnotes of material cited, which the author rightly says 'must be treated with caution'; G. R. Strauss interview transcript, pp. 25–8.

spoke of resignation to Michael Foot, to his wife, Jennie Lee, and others.[90] It is often commented that on 15 February 1951 Bevan made a speech of rare brilliance in defence of the government's rearmament programme.[91] The oratorical triumph of that occasion, which drew generous applause from Churchill at the time, is beyond dispute. It seized the initiative from the Conservative opposition, and included a moving and intellectually scintillating affirmation of the values of social democracy. The Soviet Union, Bevan declared, had failed to realize that 'the most revolutionary power in the world is political democracy'. It is true that Bevan also included passing references to the need for military prepared-ness and to carrying out Britain's obligations to her allies; but a reading of his speech shows that these were incidental. The main emphasis was on the need to combat Communism in the realms of ideas and social regeneration, not through armed force. Bevan's basic reservations about the nature of the defence programme remained intact.

When Hugh Gaitskell announced that he proposed to levy charges on dentures and optical services under the NHS, it was well known that Bevan—and, in the past, other ministers such as Griffiths and McNeil—had fundamental objections to such a policy. As has been seen, Bevan had clashed fiercely with his friend, Cripps, over proposed NHS charges in March–April 1950, and had forced the Chancellor then to drop the charges in favour of a ceiling on Health Service expenditure, plus a Cabinet Committee to review NHS finance. There was general agreement that expenditure on the Health Service, especially by the regional hospital boards, had got out of hand, and must be pruned at a time when housing, education, industrial investment, and other priorities were being cut back in the interests of the post-devaluation export pro-gramme. Bevan's own inquiry by Sir Cyril Jones had made major proposals in July 1950. In particular, Jones pointed out the inflating costs of the hospital services which accounted for £254m. out of £426m. in the NHS budget for 1950–1. His proposal was that Regional Hospital Boards should be relieved of direct, but undefined, control of hospital

[90] Private information.
[91] *Parl. Deb.*, 5th ser., vol. 484, 728–40 (15 Feb. 1951).

management, and that Hospital Management Committees should become agents of the Ministry itself.[92] Jones called for more centralization, not less—much as Bevan himself had argued in 1945. The Ministry should concern itself far more closely with monitoring the financial administration of the hospital service than had hitherto been the case. The Cabinet Committee, chaired by Attlee, which surveyed the financing of the Health Service from the time of its appointing in April 1950, drew attention to many alarming features of rising expenditure, including a £6m. deficit due to the withdrawal of Cripps's proposed 1s. prescription charge, rising costs due to petrol price increases, and wage advances to Health Service workers. Bevan himself accepted all these points.[93] On 16 November he told the Committee that the loss of £5m. a year due to the abandonment of the prescription charge was 'a heavy sum to make good out of other savings', while there was likely to be a deficit in hospital expenditure after the Whitley awards on wages and salaries. There would be difficulty in keeping to the ceiling of £392m. on NHS expenditure in 1950–1.[94] All this was admitted.

But, Bevan argued, there were other ways of securing economies in the Health Service than by imposing Gaitskell's controversial charges, which in any case were only estimated to bring in the relatively tiny sum of £23m. in a full financial year. Gaitskell rightly emphasized to Marquand the cost of raising Old Age Pensions, which would amount to an additional £20m.[95] But the decision to consider higher NHS charges ante-dated the increase in pensions and was related to wider issues. The underlying cause, without question, was the rising cost of the rearmament programme which was likely to cast its sombre shadow over the Health Service as over everything else. On his first day as Chancellor on 4 October 1950, Gaitskell stressed to Attlee that the large increase in defence expenditure (at that time £3,600m., not the £4,700m. agreed

[92] Enquiry into Financial Working of the Health Service, by Sir Cyril Jones, 15 July 1950 (PREM 8/1486).

[93] Memorandum by Bevan, 'National Health Service compared with Expenditure', presented to Cabinet Committee on the National Health Service, 16 Nov. 1950 (ibid.).

[94] Ibid.

[95] Gaitskell to Hilary Marquand, 21 Feb. 1951 (ibid.).

to in January) meant taking a close look at all resources. National Health Service costs should not exceed the figure included in the estimates. On 'major issues of policy', including charges on NHS services, he needed the Prime Minister's guidance.[96] Bridges warned Eady on 13 January 1951 that gaining additional borrowing powers from parliament to meet the lack of balance in the budget 'would involve the Chancellor in political difficulties'.[97] The decision on 25 January to increase the defence budget still further, beyond the £4,700m. agreed to, imposed a still greater strain. Shinwell had spoken on 21 December of defence estimates of £1,112m. in 1951–2, compared with the £830m. being spent in the current year. Gaitskell's estimate was now £1,250m., excluding the cost of strategic stockpiling.[98] On 23 January, Gaitskell told the Cabinet Defence Committee, of which Bevan was now a member as Minister of Labour, of the colossal problems of diverting men and resources from civilian to defence programmes, at a time of growing difficulty in the terms of trade, and shortages of raw materials and of machine tools. Direction of labour, he suggested, might even be necessary.[99] All this formed the essential background to the debates on Health Service charges the following month.

In the interim there was one embarrassing episode for Labour in a by-election at Bristol West, a safe Conservative seat, on 15 February. Here, the local party selected as Labour candidate a pacifist and conscientious objector, whom Attlee and Transport House refused to endorse, but for whom Silverman, Emrys Hughes, and Crossman spoke during the campaign. The 17.0 per cent swing to the Conservatives here was an aberration, more than twice as large as any other swing in a by-election in the 1950–1 parliament. In the neighbouring Bristol South-East constituency, where a by-election had taken place in November after Cripps's resignation, the swing against the Labour candidate, the twenty-five-year-old Anthony Wedgwood Benn, was only 7 per cent.

[96] Gaitskell to Attlee, 4 Oct. 1950 (ibid.).
[97] Bridges.to Eady, 13 Jan. 1951 (T 225/123).
[98] Minutes of Cabinet Defence Committee, 21 Dec. 1950 (CAB 131/8).
[99] Minutes of Cabinet Defence Committee, 23 Jan. 1951 (CAB 131/10).

Battle was joined in the Cabinet Committee on expenditure on the Health Services on 15 March, with Attlee in the chair, and Morrison, Gaitskell, Addison, Griffiths, Isaacs, Bevin, Dalton, Bevan, McNeil, Summerskill, and Marquand present.[100] It was already clear that Marquand, Bevan's successor on Health and a professional economist, was prepared to give way on the issue of Health Service charges. He had proposed a charge of half the cost of dentures, a shilling charge on prescriptions, and £10m. cuts in the hospital services beforehand.[101] Gaitskell on 15 March now advocated, in addition to holding NHS expenditure at the present year's level of £392m., a charge of half the scale fee for dentures, a charge of £1 per pair of spectacles (other than for children), and of a shilling on prescriptions as well. There were divided opinions in the Committee. Some ministers felt that more hardship would be relieved by the increase in pensions than would be imposed by the new NHS charges. However, Bevan spoke out strongly against a breach in the principle of a free health service. He asked also whether the huge sums earmarked for defence would in fact be spent at all. Morrison, Marquand, McNeil, Summerskill, and Addison seem to have backed Gaitskell; the balance of opinion in the Committee was clearly against Bevan, with Griffiths his only (and rather shaky) supporter. The issues then went formally to Cabinet, and it stayed there for some considerable time.

On 22 March the first major debate in Cabinet took place.[102] Gaitskell repeated the need for a ceiling of £392m. on NHS charges, but the ministers accepted a compromise offered by the ailing Lord Privy Seal, Ernest Bevin, that a ceiling of £400m. be accepted. This would mean retaining the charges on dentures and spectacles but dropping the prescription charges. Bevin declared that the public would accept charges on dentures and spectacles, as 'there was a widespread impression that some abuses had occurred in this part of the health service'. Morrison, Shinwell, Marquand,

---

[100] Cabinet Committee on the Social Services, 15 Mar. 1951 (CAB 130/66); Cabinet Committee on the National Health Service, 1951 (CAB 134/519).

[101] Ibid., 14 Mar. 1951 (ibid.).

[102] Cabinet Conclusions, 22 Mar. 1951 (CAB 128/19); memorandum by Gaitskell on the 1951 budget, Mar. 1951 (T 171/403); Attlee to Gaitskell, 20 Mar. 1951 (ibid.). The figures were £13m. for 1951–2, £23.3m. for a full year.

and McNeil all supported him. Griffiths also accepted the charges now, though with reluctance. Attlee added the somewhat fatuous point that the charges should be presented 'as a means of eliminating waste from the services and not solely as a matter of raising revenue'. The critics were Aneurin Bevan and, more surprisingly, the President of the Board of Trade, Harold Wilson. The latter, to some degree an apostle of decontrol at that department, is said to have told Woodrow Wyatt that he feared being made a scapegoat for losses in the overseas trading account; but he had also vigorously condemned American stockpiling of raw materials.[103] Wilson urged the need for cuts in the defence budget instead of undermining the welfare state. Bevan launched an impassioned attack on the proposals—and on Gaitskell personally. 'He thought it deplorable that for the sake of £23m. in a very large Budget the principle of a free health service should be abandoned. . . . The Government were now proposing to depart from Labour principle, for the sake of a paltry increase in revenue.' It was quite wrong to represent the charges as needed to finance old age pensions. 'The real cause was the cost of the increased defence programme', in which shortages of raw materials would in any case mean the sum allocated for defence could not be spent. Why could not £23m. be trimmed off the huge defence budget instead? With Bevan and Wilson recording their dissent, the Cabinet accepted the NHS charges as part of Gaitskell's budget.

On 9 April, the battle was resumed with even more fury.[104] In the interim, Bevan had delivered his notorious off-the-cuff (and perhaps unpremeditated) statement to the Bermondsey dockers about possible resignation. In a talk with Dalton on 6 April, Bevan had revealed the depths of his bitterness towards Gaitskell, whom he described as 'a second Snowden'. Gaitskell had accepted an impossible rearmament programme quite blindly, because 'he was wildly pro-American and anti-Russian'.[105] Meanwhile Gaitskell had let it be known that he would stick to his charges or else resign. 'Nye's

[103] Woodrow Wyatt, *Turn Again, Westminster* (London, 1973), p. 150; minutes of Cabinet Economic Committee, 5 Dec. 1950 (CAB 139/224).
[104] Cabinet Conclusions, 9 Apr. 1951 (CAB 128/19).
[105] Dalton's diary, 6 Apr. 1951.

influence was much exaggerated', he told Dalton, who thought this a most serious misjudgement.[106] In the Cabinet on 9 April, Bevan launched another passionate attack on the NHS charges. The defence budget was quite impractical; the Health Service charges were 'a serious breach of Socialist principles'. If they were implemented, he would resign from the government. Wilson again supported him with cogent economic arguments. Gaitskell, however, stood firm and reasserted that the rising cost of the defence budget would make reductions in government expenditure impossible. He resisted Bevan's alternative suggestion of either reducing the budget surplus by £13m., which would be inflationary, or else transferring money from the National Insurance fund. The tension was made even worse because Attlee was at this time in St. Mary's Hospital for an operation for a duodenal ulcer, and Bevan's old adversary, Morrison, now took the chair at Cabinet meetings. In the afternoon of 9 April, Morrison visited Attlee in hospital. But as in August 1947 he found that the Prime Minister could offer little initiative or advice when faced with a major internal crisis. Attlee's message, read out to the Cabinet at another meeting at 6.30 p.m. on the 9th, emphasized the political dangers of Cabinet disagreement.[107] He warned that it was unusual for a minister to resign over the budget: he added the (unhelpful and misleading) analogy of Lord Randolph Churchill's resignation in 1886. It would also be damaging for the party to have an election now. Later in the summer, 'conditions might be more favourable—the meat ration might be increased, the weather might improve and there might be a change in the international situation'.

Attlee's remarkably vacuous letter dealt with none of the substantive points at issue. Bevan, reasonably enough, retorted that it was a question of principle not of political expediency. 'He had given five years to building up the Health Service; he had proclaimed it on many public platforms as one of the outstanding achievements of the Labour Party in office; he had, in particular, upheld the conception of a free service as the embodiment of Socialist principles.'

[106] Ibid., 5 Apr. 1951.
[107] Cabinet Conclusions, 9 Apr. 1951 (CAB 128/19).

He added, ominously, that 'latterly he had come to feel that he could bring more influence to bear on Government policy from outside the Cabinet than he could ever hope to exercise within it; and, when a Minister reached that position, it was time for him to go'. Privately, Bevan spoke to Dalton of 'rootless men like Gaitskell and Gordon-Walker who are dismantling the welfare state'.[108] Ministers asked the Cabinet whether some alternative could not be found, perhaps by postponing the charges for six months, to see whether the money allocated for defence could profitably be spent. Perhaps Gaitskell would be content with the ceiling on expenditure of £400m. alone? The Chancellor remained adamant that these measures would not produce the necessary savings. Bevan therefore warned that he would have to resign. He added that he was also concerned with the wider issue of 'the pace and volume of the rearmament programme', and how the western democracies were in danger of undermining their economies in response to American pressure. Wilson also declared that he, too, would have to resign in protest at the economic implications of the defence budget. All other ministers pronounced their support for Gaitskell, except for George Tomlinson who felt that £13m. was a small economy for which to pay so high a price, and who hoped that 'the majority would not press their view to a point which would make these resignations inevitable'. Gaitskell, for his part, declared that if the Cabinet reversed its view on NHS charges, then he would have to resign instead, but 'would make no trouble whatever'.

Bevan had spoken of resigning the next day, and making a personal statement in the Cabinet on the 11th. In fact, at a party meeting that day, he was persuaded not to do so immediately. Perhaps he was swayed in part by a letter urging him not to resign, sent by a group of right-centre ministers, Robens, Callaghan, Michael Stewart, Fred Lee, and Arthur Blenkinsop.[109] It was generally taken that Bevan would not now resign. 'The resignations have been avoided', declared *The Times*. Geoffrey Cox, the political

---

[108] Dalton's diary, 9 Apr. 1951.
[109] Dalton's diary, 10 Apr. 1951. The letter is printed in Michael Foot, op. cit., p. 322.

correspondent of the *News Chronicle*, wrote on 12 April that 'the dispute can be regarded as ended', though he did not elaborate. 'There will be no resignations from the government', wrote the correspondent of the *Daily Herald*, and the *Manchester Guardian* commented in similar terms.[110] In fact, the dispute was now to reach a more serious level still, interrupted only briefly by the death and funeral of Ernest Bevin three days later. At a Cabinet meeting to discuss the NHS Bill at 11.0 a.m. on the 12th,[111] Bevan announced again that he could not, as a minister, vote in favour of a bill which would authorize charges for NHS dentures and spectacles. Despite protests from Bevan and Wilson, Morrison announced that there could be no delay and that the NHS Bill must go ahead. In fact, Gaitskell's budget speech on 10 April had been relatively well received on the Labour side as being less severe than had been feared. Its main features, apart from the NHS charges, were an increase of 6*d.* in the pound on income tax, raising purchase tax on many items from $33\frac{1}{3}$ per cent to $66\frac{2}{3}$ per cent, and a tax on distributed profits of up to 50 per cent. Also Cripps's initial allowance on industrial investment, begun in 1949, was abolished. It was acknowledged as technically an excellent performance, the first wholly Keynesian budget. The announcement of the NHS charges brought a solitary muffled cry of 'Shame!', believed to come from Jennie Lee. In the period 14–18 April there were desperate moves, in which Dalton was prominent, to try to fudge up a compromise, perhaps on the basis of including only the principle of the charges in the budget, or else announcing that they would apply for only a temporary period. Desmond Donnelly, the member for Pembrokeshire and at the time a young supporter of Bevan's urged him not to dither, as he had done after the irrelevant issue of President Truman's dismissal of General MacArthur a few days earlier. Donnelly, who later moved to the far right and finally left the Labour Party altogether, wrote twenty years later of his 'feeling that he [Bevan] was discrediting himself by these vascillations [*sic*] and that he had gone too

---

[110] *The Times*, 12 Apr. 1951; *News Chronicle*, 12 Apr. 1951; *Daily Herald*, 12 Apr. 1951; *Manchester Guardian*, 12 Apr. 1951.
[111] Cabinet Conclusions, 12 Apr. 1951 (CAB 128/19).

far to pull back'. He wrote to Bevan on 14 April, 'I was against your resigning on Tuesday. I now realise how wrong I was & that Mike Foot's view that you can pack up if they still bring in the Health Act Amendment is right. *Dalton & co. of course are desperately keen for you to stay and that is the final argument for going*!!' Donnelly added a warning about those to whom Bevan chose to talk. 'I saw you talking to Eric Fletcher [member for Islington East] who has doubtless reported it all to Herbert as he did me on German rearmament. A lot of other chaps who are your well meaning friends are very indiscreet. Mike Foot is the opposite though.' Ironically enough, Donnelly himself was later accused of revealing the secrets of meetings of Bevan's followers to eager journalists.[112]

All these compromise moves failed. Gaitskell's suggestion of a formula to the effect that the NHS charges 'should not necessarily be permanent' was rejected by Bevan as it left the principle still wide open. Mediation by Dalton, Isaacs, and Griffiths failed.[113] On the 19th, Bevan, in the last Cabinet meeting that he ever attended, announced that he could not vote for the NHS Bill on the second reading.[114] Gaitskell, Bevan, and Marquand were asked to hold desperate eleventh-hour discussions to see whether a form of words could be concocted to allay fears among government supporters about a permanent ceiling on NHS expenditure. It is very doubtful whether these could have led anywhere. In fact, the temperature was raised even further by a ferocious personal attack on Gaitskell in *Tribune* on 20 April. For many years, *Tribune* had been remarkably loyal to the government. For over a year it had official financial links with Transport House, which gave it some money in return for publicity in its pages. On 1 December it had deprecated suggestions in the Beaverbrook

---

[112] Desmond Donnelly to Aneurin Bevan, 14 Apr. 1951; Donnelly to F. J. Calderon, 5 Dec. 1978. Defence statement drawn up by Leon Brittan QC, Desmond Donnelly v. Michael Foot, Davis Poynter Ltd, 20 Nov. 1973 (National Library of Wales, Donnelly papers, Box 3). Foot's biography of Bevan had accused Donnelly of improperly communicating proceedings of the Bevanites to journalists. Donnelly had to withdraw his prosecution.

[113] Dalton to Attlee, 15 Apr. 1951 (Dalton papers 9/18/20); Williams, op. cit., p. 256.

[114] Cabinet Conclusions, 19 Apr. 1951 (CAB 128/19).

press that there was a Cabinet split over rearmament, involving Bevan. As recently as 9 February, it had urged that 'the Labour movement should rally its strength to keep this government strong and in power'. It had been expressing concern both about the government's excessive involvement in American policy in the Far East, and towards the cost of the defence programme. Yet Roy Jenkins, Attlee's PPS, had written in *Tribune* on 9 March that 'the impact of the rearmament programme upon our standard of living is likely to be less dramatic than many people at first believed, since much of the resources would come from increased production'.[115] But the leading article in *Tribune* on 20 April, written by Michael Foot, launched a philippic against 'A Dangerous Budget'; it obviously bore the stamp of approval from Bevan himself. The budget, it claimed, had ignored such socialist policies as Roy Jenkin's proposed capital levy (advocated in a Tribune pamphlet entitled *Fair Shares for the Rich*), or higher death duties. Instead, Gaitskell had 'delivered a frontal attack on the Health Service'. He was compared with Snowden— second only to Ramsay MacDonald in Labour demonology. Labour's unity had to be resolved 'before we are led back to another 1931'. The approval of the Stock Exchange for the Budget was noted sarcastically. Dalton, on good personal terms with Bevan down to 19 April, was now livid. 'This makes me see *very red*!' In his hospital bed, Attlee called Bevan 'a green-eyed monster'.[116] Bevan promptly wrote a letter of resignation from the Cabinet on Sunday 22 April, shortly after the *Tribune* article appeared. His letter, and Attlee's reply, were published the next day. Harold Wilson's resignation followed later on the 23rd. There were no other departures, apart from John Freeman, a junior minister at Supply. He had resisted strong pressure from Hugh Dalton, who regarded the handsome, red-haired young officer as one of his special protegés. At Supply, Freeman had first-hand knowledge of the escalating cost of raw materials.

Aneurin Bevan then made his personal statement in the House on the 23rd.[117] It was a political disaster, the worst

---

[115] Roy Jenkins, 'Arms and the Social Services', *Tribune*, 9 Mar. 1951.
[116] Dalton's diary, 20 Apr. 1951.
[117] *Parl Deb.*, 5th ser., vol. 487, 34–43 (25 Apr. 1951).

of his career, his speech being shot through with personal bitterness towards Gaitskell. He made a broad assault on the government's foreign and defence policies, 'dragged behind the wheels of American diplomacy'. But it was his comments on the budgetary arithmetic that underlay Gaitskell's imposing charges of, in the end, a mere £13m. on the Health Services which captured attention—'the arithmetic of Bedlam'. Bevan's comments on having to 'manœuvre' to prevent cuts in the housing programme or prescription charges were received unsympathetically by the House, especially on the Labour benches. The speech was heard in virtual silence, and was a parliamentary failure in every respect. By contrast, Wilson's resignation statement the next day, a much more dignified and moderate affair which dwelt presciently on the economic consequences of the rearmament programme for the balance of payments and strength of sterling, met with a far warmer reception. It won some personal sympathy from Churchill for the young ex-minister.[118]

At a meeting of the Parliamentary Labour Party on 24 April, Bevan raged almost uncontrollably at Gaitskell's attacks on 'my Health Service'. Dalton whispered (at the top of his voice) to Morrison, 'This is Mosley speaking.' Roy Jenkins thought it 'sub-human'.[119] Only a handful of MPs supported Bevan. The government soon restored its ranks and beat down this rebellion. The National Executive, adroitly marshalled by Morgan Phillips, took the unusual step of declaring its support for Attlee, Gaitskell, and the Cabinet in standing firm against Bevan. The left-wing members on the NEC—Bevan himself, Driberg, Mikardo, and Barbara Castle—wrote to Phillips protesting against what they considered was an unconstitutional action on the secretary's part, but Phillips firmly rebuffed them.[120] In the Cabinet, there were consequent ministerial changes. Shawcross succeeded Wilson at the Board of Trade, Robens followed

[118] *Parl. Deb.*, 5th ser., vol. 487, 228–31 (24 Apr. 1951); cf. Harold Wilson, *A Prime Minister on Prime Ministers* (London, 1977), p. 268.

[119] Dalton's diary, 24 Apr., 11 May 1951; *News Chronicle*, 25 Apr. 1951; *The Times*, 25 Apr. 1951.

[120] Bevan, Castle, and Mikardo to Morgan Phillips, 26 Apr. 1951; Phillips to Bevan, Castle, and Mikardo, 27 Apr. 1951 (Labour Party archives, GS 28/7).

Bevan at Labour, and the industrialist, Richard Stokes, headed a new department of raw materials as Lord Privy Seal, to cover Bevan's criticisms in his resignation speech on the international scarcity of raw materials. In his constituency in Ebbw Vale, Bevan had a far friendlier reception than in London. He attacked American foreign and economic policy, and the huge inflation in raw materials as the result of American stockpiling. But he insisted that there was no split in the Labour movement. The passion for unity remained and should never be underestimated.[121] But that passion was becoming increasingly muted in reality. The original 'Keep Left' group had remained in somewhat shadowy existence throughout 1950–1. On 26 April, fifteen Labour MPs met privately. They included Richard Acland, Barbara Castle, Richard Crossman, Harold Davies, Michael Foot, Leslie Hale, and Ian Mikardo of the 'Keep Left' group, along with Hugh Delargy, Will Griffiths, Jennie Lee, 'Kim' Mackay, and Tom Driberg. The last-named had recently been in official disfavour for making a lengthy three-month tour of the Far East, unpaired, while the government's majority was in single figures. There were three others present —Bevan, Wilson, and Freeman, the three ministers who had resigned. Ian Mikardo took the chair, and his assistant, Jo Richardson, the secretary of 'Keep Left' for some months, again took the minutes. The 'Bevanites' had come into existence. Gaitskell felt that 'a fight for the soul of the Labour Party' was under way.[122] The internal peace of the Labour Party would never again be the same.

Aneurin Bevan's resignation was the dramatic climax of months of passionate argument within the government on international and industrial policy. But, of course, its focus was the question of Health Service charges, and their relationship to an expanded defence budget. Many solid points can be made to justify Gaitskell's arguments. The finances of the Health Service were out of control. Sacrifices had been made elsewhere—on housing, education, national insurance.

[121] *The Times*, 30 Apr. 1951.
[122] Gaitskell's diary, 4 May 1951; Mark Jenkins, op. cit., pp. 152–4. For Driberg's travels, see T. Driberg, *Ruling Passions* (London, 1977), p. 252, and J. Howe (Maldon Labour Party) to Morgan Phillips, 5 Dec. 1950 (Labour Party archives, GS 23/7).

Why should the Health Service alone be made a sacred cow? The future difficulties of the government's rearmament programme could not, perhaps, be foreseen in the early spring of 1951. Certainly, the deteriorating balance of payments picture owed much to later factors that summer, notably the pressure exerted by the Persian oil crisis which led to a sharp rise in the cost of fuel imports. Bevan's criticisms of the economic implications took many varying forms, as Gaitskell's distinguished biographer has rightly pointed out.[123] Not all these criticisms were consistent; not all of them were organically related. Sometimes Bevan focused on the high cost of imported raw materials; sometimes, on the shortage of machine tools; sometimes, on the problems of the engineering or metal trades; sometimes on the shortage of skilled labour and the problems of directing labour to other employment. Not all Bevan's prophecies were borne out. And, of course, the entire argument was overlaid with the personal antagonism between Bevan and his Tribunite supporters, and Gaitskell whom they viewed as a second Snowden. Gaitskell was distinctly less right-wing, and Bevan much less left-wing than current polemics and posturings tended to suggest.

Even so, it cannot reasonably be disputed now that on the main issue Bevan and Wilson were right, and Gaitskell was wrong. The Budget of April 1951 may fairly be considered a political and economic disaster, for all the immense talent of its author. Indeed, the entire affair reflects on Gaitskell's relative political inexperience as a senior minister, and his doctrinaire stubborness, a trait he was to show again in the controversy over Clause Four after the 1959 election. Dalton commented in 1951 that his protégé thought 'too little about the Party & too much about the electorate in general'.[124] Perhaps Gaitskell was also unduly swayed by the applause of Bridges, Plowden, and other leading civil servants. The episode reflects badly, too, on Attlee's failure to lead, and his wanton sacrifice of a valuable and charismatic minister as a result.

The defence programme was not, in fact, carried out. Indeed,

---

[123] Williams, op. cit., pp. 279–80.
[124] Dalton's diary, 5 Apr. 1951.

Douglas Jay had emphasized to Attlee back in August 1950 the immense problems inherent even in the original £3,400m. programme. The difficulties Jay itemized then—shortages of labour, the scarcity of machine tools, the particular burden imposed by defence spending on the chemical, textile, and metal-using industries—were all spelt out in detail again by the *Economic Survey for 1952*. So, too, were the problems in directing skilled workers to the aircraft and machine tool industries. Gaitskell himself had warned the Cabinet Economic Policy Committee of the grave shortage of machine tools as early as 3 April—seven days before the budget. He spoke hopefully then of ordering 6,000 of the 32,000 needed from the United States: on 24 July he was to tell the Committee of his pleasure that 250 had now been received from across the Atlantic.[125] There were, by the summer, evident problems with the deteriorating balance of payments; many of them were the result of the defence programme with its consequent loss of earnings for manufactured exports of which Gaitskell was now giving somewhat belated warning to the Cabinet Defence Committee.[126] The further severe deterioration of the balance of payments in the summer of 1951, which led to Gaitskell's emergency visit to Washington and Ottawa, was superimposed on difficulties that were already critical, with a continued high volume of exports nullified by a huge rise in the cost of imports in the second quarter of 1951 between 1 April and 30 June.[127] The financial projections that had been offered in Gaitskell's budget were already becoming out of date, even while the Finance Bill was making its way through parliament. Another disastrous feature of Gaitskell's budget for the long term, as Andrew Shonfield has pointed out very clearly, was its abolition of Cripps's initial investment allowances to businessmen

[125] Jay to Attlee, Aug. 1950 (Attlee papers, Box 9); minutes of Cabinet Economic Committee, 3 Apr., 25 July 1951 (CAB 134/228); *Economic Survey for 1952* (PP 1951-2, XXV), Cmd. 8509, pp. 19-22.

[126] Minutes of Cabinet Defence Committee, 31 July 1951 (CAB 131/10). Gaitskell observed that 'the balance of payments situation was now far less favourable than when we had first undertaken the £4,700m. programme'. Cf. Gaitskell's diary, 10 Aug. 1951.

[127] *The Economist*, 7 July 1951.

for re-equipment.[128] This meant a fatal assault on the productive investment capacity of British industry, and a declining level of industrial investment through the fifties. The entire financial basis of the defence programme was quite misconceived, not least because the major American contribution that had been visualized, both in terms such as machine tools, and in 'budget-sharing' financial assistance, was not, in practice, forthcoming. The relative lack of growth in the British economy, compared with such nations as France, Germany, or Japan, and its declining share of world trade in the fifties, had many sources, some of distant historical origin. But they can be traced, at least in part, to Gaitskell's one and only budget.

Nor were the Health Service charges necessarily effective in achieving their objective. By 26 April Marquand was pleading with the Cabinet to hurry on the bill which authorized the charges.[129] Otherwise, the costs incurred by the last-minute rush to get spectacles and false teeth while they were still free would partly nullify any savings in revenue obtained. Applications for dentures had doubled and for spectacles had risen by a quarter: there might be a loss of revenue of £5m. to £6m. Marquand pointed out that 'those who criticised the charges had claimed that the amount actually received would not be sufficient to justify what they regarded as a retrograde step'. Bevan seemed to be winning a posthumous triumph. For this and other reasons, five Labour MPs voted against the government's NHS charges, and a further 35 deliberately abstained.[130] Gaitskell had to bring in a belated element of concession to state that, in the first instance, the charges would last for only three years.[131] In the maelstrom of defence expenditure, the £13m. notionally collected from the Health Service charges seemed pathetically small. A broad socialist principle had been fundamentally eroded in the process.

When the Conservatives under Churchill returned to power in October 1951, they immediately began to review the

[128] Andrew Shonfield, *British Economic Policy since the War* (Penguin edn., Harmondsworth, 1958), pp. 89 ff. and 173 ff.
[129] Cabinet Conclusions, 26 Apr. 1951 (CAB 128/19).
[130] Discussed in Cabinet Conclusions, 7 May 1951 (ibid.).
[131] Cabinet Conclusions, 30 Apr. 1951 (ibid.); Gaitskell's diary, 4 May 1951.

defence programme, on something like Bevanite lines. The original three-year programme was seen now to be obviously impractical. Duncan Sandys, the new Minister of Supply, recorded on 26 November 1951:

This three-year plan was formulated on the unrealistic assumption that all necessary labour, materials and machine tools would be available when and where required. . . . By the summer it was clear that, owing mainly to rising prices, the cost of the programme would considerably exceed the estimate of £4,700m. It was also evident that the assumptions about the availability of labour and materials would not be fulfilled, and that the programme would not be completed within the three-year period.[132]

In the Treasury, Ian Bancroft criticized the original costing of the defence programme adopted by the service departments earlier in 1951. 'The sort of things which emerge at the preliminary stage bear absolutely no relation to their changes of being achieved (physical and production limitations etc.). But this year at any rate it looks as though the blooms nurtured in the Service Department's hot houses will very soon wilt when exposed to the chilliness of the world as it is.'[133] Churchill promptly addressed his mind to 'the world as it is'. In a defence debate in the Commons on 6 December 1951, he announced, briefly and almost casually, that the £1,250m. allocated for defence in 1951-2 simply could not be spent, and that the £4,700m. programme was being spread out over a longer, undefined period.[134] When pressed on the point by Bevan, he remarked, ungenerously, that the honourable member need not take credit for being right by accident.[135] The Churchill government relentlessly slowed down defence expenditure from its original proportion of 9-10 per cent of the gross national product. In the Churchill Cabinet in November 1952, Lord Alexander, the Minister of Defence, announced a reduction in the estimates from £1,838m. to £1,645m. for 1953-4. The Chancellor, Butler, supported by Churchill, had this reduced still further to a proposed £1,610m. In the *Economic Survey for 1953*, it

[132] Memorandum on 'The Progress of Rearmament Production' by Duncan Sandys, 26 Nov. 1951, CP (51) 27 (CAB 129/48).
[133] I. Bancroft to Humphrey Davies, 3 Nov. 1951 (T 225/124).
[134] *Parl. Deb.*, 5th ser., vol. 494, 2601-2 (6 Dec. 1951).
[135] Ibid., 2663.

was revealed, without flourish, that defence expenditure had run at only £1,129m. for 1951–2, and was projected for £1,513m. for 1952–3 and £1,637m. for 1953–4, a total of £4,279m. for the three-year period and far less than the £4,700m. allocated in January 1951.[136] Actual expenditure in fact fell well short even of this reduced total: it totalled £3,878m. for 1951–4.[137] No expansion of defence production in the metal-using industries was visualized for 1953–4. The main emphasis would be placed on the export of plant and machinery, and the re-equipment of home industry for civilian requirements. Truly, it could be observed in 1953, even if a little late, that we were all Bevanites now.

Bevan's resignation, however, had an impact far beyond the technical and economic shortcomings of Gaitskell's budget and the government's rearmament programme. It suggested to the general public that the administration, after six exhausting years in power, was running out of energy and out of ideas. Bevin and Cripps had gone; Attlee, Morrison, and Dalton were ageing sexuagenarians. Dalton told Attlee that they looked like a government of pensioners. Even Addison, almost eighty-two though still remarkably vigorous, was still a senior minister. There were new faces in the government such as Robens, Younger, and Marquand, but talented younger men like Callaghan, de Freitas, or George Brown remained in minor posts. Men such as Mikardo and Albu were excluded (so Dalton alleged) on anti-Semitic grounds.[138] The government now seemed almost broken by shattering crises, the war in Korea, troubles in Europe and Africa, industrial disputes, problems over finance, and the resignation of leading ministers. The Festival of Britain, based on the South Bank of the Thames a short way downstream from Westminster, was launched on 1 May with a keynote speech by the Foreign Secretary, Herbert Morrison. But its brilliant display of science, design, and technical ingenuity, reinforced by the Battersea fun-fair, was offered

---

[136] Cabinet Conclusions, 7 Nov. 1952 (CAB 128/25); *Economic Survey for 1953* (PP 1953–4, XXIV), Cmd. 8800, 48–9.

[137] A. Seldon, op. cit., p. 335.

[138] Dalton's diary, 21 Feb. 1951. He quotes Attlee as saying that Mikardo and Albu 'both belonged to the Chosen People & he didn't think he wanted any more of *them*!'

to a nation that felt little enough gaiety within itself, and certainly none of the Victorian *joie de vivre* of 1851. Indeed, the delays in opening parts of the exhibition, with exhibits and stands surrounded by débris and puddles of liquid mud —the legacy of a wet spring and unofficial strikes by building workers—were more in tune with the mood of that desperate summer. Government, party, people all had their backs to the wall and there seemed no way out.

11

The Retreat from Jerusalem

In the summer of 1951, the Attlee government seemed to be cabined and confined within a kind of siege mentality. It was barely hanging on with its tiny majority. Its parliamentary supporters were pulverized by late-night sittings and filibustered debates, its ministers exhausted by intractable problems at home and abroad. It had no legislative initiatives to offer. Morrison had recently told the Cabinet Legislation Committee that the chief whip 'was having difficulty in finding enough legislative business to occupy the available Parliamentary time'. He appealed for 'several *additional Bills*' on any subject.[1] The party seemed in remarkably good heart throughout the country, with individual membership still rising in spite of the resignation of two Cabinet ministers. There were still ingenuity and optimism in Morgan Phillips's office in Transport House. But in general the government seemed firmly on the defensive, protecting its redoubts like the British army at Quatre Bras and Waterloo, but incapable of advancing to occupy any new ground, and with no potential Blucher on the horizon. Within the parliamentary party and the movement in the country, the divisions opened up by the rise of the 'Bevanites' grew ever wider. In fact, the original group which had convened on 26 April was casual in its activities; Bevan himself had a poor attendance record, while Harold Wilson and John Freeman kept their distance. Bevan was anxious not to embarrass his former colleagues, and kept silent in the House. However, some *frisson* was caused on 14 July by the appearance of a 'Keep Left' pamphlet, *One Way Only*, which named Bevan, Wilson, and Freeman amongst its authors. The general drift of this publication ('an essay in qualified judgements', in Michael Foot's words) now seems remarkably moderate. There was much emphasis on the world-wide crisis in raw materials, on the need to keep down prices at home and to increase

[1] Minutes of Cabinet Legislation Committee, 7 Nov. 1950 (CAB 134/336).

expenditure on the social services. A good part of the pamphlet consisted of quite unexceptional pleas for dealing with world poverty through overseas aid programmes of the kind initiated in the Point Four Programme and the Colombo Plan in 1950. However, the pamphlet also included some passages, apparently written by Bevan himself, which urged a scaling down of the rearmament programme and the need to restrain the United States in its foreign policy especially over arming Germany. Despite the hostility of the book-sellers' trade, it sold over 100,000 copies according to Peggy Duff.[2] The pamphlet was taken as a shot across the bows of the Labour leadership. *Tribune*, by now far more critical of the government since Bevan was no longer a member of it, continued a series of harsh attacks on Gaitskell, over his budget, his calls for wage restraint, and his endorsement of the defence programme. It was known that Ian Mikardo and others were mobilizing opinion in the constituencies with a view to achieving a shift to the left in the elections for the constituency section of the National Executive at the annual party conference in October.[3] The 'Bevanites' were at this period a shifting group with perhaps a hard core of no more than ten regular members. Whether Bevan himself was truly a 'Bevanite' was a nice question. Certainly the group were far short of being the 'party within a party' that was to be condemned by the right wing of the party from 1952 onwards. But they were clearly a potentially divisive element, which kept the dispute between Bevan and Gaitskell in April embarrassingly prominent and alive.

In policy-making, too, the government faced many grave difficulties. The Korean War remained a source of anguish, though it was less divisive in the Labour Party after President Truman dismissed General MacArthur in early April. The war entered a period of prolonged stalemate, with the threat of further US attacks on the Chinese mainland, whether by sea or air, increasingly remote. Nor was anything heard further of the possible use of the atomic bomb. German rearmament continued to be a running sore throughout the summer, but

[2] Foot, *Bevan*, vol. ii, p. 342; Peggy Duff, *Left, Left, Left* (London, 1971), p. 36; *The Times*, 10 July 1951.
[3] *Tribune*, 10 Aug., 7, 14, 21 Sept. 1951; Dalton's diary, 4 Oct. 1951.

it was clear that the proposed 'European Army', the EDC, was being put into motion, however great the opposition from Dalton and other ministers. On 4 September, the Cabinet reaffirmed its support for the European Army in principle.

There were, however, other foreign difficulties to torment the Attlee government. Above all, an unexpected crisis erupted in Iran when the nationalist government there, now under the eccentric and serpentine leadership of Dr Mussadiq, nationalized the oil refineries of the Anglo-Iranian Oil company at Abadan on 2 May. It had announced its intention of doing so since 20 March. It also took over the assets of the British-owned company which had held a forty-year lease. The British reaction to this provided an immediate hazard for Herbert Morrison, who had succeeded Bevin at the Foreign Office as recently as 9 March. Attlee had been very hesitant to appoint Morrison whom he felt to be out of his depth in foreign affairs. Other candidates had been discussed, notably James Griffiths, a trade-unionist, as has been seen. Aneurin Bevan was not seriously considered. However, Morrison had incontestable claims for the second-ranking post in the government. With many misgivings, Attlee appointed him to succeed Bevin.

Morrison's seven months' tenure of the Foreign Office has been much criticized. Dean Acheson later wrote derisively of the new Foreign Secretary's ignorance of foreign affairs, and his London parochialism. He also found Morrison abrasive and quarrelsome, and less sympathetic than Bevin (whose own strong temper was notorious).[4] Kenneth Younger, the Minister of State, condemned Morrison's 'ignorance and essential vulgarity of mind' as Foreign Secretary.[5] His first action after his appointment was to send his secretary off to the Commons library to take out a life of Palmerston. Dalton was another critic of Morrison's performance, partly on the simple, snobbish grounds of his colleague's ignorance of diplomatic protocol. Morrison he found 'cocky and reactionary' at the Foreign Office, a 'pseudo-Pam' anxious to send troops to Iran and to arm the

---

[4] Dean Acheson, *Present at the Creation*, p. 505.
[5] Kenneth Younger, transcript interview, p. 72.

Germans.[6] Attlee, in similar vein, confided to Dalton in September that sending Morrison to the Foreign Office had been a great mistake. 'His ignorance was shocking. He had no background and knew no history', Attlee complained. 'H. M. always read off a sheet of paper in Cabinet; he hadn't got any of it in his head.'[7] Foreign Office personnel were not impressed either; Sir David Kelly, the ambassador in Moscow, criticized him for giving an interview to *Pravda*; Gladwyn Jebb wrote that Morrison's 'whole outlook was parochial'.[8] Conservatives reacted with joy when in the Commons Morrison pronounced 'Euphrates' with two syllables rather than three; this drew defensive comments from the sensitive Foreign Secretary about critics from wealthier, better-educated backgrounds. It was said at the time that Bevin couldn't pronounce the names either—but at least he knew where they were. This criticism of Morrison, mainly from middle-class university-trained observers, seems excessive; the critics protested too much. Morrison had to handle a sequence of difficult problems—Korea, Formosa, Anglo-Soviet relations, German rearmament, Iran, Egypt— in a short space of time. On balance, no serious errors were made, and he dealt with complex issues with composure and some judgement. Matters of protocol and public style were of no importance. However, Morrison just wasn't Bevin. Compared with his titanic predecessor, his instincts were less sure and his feel for international diplomacy less instinctive. Inevitably, British foreign policy lost some of its authority from March 1951 onwards.

This emerged in full measure during the Iranian oil crisis. In the early stages, Morrison was seriously deflected into the controversy involving Gaitskell, Bevan, and the Health Service charges; he was acting chairman of the Cabinet during Attlee's absence in hospital. When he applied his mind fully to the problem of Iranian oil after the budget, the effect was not reassuring to his colleagues. The nationalization of the Anglo-Iranian Oil Company was very difficult and

---

[6] Dalton's diary, 16 Sept. 1951.

[7] Ibid. Attlee told Dalton, '*I* am handling Persia.'

[8] Material in FO 371/94837–8, and Sir D. Kelly to K. Younger, 17 Aug. 1951 (FO 371/94839); Gladwyn, *Memoirs*, p. 251. He would have preferred Shawcross or McNeil as foreign secretary.

embarrassing for the British government for many reasons. There was, of course, the perceived centrality of the Middle East, including the Persian Gulf, as Britain's 'lifeline' in the Commonwealth strategic defence system. This was reaffirmed by the Chiefs of Staff Committee on 30 March which emphasized again the vital aspects of British defence considerations in the Middle East, in terms of the air and sea communications links in the area; the treaty obligations Britain had towards Iraq, Jordan, and other Arab states; the need to preserve North Africa from Communism or Russian aggression; and the role of Middle East air bases as a spring-board for offensive and strategic air action in the event of global war.[9] This premiss remained as unshakeable in the minds of the Foreign Office and Ministry of Defence as it had been in 1945. Equally crucial, the role of oil in Britain's energy requirements was getting more vital year by year, as domestic and other coal supplies became ever more expensive and inadequate in quantity. The oil refinery at Abadan was the largest in the world, and Iran easily the largest Arab oil producer. In addition, naturally, a Labour government which had nationalized 20 per cent of the industry in its own country could hardly raise objections if a foreign third-world government did the same to its central economic asset. Relations with the United States, already difficult over policy towards China and a European Army, were another complicating factor. The Americans were a rival force in the affairs of Middle East oil, where they were making vast inroads. The Aramco Oil Company, American-based, had recently concluded an agreement with the Saudi Arabian government; the US State Department (notably the Assistant Under-Secretary, George McGhee) was putting pressure on the British Foreign Office to conclude a new oil agreement to replace that 'supplemental agreement' made between Anglo-Iranian and the then Iranian government in July 1949.[10] Negotiations went badly. Anglo-Iranian ('confused, hide-bound, small-minded and blind' in the view of one

[9] 'Basic Assumptions for a re-examination of Middle East Strategy', 30 Mar. 1951, annexed to Chiefs of Staff Committee minutes (DEFE 4/41.).

[10] B. A. Burrows, British Embassy, Washington, to G. Furlonge, Foreign Office, 3 Jan. 1951 (FO 371/91521) EP 1531/16.

knowledgeable observer)[11] dragged their feet repeatedly. They claimed that a fifty-fifty sharing of profits on the lines of the Saudi–Aramco deal was less feasible in Persia because of the technical problem of separating the Anglo-Iranian company's interests from its other concerns. The Iranian Majlis, meanwhile, had voted down the July 1949 'supplemental' agreement in December 1950, and proceeded to call for nationalization. There was widespread popular hatred of Anglo-Iranian as an autocratic company which had passed into British control through commercial trickery, and which habitually made larger payments to the British Treasury than to the Iranian government. The 4,500 British community around the Abadan refinery and in the southern Iranian oil-fields were a totally segregated group, cut off from contact with Iranian society. At this critical time, the Iranian Prime Minister, General Razmara, admired by the British as a supposedly progressive nationalist, was assassinated on 7 March 1951 by members of an extreme Muslim sect, Fidayan-I-Islam. After a period of confusion, he was succeeded as prime minister on 27 April by the extreme nationalist Dr Mussadiq, whose bizzare, pyjama-clad appearance belied much tactical subtlety. Anglo-Iranian was then formally nationalized on 2 May.

Negotiations during May over a deal between Britain and Iran continued to go badly. Tension promptly arose around the oil installations at Abadan, with fears of harm to British property and personnel. Morrison adopted an approach of qualified sabre-rattling; he was much irritated by pressure from Dean Acheson, George McGhee, and the US State Department, for an early British withdrawal from Iran and a total surrender to Mussadiq. As early as 10 May the Cabinet considered the option of possible military intervention. 'Our strategic decisions in the Middle East were dependent on our ability to maintain our position in Persia.'[12] The Treasury pointed out the vital part of Iranian oil in the British balance of payments, which were already under some threat. For his part, Morrison criticized the proposals of a Treasury working

[11] The views of Sir Frederick Leggett, Labour Adviser of AIOC, given to L. A. C. Fry, Foreign Office, 6 Feb. 1951 (FO 371/91522) EP 1531/47.
[12] Cabinet Conclusions, 10 May 1951 (CAB 128/19).

party for a solution of Iranian oil problems as 'going too far
in the Persians' favour'. He urged that an arrangement be
made which gave Mussadiq 'the shadow of nationalisation but
would still leave the Company in firm control'. In reply, the
Treasury pointed out that all schemes proposed by Britain to
date, such as a British incorporated company to handle
AIOC's affairs, had been rejected by Iran since ultimate
control would still remain in the hands of the company. The
Treasury also warned of the dangers of landing Britain in a
state of economic warfare with Iran 'which would almost
certainly lead to internal chaos and would probably lead to
Russian domination'.[13] Gaitskell found himself trying to
moderate the bellicose pronouncements of Morrison and
Shinwell. The latter, as Minister of Defence, was the most
hawkish member of the Cabinet. 'Throwing up the sponge'
in Iran, he argued, could lead to the nationalization of the
Suez Canal and the collapse of British power throughout
the Middle East.[14]

By the start of June it seemed increasingly likely that
Britain would drift into a state of near-war with Iran. The
British minister in Teheran, Sir Francis Shepherd, an imperialist of the Curzon school, complained angrily about 'the
Americans butting in on this question without consulting
us. . . .'[15] By 21 June, Morrison was telling his Cabinet
colleagues that all negotiations with Mussadiq had broken
down, and the possibilities of military and naval action at
Abadan were now solemnly discussed.[16] E. A. Berthoud of
the Foreign Office Eastern Department minuted that 'the
removal of Mr. Moussadek [*sic*] is now objective number
one, and action is likely to be taken accordingly'. The Joint
Planning Staff had been actively considering military intervention since April. By June a plan had been evolved, code-
named 'Midget', later replaced by 'Buccaneer', to hold
Abadan island indefinitely by military force, backed up by

[13] M. T. Flett, Treasury, to R. J. Bowker, Foreign Office, 24 May 1951 (FO
371/91540).
[14] Gaitskell's diary, 11 May 1951; Shinwell's views in annex to Chiefs of
Staff Committee minutes, 23 May 1951 (DEFE 4/41).
[15] Sir F. Shepherd, Tehran, to Foreign Office, 1 June 1951 (FO 371/91540).
[16] Cabinet Conclusions, 21 June 1951 (CAB 128/19); minute by E. A.
Berthoud, 21 June 1951 (FO 371/91550).

HMS *Mauritius* and perhaps other vessels in the Persian Gulf. The government were asked to consider sending a detachment of troops to Bahrein, for early dispatch to Abadan.[17] The Chiefs of Staff were in tough mood. At a meeting on 17 July 1951, Field Marshal Slim, the CIGS, urged the need to retain military control at Abadan as long as possible. The alternative would be a massive loss of British prestige, which would play into the hands of the Russians. Lord Fraser, the First Sea Lord, impatiently declared that 'the Persians were becoming increasingly impossible, intolerable and impudent'. Fraser went on, in heady vein, 'Withdrawal would lead to a great outcry from the British public who were tired of being pushed around by Persian pip-squeaks. The present situation was having a thoroughly bad effect on morale, not only of the forces and of those in Persia but country-wide. Firm action would give everyone a fillip and dispel the dumps and doldrums into which they were rapidly falling.'[18] Fraser's cure for the 'dumps and doldrums' was to dispatch the entire Home Fleet into the Mediterranean, aircraft carriers and all, as a preliminary to large-scale military invasion of Abadan. It would be fair to add that Fraser later calmed down and his interventions in the Iranian crisis became distinctly more balanced. But this indicates the kind of emotion evoked by the nationalization of Iranian oil in the summer of 1951.

Morrison, in Gaitskell's words, 'was something of a fire-eater'. He felt that Britain was 'far too United Nationsy'.[19] Shinwell also demanded 'a show of force' and solidly backed up the Chiefs of Staffs' arguments in favour of plan 'Buccaneer'. However, at a crucial Cabinet meeting on 2 July, the bulk of opinion was clearly against such a hazardous policy, with Attlee, Gaitskell, Dalton, Noel-Baker, and Griffiths all urging caution.[20] Griffiths emphasized the need to consider the impact on Asian opinion of military action. By 12 July, Morrison also seemed to be coming round to the view that military intervention in Iran to protect British property

[17] Confidential Annex to meetings of Chiefs of Staff Committee, 11 July 1951 (DEFE 4/45).
[18] Confidential Annex to meeting of Chiefs of Staff Commiteee, 17 July 1951 (ibid.).
[19] Gaitskell's diary, 11 May 1951; Younger, interview transcript, p. 71.
[20] Cabinet Conclusions, 2 July 1951 (CAB 128/20).

would probably be unwise. He now urged a phased withdrawal from Abadan, with a message to the American government that Britain was now considering acceptance of the
interim ruling of the International Court of Justice at The
Hague. Attlee warned against Britain's associating herself
with 'a corrupt and undemocratic regime in Persia' and
emphasized the need to accept the fact of nationalization as
the basis of friendly partnership with the Iranian government.
At a further Cabinet meeting on 23 July, Morrison circulated
a paper which contemplated using British forces at Abadan
in order to safeguard British lives. He argued that a British
show of force would arouse respect among the Arab peoples.
This came under heavy fire. The Attorney-General, Sir Frank
Soskice, sharply criticized the basis of Morrison's argument
in international law. Military force, he argued, could be
allowed only in the last resort, if lives were visibly in physical
danger.[21] On 26 July, the Cabinet agreed to resume negotiations with Iran. After a mission to Teheran by the US envoy,
Averell Harriman, the British government began an evacuation of technicians and other personnel and their families
from Abadan. On 1 August Fraser approved the withdrawal
from HMS *Mauritius* from the Persian Gulf, and 'Buccaneer'
effectively went into cold storage.[22] The Iranian oil crisis
gradually receded from prime attention. The company was
nationalized, but Britain in due course received her flow of
oil from the Iranian oilfields just the same. A further attempt
at mediation on 4–22 August, by the breezy Lord Privy Seal,
Richard Stokes, a businessman who knew the region at first
hand through his engineering firm, Ransome and Rapier,
failed to make any headway.[23] Operation 'Buccaneer'
remained, at least theoretically, under consideration by the
British government until September. Morrison continued to
be attracted by the prospect of sending a British strike-force
to occupy the island of Abadan, as did Shinwell. Attlee,
however, as well as most of his Cabinet, argued strongly

[21] Cabinet Conclusions, 23, 26 July 1951.
[22] Confidential Annexes to meetings of Chiefs of Staff Committee, 1 Aug.
1951 (DEFE 4/45) and 8 Aug. (DEFE 4/46).
[23] Richard Stokes diaries, 4–22 Aug. 1951 (Bodleian, Stokes papers); Stokes's
record, 5 Aug. 1951 (FO 371/91557) EP 1531/339. One of Stokes's recent
responsibilities had been to organize the Festival of Britain.

against the use of force. More important still, pressure from Acheson and the American State Department against British military intervention was overwhelming. In the end, the Cabinet firmly rejected the military option. At a meeting on 23 September it was finally ruled out. By 4 October the last of the British personnel had been evacuated from Abadan. The 'lunatic' Dr Mussadiq remained in power in Iran until overthrown in mid-1953. However the Iranian oil crisis was a very serious one and added notably to the tension at a key period and again suggested how the enduring call of empire exercised its siren effect on elements within the Labour government. Fortunately it was resisted this time, as on other occasions. Britain, heavily committed in military action in Korea and Malaya, had already problems enough.

Another crisis in the Middle East concerned relations with Egypt where Britain had maintained a military presence in the Suez Canal Zone since the treaty of 1936, and historically since 1882. Back in 1946, a mission to Cairo by Lord Stansgate, the Air Minister, had seemed to bring agreement between Britain and the Wafd regime in Egypt somewhat closer. Bevin was anxious, as he wrote to Attlee on 25 May 1946, to withdraw troops rapidly from Egypt for financial and other reasons, despite the protests of Smuts at the Commonwealth Prime Ministers' conference who feared that the floodgates of Soviet penetration would be opened as a result.[24] Agreement seemed to have been reached at talks between Bevin and the Egyptian Prime Minister, Sidky Pasha, in London in October 1946; but then Sidky on returning to Cairo uttered interpretations of the treaty terms which implied Egyptian sovereignty over the Sudan. This was a vital region for Egyptians, with the Nile waters essential for their irrigation, but opinion in Sudan reacted strongly against fears of Egyptian domination. The British themselves had sedulously been cultivating Sudanese nationalism. In the end, Bevin had to tell the Commons, on 27 January 1947, that negotiations between Britain and Egypt

[24] Memorandum by Bevin on Revision of Anglo-Egyptian Treaty of 1936, 18 Jan. 1946; Smuts to Attlee, 8 May 1946; Bevin to Attlee, 25 May 1946 (PREM 8/1388, pt. 1).

had broken down.[25] Matters remained in this unsatisfactory condition for the next four years, complicated by the turmoil in neighbouring Palestine. Bevin himself was anxious to stress that the Canal Zone was far from being vital for Britain as a military base.[26] Cyrenaica, with airfields such as that at Derna, would make 'the best aircraft carrier', while stores could be retained at Aden and in British Somaliland instead. There were also valuable British air bases nearby in Iraq and Cyprus. But relations with Egypt remained ambiguous. Indeed, Egypt, like Iran, has sometimes been considered an area where Bevin somewhat let things drift in his declining period as Foreign Secretary in 1950–1.

But Morrison, installed at the Foreign Office in March 1951, found his attention increasingly caught up by the problem of Egypt. British troops were due to leave the Canal Zone by 1955 in any case, and he suggested opening new negotiations with the Egyptian Prime Minister, Nahas Pasha. For the moment, however, British troops would stay at Suez. The Cabinet warned on 5 April that the British public would not tolerate any further weakness or appeasement of Egypt.[27] The situation was complicated by American pressure for the creation of a Middle East Command, that would include Egypt. The Americans felt that Britain had underestimated the force of Egyptian nationalism (still smarting from military defeats by the Israelis in 1948) and that retaining a military base in the face of Egyptian hostility would be impossible. Morrison protested that a British base in Egypt was essential. 'No question of imperialism exists', he wrote to Acheson on 14 August 1951.[28] But, here again, his judgement was being overruled. It was agreed in principle by the United Kingdom and the United States Chiefs of Staff jointly on 14 September that a new Middle East command, to include Egypt, should be created, presupposing

[25] H. J. Huddleston, Governor-General in the Sudan, to Attlee, 9 Nov. 1946 (PREM 8/1388, pt. II); Stansgate to Attlee, 10 Dec. 1946, draft statement by Bevin, 21 Jan. 1947 (PREM 8/1388, pt. III).

[26] Discussion at the Foreign Office, 10 Jan. 1947, citing Bevin's views (PREM 8/1388, pt. II).

[27] Cabinet Conclusions, 5 Apr. 1951 (CAB 128/19); memorandum by Morrison on 'Egypt: Defence Negotiations', 30 Mar. 1951 (PREM 8/1388, pt. III).

[28] Draft letter, Morrison to Acheson, 14 Aug. 1951, annexed to Chiefs of Staff Committee minutes (DEFE 4/45).

Britain's withdrawal of her forces from the Suez Canal Zone.[29] At the time, these included three infantry battalions, along with armoured, armoured-car, field artillery, light anti-aircraft, heavy anti-aircraft, and field engineering regiments; all would have to be moved to other bases in Malta, Cyprus, Aden, Sudan, and British Somaliland, which would mean a considerable redeployment of British forces. In a major war, the Middle East would henceforth become an Allied rather than a purely British responsibility, although 'it will remain a British sphere of influence'. The retreat from empire was visualized as going on apace.

However, the fanfares of departure had not yet been sounded, in Egypt at least, in October 1951. In the very last weeks of the government, indeed during the election campaign itself, Nahas Pasha, supported by the Egyptian parliament, announced on 8 October that the 1936 Anglo-Egyptian treaty was being unilaterally abrogated, as was its predecessor of 1899 for the condominium of the Sudan. The privileges enjoyed by the British forces of occupation would be abolished, and attacks both on British forces in the Canal Zone and in Khartoum were threatened.[30] Morrison's instinctive response was again belligerent; echoes of Wolseley and General Gordon were heard in the land. He began urgent talks on 9 October with the Chief of the Air Staff and the Vice-Chief of the Imperial General Staff on military preparations in the Canal Zone. The implication, as Morrison bluntly put it, was 'that we stay in Egypt'.[31] The Parachute Brigade would be flown in from Cyprus. In the Chiefs of Staff Committee, Field Marshal Slim urged that immediate action be taken to convince the Egyptians that Britain was not too 'spineless' to use force. Unlike in Iran, Britain with 38,000 troops in the Canal Zone, could act from a position of strength. It was proposed that 2 Infantry Brigade be moved to Egypt at once, and that 1 Guards Brigade in Tripoli and 19 Infantry Brigade stationed in Britain be put on active stand-by. Again, Attlee himself was reluctant to use military force. He minuted on 9 October 'the need to avoid

[29] Meeting of Chiefs of Staffs Committee, 10, 14 Sept. 1951 (ibid.).
[30] Material in PREM 8/1388, pt III.
[31] Morrison to Attlee, 12 Oct. 1951 (ibid.).

provocation'. Again, Morrison, in the opinion of Dalton at least, was as anxious to dispatch troops to Suez as he had been to Abadan—'bloody little fool'.[32] Attlee, however, overruled him; since he was chairman of the Chiefs of Staff Committee, this was decisive. On the other hand, it could be argued by some that limited military intervention was reasonable, at least to protect Sudan from Egyptian invasion and unwanted occupation. The entire problem remained in the melting-pot until 26 October when Attlee formally tendered his resignation to the King. Subsequently, Eden, the Conservative Foreign Secretary, pursued a policy of withdrawal, and the last detachment of British troops left the Canal Zone in 1954.

In a quite different region, the Labour government was also plagued by a post-imperial problem, although one very much in limbo when the administration fell from power. This was the proposal, pushed hard by the Colonial and Commonwealth Relations Office since the end of 1949, of a federation in Central Africa to take in Northern and Southern Rhodesia and Nyasaland. The situation was much influenced by the fact that, whereas Nyasaland and Northern Rhodesia were overwhelmingly black African, Southern Rhodesia contained a substantial white emigré population of 223,000, very close in their political and racial attitudes to the apostles of apartheid in South Africa. This remained a departmental matter for much of 1950 with Andrew Cohen, the Colonial Office's 'King of Africa', becoming a passionate advocate of federation on political and economic grounds, with all the zeal of a convert. There was some tension between the Commonwealth Relations and Colonial Offices on the issue. James Griffiths, the warm-hearted ex-miner who was now Colonial Secretary, emphasized African fears about the idea of federation. However, Patrick Gordon-Walker, the right-wing Commonwealth Relations secretary, who had recently banished Seretse Khama from

---

[32] Memorandum of 19 Oct. 1951, 'Top Secret' (PREM 8/1388, pt. III); minutes of Chiefs of Staff Committee, 15, 16 Oct. 1951 (DEFE 4/46, 47); Morrison's minute of 18 Oct. 1951 (FO 371/90143); Dalton's diary, 27 Sept. 1951.

his homeland, was a firm advocate of the scheme.[33] But their views tended to merge, with a common belief that an integrated federation in Central Africa might become a counter to what was believed to be growing South African influence —even though Garner at the CRO pointed out that, in any case, the putative federation would be totally dependent on South African goodwill for transport and capital investment.[34] Progress was made in 1950, aided by the good personal relationship struck up between Griffiths and Roy Welensky, the Southern Rhodesian leader, a former railway trade-union organizer and ex-boxer. On 8 November 1950, Griffiths agreed that the African peoples concerned should have a meeting with British government officials in London to consider the feasibility of a federation. This met in the Commonwealth Relations Office in March–May 1951; its report came out strongly in favour of what was called 'Closer Association'.[35] It was noticeable that the reception of the report was most favourable amongst Southern Rhodesian whites; while black African opinion was unanimous in its hostility to what they regarded as a more subtle form of white racial domination. Dr Hastings Banda, the London-based president of the Nyasaland African Congress, and a member of the Labour Party, was especially vehement and sent his protests to the former Colonial Secretary, Creech Jones.[36]

There is no doubt that both Gordon-Walker and Griffiths were by now enthusiastic supporters of the idea of a Central African Federation. Gordon-Walker toured Southern Rhodesia in September to gauge opinion, while Griffiths visited the largely African territories of Nyasaland and Northern Rhodesia to campaign in favour of 'closer association'. Finally, a second conference was held at Victoria Falls on the Zambesi on 18 September 1951. It was not a success.

[33] Memorandum of conversation between Griffiths and Gordon-Walker, 25 Apr. 1951 (DO 121/136); memorandum by Andrew Cohen, 18 Apr. 1951 (CO 537/7203); Blake, op. cit., pp. 248 ff.

[34] Memorandum, Aug. 1951 (DO 121/137).

[35] Material in CO 537/7201; *Central African Territories: Report of a Conference on Closer Association, 1951* (PP, 1950–1, x, 417 ff.) Cmd. 8233.

[36] Hastings Banda to Creech Jones, 23 June 1951 (Creech Jones papers, ACJ/ 7/1/339–44).

African opinion from the two northern territories was totally hostile. Black Southern Rhodesian opinion was not heard from at all, since the blacks there were allegedly 'represented' by a white Minister for Native Affairs. On the other side, Sir Godfrey Huggins from Southern Rhodesia expressed much irritation at African objections. After a public dispute with Griffiths, he was forced to concede that Northern Rhodesia and Nyasaland should remain protectorates even after federation, while the land distribution for blacks, and their political advancement in the two northern territories should be left to their respective governments.[37]

It was very clear that blacks throughout the territories feared that the proposed federation would mean a loss of land, the endangering of their political advancement, and their legal subjection to the quasi-apartheid of the Southern Rhodesian regime in Salisbury. Nevertheless, Griffiths and Gordon-Walker both came out firmly, in a joint report published on 5 October, in favour of support for the principle of federation on both political and economic grounds.[38] It was hoped that Africans would give the idea further consideration and that another conference would be held. In fact, it became clear that the fall of the Labour government on 26 October removed it from a serious dilemma in central Africa. Black African opposition continued to be unrelenting. By the time that Griffiths divided the House of Commons against the idea of federation on 4 March 1952, it was clear that any prospect of bipartisanship over the proposal was dead. In any case, the entire notion was complicated by such factors as Britain's highly ambiguous relationship with the government of South Africa, and by anxiety for the chromium supplies of Southern Rhodesia (so it has been claimed) to further the production of Britain's nuclear weapons programme. From March 1952, led by Griffiths, the Labour Party was firm against a Central African Federation. Only a handful, including Gordon-Walker and George Brown, remained enthusiastic still. The later, abortive history of the Federation, until it was wound up by R. A. Butler

[37] Blake, op. cit., p. 258.
[38] Joint memorandum by Griffiths and Gordon-Walker. 'Closer Association in Central Africa', 5 Oct. 1951 (DO 121/138).

in 1963, was a commentary on how Labour ministers had radically misjudged a crucial aspect of post-imperial settlement in Africa.

But the main immediate problem for the Attlee government in the summer of 1951 concerned neither Asia nor Africa directly. It related once again to the balance of payments and other economic difficulties. In the words of the *Economic Survey for 1952*, 'a violent and disastrous change took place during 1951 in the overseas balance of payments of the United Kingdom'.[39] The problem was fully evident in the first half of the year, when the deficit reached £93m. In the latter part of 1951, starting with extreme severity in August, the deficit climbed to the extraordinary total of £428m., with a total of £521m. for the year as a whole. In part, this was because the exceptional surplus of the autumn of 1950 was leading to a reaction. But the most notable feature was the huge increase in the cost of imports, over £1,100m. more than in 1950. In June alone, the excess of imports over exports reached a record £151.2m. A large rise in imports from OEEC countries resulted in a loss of dollars and gold to the European Payments' Union. In addition, net income from invisible transactions fell by £120m., partly due to the Iranian seizure of the Abadan oil refineries. A catastrophic factor in August and September was that other countries in the sterling bloc, held down since devaluation, vastly increased their dollar purchases and thus produced a large dollar deficit rather than a surplus.[40] Again, it could hardly be denied that by the summer the rigours of the rearmament programme were having serious effects, both on home production and on exports. Problems such as the shortage of machine tools, of which Bevan had often spoken in March and April, were being underlined. Everywhere there seemed to be a sudden loss of confidence. The *Financial Times* Ordinary Share Index, which had stood at 139.7 on 8 June, almost an all-time record, had fallen by 27 July to

[39] *Economic Survey for 1952*, p. 7.
[40] Ibid., pp. 8 ff.; minutes of Cabinet Economic Committee, 26 June–31 July 1951 (CAB 134/228); *The Economist*, 21 July, 18 Aug. 1951. A good monograph is Joan Mitchell, *Crisis in Britain, 1951* (London, 1963).

128.3.[41] By 31 July, Gaitskell was having to tell the Defence Committee of the immense strain imposed by the arms budget on the economy. The sum of £4,700m. should be regarded as the absolute maximum; he had to restrain Shinwell who sought a further increase still. It was agreed that Shinwell's programme should be cut by £150m. and that the Americans should be approached for help with the provision of finished military equipment.[42] Among the further miseries of home consumers were the impact of higher taxes after the budget, and cuts in the already meagre rations of foodstuffs. On 3 September, the butter ration was cut to three ounces, bacon to three ounces, and cheese to one and a half. The financial calculations of the winter months, so hurriedly made during the planning of the rearmament programme, were in total disarray. The British public after years of austerity were now being faced with new and even more insupportable burdens.

Gaitskell reacted to these new financial problems, some foreseeable, some unexpected, with great energy. He urged the TUC at Blackpool to pursue wage restraint, since the external situation was being compounded by an upward curve of wages at home in the aftermath of the wage-freeze policy. Rather surprisingly, he also mentioned industrial copartnership schemes, and the distribution of bonus shares to workers. Gaitskell's speech was very well received, not least because on 26 July he had proposed, in defiance of City criticism, a limitation of dividends for three years.[43] The maximum dividend allowed would be the average distributed in the last two years, plus 7 per cent for new companies needing to raise capital. But the bad news marched on. A record trade deficit of £150m. for June 1951 was followed by a further deficit of £127m. for July and more bad tidings on all fronts in August and September. The balance of payments crisis on current account led to a crisis on the capital account. The gold and dollar deficit for July–September 1951 was $638m., worse even than the same period in 1949 though not as grim as in 1947. In

---

[41] *Financial Times*, 23 June–28 July 1951.
[42] Minutes of Cabinet Defence Committee, 31 July 1951 (CAB 131/10).
[43] *The Times*, 27 July, 5 Sept. 1951; *News Chronicle*, 5 Sept. 1951.

desperation, Gaitskell flew to North America on 4 September for urgent financial talks in Washington and Ottawa.[44] Here, he told the US Treasury and State Department officials of the mounting dollar deficit and of renewed balance of payments crises, with the world-wide problem in the inflating cost of raw materials a central theme. Talks with the US Treasury went badly. Snyder, the Secretary to the Treasury, revealed himself, in Gaitskell's view, as 'a pretty small minded, small town semi-isolationist'. Dean Acheson ('a sensitive and cultured mind') and the State Department were more sympathetic on stockpiling and on US aid.[45] A programme of 'burden-sharing' was finally agreed to assist with the costs of rearmament. But it would take many months to have effect, while Congressional leaders would be swayed by electoral considerations. The situation may not have been quite as bleak as the British Treasury team implied. Robert Hall felt that the crisis of July–September 1951 had been caused in part by purely short-term factors, such as an unusually high rate of United Kingdom imports, and short-term outflows of capital. Hall added that, despite the loss of Iranian oil, 'if we could only get more coal and steel, I do not myself consider it beyond our powers to deal with the situation'.[46] For all that, the statistics, in the late summer of 1951, were frightening enough, almost as alarming as in the gloomiest period of the Cripps era. It led Gaitskell to proclaim with new fervour the economic difficulties created by the rearmament programme which he had himself so passionately endorsed, in terms similar to those of Bevan himself. *Tribune* ran a headline on 21 September, 'Has Gaitskell joined the Bevanites?'

It was during Gaitskell's absence abroad, with the government harassed by problems in Iran and Egypt, divided over German rearmament, anxious over the TUC's response to the call for wage restraint, apprehensive over the balance of

[44] Material in T 230/186.

[45] Gaitskell's diary, 9 Nov. 1951.

[46] Memorandum on Discussion in Washington and Ottawa on Balance of Payments and Defence Contracts', 26 Sept. 1951, and memorandum by Hall (T 230/186). It might be noted that the export target for 1951 was virtually achieved (£2,748m. instead of a target of £2,750m.).

payments crisis, that Attlee unexpectedly announced the
dissolution of parliament and the calling of a general election.
Attlee had discussions with Morgan Phillips and Dalton from
16 September onwards. Dalton (who, like Bevan, wanted an
October election) made the point that the announcement of
an election would divert attention away from a forthcoming
second Bevanite pamphlet, *Going our Way*.[47] Willie Whiteley,
the chief whip, was another key adviser. On 19 September,
Attlee told a Cabinet meeting that he had decided to dissolve.
It was a thin Cabinet and a gloomy finale. Only seven ministers
were present, including the ageing Addison, now visibly
breaking up in health, 'a very quick and final decline'. The
ministers present—Dalton, Ede, Alexander, McNeil, Addison,
and Jay (deputizing for Gaitskell)—all agreed with Attlee.
Morrison, away in Ottawa, discussing western defence, and
thus again excluded from the final decision of timing a
general election as he had been in February 1950, sent a
message which read 'Still, no comment'—to indicate his
displeasure.[48] Gaitskell (whose personal relationship with
Attlee had become less cordial since May) also viewed the
decision to hold an election with dismay. The timing was
bad on economic grounds, while there was no prospect of
a breakthrough either in Korea or Iran. 'To Hugh it came as
a thunderclap. He was very upset by it', his private secretary
recalled.[49] Attlee then announced the election in a radio
broadcast, the first Prime Minister to choose this method
of communication. In the end, it seems to have been a
wholly personal decision by Attlee, largely determined by
the need to have an early election before the King began
a lengthy tour of Africa.[50] In the event, the King's illness
was to prevent his going at all; indeed, he died in early
1952, so Attlee's major consideration did not in fact apply.
On tactical grounds, the election was surely a mistake, with
bad news about the balance of payments, unresolved difficulties in the Middle and Far East, and the impact of the
Bevanites still very present in the public consciousness.

[47] Dalton's diary, 4, 16 Sept. 1951.
[48] Cabinet Conclusions, 19 Sept. 1951 (CAB 128/20); Dalton's diary, 19 Sept.
1951; Donoughue and Jones, op. cit., pp. 501–2.
[49] Philip Williams, op. cit., p. 283; Hugh Gaitskell diary, 16 Nov. 1951.
[50] Kenneth Harris, op. cit., pp. 486–7.

Two days later, on 21 September, *Going our Way* was published, with its sharp attacks on the TUC leadership, receiving much attention in the right-wing press.[51] Had the government been able to soldier on through the winter, there would have been perhaps better financial news in the spring, and both Egypt and Iran would have calmed down. In mid-1952 the British economy began a steady advance, a beneficial legacy of Crippsian austerity perhaps. There was a boom in private investment. Living standards rose generally from which the Conservatives were to derive sustained electoral benefit. But Attlee and his colleagues, exhausted by interminable crises at home and abroad, after eleven almost continuous years in office in some cases, were in no mood to continue. The decision was made, and it had to be resolutely followed up.

Despite all their problems, the Labour government and the party were by no means downcast as the election approached. Morale in the parliamentary party, as George Strauss later recorded, had remained high throughout 1951. Morgan Phillips and the Tapers and Tadpoles of Transport House were fully prepared for battle; the party organization was boosted in marginal constituencies, helped in some cases by the use of privately-commissioned opinion polls. The party conference at Scarborough on 1–2 October, an abbreviated affair, was suffused by a profound mood of party unity, endorsed by Bevan as enthusiastically as anyone. Attlee himself received a warm reception; he responded by including in his speech a moving, inspirational passage from Blake's 'Jerusalem'. The effect was somewhat modified the next day when it transpired that the NEC constituency section elections had seen Bevan's supporters capture four places out of seven, with Bevan himself heading the poll and Mrs Castle (who had wisely switched from the women's section of the NEC), Driberg, and Mikardo joining him, and only Griffiths, Morrison, and Dalton as non-Bevanites on the NEC constituency section. Dalton recorded that this was the result of active canvassing amongst the delegates by Mikardo and Geoffrey Bing.[52] In these circumstances, Bevan's final

---

[51] *The Times*, 21 Sept. 1951; *Tribune*, 28 Sept. 1951.
[52] Dalton's diary, 4 Oct. 1951. On this, see Leslie Hunter, *The Road to Brighton Pier* (London, 1959), pp. 53 ff. Hunter was a journalist close to Herbert Morrison.

oratorical appeal for a joyous fight and a united campaign
fell a shade flat.

The party manifesto had also provoked some argument.
There had been some controversial policy proposals, notably
a document on 'The Distribution of Wealth and Income'
which the NEC had considered on 27 June, with Attlee,
Morrison, Dalton, and Bevan all present. This paper outlined
the relatively minor shift of wealth that had taken place
during the years of Labour government.[53] Even in 1947, the
wealthiest 10 per cent of adults still owned 80 per cent of
private property (in 1937, the figure had been 87 per cent).
Death duties were too slow in having an effect and could be
circumvented by the ingenious rich; capital gains taxes were a
feeble instrument. The conclusion reached was the need for
a capital levy—which, indeed, right-wingers such as Roy
Jenkins, as well as the Bevanite left, had long favoured. The
draft policy statement on 25 July was much watered down,
and had been opposed by Bevan and Mikardo, while Mrs
Castle drafted a statement which claimed that it was just
a blanket defence of the government on every aspect, including the rearmament proposals, world mutual aid plans, and
the principle of a free health service.[54] Again, on 12 September
Bevan and Mikardo had strongly attacked the defence
sections of the NEC report to be considered by the party
conference, under the title, 'Our First Duty—Peace'.[55]
Dalton records how the discussion of the manifesto for the
election later produced a great row on the new National
Executive, with the Bevanites raging for more socialism and
the trade-unionists denouncing the *Tribune* pamphlet, *Going
our Way*, for its attacks on trade-union leaders like Sam
Watson, and Jock Tiffin of the TGWU.[56] In the end, a compromise was patched up. Dalton gloomily concluded afterwards that 'we shall be badly beaten at this election'.[57] Still,
for all his personal links with Gaitskell, he was now significantly closer to the Bevanites on foreign-policy and social
issues, and sometimes thought of in the press as a new leader

[53] Minutes of National Executive Committee, 21 Mar., 27 June 1951.
[54] Ibid., 25 July 1951.
[55] Ibid., 12 Sept. 1951.
[56] Ibid., 2 Oct. 1951; Dalton's diary, 4 Oct. 1951.
[57] Dalton, ibid.

of the Labour left. In fact, the new manifesto was not unimpressive. It included some new features, including suggestions on dividend limitation and a modified levy on capital,
and such social demands as comprehensive secondary schools
and the enfranchisement of occupiers of leasehold property.
There was no shopping-list on nationalization this time,
merely a vague pledge to take over (unnamed) industries
which were 'failing the nation'. Drafted by a somewhat ill-
assorted committee consisting of Dalton, Bevan, Mikardo,
and Morgan Phillips, it made the best of a difficult situation.

In the campaign, Labour fought hard and well. Despite
the untimely death of the national agent, Dick Windle, in
September, the organization under his successor, Len
Williams, remained very sound. As in 1950, Attlee's gentle
motorized progress through the shires was a personal triumph.
The only excitement of note came from the driving eccentrici-
ties of Mrs Attlee; the Prime Minister himself quietly worked
on crossword puzzles in the back of the car. Dalton was
heartened by his own boisterous election meetings, even
though he wrote on 13 October 'I think we're out.'[58] The
Gallup Polls were depressing on 5 October at the start of the
campaign, with a large Tory lead over Labour of 50.5 per
cent to 43.5 per cent. This was attributed by Labour, with
some justice, to the middle-class housewives who largely
conducted the interviews with the sample of voters and
built in their own right-wing prejudices. When the 'don't
knows' were allocated, there was a revised result at the end
of the campaign of Conservatives 49.9 per cent and Labour
47.0 per cent.[59] In fact, this much under-represented the
Labour vote since the eventual result was to show Labour
polling 48.8 per cent (a higher proportion than 1945) to the
Conservatives' 48.0 per cent. The Conservatives deliberately
fought a restrained and moderate campaign. Churchill bid
hard for Liberal votes, and even offered Conservative support
for Lady Violet Bonham-Carter, the Liberal candidate at
Colne Valley. Lady Violet had earlier suggested to Clement
Davies that Liberals and Conservatives make an anti-socialist
pact in constituencies where Labour MPs had been elected

[58] Ibid., 13 Oct. 1951.
[59] *News Chronicle*, 25 Oct. 1951.

on a minority vote.[60] At Bolton West and Huddersfield West, the Liberal candidates, Arthur Holt and Donald Wade, were themselves beneficiaries of such a pact under which the Conservatives stood down. Clement Davies himself had no Tory opponent in Montgomeryshire, nor did Roderic Bowen in Cardiganshire. There were even rumours that Clement Davies might be offered a post in a Churchill Cabinet after the election (as, in fact, he was).[61] Churchill himself kept up a moderate image by affirming that there would be no anti-trade-union legislation, even on the closed shop, by a future Conservative government. The general tone was tranquil, with public meetings generally quiet and orderly, and rapt attention paid to party election broadcasts on the radio. Morgan Phillips told Walter Nash, the New Zealand Labour leader, on 17 October, that it was a difficult election to predict. 'People are quiet and thoughtful; but there are no apparent signs of exciting or enthusiastic electioneering.'[62]

The temperature was raised sharply in the last days of the campaign when Morrison, of all people, raised the cry that Churchill was a warmonger who might dispatch British troops to Iran and Egypt. Shinwell, Bevan, and Strachey joined in the outcry. Churchill repelled this 'cruel and ungrateful accusation', but he himself had first raised the Iranian issue on 2 October and had condemned the government's weakness. The warmongering cry was taken up with enthusiasm by the pro-Labour tabloid, *Daily Mirror*, edited by Sylvester Bolam, with its peace-mongering slogan, 'Whose Finger on the Trigger?' featured in the paper on 23–5 October. This led to Churchill later suing the paper for libel. Woolton was to say after the election that 'he found it a very saddening thing to think that the Goebbels technique, lie following lie, should have been able to grip the people of this country as it had done during the election', dividing the nation into two classes.[63] Indeed, a notable feature of the campaign was the

[60] Lady Violet Bonham-Carter to Clement Davies, 15 Nov. 1950 (Davies papers, J/3/45); Davies to Bonham-Carter, 11 Jan. 1951 (ibid., J/3/53).
[61] Davies to Gilbert Murray, 9 Nov. 1951 (ibid., J/3/65). In response to much pressure within the party, Davies reluctantly turned down Churchill's invitation.
[62] Morgan Phillips to Walter Nash, 17 Oct. 1951 (Labour Party archives, GS 29/1).
[63] Minutes of Executive Council of Conservative National Union, 8 Nov. 1951 (Conservative Central Office); cf. *Daily Telegraph*, 29 Oct. 1951.

impact of foreign events, to a degree unusual in a British general election. This was in part the result of unexpected factors in October including the new crisis in Egypt from 8 October onwards, and the assassination of Liaquat Ali Khan, the Prime Minister of Pakistan. The Conservatives were far from blameless, linking as they did the three disasters of 'Abadan, Sudan, and Bevan'. They also made much of Labour's mishandling of the economy, the rising cost of living, and the defects of nationalization, including steel. Labour emphasized full employment, planning, and social welfare. On housing, the Conservatives (more specifically Harmar Nicholls on behalf of the 'One Nation' group) had stampeded the leadership in the 1950 party conference into including a pledge in the manifesto that 300,000 houses a year would be built; the chairman of the conference momentarily lost control in the face of Nicholls's persistence and Woolton had to yield.[64] Overall, the verdict of Charles Wintour in the *Evening Standard* was a fair one. 'The fire of 1945 has been lacking. Six years ago real venom and hatred were abroad.'[65] There were no Laski scares or Beaverbrook stunts this time.

In the event, the results showed only a small shift of opinion compared with February 1950. The turn-out of voters was again remarkably high—82.6 per cent as against 83.9 per cent in 1950. As before, Labour won more votes, almost 14 million in all (to be precise, 13,948,883). It had gained its highest poll and the largest vote ever won by any British politician party. Morgan Phillips could justifiably tell the NEC in November that 'the party is in good fettle'.[66] The Bevanite divisions evidently had little, if any, effect. There were actually Labour gains in North Wales, where both Anglesey and Merioneth were captured from the Liberals: ironically enough, the two defeated candidates there, Lady Megan Lloyd George and Emrys Roberts, had voted consistently with the Labour Party in the previous parliament. But the shift in votes was enough to bring about a change of government.

[64] Percy Cohen, 'A History of the Conservative and Unionist Party Organization, (unpublished MS in Conservative Central Office, 1964), p. 488.

[65] *Evening Standard*, 24 Oct. 1951. Wintour believed that 'the Tories have not fought a good election'.

[66] National Executive Committee minutes, 7 Nov. 1951.

Labour ended up with 295 seats, as against 321 for the Conservatives. With a mere six Liberals (who put up only 109
candidates compared with 475 in 1950), there was an absolute
majority for the Conservatives. The Conservatives made 23
gains, 21 from Labour and two from the Liberals, to confirm
the previous pattern of the distribution of party support. Just
three of the Conservative gains were in Yorkshire (Doncaster,
Darlington, and West Middlesbrough), and four in Lancashire
(Bolton East, Oldham East, Rochdale, and Manchester,
Blackley) where Labour also lost Bolton West to a Liberal
running with Tory support. Eleven of the twenty-one Conservative gains from Labour were in London and the south-
east of England. South Battersea, Camberwell, and Dulwich
fell amongst London boroughs, while there were further
gains in Bedfordshire, Buckinghamshire, and Berkshire. Only
two junior ministers were defeated, Aidan Crawley in Buckingham and David Hardman in Darlington. The European
federalist, 'Kim' Mackay, fell at North Reading, though Ian
Mikardo hung on to the other Reading seat. There had been
a swing of just 0.9 per cent in votes from Labour to the Conservatives. Had it not been for a much-reduced tally of
Liberal candidates, Churchill would not have won at all.
By a six-to-four proportion, Liberals voted Conservative in
seats where there was no Liberal candidate this time. Still,
it was enough. Attlee resigned on the evening of 26 October.
Morrison then bombarded his colleagues on the NEC with an
analysis of the losses in marginal seats, and the need for
a much more vigorous programme of political education.
Labour, so Morrison, the constant apostle of caution and
consolidation, argued, needed 'the propaganda zeal of the
pioneers'.[67] Thirty-six years on, the spirit of Keir Hardie and
the ghosts of Labour's past could still haunt and inspire those
anxious to rekindle Labour's future.

When parliament reassembled, Richard Crossman wrote in his
diary for 21 October that 'everyone is so enormously relieved
at having got back that they are in the highest spirits'. Dalton,
who had feared a massacre, felt that the 'Octobrists' had been

[67] Memorandum by Herbert Morrison, 'Considerations arising out of the
General Election, 1951', 12 Dec. 1951 (Labour Party archives, GS 29/1).

justified. 'The election results are wonderful.'[68] The party continued to display its intellectual vitality in early 1952, with the publication of the *New Fabian Essays* (including essays by Crossman, Crosland, Jenkins, Mikardo, Healey, and Strachey), the founding of the right-wing monthly *Socialist Commentary* under the devoted editorship of Rita Hinden, and the appearance of Aneurin Bevan's remarkable volume, *In Place of Fear*, written in part during a visit to Yugoslavia as a guest of Tito. Labour was manifestly very much alive. But the post-election euphoria did not last. At the end of November 1951, thirty-five Labour MPs had defied the party whips to vote against a Japanese peace treaty, while another 100 abstained. On 5 March 1952, an amendment put forward by Bevan and his supporters, which condemned the rearmament programme, produced 57 rebels against Attlee and the official leadership. The rebels included Bevan, Wilson, and Freeman: James Callaghan rebuked them for their 'intellectual hypocrisy'. From that time onwards, Labour was to be racked by prolonged civil war. The Morecambe conference in a dismally wet week in October 1952 was a disastrous occasion for internecine civil war and bad temper. In the end, the Bevanites captured six of the seven seats in the constituency section of the NEC, with only James Griffiths of the party right wing escaping the whirlwind.[69] Relations between Bevan and Gaitskell and his followers became increasingly hostile. The moderate 'Keep Calm' group (headed by Strachey) could do little. The party was torn by endless tensions— over German rearmament in 1953-4, and over British membership of the South-East Asia Treaty Organization in 1955. There were also frequent tensions over Britain's nuclear weapons programme. In April 1955, Bevan was briefly expelled from the parliamentary Labour Party. Attlee, an ageing, withdrawn figure, was unable to stem the tide. The party suffered further defeats in the 1955 general election when the Conservative majority over Labour now rose to sixty-seven.

[68] Dalton's diary, 27 Oct. and 'end of October' 1951; *The Backbench Diaries of Richard Crossman*, p. 30.

[69] Philip Williams, op. cit., pp. 302-4, is excellent on these developments. Also *Report of 51st Annual Conference* held at Morecambe, 29 Sept.-3 Oct. 1952, pp. 123 ff.

Further acute dissension followed from 1957 onwards over Britain's possession of an independent nuclear weapons system. After the trauma of the Suez invasion in October–November 1956, this led to widespread rank-and-file demands, by no means confined to the Bevanites, for Britain to reassess NATO and perhaps break with the American alliance. The reluctant partnership created anew between Gaitskell, now the party leader, and Aneurin Bevan in 1957, when Bevan strongly attacked the unilateralists for wanting Britain to go 'naked into the conference chamber', did not improve matters. Labour duly lost the 1959 general election as well, thus losing ground at four successive elections. It now held only 258 seats to the Conservatives' 365, while Labour's share of the poll fell to 43.9 per cent. Even more bitter disputes followed, first over Gaitskell's attempt to renounce Clause Four, with its commitment to nationalization, more damagingly still over the revolt led by CND against the party's defence policy. CND was assisted by a change in the leadership of major unions. In the Transport Workers, Arthur Deakin, long the scourge of the left, had died; he was followed, after an interlude, by the leftish figure of Frank Cousins, a unilateralist. Gaitskell's defeat at the 1960 party conference, and his subsequent victory at the 1961 party conference were both accompanied by intense party bitterness. The issue of the European Common Market in 1962 added further tension, which Gaitskell managed this time to defuse. Not until the spring of 1963, by which time both Bevan and Gaitskell were dead, and the party reunited under the reformed quasi-Bevanite, Harold Wilson, did Labour again appear a credible challenger for power. It narrowly won the general election of 1964. Now there was a real hope that the demons of division present throughout the thirteen years of opposition since 1951 had been purged. Labour's long march, so wantonly interrupted, could perhaps be resumed.

Yet it would be wrong to read this saga of division and bitterness back into the years of the Attlee government in 1945–51. These divisions, in any case, largely concerned foreign policy and defence questions. Apart from the symbolic fight over Clause Four, there was far less disagreement about the idea of socialism or the priorities of domestic social and

economic policy. By the later fifties, Gaitskell, Bevan, and
Wilson were largely united on a much more flexible definition of nationalization, which did not rule out further public
ownership but emphasized also other methods of gaining
control of 'the commanding heights of the economy' and
stressed the need for public corporations to become more
competitive and enterprising. This was a visible shift of party
opinion, brilliantly demonstrated in Anthony Crosland's
Future of Socialism in 1956. It was argued here that Labour
should henceforth concentrate on the promotion of social
equality through fiscal measures, changes in the distribution
of ownership, reforms in education and the like, rather than
pursue a time-worn and unnecessary debate on nationalization. Towards the achievements of the Attlee government,
there remained an air of respect, even of reverence, in the
fifties. Attlee himself remained an honoured figure, long after
he retired from the party leadership in the autumn of 1955.
In the 1964 general election, he emerged from retirement,
at Harold Wilson's request, to take an active and effective
part in Labour's programme of public meetings. Even in the
1966 election, as a very old man, afflicted by the effects of
a stroke, he made a brief television appearance to appeal for
Labour votes. Wilson's handsome electoral victory in 1966,
which saw Labour winning 364 seats against the Conservatives'
253, was seen as being very much in the mainstream Attlee
tradition. Otherwise, supporters of Gaitskell and Bevan alike
in the fifties, whatever their differences over contemporary
questions, were united in looking back with pride at the great
administration of 1945–51 in which they had all proudly
served. After all, until April 1951, there had been no significant
rebellions; unity and solidarity had largely prevailed. The
Attlee government marked for them the climax of British
democratic socialism. Similarly, the rival followers of both
Denis Healey and Tony Benn appealed to the great tradition
of 1945 and of Attlee himself, during the deputy-leadership
contest in 1981. Michael Foot made much of it during the
election campaign of May–June 1983. Unlike the Lloyd
George administration in 1918–22, this was a post-war
government whose ministers took pride in their involvement.
It was regarded as dynamic and creative in most aspects of

policy, and hailed as such throughout the Labour movement. Further, it was lauded throughout much of the world as the embodiment of Britain's 'middle way', nowhere more so than in the African and Asian third world where the British Labour Party supplied so much ideological inspiration.

There was the further, ambiguous compliment (naturally enough, one much suspected on the Labour left) that the Conservatives after 1951, for all their rhetoric about 'setting the people free', pursued in office a broad policy of continuing the main lines of their Labour predecessors. Butler, Eden, Macmillan, the main Conservative ministers of these years, were all committed to the middle way of social reform and moderation. Churchill himself was anxious to preserve domestic peace in 1951–5, to pave the way for achievements in world diplomacy and to exorcize working-class memories of Tonypandy and the General Strike.[70] At home, the Conservatives followed a highly conciliatory policy towards the unions. Sir Walter Monckton, Churchill's Minister of Labour, was notorious for his solicitude for the wishes of the TUC high command. But his successors, Macleod, Heath, Hare, and Godber, were scarcely less diplomatic. On economic and social policy, civil service pressure alone helped towards ensuring a broad continuity between Labour policies after 1945 and Tory policies after 1951. Apart from iron and steel, and road haulage, both denationalized in 1953 without much outcry, the industries nationalized by Labour were all left intact. There were no sharp reversals in social policy either, with the broad fabric of the welfare state fully sustained, and many appeals to Disraelian traditions of social reform and of 'one nation'. Prescription charges were introduced on the National Health Service, but the first breach in a free service, after all, had been made by Gaitskell in April 1951. Expenditure on the NHS, given a broad endorsement by the 1956 Guillebaud inquiry, went steadily upwards, in the mood of consumer affluence, growing prosperity, and social peace that marked British life for most of the period from 1951 to 1964. Nor was there any great change in fiscal management as the presence of that amiable bipartisan hybrid, 'Mr Butskell',

[70] On this, see Anthony Seldon, *Churchill's Indian Summer* (London, 1981), *passim*.

suggested. The Conservatives generally tended to rely more than Labour on fiscal weapons, which helped account for the sharp slump in the stock-market following the Conservative election victory in October 1951, a slump that continued until well into the new year. Bank rate, steady at 2 per cent during the Attlee period, rose to 4 per cent by March 1952. But the general pattern remained a broad commitment to a mixed economy, and to Keynes-style budgetary planning and demand management. On such matters as the distribution of industry, the Conservatives were zealous to build on Labour's regional policies; there was a marked impetus in the Conservatives' regional programmes during the mild slump of 1959-60, despite the party's known electoral weakness in Wales, Scotland, and the North of England.

In colonial policy, Labour's pursuit of the ideal of a self-governing free Commonwealth was pursued avidly by the Conservatives in Africa, Asia, and South America. In the end, embarrassing and costly colonial wars in Kenya and Cyprus were wound up in good time for the 1959 general election. Jomo Kenyatta and Archbishop Makarios were both released from British gaols to become presidents of Kenya and Cyprus respectively. Colonial Office personnel worked to ensure a broad continuity with the policies of Creech Jones and Griffiths under Labour. Butler duly wound up the Central African Federation in 1962-3, to the dismay of the residual Tory imperialist right wing, while Macmillan spoke in 1960 of the 'wind of change' blowing through Africa and the Commonwealth at the time of South Africa's expulsion from it, very much in tones used by Labour ministers in the past. In foreign affairs, apart from the abberation of Suez in 1956, which was rapidly suppressed, the Conservatives followed a policy, based on the Atlantic alliance, of international conciliation and the search for a diplomatic solution 'at the summit', from Churchill's campaign for 'summit diplomacy' in the early fifties, down to the atomic test-ban treaty in Moscow in 1963. Relations with post-Stalin Russia showed a gradual thaw. No stronger confirmation could have been found of the broad wisdom of the policies pursued by Attlee and his colleagues than in their Conservative successors' respectful affirmation of them.

The record of the Attlee government of 1945–51 can be assessed by varying criteria, absolute or relative. In absolute terms, of course, a socialist revolution did not take place, and British society in general showed remarkably little outward change. This became a standard line of attack from 'the angry young men' of literature and the drama in the fifties. John Osborne in his various plays from 1955 onwards denounced the treachery of Labour leaders for failing in their pledges after the war and ignoring the socialist passion of the workers. Instead, a shabby, reformist compromise had been created, neither inspiring nor efficient. Arnold Wesker's trilogy of plays was an even more powerful affirmation of this line of argument, drawing on the historic socialist roots of Jewish families in London's East End to point the contrast between their faith and the reality of Attlee and Gaitskell's Britain. But, then, Wesker was 'talking about Jerusalem'. Without endorsing this cultural critique, always strong on passion, weak on economic and political analysis, it is certainly possible to agree that the Labour government after 1945 had serious limitations in many aspects of its policy. Nationalization did not proceed beyond the list dictated by the party's manifesto in 1945. It was losing its appeal as early as 1947, and played less and less part in Labour's economic programme thereafter. Labour leaders were now showing a new concern at the dangers of size and of statist centralization; Crossman in 1956 was to write on 'Socialism and the New Despotism', in terms reminiscent of Lord Chief Justice Hewart in the past. Planning, in any meaningful sense, played no prominent part in the government's economic strategy either in the cheap money period of Dalton or the corporate industrial partnership of the Cripps era from late 1947. The means of control, and, even more, the plan itself were lacking. There was no attempt either to democratize industry on the basis of workers' control, copartnership or any other method. Nor, it must be said, did the unions show any particular enthusiasm for this. The drive for exports in the 1948–51 period was impressive and enduring in its effects; but it led to distortions, to a rigidity of the industrial structure based on a small range of traditional over-manned heavy industries, and to a neglect of long-term capital investment and re-equipment which extended its long shadow over Britain's sluggish economic performance from the later fifties onwards. Not until 1953 did new capital investment in Britain reach the level of 1938, back in the 'bad old days' of the thirties.[71]

On the social side, the welfare state did not significantly modify the class system. Indeed, so some have argued, through the benefits conferred on middle-class citizens, it might even have widened the gulf between wage- and salary-earners. Real poverty survived the reforms of 1945–51, long before it was publicized by the searching academic inquiries of Peter Townsend, Brian Abel-Smith, and Dorothy Cole (into such problems as the circumstances of old people) from 1957 onwards.[72] The idea that the welfare state had extended the notion of a basic minimum within the national assistance scheme was effectively exploded; such works as Seebohm Rowntree's optimistic final edition of his study of poverty in York (1951) were seen to be impressionistic and uncritical. The fiscal base for social reform remained a fragile one; indeed, Abel-Smith and others were to show that the notion that the British were taxed with greater severity than their European neighbours was a myth.[73] Between 1945 and 1951, there was no serious taxation of capital gains or of industrial dividends; company profits rose by £276,000,000 (25½ per cent) even in the period January–August 1951.[74] No real effort was made to eliminate, or even partially modify, the maldistribution of wealth and property which remained very pronounced in Britain even after six years of supposedly socialist government. In the early fifties, 1 per cent of the population owned 50 per cent of the private capital in England and Wales. There was no wealth tax; conversely wages for wage-earners gained over prices by perhaps 1 per cent a year between 1946 and 1951. The Labour government, too, displayed much institutional caution. It showed

[71] Andrew Shonfield, op. cit., pp. 173 ff.

[72] See Peter Townsend, *The Family Life of Old People* (London, 1957); Dorothy Cole, *The Economic Circumstances of Old People* (London, 1962); Brian Abel-Smith and Peter Townsend, *The Poor and the Poorest* (London, 1965). Material from the Diamond Commission (above, Chapter 4, note 78), somewhat goes against this.

[73] Brian Abel-Smith, *Labour's Social Plans* (Fabian Tract, 369, 1966), pp. 18–19.

[74] *Financial Times*, 8 Sept. 1951.

a conservative attitude towards the civil service, and almost a reverence for the constitution, from the monarchy and the House of Lords to the fabric of local government which remained much as Lord Salisbury had left it in 1888. In foreign policy, the government found itself caught up in cold-war postures, often to defend old imperialist commitments in Africa and Asia. It took its stand on the premise of a direct Russian military threat to western Europe which later years (after Stalin's death) seemed to show to be increasingly illusory. At the end, the Attlee government committed Britain to a rearmament programme which was economically damaging and politically naïve. The secret decision to commit the country to an independent nuclear weapons programme, which no government minister had the scientific expertise to understand, consorted ill with the proclaimed desire to promote world peace and disarmament.

But it is easy to go too far in criticizing or debunking the Attlee government. Arguments from hindsight often neglect the realities actually confronting the administration in the very different world of 1945. Critiques of that government in particular tend to underestimate the overwhelming financial and economic pressures resulting from the loss of overseas assets, the imbalance of trade, the loss of markets, the shortage of raw materials, and the vast dollar deficit which was the government's *damnosa hereditas* from the war years and from the pre-war heritage of industrial decay. In large areas of policy, the Attlee government had a clear record of achievement and of competence, which acted as a platform for successive governments, Conservative and Labour, throughout the next quarter of a century. The advent of a monetarist Conservative government under Mrs Thatcher in 1979 signalled the first real attempt to wrench Britain out of the Age of Attlee. It received a huge endorsement at the polls in 1983. Yet until late 1983 at least, the economic record of well over three million unemployed, a severe contraction of manufacturing industry, eroding public and social services, and some threat of social and racial disorder, did not suggest that this alternative ideological approach had so far provided more coherent or acceptable answers to Britain's acknowledged problems. The 'new left' critique, adopting some of the rhetoric of the Bevanites of the fifties, but really offering a neo-Marxist diagnosis very different in tone and method, perhaps more akin to the democratic centralism of eastern Europe, with rigid party control, than to the British parliamentary model, had still to be tried. It had not so far seemed likely to command widespread public support, while its effects on the Labour Party had, down to the June 1983 general election, been divisive rather than creative.

In contrast, the Attlee government offered a record of sustained, if erratic, economic growth. It provided a base for the era of affluence from 1952 onwards when much improved terms of foreign trade accompanied a domestic investment boom. Full employment, an abiding priority for the government, involved an immense economic and social shift from the defeatism and stagnation of the twenties and thirties. The welfare state, while conceived to some degree in terms of bipartisan wartime blueprints, meant a substantial reinforcement of the social egalitarianism of the war years, and a recasting of the fiscal system for social ends. Overseas, there was the notable creation of a new Commonwealth founded on the basis of self-government and multiracial equality. The transfer of power in India and Pakistan, very much Attlee's own work, was the outstanding legacy here, a notable contrast to the retreat from empire conducted by governments in France, the Netherlands, Belgium, or Portugal in the forties and fifties. The foreign policy of the Labour government was firmly Atlanticist in emphasis. Since the commitment of the United States to the defence of western Europe was a vital component of that policy, Bevin's creation of the fabric of transatlantic collaboration, from Marshall Aid to NATO, must rank as one of the outstanding achievements by any British foreign minister since the days of the Elder Pitt.

Neither can these policies be reasonably characterized by mild centrism, a precursor of the SDP of the 1980s, nor by a betrayal of the inheritance of socialist convictions through the constraints of office and the blandishments of an allegedly right-wing civil service and the social establishment. On the contrary, the consensual or bipartisan nature of the Labour government's programmes can be exaggerated. The

National Health Service, several nationalization measures, the independence of India were all fiercely resisted at times by the Conservatives or outside pressure groups. In many cases, the most radical ˙available option was taken up. Cripps as Chancellor retained a commitment to high social spending, for all the rigours of austerity. Attlee himself, from the nationalization of hospitals to the recognition of Communist China, often confirmed Kenneth Younger's, perhaps surprising, view of him as 'the outside-left member of the Cabinet'.[75] It was a gifted administration, a government of prima donnas in many ways, but one in which the broad vision of Bevin, the managerial skills of Morrison, the spartan intensity of Cripps, the ebullient authority of Dalton, the charismatic appeal of Bevan, the intellectualism of Gaitskell, the experience of Addison, the administrative flair of Wilson, and the gut class loyalty of Griffiths, Isaacs, Shinwell, and others all welded into some kind of coherent whole. The socialist ideal still retained its validity for all these men and women, with Attlee himself anxious to reinforce it. But this ideal was combined with executive competence in most areas and a zest for power rare in the annals of the somewhat innocent world of the British left.

A contrast can be fruitfully drawn both with the experience of other European countries in the post-1945 period, and with Britain's own earlier post-war experience after 1918. Compared with other countries, the pattern and rhythms of British society showed fewer changes than most, inevitably so as Britain had escaped the rigours of wartime occupation. The performance of the British economy after 1945 was later discussed, unfavourably, at much length by foreign critics. It was noted that, between 1953 and 1960, Britain's share of world manufactured exports fell from 20 per cent to 15 per cent, while West Germany's rose from 15 per cent to 19 per cent. In that period, France increased her exports three times as fast as Britain, and Germany and Italy six times as fast. A British financial journalist wrote a powerful condemnatory work on *The Stagnant Society* in 1961. Of course, in the years since then Britain's economic performance has become

[75] Kenneth Younger, interview transcript, p. 77.

progressively more dismal.[76] In the period 1945–51, however, the performance of the British economy seemed far more dynamic. For much of this six-year span, as has been seen, the nation showed a picture of growth, rapidly rising production, and an export-led boom. Inflation was not a problem (except briefly in 1951) while Bank Rate never rose above 2 per cent. In any case, those who governed Britain in the Attlee years were always anxious to balance economic advance with social and political liberty, as the writings of Evan Durbin and others had proclaimed.[77] The pattern of *dirigiste*-style industrial growth and technical modernization in post-war France was accompanied by an enduring social division and class inequality, symbolized by the continuing strength of the Communist Party, and the alienation of large sections of the working class from the processes of government from 1946 down to Mitterrand's electoral victory in 1981. The events of 1958 and the riots of 1968 were evidence of this. Much the same could be said of Italy with its immense regional disparities. In West Germany the economic performance by the fifties was no doubt miraculous. Industrial production attained heights of expansion Britain had not achieved since the mid-nineteenth century. But Britain's industrial heritage retained deep-rooted problems, quite apart from an institutional conservatism within the worlds both of the trade unions and of management. In addition, as has been noted, the Labour government made a major priority of relating central economic direction with the full panoply of individual liberties and of democratic procedures. Britain in the fifties emerged from the post-war period with its economy comparatively less buoyant, but its political liberties more secure and its intellectual life less fettered than in a West Germany still emerging from the

---

[76] Michael Shanks, *The Stagnant Society* (Penguin edn., Harmondsworth, 1961); for an excellent comparative analysis on this theme, see Henry Phelps Brown, 'What is the British Predicament?', reprinted in C. Feinstein (ed.), *The Managed Economy* (Oxford, 1983), pp. 207–25, in which the slowness of adaptation of our economy to the manufacturing and trading requirements of the western world is shown to be the main constraint on modern British economic development.

[77] Cf. Evan Durbin, *The Politics of Democratic Socialism* (London, 1940), and his chapter in Donald Munro (ed.), *Socialism: the British Way* (London, 1948), pp. 3–29.

trauma of Nazism. British society did not take naturally to the corporate style. Contrasts were also drawn between Britain and smaller thriving European nations such as Austria, Sweden, or Switzerland. But their neutrality rested to some degree on evading the kind of international commitment that the British government felt compelled to make. In putting the memories of appeasement behind it, the Attlee government believed it was undertaking an involvement in world leadership that was inescapable. It flowed from Britain's historic role in the Middle East, from its headship of a world-wide Commonwealth, from its central place in the economic and military union of western Europe, and above all from its relationship with the United States. It was in a multiplicity of roles, so it was believed, that Britain's essential strength lay. The post-war problems of the British economy should always be related to the belief, as widespread in Washington and Moscow as in London, that Britain between 1945 and 1951 was still a great power, and the leader of a struggling, exhausted continent in trying to generate a new and more stable international political and economic order. By this test, Britain in the Attlee years does not emerge badly. If the public mood between 1945 and 1951 was not complacent, neither was it paralysed by defeatism.

There is a great contrast to be drawn also between Britain after 1945 and the experience of the post-1918 Lloyd George coalition, of which the venerable Lord Addison could remind his colleagues with extensive personal recollections. In some ways, the contrast between Britain's government after 1918 and that after 1945—between the 'hard-faced men' of the coupon election and the socialist crusaders at the end of a 'people's war'—may not be as extreme as is sometimes argued. Lloyd George's government was not as reactionary, nor was Attlee's as radical, as is often popularly believed. In social policy, Lloyd George began with a whirl of activity on health, housing, and other matters until deflation and the Geddes Axe descended. On labour policy, the earlier coalition tried to build up the official trade-union leadership and to preserve freedom of access between Downing Street and Unity House. In colonial policy, the Lloyd George government began the policy of disengagement, for instance in Egypt and to some degree in post-Amritsar India. In foreign affairs, Lloyd George himself pursued a policy of peace, in trying to bring the great pariah nations, Germany and the Soviet Union, into the comity of nations, modifying the system of Versailles, and creating a new framework for international reconciliation and economic intercourse.

But, for all that, there remain undeniable contrasts between one post-war government and its successor; they almost all tell heavily in favour of the Labour ministers after 1945. Even before the Lloyd George government fell into final disarray, it was all turning sour, its social policy wrecked by Geddes, its labour policy made a mockery by Black Friday, its imperial policy besmirched by the bloody 'retaliation' in Ireland, its foreign policy mocked by the jingoism of Chanak. Both post-war governments, that of 1919 and of 1945, derived their momentum—indeed, their very existence —from the social radicalism of wartime. The Attlee government, unlike its predecessor, actually kept the momentum going, and added new elements (notably in health) drawn from Labour's own programmes of the thirties, rather than spearheading a reaction against it. A far higher priority was given to social expenditure than after 1918. A prime emphasis was placed on full employment. A decisive commitment was made to removing the discredited managements of the coal and other industries, instead of returning to the follies of 'decontrol' and private capitalism. One corollary was relative industrial peace. In the five years 1918–23, 178,000,000 working days were lost in industrial dispute; in the five years 1945–50, the total was only 9,730,000. Overseas, the contrast between the handling of Ireland after the first world war and the far more sensitive course of policy in India after 1945 is highly suggestive. Britain after 1945 was a less tension-ridden, more unified society than that which emerged after the Lloyd George era after 1918, overlain as the latter was by the aura of corruption and adventurism. This time, the vision of a 'land fit for heroes', so ironically recalled by Aneurin Bevan in *Why not Trust the Tories?* in 1944, was not wantonly forgotten or betrayed. In an area like South Wales, the despair and disillusion that crucified the valleys in the twenties and thirties is in stark contrast to the buoyant optimism after 1945. 'Red Maerdy', a citadel of class bitterness in the twenties, was in the later forties alive with hope and industrial renewal. Britain after 1945 is a part of the usable capital of Britain's political heritage. Britain after 1918 is a world well lost, and lost in a fashion highly damaging to the radical reputation of the Prime Minister of the day.

The Attlee government, then, was a landmark in the history of modern Britain. It may also be concluded, finally, that it was a rare episode in the battle-scarred history of the Labour movement. It offered a crowning achievement of unity and fraternity; in that sense, the perception of Tony Benn, with which this book began, is wholly correct. Throughout its eighty-odd years, the Labour Party has been plagued by the rival tensions of grass-roots pressure for a socialist society and the alternative demands of the realities of power. This dualism has been symbolized, on the one hand, by movements in the constituencies and sometimes in the unions, for socialist advance, and on the other by the control usually imposed by the parliamentary leadership, through the PLP, the conference, the NEC, and the party machine, in ensuring that the party's reforming zeal is duly tempered by realism. In practical terms, this is often expressed through the tension between the party conference, with its activists' cries for more socialism, and the PLP, with its appeal to gradualism. Bevanite 'advance' and Morrisonian 'consolidation' seem to embody these two impulses, as do perhaps Bennite radicalism and Healeyite moderation in a later age. In fact, the structural problem for the Labour Party is uniquely difficult and has often led to schism and crisis. Neither of the two standard models used to explain the operation of the Party can be accepted. The left-wing claim that Labour is a uniquely democratic party, different in character from the authoritarian model of the Tories, flies in the face of much of the party's history from 1900 onwards. Equally, the view of Robert McKenzie that the idea of inner party democracy is basically a fraud, and that in its authoritarian structure the Labour Party is virtually identical with the Tory enemy, also conflicts with key

features of the history of British twentieth-century democratic socialism.

The truth may be that Labour has had two different
impulses within it, almost impossible to reconcile. The party
conference and the parliamentary party embody them both
—the streak of populist protest contrasted with the urge for
power. The dualism was institutionalized for ever in the 1918
party constitution. In Michael Foot's perceptive words, the
party created two sovereign bodies, neither willing to bow
the knee to the other.[78] In the early 1980s, under Foot's
leadership, the problem remained unresolved. Historically,
the Labour Party always functioned best in a system of
pluralism, with the divergent tendencies and pressures recognized but neither allowed to dominate. In Keir Hardie's wise
words, back in 1907, applicable both to the idea of a Labour
alliance between socialists and trade-unionists, and to the
structural relationship between the party conference and the
party in parliament, 'there must be free play between the
sections'. Otherwise, Hardie added, 'they would be in for
a spill'.[79] There have been 'spills' aplenty in Labour's history.
After the creation of the 'federal hybrid' in 1918, tension
continued throughout the twenties between a parliamentary
phalanx under MacDonald and external grass-roots pressures,
most spectacularly in the General Strike. In the crisis of
August 1931, the external influence of the TUC brought
down the second Labour government, despite the existence
of a clear majority in the Cabinet in favour of cuts in unemployment benefit. In the thirties, the stresses between
political and industrial militancy—often of a Popular Front
type—and a centrist parliamentary party and TUC continued
unabated. Again, the years after 1951 saw the problems
recur with greater ferocity. The explosion over CND at the
party conferences in 1960–1, the growing lack of authority
of Labour governments under Wilson and Callaghan, in the
face of trade-union unwillingness to act politically and
a rising left-wing tide in the constituency parties, all testified

[78] Michael Foot, 'My Kind of Socialism' (*Observer* publications, London,
1982), p. 7; cf. *idem*, 'The Labour Party and Parliamentary Democracy', *The
Guardian*, 10 Sept. 1981.
[79] Keir Hardie's speech to Labour Party conference, 1907, cited in Kenneth O.
Morgan, *Keir Hardie: Radical and Socialist*, p. 168.

to the growing disorder in the party. The emergence of Bennite-type left-wing activism in the seventies, and the insistence that party leaders be curbed at every point—shadow Cabinet elections, the drafting of a manifesto, the selection of candidates, the election of a leader, the policies to be enacted by a future Labour government—was the apotheosis of a populist strain basic to Labour's outlook. It was countered by the more traditional centrism avowed by the Labour Solidarity Committee associated with Healey, Shore, Hattersley, and others.[80] The outcome remained uncertain down to June 1983, with Michael Foot, as a left-wing leader with a Tribunite, Bevanite, unilateralist background, committed to enforcing the stamp of the parliamentary leadership. The old rebel now became, to some degree, the advocate of moderation, solidarity and discipline. Labour's very future as a party often seemed in doubt. The 1983 general election, which saw Labour's total of seats fall to 209 and its share of the poll slump to 27.7 per cent, the lowest since 1918, reinforced these fears. But the fault lay neither in the malign, neo-Marxist designs of Benn, nor in the blinkered parliamentarism of Healey and Shore, nor again in any lack of skills of leadership shown by Foot. All could legitimately claim to be custodians of the movement's heritage. The problem was inherent in the very ambiguity and fluidity of Labour as an organized party. It would confront Neil Kinnock, another traditional left-winger elected to succeed Foot as party leader in October 1983, as it had confronted all his predecessors since the days of Keir Hardie back in 1906.

In the years 1945–51, everything suddenly worked, and with remarkably little difficulty. A number of different factors gave the Labour movement a purpose and united quality it had never possessed before, or perhaps showed again. There was the existence of a powerful, respected, experienced group of dominant leaders, Attlee, Bevin, Morrison, Dalton, Cripps, whose authority was almost unquestioned. There was the unifying influence of the war years with their drive for social equality and radical reform. There was the uniquely close relationship between the major unions

[80] See David Kogan and Maurice Kogan, *The Battle for the Labour Party* (London, 1981), especially pp. 136 ff.

and the political leadership at all levels of the party. There were clearly defined priorities on policy embodied in the crisp, precise manifesto of 1945. There was a large homogeneous, self-conscious working class, with perhaps two-thirds engaged in manual work in manufacturing or other industry, or in service employment. Home-owning skilled workers (the C2s of sociologists in the 1980s) were a relatively small, if growing, minority. Finally, there was the overwhelming mood of popular idealism released by the ending of six years of total war, an overpowering urge that a people's war should this time be followed by a people's peace. These imperatives for unity served broadly to unite the Labour Cabinet, despite all policy arguments and economic hammer-blows, down to Bevan's tragic, and perhaps unnecessary, break with his colleagues in 1951. They served to make the parliamentary leadership, the national executive, Transport House, and activist opinion in the constituencies identified with one another as never before. There was an urge for power as vigorous in the heart, mind, and soul of Aneurin Bevan as in the case of Herbert Morrison. The Attlee government was thus unique in its structural cohesiveness and in its legislative vitality. Its legacy lived on in a broad influence over the Labour and progressive left, over political and economic thought and, indeed, over much of British intellectual and cultural life for a full quarter of a century after 1951. It was without doubt the most effective of all Labour governments, perhaps amongst the most effective of any British government since the passage of the 1832 Reform Act and the first partial advance of the dynamic of democratization in our political processes. It helped merge its philosophy of social democracy with older strains in a native libertarian tradition, just as Aneurin Bevan was able legitimately to quote Colonel Rainboro of the Levellers of 1647 in analysing the constant ferment between democracy, property, and poverty.[81] It brought the British Labour movement to the zenith of its achievement as a political instrument for humanitarian reform. But it did so by evading, rather than resolving, those dilemmas inherent in the potent, beguiling vision of socialism in our time.

[81] Aneurin Bevan, *Why not Trust the Tories?*, pp. 88–9.

Appendix I
Members of the Cabinet, July 1945–October 1951

Prime Minister: C. R. Attlee

Lord Chancellor: Lord Jowitt

Lord President: Herbert Morrison
(from 9 Mar. 1951) Lord Addison

Lord Privy Seal: Arthur Greenwood
(from 14 Apr. 1947) Lord Inman
(from 7 Oct. 1947) Lord Addison
(from 9 Mar. 1951) Ernest Bevin
(from 26 Apr.) Richard Stokes

Chancellor of the Exchequer: Hugh Dalton
(from 13 Nov. 1947) Sir Stafford Cripps
(from 19 Oct. 1950) Hugh Gaitskell

Minister of Economic Affairs:[1]   (29 Sept.–13 Nov. 1947) Sir Stafford Cripps

Foreign Secretary: Ernest Bevin
(from 9 Mar. 1951) Herbert Morrison

Home Secretary: Chuter Ede

First Lord of the Admiralty: A. V. Alexander (post not in Cabinet from 4 Oct. 1946)

Minister of Agriculture and Fisheries: Tom Williams

Secretary of State for Air: Lord Stansgate (post not in Cabinet from 6 Oct. 1946)

Minister of Civil Aviation: (31 May 1948 to 28 Feb. 1950) Lord Pakenham (post not in Cabinet from 28 Feb. 1950)

Colonial Secretary: George Hall
(from 4 Oct. 1946) Arthur Creech-Jones
(from 28 Feb. 1950) James Griffiths

[1] Post combined with Exchequer, 13 Nov. 1947. Held by Hugh Gaitskell but outside the Cabinet, 28 Feb. to 19 Oct. 1950.

Secretary of State for the
   Dominions (renamed
   Secretary of State for
   Commonwealth Relations,
   7 July 1947):   Lord Addison
                                (from 7 Oct. 1947) Philip Noel-Baker
                                (from 28 Feb. 1950) Patrick Gordon-
                                     Walker

Minister of Defence: C. R. Attlee
                                (from 20 Dec. 1946) A. V. Alexander
                                (from 28 Feb. 1950) Emanuel Shinwell

Minister of Education: Ellen Wilkinson
                                (from 10 Feb. 1947) George Tomlinson

Minister of Fuel and Power: Emanuel Shinwell (post not in Cabinet
                                     from 7 Oct. 1947)

Minister of Health: Aneurin Bevan (post not in Cabinet
                                     from 17 Jan. 1951)

Secretary of State for India
   and Burma: Lord Pethick-Lawrence
                                (from 17 Apr. 1947) Lord Listowel
                                (post abolished, 4 Jan. 1948)

Minister of Labour and
   National Service: George Isaacs
                                (from 17 Jan. 1951) Aneurin Bevan
                                (from 24 Apr. 1951) Alfred Robens

Chancellor of Duchy of
   Lancaster:[2]   (from 31 May 1948) Hugh Dalton
                                (from 28 Feb. 1950) Lord Alexander

Paymaster General:[3]   (9 July 1946 to 5 Mar. 1947) Arthur
                                     Greenwood
                                (2 July 1948 to 1 Apr. 1949) Lord
                                     Addison

Minister without Portfolio: (4 Oct. to 20 Dec. 1946) A. V. Alex-
                                     ander

Secretary of State for
   Scotland: J. Westwood
                                (from 7 Oct. 1947) A. Woodburn
                                (from 28 Feb. 1950) Hector McNeil

[2] Post not in Cabinet previously.
[3] No appointment previously; Lord MacDonald, Paymaster-General from
1 Apr. 1949 not in the Cabinet.

*Minister of Town and Country
Planning* (renamed Local
Government and Planning,
31 Jan. 1951):   (from 28 Feb. 1950) Hugh Dalton

*President of the Board of
Trade*:   Sir Stafford Cripps
(from 29 Sept. 1947) Harold Wilson
(from 24 Apr. 1951) Sir Hartley Shawcross

Secretary of State for War: J. J. Lawson (post not in Cabinet from
4 Oct. 1946)

Appendix II
Contested By-elections,
July 1945–October 1951[1]

Date	Constituency	Result	Swing from Lab. to Cons.
1945			
1 Oct.	Smethwick	Lab. hold	−2.9
2 Oct.	Ashton-under-Lyne	Lab. hold	−3.1
3 Oct.	East Edinburgh	Lab. hold	−2.1
30 Oct.	Monmouth	Cons. hold	8.2
31 Oct.	City of London	Cons. hold	
14 Nov.	Bromley	Cons. hold	−0.2
15 Nov.	Bournemouth	Cons. hold	
20 Nov.	South Kensington	Cons. hold	
13 Dec.	North Tottenham	Lab. hold	8.2
1946			
31 Jan.	Preston	Lab. hold	2.3
7 Feb.	South Ayrshire	Lab. hold	2.3
12 Feb.	Glasgow, Cathcart	Cons. hold	1.1
21 Feb.	Heywood and Radcliffe	Lab. hold	0.5
13–18 Mar.	Combined Eng. Universities	Cons. gain from Ind.	
4 June	Ogmore	Lab. hold	
6 June	Down	Cons. gain from Ind. Cons.	
22 July	Bexley	Lab. hold	11.1
23 July	Pontypool	Lab. hold	4.1
25 July	Battersea North	Lab. hold	4.1
29 Aug.	Glasgow, Bridgeton	ILP hold	
19 Nov.	Rotherhithe	Lab. hold	
20 Nov.	North Paddington	Lab. hold	5.9
22–7 Nov.	Combined Scots. Universities	Cons. gain from Ind.	
26 Nov.	South Aberdeen	Cons. hold	2.6
5 Dec.	Aberdare	Lab. hold	
5 Dec.	Kilmarnock	Lab. hold	−4.2

[1] The term 'Conservative' includes National, National Liberal and Conservative, National Liberal, Unionist, and other variations.

Date	Constituency	Result	Swing from Lab. to Cons.

1947

11 Feb.	Normanton	Lab. hold	3.3
7 May	Jarrow	Lab. hold	5.1
11 Sept.	Liverpool, Edge Hill	Lab. hold	10.2
25 Sept.	West Islington	Lab. hold	8.6
26 Nov.	Gravesend	Lab. hold	6.8
21 Nov.	Howdenshire	Lab. hold	5.9
27 Nov.	East Edinburgh	Lab. hold	1.5
4 Dec.	Epsom	Cons. hold	8.8

1948

28 Jan.	Glasgow, Camlachie	Cons. gain from ILP[2]	
18 Feb.	Paisley	Lab. hold	4.7
4 Mar.	Wigan	Lab. hold	6.5
5 Mar.	Armagh	Cons. hold	
11 Mar.	North Croydon	Cons. hold	8.2
24 Mar.	Brigg	Lab. hold	4.3
29 Apr.	Central Southwark	Lab. hold	6.5
30 Sept.	Glasgow, Gorbals	Lab. hold	17.0[3]
7 Oct.	Stirling and Falkirk Burghs	Lab. hold	2.9
13 Nov.	Edmonton	Lab. hold	16.2
25 Nov.	Glasgow, Hillhead	Cons. hold	6.0

1949

17 Feb.	Batley and Morley	Lab. hold	5.6
24 Feb.	South Hammersmith	Lab. hold	5.2
10 Mar.	North St. Pancras	Lab. hold	5.6
16 Mar.	Sowerby	Lab. hold	6.9
21 July	West Leeds	Lab. hold	10.5
8 Dec.	South Bradford	Lab. hold	5.3

1950

5 Apr.	Sheffield, Neepsend	Lab. hold	0.8
25 Apr.	West Dunbartonshire	Lab. hold	0.4
4 May	Brighouse and Spenborough	Lab. hold	1.7
28 Sept.	North-East Leicester	Lab. hold	3.7
25 Oct.	Glasgow, Scotstoun	Cons. hold	1.6

[2] The Revd Campbell Stephen, elected as ILP member in 1945, had joined the Labour Party before his death.

[3] A Communist candidate intervened in the by-election to take 16.8 per cent of the vote.

Date	Constituency	Result	Swing from Lab. to Cons.
1950 (Cont)			
2 Nov.	Oxford	Cons. hold	4.4
16 Nov.	Birmingham, Handsworth	Cons. hold	5.6
29 Nov.	West Belfast	Cons. hold	
30 Nov.	South-East Bristol	Lab. hold	7.2
30 Nov.	Abertillery	Lab. hold	0.6
1951			
15 Feb.	West Bristol	Cons. hold	17.0
5 Apr.	Ormskirk	Cons. hold	6.2
21 Apr.	Harrow West	Cons. hold	7.5
14 June	East Woolwich	Lab. hold	3.7
21 June	Westhoughton	Lab. hold	1.9

Appendix III

United Kingdom Balance of Payments, 1946–1953 (in £ millions)

	1946	1947	1948	1949
Current account debits:	1,836	2,212	2,347	2,545
Current account credits:	1,538	1,769	2,348	2,576
Balance	−298	−443	+1	+31

	1950	1951	1952	1953
Current account debits:	2,925	4,259	3,741	3,640
Current account credits:	3,225	3,852	3,871	3,718
US defence aid (grant less US share of counterpart)		+4	+121	+102
Balance	+300	−403	+251	+180

Source: *United Kingdom Balance of Payments, 1946 to 1955* (Cmd. 9585), PP (1955–56), xix, 221 ff.

Appendix IV

United Kingdom Net Gold and Dollar Deficit/Surplus, 1946–1952 (in £ millions)

1946:	January–June	−80
	July–December	−146
1947:	January–June	−469
	July–December	−555
1948:	January–June	−254
	July–December	−169
1949:	January–June	−239
	July–December	−142
1950:	January–June	+78
	July–December	+209
1951:	January–June	+148
	July–December	−564
1952:	January–June	−232
	July–December	+57

Sources: *Annual Statements on United Kingdom Balance of Payments*

Appendix V

Gross Domestic Fixed Capital Formation
at Current Prices, 1945–1952
(in £ millions)

	Ships	Vehicles	Plant & Machinery	Houses	Other New Buildings	Total
1945	40	50	120	140		350
1946	50	120	200	550		925
1947	70	160	360	330	280	1,199
1948	86	163	500	337	336	1,422
1949	80	192	562	332	411	1,577
1950	74	188	643	331	464	1,700
1951	59	197	752	376	505	1,889
1952	57	203	795	494	557	2,106

Source: C. H. Feinstein, *National Income, Expenditure and Output of the United Kingdom, 1855–1965* (Cambridge, 1972) table 39.

Select Bibliography

A. MANUSCRIPT COLLECTIONS

1. *Public Records*

Cabinet: CAB 21 (Registered files; Prime Minister's briefs)

CAB 87 (War Cabinet Committees on Reconstruction)

CAB 124 (Lord President of the Council secretariat files)

CAB 128 (Cabinet Conclusions, 1945–52)

CAB 129 (Cabinet Papers, 1945–52)

CAB 130–134 (Cabinet committees: minutes and memoranda)

Colonial Office: CO 537
Defence: DEFE 4, 6 (Chiefs of Staff)
Dominions Office: DO 35

DO 121

Foreign Office: FO 371

FO 800 (Bevin Papers)

Health: MH 77
Home Office: HO 45
Housing: HLG 102 (Miscellaneous files)

HLG 104 (Planning and Development files)

Labour: LAB 10 (Industrial Relations)

LAB 16 (Solicitors' Department)

LAB 43 (Private Office papers)

Prime Minister's Office: PREM 4 (1945)

PREM 8 (1945–51)

Treasury: T 161 (Supply files)

T 171 (Budget and Finance Bill papers)

T 222 (Organization and Methods Division)

T 225 (Defence Policy and Material Division)

T 227 (Social Services Division)

T 228 (Trade and Industry Division)

T 229–238 (Central Economic Planning Staff)

T 247 (Keynes Papers)

2. *Private Papers*

Lord Addison papers (Bodleian Library, Oxford, and in private hands).
A. V. Alexander papers (Churchill College, Cambridge).
Lord Ammon papers (University of Hull), courtesy of Mr N. Higson.

C. R. Attlee papers (Bodleian Library, Oxford, and Churchill College, Cambridge).

Ernest Bevin papers (Churchill College, Cambridge).

Lord Citrine papers (British Library of Political and Economic Science).

G. D. H. Cole papers (Nuffield College, Oxford).

Arthur Creech Jones papers (Rhodes House Library, Oxford).

Sir Stafford Cripps papers (Nuffield College, Oxford). Mr Maurice Shock has kindly assured me that the Cripps papers in his possession at the University of Leicester contain no material of significance for this book.

Hugh Dalton papers (British Library of Political and Economic Science).

Clement Davies papers (National Library of Wales, Aberystwyth).

S. O. Davies papers (University College, Swansea).

Desmond Donnelly papers (NLW, Aberystwyth).

Tom Driberg papers (Christ Church Library, Oxford).

J. Chuter Ede papers (British Library and Surrey Record Office).

Huw T. Edwards papers (NLW, Aberystwyth).

Hugh Gaitskell papers (Nuffield College, Oxford), courtesy of Dr Philip Williams.

Victor Gollancz papers (University of Warwick: Modern Records Centre, MS 157).

Arthur Greenwood papers (Bodleian Library, Oxford).

James Griffiths papers (NLW, Aberystwyth).

Lord Inverchapel papers (Bodleian Library, Oxford).

Harold Laski papers (Labour Party headquarters).

Lady Megan Lloyd George papers (NLW, Aberystwyth, MSS 20485C–20491E).

R. W. G. Mackay papers (British Library of Political and Economic Science).

Herbert Morrison papers (Nuffield College, Oxford).

Philip Noel-Baker papers (Churchill College, Cambridge).

Morgan Phillips papers (Labour Party headquarters).

Richard Stokes papers (Bodleian Library, Oxford).

George Strauss interview transcript (Nuffield College, Oxford).

Lord Woolton papers (Bodleian Library, Oxford).

Kenneth Younger interview transcript (Nuffield College, Oxford).

3. *Other Papers*

Ivor Bulmer-Thomas: Correspondence with the author, 1982.

Conservative Party
(Central Office):   National Union minutes, 1945–52.
                      Sub-Committee on Political Education minutes, 1945–52.
                      CPC material.

Labour Party
(Walworth Road):   National Executive Committee minutes, 1940–51.

Policy Committee minutes, 1940–55.
General Secretary's correspondence (GS 1–35),
1944–52.
International department archive, 1944–52.

The Queen's College, Oxford: Governing Body Minutes, 1947–8.

University of Warwick
Modern Records
Centre: MS 126 Minutes and Record of General Execu-
tive Council, Transport and General Workers'
Union, 1945–51.
MS 127 Reports and Proceedings, National
Union of Railwaymen, 1945–51.
MS 175 Minute books and papers, National
Union of Seamen, 1947–9.

B. OFFICIAL PAPERS

Hansard, *Parliamentary Debates*, Fifth Series.
Census of England and Wales, 1951: Report with Appendices.
Annual Reports of the Ministry of Health, 1946–52.
Annual Reports of the Ministry of Labour, 1946–52.
Annual Statements on United Kingdom Balance of Payments, 1946–52.
Housing returns (quarterly), 1945–51.
Memorandum on Ministry of Education estimates for 1945 (Cmd. 6629), PP (1944–5), ix. 63.
Report on Standing Committee C on the National Health Service Bill, PP (1945–6), viii. 369.
Report of the Bank of England Commissioners (Cmd. 7115), PP (1946–7), x. 105.
Statement on the Economic Considerations affecting relations between Employers and Employed (Cmd. 7018), PP (1946–7), xix. 1195.
Housing Programme for 1947 (Cmd. 7021), PP (1946–7), xix. 567.
Annual Report of the National Coal Board for the year ending 31st December 1946, PP (1947–8), x. 351.
Annual Report of the National Coal Board for the year ending 31st December 1947, PP (1947–8), x. 387.
The Colonial Empire (1947–1948) (Cmd. 7433), PP (1947–8), xi. 47.
Statement on Personal Incomes, Costs and Prices (Cmd. 7321), PP (1947–8), xxii. 1007.
Economic Survey for 1948 (Cmd. 7344), PP (1947–8), xxii. 733.
Total Provision of Housing Accommodation in Great Britain as at 31st July 1948 (Cmd. 7507), PP (1947–8), xxii. 1.
Economic Survey for 1949 (Cmd. 7647), PP (1948–9), xxix. 509.
The House of Lords' reasons for insisting on Amendments to the Iron and Steel Bill, PP (1948–9), iii. 329.
Events leading up to the Signature of the North Atlantic Treaty, with a Commentary on the Text (Cmd. 7692), PP (1948–9), xxxiv. 665.

The Colonial Territories (1949–50) (Cmd. 7958), PP (1950), viii. 415.

Economic Survey for 1950 (Cmd. 7915), PP (1950), xix. 577.

Annual Report of the National Coal Board for the year ending 31st December 1950 PP (1950–1), x. 129.

Economic Survey for 1951 (Cmd. 8195), PP (1950–1), xxvii. 73.

Central African Territories: Report of Conference on Closer Association, 1951 (Cmd. 8233), PP (1950–1), x. 417.

United Kingdom Balance of Payments, 1946–50 (Cmd. 8201), PP (1950–1), xxi. 93.

United Kingdom Balance of Payments, 1948–51 (Cmd. 8379), PP (1950–1), xxi. 133.

Annual Report of the National Coal Board for the year ending 31st December 1951, PP (1951–2), viii. 675.

Report and Statement of Accounts for the period ending 30th September 1951: Iron and Steel Corporation of Great Britain, PP (1951–2), xvi. 1.

Economic Survey for 1952 (Cmd. 8509), PP (1951–2), xxv. 203.

United Kingdom Balance of Payments, 1946 to 1955 (Cmd. 9585), PP (1955–6), xix. 221.

C. NEWSPAPERS, PERIODICALS, AND REPORTS

1. *Newspapers*

Baner ac Amserau Cymru
Daily Herald
Daily Telegraph
Daily Worker
Evening Standard
Financial Times
Manchester Guardian
News Chronicle
Sunday Times
The Times
Western Mail

2. *Periodicals*

The Banker
British Medical Journal
The Economist
Foreign Affairs
Horizon
International Affairs
The Lancet
The Listener
Lloyds Bank Review
Local Government Chronicle
Local Government Journal
The Medical Officer

Medicine Today and Tomorrow
New Statesman and Nation
Political Quarterly
The Practitioner
Socialist Commentary
Socialist Outlook
The Spectator
Tribune

3. *Reports*

Annual or Quarterly Reports of the Following Organizations:

Conservative Party
Council for Wales and Monmouthshire
Federation of British Industries
Iron and Steel Confederation
Labour Party
National Coal Board
National Union of Railwaymen
Trades Union Congress
Transport and General Workers' Union

D. BIOGRAPHIES AND MEMOIRS

Arranged in order of subject; place of publication London unless otherwise stated.

Acheson, Dean, *Present at the Creation: My Years at the State Department* (1970).
Addison, Lord, *Portrait of a Progressive: the Political Career of Christopher, Viscount Addison*, by Kenneth and Jane Morgan (Oxford, 1980).
Attlee, Clement, *Mr. Attlee*, by Roy Jenkins (1948).
— *Labour's Big Three. A biographical study of Clement Attlee, Herbert Morrison and Ernest Bevin*, by J. T. Murphy (1948).
— *As it happened* (1954).
— *A Prime Minister Remembers*, by Francis Williams (1961).
— 'Clement Attlee', in *A Prime Minister on Prime Ministers* by Sir Harold Wilson (1977).
— *Attlee*, by Kenneth Harris (1982).
Beaverbrook, Lord, *Beaverbrook*, by A. J. P. Taylor (1972).
Bevan, Aneurin, *Aneurin Bevan*, by Vincent Brome (1953).
— *Aneurin Bevan*, vols. i and ii, by Michael Foot (1962, 1973).
— *My Life with Nye*, by Jennie Lee (1980).
Beveridge, Sir William, *William Beveridge: a Biography* by José Harris (Oxford, 1977).
Bevin, Ernest, *The Life and Times of Ernest Bevin*, vol. ii (1967), and *Ernest Bevin: Foreign Secretary 1945-1951* (1983), by Alan Bullock.
Blackburn, Raymond, *I am an Alcoholic* (1959).

Bracken, Brendan, *Brendan Bracken*, by C. E. Lysaght (1979).
Brown, George, *In my Way* (1971).
Byrnes, James, *Speaking Frankly* (1947).
Cadogan, Sir Alexander, *The Diaries of Sir Alexander Cadogan, 1938–1945*, ed. David Dilks (1971).
Chandos, Viscount, *The Memoirs of Lord Chandos* (1962).
Citrine, Lord, *Two Careers* (1967).
Cole, G. D. H., *G. D. H. Cole and Socialist Democracy*, by A. W. Wright (Oxford, 1979).
Cripps, Sir Stafford, *The Life of Richard Stafford Cripps*, by Colin Cooke (1957).
Crosland, Anthony, *Tony Crosland*, by Susan Crosland (1981).
Crossman, Richard, *Palestine Mission: a personal record* (1947).
Dalton, Hugh, *Memoirs, 1931–45: the Fateful Years* (1957).
— *Memoirs, 1945–60: High Tide and After* (1962).
Dash, Jack, *Good Morning Brothers!* (1969).
Davenport, Nicholas, *Memoirs of a City Radical* (1974).
Deakin, Arthur, *Trade Union Leadership*, by V. L. Allen (1957).
Dixon, Sir Pierson, *Double Diploma: the Life of Sir Pierson Dixon*, by Piers Dixon (1968).
Driberg, Tom, *Ruling Passions* (1977).
Duff, Peggy, *Left, Left, Left* (1971).
Eden, Anthony, *Anthony Eden, a Biography*, by David Carlton (1981).
Foot, Michael, *Michael Foot*, by Simon Hoggart and David Leigh (1981).
Forrestal, James, *The Forrestal Diaries*, ed. W. Millis (1952).
Gaitskell, Hugh, *Hugh Gaitskell, 1906–63*, ed. W. T. Rodgers (1964).
— *Hugh Gaitskell*, by Philip Williams (1979).
— *The Diary of Hugh Gaitskell, 1945–1956*, ed. Philip Williams (1983).
George VI, *King George VI*, by J. W. Wheeler-Bennett (1958).
Gladwyn, Lord, *The Memoirs of Lord Gladwyn* (1972).
Griffiths, James, *Pages from Memory* (1969).
— *James Griffiths and his Times*, by J. B. Smith *et al.* (Cardiff, 1977).
Healey, Denis, *Denis Healey and the Politics of Power*, by B. Reed and G. Williams (1971).
Hopkinson, Tom, *Of this our Time* (1982).
Horner, Arthur, *Incorrigible Rebel* (1960).
Isaacs, George, *George Isaacs*, by G. G. Eastwood (1952).
Jay, Douglas, *Change and Fortune: a Political Record* (1980).
Keynes, J. M., *Essays on John Maynard Keynes*, ed. Milo Keynes (Cambridge, 1975).
— *The Collected Writings of John Maynard Keynes*, ed. D. Moggridge, xxiv–xxvii (1979).
Kilmuir, Lord, *Political Adventure: the memoirs of the Earl of Kilmuir* (1964).
Kirkpatrick, Sir Ivone, *The Inner Circle* (1959).
Laski, Harold, *Harold Laski*, by Granville Eastwood (1977).
Lee, Jennie, *This Great Journey* (1963).

Longford, Lord, *Born to Believe* (1953).
Macleod, Iain, *Iain Macleod*, by Nigel Fisher (1973).
Macmillan, Harold, *Tides of Fortune, 1945–55* (1969).
Mallaby, George, *From my Level* (1965).
Manning, Leah, *A Life for Education: an Autobiography* (1970).
Maudling, Reginald, *Memoirs* (1978).
Montgomery, Lord, *Lord Montgomery of Alamein*, by Alun Chalfont (1976).
Morrison, Herbert, *Autobiography* (1960).
— *Herbert Morrison: Portrait of a Politician*, by Bernard Donoughue and G. W. Jones (1973).
Nehru, Jawaharlal, *Jawaharlal Nehru: a Biography*, vol. i, by S. Gopal (1975).
Nicolson, Sir Harold, *Harold Nicolson: a Biography*, vol. ii. 1930–68, by James Lees-Milne (1981).
Nkrumah, Kwame, *Autobiography* (1957).
Orwell, George, *George Orwell: a Life*, by Bernard Crick (1980).
— *George Orwell, a Personal Memoir*, by T. R. Fyvel (1982).
— *Collected Essays, Journalism and Letters of George Orwell*, vol. iv, 1945–50, ed. Sonia Orwell and Ian Angus (rev. edn., 1981).
Parker, John, *Father of the House* (1982).
Prothero, Cliff, *Recount* (Ormskirk and Northridge, 1982).
Redcliffe-Maud, Lord, *Experiences of an Optimist* (1981).
Shinwell, Emanuel, *Conflict without Malice* (1955).
Silverman, Sidney, *Sidney Silverman, Rebel in Parliament*, by Emrys Hughes (1969).
Strachey, John, *John Strachey*, by Hugh Thomas (1973).
Strang, Lord, *Home and Abroad* (1956).
Summerskill, Edith, *A Woman's World* (1967).
Swinton, Lord, *Lord Swinton*, by J. A. Cross (Oxford, 1982).
Tawney, R. H., *R. H. Tawney and his Times*, by Ross Terrill (1974).
Tomlinson, George, *George Tomlinson: a Biography*, by Fred Blackburn (1954).
Truman, Harry S., *Memoirs*, vol. ii, *Years of Trial and Hope* (1956).
Wavell, Earl, *The Viceroy's Journal*, ed. Penderel Moon (Oxford, 1973).
Wigg, George, *George Wigg* (1972).
Wilkinson, Ellen, *Ellen Wilkinson*, by Betty D. Vernon (1982).
Williams, Lord, *Digging for Britain* (1965).
Wilson, Sir Harold, *Sir Harold Wilson: Yorkshire's Walter Mitty*, by Andrew Roth (1977).
Winterton, Earl, *Orders of the Day* (1953).

Biographical information was also obtained from the *Dictonary of National Biography* (supplements for 1941–50, 1951–60 and 1961–70); *Dod's Parliamentary Companion; The Times: the House of Commons* (for 1945, 1950, 1951 and 1955); and *Who's Who*.

E. OTHER PUBLISHED WORKS

Place of publication London unless otherwise stated.

Abel-Smith, Brian, *The Hospitals, 1800–1948* (1964).
Addison, Paul, *The Road to 1945* (1975).
Alexander, G. M., *The Prelude to the Truman Doctrine* (Oxford, 1982).
Anderson, P., and R. Blackburn (eds.), *Towards Socialism* (1965).
Attlee, C. R., *The Labour Party in Perspective* (1937).
— *Purpose and Policy* (1946).
Barker, Elizabeth, *Britain in a Divided Europe, 1945–1970* (1971).
Barker, Rodney, *Education and Politics, 1900–1951* (Oxford, 1972).
Barry, E. Eldon, *Nationalisation in British Politics* (1965).
Bartlett, C. J., *The Long Retreat* (1972).
Beer, Samuel, *Modern British Politics* (1965).
Beloff, Max, *New Dimensions in Foreign Policy* (1961).
Bentley, Michael, and John Stevenson (eds.), *High and Low Politics in Modern Britain* (Oxford, 1983).
Bethell, Nicholas, *The Palestine Triangle* (1979).
Bevan, Aneurin, *Why not trust the Tories?* (1944).
— *Democratic Values* (1950).
— *In Place of Fear* (1952).
Blake, Robert, *A History of Rhodesia* (1977).
Bonham, J., *The Middle Class Vote* (1955).
Boyd, Francis, *British Politics in Transition, 1945–63* (1964).
Brady, R. A., *Crisis in Britain* (Cambridge, 1950).
Brogan, Colm, *Our New Masters* (1948).
— *Patriots, my Foot!* (1949).
Brown, E. H. Phelps, *The Origins of Trade Union Power* (Oxford, 1983).
Burn, Duncan, *The Steel Industry, 1939–1959* (Cambridge, 1961).
Burridge, T. D., *British Labour and Hitler's War* (1976).
Butler, David, *The British General Election of 1951* (1952).
Butt Philip, Alan, *The Welsh Question, 1945–1970* (Cardiff, 1975).
Cairncross, A. K. (ed.), *The Scottish Economy* (Cambridge, 1954).
Cairncross, A. K., and B. Eichengreen, *Sterling in Decline* (Oxford, 1983).
Calder, Angus, *The People's War*, Panther edn. (1971).
Calvocoressi, Peter, *The British Experience*, 1945–75 (1978).
— (ed.), *Survey of International Affairs, 1939–52* (1952–4).
Catlin, G. (ed.), *New Trends in Socialism* (1935).
Chester, D. N., *The Nationalized Industries* (1951).
Clarke, Sir Richard, *Anglo-American Economic Collaboration in War and Peace, 1942–1949* (Oxford, 1982).
Cleary, E. J., *The Building Society Movement* (1965).
Clegg, Hugh, and T. E. Chester, *The Future of Nationalisation* (Oxford, 1953).
Cohen, Sir Andrew, *British Policy in Changing Africa* (1959).
Cole, G. D. H., *The National Coal Board* (1948).
— *Facts for Socialists* (rev. edn., 1949).

—— *Labour's Second Term* (1949).
—— *The Post-War Condition of Britain* (1956).
Cole, Margaret, *The General Election of 1945 and After* (1945).
—— *Miners and the Board* (1949).
Cook, Chris, *A Short History of the Liberal Party, 1900–1976* (1976).
Cook, Chris, and J. Ramsden (eds.), *Trends in British Politics since 1945* (1977).
Cowles, Virginia, *No Cause for Alarm* (1949).
Cripps, Sir Stafford, *et al.*, *Problems of a Socialist Government* (1933).
Cronin, J. E., and J. Schneer (eds.), *Social Conflict and the Political Order in Modern Britain* (1982).
Crosland, C. A. R., *The Future of Socialism* (1956).
Crossman, Richard, *Socialist Values in a Changing Civilization* (1951).
—— *Socialism and the New Despotism* (1956).
—— (ed.), *New Fabian Essays* (1952).
Currie, Robert, *Industrial Politics* (Oxford, 1979).
Daalder, Hans, *Cabinet Reform in Britain, 1914–1963* (Palo Alto, USA, 1964).
Dalton, Hugh, *Practical Socialism for Britain* (1935).
Donnison, D. V., *Housing Policy since the War* (Welwyn, 1960).
Dow, J. R. C., *The Management of the British Economy, 1945–60* (Cambridge, 1964).
Durbin, Evan, *The Politics of Democratic Socialism* (1940).
—— *The Problems of Economic Planning* (1949).
Eatwell, Roger, *The 1945–1951 Labour Governments* (1979).
Eckstein, Harry, *The English Health Service: its Origins, Structure and Achievements* (Cambridge, Mass., 1959).
—— *Pressure Group Politics: the case of the British Medical Association* (1960).
Epstein, Leon D., *Britain—Uneasy Ally* (Chicago, 1954).
Fienburgh, W., and R. Everly, *Steel is Power: the Case for Nationalisation* (1948).
Flanders, Allan, *A Policy for Wages* (1954).
Fleming, D. F., *The Cold War and its Origins*, vol. i (1961).
Foot, Michael and D. Bruce, *Who are the Patriots?* (1949).
Gaddis, J. L., *The United States and the Origins of the Cold War, 1941–7* (New York, 1972).
Gaitskell, Hugh, *Socialism and Nationalisation* (1956).
Gardner, Lloyd C., *Architects of Illusion: Men and Ideas in American Foreign Policy, 1941–1949* (Chicago, 1970).
Gardner, R. N., *Sterling–Dollar Diplomacy* (New York, new edn., 1969).
Gimbel, John, *The Origins of the Marshall Plan* (Palo Alto, USA, 1976).
Glennester, H. (ed.), *The Future of the Welfare State* (1983).
Goldsworthy, D. J., *Colonial Issues in British Politics, 1945–1961* (Oxford, 1971).
Gordon, M. R., *Conflict and Consensus in Labour's Foreign Policy, 1914–65* (1969).

Gowing, Margaret, *Independence and Deterrence: Britain and Atomic Energy, 1945–1952* (1974).

Graebner, Norman (ed.), *An Uncertain Tradition: American Secretaries of State* (New York, 1961).

Gupta, Partha Sarathi, *Imperialism and the British Labour Movement, 1914–1964* (1975).

Hall, J. D., *Labour's First Year* (1947).

Halsey, A. H. (ed.), *Trends in British Society since 1900* (1972).

Harrington, W., and P. Young, *The 1945 Revolution* (1978).

Harrison, Martin, *Trade Unions and the Labour Party since 1945* (1960).

Harvie, Christopher, *No Gods and Precious Few Heroes* (1981).

Haseler, Stephen, *The Gaitskellites* (1969).

Henderson, Sir Nicholas, *The Birth of NATO* (1982).

Hewison, R., *In Anger. Culture in the Cold War* (1981).

Hoffman, J. D., *The Conservative Party in Opposition, 1945–51* (1964).

Hopkins, Harry, *The New Look* (1963).

Howell, David, *British Social Democracy* (1977).

Hunter, Leslie, *The Road to Brighton Pier* (1959).

Hyamson, A. M., *Palestine under the Mandate, 1920–1948* (1950).

Jackson, Robert, *Rebels and Whips* (1968).

Jay, Douglas, *The Socialist Case* (new edn., 1947).

— *Socialism in the New Society* (1962).

Jenkins, Mark, *Bevanism: Labour's High Tide* (1979).

Jones, Bill, *The Russia Complex: the British Labour Party and the Soviet Union* (1977).

Jouvenel, Bertrand de, *Problems of Socialist England* (1949).

Kavanagh, Denis (ed.), *The Politics of the Labour Party* (1982).

Kirk, G. (ed.), *Survey of International Affairs: the Middle East* (1954).

Knapp, Wilfred, *A History of War and Peace* (Oxford, 1967).

Leff, S., *The Health of the People* (1950).

Leruez, Jacques, *Economic Planning and Politics in Britain* (1975).

Lewis, Roy, and Angus Maude, *The English Middle Classes* (1949).

Lindsay, Almont, *Socialised Medicine in England and Wales* (Oxford, 1962).

Luard, Evan (ed.), *The Cold War: a reappraisal* (1964).

McCallum, R. B., and A. Readman, *The British General Election of 1945* (Oxford, 1947).

McKenzie, R. T., *British Political Parties* (new edn., 1963).

Mackintosh, J. M., *Trends of Opinion about Public Health, 1901–51* (Oxford, 1953).

Mallalieu, William, C., *British Reconstruction and American Policy 1945–55* (New York, 1956).

Mansergh, Nicholas, *Survey of British Commonwealth Affairs: Problems of Wartime Co-operation and Post-war Change, 1939–1952* (Oxford, 1958).

Martin, David E., and D. Rubinstein (eds.), *Ideology and the Labour Movement* (1979).

Marwick, Arthur, *Britain in the Century of Total War* (1968).
— *British Society since 1945* (1982).
Mikardo, Ian, *The Second Five Years: a Labour Programme for 1950* (1948).
— *The Labour Case* (1950).
Miliband, Ralph, *Parliamentary Socialism* (1961).
Mitchell, Joan, *Crisis in Britain, 1951* (1963).
Monroe, Elizabeth, *Britain's Moment in the Middle East, 1914–1956* (1964).
Moore, R. J., *Escape from Empire* (Oxford, 1983).
Morgan, Kenneth O., *Rebirth of a Nation: Wales, 1880–1980* (Oxford and Cardiff, 1981).
Munro, Donald (ed.), *Socialism: The British Way* (1948).
Murray, D. Stark, *Health for All* (1942).
Nicholas, H. G., *The British General Election of 1950* (1951).
— (ed.), *Washington Despatches, 1941–45* (1981).
Panitch, Leo, *Social Democracy and Industrial Militancy* (Cambridge, 1976).
Parker, Julia, *Local Health and Welfare Services* (1965).
Pimlott, Ben, *Labour and the Left in the 1930s* (Cambridge, 1977).
Priestley, J. B., *The Arts under Socialism* (1947).
Pritt, D. N., *The Labour Government, 1945–51* (1963).
Pelling, Henry, *Britain and the Second World War* (1970).
Rhodes, H. T. F., *The Lynskey Tribunal* (1949).
Roberts, B. C., *National Wages Policy in War and Peace* (1958).
Robson, W. A. (ed.), *Problems of Nationalized Industry* (1952).
Rogow, A., and P. Shore, *The Labour Government and British Industry, 1945–1951* (Oxford, 1955).
Rosecrance, R. N., *Defense of the Realm* (1968).
Ross, Alan, *The Forties* (1950).
Ross, G. W., *The Nationalization of Steel* (1964).
Ross, J. S., *The National Health Service in Great Britain* (Oxford, 1952).
Rothwell, Victor, *Britain and the Cold War, 1941–1947* (1982).
Schaffer, Gordon, *Labour Rules* (1946).
— *Russian Zone* (1947).
Seldon, Anthony, *Churchill's Indian Summer* (1981).
Shinwell, Emanuel, *The Labour Story* (1963).
Shonfield, Andrew, *British Economic Policy since the War* (Harmondsworth, Penguin edn., 1958).
Sissons, M. and French, P. (eds.), *Age of Austerity, 1945–1951* (1963).
Stewart, Margaret, *Taking Work to the Workers* (1946).
Thomas, Brinley (ed.), *The Welsh Economy* (Cardiff, 1962).
Thomas, Ivor, *The Socialist Tragedy* (1949).
Titmus, R. M., *Essays on the Welfare State* (1958).
Toynbee, Arnold (ed.), *Survey of International Affairs: Four-Power Control in Germany and Austria, 1945–46* (1956).
Watkins, Ernest, *The Cautious Revolution* (1951).
Watt, D. C., *Personalities and Policies* (1965).

Weiner, Herbert E., *British Labour and Public Ownership* (1960).
Williams, Francis, *The Triple Challenge: the Future of Socialist Britain* (1948).
Wilson, Harold, *Post-War Economic Policies in Britain* (1957).
Winter, J. M. (ed.), *The Working Class in Modern British History* (Cambridge, 1983).
Worswick, G. D. N., and P. H. Ady (eds.), *The British Economy, 1945–50* (Oxford, 1952).
— (eds.), *The British Economy in the Nineteen-Fifties* (Oxford, 1962).
Young, Michael, *Labour's Plan for Plenty* (1947).
Youngson, A. J., *British Economic Growth, 1920–1966* (1967).

F. ARTICLES

Mark Abrams, 'Social Trends and Electoral Behaviour', *British Journal of Sociology*, xiii (1962).
R. K. Alderman, 'Discipline in the Parliamentary Labour Party, 1945–51', *Parliamentary Affairs*, xviii. 3 (Summer 1965).
Thomas Balogh, 'Britain's Foreign Trade problem: a Comment', *Economic Journal*, lviii (1948).
Caroline Benn, 'Comprehensive School Reform and the 1945 Labour Government', *History Workshop*, 10 (Autumn 1980).
Alan Booth, 'The "Keynesian Revolution" in Economic Policy-Making', *Economic History Review*, xxxvi. 1 (Feb. 1983).
E. H. Phelps Brown, 'Levels and Movements of Industrial Productivity and Real Wages internationally compared, 1860-1970', *Economic Journal*, lxxxiii (Mar. 1973).
Donald Bruce, 'A review of Socialist Financial Policy, 1945-1949', *Political Quarterly*, xx. 4 (Oct.-Dec. 1949).
A. K. Cairncross, 'The Relationship between Monetary and Fiscal Policy', *Proceedings of the British Academy* lxvii (1981).
G. D. H. Cole, 'The Dream and the Business', *Political Quarterly*, xx. 3 (July–Sept. 1949).
Arthur Creech Jones, 'British Colonial Policy with particular reference to Africa', *International Affairs*, xxvii. 2 (Apr. 1951).
W. Manning Dicey, 'The Cheap Money Technique', *Lloyds Bank Review*, new series, 3 (Jan. 1947).
Leon D. Epstein, 'Socialism and the British Labour Party', *Political Science Quarterly*, lxv. 4 (Dec. 1950).
W. N. Ewer, 'The Labour Government's Record in Foreign Policy', *Political Quarterly*, xx. 2 (Apr.-June 1949).
John T. Grantham, 'British Labour and the Hague "Congress of Europe"', *Historical Journal*, 24, 2 (June 1981).
Margery Fry, 'The Criminal Justice Bill', ibid., xix. 2 (Apr.-June 1948).
Gary R. Hess, 'The Iranian Crisis of 1945-46 and the Cold War', *Political Science Quarterly*, 89, 1 (Mar. 1974).
Billy Hughes, 'In Defence of Ellen Wilkinson', *History Workshop* 7 (Spring 1979).

Howard C. Jones, 'The Labour Party in Cardiganshire', *Ceredigion*, ix. 2 (1981).

H. D. Jordan, 'The British Cabinet and the Ministry of Defense', *American Political Science Quarterly*, xliii. 1 (Feb. 1949).

N. D. Joy, 'Fair Compensation and the British Labor Government', ibid., lxv. 4 (Dec. 1950).

Kenneth Knowles, 'The Post-war Dock Strikes', *Political Quarterly*, xxii. 3 (July–Sept. 1951).

Y. Krishnan, 'Mountbatten and the Partition of India', *History*, 68, 222 (Feb. 1983).

John McHugh and B. J. Ripley, 'The Neath By-Election, 1945', *Llafur*, 3, 2 (Spring 1981).

Donald MacRae, 'The Domestic Record of the Labour Government', *Political Quarterly*, xx. 1 (Jan–Mar. 1949).

William C. Mallalieu, 'The Origins of the Marshall Plan: a study in policy formulation and national leadership', *Political Science Quarterly*, lxxiii. 4 (Dec. 1958).

F. M. Martin, 'Social Status and Electoral Choice in Two Constituencies', *British Journal of Sociology*, iii (1952).

Arthur Marwick, 'The Labour Party and the Welfare State in Britain 1900-1948', *American Historical Review*, lxxiii. 2 (Dec. 1967).

Christopher Mayhew, 'British Foreign Policy since 1945', *International Affairs*, xxvii. 4 (Oct. 1950).

R. Ovendale, 'Britain, the U.S.A. and the European Cold War, 1945-8', *History*, 67, 220 (June 1982).

Henry Pelling, 'The 1945 General Election Reconsidered', *Historical Journal*, 23, 2 (June 1980).

Peter G. Richards, 'The General Election', *Political Quarterly*, xxi. 2 (Apr.–June 1950).

Lionel Robbins, 'Inquest on the Crisis', *Lloyd's Bank Review*, new series, 6 (1947).

— 'The Sterling Problem', ibid., 14 (1949).

David Rubinstein, 'Ellen Wilkinson reconsidered', *History Workshop*, 7 (Spring 1979).

R. V. Sampson, 'The Dilemma of British Labour', *Foreign Affairs*, 30, 3 (Apr. 1952).

John Saville, 'Labour and Income Redistribution', *Socialist Register* (1965).

Peter Self, 'A policy for Agriculture', *Political Quarterly*, xix. 2 (Apr.–June 1948).

Jacob Viner, 'An American view of the British Economic crisis', *Lloyd's Bank Review* new series, 6 (Oct. 1947).

D. C. Watt, 'American Aid to Britain and the problem of Socialism', *The American Review*, 11, 4 (Mar. 1963).

Peter Weiler, 'The United States, International Labour and the Cold War: the Break-up of the World Federation of Trade Unions', *Diplomatic History*, v (Winter 1981).

H. D. Wilcock, 'Public Opinion: Attitudes towards America and Russia', *Political Quarterly*, xix. 1 (Jan.-Mar. 1948).
Philip Williams, 'Foot-Faults in the Gaitskell-Bevan match', *Political Studies*, xxvii. 1 (Mar. 1979).
Barbara Wootton, 'The Record of the Labour Government in the Social Services', *Political Quarterly*, xx. 2 (Apr.-June 1949).

G. UNPUBLISHED THESES

J. A. Chenier, 'The Development and Implementation of Postwar Housing Policy under the Labour Government' (Oxford University, submitted for D. Phil., 1982).
Jane Morgan, 'The Political Career of Christopher, Viscount Addison, 1869-1951' (University of Leicester, Ph. D., 1979).
D. M. Roberts, 'Clement Davies and the Liberal Party, 1929-56' (University of Wales, Aberystwyth, MA, 1975).
Gillian Susan Roberts, 'A Study of the Protection of Public and Essential Services in Labour Disputes, 1920-1976' (Cambridge University Ph.D., 1977).
C. R. Rose, 'The relation of Socialist principles to British Labour foreign policy, 1945-1951' (Oxford University D. Phil., 1959).
I. H. Taylor, 'War and the Development of Labour's Domestic Programme, 1939-45' (London School of Economics Ph. D., 1977).
Jonathan Wood, 'The Labour Left in the Constituency Labour Parties, 1945-51' (University of Warwick MA, 1977).

Index